W9-BGN-197

From Vagabond to Journalist

From Vagabond to Journalist

Edgar Snow

in Asia

1928–1941

Robert M. Farnsworth

University of Missouri Press
Columbia and London

B
S6726 F

Copyright © 1996 by
The Curators of the University of Missouri
University of Missouri Press, Columbia, Missouri 65201
Printed and bound in the United States of America
All rights reserved
5 4 3 2 1   00 99 98 97 96

Library of Congress Cataloging-in-Publication Data

Farnsworth, Robert M.
    From vagabond to journalist : Edgar Snow in Asia, 1928–1941 /
Robert M. Farnsworth.
        p.   cm.
    Includes bibliographical references and index.
    ISBN 0-8262-1060-0 (alk. paper)
    1. Snow, Edgar, 1905–1972.   2. Foreign correspondents—United
States—Biography.   I. Title.
PN4874.S5715F37   1996
070'.92—dc20
[B]   96-777
                                                        CIP

⊗™ This paper meets the requirements of the
American National Standard for Permanence of Paper
for Printed Library Materials, Z39.48, 1984.

Designer: Stephanie Foley
Typesetter: BOOKCOMP
Printer and Binder: Thomson-Shore, Inc.
Typeface: Hiroshige

All photographs are courtesy of the Edgar Snow
Collection, University of Missouri–Kansas City.

JUN 2 8 1996

Contents

Acknowledgments

I BEGAN RESEARCHING THIS BOOK in 1984, just before going to China for an academic year as a Fulbright lecturer in American Literature. It has taken long to write in part because the history Edgar Snow lived through is not part of the general education of a professor of American Literature. I had much learning to do. I should also note, however, that approximately two of the intervening years were spent editing a collection of Snow's early travel articles throughout Asia, *Edgar Snow's Journey South of the Clouds*, which was published in 1991.

I was well aware that Edgar Snow held a very special role in Chinese history and politics; nevertheless, I was unprepared for much that quickly followed after my wife and I arrived in China in 1984. I was almost immediately invited to become a member of a new society honoring the roles of Anna Louise Strong, Agnes Smedley, and Edgar Snow in China's national revolution. Liu Liqun, then secretary of that society, arranged a memorable tour for me to Yenan and Pao An. He also introduced me to many who once knew Edgar Snow and now were honored for their own achievements in China. Rewi Alley opened his private library to me and over lunch often tried to straighten out the confusing tangle of history and politics that marked Snow's China years. Irving Epstein lived in the same hotel compound as we and was generously ready to answer questions. George Hatem was a friendly but more elusive and distant presence. Huang Hua shared memories of his student days at Yenching when he first met Ed and Peg Snow in a private interview in a spacious chamber of the Hall of the People. I was invited to numerous conferences and public receptions.

But looking back at these early days of research, I am a little embarrassed by the opportunities wasted, because I was yet so ill-prepared. My awareness of modern Chinese history, like that of most Americans, was vague and confused. My principal job at the time was to teach Chinese students about American literature. To heighten my sense of frustration it was obvious that the memory of Edgar Snow was frequently evoked for contemporary political purposes that were not always clear to me. Too often the conferences I attended seemed more obviously public showpieces than serious efforts at historical inquiry.

I returned to the University of Missouri–Kansas City to work among the papers of the Edgar Snow Collection with a sense of relief. Slowly but surely I found my story there. Meanwhile I continued to read as widely as I could in the writings of Snow's contemporaries who viewed the same historical events but from different personal angles. I was surprised and gratified by the talent and achievements of many about whom I previously knew so little.

But there was yet another reason why this book took so long to write, and that had to do with Edgar Snow and his profession. Throughout his career Snow felt a close kinship between journalism and literature. He occasionally tried his hand with fiction and certainly read widely and enthusiastically among novelists and short-story writers, not just for personal enjoyment but also for instruction about the art of writing itself. But his claim to fame rests upon his ability to explain complex historical events in a foreign land in passionate words that a concerned, intelligent American citizen can understand and feel. This task carried for him a lode of civic urgency. Democracy does not work unless the people care and are informed.

As Snow's deep professional pride became clear to me, it became more and more a conscious challenge to my own long-engrained academic habits of writing. I slowly learned a new respect for the achievement of clarity in the face of the confusion and ambiguity that commonly clouds trivial as well as historical events. I also learned a new respect for an honest balance between recognizing that writing is intrinsically and inevitably personal, and hence editorial, but that a reader's trust depends upon his faith in the journalist's willingness and ability to report events fairly and objectively. Establishing a trusted personal perspective for a journalist is the task and challenge of a lifetime. That trust may be damaged, even destroyed, by factual mistakes or faulty arguments, but in the long-term it is even more deeply challenged by the danger of contradiction from history with all its surprisingly abrupt twists and turns. As my respect grew for the skill and passion needed to communicate with an intelligent, concerned popular audience, I tried to discipline my own writing accordingly.

Thus I have many debts of gratitude to acknowledge. Three times I have been privileged to live and work in Asia as a Fulbright lecturer in American Literature: in India, 1966–1967; in Turkey, 1974–1975; and in China, 1984–1985. I have not become an academic expert on Asia, but I believe these experiences prepared me to read the story of Edgar Snow's Asian journeying with an unusual empathy. And I shall always be grateful to the Fulbright program for these opportunities.

Closer to home Mary Clark Dimond and her husband, E. Grey Dimond, founder and respective chairs of the Edgar Snow Memorial Fund, were responsible for bringing the collection of Edgar Snow's papers to the University of Missouri–Kansas City. For several years before and during my research on Edgar Snow I served on the board of the Snow fund. My association with the fund made many of my contacts with Snow's friends possible both here and in China. But it is chiefly for the presence of the Edgar Snow Collection at the university that I am most indebted. I could not have written the story I have drawn from the Snow papers without the ability to return to the papers again and again to check the significance of information I did not immediately understand. I owe a special thanks to Marilyn Burlingame, archivist of the Edgar Snow Collection, who frequently found what I could not and sometimes led me to material whose value I did not recognize.

When I began this project, the late Henry Mitchell, another board member and associate vice chancellor of the university, was to coauthor this book with me. He early located and acquired important Snow documents and encouraged my early efforts to put our research into writing. Under the press of his administrative duties and probably impatient with my slowness at putting the story together, but before learning of his fatal illness, he withdrew from the project. His encouragement and continued support meant much to me.

I early met Helen Foster Snow and corresponded frequently with her over the years of my research. The collection of her papers at the Hoover Library and her voluminous writing about her years in China when she was married to Edgar Snow are a major source for the story I have written. However, even as I have written a story that differs from that of her husband, so does my story differ from hers.

Lois Wheeler Snow figures far less prominently in my story since it principally focuses on Snow's years in China before he met her. However, she has been very generous in granting me access to and use of her husband's papers and photographs, and my account of Snow's final days draws heavily from her book, *A Death with Dignity*.

After I had written a great number of pages, but still had not completed a first draft, I strongly felt a need for assurance from someone knowledgeable that what I was writing was worth continuing. I asked John S. Service to read my manuscript, and he graciously consented. At that point Service pointed out that my story badly needed shape and focus, but he also took the trouble to correct some minor geographical and historical mistakes and even to suggest added information and to encourage me. He has since read the revised manuscript, and his advice and encouragement have been invaluable. A. Tomas Grunfeld also generously provided useful advice.

I am also indebted to the Faculty Research Council of the University of Missouri–Kansas City for the travel grants that made much of my early research possible.

It would be an imposition on readers and the publisher to list all to whom I owe gratitude. I hope the published book offers some return for their generosity and courtesy, but I also retain many vivid memories that someday I hope to translate into more private opportunities to show my thanks.

Since my story is so heavily concerned with Snow's years in China from 1928 to 1941 when the Wade-Giles system was the most commonly accepted method of representing Chinese words in English, I decided it was appropriate to use that system consistently rather than to change all of Snow's references to pinyin.

From Vagabond to Journalist

Introduction

I N HIS AUTOBIOGRAPHY, *Journey to the Beginning,* Edgar Snow declared he had already lived three lives. The first, in Kansas City, where he was born and grew up, also included early adult years in New York, where he followed his older brother to pursue a career in advertising.

The second began at twenty-three, when he abruptly left New York to sign on board a freighter bound for the South Pacific, the first stage of a journey around the world to satisfy a craving for adventure and test his ability to earn a living as a writer. His journey stalled in Asia for thirteen years, during which he wrote his way to world recognition in the *Saturday Evening Post* and four books, *Far Eastern Front, Living China, Red Star over China,* and *Battle for Asia.*

His return to the United States in 1941 began a third life as a popular and distinguished foreign correspondent during World War II for the *Saturday Evening Post.* But following the war the United States and the Soviet Union engaged in a Cold War that Snow considered a tragic mistake. He dropped from public favor and published his autobiography in part to reclaim his public authority.

Snow recognized in his autobiography that his second life was the key to the Edgar Snow the world once knew and was then in danger of forgetting. He minimized the story of his first life in Kansas City and built the story of his third life during World War II and the Cold War that followed on what he had learned during his maturing years in Asia from 1928 to 1941. Even during the Cold War, his *Red Star over China* continued to win recognition as a classic of historical journalism.

Since Snow published his autobiography, John Maxwell Hamilton has written a distinguished and detailed biography of Snow. With these two books published, the question arises why yet another about the life of Edgar Snow.

Hamilton's book is the result of years of painstaking research and mature consideration. Often insightful biography, it focuses principally on the difficult dialogue the mature Edgar Snow had with American public opinion and foreign policy. Inherently this makes Snow's formative and most productive years in China incidental to Snow's long struggle against American foreign policy in later life. Hamilton treats Snow's personal life with marked reticence, minimizing the role it played in his professional development. Perhaps as a by-product of his respect for Snow's privacy, Hamilton also accepted what Edgar Snow publicly wrote about himself, particularly in *Journey to the Beginning,* as if it were fact.

A close examination of the very extensive personal papers of Edgar Snow and his first wife, Helen Foster Snow, housed respectively at the University of Missouri–Kansas City and at the Hoover Library on the campus of Stanford University, has made clear to me Edgar Snow was in fact more troubled, vulnerable, and consequently more interesting, than the poised, purposive, but often too blandly romantic persona Snow created in *Journey to the Beginning.*

The Kansas City family in which Snow grew up was always important to him, but he had great difficulty acknowledging some of his negative feelings about that family. His lengthy and detailed letters to father, mother, sister, and brother, particularly during his first few years abroad, are rich in sentiment, but in frequent contradiction to his behavior. He promised repeatedly to come home, but after New York he never seriously considered living in Kansas City again. In *Journey to the Beginning* he acknowledged his youth was troubled by the conflict between his father's atheism and his mother's Catholicism. The pain of this memory became fixed in his memory by the circumstances of his mother's death while he lingered in far-away Shanghai. He still found this story too painful to tell in *Journey to the Beginning.*

During Snow's Asia years his elder brother, originally a role model for his independence from his Kansas City family, worked his way toward the middle-class conservative success from which Snow fled when he left New York's advertising community. He married, established a family, and moved into a notably responsible position in the American business world. Their contrasting success made the brothers a little competitively suspicious for a time, yet on Snow's return to America they readily restored their close fraternal bond.

The marriages of both Snow's brother and sister followed close upon the death of his mother and his own renewed determination to resume his world journey homeward. But eighteen months later in India, struggling to understand the history of yet another ancient and proud civilization's rebellion against European colonialism and its own feudal past, and burdened with more and more foreboding news about the prospect of a job in a United States mired in deep economic depression, Snow precipitately decided to return to Shanghai. The bachelor apartment he once shared with his brother in New York was no longer available, and silently he admitted he felt no desire to return to his family in Kansas City.

Instead he returned to Shanghai lonely, suffering from malaria, and questioning his own bachelor's life following his brother's and sister's marriages. His ego was soothed and restored when a bright and beautiful young American woman, who landed in Shanghai only a few days after he did, arranged to be introduced to him and unabashedly declared herself a fan of his writing.

A long and complicated courtship led to a troubled, but challenging, modern marriage of ambitious writers. Sometimes in spite of and sometimes because of their troubled emotional relationship, their marriage significantly influenced Snow's growth as a writer and as a person, but their marriage also drifted toward disaster as the world drifted toward global carnage. In 1941, at the end of his long residence in Asia, Snow, deeply troubled by the failure of his marriage, the renewed threat of civil war in China, and the breakdown of international reason, dramatically aborted a final effort to complete his round-the-world journey and suffered a painfully severe middle-age crisis as he journeyed homeward in a final effort to redeem his marriage.

During these eventful years away from home Snow also developed strong, but often discreetly guarded, ties with a group of other foreigners who came to play a significant role in the shaping and reporting of the story of China's revolution. Two of these, Rewi Alley and George Hatem, unlike Snow, chose eventually to become Chinese citizens. Their friendship and the recognition of their contributions to China made them significant hosts and sources of information on Snow's later visits to China. Three others, Evans Carlson, Agnes Smedley, and James Bertram, all publicly shared Snow's empathy with the revolutionary aspirations of the Chinese people in books appealing for the world's support. Looming significantly in the background of these friendships was the vivid and inspiring presence of Soong Ching-ling, the widow of Sun Yat-sen. All became lifelong friends, almost another kind of family for Snow. Each lived an extraordinary story of his or her own, but each also formed a deep and substantial personal relationship with Snow based on mutual trust, respect, and shared commitment. There were many other notable friendships that lasted throughout Snow's life, but this group is exceptional in their personal achievements and the close working relationship they had with Snow.

The years 1928–1941 were eventful in world history as well as in the personal and professional life of Edgar Snow. Throughout Asia burgeoning national movements challenged European colonial control. Snow early identified two dynamic new forces that cut across national boundaries and impinged on these revolutions. Japan early grasped many necessary lessons for industrializing from Western nations, and then moved militantly to replace them in Asia with a new form of colonialism masked by an appeal to pan-Asian brotherhood. The Communist revolution in Russia promised a whole new system of ordering national and international economic and political power. By identifying imperialism with capitalism and the people with the proletariat it strongly appealed to Asian national rebellions against colonial rule.

European democracies, also colonial powers, were unwilling or unable to face the challenge Asian nationalism posed to their own democratic traditions. Critical challenges closer to home arose and obscured the challenges from faraway Asia. An aggressive Italy insisted on a bigger share of the colonial pie in Africa. A civil war that quickly turned into a training ground for World War II broke out in Spain. And finally Nazi Germany threatened to take over all Europe. The United States spent the early thirties in a devastating economic depression that encouraged America's willingness to believe, falsely, in the security of its geographical isolation and hence to insist the troubles of the rest of the world were only matters of curiosity, not of basic self-interest.

The romantic world a twenty-three-year-old Edgar Snow set out to view in 1928 as a carefree vagabond traveler proved far more sinisterly engaging than he expected. The sufferings of the Chinese people quickly brought home to him the right and the need for this once-proud people to establish a modern nation state. He early witnessed firsthand the deception behind Japan's mask of pan-Asian fellowship. However, determined to remain true to his original motive for travel and bound by the promises he had made to his Kansas City family, he left China after his mother's death for a leisurely trip through Southeast Asia that further educated him on the depth and sweep of the Asian rebellion against colonialism.

He returned to China just before Japan invaded Manchuria and made a mockery of the international agreements world leaders had designed to keep international peace following World War I. He quickly recognized the threat of global war and told a growingly respectful audience in Europe and America why. Then just as he was beginning to despair of China's national revolution, he met the Communist forces that eventually led the Chinese people to effective national rebellion. *Red Star over China* became Snow's major journalistic achievement.

Japan invaded China as Snow finished *Red Star over China*. Combined with Italy's invasion of Abyssinia and the Spanish civil war, it made World War II increasingly undeniable. As an authoritative Asian reporter Snow now held a uniquely privileged and respected position. China became a touchstone for the fate of other nations in Asia and ultimately for a new world order or disorder to be shaped by international war and its victors.

During China's darkest years of occupation by Japan, Snow felt China's danger too strongly to be simply a witnessing journalist. Struggling to imagine and write a fitting sequel to *Red Star over China*, he worked long and diligently to establish an industrial cooperative movement designed to preserve as much as possible of China's industrial capacity from loss to the Japanese. He raised substantial international support for Indusco, but ultimately it was strangled by bitter national politics.

Once written and published, *Battle for Asia* was widely received as a fitting sequel to *Red Star over China*, but its challenge to America to clarify its position on colonialism before entering World War II came too late. The Japanese attacked Pearl Harbor within months of its publication.

Edgar Snow absorbed a crash lesson in world history while wrestling with troubled personal commitments to family and nation. No matter in what country he lived, he assumed his own Americanness as given. In his autobiography he represented his journey to Asia as part of a deeply ingrained historical predisposition in the American experience to go west to discover the East. Once in China he readily embraced the easy anticolonialism of his American journalistic mentors. He assumed any red-blooded American would want China, or any nation, free from European colonial intrusion and Japanese aggression.

He was early and deeply moved by the terrible suffering of the Chinese people as a result of massive and relentless natural disasters such as flood and drought as well as from the more humanly culpable economic exploitation of landlords, warlords, and sweatshop owners. His feelings bound him, reluctantly, to these people. By the time he wrote his autobiography he clearly recognized that during his thirteen years in Asia, China had become his second national home, and it remained so the rest of his life no matter where he lived.

Trying to summarize the sobering wisdom he had learned from this long Asian journey in his autobiography he reached for the image of Ishmael used by two other troubled questers, T. E. Lawrence and Herman Melville.

Perhaps the authority of this romantic tradition could help explain why, while acknowledging a deep sense of brotherhood with the Chinese people, he nevertheless had to return to his native land:

> Yes, I was proud to have known them [the people of China], to have struggled across a continent with them in defeat, to have wept with them and still to share a faith with them. But I was not and could never be one of them. A man who gives himself to be the possession of an alien land, said Lawrence in his *Seven Pillars,* lives a Yahoo life; and I was tired of being a Yahoo. I was an American, I told myself, and now at last I saw myself as I was, an Ishmael in a foreign land, and drew back to avoid being engulfed in the deep.

But coming home did not end Snow's role as Ishmael. His autobiography is steeped in his sense of alienation from the Cold War politics of his native land, and he soon moved with his family to Switzerland. He continued to mine the mother lode of his early years in China and concluded a distinguished public career playing a notable role in the restoration of civil relations between the nation he identified with by birth and heritage and the nation he adopted by choice and commitment.

1

Setting Out on a Second Life

E DGAR SNOW OPENED HIS autobiography with "When I first reached Shanghai I was every youth, full of curiosity and wide open to the world." The youth he described was born in the self-conscious discovery of history, of his awakening to a role in a particular time and place. Snow had already told much of that story in *Far Eastern Front, Red Star over China, Battle for Asia, People on Our Side,* and the pages of the *Saturday Evening Post,* and the world had paid respectful attention. But after World War II what seemed to Snow a lunacy, called the Cold War, had spread across the world and cast doubt on his journalistic authority. Perhaps if he told the story of how he had earned *author*ity, of his intensive education in world history, and particularly the national aspirations of Asia, he could alleviate the Cold War hysteria and restore some of his own compelling professional power.

Thus *Journey to the Beginning,* his autobiography, was only in part a personal story. What followed his landing in Shanghai was an experience for every man, certainly for all those Western men who knew and understood so little of their Eastern brothers. He played down the personal, giving only a brief account of his youth in Kansas City and his early adult years in New York and folding that little into the narrative of his Asian years. His brief references to his family, particularly to his father and mother, suggest an ambiguous mix of care, guilt, and resentment that he never fully clarified or resolved. Indeed the golden years of his public Asian odyssey were threaded with personal anxieties and pain he deliberately hid from the view of his readers, and sometimes even from himself.

In *Journey to the Beginning* he noted his father, James Edgar Snow, came from a long Protestant, anti-Papist tradition. After becoming a freethinker, his father fell so in love with a beautiful, redheaded, strictly Catholic girl, Anna Catherine Edelmann, he readily promised to take instruction in the Catholic faith and raise and baptize their children as Catholics if she would marry him.

Their third and last child, Edgar, was born July 19, 1905. By this time the father's instruction in Catholicism had soured, providing instead restocked ammunition for his original views as a freethinker. Mildred and John Howard, Edgar's older sister and brother, were educated in Catholic schools, but father insisted Edgar go to public schools. Edgar continued to attend Mass with his mother on Sunday mornings, but in the afternoon he also had to listen to a second catechism composed of well-chosen lines from Robert Ingersoll or other writers on the Roman Catholic Index.

By the time Snow wrote *Journey to the Beginning* he had become an avid reader of Mark Twain and insisted he lost his religious faith in adolescence, not because of Ingersoll's arguments but because of an older altar boy who disrespectfully ate some Communion wafers without being struck by lightning. Nevertheless, Snow remembered continuing to attend Mass out of consideration for his mother.

Snow's father ran a small printing business in Kansas City. A passionate reader with a strong sense of personal integrity, he was an earnest, if somewhat impractical, idealist. In his college years he once wrote, "How strong must that student feel who can walk through a library with the consciousness that he knows the plans and purposes of all the leading books!"

Snow's mother was more personally forgiving and comfortably accepted the authority of tradition. Intellectually, Snow sided with his father, but emotionally he bonded with his mother. He frequently associated her with the pleasures of his youth in later letters. Her unexpected death in 1930, while he was away in Shanghai, troubled him for much of the rest of his life. He did not tell the painful story he learned from his father's letters in *Journey to the Beginning*. Instead he noted only, "It never occurred to me that I would not see her again. The letter from home which would within a few weeks report her illness to me did not reach me until two weeks after a cable told me of her death." He claimed the memory of his mother's goodness and loving kindness kept him from ever becoming a militant anti-Catholic, but it took years to work his way to that tolerant position.

Snow tells two other meaningful stories about his youth in *Journey to the Beginning*. One day, while Mildred's boyfriend was visiting, Snow borrowed the boyfriend's Stevens without permission for a drive around the neighborhood. Unfortunately his family all came out on the front porch just as he was returning from an up-till-then glorious drive. The resulting scene could have been sketched by Norman Rockwell. His mother's excited gestures and shouts distracted him as he pulled into the driveway, and he ran the car into a tree. His father made him pay for the damage. To do so he had to sell a much valued saxophone. So ended the promising musical career of the leader of the Kansas City Blue Bells Jazz Band, "Out of Town Jobs a Specialty."

The second story took place in 1922, when he turned seventeen. With two fellow students at Westport High School, Bob Long and Charlie White, he shocked wheat in Kansas to earn enough money for a trip to California. Long owned a Model T Ford. Snow kept his travel plans from his parents.

Roads and maps in those days were primitive and scarce, so travel in the Model T was indeed adventurous. Once, in the desert, the car's motor became so hot a cylinder was scored. Their water gone, the young travelers used their last bottle of soda pop to keep the car running. When they got to California they were broke. One night they stayed with Buddy Rogers, whom Snow knew as a fellow teenage jazz musician from Olathe, Kansas. Rogers was then in acting school. Long sold his damaged car, then wired his family. *His* family knew of the trip from the beginning, and his mother and brother came out and brought him back to Kansas City by train.

Snow and White hoboed their way back—first, however, mistakenly choosing a train that took them away from rather than toward home. Near Sacramento the two worked for a short time serving food to Mexican workers in a labor camp. Finding their work and the accumulation of money equally tedious, they soon chose to ride the rails again, casually risking life and limb, to make their way home. They were caught, arrested, and separated. Snow quickly forgot the danger and pain, while the excitement and sense of achievement endured and fueled a later grander ambition to circle the world.[1]

Two years after this western trip Snow headed east. He announced to his classmates at Kansas City Junior College he was leaving home to enter an advertising program at Columbia University. He followed the footsteps of his brother, Howard, who invited him to join several other ambitious and fun-loving young men, most of whom were from the Kansas City area. Beside his regular advertising work, Howard, who strongly resembled his younger brother, appeared as a model for Spur bow ties in the *Saturday Evening Post*. The brothers lived in various apartments with changing Midwest partners, eventually settling at 56 West Fifty-fifth Street, intentionally close to the Ziegfeld Follies Theater. Buddy Rogers, from Olathe, Kansas, on his way to movie stardom and eventually to marriage with Mary Pickford, lived with them for a time. Bette Davis, yet relatively unknown, was one of several actors and actresses that partied there.

That the begrizzled author of *Red Star over China* was originally drawn to journalism through ambition to enter the glitzy new American profession of advertising hardly seems appropriate, but so it was. He early found work with the Medley Scovil Company but delayed enrolling at Columbia until the spring semester. He then took two evening courses in advertising and completed one, still working for Scovil. He also enrolled in summer courses at Columbia University but apparently never finished any of them.

In 1925 he returned to his home state to attend the University of Missouri School of Journalism for a year. That year provided a key to doors he had no idea of knocking on at the time. Later in China, mentored by Missouri journalists, he proudly claimed Missouri his alma mater, despite his limited attendance. One of three journalism courses he took was in advertising. Although he was a stringer for the *Kansas City Star* during that year, his primary interest apparently was still to strengthen his skills and credentials for his advertising job. He returned to work at Scovil the next summer.

From New York, Snow began a remarkably extensive and carefully preserved correspondence with his family in Kansas City. While he may well have found it difficult to live with the religious tension between his mother and father, he clearly respected both and earnestly sought their approval. For years he wrote lengthy and detailed letters to his father, mother, sister, and, after he left New York, to his brother, letters rich in sentiment and suspiciously redundant in promises to return home. Each new promise was almost inevitably accompanied by another apology or explanation for his failure to keep his last.

After he returned to New York from his stint at the University of Missouri his letters indicate he was still unsatisfied. He wrote his sister, Mildred:

> Buddy just got the shocking news that he's to have the lead in a great new Paramount picture called "Wings." Among the things he may have to endure are the wiles and witcheries of Clara Bow, the heroine, the trials and tribulations of learning to fly, [and] Paris, London, Arizona, Kansas and various other "locations" to which he will be dispatched. . . . It might also be worth mentioning that for these diverse performances he will probably receive about five hundred per week. Such popularity must be deserved! Buddy is a very personable and handsome young man.

Snow wrestled earnestly with his envy: "Proximity to such grandiose success is apt to be discouraging at times. Still it is not difficult to look around and realize that his is the exceptional case indeed; that my own position is not unequal to the average and that I have a chance of making a milder success of my own."

He tried hard to stay focused on winning his own "milder success," but by March 1927 his impatience began to show in his letters home. He wrote his father: "But I *will* succeed. I am determined to raise my head above the crowd and to amount to something in a larger way than at present seems possible in Kansas City." He was twenty-one and in debt to his parents. He probably had borrowed money from them for his previous year in journalism school. He summarized his weekly budget of forty-one dollars to explain to his father why he had so little money to spare. But it was not just the money that made him unhappy with his job: "if a suitable opportunity presents, I shall make a change—possibly for less money. This I know: That I should get as much experience as possible—experience of a broad expanding nature—while I am still young. I intend to do this even at the sacrifice of earnings and position."[2]

In October 1927, still concerned with small separate debts to his mother and father and to Howard, Snow finally was able to announce a milder success of his own. He won the World Wide Letter Writing Contest sponsored by the *Savings Bank Journal*. The prize was a brand new Remington portable typewriter, "a machine I have been yearning to possess for some time." His picture and biography were to appear in all the banking publications. When it did, however, he was disappointed with the changes the editor had made in the biographical information that Snow had sent him. It was only the first of many skirmishes with editors.

About this time he thought of enrolling in New York University Law School, but it would have taken three years of evening courses to finish a degree. Two projects he had just started for Scovil were very promising. He had submitted a twenty-thousand-dollar advertising campaign to the Canadian Bank of Commerce that was favorably received, and Kelly Graham, president of First National Bank of Jersey City, had given Snow an early, but most encouraging, signal of an eventual favorable reception for an ambitious project Snow planned for Graham's bank. Graham invited Snow to dinner at the Baltusrol Club with Senator Edward I. Edwards, then considered a 1928 presidential candidate, and Harvey Black, newly elected president of Standard Oil of New Jersey.[3]

A few weeks before Christmas, Snow was surprised to learn he was not to expect a raise for the coming year. At first he doubted the message. He proudly concluded the sale of his ambitious plan for First National Bank, but when he brought the news to Scovil, the latter's only comment was a grudging, "Perhaps we shall make some money on this account yet!" Snow said little or nothing to Scovil, but he wrote Mildred, "The saphead. Does he think I don't realize we make more off this client, in a year, than my salary for the same period?"

It was a minor instance in the world of commerce but a fateful moment in the career of Edgar Snow. He gave Mildred a hint that would later prove prophetic: "I think often of you, Sis, and wish to goodness knows what ends, that you were here. Still, think how interesting I may become to you someday, after we've been separated for a long time—and I've got adventurous achievements to charm your imagination."

Early in December he also wrote his mother about another friend who had landed a good job taking him to South Africa and Australia and then to Paris for Christmas. His friend's good fortune and his own disappointment tinged his writing with purple-patched poignancy:

> The "Blue Peter" flies on the mast of the good ship Sentinel, a United Fruit Company boat, which lies across the street from me, at the edge of the pier. . . . It beckons urgently to the passerby and expensively taunts him, jeering at his sane solidity of domestic existence. . . . A ferry boat, crowded with Sunday commuters, noses intimately alongside and flaunts its fat sides temptingly against the trim, sea-going vessel. Yet the Blue Peter looks out to the sea and still waves bravely and joyously. And in a little while the stout hearted ship pulls quietly away from shore and leaves the pulsing, throbbing city with its cares and its woes, behind. Let us praise the Blue Peter, for its youth and freedom!

Two weeks later Snow noted to his father, "I see Charles Lindbergh is spending the holidays in Mexico or parts south. Eventful lad, that, isn't he?" He also thanked his father for sending him the *Saturday Evening Post* article about Stilwell, a then-unrecognized looming of Snow's later career.

On Christmas Day he telegrammed his mother, "This is the last Christmas I will be away from home."

By early January he learned "Mr. Scovil deferred my raise because I have been consistently late in arriving at the office in the morning." He tried to accept the rebuke in good faith, "I suppose I needed the lesson. So I purchased a Big Ben which, when it goes off, shakes the walls." His conscientious effort at reform, however, did not take. Complaints about his tardiness followed him the rest of his life. But in the same letter he stated flatly he did not expect to be with Scovil longer than two more months: "I shall either go with another agency or secure a position as advertising manager in a large corporation. I am worth far more money than Scovil will ever pay." At the time he was being considered for a position as assistant to Arthur Hornblow Jr., the head of Samuel Goldwyn Motion Picture

Company. He had interviewed three times and submitted writing samples but was uncertain about what Hornblow was looking for when he demanded "dramatic instinct!"[4]

While Edgar Snow looked for some new glamorous, well-paying job, he must have already begun planning the fundamental change in his career that would eventually lead him to fame and extraordinary achievement, if not great fortune. By January his plans to leave New York and work his way around the world, writing of his adventures along the way, were well advanced. He did not tell his parents until it was too late for them to protest or intercede. The business of establishing an independent life required certain privacies, or even evasions, from his family. He did, however, give his mother a broad clue: "Yesterday I was down to see Kermit Roosevelt—Theodore's (sr.) son. He is president of the Roosevelt Steamship Lines, a company with whom it is just possible I may soon become affiliated."

Only on February 17, safely on board ship and expecting any moment to sail, was he ready to break the news:

> My dream of seeing the world has prospects of realization. When recently I told you I expected to join the organization of the Roosevelt S. S. Lines it was no idle threat. But I am sure you cannot have conceived of the manner in which I am now employed by the company. Your unworthy son is now a Deck Boy on the *S. S. Radnor,* sailing under the Roosevelt supervision and operated by the Merchant Fleet Corporation.

The *Radnor,* however, did not leave New York for the South Pacific and the Far East until February 26, so Snow cagily delayed sending his letter to his parents for a few days. He reassured them his decision was not "a rash and hasty action which I have taken with no forethought." They would be happy to learn Alvin Joslin, a schoolmate from Kansas City whom they knew, was signed aboard with him. So he was not without friends. Dean Walter Williams from Missouri had provided several letters of introduction to alumni scattered along the path of his extensive voyage. Even Kermit Roosevelt, president of the lines on whose ship he was serving as a deck boy, had given him a letter of introduction.

He also had been introduced to Mrs. Marie Meloney, editor of the *New York Herald Tribune Magazine,* and she had given him "several suggestions for stories which the *Tribune* would be glad to get from the Far East." He had written to W. L. Dickey and George B. Longan, editors of the *Kansas City Journal-Post* and the *Kansas City Star* respectively, and both expressed interest in his stories. Charles Hanson Towne, editor of *Harper's Bazaar,* not only encouraged him to submit stories but also offered to serve as his agent, along with Howard, in placing stories unsuited for *Harper's Bazaar*. And finally to cap his rather extensive arrangements, if his writing ambitions all proved fruitless, he had the promise of a job with the Blackman Advertising Agency when he returned.[5]

Many years later Snow prepared a brief biographical sketch for Paul Freye who was then interviewing foreign correspondents on Armed Forces Radio Network from Tokyo. He remembered his job with a "Wall Street advertising firm":

> I wrote copy for paltry sums, which my friends invested for me when the stock market was still booming. One night I had a bad dream. I saw myself old and practically worthless at the age of 30, holding a check for $100,000 and hanging on to a crutch with the other. I decided it was just as easy to make $100,000 after 30 as before it, but not as easy to see the world. . . . I sold out my three shares of stock, took my profits, and went to sea as a sailor.

Over the years he threaded fanciful stories such as this into his vita. There is no mention of such stock-market profits in his many letters home during the early months of his voyage, perhaps because he still had not yet cleared up all of his debts to his family. If he truly had stock-market profits, he kept them quietly in reserve, for he worked his way to Hawaii and then, unable to find a berth and short of funds, brazenly, but successfully, stowed away from Honolulu to Yokohama.

In the autobiographical sketch he did for Freye he more convincingly remembered feeling he must seize the day before he lost his youth. From the *Radnor* he wrote his parents of his "intense eagerness to visit the more interesting countries of the world . . . before the imagination and spirit of my youth had dimmed." He had been "somewhat depressed by the monotony of existence and the thought I labored, a cog in the gargantuan machine, while youth, life, was slipping by. I wanted to fill my youth with something more than the pious, pitiful platitudes which I felt surrounded me."[6] His ardor suggests he may well have been just as frightened by the prospect of professional success when he sold the new advertising program to First National Bank of Jersey City as he was angered by Scovil's pinchpenny concern with his being on time.

Vagabond

2

First Success—and a Great Job

EARLY IN MARCH 1928 the *Radnor* reached Panama where it was delayed several days for engine repairs, giving Snow an opportunity to explore Panama City. When some paint fell in his eye, his captain sent him ashore to see a doctor. He immediately tried his hand at writing two articles about his experiences in Panama for Charles Hanson Towne, but neither reached print. He was able, however, to assure his parents, "I am healthy and happy. I am sunburned; my muscles are hardening; I never looked nor felt better in my life. The work on the ship is hard—but not always dull. My eyes and ears are weary with over-exertion."

Six days out of Panama trouble with two boilers caused the *Radnor* to limp along at six knots. The ship was originally scheduled to reach Honolulu March 25, but he now thought it would be fortunate to arrive by the end of March. His typical day was demanding: painting, sweeping, chipping paint, sandpapering from eight until noon; free from noon until eight, when he took a bath, rested, read, wrote, and spun yarns with the crew; dinner at five; and on lookout at eight, "standing in the 'eyes' (the prow) of the ship and watching for lights on the horizon." After four hours of this he lost no time in bedding down, and the open sky provoked him to ponder his true identity:

> In this clean, crisp, salty air one sleeps like a child again. Under a cerulean canopy, broken by bright, languid stars so near one feels one could reach out and grasp a handful to one's breast, I lie and marvel at the thought of my being here at all. I seem strongly to have been transferred to another

16

world. This sea, lulling me to sleep! That open starry sky above me and deep, deep silence aboard ship—how come I here and *am* I here, or is it some second self which I have sent out to find romance for my senses? Is the real Edgar drowsing in some office building in Manhattan, vicariously enjoying himself through this *me* on the *Radnor*?

Robert Johnson, son of Owen Johnson, author of *Stover at Yale* and other novels, was a passenger on board the *Radnor*. Johnson was going to Shanghai to understudy the correspondent of the *New York Times*. Snow then considered this "a tame ambition" and suspected Johnson had other plans he was not revealing. When Snow reached Shanghai early in July, he and Johnson would share a room at the YMCA.[1]

By March 26 the *Radnor* had not yet reached Honolulu but was expected to by the end of the week. Snow wrote his brother that he and Al were both putting on weight, and he was growing a mustache. His fellow sailors made him envious with their "sound, hard-muscled bodies, carefree blithesome spirits and their utter content in the unglorified lives they live." A particular veteran, named Morgan, at sea for twenty-two years, fascinated him. Morgan lived and traveled in "the Fiji Islands, the West Indies, Sumatra, Java, West Africa (the Belgian Congo), Afghanistan, Samoa, Pago-Pago, Calcutta, Egypt and Southern Spain. He keeps my brain whirling as I try to follow his stories which are laid one moment in the Far East and the next in a directly antipodal region. But always there is one breath-taking tale about Singapore—a spot which he seems to cherish more than any place else on earth." For this reason he was known among the sailors as Singapore Sam.

Snow was more willing to admit to Howard than to his parents that his travel was not all wonder and adventure, but even to Howard, at least this early, he deliberately emphasized the positive: "You will say I am omitting the 'sordid details'—giving a picture which is only half-true. Yes, there is plenty of unpleasantness—but why bring that up? One easily forgets the pain when any pleasurable sensation quickly follows it."

He told his family about meeting a twin to Aphrodite named Doris at a dream-cottage just off Waikiki: "She smiles like Janet Gaynor and plays golf like Miriam Burns. She has the imperiousness of proud young beauty, yet she is as naive, sweet, gentle, amiable—oh hell! I'd like to marry her! Unfortunately polygamy is not practiced any longer in the islands, or I might become her enslaved bread-winner. You see she is already married to my host of the second evening."

He described a Saturday evening of dancing, swimming, gardenias, and moonlight that carried into six o'clock Sunday morning and added up to "the most incomparably divine night of my life." Reluctantly, however, he also admitted, "We are working hard on the *Radnor:* chipping paint *sempre et sempre!*" Then he quickly glossed, "but who cares when Honolulu breathes on one every minute of the day and night."

The breath of Honolulu was sufficiently enticing for both he and Al to let the *Radnor* sail on without them. Joslin was ready for a vacation and then a return to Kansas City, while Snow was happy to have an interlude before pushing on to see more of the world.

He tried his hand again at an article for Towne. Like his letter to his family, "In Hula Land" is a fluffy, mildly humorous rhapsody to Hawaii as a tropical paradise. He gave no hint of being aware the American naval base in Hawaii was already the center of a dramatic competition shaping up for some time in the Pacific between American and Japanese national interests. Thirteen years later, finally on his way home, he would see Hawaii with very different eyes.

By May 11 the two Kansas Citians had opened a neat little stand on the grounds of the YMCA positioned to catch the attention of the sailors of the U.S. Pacific Fleet then on maneuvers in the area. They sold pineapple juice and fresh pineapples, whole and sliced, for the Hawaiian Pineapple Company. Each cleared between seven and eight dollars a day profit. There is no mention of such mundane activity in the *Harper's Bazaar* article, nor is there any hint the author had crudely worked his way to Honolulu as a lowly deck boy. Realism, like history, was not yet welcome.

He wrote his parents he was uncertain whether he would remain one more day or one more month. He was even then looking for a berth that would take him on toward Japan or the Philippines, but he grew more and more frustrated as his money ran out. Just when he had decided on the daring, but desperate, measure of stowing away on a Japanese liner for Yokohama, he received the kind of news from Towne that happened "only in Alger books" and that quickly had him "treading with winged sandals on clouds of pink bliss!" Towne accepted "In Hula Land" and paid handsomely for it: three hundred dollars. Snow's high hope had early turned into tangible success. His elation sustained him through his adventure as a stowaway, an adventure he would quickly turn into a second published success. As soon as he arrived in Japan he sent his parents the good news, remarking, "The Gods are infinitely gracious."[2]

His second article points more clearly to his later journalism, an adventure story combined with a contemporary event of potential historical interest. He added a touch of pathos by representing his decision to stow away as a sudden impulse triggered by his disappointment at learning the berth he thought he had on the *Yomachichi* had been given to another. Cursing his luck, he supposedly was about to return to the YMCA when he remembered a friend, Dan Crabbe—Dan Hopkins in the published accounts—was sailing that day on the *Shinyo Maru* as a passenger.

In fact he took sufficient time on June 12, the day of his departure, to get his first U.S. passport with Al Joslin as witness. His intention to depart on the *Shinyo Maru* the same day is written in his passport. A letter to Towne describing his adventure mentions no promised berth on the *Yomachichi*. He describes boarding the *Shinyo Maru* with Crabbe and sitting in his cabin uneventfully until the harbor pilot left the ship. He later gave the room boy a ten-yen bribe to overlook his presence.

The daughter of Tsuneo Matsudaira, the Japanese ambassador to the United States, with her parents, was also a passenger. She was engaged to marry Prince Chichibu of Japan. According to Snow's later story, he literally bumped into Ambassador Matsudaira one night and so made his acquaintance. That chance meeting led to an impromptu bridge game between Crabbe, Snow, Mrs. Matsudaira, and the princess-to-be.

On June 21, the day before landing at Yokohama, Snow wrote to Al Joslin from the first-class library. He cleared up the financial questions of their partnership in the pineapple-juice stand and explained his circumstances on the *Shinyo Maru*, particularly his danger of discovery: "Tomorrow morning at 9:00 the ship is due in Yokohama. If I can carry on the deception for another 24 hours there is a chance that I may get through undetected. I shall mark 'safe' on the outside of the envelope if I succeed. If not there will be a fancifully designed noose for a decoration of the envelope flap. . . ."

As Snow later developed his story the room boy warned Snow and Crabbe a search of the cabins was to be made because there was fear enemies of the Matsudairas were aboard. Snow successfully evaded discovery by spending the night in the shower room. He wrote Towne: "I managed to make the entire trip without once being questioned. . . . The only discomfort I suffered during the entire trip was one purely gastronomical." He referred to living on the one meal a day Crabbe could order served in the cabin, a breakfast of ham and eggs.

The ship's landing presented a dilemma. Passengers had their passports stamped by Japanese customs with a landing visa, but Snow could not submit his passport for fear of discovery. He later wrote, "Black failure smirked at me, grinned at me evilly. Visions of Japanese jails flooded my imagination." But a way out presented itself in the person of Charles Williamson, an English reporter for a Yokohama paper. Reporters did not need a landing visa to get off. A few minutes later Snow walked down the gangplank scanning the notes Williamson loaned him. Another reporter, in on the plot, walked close behind. As Snow came abreast of the customs authority, he showed his notes and stated, as if preoccupied, "Japan *Times.*" It worked.

Once on land he marked "SAFE" on the outside of his sealed letter to Joslin and sent it off. He then wrote up his adventures on board the *Shinyo Maru* and gave his story to O. D. Russell, news editor of the *Japan Advertiser,* to publish after his departure from Japan.

Two years later he published a portrait of Shanghai in *American Mercury* tailored to fit the satirical predilections of its editor H. L. Mencken. It produced indignant reaction in the *Shanghai Evening Post and Mercury.* One letter signed "Iowan" brought up Snow's earlier publication of the stowaway story in journalistic retaliation: "What harm can the story of [a] stowaway on a Japanese liner do? Sometimes nothing, but in this instance, the cabin-boy who brought the young fellow his meals was discharged from the service of the steamship company and was reduced to beggary. Because of the black mark against him, he was unable to find work." The freedom of the vagabond did not always square with his social responsibility.

Randall Gould, the editor of the *Shanghai Evening Post and Mercury,* also later remembered that Edgar Snow on a return voyage from India to Shanghai found himself on board a Japanese ship captained by the same man who had captained the *Shinyo Maru* on which Snow stowed away. This time the captain made very certain that Snow had a legitimate ticket.[3]

By June 29 Snow was in Tokyo writing a letter to his parents that was interrupted by contemporary history, in the form of a Japanese detective, knocking on his door. He was traveling in Japan with Dan Crabbe. In Tokyo he had put down *journalist* as his vocation on the hotel register. Japan's national ambitions on the Asian continent were already making the authorities very sensitive to the reports of foreign journalists. Hence the detective's call. The detective wanted to know how and where he had arrived in Japan. Snow answered by way of the *Shinyo Maru* at Yokohama. As soon as the detective left, he and Crabbe realized they must leave Tokyo immediately in case the detective decided to check the *Shinyo Maru*'s passenger list.

He and Crabbe traveled back down the coast without police interference to Yokohama, Fuji, Nagoya, Kyoto, Kobe, and finally Nagasaki, from which Snow shipped to Shanghai just a few days before finishing his letter.[4] He was heartbroken to find much of his first mail from home had been sent on to Manila for reasons he did not understand. Fortunately he had received a few letters before leaving Honolulu. Among them was Towne's informing him of the success of his Honolulu article.

He was uncertain whether he would stay three weeks or three months in Shanghai. If a berth on a boat sailing for the Philippines or India were available he might leave at once. Otherwise he would try to get a job and remain until fall. Meanwhile he was staying at the Navy YMCA.

By late July, Snow had received a very worried letter from his mother. His letters could not always be promptly mailed. There had been a dearth of mail from him before she began receiving detailed news of his stowaway trip aboard the *Shinyo Maru* and his later travels throughout the islands of Japan. He sent her a cable at a cost of nine dollars, a prohibitive expense, and then wrote a longer reassuring letter:

> I am the luckiest person. Not only do I get articles printed in *Harper's Bazaar*, manage to be the only individual who ever stowed away success- fully on a Japanese liner to Japan and lived to tell the story in Shanghai, but when I arrive in latter port succeed in getting one of the prize jobs of the year! I have just been taken on the staff of *The China Weekly Review*, at $Shanghai 400 [*sic*] per month, a princely salary on which one can become simply filthy with luxury out here on the fringes of the world.

He quickly warned his parents against inferring he intended "to fertilize in China for the next ten thousand years." He planned to remain only until "the torrid heat of the tropics" subsided. Then he would "leave the heathen and go forth to conquer such fantastic names as Malaysia, Burma, Siam, Afghanistan, Persia, Arabia," all places he had named to them before. At the latest he expected to be back in New York by next May.

He was happy to report Joslin "got a job on the *City of Honolulu*, as waiter, and worked his way back to the coast." Snow assumed he was back in Kansas City by this time and suggested his mother "Make him come round to see you and tell you what a dreamy place Hawaii is—and how it feels to be broke there." He also asked for news of what happened to the pineapple stand.

His finances were below nothing, so he simply could not afford sending presents from Japan. If he was traveling on stock-market profits his parents were clearly not in the know. He borrowed money from Crabbe, his traveling companion in Japan, and still had to pay him back. But in addition to now having a well-paying job, he still luxuriated in the news of receiving his first substantial fee for his writing and even more in Towne's praise: "There are really very beautiful passages in this manuscript." But he worried that his success in this article was wholly due to the exceptional nature of his subject: "Hawaii is such an unearthly beautiful place that anyone who writes at all should write of it only in an immortal vein. I feel convinced that I shall never be able to write so enthusiastically again."[5]

3

The China Maelstrom

E DGAR SNOW'S "PRIZE JOB" in Shanghai was assistant advertising manager of the *China Weekly Review*. He was hired by an experienced China observer and University of Missouri alumnus, J. B. Powell, who had come to Shanghai before America entered the First World War to assist another Missouri graduate, Thomas Fairfax Millard, in publishing a weekly paper, *Millard's Review of the Far East*. Powell had assumed control of the weekly in 1923 and renamed it the *China Weekly Review*.

Soon after arriving in Shanghai, Snow wrote his father with pride, listing nine new accounts he had acquired for the *China Weekly Review*. Since the staff was small, it was understood from the beginning that Snow would be expected to do more than solicit advertisements. He soon wrote his brother he was regularly contributing to articles as well as working on the advertising. He had three in the last issue, and "last week I contributed my first editorial."

Powell was then planning a special "New China" edition "to show the diehards that the nationalists are here to stay." During the near panic in the international settlement in Shanghai created by the Northern Expedition's capture of Hankow and Nanking in 1927, the American Chamber of Commerce had held a hurried meeting and contrary to its own bylaws had tried to expel Powell from its ranks. Powell early supported Chiang Kai-shek, while many in the American community still considered him a bolshevik.

Snow's first signed article, "Lifting China out of the Mud," appeared in the "New China" issue. It was the traditional break-in for a young journalist: a statistical report of the extent of paved roads in China. He boasted to Howard: "The New China Number is the most successful special issue we have ever produced." Its one hundred advertisers and total revenue of fifteen thousand dollars were particularly gratifying to Mr. Powell, who "has been under a boycott from all foreign advertisers, because of his independent attitude as expressed editorially during the recent unpleasantness in Shanghai." Snow might later disagree with Powell about Nationalist politics, but he enthusiastically applauded his belief in the democratic responsibility of the journalist to report news the people *needed* to know whether they *wanted* to or not.

Snow also explained to his father: "You see J. B. is the one English-speaking foreigner who is more or less pro-Chinese in every dispute between the 'peaceful invaders' and the yellow men. He is the champion of their every cause. This not only arouses the ire of the British, but plagues the American money-grabbers as well."

Snow was happy to find the American press represented primarily by Missouri graduates and consequently attracting the brunt of criticism from prominent business and banking interests, particularly the British. Finding the Missourians impossible to control, such interests took to "calling us all sorts of names; among them such diverting appellations as 'The Corn-Cobbers,' 'The Prize Pumpkins from Missouri,' and, [most] priceless of them all, 'The Cowboy Correspondents.' " While it might be true "that the spirit of the Missourians is essentially that of mule-drivers and corn-cobbers," it is even more undoubtedly true that "we have a deep and fundamental dislike of the superiority complex of the British in the East, as manifested by their colonial policies and further imperialistic ambitions." He also proudly insisted it could not be denied "there are a number of gentlemen from the Show-me state who persist in serving as goddam good journalists."

A few weeks before his first article appeared and only about four weeks after he had arrived in Shanghai, Snow was offered the position of editor of the *Hankow Herald*. He wrote his mother: "Of course I refused the job . . . on the basis I was obligated to Mr. Powell, that I was uncertain as to how long I'd remain in China and that I had no fancy for being buried in a god-forsaken dump controlled by the slant-eyes."[1] This is a rare instance of a crude stereotype in Snow's letters from China, but it is worth noting to measure the distance in understanding he soon traveled.

There was a substantial history lesson for Snow to absorb behind the quarrel between Powell and the American business community. China was in the midst of a convulsive effort to give birth to a modern nation. Despite his unwavering self-identification as an American, J. B. Powell witnessed this birth as a sincere friend of China and was inevitably deeply involved in the trauma. By World War I the Manchu dynasty had clearly demonstrated its incapacity to reform the nation. Dr. Sun Yat-sen articulated the case for more revolutionary change with broadly compelling cogency but showed little talent for the extraordinary task of organizing his ideas into practical revolutionary action.

Intellectuals and students were attracted to democratic ideas from the West but felt deeply the shame of the Western nations' extraterritorial presence in China. The Versailles peace treaty of 1919 ignited an explosion of national pride and anti-Western resentment. Since China had declared war on Germany in 1917, and since President Woodrow Wilson's Fourteen Points included the principle of national self-determination, it had been widely expected the German possessions in Shantung Province taken over early in the war by the Japanese would be returned to China. When these possessions were awarded to Japan as a consequence of British and French agreements designed to bring Japan to the side of the Allies in the war, Powell witnessed China's sense of betrayal. University students throughout China took to the streets in clamorous protest, initiating what is celebrated today as the May Fourth Movement.

Just two months later the young revolutionary Soviet government of Russia, recognizing the opportunity to extend its influence to the peoples of Asia increasingly rebellious against European colonialism, dramatically proclaimed its intention to: return to China all territory seized by the former czarist government; return the Chinese Eastern Railway to China without asking for compensation; refuse all further indemnity payments from the Boxer rebellion; renounce all extraterritorial privileges; and render null and void all unfair agreements forced by the former czarist government. The contrast between this initial Soviet response to those of Western nations from the point of view of the Chinese nationalist was striking. Thus communism gained credence as an anti-imperialist force, and close ties were developed between the revolutionary new Soviet government of Russia and the struggling nationalist movement in China.

Powell was deeply suspicious of this developing relationship, and he, along with a significant portion of the American press and Congress, disapproved the ceding of the rights formerly held by Germany in Shantung to Japan in the Versailles peace treaty. That proved a significant factor in the U.S. Senate rejection of American participation in the League of Nations, and in 1922 it was in part responsible for an international conference to be held in Washington at which Japan agreed to withdraw its troops from Shantung, restore German interests in Tsingtao, and cede control of the port and railways to China. Powell played an active role in the Washington conference. The verbal agreements of the conference were for the most part welcomed in China, but the Chinese had good reason to be skeptical of such paper proclamations.

Sun Yat-sen, finally presiding as president of a government in Canton still unrecognized by most foreign nations, sent Chiang Kai-shek to Russia in the fall of 1923. Chiang, like Powell, was early skeptical of Soviet promises of support and deeply suspicious of the intraparty quarrels he could readily observe there. While Chiang was in Russia, Mikhail Borodin, Comintern representative, arrived in Canton and quickly won Dr. Sun's respect. Dr. Sun himself visited Russia in 1924. Upon Chiang's return to Canton he deeply impressed Borodin and in the fall of 1925 moved from his position as director of Whampoa Military Academy to command the Cantonese Army. Dr. Sun died in March of that year. Chiang's reservations about proletarian revolution were subsequently clearly signaled, though not openly declared, by his permitting a warlord ally to organize hoodlums in Canton into a "Central Labor Union" during the famous Canton–Hong Kong strike that paralyzed British shipping with astonishing effectiveness in early 1926. This phantom Central Labor Union was then used to break the strike.

Chiang Kai-shek soon became chairman of the Kuomintang Central Committee. The committee at the time was composed predominantly of leftists. While all the key players claimed to operate under Sun Yat-sen's revolutionary mantle, a deadly power struggle was waged under its folds. In the summer of 1926 the Northern Expedition set out from Canton to defeat the warlords and unify the country under the Kuomintang. The most aggressive military forces, those that marched on Hankow and Nanking, were led by generals sympathetic to the Left. Chiang Kai-shek characteristically husbanded the strength of his forces by refraining from aggressive combat. The capital was moved from Canton to Wuhan, the collective name for the adjacent cities of Hankow, Wuchang, and Hanyang and a much more central position in China than Canton in the extreme south. Eugene Chen, Sun Fo (the son of Sun Yat-sen), Soong Ching-ling (Sun Yat-sen's widow), and Mikhail Borodin were among the first political leaders to move to Hankow from Canton.

Mao Tse-tung seemed peripheral at the time. He attended the Second Congress of the Kuomintang that met in Shanghai in May 1926, but in December he was sent to Hunan, where as inspector of the peasant movement in the remote interior he was eventually to build a more substantial Communist base than his more prominent urban-oriented comrades in the Wuhan government. By the early months of 1927 Borodin's highly visible role in the government, plus some very real, but much sensationalized, threats to the foreign community during the fall of Nanking, and the surprising meekness of the British surrender in Hankow, all made the International Settlement in Shanghai very uneasy about the leadership of the Kuomintang government, as indicated by the angry reaction to the news reports and editorials of the *China Weekly Review.*

Shanghai had a particularly confusing and troubled history during these events. There was massive leftist sympathy among the workers and students, but opposing them were the leaders of the Green Gang, who after many years of suspicious coexistence had reached a tacit understanding with representatives of foreign governments and business interests in the International Settlement and with heads of Chinese banks, many of which they had penetrated. Chiang Kai-shek recruited and then worked closely with Green Gang leaders to undermine an effort to seize control of Shanghai by Communist-led workers in October 1926. The first massacre of striking workers followed.

Chou En-lai arrived in Shanghai immediately after this fiasco on assignment from the Kuomintang to rebuild the power of the labor unions and the students. By February 19, 1927, he had succeeded sufficiently for the unions to call a general strike in anticipation of the Kuomintang army's entrance into the city three days later. But Chiang Kai-shek's forces were still safely settled in Nanchang. On the day of the strike Chiang gave a broad public hint of his intentions toward the Communists by publicly blaming the failure of Dr. Sun Yat-sen's revolution on there being too many disparate elements within the Kuomintang and announcing, "The time has come to expel them [the counterrevolutionaries] since they are not true believers."

The Left in retrospect seemed almost willfully and suicidally naïve in trusting Chiang so long, but it was also seriously handicapped by the authority Comintern agents held within the government. Stalin was isolating Trotsky within the Communist Party. The two deeply disagreed about the strength of Chiang Kai-shek and the necessity of Chinese Communists working with him. The Stalin-controlled Comintern insisted on seeing Chiang Kai-shek as the only effective leader of the Chinese revolution and so directed its agents in the Hankow government. Stalin's persistent support of Chiang Kai-shek would continue to amaze and anger Edgar Snow throughout his years in China.

The February 19 strike in Shanghai quickly became another murderous fiasco. British, American, and French police in the International Settlement arrested students handing out leaflets and turned the students over to the soldiers of the ruling warlord. The *New York Herald Tribune* carried the story of their grim fate and the gruesome consternation caused by the public display of their severed heads. This immediate bloody reaction to the strike was only the initial horror. Even while concluding arrangements with the Shanghai bankers and the leader of the Green Gang, Huang Ching-yung, better known as Huang Mapi, or in English as Pock-marked Huang, Chiang Kai-shek was hailed by communists around the world. The Russian newspaper *Pravda*, the German *Rote Fahne*, the French *L'Humanité*, as well as internationally recognized Red leaders—Earl Browder of the United States, Jacques Doriot of France, and Tom Mann of England—all praised Chiang Kai-shek, as did Joseph Stalin in Moscow. One can understand how such endorsements might linger in the minds of the Shanghai American business community.

Chiang's deal concluded, the famous April massacre was unleashed. Chou En-lai estimated the toll at five thousand lives in a later interview with Edgar Snow. Chou himself was captured by General Pai Chung-hsi and ordered executed. But the general had a brother who had been Chou's student at the Whampoa Military Academy, and the brother helped Chou escape.

In his autobiography published in 1945 J. B. Powell retold a story of Stirling Fessenden, the American chairman of the International Settlement. Fessenden told Powell how he worked with the Green Gang and French officials in the last days of February 1927 to thwart the ambitions of the Reds. Tu Yueh-sheng, another Green Gang leader then ascending to extraordinary power, demanded at least five thousand rifles and ample ammunition from the French and permission from Fessenden to move his trucks through the International Settlement. Tu got what he wanted. Even in 1945 Powell told this story with firm and righteous relish. He never wavered in his faith in Chiang Kai-shek.

In *Journey to the Beginning*, Snow told of learning about the deal Tu cut with Fessenden, not from Powell, but from Ho Chih-hsiang, the Chinese editor of the *China Weekly Review*. He also added that Lin Yu-tang, with whom Snow later developed a friendly, but contentious, relation, pointed out to him the irony of Chiang Kai-shek's subsequent appointment of Tu as chief of the bureau of opium suppression. Tu held a "virtual monopoly of the opium business in the lower Yangtze area." But these early insights into the murky intrigue of Kuomintang politics were as yet only seeds. They would blossom into significant differences between him and Powell only some time later: "In the Thirties we foreigners and respectable Chinese alike felt that Mr. Tu and Mr. Chiang had saved China from 'the mob.' Talking it over with business men and with J. B. Powell, I concluded that the sacrifice had been necessary and that the *Review*'s policy was right. Powell believed that this one quick firm action had 'saved China from the Communists.'" Snow, writing years later, then added with pointed irony, "By China we meant, of course, Shanghai."

Despite the differences between Snow and Powell that would eventually emerge and later widen significantly in their assessment of Chiang Kai-shek and the menace of the communist threat, a strong bond of professional and personal respect formed very early between them and endured through Snow's China years. It is perhaps a curious indirect testament to this respect that Powell's memory plays a trick upon him in his memoir when writing about Chiang Kai-shek's 1927 attack upon the Left in Shanghai. He refers to Snow's account in *Red Star over China* but indicates Snow was at the time of the Shanghai incident already on the staff of the *China Weekly Review*.[2] Snow, of course, did not arrive in Shanghai until more than a year later.

4

Manchuria and the
Threat from Japan

SNOW WAS A QUICK learner. Only three weeks after arriving in Shanghai he wrote his mother of the danger posed by the extraordinary concentration of international political forces in China. A very critical situation already existed between the new Nationalist government and the Japanese: "War over Manchuria is quite apt to be the outcome. These activities will be centered beyond the Great Wall and will, of course, in no way conflict with my peace of corpus. I could scarcely have chosen a more interesting period in which to arrive in China." Snow's reassurance was sincere, but he was very soon professionally involved in China's conflict with Japan.

Japan's triumph over Russia in 1905, the first victory of an Asian over a European nation in modern times, gave substantial stimulus to its budding ambition to challenge Western encroachment in Asia by replacing it. When Germany became preoccupied with fighting the Allies in World War I, Japan seized its opportunity, invaded Shantung, and captured Tsingtao, Shantung's major port. To China's great indignation, as noted earlier, the Treaty of Versailles awarded the German Shantung concessions to Japan, implicitly endorsing the Alice-in-Wonderland view that Japan had attacked German forces there in the interest of protecting China.

Japan dragged its feet on the agreements made in Washington in 1922 to withdraw its troops from Shantung, restore German interests in Tsingtao, and cede control of the port and railways to China, and it openly continued to develop its naval power contrary to its pledge to limit its navy to three-fifths the size of the separate British and American navies. The United States apparently saw no means of enforcing the Washington agreements and was reluctant to spend the money to maintain its agreed-upon naval superiority. Many, including J. B. Powell, saw the attack on Pearl Harbor nearly twenty years later as a direct consequence.

For years there had been contention within Japan between a relatively liberal, internationally minded political party and an aggressively nationalistic set of military officers. From 1927 to 1929 the military officers, led by Baron Giichi Tanaka, were in power. Late in 1927 the Chinese press published the infamous Tanaka Memorial, ostensibly a report by Baron Tanaka to the emperor rationalizing the need for Japanese expansion into Manchuria and eventually into other areas of the Pacific to challenge the American presence. Snow had probably picked up on the concern generated by this alleged document when he wrote his mother of the Japanese danger. The memorial has never been unquestionably authenticated, but its broad outlines proved sufficiently accurate to give it wide credence, particularly in China, from late 1927 through World War II. In *Far Eastern Front*, Snow warned the public at large of the dangers outlined in the Tanaka Memorial. Under Baron Tanaka's rule Japan moved back into Shantung in 1927.

Thus in May of the next year, when Chiang Kai-shek's armies moved into Tsinan, the capital of Shantung, on their Northern Expedition against the warlords, and while Edgar Snow was minding his pineapple stand in Honolulu, the Japanese were still there. A clash occurred, probably initiated by rowdy Nationalist troops violating their orders. But the conflict that followed degenerated into flagrant mutual atrocities. This provided an excuse for the Japanese quickly to bring in a superior force and occupy Tsinan, declaring it a neutral territory. On June 4 the Japanese added a most ominous message by blowing up the railway car of Chang Tso-lin, the warlord ruler of Manchuria, on his way to Mukden from Peking.

Months after the fighting in Shantung had stopped, charges were made that the Japanese had again violated the agreements reached at the Washington conference by impounding much of the rolling stock of the Chinese railways that passed through Tsinan and interrupting the flow of railway traffic. The charges were commonly accepted as true. Hence, there was considerable surprise when the Japanese legation in Peking on December 9 issued the uncompromising denial: "The Japanese have not in the past held up any rolling stock nor have they any intention of doing so or of interfering in any way with the administration of the railway."

Sun Fo, who was then minister of Railways, immediately saw the opportunity and announced a public test of the Japanese statement. He arranged a special railway car to travel from Pukow to Tsinan. He invited J. B. Powell to be on the car. Powell could not leave Shanghai at the time and sent Snow, now five months in China, in his place. Snow joined two other Western witnesses: A. J. Hearne, chief engineer of the southern division of the Tsinpu Railway, who was British, and Alfred Batson of the *North China Daily News*. Snow's first published story with significant international implications appeared in the *China Weekly Review* on January 12, 1929.

Their train was stopped many times, usually by Chinese railway officials obeying Japanese orders. Finally at Taianfu, twenty-five miles south of Tsinan, their train was allowed to proceed no further. Another locomotive was dispatched from Tsinan to carry Hearne alone to Tsinan. The two American journalists were to be driven by auto. Hearne refused such terms and insisted the special car with all three aboard be taken to Tsinan. He seemed to win his point. But after numerous delays, the train was finally stopped at Hsiachung, just three miles south of Tsinan for final permission to enter the city. The party then decided to walk the final three miles rather than wait through another delay. They had left Pukow at 9:00 A.M., Saturday, December 29. It was now noon, Monday, December 31. The trip ordinarily would take less than half that time.

Just north of Hsiachung they passed the repair depot where they could see a large number of railway cars parked. Snow talked to the manager of the yard who said there were 51 locomotives, 33 passenger cars, 9 service cars, and 492 goods wagons in the yard. All but 10 percent could roll. Hearne tried to negotiate the release of the railway cars with the Japanese in charge to no avail. Finally he asked what the Japanese would do if he ordered the rolling stock released. Mr. Nishida replied, "In that event it is quite possible you might be prevented—by military force if necessary." Snow concluded his account with obvious irony, "And yet the Japanese continue to claim they never have interfered with the administration of the railway nor have they any intention of so doing."

In world politics the incident at Tsinan is a minor affair. But it was Edgar Snow's first firsthand experience of how the Japanese blandly covered aggression with a big lie. Still the full gravity of what he witnessed had to compete for his attention with a reminder of the desire for youthful adventure that brought him to China. He wrote his brother at length about his fellow correspondent Alfred Batson. Besides being an "ex-Canadian army officer, ex-Nicaraguan revolutionary, ex-seaman, ex-cross country walker, ex-actor, ex-oh, a score of different high sounding things," Batson had been a personal advisor to Sandino for sixteen months. Forced to flee when the marines moved in, Batson retreated through Central America and Mexico, beginning with only $1.88 in his pocket. He was "royally entertained by presidents and generals, captured by bandits, fed upon bananas and tortillas, attacked by giant cobras, seduced by glowing senoritas, pursued by the Mexican army and, finally, escorted with a guard of honor, across the Rio Grande." His experiences were to be published that spring under the title *Beating Back through Central America*. Snow did, however, find one of his traits most objectionable, "he simply cannot forget that he went to Harvard."

Besides becoming acquainted with Batson, this Tsinan trip gave Snow a good bit of exposure in the Chinese press: "Newspapers all over the country played it for front page stuff. . . . You see it was reported that we had been arrested and were arbitrarily being detained by the Japanese military authorities." Editorials protesting their supposed arrest followed. Snow for the first time became widely identified in the Chinese press by the character meaning "white cloud."

Snow's article on the trip to Tsinan served Sun Fo's purpose admirably. It is therefore not surprising that Snow was soon writing home of his hopes for an invitation from Sun Fo to make an extensive trip over China's railways to report on the scenic and historic wonders still available to tourists. His reports were to be put together in special issues of the *China Weekly Review* and also collected as independent booklets. Such a trip also offered attractive possibilities for independent travel stories.[1]

When fighting broke out again in the area of Wuhan, Snow's railway trip seemed out for the time, but he made clear to his father he was at no loss for opportunities. He was offered a consulate job in Sourabaya, Java, for five months but declined: "What do I know about signing treaties?" A more tempting offer arose from Millard's decision to become an adviser to the National Government and resign his position as correspondent for the *New York Herald Tribune*. Snow later often acknowledged Millard, along with Powell, as an early China mentor. Powell recommended Snow as a replacement for Millard, and the position was offered on a trial basis. "But of course I shall have to refuse it. I am determined not to be sidetracked, even by so luscious a plum, from the goal I am supposed to be striving toward."

Finally, Powell offered him the post of associate editor of the *China Weekly Review* at an increased salary. George Missemer, another member of the editorial staff, was to be away on a long trip. "I cannot, simply cannot accept. And yet I do hate to refuse J. B. for he has been incredibly kind to me. But if I permit myself to become harnessed in this job (which, by the way, I could handle in addition to the *H-T*'s work), I know the grim future that is ahead of me."

He clearly had to be vigilant to retain his freedom and independence:

> Wotta life. It is a grand scheme to defeat one's purpose; an outrageous alliance of the gods to blind one with inconsequentials that lash one to mediocrity. As soon as we stand still very long, life seems to have a way of placing us, of gently but inevitably forcing us into a respectable groove.
> So you see, I've *got* to get out of here. Or very soon I shall find myself bound to a promise that I shall despise. I think that I shall leave here, regardless of any plans or hopes unrealized, by May 1st. I cannot endure the thought of being away from home any longer than such a date of departure will mean.

But again Snow did not go home. Often lonely and deeply valuing his family's letters, he seemed more reluctant to return than he was ready to acknowledge, even to himself. His letter hinted why.

Acknowledging that his and Howard's absence was no cause for happiness, he nevertheless hoped his father and mother might use the occasion to grow dearer to each other and to rediscover "the zest of the young dream of faith that you had before you were burdened with children." He assured his father: "Nothing can make me more aware of life's values than the assurance that you and mother still are very important to each other. Nothing can make me more despondent than the fear that you are inadequate to the point of unhappiness."

Shortly after arriving in Shanghai, Snow wrote his mother reassuringly that he had attended mass at St. Joseph's, "the church nearest to my present address." But his letter gave far more attention to the beggars he encountered outside the church than to the mass held within. It typified his internalization of the conflict between his father's hard-searching skepticism and his mother's warmly personal, but unconvincing, faith. He closed his long letter to his father apologizing for his open and earnest sentimentalism: "But I do want you to know that I love you, and I love mother, and that together you are a something to me, a meaning, a truth on which I lean and nourish myself, and in you and your love and faith I replenish all the dreams that I am capable of conceiving. I confess that I am proud that you are my dad, and I want to make you proud that I am your son."[2]

By April his ambitious railway trip was on again, and Snow soon traveled the Shanghai-Hangchow-Ningpo line to write the first of his four installments. His trip took him through Shaohsing, the birthplace of Lu Hsun, whose writing within a year would begin to make a marked impression on him.

His second trip was on the Shanghai-Nanking line, again made in April, though the account was not published until August 10. In accord with his eagerness to see China modernized he gave special attention to Wusih as an industrial center comparable to Manchester, England. Although Wusih had few of the scenic or historic attractions of Soochow, ancient capital of the Kingdom of Wu, or of Yangchow, the city ruled by Marco Polo to which Snow traveled by auto on a side trip, he insisted the traveler "will leave Wusih with a light heart, in which has been born a new feeling of confidence and of hope. Do not forget it when you are faced with the more depressing scenes of ignorance and helplessness that are bound to greet you in your travels through less enlightened districts of China. . . . In Wusih, we repeat, is the concrete evidence of the dawning of New China."

As for Nanking, only recently again proclaimed capital of China by Chiang Kai-shek, Snow was studiedly neutral in his observations. He reviewed its legacy from the Ming dynasty and acknowledged it was the choice of Sun Yat-sen for a capital as well as now the site of his impressive tomb. Although he passed through Nanking a month prior to the ritual interment of Sun Yat-sen's remains in the tomb, a significant effort by Chiang Kai-shek to cloak himself in Sun's mantle, he gave no hint of such political implications.

At the end of this second trip Snow received a letter from his brother announcing the latter had placed an article of his in the professional magazine *Advertising and Selling* and also announcing that Howard had now assumed a very well-paying position as eastern manager of advertising for the *Chicagoan*. The letter made him feel once more the light goad of sibling rivalry: "Of course I am glad for you; happy to know that you are getting on. Your wonderful salary truly awes me, and in a way the news is a little depressing, it is only natural for me to have the selfish reaction that causes me to catch up with you when (if ever) I return." He hastened to add that Howard should not take his parenthetic comment seriously: "I am going to leave China as soon as this trip is done. Nothing will persuade me to stay away from home any longer than that will necessitate."

Howard's letter contained a peroration on leaving their old apartment on 56 West Fifty-fifth Street that drew Snow's praise: "I could not have uttered a better elegy. All those long seasons' dreams that I have brought away from that place!" Although some of their experiences were not pleasant, he still believed "they were perhaps the best years we've thus far had together." But the memory of Jack's inevitable evening greeting, "Back again the same day, eh?" still symbolized the "world of puerile half-living, of triteness and banality" from which he had fled.

Snow's third railroad trip was a long journey northward on the Blue Express that began in Pukow and ended in Tientsin. Two-thirds of this journey was a repeat of the trip Snow had made only a few months earlier to test the Japanese statement of noninterference in railway affairs. This time he left

Shanghai on May 27 and passed through Tientsin to arrive at Mukden on the fourth leg of his trip by June 2. There was now sufficient understanding between Chinese and Japanese authorities in Shantung so that Snow's train proceeded through Tsinan without trouble.

These railway journeys, first through the southern region of the fertile Yangtze valley and then northward to the harsher climate and geography of the land of ancient pride and contemporary military conflict, were for Snow a valuable primer to China's history and culture and a brief exposure to the hopes and possibilities of its industrial progress.

The fourth and last leg of his journey, however, through Manchuria, introduced him to a coveted land simmering with the international conflict he had already noted in his letters home. The Trans-Siberian Railway was in those days a modern marvel. It brought Peking within twelve days of Paris, "a feat of transportation which it has taken the world some hundreds of years to accomplish. It is a saving of 200% in time over the old water route through Suez, and the economy in cash is almost as great." It made Manchuria the eastern gateway to Europe. But Manchuria was also a land of great "expanses of fertile magnificent plains, so like the picture with which every middle-western American is familiar and for whom this country will naturally have a special endearment."

Many European nations and the United States had substantial economic and political interests in Manchuria, but it was the immediate backyard of Russia, Japan, and Korea, while officially acknowledged as belonging to China. Korea was then completely under the control of Japan. In his article on the railway trip Snow recognized that "the casual tourist (for whom this is primarily written) will scarcely have time to delve very deeply into the labyrinthine channels of a situation so complex and fraught with difficulties even for the deeper student of Far Eastern conditions."

But he detailed these labyrinthine international interests before focusing on those of the United States in a letter to his mother from Mukden. Few knew that "we held a dominant rank in countries exporting to the provinces of Kirin and Fengtien" or that "our financial interest in the Peiping-Mukden Railway has been responsible for our keeping American marines stationed along points of that line ever since the Boxer Days." He sympathized with "poor chaotic China" who was "trying her best to control this territory, over which she nominally has full sovereignty." He closed, noting it was difficult to forecast what was to happen to the territory then "governed" by "the bland young man" he was to meet the next morning.

The next day Snow had an appointment with Chang Hsueh-liang, popularly known as the Young Marshall. In *Journey to the Beginning*, Snow indicated he first met W. H. Donald, the legendary Australian journalist, on this trip to Mukden and acknowledged him as the source of an article he later published in the *China Weekly Review* that covered much the same ground as his letter to his mother.

In 1929 Chang Hsueh-liang, not yet thirty, was seen as an opium-addicted playboy who still had to prove he was capable of filling the shoes of his bluff and cagy warlord father, Chang Tso-lin, the Old Marshall, whose railway car was blown up by the Japanese almost precisely one year earlier. Snow published his interview with Chang Hsueh-liang separately, but in his railway article he commented graphically on what the Young Marshall inherited from his father. He first described the former as having "a fine, intelligent forehead, a strong straight nose that suggests Manchu blood, and the boldly chiseled features of an aristocrat." His Western clothes and outlook made him "known as the Chesterfield of China." Then, however, he quietly noted, "the recent execution of two subordinate generals, whom he summarily dispatched, after having invited them to his home for a mahjong party" made it clear "he has the determination of his father."[3]

Snow returned to Shanghai and as acting editor published the article he wrote from Donald's briefing. In *Journey to the Beginning* he described the early prediction he made of Japanese aggression in this article as rash. It was rash in that it took two years to be fulfilled, but the article nevertheless is an early example of the predictive journalism that ultimately won him an international reputation. It asked, "Which Way Manchuria?" and is in effect an unintended preface to his later book on the Japanese aggression in Manchuria, *Far Eastern Front*.

Japanese ownership and management of the South Manchurian Railway had led to striking economic development and prosperity in southern Manchuria, a development and prosperity that almost certainly would not have occurred under Chinese ownership and management, given the chaotic history of the government of China during the years of Japanese control of the railway. Japan had wrung the rights to this railway from China in the treaty of 1905 that followed Japan's defeat of Russia. That same treaty forbade China the construction "of any main railway in the neighborhood of or parallel to" the South Manchurian Railway, "or any branch line which might be prejudicial to the interests of the above railway." These treaty rights were reconfirmed in the Washington conference of 1922 despite the efforts to curb Japanese power and influence in other areas.

Japan repeatedly insisted her economic activities in China were without political ambition, "her aim was simply and solely to make Chinese Manchuria prosperous and progressive, to create a new source or supply of raw materials for Japanese industry, and a new market for Japanese goods, as well as those of other countries." Snow saw Japan's economic power over this prosperous area of Manchuria in fact making it into another Korea, already politically as well as economically a Japanese colony. Recognizing this threat, Nanking and Chang Hsueh-liang belatedly planned to develop railways both to the west and to the north of the South Manchurian Railway. Some of these plans almost certainly involved violations of the existing treaties. In addition there were vague, if not forlorn, hopes of developing the Chinese port of Hulutao. Japan had tightened its economic control of the railway with loans to a corrupt national government of China that had quickly dissipated the funds.

It was this knot of economic and political interests that caused Snow to ask "Which Way Manchuria?" Since China's debts were great and its government as yet weak, he saw little prospect of China being able to buy her way out of this dilemma by paying off her loans through her own efforts or sufficiently borrowing to do so from outside sources. As a consequence

> the presence of such large Japanese capital in Manchuria must remain the most dangerous existing threat to China's sovereignty. To say this, it is not necessary to overlook the numerous benefits resulting from the introduction of that capital. It has been indelibly impressed upon the world that the gifts of the conqueror to the conquered are ever bitter—and in the end costly. This is peculiarly so in Manchuria. . . . Let her interests be endangered in the slightest, and it is difficult to believe Japan would hesitate to invade Manchuria, placing her military machine in control.

Snow observed that anyone who has traveled the railway zones and talked with the Japanese in Manchuria must feel a pervasive conviction among them that "until the Rising Sun floats unrivalled across South Manchuria, Japan cannot rest." He closed his article by speculating on the conditions under which Japan would create an incident as an excuse for invasion. Two years later, on September 18 and 19, 1931, such an incident was created in Mukden, and the Japanese invasion that followed was swift and effective.[4]

When Snow published this article in the *China Weekly Review*, J. B. Powell was in Manchuria covering the threat of war *not* between China and Japan, but between China and Russia. Baron Giichi Tanaka's ministry in Japan fell that same month primarily over his failure to persuade the army to punish the officers who were responsible for the assassination of the Old Marshall, Chang Tso-lin. Baron Tanaka died September 29, 1929. But the Chinese-Russian crisis Powell covered was eventually resolved, and the militaristic nationalism of Baron Tanaka lived on. When war did come in Manchuria, it was between China and Japan.

5

The Cost of "a line or
two that may not die"

F ROM MUKDEN AT THE end of his railway tour Snow tried to explain
to his mother why the three weeks he had originally allotted to China
had now stretched to nearly a year:

> In another 47 days I shall be 24 years old. (This is not a reminder to
> send me a greeting card with forget-me-nots and roses, inscribed with
> the conventional mother-to-son-on-his-birthday slush.) A little less than
> a year ago I was fretting in Honolulu, worrying about when I could get
> the next boat that would take me home in 60 days. Never, in my remotest
> dreams, did I imagine that this month would find me in this hinterland
> of civilization, miles away from my friends, and a three day journey to
> even the nearest of my Far Eastern acquaintance. And yet men speak
> of planning their lives. Well, I suppose we do, to a certain extent. But
> certainly I have not willed to stay away from home so long. There is some
> larger influence behind it all, someone else who pulls the strings. Of this
> I cannot but think, as I plan today (as I planned six months ago) to take
> my leave of China, and all things, Sinoese, in the very near future.

From Manchuria, Snow returned to Peking for a holiday. But the awaiting
mail brought him news that initially destroyed any sense of celebration. It was
an experience that for a brief time made the vanity of human planning very
personal. At the beginning of his railway journey he had toured University
Hospital in Soochow. In a tuberculosis ward a Chinese "supported on either
side by a distraught concubine" staggered in. "Quite obviously the poor devil
was in the last reaches of consumption." The doctor coolly "estimated the

number of days the old pipe-hitter would last." The incident impressed Snow enough that he invested twenty dollars in an X ray of his chest.

Once outside in the sun his fears of tuberculosis seemed absurd, and he confidently looked forward to the doctor's report confirming the good health he felt. The report was supposed to reach him in Nanking, but it was delayed, only finally reaching him in Peking with a large batch of other private and business mail. Impatiently he searched through the medical jargon to read with disbelief: "So you see it is urgent. . . . That you put yourself in the care of a physician at once . . . suggest Dr. Dunn . . . those are marks which indicate old lesions of tuberculosis . . . and the shadows at present in your lower lungs, particularly your right . . . show very suspicious signs of tubercular activity."

On receipt of the news Snow numbly went the following Tuesday to the Peking Union Medical College. More extensive X rays and a much fuller personal medical history were recorded. For the next forty-eight hours he was alone and fearful. During his anxious wait he found new cause to sympathize as never before "with all the miserables of the world. I bore their pain, I suffered with them."

On Thursday he did not find Dr. McIntosh wearing the broad smile he looked for, but his sober words were even more welcome. The X rays indicated Snow probably had active tuberculosis when he was young, but now he had "nothing more than an inflammation due to bronchial trouble. . . . I am quite sure there is no active TB in your system."

No longer grimly confronted with his own mortality: "How dear the babbling brooks, how delicious the wine of the air, how blue the sky, how perfectly adorable the freckles on nurse's nose! Strange that before I had not thought how worthwhile would be the effort to kiss them!"

Snow made some new American friends who invited him to join them the next weekend at the Kanlu Hotel, the former hunting lodge of the emperor, in the Western Hills of Peking. In the party was a delightful American girl who had known many of Snow's friends in Honolulu. The party traveled from the Kanlu to the palace in rickshas. On their return Snow's new lease on life inspired him impulsively to change places with his "ricksha boy" and challenge his companion's boy to a race. He took the lead for three or four hundred yards, but then "the Chesterfields began to tell." English tourists frowned their disapproval but amused Chinese cheered the spectacle. His boy, apparently riding in a ricksha for the first time in his life, seemed scared to death.[1]

The shadow threat of his personal death dissipated in a day of celebration, but it was soon followed by another and different encounter so grimly undeniable that he subsequently represented it in his autobiography as changing the course of his life. His railway tour was essentially completed, but his instructions from Sun Fo, the Railway minister, entitled him to travel the entire railroad. There was famine in nearby Inner Mongolia. As Snow explained in *Journey to the Beginning*, his travel companion, there given the fictional name C. T. Washington Wu, pointed out famine was not a proper tourist attraction. Probably sparked by his own recent brush with mortality and his sudden sense of kinship with "the miserables of the world," Snow insisted nevertheless on visiting the area.

C. T. Washington Wu's real name was S. Y. Livingston Hu, and he in fact had a reasonably impressive list of business and academic credentials. He graduated from Northwestern University in the United States in 1922, following which he went to Harvard for his master's degree. After working for a variety of American banks and trust companies, he returned to China in 1926 to join the faculties of Nanyang and University Utopia. In 1927 he joined the Nationalist Government at Hankow as secretary in the Ministry of Communications under Sun Fo. Snow took photographs of Hu and referred to him occasionally in his letters home. His references are neutral and casual. Hu is listed as coauthor with Snow of the tourist brochures, but he seems to have had little to do with the writing. Apparently his name was added principally to give credence and authority to the work of the as yet relatively unrecognized Snow. Hu had published several articles in the *China Weekly Review* on his own.

But in *Journey to the Beginning*, Snow transformed Hu into a caricature of exploitation to give added point to the moral indignation that had grown within him. C. T. Washington Wu is described as an American-returned student who knew nothing about the railway but "was one of thousands of hangers-on" with whom Kuomintang officialdom always seemed encumbered. He not only resisted Snow's effort to see the famine but also snubbed Rewi Alley, whom Snow was surprised to find traveling among the third-class passengers. Worst of all, though of little value to Snow as a railway expert, his title awed minor officials, and he repeatedly took advantage of that awe to enjoy banquet delicacies and the sexual service of young girls provided on command. The latter became particularly sinister when Snow linked it with the memory of goods wagons their party saw just outside the Great Wall city of Kalgan filled with girl-children headed for factories and brothels.

Wu's exploitation is pictured in sharp contrast with the tough compassion of Alley, who in 1929 was doing volunteer work while on vacation from his job inspecting Shanghai's notorious factories. Alley, experienced in the underside of Shanghai's wretched labor conditions, tutored the young journalist in the sinister marketing of the girl-children. Snow at one point gently pulled a bewildered young boy, scarcely six years old, away from the emaciated corpse of his father to make sure "at least one empty stomach was well fed that day." He later learned Alley had quietly outdone his gesture by making another of the abandoned and starving young boys they had come across his first adopted son.

In 1929 Snow focused his indignation on the insouciance of a Shanghai readership that casually dismissed the horrors he witnessed as a "so-called famine." But this famine experience remained vivid in his memory and reappears in his later writing as a barometer of his changing social reflections. In *Red Star over China* he shifts the focus of his indignation from the insouciance of the Shanghai foreign community to the callousness of rich men and officials—with armed guards to defend them and singsong girls to entertain them—who hoarded plentiful stocks of grain to profit from the terrible demand. These merchants of death were substantially abetted by the political rivalry of warlords who would send no railway cars westward, even to starving people, lest the cars be seized by their rivals.

When the memory of this experience appears even later in his autobiography the target of his indignation becomes the tendency of Westerners to dismiss such horrors with offensive stereotyping that blamed the victim. Foreigners often spoke with unwitting self-incriminating righteousness: "These Chinese are heartless: they think no more of selling a child than a pig." But when he penetrated into the heart of the famine area he remembered seeing in fierce and macabre detail there were even "worse fates than living to be sold into service." The sale of children and women was not a sign of some fault in the Chinese character but a consequence of a combination of natural disaster and exploitative economic practice.

By the time he wrote his autobiography he realized a new man had begun to grow within himself from his appalling experience at Saratsi (present day Hohhehot) and Kalgan, a new man unwittingly bound to a distant land and people by haunting images of human helplessness coupled with contrasting images of human vulturism that over the years compelled his imagination again and again to seek remedies for the needs of such victims, even revolutionary remedies if necessary.[2]

Before Snow left Peking in 1929 tensions between Russia and China increased significantly over a Harbin police raid on the Soviet Consulate, probably ordered, though publicly denied, by Chang Hsueh-liang. Powell wired Snow he should return immediately to Shanghai, he was promoted to assistant editor, and was thus temporarily in charge of the *China Weekly Review*. Powell apparently gave Snow no choice this time. The *Chicago*

Tribune had ordered Powell to Manchuria, so Snow would also serve while Powell was away as South China correspondent for the *Chicago Tribune*. George Missemer, the veteran copy editor, was still in the United States. Snow was also to move into the Powell household to offer protection to Powell's sisters. Powell's wife and children lived in the United States. Snow, however, continued to insist in his letters home he had no intention of being a journalist in China for long.

Early in 1929 Gertrude Binder became the youngest member of the *China Weekly Review*'s staff. Agnes Smedley's challenging autobiographical novel, *Daughter of Earth,* which opens with the story of her harsh upbringing in the mining camps of Missouri, was just then reaching publication. Smedley herself came to China from Germany searching for new causes and a new life. She and Snow crossed paths without meeting as she stayed for some months in Mukden and Nanking before heading for Shanghai and promptly moving into an apartment with Binder in May. The latter remembered with a chuckle when Snow became acting editor. He immediately gave everyone a raise. Perhaps this was a means of getting even with Powell for giving him no choice but to assume the previously refused editorial position.

Snow himself remembered another incident at this time that he turned into a tribute to Powell. An official Chinese visitor was denied the use of an elevator reserved for white men while Powell was away. Snow wrote a satirical editorial about it, and the British owners of the building promptly changed their discriminating policy. However, when the *Review*'s lease expired, Powell was refused renewal. Although he knew the reason, he spoke no word of blame to Snow.[3]

Snow's first signed editorial, "The American College Boy Vagabond in the Far East," was about a gray-haired, iron-jawed American consul who had recently arranged the release from jail of three "romancing rover boys," who "had tried to kidnap a traffic cop and take him for a midnight ride in a 'borrowed' ricksha." One of these young men reported he had been shot in the hand upriver on a Yangtze boat. It later developed that the young man gave himself a surface wound to create public concern that would serve as very favorable publicity for the book he was about to publish.

With suspicious righteousness, considering he was only a year away from his stowaway voyage on the *Shinyo Maru,* Snow described such vagabonds as "an embarrassing nuisance in the orient." They "frequent all kinds of establishments, because they are looking for the 'color of the East,'" but they often get into trouble, "and seldom are able to take care of themselves when they find it." His tone is also surprising because even after the editorial he persisted in referring to himself as a vagabond in his letters home and assuring his family he would soon resume his journey and see them again in a matter of months.

His parents, apparently in response to his interest in vagabonds such as Singapore Sam Morgan and Alfred Batson, a few months later sent him a news clipping about an aspiring young rival to Richard Halliburton, John Marshall, "champion vagabond of the world." Marshall turned out to be the very young man who claimed to be attacked by bandits on the river to create publicity for his forthcoming book. Snow admitted after listening to Marshall's "romantic story" he had "bit" to the extent of supporting him with twenty dollars. Besides borrowing a typewriter that he never returned from a United Press man, Marshall subsequently sponged off Snow's friends in Java and Japan. Thus the editorial, seemingly indicating a change of heart, probably grew out of Snow's personal pique at being taken.

But world events continued to conspire against his halfhearted promises to head homeward. The Chinese-Russian crisis in Manchuria had thrust him into a heady position of authority. Being an editor in charge of a magazine and holding press credentials from the *Chicago Tribune* was in part a satisfyingly maturing experience for a young man of barely twenty-four. He proudly explained to his parents that he worked from ten in the morning until ten or eleven at night with leisurely time for "tiffin" and dinner. He wrote articles and editorials himself and bought, rejected, and encouraged articles by others. He had "two or three interviews a week with high government officials, such as Chiang Kai-shek, C. T. Wang, T. V. Soong and others. As a representative of the *Trib* I have no difficulty seeing them."

Yet to his sister he confided a dream of a different, freer world:

> I sit in an office, Mil, that is literally filled with books. Fiction, biography, travel, adventure, mostly stories about China or the other lands of the Orient. It is painful to record that I have read precious few of them, but the very atmosphere seems redolent with things I love and I fancy some of it seeps down from the shelves and is the thing that keeps me satisfied with this drivel I have to turn out. In a corner is an ancient leather armchair and a broken reading lamp beside it. And here I sit many a night, long after others have taken the din of office hours with them and gone home, smoking unnumbered cigarettes, and turning the pages of books I should like to read if I had time. I will just get started in something I like, when the cables start coming in and I will have to give it [up] and immerse myself in the storm of the news.

His restlessness was also stirred by meeting Theodore and Kermit Roosevelt in Shanghai on their way back from an expedition to Yunnan in search of the giant panda. He had two long talks with Colonel Roosevelt, who told him of "crossing the Yangtze on a single thread of rope and the Mekong on

As an editor of the China Weekly Review, *Snow regularly met senior Kuomintang officials. Here J. B. Powell, Randall Gould, Victor Keen, and Snow, along with other Japanese and Chinese correspondents, are pictured with Generalissimo Chiang Kai-shek (center) and Foreign Affairs Minister Wang Fu-chao (far left).*

an improvised raft. He mentioned a near encounter with bandits and a visit with the Abbot of Yungning. He told of the golden monkeys they had got in Szechuan and of the blue sheep in Yunnan." Snow also read with great interest accounts in the *National Geographic* of the strangely peopled land where Yunnan fades into Tibet by Dr. Joseph Rock, a man with whom in less than two years he would share a troubled caravan adventure. And he found a wonderful decades-old map of the region by Major H. P. Davies over which he plotted to leave China for home through a portal of romantic adventure.[4]

Late in October panic abruptly seized the New York Stock Exchange. But the impact of the stock market crash was quickly eclipsed for Snow by the more disturbing news that his mother was ill, and the doctors suspected cancer, the "dreadful, unmentionable disease" Snow rightly feared even more than the tuberculosis he had only recently escaped. He received the news November 2 in a letter from his father dated October 11. He wired home immediately, "How's mother?" Follow-up letters dated October 13 and 14 from his father explaining that his mother had had a minor operation, that tests indicated no cancer and all was well, arrived the next day.

On November 3 he wrote his father: "This news from you had a shocking effect on me. I am not sorry you mentioned it, even if it turns out to be utterly a baseless alarm. For it made me realize how vital it is that I come back to you and be with you again as soon as possible. I am going to terminate my wanderings now as early as satisfactory arrangements can possibly be made." Relieved to learn his mother was not seriously ill, he explained to her a new realization of his family's importance to his work. Approval from others was always pleasing, but his family's praise was "life-giving nourishment." It was for them he strove to "make a new line or two that may not die."

Later in November he wanted his family to know his prolonged stay in Shanghai was not by choice. J. B. Powell was still in Manchuria. Why, considering his important Shanghai interests, was beyond understanding. If he did not know Powell's Presbyterian habits well, he would be tempted to think he had acquired a Russian concubine, which were very inexpensive in Harbin. In any case he had informed Powell that "his extended stay has . . . 'shot my plans to hell.' "

Despite complaining to his sister that his editorial duties severely limited his freedom to enjoy the well-stocked library of the *Review,* the twenty-four reviews he published during his two years on the staff indicated he read broadly and intensely. John "Bill" Powell, J. B.'s son, many years later remembered the library as "one of the best newspaper libraries in the Far East, filled with books on Asia and the Pacific. . . . The *Review* office became a gathering place for foreign newsmen and writers, partly because it was a good place 'to look something up.' " Roughly half Snow's reviews were of books on China.

About the same time he was coping with the news of his mother's visit to the hospital he also wrote a sharply critical review of *Chiang Kai-shek: The Builder of New China.* Beginning to assert his independence from the political views of his mentor, Powell, he attacked the three authors' trite and empty praise of Chiang's guiding policy as one of "Peace, peace at any price." Chiang was a soldier, and "few soldiers believe in peace at all, and none in peace at any price." While admitting "Chiang Kai-shek is neither the villain that his Left Wing opponents would make him appear to be," nor "the 'man of steel' which his more ardent admirers would have us understand," he was particularly disappointed the authors failed to explain such conundrums as how "this inadequately educated, poorly born, unsophisticated gentleman from Ningpo . . . has been able to hold the spotlight on himself in Chinese politics for more than two years"; how "though surrounded by minions of far superior intellect [Chiang] still manages to dominate them"; and how "though essentially a military man and inexperienced as a government official [Chiang] yet has no army of significance under his personal banner, but despite the fact continues to hold his power against opposition perhaps more overwhelming than that which faced anyone who has gone before him?"[5]

He did not wait for Powell's return to move into a small apartment with a young man from Nebraska, then branch advertising manager for General Motors in Shanghai. John Allison had only recently taught English in Japan for two years. Within a few months he joined the U.S. Foreign Service and eventually worked closely with John Foster Dulles in drafting and winning acceptance for the enlightened peace treaty Japan and the United States signed following World War II. After Dulles was named Eisenhower's secretary of state and during the years of crucial recovery for Japan, Allison was named American ambassador to that country. But for now he and Snow were happy to move into 81 Seymour Road chiefly because of its very low rent, about twenty-five dollars a month in American money. Snow assured his mother, however, "It is furnished well, has a bath, kitchen and breakfast room in addition to the living room."

There was yet another advantage, or rather two: "For $25 Mex [Chinese money] we get an experienced boy who cooks only second to you, and also combines the luxury of valet, servant and, if necessary, nurse. What Howdy and Bert would give to have such a treasure as our I-Sung in New York!" I-Sung also had a nephew who wanted to "learn coolie" badly enough to work only for food and board. Besides dusting the furniture, washing the dishes, and generally making himself useful, he gave face to his uncle. Allison and Snow eventually insisted on paying him a dollar a month to satisfy the various proprieties of all concerned.

As another Christmas away from home approached, Snow assured his family, though he was not in love, his life was rich in romantic interest:

> You would be amazed at the heterogeneous character of my acquaintances in Shanghai. They include members of every race that is found in any numbers in the Orient. There is a German newspaper man and a woman author of Deutschland [probably Agnes Smedley]; a Soviet Russian whose Polish wife has a voice like a bell; a Chinese who loves English poetry; an American marine officer [Evans Carlson] whose wife is a lovely southern girl whose specialty is tea with raisin crumpets; a Georgian from the Caucasus, and Georgians are the most entrancing of all women; a young Chinese couple who are my favorites, though they live like mice on a government salary that wouldn't buy your lettuce; a Japanese girl with gold teeth and a brain—a rare combination in Nihon— who is teaching me something of her language in exchange for my criticism of her English and applause for her divine sukiyaki; an Indian poet married to a Japanese, who together own a garden that is a miniature

Arcadia, and an American Jewess who looks like an Irish girl—"all these,"
as Rupert Brooke would say, "have been my loves." Figuratively speaking,
of course.

Allison confirmed that Snow "got around and knew all sorts of interesting
people," not least of whom was Smedley.

Snow's letter to his mother celebrating the ethnic diversity of his friends in
Shanghai apparently did not sit well with his father. About four months later
the elder Snow made it quite clear he did not approve of how life in the big
city had changed his sons: "It appears from what you say that New York is
a bunch of Jews and foreigners, so massive and strong that it has swept you
fellows off your feet and you have been so close to it that you imagine it is
America. Its ideals are America's, you think. It is only about 5% of America
and when you get back to the United States, I suggest that you see America
first. Do not forget the 11th commandment."

Snow wrote his mother about a date with an American Jewish girl who
looked like she was Irish that he later used to strong effect in *Journey to the
Beginning*. He was walking with her one evening just after the New Year on
Bubbling Well Road. Dressed formally in his tux and carrying his camel-
hair coat on his arm, he saw three sheets of flame burst from a house down
the road and come at the couple as hoops of fire. When one of the three
reached within a hundred yards, he realized it was a human torch: "A crowd
of Chinese soon gathered to watch the poor devil incinerate. None of them
made any effort to save him." He reached for an explanation, "In order to
forgive this you must understand that Lao Tse taught that when a person
saves another's life he must assume full responsibility for him from then on.
Every Chinese believes this."

Although he did not relish losing his sixty-dollar camel-hair coat, Snow
wrestled the man to the ground, wrapped his coat around him to snuff
the flames, and saved his life. The Chinese onlookers were wide-eyed with
surprise. "The logical conclusions for the Chinese to reach were either (a)
that I was insane or (b) that I had so much money that a mere rag worth
6 tens of dollars was inconsequential." In *Journey to the Beginning*, Snow
gave the story sharper point by having a ricksha coolie demand that Snow
pay for the water he ordered to throw on the burning man. To his mother, he
described only being besieged by beggars asking for "kumsha."

He assured his mother the man was saved. He had probably been asleep
when the boardinghouse he was staying in caught fire. Instinctively the
man ran into the street as fast as he could. But even as Snow later calmly
explained much of the incident, he still found the crowd's reaction difficult to

understand: "How incredible is the suffering of the people of this benighted land!" The tragic human ordeal that so disturbed him in remote Saratsi just a few months earlier now had a Shanghai complement.

In *Journey to the Beginning* he broadly caricatured his female companion as previously he had S. Y. Livingston Hu, and he conspicuously linked the two by having the girl complain vacuously with the identical words used by Wu, "What a miserable, miserable country China is," words incidentally not far from his own youthful reference to "this benighted land." Cynically she advised Snow that "always happens when an outsider tries to interfere with fate in China. . . . They let you burn your fingers, take your coat, and then want to be paid for it." He leaves her forever with a parting shot, "Very smart, but I hope that I never get that cynical."[6]

In his autobiography this incident implies he left Shanghai no longer able to tolerate the indifference of both Chinese and foreigners to human suffering. The incident occurred early in January 1930. He did not leave Shanghai until late September. The experience obviously was sufficiently moving to remain vivid in his imagination, but between that January and September he experienced a personal tragedy that layered his departure from China with a heavy sense of family guilt he found difficult to acknowledge in his autobiography. He did, however, write several other pieces during these months. In one of these he would directly indict the Shanghai American community with the indifference he later caricatured in his date.

6

Mother's Death and Escape

J B. POWELL RETURNED to Shanghai at the end of November 1929. Snow immediately resigned from the *China Weekly Review* and quickly ◆ accepted an offer to become a correspondent for Consolidated Press beginning January 1, about the time of the human torch incident. His new job with Conso Press, a foreign news service that had been recently started up by David Lawrence and Drew Pearson, seemed the answer to his dreams. It gave him sufficient money to live on, a ready outlet for his writing while still allowing him to publish lengthier work elsewhere, and much personal freedom to travel and find his own stories. He confidently expected to resume his world travel soon.

He was therefore surprised when his new leisure made him feel melancholy and shelved. But such feelings soon passed. He had plenty to do. He was already mulling through his recent experiences for stories and feature articles he might put on the market. He hoped to travel through Europe by way of Russia, but he advised his family he probably would not leave Shanghai until late in spring. Winter in Moscow was not an attractive prospect.

Shortly after Powell's November return to Shanghai, a crisis in Nanking demanded Powell's presence, and he persuaded Snow to resume his editorial duties for a few weeks. This brief return to the *Review* reenforced Snow's determination to be on his own. By January he was again free. Late in February he suggested to Horace Epes, vice president of Consolidated, that he file stories on a trip through Russia from east to west. It was to be the first leg on his trip home. Consolidated quickly accepted and supported his plan.

The thought of resuming his round-the-world voyage and a gloomy letter from Howard provoked him to review his original ambitions and examine how his two-year experience had modified them. Just short of two years after he sailed from New York he wrote his father that his brother's unhappiness reminded him money ruled in America, and money was not the reward of virtue, intelligence, or culture. A little self-servingly, he generalized, many fail in such a land simply because "they have used their intellect for unorthodox purposes, sent out tentacles from their brain into fields other than those strictly concerned with the American duty of making more money than one really needs, violated the principle of our prosperity, [and] humiliated the ritual of 'getting on.' "

He warned his father not to conclude "that I have been reading Nathan or Mencken. This has been my opinion for a long time." Howard probably will achieve his dream "to wrest a fortune from business and, while still young, to retire and use his maturer years in search of knowledge, experience, adventure, perhaps happiness," but probably not as quickly as he hoped.

During his New York years he had tried the path Howard chose, stamping out "the fires of other loves" infinitely more precious, but he grew weary. So he resolved "to devote two, three, perhaps four years to experiment with another kind of existence." An "older pantheism" beckoned from across sunlit seas. "Meanwhile in my heart were cravings, avidities, tendencies which I wanted to test, shape, perhaps give expression, perhaps satiation."

Two years later he might not be nearer the truth, but he was conscious of "greater breadth of interest, an almost unbearable impatience with my faculties for absorbing knowledge, a keener appreciation of the swiftness of one's passing." The new influences and ideas had not yet fused coherently. He apologized for his verbal awkwardness, if not sophistry, but then made a final stab at explaining the conflict between his heart and his head: "Perhaps this eerie thing within one, that I foolishly dream of somehow making apparent on paper, is merely an expiring memory of golden, island happiness, of that simple, idyllic existence which all men believe once was, and devout persons absurdly believe will be again."[1]

He was preparing to leave Shanghai with many of the same feelings with which two years before he more precipitately left New York. Although he denied Nathan and Mencken as sources for his feelings, he was soon to write a controversial piece on "Americans in Shanghai" at Mencken's request for the *American Mercury*. He could share Mencken's skepticism with his father.

His self-proclaimed romantic mission to define "an expiring memory of golden, island happiness," however, was shockingly interrupted by the very personal tragedy he recently feared, but thought he had escaped. On March 22, 1930, his mother died. He did not know about her recent illness or her reentry into the hospital. The news stunned him and stirred again his feelings of guilt about his extended absence from his family. By March 28 he received two letters from his father that made it clear "that mother's sanity was really on the brink." He imagined the distress of his father and sister and described his own: "What a period you must have been through, you and dear sis. It was terrible enough for me to get such tragic news, so far away, so important to aid; but you and Mildred, through it all, until the last breath! . . . I am sorry, O I am sorry that I was not with you to share my part of your pain, and distress."

But the letters from home were sufficiently ambiguous about the details of his mother's final illness and death that he grew increasingly anxious and insistent on the facts. On May 12 his father wrote a sadly reluctant letter that began: "You have asked me to fill in the gap between my letter of March 18th and my letter of March 25th, the former saying that your mother was physically sound and having excellent care; the latter consoling you for her death, assuring you that you were not to blame."

To fill in the gap his father told a troubled story with no conclusive evidence of blame but charged with deeply resentful suspicions. His father tried hard to maintain a semblance of dignity and objective honesty: "Personally I was treated courteously by all the attendants at the hospital and conducted myself in a gentlemanly way. It was some time afterwards that Mayme [Snow's aunt] let me know that a nun from the office had come into your mother's room and demanded we pay the hospital bills."

There had been a concerted family effort to reduce and help pay for the sudden rush of medical expenses, but the hospital bill in particular was given low priority. After the first week, however, Mayme asked him to pay something on the bill. He paid fifty dollars. During the third week the expensive special nurse was relieved by relatives from noon to five o'clock. While another aunt, Katherine, was taking her turn, a nun came into the room and spoke so roughly about the bill within mother's hearing that Katherine immediately went to the office and wrote a check to pay the bill to quiet her. Snow's mother, upset and ashamed, rose from her bed and tried to follow but fell. "This, mind you, while I was writing you that your mother was having the best of care."

To spare his feelings Mayme first gave Snow's father a more blandly forgiving story of events but eventually told the truth about Katherine's experience and mother's fall. Snow's father went immediately to the doctor and on the next or same day wrote him "as per copy of letter enclosed." The enclosed letter does not survive. When told about the father's letter, Katherine called, weeping, and asked him not to send the letter. She "did not wish to say anything evil about anyone or did not wish to hurt anyone's feelings. I told her if what she said was the truth she ought to have told it and told it sooner and that it was not she but I that was doing this."

"Your mother knew that I was not flush financially. It occurred to me that this might have caused her to get the last fall and the last fall might have resulted in her death."

Snow's father gave a vivid picture of the final sequence of events from Friday evening when his wife began to run a fever to her death at 4:30 A.M., Saturday morning. But the immediate shock of her death had worn off, and he now struggled with its aftermath. With all the suspicions born of what he learned subsequent to his wife's death, he thought of suing the hospital. But Harry's wife "is not well . . . she cannot stand it to go on a witness stand." He quickly dismissed the idea. He was in no position to sustain such legal action.

Frustrated and angry, he could get no information about the autopsy from Dr. Miller, the attending surgeon. Miller put him off with the excuse he was still doing lab work. He concluded, "Miller is lying to hide somebody or something. I have wakened many times in the night, wishing that I might find out the facts and in your mother's name, do something that would prevent other mothers from meeting a like fate."

He tried to accept his own helplessness and clear his son from any unnecessary feelings of responsibility. "All of us did all we could for your mother. You did the best you knew. Do not condemn yourself in any way. If you had been here, you would have received no more consideration than Mildred and I." Then his festering resentment broke through his effort at resignation: "Your mother taught you to lift your hats to priests and nuns and that all of them were good and kind. This was the result of her teachings and environment. Fate chose a cruel and tragic time to disillusion her." Seeing nothing else to do he "will try to dismiss the matter until further developments compel my attention." He suggested his son do the same.

Ironically the autopsy and medical records of the hospital denied the father's view and indicate strongly most of the fears and suspicions he shared with his son were not justifiable. When she entered the hospital, Anna Snow was incoherent. The hospital staff's euphemistic references to a nervous disorder and the father's and son's fears of insanity are not supported by the autopsy. Her feverish state is most readily explained by real physical disease, not "womanly weakness." Her death was caused by significant infection in the abdomen and urinary tract. The autopsy contains no indication the fall the father wrote of was a significant factor in her death.

Snow probably carried many of his father's fears and suspicions with him the rest of his life. In one respect at least his mother's death left Snow more exclusively his father's son. He had lost his faith in his teens but did not immediately become hostile to the church as a consequence. Now his attitude hardened, and he later declared the circumstances of his mother's death his reason for never attending Mass through the remainder of his stay in China.[2]

Early in May he visited the American Embassy in Tokyo for help in obtaining visas to cross Russia, but he also wrote Howard he had treated himself to a vacation, first visiting friends in Yokohama, then to the garden island of Enoshima, "nestling in a little bay that coils around the base of Fujiyama," and finally to Atami, one of the "eight beauty spots" of Japan, where for three days he "slept, ate, bathed a la Japonaise."

This vacation seems to have been an escape from more than the demands of his writing. His diary makes clear that besides its extraordinary natural beauty Atami also had the attraction of geisha and young women from Oshima (sleeping partners) strolling up and down the beach walk. He discreetly described playing games and learning the lyrics to Japanese jazz from a young woman named Nasam. At the Uwanaton Hotel in Enoshima he also enjoyed having a little *Hana-san* play for him on her *sanisen* while he ate "Japanese chow." He learned the trick of appearing a little deaf from a Japanese friend to draw these women physically closer.

He did not openly try to explain to himself, to his brother, and certainly not to his later reading public just how such pleasures offered relief from his grief over his mother's death. But there is a suggestive hint in his review of *Infidels and Heretics*, an anthology for agnostics edited by Clarence Darrow and Wallace Rice, published just before he left Shanghai. He complained of many omissions in the collection, but particularly that the editors meant "to confine their treasury to western writers." Then he cited a passage of Hafiz notable for its rich cynicism as an example of what the anthology lacked:

> Then from the fragile table seize a tass,
> And drain the wine of life before the glass
> Shall crumbling all, with table and with you,
> And with your god into oblivion pass. . . .

He had lost faith in his mother's Catholicism long ago. His father's skepticism provided only cold comfort. Groping for answers to emotional needs he could not completely explain, he apparently reached for the "expiring memory of golden island happiness" he hoped to find in an "older pantheism."

The entries in Snow's diary for this period are sketchy and haphazardly organized. But on leaving Shanghai in September to resume his round-the-world journey, he also noted his disappointment that Chiyako was not there to see him off. Chiyako is not clearly identified, but she seems to have been Japanese and a close friend for some time prior to his departure. She probably is the Japanese girl with the rare combination of gold teeth and a brain teaching him her language and feeding him "divine sukiyaki" listed figuratively among his loves in the letter to his mother. At any rate the romantic memories he recorded in his diary after leaving Shanghai suggest that at some time prior to his departure his relation to Chiyako, sometimes spelled *Chiyeko*, had become intimate.

Snow's acknowledgment of his mother's death in *Journey to the Beginning* is very brief and chronologically vague. It comes early in his narrative, and he linked it tenuously with his experience of famine at Saratsi. He did not mention his mother's death again in his autobiography and particularly did not place it in the context of his planned departure from Shanghai. Instead he implied the reason for his Shanghai departure in the dramatic story of his cynical date and the human torch reviewed above. However, he began the next chapter, "The Banker's Daughters," with a rather hard to believe story of a friend Larry's taking a naïve young Snow to visit a well-appointed geisha house under the pretence of introducing him to two young Japanese "modern girl" banker's daughters. The memory of this visit is supposedly triggered by a conversation about *modan garu* (modern girl) on a Japanese ship on his way from Shanghai to Formosa.

It is possible the incident actually happened as described on the May visit to Yokohama that Snow mentioned in his letter to Howard. But if so, it also seems the kind of story he would have shared with his brother, but he did not. There is no hint of the banker's daughters in his diary. In *Journey to the Beginning* one of the two geisha is named Chiyeko, the name of his Shanghai friend, who otherwise does not appear in his published writing. Thus this story seems a likely fiction designed to memorialize publicly, but discreetly, a privately valued visit to Atami and Enoshima after his mother's death and his subsequent relation with Chiyako, or Chiyeko. His mother's death seems to have marked a new aggressive freedom in his sexual life. The later story of his nurse-lover, Batala, in Burma is a more convincingly documented similar example of such coded fiction.

A final footnote about his anticipated journey homeward: He also raised the question with his brother of their once more sharing an apartment, "When

I return to New York next fall, where will I live? Have you room at your place? But no, four men in an apartment is too many. Let us get a flat together." However, before he left Shanghai he was chagrined to learn his brother had married. There would be no bachelor apartment waiting for him in New York.[3]

7

Good-bye Shanghai

J UST BEFORE SNOW RECEIVED news of his mother's death he wrote
an article about the U.S. Marines as a peace-keeping force for which he
used a pseudonym, John Fairnsworth. He sent the article to Howard to
circulate for him, but Howard found it "critical, sarcastic." Acknowledging
that he wrote "out of indignation" and aware also that such an article might
do him no good, he still insisted, "it was something which I felt ought to be
written and I have not changed my belief in this respect." He may well have
used the pseudonym to protect the *China Weekly Review* from any backlash
to his criticism of American foreign policy since he had just stepped down
from being its active editor for months. Or possibly he wanted to protect his
marine friend Evans Carlson, who may have been its source or who might
well have been accused of being one even if he was not. In any case the
article was never published.

The principal concern of the article was the continuing presence of a
marine contingent sent to Shanghai in 1927 in response to resident American
fears of the imminent takeover by Chiang Kai-shek's nationalist troops.
"These marines have never fired a shot in China—and they never will."

Two particular incidents indicated serious problems with the marines' continuing presence. One involved the apparent callous murder of two Chinese
boatmen who would not cooperate with the illicit plans of the marines who
hired them. The second involved a marine officer whose wife's body was
found badly mutilated after a fire in their apartment and following a drunken

quarrel over the wife's alleged promiscuity. Snow used these incidents to examine the dilemma of a marine force assigned a boring, pointless task in a foreign city noted for the ready availability of sex, drugs, and smuggling. While marine behavior raised real issues, Snow made a grand leap in logic to attack the foolish pretence "with which our State Department expounds a policy of peace and good will toward all nations, including the Chinese," while spending large sums of American taxpayers' money to preserve "this melancholy portrait of marines at peace." He protested "this offense against 'American dignity and prestige' . . . born of the hypocrisy of our foreign policy."[1]

Although this indictment was never published, another criticism of the American presence in Shanghai was, and it brought quick public notoriety. After he had received the telegram informing him of his mother's death, but before he knew the disturbing details, Snow indicated to his father he was going to "write Mr. Mencken an article on Shanghai, as he suggests. It is an assignment to which I feel scarcely adequate. I can only hope he will also find it 'full of excellent stuff.'" Mencken not only accepted "Americans in Shanghai" but also invited a follow-up.

In August the *China Weekly Review* announced Snow's soon-to-be published article with obvious misgivings: "Evidently Mr. Snow, by his acceptance in *The Mercury*, will do for China what Olan D. Russell has been doing for Japan. *The Mercury* dedicates itself to debunking American scenes. This has become tiresome after six years; so nowadays *The Mercury*, which has lost its former sting, is considered puerile by the critical group, but it is still read by young intellectual upstarts and college freshies giddy over the new freedom." The *Review* suggested that the *Mercury*, *Plain Talk*, the *Haldeman-Julius Monthly*, and the more radical *New Masses* made up a ready market for this "debunking" of Yankees in China that Snow was belatedly initiating. "All these avenues enjoy 'taking' religion 'for a ride.'"

A scrapbook Snow kept of his early publications indicates the market for such writing was much broader than the *Review* wanted to believe. The scrapbook contains excerpts from his *Mercury* article reprinted in the *Kansas City Times*, the *Lincoln (Nebr.) Star*, the *Sioux City (Iowa) Tribune*, the *Omaha (Nebr.) World Herald*, the *Chickasha (Okla.) Express*, the *Santa Fe New Mexican*, the *Enid (Okla.) Eagle*, and the *Mexico (Mo.) Ledger.*

Snow began his article noting Shanghai's ostensible Americanization. He recited a long list of readily available American home comforts, headed by Clara Bow and Buddy Rogers, public icons with a special personal reference. But the list was deceiving. The presence of these American symbols indicated no real cultural confraternity between "Chinese and Americans, except the common bond of making money, which both are too busy doing." This concern with money, making everything for sale, gave the city a revealing kind of excitement:

> Repugnant to some, its [Shanghai's] fascination for others lies in its very crudities, its stark and frank carnalities. Over it hangs the promise of gold and Gehenna. Never drab, it burns with the primal longings of an animal heart. It is as swift, as sudden, as elemental as the jungle, its appetite ever-ravishing, always unappeased. It has at once the charm and the futility of a mistress who never knows repletion.

The right to vote in Shanghai was determined by property ownership. Ninety percent of the population of the International Settlement was Chinese, but they were disenfranchised. A small group of wealthy Britons in reality "rule the Settlement as one of the narrowest oligarchies surviving in the world today. . . . Yet Washington naively accepts dual responsibility with London for what is done, while virtuously assuring the plain people that America has and wants no concessions in China."

Snow wrote with disdain of the "American Mayor" of the International Settlement, who received twenty-five thousand dollars a year for wearing the grandiloquent title of director-general of the International Settlement and for journeying to Washington "to propagandize against the withdrawal of American marines and sailors, and against the abolition of extra-territoriality." But "his British employers deceive no one—at least no one in Shanghai." This is the same Stirling Fessenden who proudly told J. B. Powell of his role in striking the deal between the Green Gang leader, Tu Yueh-sheng, and French officials that doomed the leftist-led takeover of Shanghai in 1927.

Snow pointed particularly to prostitution and missionary activity to illustrate the moral pretentiousness of the American presence in Shanghai. While he gave specific addresses and names of the proprietors of houses employing "American and Russian talent," he nevertheless explained that the prevalence of prostitution in Shanghai was principally attributable to the male population being so greatly in the majority. Having by far the highest ratio of prostitutes to total population of any city in the world, "Shanghai is a man's town." It was not without wholesome American women, but for the "fewer than 600 females, there are some 3,000 males . . . exclusive of the 1,200 marines, and the gobs, who vary from 2,000 to 3,000." Most of these women married before they came to Shanghai; "if not, they marry soon afterward. It is safer that way."

But if there were more sinners in Shanghai than anywhere else in the world, there were also more missionaries. Snow crudely caricatured missionaries and their activities. Memories of the starving at Saratsi ignored by complacent Shanghailanders probably merged with his father's representation of an overly zealous nun causing his distraught mother's fall to sharpen his animus. He described a cross-eyed evangelist who stopped him in the lobby of the Navy YMCA and asked, "My friend, excuse me for this intrusion, but may I ask if you know your Saviour?" Snow deadpanned that the man's crossed eyes contributed to his evangelistic success, for every time he asked if a man "will stand up for Jehovah, two men rise from their seats."

His harshest indignation was reserved for "the amalgamated Christian holy men" to be found in the six-story Missions Building. Among these are "wealthy hierarchs, rivaling the exploiters who looted the Hawaiians while confounding them with the wonder of 'salvation from sin through the Son of God, our Saviour, Jesus Christ.'" While these men "smoke large cigars and grow to resemble them in girth and mentality," make "money in Shanghai real estate, . . . provide fashionable weddings for their daughters and furnish them with rich dowries, insuring marriage with the Best Families," just a few hundred miles to the northwest "20,000,000 Chinese are waiting to be 'delivered'—*not* via the glorious pathway of our Lord." They seek only rescue from starvation. "They plead only for a meagre cup of millet a day."

His final and most telling indictment of these Americans, whether businessmen or missionaries, was that they "little bother themselves about what is happening in the hearts and minds of the multitude around them." They lived in "a hermetically sealed glass case." This seems the source of the coldly caustic dialogue he attributed to his date in the aftermath of his rescue of the human torch in *Journey to the Beginning*.

The *Shanghai Evening Post and Mercury* quickly responded to Snow's article with an editorial. He did not paste it into his scrapbook. Apparently aware of his near exit from Shanghai, the editors asked: "How many of these traveling, hustling, prurient journalists have we had with us for a season, peering at us from the outside rim, and from the particular section of that rim that suits their tastes, (or the tastes of the magazine to which they hope to sell their stuff) broadcasting with authority to the world?" The editors then attacked this "golden youth, all glamorous with wickedness," for his lack of proportion in failing to report the more decent and virtuous aspects of American life in Shanghai:

> We quite understand that you and Henry [Mencken] would not think much of the Community Church that these uninteresting Americans keep up; or the two American units of volunteers, and many other things too wholesome to be quaint which your investigations on Soochow Road kept you too busy to find. But busy as you are, did you never meet

an interesting missionary? . . . Well, well, Edgar, it's so hot and sticky—and the decent people are concealed, you say. And besides they're dull. Maybe Mr. Mencken wouldn't even buy a story about them.

The very next day Snow replied to the editorial by ironically noting the paper was really very liberal: "in other days I might have looked for a rope and a swing high in the trees from a gang led by such men as you." Instead he had been treated as an adolescent to a pants-down whipping. Following up this image, he verbally mooned the editors with deliberate euphemism: "I am sanguine enough to believe that your verbal posterior attack will not wholly incapacitate that part of me for your especial reference when in the future your virtuous indignation is again aroused."

He suggested the charge of adolescence was more properly attributable to this two-year-old paper than to a twenty-five-year-old journalist. But he struck a more earnest and less defensive note when he protested, "As for finding Americans in Shanghai dull, or the city itself uninteresting, I made no such statement. On the contrary, a more engaging and instructive community would be hard to find, and I shall soon bid my temporary farewell with reluctance." It is not clear whether the word *temporary* was simply a politic gesture or in fact he harbored some thought, even before he left, of his eventual return to Shanghai.

But the dialogue did not end there. On August 21 another letter to the editor, this time signed "Iowan," appeared. It was this letter that recalled Snow's story of his stowaway on board the *Shinyo Maru*. Pointing out that Izawa the cabin boy was discharged, blacklisted, and reduced to beggary because of the publication of Snow's story, the Iowan draws a parallel between Snow's betraying his friend for a few dollars and his "lambasting his acquaintances and his friends" in Shanghai for the satisfaction of "seeing his name over an article in *The American Mercury*." However, "The American Mercury played a dirty trick on him. Edgar says so himself. His article was published before he had a chance to straighten out his affairs and get out of town."[2] At this point Snow apparently decided continuing the argument was a mistake.

By early June, Snow knew Russia had refused his application for a visa. He suspected it was because of his close association with Powell who had written articles very critical of Russia after a recent short visit. He changed his planned route home to go through Southeast Asia and wrote Conso Press for approval. He also suggested a short trip to the battlefront in Honan. Horace Epes approved both suggestions. His visit to the front was apparently not very productive. Only a brief article in the *China Weekly Review* is clearly traceable to this experience.

Neither Snow nor Smedley ever published an account of their early acquaintance, though in 1959, by then named one of Smedley's three literary executors, Snow indicated to James Bertram that among thirty thousand words he cut from *Journey to the Beginning* to suit Random House were "some 5,000 words . . . about Agnes—three or four short chapters—and her influence on me as well as others."

Soon after she arrived in Shanghai, Smedley, probably through Gertrude Binder, made herself known to Powell. Her long commitment to Indian nationalism prompted her early to contact Shanghai's large Sikh community. She probably played a role in the *China Weekly Review*'s substantial airing of Sikh arrests and murders in the British concession of Shanghai while Snow was concluding his northwest railroad tour.

But Smedley's already long and varied passionate radicalism in class and gender politics—she was thirteen years older than Snow—probably made her at least initially a little disdainful of Snow's political naïveté and his youthful insistence on keeping himself unattached, free to wander. Soon after arriving in Shanghai, Smedley sought out Lu Hsun. Ten months later, in September, just prior to Snow's departure from Shanghai, Smedley helped arrange a daring and secret fiftieth birthday celebration for Lu Hsun attended by a number of radical writers and intellectuals marked for arrest by the Kuomintang. Snow knew of Lu Hsun by this time. He mentioned him as one of the dangerous authors French security police looked for when they examined the books he carried as he entered Haiphong a couple of months later. There is no indication Snow was invited to the party.

But when he left Shanghai that same month, Snow carried a letter of introduction to Nehru from Smedley. And once in India the remarkable members of the Chattopadhyaya family, the family of Smedley's former husband, Virendranath, the fiery Indian nationalist, were among his most prized contacts. Smedley was at least willing to steer the young journalist to the right people.[3]

About this same time Snow interviewed a more marketable subject, Mei Lan-fang, fresh from winning international acclaim on an American tour for his classic portrayal of feminine roles in Chinese opera. Even Mei, however, recognized it was time for revolution in China: "We are beginning to learn the stimulative force of plays which deal with the problems of contemporary life. . . . Until the advent of our modern, but wretched, proletarian plays, we had completely ignored the revolutionary changes that began even before the collapse of the Ch'ings." But he argued for keeping the singing, orchestra, and dancing of classic Chinese plays "pure and perfected as they are in the Western opera." The development of a popular theater would inevitably reflect current social values. But "the old type of drama should be preserved as our opera, while the spoken drama evolves along foreign lines, tempered by Chinese environment."[4]

Snow wrote yet another article before leaving Shanghai that suggests a more significant shared interest with Smedley. On July 27 the Communist forces that had regrouped in the mountains of Kiangsi attacked and occupied Changsha. It was the first major city to come under Communist control since the abortive capture of Shanghai in 1927. Snow had begun gathering information for his article prior to the taking of Changsha. He wrote the editors of *Current History,* "Some months ago I cultivated the friendship of a few local members of the C. P., with the hope of cutting through the secrecy with which it is necessarily surrounded. This acquaintanceship, together with a study of the Red activities over recent months, has helped me to form certain concepts which I believe you may find of interest."

On September 1 he wrote a follow-up letter asking the editors to omit a reference to two Communists he knew personally who received thirty dollars monthly from Russian sources and a bank clerk who told him he regularly endorsed 250 to 300 small checks "made out to Chinese workers by a Sino-Russian trading company that legitimately employs only a Chinese clerk and some office coolies." He feared questioning by the British C.I.D. and the Chinese police if these references appeared. Since he was in fact rather certain to be leaving Shanghai within a month of his letter, he more probably wanted to protect those he referred to or protect his later freedom of movement in British-controlled Burma and India.

He declared his political neutrality: "In no instance have I consciously overstated the case for communism, or against it." Whether he achieved objectivity or not may be argued, but the Communists he described were no Robin Hood's band:

> During the last 12 months the Reds have captured, looted and pillaged over 350 cities and towns in the provinces mentioned above. In Fukien province 14 hsien or county districts have been ravaged; in Kwangtung 16 hsien; in Chekiang 12 hsien; in Anhwei 18 hsien; in Hunan 28 hsien; in Kwangsi, Hupeh and Honan, lawlessness has prevailed over such wide areas that it is impossible to estimate the extent of the damage actively directed by communists.
>
> Worst of the sufferers has been Kiangsi province, where out of a total of 83 hsien, 45 have been taken by the Reds. An itemized report issued not long ago from the Kiangsi capital listed the estimated losses in districts occupied by communists as approximately $215,000,000, including a total of 37,000 houses burned. Incidentally, 82,000 Chinese, mostly merchants and "long gown" men and women, have been murdered.

This quote is from his typescript. *Current History* significantly changed his numbers and even some of his statements.

After giving all the information he had gathered about the Kiangsi Communists, Snow ended his article by speculating about the implications of the strength of the Communist movement. *Current History* also cut these editorial speculations, which was more properly within its right. But these speculations indicate even at this early date Snow was beginning to focus on the major theme of his professional life as a journalist: the role of Communism in the Asian revolt against colonialism.

He saw Chiang Kai-shek engaged in a fruitless struggle with the northern warlords, Yen Hsi-shan and Feng Yu-hsiang. Unable to buy them out or militarily defeat them, he saw the most probable result: "the creation of deeper hatreds and estrangements among members of the only group capable of establishing a stable, democratic government, and the physical and financial exhaustion of both north and south."

He was even more concerned with the attitude of the "imperialistic" powers, "among which the Chinese now include the United States." If the Communists began to challenge Kuomintang power in the cities, Western governments would feel the pressure to intervene. At Changsha, "after Americans and other foreigners were evacuated, the U.S.S. *Palos* returned and engaged the Reds, tallying over 30 casualties against them. British and Japanese gunboats participated in similar affrays." If the Communists won sufficient strength to attack Hankow, naval retaliation from the foreign powers was even more likely and probably would be much heavier. To highlight the danger Snow then offered his own early version of a domino theory, but he offered it as a factor in the struggle between Asian nationalism and European colonialism, not between freedom and communism:

> For should China go Red, the repercussion among other Asian peoples might be disastrous for world peace. Indo-China, where the French are having their difficulties with revolutionaries, India, where British rule is gravely imperilled, the Philippines, where nationalism is struggling out of infancy, the Dutch Indies, Korea—all through the East the structure of colonial capitalism would be severely rocked by a thorough-going People's Revolution in China.
>
> Russia is in the background now, but would she remain there in face of an "imperialistic invasion," directed against her Chinese proteges? It is debatable. Certainly she might be expected to worry the Nanking government, after the Manchurian pattern of "unofficial war," if she perceived that the Chinese Reds were being robbed of triumph through foreign interference.
>
> Thus, a great war of Asia, and a mighty world conflagration such as the more fervid Russian leaders have constantly sought to ignite, lies ever embryonic in the Chinese revolutionary arena. It is a spectacle that can

be averted. But merely laughing it off as a bugaboo will not dispel the ominous thrust of the threat.[5]

The Communists' move into Changsha in fact proved a mistake. They could not sustain control of the city, and it did not lead to attacks on other cities. Yet the mistake in the long run was only tactical. The Communists were eventually to lead a successful national revolution ridding China of foreign control. The nationalist struggles in Asia against colonial rule would take many different shapes. The role the international communist movement intended and in fact did play among these various nationalist struggles would be complicated, ambiguous, and much debated.

But the remarks *Current History* chose not to publish suggest that Edgar Snow had staked out a serious journalistic claim on an issue that would become critical in world history. *Red Star over China* and *Battle for Asia* would ultimately prove the rich value of his claim and establish Snow among the foremost journalists of his time. As he now prepared to leave Shanghai and explore Southeast Asia, his nearly two-year apprenticeship with the *China Weekly Review* had at least vaccinated him with a sense of political reality and consequence noticeably missing two years earlier when he slipped aboard the *Shinyo Maru* from Hawaii to be unexpectedly delighted by the opportunity to play bridge with a soon-to-be Japanese princess.

8

Formosa, Canton, Hong Kong, and Macao

ON SEPTEMBER 17 SNOW OUTLINED to Horace Epes of Conso Press his itinerary for resuming his round-the-world journey and returning home. He listed Formosa, Canton, Macao, Hong Kong, Hanoi, and Yunnanfu (present day Kunming) in that order. Although the dates he assigned were admittedly tentative, he expected to leave Shanghai on September 24 and arrive in Yunnanfu late in October. He allowed about six weeks for a caravan trip from Yunnanfu to Bhamo, Burma, from November 1 to December 15. He hoped to arrive in Calcutta early in January and planned approximately three weeks in various Indian cities.

He then added, "I will furnish you another itinerary when I reach India, to cover my trip through Persia and Arabia." He also mentioned the possibility of adding side trips in India to "Tiger Hill (for Mt. Everest)," a week's boat trip through the Kashmir valley, and a possibly longer stay in Calcutta. If he was unable to get a British visa for Burma, he would have to proceed through Indo-China, the Malay states, and the Dutch East Indies.

On September 26, two days later than he anticipated, he began a new diary with this desultory comment: "Left Shanghai at 12:15. Only John [Allison] at the ship. I look in vain for Chiyeko who promised to come. Apparently she feared other friends would be there & she might be embarrassed." Chiyeko had sent a letter he asked the captain of the *Chosa Maru* to translate. He did not indicate its contents but complained about the captain's poor translation. That evening, however, he reminisced about his and Chiyeko's first days together on Scott Road, insisting in the privacy of his diary that he "loved her very, very much."

The *Chosa Maru* was little more than a ferry, but it was the only ship Japan permitted to take passengers from Shanghai to Formosa, and it took four long days, with an overnight stop at Foochow. About four hundred years earlier Portuguese had come upon the island and named it *Ihla Formosa,* or "Beautiful Island." The Dutch who followed were more successful in establishing a lasting settlement, but a legendary local hero, Koxinga, led an early successful revolt against European colonialism in 1661. From 1683 to 1895 the island was part of the nearby mainland nation of China and was known as Taiwan. The Japanese then claimed the island as a prize of conquest following the Chinese-Japanese war of 1895.

Formosa was not much in the news at the time of Snow's planned visit. There was little reason to anticipate the controversial role it would begin to play in world affairs at the end of the Chinese civil war in 1949. At the time the island held a double attraction for Snow. Its remoteness held the promise of unknown adventure thus satisfying his original travel ambition, and he was interested in seeing the island as a test of what "the little Mikado-worshipers from the north" could do when they assumed "the white man's burden."

Three years after Snow left Shanghai he would conclude *Far Eastern Front* by noting that there were then in Asia two political driving forces "destined to be historically great," forces requiring "a workable ideology, with strong evangelical leaders and a vast amount of faith from followers ready to die for their beliefs. These two forces are Japan, and Soviet Russia as an Asiatic Power. Both are vital, dynamic, and inherently aggressive. Both menace the western imperialist system (behind which, in the West, lies no similar faith) as it functions in the Orient."[1]

He arrived in the port city of Keelung at 6:30 A.M., apparently the only white foreigner in town. After breakfast he took a train to Lake Jitsugetsutan, "Lake of the Moon and the Sun," which he would long remember as one of the natural wonders of the world. The impressive scenery of the last ten miles, on a midget train pulled by coolies through lush mountains, was hardly sufficient reward for the exhausting day-and-a-half trip. From a teahouse in Gojo a Japanese engineer finally led him up a steep three-mile trail to an inn perched on a sheer cliff overlooking the imposing lake he had come to see.

His stay was brief and disappointing. After a nap he was awakened to receive a delegation of bedraggled tribals from Kaban. These once fierce headhunters sang a chimelike fugue punctuated by pounding wooden poles into hollowed rocks embedded in the earth. He later wrote a more attractive story of his stay at the inn and his meeting with the tribals for the travel section of the *New York Sun*. He also later noted in *Journey to the Beginning* that the "very peaceful frontier town on the edge of the reservations in which the Japanese had confined those wild men of the mountains would, within a week of my visit, be the scene of the bloodiest aboriginal uprising of a decade. Nearly every Japanese in Jitsugetsutan was murdered in his sleep."[2]

Two days later in Taihoku he had breakfast with the American consul and then interviewed the Japanese chief of foreign affairs. These interviews and what independent investigations he could make the next day became the basis for four articles in which he challenged the moral pretentiousness behind Japanese appeals to Pan-Asian sentiment as justification for its own colonial ambitions.

He noted that thirty-five years after the Japanese assumed control of the island, "in the official language, and in the common speech of all Nipponese here, there are no 'Chinese' inhabitants. There are only Formosans, or *Honto-jin*—'Island Men.' " Schools were conducted in Japanese, with some teaching in English. Those who wished their children to have a Chinese education were only grudgingly permitted to send them to China. Even on the streets "Chinese exchange low bows, grin and—actually draw in their breath through their teeth in that irritating Japanese fashion!"

The Japanese banned public dancing on Formosa, though it was permitted in Japan. They imperiously rationalized: "If a civilization is strong enough, as ours is in Japan, the evil effects dancing may produce on the unsophisticated can be resisted." No restrictions, however, were placed on either Chinese singsong girls or Japanese geisha. They paid fat license fees as entertainers.

Much publicity had been given to Japan's "enlightened experiment" with opium eradication on Formosa, but Snow's efforts to obtain hard information about it were thwarted. Not allowed to visit opium factories, he became skeptical of the vaunted value of licensing twenty-seven thousand users. He particularly questioned the daily allowance of nearly two ounces permitted licensees, since "few addicts use more than two ounces in 24 hours." He could find neither an education program nor a house of refuge to meet addicts' needs.

Finishing his brief investigation into Japan's colonial rule, he found his only means of travel to Hong Kong was again a single ship, this time the *Canton Maru*, sailing on Sunday, October 5. First class was booked up. Second class meant "a ten-by-eight cabin stuffed with either sex, who share a common delight in sleeping with the windows closed." In his cabin a Chinese woman was seasick, a young Japanese woman was melancholy because her engagement had just been broken, and three Japanese men talked or read love stories into the night without regard for Snow's need for sleep. When the wives of these men appeared from steerage to feed them, Snow seethed. But neither anger nor guile enabled him to prevail on his fellow passengers to open the porthole for fresh air.[3]

On a map of Asia, Canton, Macao, and Hong Kong all sit close to each other on the southeastern curve of the continent. Each is a natural port. Canton and Macao sit further up a wide-mouthed estuary from Hong Kong. Maritime merchants and explorers from the West visited early and left their calling cards with varying success. Snow was going out the way the West had come in. Despite logging an impressive number of miles traveling throughout China during his first two years, he had never gone south to Canton from Shanghai. He was curious to see the original seat of the modern Chinese national movement that aroused in him such strongly mixed feelings. Dr. Sun Fo, the son of Dr. Sun Yat-sen, had proudly advised him, "In Canton you will see how a progressive and modern city can be run by our party."

Canton was rich in Kuomintang history and a base of strength for the Sun family. Snow was skeptical of the mythicizing of Sun Yat-sen then in progress. Chiang Kai-shek's political effort to assume and spread the mantle of Sun Yat-sen through his courtship and marriage of Soong Mei-ling, the sister of the widowed Mme. Sun, his efforts to identify the latter with his cause despite her explicit public repudiations, and his building of the Sun Yat-sen memorial in Nanking—Chiang's choice of a national capital in repudiation of the former governing body at Wuhan—ripely merited the critical comments of Shanghai's foreign press during Snow's residence there. Thus Snow was happy to find and write about another Cantonese doctor who was a very loyal friend to Sun Yat-sen and who left a heritage of more immediately beneficial public service. The Wu Hon Memorial Hospital was at this time more clearly a success than the realization of Sun Yat-sen's airy "Three Principles," *San Min Chu-i.*

But Snow also learned much that was disillusioning about Sun Fo, the man who had early provided him some prized journalistic opportunities. In *Journey to the Beginning,* Snow indicated he learned about Sun from Kan Teh-yuan, a crusading journalist persecuted by the politicians he sometimes publicly exposed. In his diary, however, Snow also expressed severe reservations about Kan because of his willingness to extort money from people of various nationalities he threatened to expose. Nevertheless Snow found the evidence against Sun Fo overwhelming:

> Sun now has 3 houses in Nanking & 2 in Shanghai. He was removed from office in Canton by his father because of official corruption. In Canton he has reputation of being worst embezzler in the gov. One thing— many ancient temples destroyed by him during time he was mayor of

Canton. No account ever made of use of money received for sale of temple property. But, for that matter, little account is made of any money received by local gov.

Canton's Sun Yat-sen memorial gave him an opportunity to express some of his mixed feelings about the patchwork nature of the Chinese nationalist movement. He noted the incongruity of combining on a carved pavilion both an Egyptian obelisk and a stone reproduction of the Liberty Bell. Behind was a building reminiscent of the Trianon of Versailles with a heavy granite pyramid roof. "Topping it all, and gazing out from almond eyes over high Mongol check bones, is a ten foot replica of Bartholdi's statue of 'Liberty Enlightening the World!'" On reflection, however, the monument was more appropriate than he first thought: "These men created something typical, a record true to China since the revolution. Nothing could be more symbolic of the far chaos and suffering, the stubborn conflict of beliefs, and the stupidity and selfishness that have torn China for the last twenty years."[4]

In *Journey to the Beginning*, Snow also reported that when Kan Teh-yuan got in trouble with his Kuomintang superiors he considered the island of Shameen, the foreign residential area in Canton, a refuge. The island, originally "only a dismal sandbar that disappeared at high tide," was first offered to the Dutch, who disdained it. But in 1859 European opium dealers accepted the concession. The French and the British, particularly, took the grant seriously, "erected high stout stone retaining walls . . . [and] dumped enough earth to fill in an area of forty-four acres." Shameen became a choice residential area for foreigners, sometimes known as the "Dutch Folly" in memory of the earlier Dutch refusal. No Chinese, save menials, could live there. No rickshas, cars, or even horses were allowed.

In 1926 the British fired on a group of Chinese demonstrators from the bridge of Shameen and sparked a strike and boycott against British goods that spread with astonishing effectiveness from Canton to Hong Kong.

> For six months the luxury-loving taipans on the island had to scramble their own eggs, sweep their floors, and light their own Havana cigars. It was terrible. Some of them found their domestic tasks so exhausting that they closed up their offices and moved to Hong Kong. By the time the strike was settled the surviving foreigners were almost willing to forfeit their cherished extraterritorial rights in exchange for Chinese cooks and some minions who would obediently answer, "Yes Mastah!" to the imperious call of "Boy!"

While Snow did not mention Kan's use of Shameen as a sanctuary in his contemporary articles, he did note in passing that "Eugene Chen, former

Minister of Foreign Affairs for the Nationalist Government, found his British passport convenient when for two days he is reported to have hid in Shameen while his enemies were scouring the alleys of Canton for him." Chen was the fiery Trinidadian who played an outspoken role in the Kuomintang from the death of Sun Yat-sen to the flight of the leftists from Hankow in 1927.

The articles Snow wrote that were not currently topical sometimes were held for later publication. The *China Weekly Review* published Snow's piece on Shameen only after he returned to Shanghai, about ten months after it was written. Eugene Chen promptly telegrammed: "Snow's references to me in article reprinted in last issue of 'The Review' is an unmitigated lie. I have never lived in Shameen, under a British passport or otherwise, for two days or for any other period of time."

Snow immediately replied:

> As the story was written last October obviously it could not have been with the purpose of injuring Mr. Chen or of jeopardizing his political career in China, since at that time he was sojourning elsewhere and supposedly had definitely left the scene. . . . However, I do not see that there is anything disgraceful in a man's utilizing any legitimate means to avoid being killed or imprisoned by his political opponent in China.[5]

Kan Teh-yuan introduced Snow to G. Edward Lyon, an American and the only foreign attorney recognized by the Canton bar association. With Lyon's help he learned a good bit about the Cantonese police force, observed a court trial, and visited a "model" women's prison. He wrote articles about each.

While Snow was very aware of how repressive and tyrannical police could be in China, he had strong praise for thirty-six-year-old General Au Yang-ku, the head of Canton's police force. Au succeeded because he introduced reforms to ensure his men were relatively "well paid, systematically educated, and satisfied with their jobs." These were hardly revolutionary acts, but they were sufficiently rare to merit special notice and praise.

The judiciary in action brought no such praise from Snow. He observed a trial presided over by noticeably young judges who could not have had more than a year or two at the bar. A lawyer friend, presumably Lyon, admitted, "They have not all had that. . . . But the Government is not worrying so much about the present as the future. They hope that these younger men, who are getting valuable experience, will form the basis for a sound, modern judicial system a few years from now." Snow listed three examples of obvious miscarriages of justice. His summary comment, "It is doubtless a fine scheme—for the judiciary. One trusts that the public will live through it."

The liberation of women from feudal customs was a significant part of the modern nationalist movement, and Snow had written sympathetic, but somewhat bemused, articles about it in Shanghai for the *China Weekly Review*. It was a legitimate litmus test of progress. Hence his visit to a model women's prison whose Cantonese name Snow rendered Hon San-so (in Mandarin: K'an-shou So). Snow found twenty-three women jailed on charges of adultery. Others were imprisoned for soliciting without a license; three for Communism; one, a concubine who fled her elder owner, for being a runaway; and several for failure to pay taxes. Many pushed notes on him. He published one from a woman whose husband charged her with adultery. Her husband was older and became jealous when he found his wife laughing and talking with his friend who was her age. The woman complained she was "put in jail, just on his word, and without any trial whatever. For four months I have been here, and no friend, not even that craven Ng Pu Shih, has made any attempt to have me set free. If I could once appear before an honest judge, I am certain that I could establish my innocence."

Snow gave Lyon the letter and elicited a commitment he would try to get her a fair trial. He recognized many of the stories he heard were likely to be distorted, even completely fabricated: "Yet it is more than probable that behind each of them there was a substance of truth. The fact that the Cantonese who accompanied me found nothing strange in the imprisonment of women for infidelity indicated that the practice is not uncommon here." Not uncommon even though the modern legal code, recently promulgated at Nanking, and supposedly functioning in this city, provided that every woman should have the same legal rights as men.[6]

Snow spent a little more than a month in Canton before sailing for Hong Kong. His stay in Hong Kong was brief. He was in Macao by mid-November. His only article on Hong Kong ended with a story of his visit with a Chinese friend to the comfortable British hotel overlooking Repulse Bay. Both, entranced with the beauty of the Chinese women on the dance floor, match poetic compliments, the friend concluding, "What I cannot understand is why a Chinese, with so much to charm him in his own race, should want to marry a foreign girl." Snow gave the story an easy O. Henry ending by remembering his friend in fact had an American wife, "a five-and-ten girl. . . . What could one say? He had made a mistake, but it was worse than that; he had to live with his mistake for the rest of his life." He was Chinese. This sentimental vignette was apparently developed from his own bachelor musings. There is no hint of such an event in his diary.

The day after his arrival in Macao he traveled by car first to Tang Kai Chuen (Mandarin, Tsuihengtsun), the home of former premier Tang Shaoyi, and nearby Choyhung, which Snow referred to as Chang Hoy, the birthplace of Dr. Sun Yat-sen. Each of these places became subjects for his travel articles. He explained how Macao's historic failure to compete with Hong Kong as a modern international port left it little more than a raffish center for gambling and a notorious "clearing house for the eroticisms." He praised Tang Kai Chuen's contrasting village cleanliness and order, but was more skeptical about the former premier's continuing ambitious entrepreneurial plans. At the former home of Dr. Sun he noted that Smedley was one of two Americans who preceded him that year. He quoted the message she left, "I am sorry that the original clay hut where Sun Yat-sen was born has not been preserved to show how he came from the poorest and humblest of people." Snow, however, giving the Sun family priority over the class from which they emerged, found their desire to put the restrictions of Sun's impoverished youth behind them quite understandable.[7]

9

The Embrace of France

T HE *CANTON MARU,* THE same ship that carried Snow from Formosa to Hong Kong, was crowded with sheep, rice, and Chinese when
it landed at Haiphong late in the morning on November 23, but on
this trip Snow was not the only Westerner. He left the ship accompanied
by Bill Smith, an engineer for Andersen Meyer and Company, and Pierre
Bloy, aviator, ex-manager of Coty's Chicago factory, and friend of chorus girls
and show people from the States and Europe. A Mr. Solomon from Standard
Oil had come to the ship expecting to meet a woman friend of his family.
Not finding her, Solomon took the three in tow and ushered them through
customs and into rickshas for the Hotel de l'Europe, where they got "slightly
squiffed" on cheap but good wine at lunch.

In a travel article about his Haiphong experience Snow claimed his trip
through customs was not as smooth as his diary indicates. He told of being
confronted by French customs officials who took his passport, advising him
he could call for it the next day at the police station. Undisturbed by his
protested wish "to go up to Hanoi that night," the officials searched through
his luggage to satisfy themselves he was not carrying "arms, ammunition,
opium, or narcotics" and his books were not by "Lenin, Trotsky, Gorky nor
Lu Hsun."

Snow had no time to interview M. Pasquier, the governor-general of Indo-
China, in Haiphong as he claimed in *Journey to the Beginning.* The information he attributed to this interview was gained instead later in Hanoi from

M. Garreau, chef de la service pour l'étrangers. The afternoon they arrived Bloy, Smith, and he went to a "second rate musical comedy with a second rate cast," then to a dance that evening. He and Bloy drove early the next morning to Hanoi.

The chorines in the musical comedy were old and haggard, but Snow was intrigued by a "middle-aged Frenchman, nearly bald, very wide at the hips . . . with a double chin," with a particularly disquieting coarse laugh. A young Annamese girl, trim and supple, sat on her feet in the seat next to him. She did not smile, even when her companion explained the show's humor. "In her eyes there was the stubborn hurt look of a sensitive child . . . made to eat something which was repulsive to her."

After noting many French colonials with their native wives, mistresses, and children in the audience, Snow suggested to his French host, "it looked as though the white men were being absorbed by the natives. Love was a leavener of color prejudice, and after all was perhaps the most disastrous weapon against imperialism."

His friend replied, "Oh ce n'est rien! These things are not enduring or important. And it is not love, my friend; it is a matter of comfort and convenience. I tell you a man gets lonely and morbid out here without a woman. If you were to live here for a while you would understand."

After the musical he, Bloy, and Smith in fact attended a dance notable for its many Eurasian women and hundreds of Frenchmen. This seems the experience that Snow later developed in *Journey to the Beginning* into a fictional party in Hanoi served by "Eurasian girls, dressed in native silk trousers only." No "shady ladies" were allowed to ply their trade at the dance, but they did operate in nearby hotels and private boardinghouses.

Snow spent only one night in Haiphong. The following evening he reported driving the ninety miles to Hanoi in an hour and forty-five minutes with Bloy. He stayed in Hanoi for ten days.

M. Garreau told him of a mutiny among Annamese troops in February that was harshly put down. A series of minor outbreaks followed. A revolutionary plot was discovered and attributed to a "few clever communists." The premature rebellion was quickly crushed. Snow later wrote in *Journey to the Beginning* he smuggled reports of these incidents to Hong Kong and thence to the United States. The source of this claim is most likely a report he filed only ten months later, after he returned to Shanghai. He kept a copy of the story in his scrapbook. It will be discussed in a later context.

Snow also learned that in June peasants demonstrated against landlords in Dalat and other cities of Cochin-China (South Vietnam). In September five thousand peasants, armed but peaceful, marched on Vinh, the provincial capital of North Annam. The French responded with bombs and machine guns. One hundred fifty were killed and six hundred wounded, but the march continued. The peasant demonstrations spread to other cities, and the French responded with troops occupying and policing the major cities. The French claimed sixty revolutionary leaders had taken refuge in Canton.

It was from Garreau he learned that sabotage prevented Governor-General Pasquier from sailing from Haiphong. The boiler of his ship was ripped out and the engine damaged. Pasquier had to return to Hanoi but soon "turned the incident to his own glory by suddenly deciding to accompany the aviators Goulette and Laouette," who were attempting to set a new flight record between Indo-China and the Continent.

Snow also read the newspaper La Volouté Indo-Chinoise and noted its strong editorial criticizing the government's policy toward the Communist movement and its report of the execution of twelve Communists over three days, from November 23 to November 25.

Despite all he learned from Garreau and La Volouté Indo-Chinoise, Snow's own strong antipathy to colonialism seems to have provoked him to over-generalize the subservient behavior he observed of the Annamese and Tonk-inese. He commented on it more than once in his diary, and at the conclusion of his Hanoi article he wrote with what retrospectively seems embarrassing assuredness and strength of feeling: "There is something about these people that hurts you. In them there is the strangely distressing quality that you see in the eyes of those who have resigned themselves to stronger men. They look as though they had never been anything but a subject race, and worse, as if it had never occurred to them, that they might be anything else." He was only at the beginning of a lengthy learning experience in the historic force of the various Asian nationalist revolts against European colonialism.

Touring Hanoi, Snow noted the yet strong cultural influence of China then being replaced by the French. He admired the graceful Confucian temple on the shore of Petit Lac and with embarrassment intruded upon a young Annamese girl at prayer before Kuan Yin. He rejected forthrightly his French host's politically complacent distinction between the French administration of Tonkin as a "protectorate," and its administration of Cochin-China as a true colony with all its advantages, a distinction that again would haunt America's later tragic war in Vietnam: "Now, it seems absurd for anyone to dispute that Hanoi is the political and commercial capital of French imperialism in Tonkin and Annam and Laos. It is to the north, with its port of Haiphong, what Saigon is to Cambodia and Cochin-China in the south. Yet the Frenchmen insist that such is not the case. Then they remind me of the Japanese."[1]

He left Hanoi early in the morning of December 4 on the railroad the French built to extend their influence into a part of China very remote from the China he had known. His train stopped uneventfully late that afternoon in Laokay and resumed its journey the next morning. He had a comfortable meal and room at the Hotel de la Gare. The next day was more exciting. Inside China, at Pishihchai, the train was invaded by Yunnanese soldiers returning from an embarrassing defeat at Nanning.

When the relative comfort of Snow's first-class passenger car became crowded with weary and hungry peasant soldiers, ragtag remnants of a force of fifty thousand men, his newsman's curiosity sensed one more story on what was becoming a lengthy list of tragic human consequences he had personally observed of the devastating traffic in opium. These men had been coerced into escorting a rich caravan of opium-laden mules from Yunnan to the consuming centers of Shiuchow, Wuchow, and Canton. The Yunnan warlords were desperate to break a blockade set up for the last year by the "Red" generals of the south. They touted their force as a "punitive expedition" against the Kwangsi bandits. But the rebel forces of Pei Tsung-hsi and Chang Fah-kwie were victorious, and on their return the conscripted soldiers were disarmed and disbanded without money and with minimal rations of rice at the Yunnan border by their own officers. They were told to report to the capital, nearly four hundred miles away, for their pay. It was a telling lesson in the corruption of the Yunnan government.

The surly soldiers were in no mood to respect the conventional restrictions of first-class travel, much to the resentment of a British colonial fresh from India also traveling in the car. But Snow quickly realized "these were good men, ending a tiresome, hazardous journey into which the world had buffeted them unwilling . . . still a long way from home, sick, with no money and no food." Since they had provided him with what he was seeking as a journalist, incident not comfort, he repaid those nearest at the end of their common journey with a basket of fruit, a box of cookies, and a Yunnan dollar for each.

On the second of his three-day train ride, from Laokay to Ami-chow, he nevertheless dispassionately admired the audacity and ingenuity of French engineering:

> Starting at Haiphong, the port city of north Tonkin, it [the train] rolls up to the foot of mountainous southern Yunnan, takes hold with talons of steel, and proceeds to pull itself up and ever upward, clinging to rocky pinnacles, burrowing through them in long tunnels, slashing into the precipitous sides nearer and nearer the clouds till at last it emerges high on the Yunnan plain and more than a mile above the delta of the sluggish Red River, back to the south and east, near the sea, where it began.

But the very challenges of the mountainous terrain that made the railway such a superb engineering feat also ironically caused the defeat of the French colonial ambition that inspired it. The sudden rise and fall of mountains isolated peoples and communities and afforded effective protection to ancient feudal corruption and arbitrary rule against the spread of the more modern corruption and arbitrary rule of European colonialism. While he admired the bold planning and ingenious engineering of the railway, he did not regret the thwarting of French imperial and commercial interests.[2]

10

Within the Shadows
of the Golden Horse
and the Jade Phoenix

S NOW ARRIVED IN YUNNANFU on December 7, 1931, ten years before the Japanese bombing of Pearl Harbor, and a little more than nine years before his own often-promised return to the United States. He was very conscious he was six weeks behind the schedule he had given Conso Press, but on his first evening in Yunnanfu he heard promising news. Harry Stevens, the American consul, called on him at the Hotel du Commerce and told him Dr. Joseph Rock, the internationally known botanist turned ethnographer, whom Snow hoped to meet, was in town preparing a caravan. Stevens also invited Snow to stay at the consulate, though he warned it was being painted and there might be no blankets for his bed. Weary of shabby colonial hotels and eager for American company, Snow quickly accepted.

Dr. Rock's famed scientific achievements along with his idiosyncratic ways publicly revealed in the pages of the *National Geographic* made him a legendary figure before and after Snow traveled with him. Colonel Roosevelt apparently did not mention Rock's more difficult traits. Snow had to learn about these during the next two months. But fifty-five years later another famous travel writer, Bruce Chatwin, reported a conversation about Rock he had with the doctor father of a Na-Khi family in a small village in Yunnan. The man Chatwin talked with had been partially trained by Rock and remembered him by his Na-Khi name, Le-Ke. He asked Chatwin, who by this time had followed Rock's career with persistent curiosity, "why was Le-Ke so angry with us?"

Chatwin replied: "He wasn't angry with you. He was born angry." Then he explained: "I should perhaps have added that the targets of his anger included the *National Geographic* magazine (for rewriting his prose), his Viennese nephew, Harvard University, women, the State Department, the Kuomintang, Reds, red tape, missionaries, Holy Rollers, Chinese bandits, and bankrupt Western civilization."

Chatwin's interest in Rock was sparked when he learned another eccentric genius, Ezra Pound, had discovered Rock's work while locked up as insane in St. Elizabeth's in 1956. Pound was probably particularly moved by Rock's persistence and courage in overcoming the loss of eighteen three-hundred-page notebooks and a four-volume manuscript, the fruits of his research on Na-Khi culture, to a Japanese torpedo at sea in World War II. He wove references to Rock's work into *The Cantos*, finally placing Rock among those historical figures giving him most inspiration and comfort:

> Yet to walk with Mozart, Agassiz and Linnaeus
>   'neath overhanging air under sun-beat
> Here take thy mind's space
> And to this garden, Marcella, ever seeking by petal, by leaf-vein
>   out of dark, and toward half-light
>
> And over Li Chiang, the snow range is turquoise
> Rock's world that he saved us for memory
>   a thin trace in high air
> And with them Pare (Ambroise) and the Men against Death
>   [13/786][1]

Happy with the prospect of meeting this legend and quickly fulfilling his dream journey, Snow moved into the Stevens's home, which turned out to be indeed "barnlike and without heat." He wrote Howard the next morning. He had not originally wanted to believe his brother's wedding announcement, but a letter waiting for him in Yunnanfu left no room for doubt. He offered deepest, heartiest wishes Howard would find his "new life interesting and rich with the rare happiness that comes to few men." His own hopes to join Rock's *National Geographic* expedition before Christmas were his compensation. Stevens took Snow to meet Rock for lunch, and Rock readily invited Snow that very day to join his caravan.

But their joint caravan would in fact not begin until January 31, almost two months later. Making the decisions necessary to travel by caravan from Yunnan to Burma with reasonable safety would prove far more difficult on the spot than when Snow dreamed about the trip in Shanghai. Neither

Snow's relations with Stevens nor those with Rock developed smoothly. Snow was originally flattered by Rock's friendliness and more than a little awed by his scholarly achievements. He also envied Rock's success at marketing his writing. He noted in his diary that *National Geographic* paid Rock fifteen hundred dollars per article and gave him a contract guaranteeing seven thousand dollars for a two-hundred-thousand-word book manuscript.

Snow had little way of knowing, however, that Rock had been sitting in Yunnanfu since October in a professional funk brought on by his failure to secure dependable funding for his work on a recent visit to the United States. Rock no more understood the economic depression spreading across the U.S. than did Snow, but Rock took his failure to win financial support as a professional insult. The sums he told Snow he had readily at command were probably a show of bravado. Rock's biographer wrote: "It was Edgar Snow, finally, who roused Rock from his stupor," even though Rock conceived an instant dislike for him.

A week after his arrival Snow noted in his diary Rock could not leave until after Christmas. By December 21 Snow also began to feel his prolonged stay with the Stevens's was resented, particularly by Mrs. Stevens. She had not been consulted before her husband invited him, and he was sure "she jealously guards her position as hostess of the house." But Stevens himself suddenly developed a "persecution complex." He insisted Snow take a pledge to write nothing at all about him. Snow could not understand what prompted his concern. At any rate Snow realized he had to move from the house and did so, back to the Hotel du Commerce, on December 23. By this time he also became privy to both Stevens's and Rock's more guarded and critical views of each other, neither of which were very complimentary.

A few days before Christmas, Rock was still unready to travel. Snow decided he would proceed on his own by caravan to Bhamo. Rock recommended Snow hire Rock's discharged cook, Ho Shi. On December 23 Rock informed Snow his caravan had arrived in the city. With Ho Shi's help Snow purchased supplies and made all the necessary arrangements to travel, but immediately listed these misgivings in his diary: "Possibility of robbery & kidnapping; chance of delay by magistrates who refuse to give permission to pass through their territory because of unsettled conditions; my inability to make self understood in Chinese; insufficient funds in case of emergencies; consciousness of having done no work since my arrival in Yunnanfu 20 days before; and likelihood of inability to do anything for next 40 days."

On December 29 he decided against going solo and enlisted the help of Stevens and Wang, an interpreter from Stevens's office, in retrieving his supplies already strapped on board the mules waiting at nearby Anningchow, the jumping-off place for the caravan.

Rock was very unhappy with Snow's sudden change of mind and the embarrassment it caused him with his former cook. He charged Snow with arbitrarily breaking his contract and failing to pay the muleteers sufficiently for their lost opportunity. In his own diary he described Snow as an "uncouth American youth . . . only learned in ill manners." As evidence Rock contemptuously noted Snow had bought potassium cyanide instead of potassium permanganate to disinfect fresh vegetables on his trip. The mistake could have killed Snow and his cook at their first meal.

Despite their differences and antipathies the two apparently respected each other's talents. As Snow learned more about Rock's personality and his past he tried to fathom his "curious mixture of conviviality & seclusiveness." He posed a question about Rock he might have asked about himself: "What force is it, unseen by us, which urges men into voluntary withdrawal from crowd and kind? It must be some trace of atavism mixed with a driving pull toward the thrills of living that are found nearest the greatness of nature which despite all men's genius, still reduced his total accomplishment to nothingness in the great high spaces of time & perpetuity."

As early as December 10 Snow began noting traits in Rock he would have to allow for in their future relation: "Susceptible to flattery. Easily led on to conversation by playing on his vanity. . . . Does not like criticism. Thinks J. B. Powell is a Bolshevik." Rock's suspicions of Powell stemmed from the latter's publishing an article by Jack Young that raised unwelcome questions about Rock's activities.

By January 3 Rock apparently had dismissed his anger at Snow's abrupt decision not to go on caravan alone. At lunch he let Snow know he expected his own caravan to leave by January 20. At first Snow said nothing, mulling over his own choices. A week later, after more candid talk between them, he decided once more to travel with Rock. Even then the question did not remain decided for long.

On January 12, the Parkers, YMCA people, invited Snow to move in with them. That same day Stevens wrote telling him two Seventh Day Adventist missionaries were traveling to Tali two days later, and Snow could travel with them. While Snow considered Stevens's note, Rock arrived and abruptly announced, "Well, I think you had better not go with me." At first Snow could not believe he was serious, but after some talk, Rock pouted, "Go with them. They're not *naturalized* Americans. . . . You don't like naturalized Americans, I understand." Then he turned on his heel and left. The son of a baker and Austrian-born, Rock was sensitive about such matters.

Snow requested an explanation, but he felt aggrieved and angry himself. When he met the missionaries he was pleased to find they were not the evangelical type, but he was not ready to leave until he received his mail and an expected check. January 13 was Rock's birthday, and at tea Rock told Mrs. Parker "an unclear story" of the cause of his previous day's behavior. At dinnertime he sent Snow a note, not mentioning his "blow-off" but again inviting Snow to travel with him. That evening at his home Rock urged Snow to let bygones be bygones. Snow agreed and noted in his diary, "Well, that's that—till tomorrow at least."

On January 20 Rock, ill in bed, postponed departure until the 25th. That same day Snow discovered to his surprise and dismay that a Japanese dentist, who had been drilling one of his teeth during more than one visit, was planning to "put a gold tooth in my head." He could only hope to have this "hideous thing" taken out when he reached Rangoon, but he feared "this devil has left very little of my tooth."

Two days later Snow wrote Mildred he planned to leave for Tali with Rock on January 25. He had purchased a seven-year-old, very animated pony for five hundred Chinese dollars (about nineteen dollars gold). He hoped to be in Tali by February 8. There he and Rock were to part: Rock north and west through Tibet into Turkestan, he south and west through Yungchang and Tengyueh to Bhamo. "I shall probably stay in Rangoon, or Calcutta for a month, writing and visiting local celebrities for material. Then a two months' trip through India, if the Consolidated Press is still willing to finance me. That should put me in Persia by the first of June."

The alarming reports he had heard of the American depression made him in no hurry to get home. He added, "What a gap has been left in things for me, now that Howard has started a new life!!" He enclosed ten dollars for some growing bit of greenery and blossom for his mother's grave. "I would like to see it there when I get home."

About that time Snow also questioned in his diary what Consolidated Press might say about all this procrastination. He despaired of being able to adequately explain his long delay or ever get sufficient copy out of his trip to make it worth their while. "My God, but it's awful—this fearful waiting, waiting. I do wish I'd gone on, the solitariness be damned. It would be better to be with bandits than biting my nails here in this filthy hole."

The caravan left on the morning of January 29, but Rock stayed in bed suffering from a bad cold. Still threatening to back out altogether, Rock finally joined Snow in driving from Yunnanfu late in the afternoon of January 31 to Laoyakuan in a car borrowed from a local official to catch up with their caravan. The car was one of only two serviceable in the city, and Rock and

Snow were the first to induce a driver to try the last fifteen miles of a short dirt highway then being built.[2]

While Snow criticized himself, probably too severely, for writing very little, he completed three articles about life in the ancient city and another about the area's commercial lifeblood, the opium trade, that would be subsequently excerpted in several magazines. He also recorded some choice material in his diary that surprisingly never reached print.

He began one article describing Yunnanfu as a city of trails' endings, the terminal of a railway and the beginning of a caravan, the last and first contact of East with West, "an absurd and hopeless confusion of nineteenth-century Chinese imperialism and grotesque young nationalism, of bewildered aborigines and a telephone system that does not work, . . . of smoldering paper prayers and electricity that gives no light, of savage dogs and furs and old embroideries." This last province to become part of China proper was ruled by a handful of war barons ostensibly loyal to the national Kuomintang government and the People's Three Principles, but in fact their rule seemed designed primarily to carry on a profitable trade in opium and to protect their barely disguised feudal power.

While Snow was in Yunnanfu, a Yi (Snow used *Lolo*, which is now considered prejudicial), Lung Yun, was the nominal governor. It was unusual for a tribal to reach such a prominent position for there had been little effort to sinicize the minority groups, who collectively made up the majority of the population. Lung had surprisingly returned to power after a military coup two years earlier. At that time he was "bound, put into a bamboo cage, carried through the streets of the capital and into the mountains, where it was planned to torture him to death." His return to office, however, was only on condition he command no troops. He served at the pleasure of Chang Feng-chung, garrison commander of the capital, and his rival, General Lu Han.

A brief postscript was attached to Snow's article announcing that after it was written Lung and Chang had fled the capital and Lu Han controlled the government. Lu Han was also the general who led the ill-fated opium caravan pretending to be an attack on the "Red" generals in Kwangsi.

This was frontier country and neither justice nor politics were likely to be argued nicely. Snow recorded in his diary that in November "52 vagabonds, loafers, & wandering coolies . . . with a few radical students," were executed "amid much beating of drums & blowing of bugles" at the East Gate. Two consuls had received threatening letters, so the government decided to reassure foreigners living in Yunnan that it had matters well in hand by contriving the mass trial and execution of these alleged Communists.

In the middle of December two men and one woman, said to be trained in Moscow, were arrested thirty *li* outside Yunnanfu. They were summarily executed without trial. On December 31 five more Communists were shot and then beheaded before a large holiday crowd outside the East Gate. Their bodies were left to lie in their own blood for three hours. This time Snow recorded, "They probably were guilty of [the] crime for which they were executed," though they were shot without trial within six hours of capture. In the midst of such official violence foreigners were ostentatiously protected.

Snow tried to visit the local prison, but found it impossible to gain admission. Women and children in Yunnanfu suffered feudal exploitation. Richard Lankester, English headmaster of a mission school run by the Anglican Church Missionary Society, told him: "Nearly every family has one or more slave girls. I should say it would be conservative to estimate the number at 20,000 in Yunnanfu alone. These are girls sold by parents at age of few months to 3 or four, or more, if family financially incapable of supporting them. Nearly all merchants have slave girls working in store. Treatment varies. Entirely up to owners. Sell from $150 to $200 Yunnan money. About $7.50 to $20.00 gold."

Snow called on the commissioner of Agriculture and Mining at 10 A.M., December 11. He was directed to a nearby singsong house from which the wealthy commissioner eventually emerged to walk back to his office with Snow. The commissioner was not a willing source of information, but Snow learned from other sources about child labor in the nearby Kochiu tin mines. Most of the four thousand laborers were children from seven to fourteen years of age. They carried 150-pound loads in wicker baskets on their backs. It was commonly said that every third of these children became hunchbacked. Child labor was also more visibly prevalent in Yunnanfu than in any other Chinese city Snow had visited. Snow wrote Richard Walsh, editor of *Asia*, of his distress at learning that for years the mine's chief engineer had been an American.

Poppies, the source of opium, were the second largest crop of Yunnan, second only to rice. The Yunnan trade was a constant source of irritation to the neighboring countries of Indo-China, Burma, and Thailand because it was illegal, conducted almost exclusively by smugglers, hence not officially regulated or taxed and also thus often an unfair source of competition. Farmers were "fined" three hundred dollars per *mou* for growing opium. This fine in effect was an indirect tax paid to the district government. A receipt was issued that then functioned as a license for the crop to be grown. The Opium Suppression Bureau, with about ten branches throughout the interior, collected the fines and thus served as minimal regulator.

Snow had a more personal brush with opium while he was staying at the Hotel du Commerce. A middle-aged French painter, Mme. Besant, whom he described as the "most engaging personality" he met in Yunnan, also stayed there. More a commercial artist than a potential Velázquez or Corot, she had a "deep sorrow in her eyes," nearly always hidden beneath long lashes.

He walked into her room once when she was painting a nude courtesan lying on a leopard robe smoking opium: "The rich contrast of her white flesh against the velvet softness of the leopard robe gave her the appearance of a kind of forbidden nocturnal flower unfolding in an erotic dream. I understood at once why Madame had chosen to paint her at night." Deep in her opium dream, the model gave no sign of resentment at Snow's entrance. Besant worked with intense quickness but gestured for Snow to remain. After about ten minutes the model finished her pipe, stretched, and fell asleep.

Besant quickly finished her painting and explained: "I didn't intend to paint her like that. I asked her for [a] simple standing nude. But she refused—said she'd be bored unless she could smoke. It was only after she started that I recognized an unusual picture. I painted it as swiftly as I could and it is finished now." She then invited Snow to dine with her, savoring the thought of her subject "lying on my bed in that supremely exhausted physical bliss."

Snow also interviewed the head of the salt gabelle. The tax on salt was a major source of government revenue, and the system set up to collect it often served as a useful informal banking and communication network for travelers. The interview led to another memorable experience. Kuo Ping-kan, the Yunnan director, invited Snow to a party on December 19. The party took place in an old-fashioned theater in a new public park. The evening scents of magnolia, tea roses, camellias, and prune blossoms drifted through the audience. The aisles within the theater were lit by colored lanterns. In front of the guests were plates of fruit, candy, and nuts, while vendors roamed the audience at large during the play. But outside the theater sat about fifty disbanded soldiers, some wounded, few with more than two items of their uniforms remaining. They sang songs and made remarks aimed at the women entering the theater.

A protégé of General Chang Hui-yuan, Hu Han-ling, played the lead, and Snow noted the staging and acting were as impressive as any he had seen outside the theaters of Shanghai. Hu played a beautiful young maiden, just what a Taoist god was looking for when he visited earth to cure the boredom he experienced in heaven. But she was in love with a monk with whom she fled. After an epic flight they were caught. She performed a dance remarkable for its jugglery of wands tipped with flashlights.

A great noise interrupted the dance. One of the proprietors rushed in to tell Chang Hui-yuan that soldiers were trying to force their way in without paying. Chang ordered his bodyguard to control them, and the play continued. A few minutes later a machine gun was heard. Then all was quiet. When the guests left the theater a half hour later there was no one hanging around the entrance. But Snow noted "a few dark forms that looked uncomfortably like corpses" in the shadow of a curved tea-house roof nearby.

Snow's nearly two months in Yunnanfu were also filled with more mundane activities such as nursing bad colds, playing tennis, riding out into the spectacular scenery of the nearby mountains, and shopping for gifts to send home. He found eight pewter mugs to send Horace Epes of Conso Press. He wrote extensively in his diary, storing experiences for later use in his writing.

He published one story just as Mr. Wang, the interpreter, told it as they were driving to Anningchow to retrieve Snow's goods and break his contracts with the muleteers after he abruptly called off his solo caravan trip. Snow was frustrated to the point of despair at the time, but later, hunched over his typewriter, he recognized he had heard a story that may well have been told to Marco Polo under like circumstances when the Venetian visited Yunnanfu, then known as Yachi. The charm of the story and its historic resonance made his current frustrations seem only the irritation needed to produce a pearl within the oyster.

A Chou prince mounted a marvelous golden flying horse on a mission to rescue two beautiful young maidens held shamelessly in concubinage by an elderly mandarin. The prince's wife was skeptical of his motives and became angrily jealous. After his return she seized an early opportunity to free the golden horse to fly away but too late realized it also carried her prized jade phoenix, the most talented bird in the world. Desperately trying to retrieve her bird, she stumbled into a nearby pond and drowned. The prince, filled with self-pity over his losses, lapsed into self-destructive debauchery. Thus the decline of the House of Chou.

Three thousand years later a great general brought Yunnan into the empire of the T'ang dynasty. Intrigued by the shape of the two distant mountains, he was told the mountains were sacred. On one the golden horse had descended and turned to stone, and on the other the jade phoenix had found a like fate. Struck by the legend the general bowed and had his men do likewise. When he rose he said to his followers: "Here where the shadows of the Chin Ma [Golden Horse] and the Pi Chi [Jade Phoenix] lengthen at the day's ending we will found a city dedicated to the wonders of the past. Let us be guided by the wisdom of our long-burried sages in creating this city which will one day be celebrated throughout the realm of the Imperial Dragon."[3]

11

On Caravan South of the Clouds

A FTER MEETING THEIR CARAVAN at Laoyakuan, Snow and Rock
spent a peaceful first night on the trail bedded down in a temple, with
Snow sleeping in the main hall beneath the "somewhat dusty gaze"
of a gaudy god of fecundity and wealth, who held in one hand a golden tael,
a symbol of prosperity, and in the other hand a gilded baby. Rock's Nashi
guardsmen's evening songs added a romantic aura to the bright moonlight.

Snow described Rock's elaborately comfortable mode of travel in his
autobiography: "He carried along everything Abercrombie and Fitch could
provide, including a folding bathtub and a complete kitchen. During the
march his tribal retainers divided into a vanguard and rear guard. The
advance party, led by a cook, an assistant cook, and a butler, would spot
a sheltered place with a good view, unfold the table and chairs on a leopard-
skin rug, and lay out clean linen cloth, china, silver and napkins." Snow, by
comparison, traveled light, but otherwise *Journey to the Beginning* gives little
hint of the tension and harsh feelings that troubled their two-week journey
to Tali.

After the first day on the trail Rock halted the caravan at Lufeng. His chest
cold had deepened, and all the reservations that had caused him to delay
starting the caravan again loomed large in his mind. The next day, February 2,
after breakfast he decided to return to Yunnanfu. Snow could go on with half
the mules and five of Rock's men. Snow also was not feeling well. He had a
line of skin eruptions on his back, arms, and legs, but after dinner he tried to

persuade Rock to continue the journey. They went to bed with Rock persisting in his decision to abandon the trip. Neither slept soundly, and sometime during the night they talked again. Snow once more tried to persuade Rock he would regret turning back from the caravan he had been so long planning. This time he succeeded. The full caravan resumed after breakfast the next morning, Rock in a sedan chair and Snow astride a stubborn beast of a mule for whom he had "no affection, no praise whatever."

They were still friendly three days later when they rested for a day at a mission at Chiu Hsiung. A Chinese nurse treated Snow's skin eruptions and brought him quick relief. Rock showed some concern by persuading Snow to hire a sedan chair to be available at need. Two days later all was still well. At Lu Ho Kai early in the afternoon a contented Snow wandered from the temple, where they pitched camp, to lay under a eucalyptus tree and pleasurably review his recent life and travels. After rolling through the names of the more exotic places he had visited since leaving Shanghai, he wrote in his diary: "All the richness of my youth seems bound forever to these names and adventure and romance, found unexpectedly with them." Years later an older, more skeptical Snow wrote in red pencil in the margin, *Merde 1951.*"

At Hungai, the last stop before Tali, an unexpected noise awakened Snow about two in the morning. He remembered that for the first time since beginning the caravan he had failed to put his gun and his purse under his pillow. He got up and with the aid of a flashlight retrieved them from a nearby table. His movements woke Rock, who demanded, "What are you doing?" Snow explained as he returned to his bed, but Rock was suspicious. He checked his own baggage with his flashlight and questioned Snow, "Why should you get up in the middle of the night to get your gun? This is funny business. . . . All right, if you are going to sleep with your gun, I'll take mine to bed with me too. What do you think of that?"

Snow recorded his surprise and resentment in his diary: "Here was a man who had lucidly exhibited his cardinal obsessions: his money and himself. . . . The facts that he had no wife, no relatives, no one who is dependent upon him, sharply accentuates this weakness of his. He has developed an instant skepticism; he is the victim of his own selfishness, his egotism. He has become, at heart, a misanthrope." It was not just the recent marriages of his brother and sister that encouraged Snow's darker thoughts about traveling alone through life.

After rising in the morning Rock asked if Snow had searched one of the men's suitcases looking for a missing book. Snow took this to be a disguised accusation of his going through Rock's own belongings. He angrily renounced Rock's suspicions, "I am astounded to think that you would think me capable of such a thing, after you have known me as you have, and slept with me, eaten with me, laughed with me over troubles we have shared together." After Rock backed off but did not apologize, nothing more was said. Snow had his own suspicions. He later added a note suggesting Rock had probably been snooping in his diary. His suspicions were sharpened by Rock's parting comment two days later.

The two barely spoke to each other again except to conclude their necessary business arrangements. They separated after arriving in Tali on the afternoon of February 13. Snow was invited to stay at the missionary home of the Kuhns, and Rock camped out on the grounds of the salt gabelle's office. Snow went to Rock's camp to settle accounts and resentfully paid what Rock said was due, though it was more than he remembered Rock originally asking. On leaving he said, "Well, I may see you again before you leave; if not, good luck! Good bye." When he reached the outer court, Rock shouted after him, "And thank you for all the trouble you've taken for me! Thank you for acting secretary to me for three weeks!"

To which Snow replied, "Yes, of course. But most of all I thank you for suspecting me of being a crook!" And he left grateful he was "no longer dependent upon such an ungracious individual for further help or guidance." The parting antipathy was mutual. Rock summarized: "a most ungrateful and impertinent individual . . . I paid all the expenses because he would not have had money enough to take him half-way to Tali. I paid all the escorts, and his parting words were 'I may see you before you go,' without even so much as a word of thanks. . . . He is a greenhorn of the first order and an impertinent sponger."[1] From Tali, Rock headed for residence among the Na-Khi people whose customs and history he eventually recorded in his ponderous *The Ancient Na-Khi Kingdom of South-west China*. These were the people Snow referred to as Nashis.

Snow appreciated the domestic comfort of his four days and five nights with the Kuhns at the China Inland Mission—a hot bath, Sunday morning breakfast in bed, a hike up to the snow line of the mountains, and even an earnest inquiry into the Kuhns' fundamentalist beliefs. These were decent, generous, dedicated people whose beliefs were literally incredible, but of considerable interest, to Snow. Amid the distractions and complications posed by the Chinese New Year celebration, Kuhn helped Snow arrange his new and more modest caravan for the next stage of his journey. When Snow's departure was delayed a day because of the tardiness of Rock's former cook, Ho Shi, and the muleteers, plus Snow's dissatisfaction with the horse they brought for him to ride, Kuhn helped Snow fire Ho Shi and offered his own mule in place of the ungainly nag. Snow was thus ready to leave Tali on the morning of February 18, rested and eager, on his own at last, free of Rock's presence, and even free of the petty thievery and lack of discipline of Ho Shi.

While in Tali, Snow also received another invitation that apparently continued to work in his mind until he wrote up a fictional variation for a travel article. Just before Snow was ready to leave, Kuhn took him to meet the magistrate of Tali and to inform the latter of Snow's departure. The magistrate prided himself upon being modern and well informed about contemporary world events. He urged Snow to stay and tutor his sixteen-year-old son, who had learned English at the YMCA in Yunnanfu. He offered good pay and excellent board. Snow could live in the magistrate's own yamen. Snow took a hasty glance into other unswept rooms of the yamen and politely declined the invitation.

Later he wrote an article describing a similar, but more attractive, offer from the *sawbwa* of Kanai, a caravan stop close to the Burma border. There is no hint of such an offer or even of a visit with such a sawbwa in Snow's diary, though his stay at Kanai is recorded in detail. The sawbwa of the article entertained Snow much more lavishly than the magistrate of Tali. Maru dancing girls appeared after an elaborate dinner, and the sawbwa suggested they were part of the pleasure Snow could expect if he settled in with the sawbwa's family. Snow wrote up these travel stories after he completed his caravan. There are other such transformations.[2]

The trip from Tali to Tengyueh where Snow again had to hire new mules and men for the final stage of his caravan proved a tough two-week test of Snow's romantic faith in travel. During the early days of this part of the trip the relief of being rid of Rock and Ho seemed enough to make Snow happy. Bandits were no longer a great fear, but the filth and disease prevalent in the backward communities that provided the only shelter along the trail became more and more difficult for him to put up with. A week from Tali, he arrived at Taipingpu in the middle of the afternoon. One "inn" was available. Snow took over the only livable room in the place and had it dusted and sprinkled. He ran four soldiers out of the next room so that his own men could use it. He was told no food, except soft-shell walnuts, was available for him to purchase for his dwindling supplies.

That evening two soldiers came for help with a great variety of pains suffered during the last two years. Snow listened to their complaints and suggested they go to bed early, quit smoking opium, and change their diet in ways he knew were next to impossible. Otherwise there was nothing he could do for them. They would not believe him and persisted in asking for medicine. Finally to get rid of them he gave one some quinine, the other some salts. Then the innkeeper and his wife, suffering from tuberculosis, syphilis, and chronic bronchitis, came begging for medicine. He tried to convince them also he had nothing adequate and that they needed to change their habits of life, but they too looked at him in disbelief. When he gave them two aspirins each to take with hot water and rice, they were grateful and astonished him by offering in return a cup of tea, a leg of chicken, and a red, white, and green ball of rice.

He wrote in his diary that day: "This afternoon I have been lonesome and homesick. And now I am discouraged, and worried over the loss of so much time. Those awful advertisements that say, 'Where will *you* be at 35' (or 40 or 60) begin to haunt me now, and I can no longer laugh at the thought of them, as always before."

At Shayang the next night he answered these forebodings with a reassertion of faith:

> There is a joy in this life; I understand Rock's love for it now. Leading one's own caravan, enjoying a special thrill of responsibility for the life of your men and yourself, riding into the morning mist, an hour ahead of the sun, driving yourself, on foot, over hills that tax the utmost strength in your limbs, and arriving toward sundown in a new valley, knowing not what room will hold your cot at night, and hoping only for quiet, well-earned sleep. These are the simple, primal thrills that no city dweller, no one who clings to the pavements can ever feel.

He recalled all the "sour advice of the stay-at-homes." He might still be selling hosiery, printing, or advertising if he had listened to their various sage and prudent advice. "I've not got but enough for three months of sparse living ahead, but I would not have missed any of the things I've blundered into for the best advertising man's job in New York!"

At Yungchang, a relatively large town, a few days later, he was distressed by the filth of the public accommodations. He called on the Booths, Canadian missionaries, but their mission was in the midst of repairs so they had no room for him. Having no other choice, he took a room at a public inn and subjected it to an epic cleaning process he later described for the amusement of his travel readers. Despite the dirty quarters he decided to lay over a day. The series of cleanings took place over both days and aroused considerable public notoriety and occasioned another notable visit.

At noon on the second day the inn master's brother called on Snow with his five-year-old son. The pale-faced boy had a cigarette hanging from his lips and a bad rash over his body. Snow gave the boy a dose of salts to be both swallowed and applied to the skin. Then he pounded the boy's chest and told the father his son would die in a month if he did not stop smoking cigarettes at once. The old man, surprised, complained that the boy cried unless he had at least two cigarettes an hour.

The man's primary mission, however, turned out to be not his son's health but to resolve a bet with his brother, the inn master, over whether all Americans really lined their coats with gold. Straightfaced, Snow told him it was true but that he had none of these coats with him since his traveling outfit was made in China. The inn master paid off his five-dollar bet, and the boy probably continued to shorten his life smoking cigarettes. Later, Snow exchanged a can of Bartlett pears, which Mrs. Booth thought a great treasure, for homemade bread, marmalade, and peanut butter and the next morning resumed his journey.

He could not always find such comic resources to frame his encounters with filth and disease for his readers. Just before reaching Tengyueh he stopped at another wayside inn, cleaner than most, for a lunch of rice, eggs, vegetables, and tea. Satisfied, he sat back to enjoy his cigarette, until he glimpsed the cook in the kitchen. He recorded what followed in his diary, but did not share it with his travel readers.

Three-fourths of the cook's face was covered with a dirty rag tied with a string to his forehead. Snow asked to look at the cook's eye, thinking it was infected and that he might offer some Argyrol to help. The cook reluctantly lifted the cloth: "Practically all the left side of his face was gone. There were maggots eating into the cheek bone, his nose had practically disappeared, there was a deep hole where the eye should have been, and part of his left lip already had been attacked. He was in the last stages of syphilis. The sight sickened me and I turned away with a shudder, hurriedly answering, 'No, I have nothing,' to his request for medicine."[3]

He arrived in Tengyueh late in the afternoon of March 2 and in sharp contrast with his public inn experiences enjoyed a three-night stay in colonial luxury, which he also did not share with his travel readers, apparently finding such luxury inconsistent with the sense of hardship and adventure he had carefully developed. The city's streets were wider and cleaner than in any other he had seen in Yunnan. He was charmed with the semitropic vegetation—roses, lilacs, jasmine, and clusters of bamboo even in the middle of town. "Against his instincts," presumably his anticolonial convictions, but happily for his sense of comfort he called at the British consulate and was invited to stay in the castlelike two-and-a-half-story structure built of handworked stone, with oiled woodwork, set on 180 tastefully landscaped acres surrounded by a foot-and-a-half-thick wall. He slept on a mattress for the first time since leaving Yunnanfu and enjoyed a leisurely breakfast in bed for two of the three mornings he stayed.

Stanley Wyatt-Smith, the British consul, was a gracious, congenial, and well-informed host. He introduced Snow to George Forrest, the pioneer botanist who preceded Rock in Yunnan and had passed on to Rock invaluable information about the culture and plant life of the province. The stout, red-faced burring Scotsman, then fifty-eight, helped Snow with the caravan arrangements for the final leg of his journey, even arranging for Snow to hire his own cook, the marvel Wang, who could produce in fifteen minutes in the heart of the jungle a five-course meal climaxed by a delicious century pudding. Snow referred to Forrest in his travel article only as an unnamed Scotch botanist. He apparently did not want to risk stirring up Rock's antipathy again by any public acknowledgment of his professional rival.

Wyatt-Smith's late and excellent dinner the first night was begun and followed by happy male drinking and storytelling, mostly about "sex and reminiscences of Shanghai cabarets." The genial company made him realize he still carried a real affection for the city he thought he was to know no more. He decided to stay a day longer, and the next evening his satisfaction reminded him of living in the China United, a modern apartment building in Shanghai, "which was after all my most pleasant experience in dwelling places in China. . . . How deeply I wish, that I could be back again in Shanghai, just for tonight."

His only published comments about Tengyueh are tacked onto a fictional episode about an innkeeper at Pupiao, two stops previous, who supposedly tried to sell her daughter to him in marriage. His comments about Tengyueh feature the suggestive cameo image of a young Chinese lady, astride a bright red dragon rug on a white-and-black pony, as elegant and beautiful as a young empress, riding out the gate as he rode in, lifting her smiling eyes as she bowed in response to his raised and flourished hat. "That is what I remember about Tengyueh."

His diary records a different probable source of this seemingly anomalous vision. On the final day of his caravan he was surprised by a quite different, but again beautiful, female apparition on horseback. This one, however, was English and dressed in a smart riding habit. She was the wife of the British deputy commissioner at Bhamo, and she was on her way to visit Wyatt-Smith at Tengyueh.[4] She became a link in Snow's imagination between an intense romantic episode he experienced at the Circuit House in Bhamo and Wyatt-Smith's comfortable male hosting.

On the morning of his departure from Tengyueh he sent the mules on ahead and had a late breakfast with Wyatt-Smith. It was 10 A.M. and two whiskies later before he took to the road. He recorded extensive notes in his diary about the Kachins that he gathered from Wyatt-Smith's library. It was Wyatt-Smith, not the fictional sawbwa, who warned him the Kachins had been raiding caravans. Wyatt-Smith also generously and wisely arranged for

Snow to have a military escort through the troubled area. On the second day out of Kanai he in fact encountered hostile Kachins.

Despite Wyatt-Smith's warning, he thoughtlessly hiked alone ahead of the caravan until he found himself suddenly uneasy about the vagueness of the trail and his distance from support. A crackle of twigs first made him aware of a lone, frightened Shan, who tersely warned him in Chinese of nearby Kachins. The Shan asked Snow to accompany him out of this dangerous spot, indicating Snow's foreignness offered them both some protection. But before moving very far they were intercepted by four Kachins running at them fiercely, apparently unimpressed by Snow's foreignness. When they came within six feet Snow fired his automatic twice in the air. The gun's noise had the desired effect. Surprised and frightened the Kachins fled.

His published account ended at this point, with him doubled up in hysterical laughter. His diary indicates both he and the Shan foolishly took to their heels. Seeing them flee, the Kachins regained their courage and again intercepted them. This time Snow, using the Shan as a translater, tried to impress the Kachins with the serious consequences of killing a foreigner and threatened them once more with his automatic. The Kachins only laughed and began warily to advance. Snow drew a line on the ground and had the Shan warn the Kachins he would shoot to kill if they crossed the line. One of the Kachins spoke at length to the Shan reducing the latter to hysterical fear. Snow could not persuade the Shan to explain the threat, but he suspected the Kachins had told the Shan in detail what would happen to him even though they would not harm the foreigner.

When the Kachins moved closer to the line, he fired near the feet of one of them. This time they did not flee but did jump back, recognizing something fearful and unknown in his weapon. Just as Snow began to wonder if he would have to shoot to kill, they all heard the sound of steps. Two soldiers hearing the shots came running. The Kachins fled at their approach and by the time the rest of the escort caught up had disappeared. Snow did not wander far from the caravan again.

His experience with the Kachins occurred on the day before he crossed the China-Burma border and three days before he met the beautiful Mrs. Clerk on her way to Tengyueh. She took the time to cordially invite him to stay at the British Circuit House in Bhamo and breakfast with her husband. Soon after meeting her Snow was again startled by a harsh sound he could not immediately identify. Unafraid, his cook explained it came from a "gas-cart." It was in fact the horn of a battered American truck. With a brief but regretful sigh Snow accepted the welcoming embrace of civilization and climbed aboard.[5]

12

Compelled by the Golden Spire

W HILE SNOW DID NOT mention meeting Mrs. Clerk on the trail in his travel piece, he did describe having tea on his arrival at the Circuit House in Bhamo with a gentleman and a lady, the lady "had the softest, darkest eyes that I have ever seen." In fact he had a prosaic lunch alone and met the obliging elderly Mr. Clerk afterward. The latter approved his wife's invitation for Snow to stay at the Circuit House and in addition invited Snow to drop in on his club. There was only one other guest at the house, a British Foreign Service auditor named Badock, a curious figure who seemed to step directly from the pages of Somerset Maugham into the memorable, but deliberately hidden, role he played in Snow's life during the next two days.

Snow's diary describes Badock as having been a sickly crippled child whom doctors had not expected to live past the age of fifteen but who clung determinedly to life while insisting as an adult he was resigned to die at any moment. Because of his physical deformity he thought himself unattractive to women of his own race, but he spoke of the beauty of Oriental women "in a voice that trembled and at times broke with the sheer loneliness of his image." Badock had a collection of "quite admirable" photographs of nude Indian and Burmese women he readily showed Snow, describing just as readily how in practice he carefully distinguished his "carnal whims" from his photography. After persuading young women to pose without clothes, he deliberately permitted "the subject to reclothe herself, step out of the room, ánd start home, before suggesting business of another sort."

The next day, March 12, Badock's Indian boy, Puddin, guided Snow through a variety of business errands before taking him to a Kachin school at the American Baptist Compound. However, the man in charge, aware of Badock's reputation, suspected Snow's motives as well and was decidedly uncordial. They returned to the Circuit House, where Wang, the cook Forrest had so superbly trained, prepared his last tiffin for Snow, and the two settled their accounts.

About three o'clock Puddin appeared with two Burmese women, "one of them stout and perspiring, the other tall, slender and with a tragic face." He thought Snow might want to take their photographs. When Snow quickly refused, he added, "If like, Mastah, can photograph without dress." He was visibly pained when his offer failed to arouse Snow's interest, but he and the women left quietly. A half hour later he reappeared with another subject. Expecting more of the same, Snow was surprised by the diminutive beauty and grace of the young woman he turned to see.

Badock meanwhile also returned. He talked to the young woman and with little difficulty persuaded her to pose nude on a wildcat robe Snow had purchased. The photos taken, she slipped into her silk *longyi* and crepe shirtwaist. Mumbling and giggling confusedly, she started back to her village. Following Badock's "nice etiquette," Snow waited until she was out the door before calling her back and suggesting "there is something else. . . ."

She came back. At 2 A.M. his knee began to swell from a mule kick he had received two days earlier. Malami applied warm compresses until his pain was soothed and he was quieted. "She is like something in burnished copper, only softened, animated by some divine power. There is something infinitely restful, comforting and preciously sweet about Malami." The young woman is usually referred to as Malami, but sometimes Ma Le, in the diary.

Malami left at 6 A.M., and Snow was grateful that Badock at breakfast was "discreetly silent about last night." But she returned that afternoon while Snow was packing his trunk and explained she intended to go with him to Rangoon. He made clear that was not possible, but she stayed to help him pack. When the packing was finished, Malami invented innocent games for them to play, until, while playing blindman's buff, she tripped over his fur robe and "bundled into a laughing, sobbing little heap of silk and flesh." When Badock, with his camera, knocked on his door an hour later, they were both exhausted, but she posed for more pictures.

After dinner Malami came along to the boat to see Snow off. In a last moment of weakness he was tempted to take her with him. He savored the prospect of flaunting British colonial propriety but feared the row the other European passengers would have created. "As it was their noses were up at a high slant because Malami walked to the gangplank and kissed me." There is no indication he ever saw Malami again after waving good-bye at the dock in Bhamo.[1]

Snow traveled by boat from Bhamo to Mandalay and by train from Mandalay to Rangoon. He spent at least a day in Mandalay, possibly two. His diary of his stay in Burma is not nearly so orderly or chronologically specific as of his caravan trip. He probably reached Rangoon sometime in the middle of March and stayed there until he took passage for Calcutta on April 22. He wrote the articles about his caravan trip from his diary while living in Rangoon. During his stay he also had a second romantic relationship with a young Burmese woman. To his travel readers he represented the two relationships as if they were one, and years later for *Journey to the Beginning* he fleshed out this story with even more extravagant fiction, representing it as a surprise "reward of hidden splendor" that followed the mishap of his being nearly crippled by the kick of his mule.

He met Ma So, a Talaing girl, at a party at a friend's house in Rangoon. Malami was eighteen, Ma So seventeen. The attraction was sudden and mutual. She came home with him that night and revisited him on several other occasions. He was as romantically lyrical writing about their relation in his diary as he had been about his feelings for Malami, but this second relation lasted longer than overnight.

His single article on Rangoon, necessarily written after he left, begins with the springtime carnival celebration of the arrival of Nat Thingyamin, the reigning spirit for that year. The Burmese were on the street gleefully cleansing each other's sins with cascades of water variously delivered. Foreigners, particularly British, were usually exempt from the damage and the fun. The heat of the day and the joy of the celebrants made Snow envious until he was suddenly engulfed by a Niagara of water delivered by slender little Malayin, who reproved him when he did not immediately recognize her, "you have forgot Bhamo so soon?" That comment may have had a double edge for Snow's private self, but he quickly explained to his readers that Malayin was sister to a young man, Meg Ba Win, whom he had last seen in Bhamo a month before.

Monday-born Malayin, with "eyes provocative in their dark merriment," supposedly came to Rangoon with her brother for her first pilgrimage to the Shwe Dagon, a storied Buddhist temple that looms impressively above the city, and to celebrate the New Year with her Rangoon relatives. Her brother "was off to a pwe, and nobody ever knew when a man would come back from a Burmese theater." So Snow tells of taking Malayin to a café, ignoring "the frigid glares and rudely audible comments flung to our table," and then pricked local colonial feeling by taking her to a movie. Malayin had a grand time, and they capped it off with a gharry ride (a Burmese horse and carriage) out along the river and finally a late-night romantic visit to the Shwe Dagon.

The temple visit Snow described corresponds very closely with what he recorded in his diary as taking place on his final night in Burma with Ma So. That afternoon he took pictures of Ma So nude on his wildcat robe, as Badock had of Malami. "Batala," the name Snow uses for his romantic partner in *Journey to the Beginning,* is inscribed in Snow's handwriting on two photographs of a nude young woman posed against a fur in the Edgar Snow Collection. They are probably Snow's photos of Ma So. At the temple Ma So explained the significance of the various shrines as they walked shoeless among a number of sleeping Burmese. He closed his diary record of this final evening: "Disturbing emotions produced by night, darkness, Ma So and self."

The sexual allusions in his description of their climb to the "flower-strewn base of the phallic spire," covered with gold and measuring 417 feet to its jewel-studded tip, take on humorous self-indulgent overtones in their extravagance. "The hill it stands on further augments its height, so that from far down the Rangoon River, long after the city itself is folded under the horizon, you still see the blazing crest of the Dagon parting the sky. It is a massive thing yet it tapers with a Grecian grace, superbly simple. The effect of its erotic symbolism is classic."

Ma So, unlike the fictional Malayin, was not from Bhamo, and there is no mention of a brother in Snow's diary. He apparently created the brother to link two separate romantic experiences. When he wrote *Journey to the Beginning,* Malayin became Batala. She also became a beautiful nurse vision he saw upon awakening from malarial fever and the pain of a mule kick to his knee that supposedly rendered him unconscious the final day of his caravan. This seems a romantic hyperbole for Malami's massaging of his injured knee at 2 A.M. on their one night together. Turning the girl-woman Malami into a professionally confident nurse made her more mature and responsible, and, in retrospect, may well have been an effort to assuage some of the disturbing doubts about his own responsibility in these relationships. In *Journey to the Beginning* he extended his two-night stay in Bhamo to more than a week for him to recover from malaria and his knee injury.

Batala, like Malayin in his article, later traveled from Bhamo to join him in Rangoon. He again enjoyed the "envious disapproval" of the British by consorting with Batala at the water festival and other social events, and together they too made a romantic nocturnal visit to the Shwe Dagon. His summary tribute to Batala is a more erotically subdued attempt to mine the romantic gold from a dubious realistic episode and probably to pay a disguised tribute to two young women who gave him more than he felt he could repay: "I had been a lonely stranger and she comforted me. I had been sick and weary and she made me whole again."[2]

One of the Westerners on board the *Taping* who witnessed his parting with Malami at Bhamo made a more personal impression on Snow once they began to talk. He was Douglas Parmentier, former New York banker and president of Harper Publishing Company, who took credit when he introduced himself to Snow for discovering John Dos Passos and Glenway Wescott as writers. Snow wrote in his diary that Parmentier had chucked everything, divorcing his wife a year or two before, to "see the world before it was completely spoilt." He had come up the Irrawaddy intending to join a caravan through western China. He had heard of Dr. Joseph Rock and hoped to join up with him. Instead he met Snow just emerging from the jungle and from happily shedding Rock's company only a few weeks previous.

Parmentier had already traveled extensively but still seemed to be searching for some illusive romance, adventure, or new spiritualism. Snow's description of Parmentier suggests he saw in the older man a haunting image of his own romantic questing, only at a more advanced age and of more privileged world-weariness:

> Parmentier reveals in his face more clearly than I have ever seen the soul of a supremely selfish man. There is a hardness to the jaw; something that suggests he has callously helped others to suffering and pain rather than experienced it himself. He is strikingly handsome. . . . Everything about him suggests the man of sensation; an individual who has starved his soul for the realization of all appetites of the body. I do not suggest lewdness; that would not suit him. He would wish his pleasures refined, artistic, richly emotional, like music or graceful movement.

Snow and Parmentier left the *Taping* at Mandalay together. They toured Mandalay until Parmentier insisted on loaning Snow a needed thirty rupees for his train ticket to Rangoon and then leaving himself for the British hill station at Maymyo. Guarding his short supply of cash, Snow traveled third class on the railway to Rangoon and delighted in the company of a husband-wife acting team who gave him a quick and rich lesson in Burmese theater, the probable source of his comment on Malayin's brother's preoccupation with the theater.

The typescript of Snow's diary at this point begins in the middle of a sentence about a romantic figure yearning for companionship who "blunders in every attempt at intimacy; and his youth, in the Orient, will not compensate the victims of his ignorance as sometimes it does in western countries."

Snow indicated he had just received a letter from Alfred Batson, the other journalist with whom he rode the train from Pukow to Tsinan a year earlier to test Japanese claims of not interfering with Chinese rail traffic. Batson had written about his recently published *Vagabond's Paradise* and John Marshall's "emetic" *Vagabond de Luxe.* The sentence fragment probably refers to one of the books' protagonists, yet the judgment made again suggests Snow at some level was questioning his own behavior.

Batson's letter complained that Marshall's book "contained one chapter after another of thinly veiled seduction of native princesses and daughters of merchant princes." This reference occurs in Snow's diary just prior to his description of the refined sensual selfishness he finds in Parmentier's face. Parmentier had probably witnessed Snow's ambivalent parting from Malami. Her provocative effort to persuade him to take her with him must have made clear to Snow she had hoped for more from their relationship than he was realistically willing to give.

As mentioned in the previous chapter Snow wrote a travel story about an innkeeper at Pupiao who tried to sell him her daughter as a bride. Nothing in Snow's diary indicates such an event actually occured, though the sale of human beings, particularly children, was notorious throughout the region. Snow's humorous account seems a more likely fictionally disguised effort to plead a case against some of the self-accusations that lingered from his relations with Malami and later with Ma So.

As Snow tells the story, Mme. Loi, the innkeeper, speaking elegant Chinese full of the old-fashioned "courtesy talk," sounds him out first about his age, marital status, and whether he has any children. When these questions are answered to her satisfaction, she motions forward her sixteen-year-old daughter and asks, "How would you like to have her for a wife?" Snow at first cannot believe the question, but, curious how this might play out, he replies, "What would I do with a wife? I am not a wealthy man. I cannot afford such nonsense." The girl's name is Me Le, suggestively close to Malami's other name, Ma Le.

Whimsically, Snow bargains with Mme. Loi. He protests the initial asking price of three hundred dollars, and when the price is finally lowered to one hundred dollars he suggests she must give him until morning to decide. A man must have a few hours to consider matrimony. Mme. Loi finds this reasonable and leaves the room, but Me Le stays. Her own curiosity by now provoked, she sat on her heels and looked him over.

> Then she took off her turban and shook her head so that her hair tumbled down over her shoulders. Slowly a wan smile crept over her face and then gradually her eyes grew radiant. She was very pretty, I decided, and like a

flower. It gratified me to believe that perhaps the prospect of our marriage was not altogether revolting to her. Suddenly, she smiled broadly, walked over to my cot, kicked off her sandals and without a word began to untie the knot of her skirt.

Alarmed, Snow could only shout, "Ai-ya!" and tell her "Tsai wei," "Sweet dreams," as he showed her the door. "Yet there was something so disturbing and provocative about the impudent little smile she gave me as she shrugged her shoulders and walked away that I decided to leave earlier next morning than I had planned."

Next morning he told his caravan driver to tie on the loads at 5 A.M. The latter, thinking they were taking Me Le, was clearly unhappy. Snow reassured him this was not the case and then asked if he could explain why Mme. Loi wanted to give him her daughter. The driver told him Me Le had secretly accepted the inn *ma-fu* (a man who takes care of horses) as her lover. They had been having a ravishing time until the matriarch discovered them yesterday morning. Angrily she made a vow by Buddha's image that her daughter would be given in marriage to the first traveler who stopped at the inn. "And I, out of 400,000,000 Chinese, happened to be that traveler." That settled it. "I would have no ma-fu's mistress for my bride."[3]

The O. Henry twist Snow gave to his fiction in the next morning's conversation with his sulking driver probably was an effort to reassure himself he was neither a cruelly selfish hedonist as he imagined Parmentier nor a complete romantic fool. Representing himself as only a pawn in Mme. Loi's effort to punish her daughter for her imprudent passion for the inn *ma-fu*, he disarmingly mocked for his readers whatever ego inflation he might have seemed to claim by describing the attentions of mother and daughter. At the same time by making Ma Le even younger than Malami and more sexually aggressive and more obviously promiscuous, he probably also in fantasy reassured himself he knew little or nothing of Malami's sexual history and therefore was justified in not taking her with him to Rangoon. He would have no inn *ma-fu*'s mistress for his bride.

When Snow reached Rangoon on March 18 there was a letter waiting for him from his new sister-in-law, Dorothy. He answered March 20, and the ingenuously frank tone of his letter suggests he felt an almost instant rapport with her. His letter also reveals, however, that his brother's marriage again raised a troubling question about his own marital future:

> Dear Dorothy:
>   Etiquette, I believe, decrees that I should have written you long ago to tell you how joyous I am that you are Mrs. Howard John [sic] Snow. But etiquette is a tedious thing. It is nearly always insincere. It conspires to reduce to formula emotions that ought to be spontaneous.

The truth is that I did not write to you because I was not glad that you were Mrs. Snow. There was of course no personal malice in this. Never having known you, how could I disapprove? But I regarded you as something which had upset the regular flow of my plans. Momentarily, you became obnoxious. The news that Howard had actually got married startled me, shocked me. I was suddenly depressed and for a great many days I felt much older than I am.

You see this was a natural, a selfish reaction. For as long as I can remember I have always thought of Howard as an entity which figured more or less constantly, directly, in my life. He was all important to me in the way that an older brother, I suppose, always is. I had never tried to imagine anything vital enough to divide the loyalty that had grown up between us.

Always I had thought that when I got back to New York it would be for a life with Howard. We would know girls, of course, after the careless way; but nothing disturbing for longer than necessary experience, nothing that would outlast its own first rapture. . . . And then abruptly you broke on the scene and it seemed to me that the whole future had to be reconstructed.

The story Snow made up of refusing the sawbwa of Kanai's invitation for him to become resident tutor to the sawbwa's son, based on his earlier refusal of the real invitation from the magistrate of Tali, probably also declared he still was not tempted to settle down, even by the added inducement of Maru dancing girls.[4] But his relations with Malami and Ma So were intensely pleasurable and likely did induce him to linger in Burma for more than six weeks before feeling compelled, even if ambivalently, to resume his journey homeward by moving on to India.

In *Journey to the Beginning,* Snow also claimed he stayed in Rangoon for a month to write the only detailed reports published in the West of the peasant revolt led by Saya San early in 1930. A report on the revolt by Snow appeared in the *New York Sun* on July 10, 1931, but was datelined June 2 from Rangoon. In early June, Snow was somewhere in western or northern India, a continent away from Rangoon. He was in Simla as late as May 29, and he wrote his father from Bombay on June 13. Nothing in Snow's diary indicates he was aware while in Burma of Saya San's revolt or of the gathering of future nationalist leaders then taking place at Rangoon University. It seems more likely he secured the story of the revolt from Indian nationalists with whom he later established close contact.[5]

13

India

The Challenge of Yet Another National Revolution

S NOW ARRIVED IN CALCUTTA April 25 in the midst of significant public political ferment over the efforts of Mahatma Gandhi to lead a broad-based national revolution even as almost three years earlier he had arrived in Shanghai amid the political turmoil that followed Chiang Kai-shek's destruction of the rival Red leadership in the Kuomintang and his swift move to consolidate and enlarge his own leadership of the revolutionary Chinese nationalist movement.

Gandhi, however, was very different from Chiang Kai-shek. On April 5, 1930, while Snow was still in Shanghai, Gandhi and a large band of loyal followers arrived at Dandi, a small community by the sea and the goal of a long public march that was to become a celebrated event in the Asian revolution against colonialism. The next day in a deliberate act of civil disobedience he challenged the world's sense of justice concerning the British tax on Indian use of salt. He was arrested in May. Boycotts and strikes followed. Other Congress leaders were jailed. Gandhi in jail proved as much of a threat to British rule as Gandhi out of jail. Consequently in February 1931, as Snow began his caravan trek from Yunnan, Lord Irwin began a series of discussions with Gandhi that led to the Irwin-Gandhi Pact. A National Congress meeting at the end of March, dominated by Gandhi, ratified the agreement. It was a limited truce in Gandhi's campaign of civil disobedience about which many on both sides had serious misgivings. But Gandhi was authorized to represent the Congress at the Round Table Conference to be held in London in the fall.

Snow arrived in Calcutta between the March meeting of the Congress and the London Round Table Conference. The city "staggered under a fierce sun and a temperature of 107." After checking various hotels, he decided on the Grand where he found the coffee particularly objectionable and everyone else dressed for dinner religiously in a "hideous combination of dinner jacket and white ducks." After two days he complained, "I have met no one. I believe it is quite possible to live here all one's life and meet no one." But the next day he indicated his time was not exactly wasted: "Finished three stories and mailed them to Consopress, also photographs." The story of his visit to the Shwe Dagon was probably among the three.

He walked to the Victoria Memorial, "the Taj of Bengal" as the British referred to it, to the Khali Ghat, and to the Burning Ghat. He found the Khali Ghat distasteful; at the Burning Ghat his distaste became disgust. He noted the fat Indian bourgeoisie with their Western educations, comfortable in their plush upholstery, driving by: "They too had worshipped the lingam stone, they had eaten of the sacred goat, they had cried to Siva for relief from the devils of pain and misfortune that assailed them. So much, ah, so much for the teachings of science and truth, the hard atheist-breeding knowledge of the West! They flick it off, as easily as they push aside a fly."

From a Hindu temple "where lecherous monks were 'purifying' some diseased women," he went to the office of Ramananda Chatterjee, seventy-year-old editor of *Modern Review*, who quickly asked after the health of Agnes Smedley. Snow questioned what did Chatterjee think of Mr. Gandhi frequently being regarded as a saint. Chatterjee answered, "A saint: yes: he is certainly a saint. Has he not brought the relations of men and rulers on a higher plane than the world has yet known? Has he not achieved non-violently what has never before been achieved without spilling blood? I think that is the accomplishment of a saint."

After Chatterjee stoutly maintained Gandhi would not compromise on the full powers and right of self-determination, Snow asked, "And if the British refuse?"

They dare not refuse. If they do not grant us these things willingly then disaster faces both of us. It is as banal as the so-called independence of women. Britain treats us like a courtesan. She gives us a house and tells us it is ours to run, except that she will keep control of the keys and the money. We older men of the party will no longer be able to hold back the tremendous tide of violence among Indian youths. . . . Hundreds of thousands of them stand ready to die for freedom if Mr. Gandhi's pacific measures fail to obtain it. Our young men want war; we older leaders do not. But if the British hold to their pig-headed, niggardly treatment of us, then we shall no longer be able to keep youth from rising.

Snow soon after visited the editors of *Liberty* and *Advance*, two Hindu nationalist newspapers, and the *Mussulmen*, "a sectarian, conservative paper with a kind of half-suppressed communalistic tone to it." Mr. Buckshee, editor of *Liberty*, impressed Snow as "the most ardent, daring, sincere and, as a revolutionary, dangerous of the lot. He tends toward communism, though wishes it to be developed in India under socialism, or some other name, and to be free from all aid or interference from Russia." When asked about religion, Buckshee commented, "We must make a religion of Nationalism to the exclusion of the barbaric survivals and superstitions bequeathed us from the dark ages. . . . Our greatest curse, our greatest weakness, the viper sucking the life blood of the Indian people, worse even than the domination of the British, is the religious fanaticism that holds our people as chattels of the vilest, most puerile superstitions imaginable."

Snow was also impressed by the "quick-speaking, dynamic" Subhas Bose, who was unhappy with the Gandhi-Irwin truce. Snow saw Bose's position paralleling that of "the liberals of China, the so-called 'reorganizationists' of Wang Ching-Wei." This was prior to Wang's notorious cooperation with the Japanese.

During the next few days he interviewed other business leaders, politicians, and editors, sometimes more than once, but he was lonely staying with the "clam-faced limeys" at the Grand. A list of books read entered in his diary is notably eclectic, including Mayo's *Mother India*, Durant's *The Case of India*, Lenin's *The Proletarian Revolution*, *The Essentials of Marx*, *The Bhagavad Gita*, *The Amanya Ranga*, *The Kama Sutra*, Rolland's *Mahatma Gandhi*, Buck's *The Good Earth*, Maugham's *Of Human Bondage*, and Conrad's *Youth and Other Stories*.

He invited a redheaded American named Weed who worked at the National City Bank to join him for a drink. Weed came around to the Grand just a few days after Snow moved to the YMCA, but fortunately that same evening Snow happened to return to the bar at the Grand. Weed invited him to his home for a meal and introduced him to other American bachelors.

Weed and his friends regularly visited "The Line," an extensive red-light district in Calcutta that catered to Westerners. Snow made a single visit with one of his new acquaintances. A drunken French girl invited them to her room to view her nude dance. "The beer was bad and the dance monotonous. 'Nancy,' as she called herself, had a large mole on her left hip. We left in disgust." They wandered to other places drinking excessively until after four in the morning. Even drunk Snow was alarmed at the money he had spent and disgusted with the coarse public sexuality. The experience did not compare to his more treasured private memories of Malami and Ma So.[1]

By mid-May, Snow was ready to move on from Calcutta. He hired a boy, Pagas Ram, to travel with him. He planned brief sightseeing stops in Benares and Agra, and then on to the summer capital at Simla where he might meet other political leaders shaping the fate of India. He found the "celebrated sacred city of Benares . . . dirtier than any Chinese city I have ever seen," though the "native" city of Yunnanfu might warrant a toss-up. The dirt and poverty seemed fitting comment on the city as a sacred religious site, but he acknowledged a new arrival in any country often missed the subtler points of beauty, and a longtime European resident might well learn to love Benares as much as Indians do.

He arrived in Agra on an overnight train without stopping in Delhi. He respectfully reviewed the Mogul history he saw reflected in the architectural wonders of the fort at Agra: "In these aisles lingered glories of a race that equally loved beauty and war, and put as much value upon a bas-relief of exquisite symbolism as upon the conquest of a new princedom."

He saved his highest praise for the Taj:

> I have not seen anything anywhere with which it might be compared or contrasted. A very few times in the East I have come suddenly upon a thing of the same rapture; once at sunset when I stood upon the Altar of Heaven at Peking; once when through a clearing mist I saw the topmost shrine of Nikko; once when moonlight flooded the golden shaft of the Shwe Dagon at Rangoon. But the cool sculptured loveliness of the Taj, so full of repose and delicacy and yet massive with a tremendous strength, dwarfs all.

The comparisons he drew between the love inspired by the Mogul Mumtaz and the Burmese Supiyalat and between the Taj and the Shwe Dagon suggest his romantic Burmese memories warmed his lyrical enthusiasm.

In *Journey to the Beginning*, Snow indicated he went to Simla to be present while Gandhi negotiated a truce in his civil disobedience campaign with Lord Irwin. Gandhi had in fact negotiated his pact with Irwin, and the National Congress had ratified it before Snow arrived in India. He took the train to Simla after a single day in Agra, arriving in summer shorts amid a hailstorm. He paid for it with a cold that put him in bed for days. He recorded a lengthy and cordial interview with Madan Mohan Malaviya, elderly Congress leader, scholar, and journalist. He wondered how Malaviya could believe so fervently in capitalism yet call himself a socialist, how he could be so sophisticated and open yet gently persist in his caste rules by dining only with other male Brahmans.[2]

Snow met another American journalist in Simla who eventually wrote his way to considerable fame, William Shirer. As foreign correspondents during World War II, their paths again occasionally crossed. Snow, according to Shirer, remained staunchly "out of sympathy for the man I revered," Mahatma Gandhi, until the latter's assassination in 1948. Snow was at Birla House in New Delhi during this tragic event. He then wrote a tribute to Gandhi for the *Saturday Evening Post* that Shirer believed "one of the classics of American journalism."

In 1931 Snow filed from Bombay the story of an interview he had on a walk with Gandhi in the hills of Simla. Snow concluded Gandhi's "power lies in his supreme justice, sincerity and purity as a man, and his exceptional shrewdness as a politician." Since such a combination was ordinarily thought impossible, many found Gandhi an enigma; his diary registers Snow was among them.

It is not clear when Snow left Simla, when he arrived in Bombay, or by what route he traveled. On May 26 he wrote Horace Epes a proposal for his travel home from Simla. Three days later he wrote Mildred indicating he might go to Kashmir that day and then on to Peshawar if he could get a check cashed. Epes indicated Conso could not pay for Snow's new travel plans, but he sent his letter to Bombay and cabled Snow the same day to eliminate Persia and Arabia and head for New York, so apparently Snow indicated an intention to go to Bombay even before he confessed his uncertainty to Mildred: "I am disheartened and tired. . . . The essence of the matter is that I am homesick. But my dilemma is that I can't quite decide whether it is nostalgia for China or for America. I am strongly inclined to believe it is China. This does not mean that I have lost affection for home and old friends and family. It means that I am afraid. I don't like the thought of going back to find familiar things that are no longer familiar. " His mother came to mind: "The other day I ate ice cream and I thought of her. She loved it. . . . She had the simplicity of a child in her capacity of enjoying trifles. A movie was an event and even going to church or taking a walk. She seemed to invest these things with glamor. Her sweetness in moments when you had done something kind for her—my God I'm afraid I'm crying." He could not convince himself she was dead "till I actually go to look for her where I last saw her. Then, when she is not there, perhaps I shall believe it. This is foolish and superstitious. Yet whenever I think of home I cannot imagine it without mother presiding."[3]

Snow most likely traveled by train from Simla to Delhi via Meerut and from Delhi to Bombay via Udaipur. However, there are surprisingly no substantial detailed diary entries that definitely establish visits to any of these cities between Simla and Bombay. He did sketch in his diary a story of Sundaram Shastri, a small merchant of Meerut, belatedly recognized as the rightful

English Lord Gardener. It is not clear how factual he believed this story. His entry begins, however, "One evening I was in a little village near Meerut. . . ."

He published an article about the trial of British Communists in Meerut. There are notes about the trial in his diary, but it seems doubtful he actually attended. The trial began March 29, 1929, and Smedley was one of those charged with "conspiracy to deprive the [British] King [and] Emperor of sovereignty." Snow was probably brought up to date on the trial by the more ardent nationalists he met with Smedley's help in Bombay, the same likely source for his earlier-referred-to story of Saya San leading a peasant revolt in Burma.

One article claims he stopped at a Swiss hotel in Delhi, meeting a well-traveled Indian, Asham Din, and touring Delhi's Red Fort. But there are no diary entries corroborating such a stop and tour. In *Journey to the Beginning,* Snow told of traveling with an Indian C.I.D. agent who suspected him of subversive activities but who left the train in Agra convinced of his innocence. There is no hint of this encounter in the diary. Udaipur, a railway stop between Agra and Bombay, appears in a list of extraordinary travel sites in his diary, and he refers to a stop in Udaipur in an article on the status of Indian women. But again there are no substantial diary entries of such a visit. The dates recorded in his diary allow for the possibility that he stopped briefly in any or all of these places traveling from Simla to Bombay.[4]

Even before Conso Press provoked his decision to return to Shanghai, he wrote his father from the Taj Mahal Hotel in Bombay:

> I am seriously considering going back to China, to remain there till next spring. I have not enough money to come home now; living in China is much cheaper than anywhere I know; and I am sure I can work better there (on articles and my book) with fewer interrupting influences, than in New York. However, it's not yet decided; I am waiting for a reply to a proposition I made to the Consolidated Press. If they accept, I may go on with my trip through Persia, and home, as planned originally. That should see me in New York by—but no more dates. I've broken enough already.

Writing in his diary under a eucalyptus tree in the mountains of south-west China, he might convince himself his romantic travel experiences were more gratifying than selling advertising, but writing his father, he reluctantly admitted the need for more tangible evidence of success:

> It seems to me important that I have something—damn that phrase—something to console you and all of us, for this endless road I've run away from you. . . . This matter of a choice as to returning to China or to America has troubled my sleep for weeks. I wish I knew whether you

would find it in the largeness of your heart to believe that I should be doing what I am convinced is to my best interest—and ultimately yours—regardless of what decision I make.

He freely shared his skeptical views of India's leaders with his father: "What particularly shocks me about them is no matter how cultured, educated and intelligent they are in mundane matters they cling to the feeblest and most childish beliefs that are in contradiction to all they know, through scientific knowledge, to be the facts of life. The one exception to this whom I have met is Jawarharlal Nehru—president of the Indian National Congress."[5]

Smedley had met Nehru, and her work on behalf of Indian Independence impressed him. She gave Snow a letter of introduction that led to him seeing Nehru twice at the palatial home of a wealthy friend, J. U. D. Naroji, in Bombay. He asked if Nehru's beliefs were "along the lines of English socialism" rather than communism. Nehru said yes but added, "I do not call myself a socialist, however, in the sense of Fabianism. I am essentially a man of action and I advocate straight-forward policies aimed at the realization of certain principles." Under Snow's probing he continued, "The state should control certain public utilities and vital industries. It would manage and operate them. Wealth of the individual should be limited and all exploitation by industrialists should be eliminated. I would like to attain the same thing as the communists of Russia with regard to an industrial policy, but through different methods."

Nehru insisted on a clean break with the British government. India could not remain within the British Empire. Relations between India and Britain should be those of sovereign friendly nations. To Snow's question about the influence of the Communist Party of India, Nehru replied:

> The Communist Party of India as such, scarcely exists. I doubt if it holds more than a hundred members. But communist ideas are largely supported by many leaders of the Nationalist movement. The thing that has kept large numbers from joining bolshevism in India is its advocacy of destruction of autocratic and imperialist government by means of violence. We are opposed to that, naturally, as all Nationalists are now convinced that it will not work in India. We are also opposed to the idea of accepting directions or instructions from Moscow, or of being under Russian influence or tutelage.

Snow pressed him on the Trade Union Congress. Nehru responded that the strength of the Congress had split into many weak factions the previous year over cooperation with the Gandhi Satyagraha Campaign. He thought the most interesting leader of the Trade Union Congress was Deshpandi who organized the first mill hands' and textile workers' strike in 1928 but who had lost most of his influence with the National Congress Party and the masses of people because of the failure of a strike he organized in 1930.

Mindful of Nehru's own Brahman caste, Snow asked what he thought of the caste system. "I think it is thoroughly rotten and corrupt to the core. It ought to be completely abolished: it is medieval and undemocratic. I like nothing about it." When asked to compare his views of Hinduism with Gandhi's, Nehru gave a depreciating smile and noted Mr. Gandhi was a very religious man. But Nehru believed the evils of Hinduism far outweighed its good points. "The sooner people are given education and knowledge in place of quotations from the Gita the better off India will be." While Nehru was persuaded Gandhi's policy of ahimsa was suited to the Indian temperament, he would have the government abolish temples, idols, and the priesthood, and put schools, books, and teachers in their place. This was Snow's kind of man, a man he could comfortably praise to his father.

Nevertheless, he saw a significant flaw in Nehru as a politician: "Fundamentally an aristocrat, secretly he is shocked or frightened by the thought of power suddenly being wrenched from the present controlling elements and administered by Indian peasants and laborers. You sense this in him at once, though he doesn't say it. This inner loyalty to the preservation of [the] bourgeoisie accounts for his renunciation of Communism, and his gradually waning influence among the proletariat."[6]

Late in June, Snow visited workers' housing in the Bombay mill districts with Yusef Meherally, president of the All-India Students' Association and secretary of the Bombay Youth League, and another correspondent, Eugenie Peterson. An open sewer ran down the lane dividing two rows of two-story tenement houses that were five feet apart. Each tenement had thirty rooms on each floor. Emaciated children ran naked through the sewer drain splashing themselves with filth. They carried it on their feet into the hovels both during the night and during the day when the heavy rains forced them inside. There was a single water tap for each tenement of sixty rooms—approximately five hundred people. This tap was the only source of water for drinking, washing, and bathing. Early in the morning the people swarmed like "caged cattle, ready for the slaughterer's knife."

Through Meherally, Snow questioned a worker with hollow cheeks and bright feverish eyes who lived in one room with his father, mother, sister, wife, and four children. He had been married nine years and had nine children, five of whom had died. It was a scene to remind Snow of the cruel poverty and hunger he had seen in the famine at Saratsi and the deadly child labor workshops of Shanghai. But in India he was visiting such scenes in the company of revolutionary leaders seriously planning and organizing to change such conditions.

The next day he went to a fashionable wedding of two professors, Chandra Bhal Yohri and Rishalakshi. Many film people were there along with Sarojini Naidu, who made a polished little talk that impressed him with its mix of saucy wit and original philosophy. Besides her effective cameo performance at the wedding Snow had watched her "manage" Gandhi's talk from her seat beside him before the Bombay Dinner Club. She seemed to advise Gandhi what to speak about and when to speak louder, and he seemed to welcome and accede to her guidance. This is apparently the meeting Snow remembered in *Journey to the Beginning* as being called by a radical group referred to as the "Young Europeans." Sarojini Naidu was the best-known of the very talented rebel Chattopadhyaya women whom Snow later wrote about in the *New York Herald Tribune Magazine*.

Snow described Naidu in his diary as "not beautiful, but her eyes are remarkable, and their soft lustre, with hidden lights changing now to fire quick-lit, now to dark wistfulness rather strange in her somewhat matter-of-fact face." She was "opinionated, strongly willed, strongly sexed," and "at deep . . . emotional." At times she appeared cunning, shrewd, and calculating. She was not a great woman, but she was witty, with an acute, well-balanced sense of humor. A brilliant conversationalist, she was highly intelligent, but not an intellectual.

He found her paradoxically very class-conscious, while completely without color, race, or religious prejudice. "She might eat with a member of the depressed class and forget that the hereditary caste barrier existed between them. But I do not think she would eat with a person whose intelligence, wealth, family, and material position were all too obviously much inferior to her own." Culture for her was something separate and more important than education. "The women of Hyderabad are in fact more advanced along the cultural planes of life than are the women of America, most of whom are literate." America is too young to have a great culture.

Snow quoted one of her sisters—probably the more radical Suhasini— "She has no political or economic logic. Her greatest service to India has been as a hostess." The student leader Meherally, however, was more generous, "She has strong influence for good. She is temperamentally incapable of doing anyone harm, but if she were to attempt it she would, I think, fail." When Snow asked Meherally about her political influence, his tribute was even more fervent: "she has a strong emotional appeal around which campaigns can be made to revolve. Through her charm on the platform, her endearment as a poet, her grace as a woman, she is a personality—

and in the long run a personality can wield far more influence than a politician."

Before leaving Bombay to return to China, not the United States, Snow noted in his diary, ironically on the morning of July 4, "Ex-colonel" Jimmie Parker stopped him in the lounge of the Taj Mahal Hotel for a private word. After they went upstairs he explained, "A high official in the Government asked me the other evening if I knew a fellow named Snow. I said yes, I did. He warned me I had better keep away from you. He simply said, 'That man travels with three passports' and raised his eyebrows significantly." In *Journey to the Beginning,* Snow gave a much more detailed account, adding he went to the American consul the next day, told him the whole story, and then heard no more about it.[7]

The colonial police had some reason to be concerned with Snow's movements and the people he met in Bombay. It was here he first came into close terms with Asian national revolutionaries whom he deeply respected.

Snow's long train ride to Madras was made even more tiresome by a Eurasian with a penchant for platitudes who shared his compartment. He recorded a visit to the Aquarium and to the ocean beach in some detail along with other historic and tourist information as if anticipating writing a piece on Madras for his travel readers, but apparently did not. At Madurai he hired a seventy-five-year-old guide coincidentally with the same name as the boy guide he hired in Calcutta, Pagas Ram. Again he took notes as if he were thinking of yet another travel piece. He stayed two days in Colombo, July 11–12, before boarding the *Chichibu Maru* for Shanghai.[8]

The leisurely trip he had planned to make around the remaining half of the world on his way home was now scotched. His brother's bachelor apartment in New York no longer waited for him. He had stayed away too long to redeem the advertising job once promised, and a major economic depression made other job prospects in the U.S. grim. But at this stage of his journey he had begun to earn credence in America as an experienced writer on China, and more recently on India. He knew he could earn living expenses in Shanghai. His caravan trip from Yunnan to Burma stirred his imagination as the subject of a salable book. Temporarily he had to retreat from his original plan to circle the world, but he still intended to write the book featured in his dream. That book could justify his long meandering journey to his home family.

14

An Attractive Woman and Hopeful Writer Lands in Shanghai and His Life

O N HIS WAY BACK TO Shanghai, Snow stopped at Canton for three days to interview Sun Fo, Wang Ching-wei, and other leaders of the latest rebel government. On the steamer to Shanghai he developed a fever that ran up to 106. The doctor diagnosed malaria. "That's attractive, is it not, that I should march safely through Yunnan bandits, relapsing fever, Burmese rebels, Indian heat and an election in Ceylon, but go to bed with malaria the day I return to Shanghai?" He spent his first three days in Shanghai in the hospital.

Writing to his father, he played down his illness, noting only that three days before he had been "subjected to an attack of prickly heat, very severe" and since then "felt like a hair shirt." The heat in Shanghai seemed as bad as anything he had experienced in India. He was happy his father's business had "not been disastrously affected by the spreading depression. . . . All I hear from friends in New York does not encourage me to go fortune-seeking there right now, tho it cannot be put off much longer. I will not be here more than a few months."

He explained to Horace Epes that "slenderness of purse" principally caused him to return to Shanghai. His trip had cost more than he planned, particularly the Indian portion. "I found myself in Bombay with only a few hundred dollars and realized that if I went back to New York it would be necessary for me to get a job almost at once. The alternative would have been living on the pater's charity, or borrowing money from him, which was distasteful to me."

But he hoped in the spring he might "return to India and perhaps even complete the Persia-Arabia end of the trip." He would plan to arrive in India after the National Congress had considered the results of the Round Table Conference in London. India might well be caught up in another round of civil disobedience or perhaps even a militant revolutionary movement, and he promised his projected Persia-Arabia venture would be "with definite time limits and minus the perils and delays of mid-Asian caravan trails." He was about six hundred dollars poorer than when he left Shanghai, and since Epes had earlier expressed a willingness to settle his extra expenses when he returned to New York, he asked for three hundred dollars, half his out-of-pocket expenses. Meantime he assumed he was still working for Conso Press.

Epes agreed to pay Snow's expenses. He was sorry Snow's change of plans prevented their meeting in New York. He wondered whether Snow expected to stay in Shanghai "for at least another year." He had received the pewter mugs Snow sent him months before from Yunnanfu and counted on a friend to fill this handsome gift with home brew, "the only thing we can get hereabouts at all suitable."

Charles Hanson Towne was quick to understand that Howard's marriage had disappointed Snow's plans to resume their bachelor apartment and invited Snow to move in with him in New York. Snow responded appreciatively:

> I have often thought how genuine must be your affection that through your busy life you have continued to be interested in me, despite my prolonged absence. Even my father writes to me now only fitfully, and always laconically. I have not heard from Howard for a long while. . . . So you are my most important source of news, and since my mother's death, of inspiration, or encouragement, or whatever spark it is that turns us back to work with new hope and determination. Candidly, now with Howard married, and sister also, and with mother dead, the strongest urge I have for hurrying to New York is to see you. Sometimes it is a very real stab when I long once again to hear your dear voice that is always so clear and sweet, and feel the envigorating contact of your radiant personality.

While Towne's "offer of a room and such luxury in your cottage, and the sharing of plans and friendship and your tennis court" lured him, he declined Towne's hospitality. In New York he would have to look for a job, and the portents were bleak. So he decided to give the East one more year, "certainly no longer." After noting he had traveled "from one end to the other of India and Burma, through Ceylon, Malay, Java, and Bali and visited a good part of Tonkin and Annam, in French Indo-China," he concluded, "The East holds few surprises for me now, but its interest somehow deepens."[1]

He was soon back at work writing. He filed a news story about a series of arrests of Red leaders that had serious implications for the Communist-led rebellion in Indo-China. This story seems the likely source for his somewhat misleading claim in *Journey to the Beginning* that he had smuggled early reports of the Vietnamese rebellion against the French out to Hong Kong.

British police in Singapore obtained important information about the rebellion with the capture of Serge Lafrance, a noted French Communist. Shortly afterward French authorities succeeded in extraditing Nguyen Ai Quoc (later better known to the world as Ho Chih Min) from Hong Kong along with a half-dozen other fellow Communist leaders. Officials in the French concession of Shanghai had arrested 185 Reds during the last twelve months, 90 since January 1. Of the latter, 80 were Chinese and were handed over to the Chinese garrison. The remaining 10 were Annamese, who were either jailed locally or returned to Indo-China for execution.

Snow drew a sympathetic sketch of the conditions that set the stage for rebellion:

> The land system in Indo-China is largely feudal, with a small percentage of the population holding more than three-fourths of the agrarian wealth; industrial conditions are pre-war, with wages on an extremely low scale, hours long, and few compensations to workmen; the political structure vests considerable power in the hands of native "mandarins," whose office is more or less hereditary, and with a decadent royalty comparable to the so-called "princes" of India, the upkeep of which is a great burden on the population. Moreover, representative government, long promised to the Indo-Chinese for their support of France during the war, has been withheld, and the ultimate supreme power in every branch of administration still rests with French officials.

He then used what he had learned from Garreau, the Hanoi chief of foreign service, ten months earlier to conclude his article: "All these conditions created a revolutionary situation, and the first oubreak of the rebellion now engaging the serious attention of France took place more than two years ago, when a company of Annamite troops mutinied and killed their French officers at the garrison of Yen Bay, on the Chinese frontier."[2]

He also mined his India experience for two substantial articles. He sent one on Gandhi to *Current History* hoping to follow up on the success of his piece on the Chinese Red forces the magazine had published in January. To the editors he noted the world hears little of the opposition to Gandhi in his own country, especially since his "surrender" in the Irwin-Gandhi Pact: "I have not gone into a discussion of this in my article, for fear of being accused of propagandism, but my belief is that neither Gandhi nor *satyagraha* will be able to survive a decisive defeat at the London conference. While zealots in America are representing him as a second Christ, intelligent men in his own environment and party are preparing to repudiate him, having realized that his piety will not get them what they want." *Current History* declined this piece.

Snow had better luck with the sympathetic editor of the *New York Herald Tribune Magazine,* Mrs. Marie Meloney. He sent her a story that opened with a young Indian woman who two years earlier had defied her Muslim parents: "I shall not marry any man till India is free!" She chose instead the cause of India as a bridegroom and became a recognized leader of women in the revolutionary Youth League.

She was not alone. The "attempt to free India from British imperialism has furnished the stimulus that history will record as the turning point in the evolution of a twentieth century woman of India." After describing many examples of extraordinary feminine leadership, Snow paid particular tribute to the Chattopadhyayas, "the most clearly emancipated from old superstitions and surely the most interesting family I have known anywhere. . . . Their place is somewhat like that of the Roosevelts in America, the Soongs in China or the Tokugawas in Japan." He saw in the strikingly various four Chattopadhyaya daughters the "pattern and precedent" required to lead the masses of Indian women out of their victimization by "a philosophy based on one of the most fundamentally corrupting of all superstitions—that the suffering one endures in this life is the result of sin in a previous existence."[3]

Even as he wrote his tribute to these strong modern Indian women another strong and very deliberately modern woman from his own country entered his life. Helen Foster landed in Shanghai on the SS *President Lincoln.* Foster carried letters of introduction to Snow's former mentors, Millard and Powell, and an envelope full of Snow's published articles she had clipped as part of her lobbying job for the American Mining Congress, including the article Snow wrote for the *American Mercury* describing the peculiar social circumstances that made it rare for attractive young Western women to remain single in Shanghai.

Snow kept a diary principally when he traveled. There are no diaries available for the period between his return to Shanghai and the beginning of his honeymoon a year and a half later. Helen Foster Snow describes their meeting and courtship in vivid detail in *My China Years,* but enough details are inaccurate to raise a warning flag about what to believe. For example, she represents Snow before beginning his round-the-world journey as a junior partner with the Scovil Advertising Agency, a promotion he may have conferred upon himself in courting her. Similarly she has Snow's father's printing company "put out the Kansas City *Star*." Whether the source of such hyperbole is her or Snow, it is clear she never came to know her husband's family or his personal history in sure detail.

But while one needs to be skeptical of her detail the broad themes she evokes are telling. There is little doubt she took the initiative to introduce herself to Snow and that she made it clear she admired his writing and hoped to build a similar career for herself. After asking him to be the subject of her first interview for Scripps-Canfield, she noted, "They won't take anything but 'golden, glamorous Orient' stuff to revive the trade—Richard Halliburton type. Did you go swimming at the Taj Mahal?"

Snow replied she was "a bit late—he'd been out of the Halliburton stage for some time. He'd had dysentery ever since he got to the Taj Mahal and was deathly sick with malaria when he got to the Shwedagon Pagoda." Snow's visit to the Shwe Dagon was untroubled by malaria, but he was in the process of shedding his Halliburton-like identity as a romantic travel writer in favor of the serious historic journalist.

She saw herself

> meeting Ed at a crossroads in his career, "the low point of my life so far," he said. He was permanently affected by his Yunnan-Indochina-Burma-India experience, not only depressed by recurring physical illness but by the hopelessness, fanaticism, and poverty everywhere. Then, arrived in Shanghai, he found a solid hostile front of Americans, irate because of his satirical article about them in *The American Mercury*—even Millard and Powell were angry. Also the British police had paid a White Russian informer to write a fictional dossier on him as a radical, and he was put on the Japanese blacklist in 1931.

Supposedly he almost immediately offered Foster, who described herself as "the unofficial plenipotentiary extraordinary without portfolio" of the Silver Lobby, a silver saddle ring he had brought back from Yunnan as a token of the "manifest *ming*" (fate) that had brought them together. Her remembered reply resonates through the relationship to follow: "I didn't come all the way to China to wear anybody's silver saddle-ring. I came here for exactly the same reason you did. I intend to become a Great Author—and to travel."

When Snow picked up her copy of "The Americans in Shanghai," his face reportedly turned grim as he described his feelings of rejection, "I really don't know why I came back to Shanghai." And when she pressed for a reason, he explained, "I got as far as India when I learned my mother had died. That took the heart out of my travels home." Her story rightly indicates the strong impact his mother's death had on Snow, but she died in March 1930, six months before he left Shanghai, more than a year before he arrived in India. He may have moved the date of his mother's death to win her sympathy, but it seems more likely she was careless of such detail.

She closed her account of this first meeting with Snow's spirits greatly revived. She told him what he wanted to hear: "Don't give up your travel book. I can't wait to read it. Don't you realize all the bright young people in America want to travel and can't?" Finally he was laughing out loud, and she drew another resonant conclusion: "It was obvious I was already taking the place of his trip home, supplying the fresh American audience he needed." That seems apt in light of his frequent statements to his family, and most recently even to Towne, that they all served as a very special private audience. Later that same day at the *thé dansant* at the French Club, he reportedly told her, "You remind me of my mother."

To which she quickly countered: "You're my first foreign correspondent. . . . But don't say things like that. I'm clad in Athenian armor. I have made a resolution not to be married till I've done some traveling, written a book, and reached at least twenty-five."[4]

Snow's account of their initial meeting is broadly consistent with hers: "Helen Foster was her real name; she was the daughter of an attorney in Utah, and no Mormon. She had studied China at home until she just decided one day, as she put it, to come out and 'become Empress of Asia.' " She dismissed his riposte it takes an emperor to make an empress by suggesting she meant "empress" only as a manner of speaking.

> But she acted like one, I noticed, as she brushed off potential conversa-
> tionalists on the subject who crowded around her. She seemed, in short,
> a Greek goddess in that town, and lovely to look at anywhere. She was
> twenty-two, with a trim, healthy body and dancing blue eyes, a surprising
> combination of beauty and brains to find adrift on Bubbling Well Road.
> Adrift was not the word; she was more purposeful than I. She had read
> prodigiously and that had fired her curiosity and imagination and an
> intense interest in learning. She passionately wanted to be a writer, she
> said, but couldn't.

He represents her as believing Helen Foster was not "a writer's name," but her correspondence suggests she wanted to hide her identity to be free to report controversial news. In any case she and Snow soon created a pen name for her, Nym Wales, the "Nym" from Shakespeare, and "Wales" representing her parents' native land. He used "Nym" to title the short chapter in his autobiography in which he concentrated the story of their meeting and subsequent marriage. His marriage to Nym Wales worked better than his marriage to Helen Foster.

Snow began his account with a quote from George Bernard Shaw: "all biographies are lies." This applied with special force, he noted, where an ex-wife was concerned. He then described their marriage as provoked by the challenge of a fanatical Asian specialist and confirmed celibate, Dr. Victor Frene, who seemed intent on recruiting Peg (as Foster was familiarly known) as his own ideal helpmate in a marriage, like Shaw's, in which sex had no part. Dr. Frene disappeared from their life once Snow persuaded Foster to marry, but he drew a conclusion very familiar to readers of Shaw: "It was a strange courtship, passion and reason all confused. And in the end the citadel did not fall to any scientific arguments—when does it?—but to the invincible musk of life. For never did clever maid more skillfully permit her adversary to win his argument and lose his heart to the ancient true needs of a man and a maid for organic—but lawful—unity." That the couple in fact took Shaw's *The Intelligent Woman's Guide to Socialism and Capitalism* along on their honeymoon for principal reading underscores Snow's point.

In 1948 Snow wrote a long private letter to Maud Russell that implicitly suggests the fictional Dr. Frene represented a real failure of sexual intimacy in their marriage. With his letter Snow enclosed a copy of a separation agreement he and Foster Snow had agreed to and signed in 1945 in the presence of a notary. He believed she had recently flagrantly violated that agreement. He thought Russell knew of the particular incident because her roommate, Ida Pruitt, was involved, and he hoped his detailed history of his and Foster Snow's relationship might persuade both Russell and Pruitt, longtime friends to him and his wife, to use their influence to persuade Foster Snow to divorce him as stipulated in the 1945 document.

The letter is relevant here because he described their marriage as troubled from the beginning: "In view of her own emphatically expressed dissatisfaction with our marriage, as early as 1933, [they married December 25, 1932] she should have deserted me then, or divorced me, for from that time on we never had a physical life together, except for a couple of very brief intervals. The last was in 1941, seven years ago, which was ended by Peg in a scene of violence."

The fiction of his contest with Dr. Frene, like the story of Batala, seems again a means of both disguising and expressing a very personal matter in his autobiography. It gives that story and both his and Foster Snow's allusions to the influence of George Bernard Shaw a deeper and more serious resonance than most readers were likely to realize. Both later published accounts agree that Foster sought out Snow as a writing mentor and only reluctantly accepted marriage principally as a form of writing partnership. Snow, having left Shanghai nearly a year before, feeling very guilty over the unexpected death of his mother while he was far from home, had returned to Shanghai anxious about losing touch with his family and his native country. The surprise appearance of this bright and beautiful American woman, who placed such high value on his writing, offered a unique and welcome opportunity, if he could woo her to the imtimacy of marriage, to unite his own strong writing ambitions with the emotional security and support of family he seemed in danger of losing. He still had lessons in realism to learn.[5]

Early in September, China suffered again from disastrous rains. The Yangtze, the Huai, the Huang, and many smaller rivers and canals overflowed their banks. Snow went up the Yangtze cruising in a small launch "over country where once green rice-fields had glistened. . . . I passed whole villages submerged except for occasional rooftops. I saw men clinging to the golden spires of temples, to the gaunt limbs of trees, to pieces of lumber, and sitting in buckets, wooden tubs, coffins, anything that would float." An area in central China larger than one and a half times the state of New York was severely flooded. More than 55 million people, at least one-third of whom were utterly destitute, were affected. Millions died.

Snow informed his American readers the natural disaster was made worse by the "predatory creatures" that roamed the land prior to the flooding:

> Certain hypocritical "republican" officials legitimize extortion on an unprecedented scale, calling it "taxation." Soldiers, following or opposing them, take their share of loot and spoils. Bandits operate widely, and while ruthless, they are generally not so merciless as the militarists who are their rivals because at least they leave the peasant his hut, his land unencumbered, and his whimsical inclination to live and propagate. The granaries are empty. All surplus has been requisitioned for the hordes of soldiers. Little silver is held by any one but the landlords and usurers, and they make no display of it. Inwardly they tremble and always are prepared to flee from the long range and thrust of the wild new cry of Communism.

Snow closed his account by recognizing his witness of the suffering caused by this flood along with the searing memories of such prior events as the drought in Saratsi and the human fireball in Shanghai were now forming a strong unwilled relationship between him and China:

> I have been in China many months, and I have a love for it, yet a deep sorrow too. I have seen so much pain and suffering here that much of it has entered my own blood. Perhaps because I am still young I have felt these things more than others; they distress and disconcert me. It seems to me that people with such fineness and robustness of character as you often find among Chinese peasants merit better treatment than they have received from the elements and from man.[6]

In September, Epes, after settling Snow's travel expenses, suggested Conso could only pay Snow a part-time rate of eighty dollars a month while he stayed in Shanghai. He was noncommittal about Snow's future travel plans but promised to take them up with Mr. Dolan later. Then he nonchalantly added a might-have-been that exploded one of Snow's most cherished bubbles: "By the way, we thought we might ask you to join the regular European staff and go into Russia if you had continued your journey around from Bombay. Since then an arrangement has been made for coverage in Russia which promises to be very satisfactory."

Snow replied, "The allowance you have made to me seems very just and is more than I expected." But with regard to the possible Russian appointment:

> That agitated me no end and, rather rashly I suppose, I at once cabled you to consider me if your arrangement was not permanent. It seemed to me ironic that, principally because the prospect at home was so unpromising, I had turned back from Bombay. Apparently the Russians have forgotten whatever grievance they had against me, too. Since my return here it has been intimated that now my request for a visa would be granted with no difficulty.

Still smarting from his lost chance, Snow then proposed expanding his work for Conso in Shanghai:

> I will open an office and display the *Sun*, copies of which, by the grace of God, have begun to arrive. I will cover all central and southern China for you, and can make arrangements for contact with Peking, if Hunter intends to stay with I.N.S. . . . . Eventually, I believe, you will be forced to do something like this. I would like to begin it. Frankly, there are opportunities here for making money, but that is not what brought me to the East, and it is not what will keep me here.

Snow's offer was supported by actual historic events. The Japanese had already begun their invasion of Manchuria on September 18, but Snow was initially professionally and personally distracted. Colonel and Mrs. Charles Lindbergh were to arrive in Shanghai on September 19 to fly over and report to the government on the disastrous flood Snow had already viewed. Snow wrote a story about the capsizing of their Lockheed-Sirius amphibian as the spring hook from the carrier *Hermes* failed to release, leaving the Lindberghs to be picked from the Yangtze, fortunately without serious injury. Late in September and early October he also courted Foster on romantic excursions to Hangchow and Soochow.

Nevertheless by the time he wrote Epes of expanding service for Conso, the serious worldwide implications of the Japanese move on Manchuria were becoming more and more ominously clear. After 1939 the Western world came to think of Munich as a symbol of appeasement leading to World War II. In 1931 many observers in Asia quickly understood that appeasement of the Japanese after the invasion of Manchuria was the first mortal blow to the post–World War I international order. As Snow wrote in *Far Eastern Front:*

> Manchuria was to become the testing-ground for the effectiveness of all peace machinery. Could Japan be made to account for a violation of her treaty pledges? If so, the governments which attempted to enforce any judgment against her would be accepting the grave responsibility of leading their peoples into war. If not, the whole peace edifice so carefully built up since the Versailles Conference seemed in imminent peril of collapse.[7]

Manchuria would also fatefully affect Snow's personal career. Within a month he was to travel there with five other correspondents. *Far Eastern Front,* the book to grow from this trip, would preempt his romantic travel story as his first published book. As Japanese encroachment in China continued even after the taking of Manchuria, and the civil conflict within China grew more serious, Snow deliberately molded himself into a serious historical journalist with increasing earnestness and pride.

15

War's Obscenities and a Secular Madonna's Grace

THE NOVEMBER 14 *CHINA WEEKLY REVIEW* announced that Edgar Snow, Victor Keen, Reginald Sweetland, and Frank P. Oliver "proceeded to Mukden during the week so as to get first hand reports of the situation in south Manchuria." By mid-November Snow took part in a press conference held by Japanese General Honjo in Mukden. Light snow was on the ground outside, but "the General's spacious quarters might have been a botanical garden in California, except for maps that papered the walls." On October 24 the League of Nations Council demanded Japan "begin immediately and proceed progressively with the withdrawal of Japanese troops into the railway zone, so that their total withdrawal be effected before the next meeting of the League Council," scheduled for November 16.

The general was asked where Japanese troops would be when the League met: "That is difficult to say. . . . Our troops certainly cannot be withdrawn from present positions held. It may even be necessary to go further inland. Under present conditions any evacuation of Japanese troops is not practicable. It is impossible." Insisting "European capitals" were near-sighted in thinking conditions in Manchuria were like those in Europe, he firmly asserted the Japanese presence was necessary to stabilize peace and order in Manchuria and to protect Japanese rights and interests.

With a look of patriarchal concern he added: "it is too bad about the League. It has a history of ten years during which it has worked for peace. We don't wish to obstruct it nor to lower its prestige. We would like to cooperate

Getting the feel of a machine gun in Manchuria.

with it. But if it does not recognize Japanese rights and interests in Manchuria there exists no basis for such co-operation."

From Mukden, Snow traveled north to Harbin. There J. B. Powell, Frederick Kuh, and Glen Babb joined Snow, Keen, and Sweetland to travel to Tsitsihar on November 19, a day after General Ma Chan-shan ended the fiercest military resistance the Japanese met. There was little left to see, but after Snow returned to Shanghai he contrasted Ma's actions with those of the Young Marshall in a letter to Howard:

> It is ironic that this Heilungkiang army, led by a sawed-off ex-bandit named Ma Chan-shan, should be the only one in Manchuria that put up any fight against the Japs. The so-called governor-general of Manchuria, Chang Hsueh-liang, fled from Mukden, his capital, without offering any resistance. At the time the Japs began their invasion of Manchuria, Chang had more than 60,000 troops in Mukden. The Mukden arsenal is the best in China and is said to be the largest in the world. Chang had many airplanes, heavy artillery, armored cars, tanks, and so on. But

when about 1600 Japanese soldiers attacked the garrison and arsenal the whole damned Chinese army there took to its heels. Chang dignified this retreat by calling it "non-resistance." That is rather thick for Mahatma Gandhi.

He later took considerable pleasure reporting Ma's making the Japanese believe they could bribe him to become one of the puppet leaders of the new state of Manchukuo. Ma was paid 2 million yen, named minister of War, and was present at the inauguration of Emperor Pu Yi, but he stayed "only long enough to collect his solatium." Late in March, dressed in coolie garb, he eluded his Japanese guards and rejoined his troops with new Japanese equipment, munitions, and artillery. Within a week he repudiated General Honjo and the puppets at Changchun and presented a report very damaging to Japanese pretentions to the League of Nations.

Snow believed Harbin to be "the key to understanding the far north." Its many nationalities and wide-open public entertainment reminded him of Shanghai. The Russian presence in Harbin was culturally dominant until relatively recent years and still marked the most notable public buildings, but it was Chang Hsueh-liang's policy before the Japanese military aggression to rapidly move as many Chinese into the northeast as possible to tie Manchuria's future to China and thus prevent its becoming once more a battlefield between Russia and Japan as in 1905. Thus, Snow reported:

> in Harbin, three virile contestants are in the arena. Japan, leading the industrialized West, with her *samurai* heart underneath excited by a dream of conquest, and accelerated by an essential economic urge for expansion; Red Russia, militant but not imperialistic, armed with a wholly new economic and social doctrine; and against them both, China, ancient but still possessed of an enormously puissant resistance, and a cultural tradition that historically has conquered all conquerors, with the erosive aid of time.[1]

Snow returned to Shanghai December 4 and continued to explain what he learned from his Manchurian trip to Howard:

> I suppose despite this colorful lesson there are still people in the West who will believe in the efficacy of prayer and the Kellogg Pact, the Nine-Power Pact, and the League of Nations to outlaw war. All of them obviously are failures. There could not be a more clearly marked case of aggressive warfare than exists against Japan in Manchuria. Yet Mr. Stimson mutters incoherently from Washington in defense of the treaties instigated by America, yet is afraid to take any action (understand that I am not recommending it), and the world statesmen at Geneva bicker over words and phrases while the Japanese army calmly proceeds to consolidate its possession of Manchuria, a country larger than France and Germany combined. What a farce.

But Howard should understand that China was not simply a victim. "Such a phantasmagoria as existed in Manchuria under the name of government did not, perhaps, deserve to survive." Manchuria's inhabitants might well "be far better off under the virtual Japanese rule already functioning there now. But the ethical problem still remains: has any nation the right to take over the land, property and government of another merely because the latter is hopelessly incompetent?"

He was surprised and grateful to receive a 12-dollar draft from his brother. That 12 dollars could be exchanged for about 51 dollars in local currency since the price of silver had recently dropped. He was living in a two-room furnished flat, conveniently located opposite a park, but near town, that cost him $225 per month. That, however, was not his main reason for not returning to New York. He did not "wish at present to be confined to a desk job. While it is true as you point out, that I am working for a reporter's salary I have great freedom and no one can make so bold as to order me here or there. . . . One has to make certain sacrifices in the world to be able to thumb one's nose at it." After having wasted much labor and money on his Gandhi piece with no luck placing it, he asked if Howard had been able to get him an agent. He recognized how busy Howard was, and he did not want him to feel obligated to continue marketing his writing.

After he returned from Manchuria a severe cold developed into sinusitis, and he was in bed for two weeks. He apologized to his father for sending no holiday gifts or cards and then gave his family their first hint of the new woman entering his life:

> The only pleasant phase of my illness has been the attention given me by my charming neighbor. She is a lovely child, not Chinese but from Salt Lake City, and in two months we have grown to be warm friends. She is 23 and she came out to China alone because she suddenly had the desire and couldn't resist it. . . . It occurred to her that she would like to be Empress of Asia, so she put on her roller skates and came out. She is quite mad, but very cheerful and quite intelligent. We get on splendidly by telling each other that we have great futures behind us.

More significantly, he then added: "She is really rather splendid because she quotes to me from my own 'works.' In Salt Lake City she read everything I ever wrote before she came out here. I feel a certain responsibility for the illusion she supports of the East."[2]

Snow chafed under his illness. He felt he was not doing his job being absent from what was happening in Manchuria, but war soon followed him to Shanghai and baptized him in what he would later remember as its "murderously exciting obscenities."

The Japanese seemed truly surprised their September invasion of Manchuria brought strong anti-Japanese reaction in China. The National Salvation movement organized demonstrations and boycotts that slowly began to bite seriously into Japanese trade with China. By January 1932 the leaders of the Japanese navy began to see an opportunity to win a share of the glory that had come to their army counterparts with the latter's successful invasion of Manchuria. On January 18, five Japanese monks wandered into Chapei, the Chinese territory of Shanghai, reportedly playing Japanese musical instruments and singing the Japanese national anthem. They drew a hostile crowd. Three of the monks were injured, and one subsequently died.

The next night about fifty Japanese, armed with clubs, pistols, and knives came to the same place where the monks were attacked and set fire to a Chinese towel factory. They resisted arrest. Two Chinese constables were killed, and one of the Japanese was fatally injured. These incidents set the scene for the Japanese consul general to present a set of four official demands on General Wu Teh-chen, the newly appointed mayor of Shanghai, and for Rear Admiral Kenkichi Shiozawa to anchor ten warships in the Shanghai harbor with their guns pointed toward Chinese territory to back up the demands. The fourth and principal demand was to end the anti-Japanese boycott. Chiang Kai-shek had made a show of resigning as president in December but retained control of the army. The Japanese demands revealed the subsequent Nanking's government's impotence and brought Chiang back into office, but he wanted no confrontation with the military power of the Japanese. The Japanese, however, were intent on military action regardless of the official Chinese response.

Late in the evening of January 28 Admiral Shiozawa, expressing concern for the Japanese nationals living in Chapei, declared his intentions to send troops into the Chinese section and expressed his earnest hope the Chinese would speedily withdraw and thus remove all hostile defences in the area. Snow covered the various official pronouncements with a growing sense of urgency and excitement. The exciting possibility of witnessing his first combat seemed good reason for not going back to a desk job in New York. He carried a copy of Shiozawa's declaration with him as he set out for Chapei to witness its effect. By 11 P.M. the declaration was cabled to cities all over the world, but Mayor Wu Teh-chen did not receive a copy until 11:25. Snow entered the north station of Chapei shortly after 11 P.M. and was surprised to find no preparations for the coming Japanese troops.

The station master at first refused to believe what Snow told him, but a young Chinese military officer arrived soon after and confirmed Snow's message. It was 11:35 and the station master quickly moved his rolling stock of railway cars to safety. The sounds of battle were heard clearly soon after.

After the first hour it was obvious the Japanese had badly underestimated the resistance they would meet. The battle raged with terrible casualties for thirty-four days. In spite of the vastly superior arms of the Japanese and such catastrophic blunders as a Chinese plane unloading its bombs on streets filled with Chinese citizens, the Nineteenth Route Army fought with gutty courage and effectiveness, and with little or no support from the government in Nanking, which retired discretely to Loyang. General Tsai Ting-kai became for Snow and the Chinese people an even more satisfying hero than Ma Chan-shan. When the Japanese finally deployed overwhelming forces to trap Tsai's army early in March, they were surprised to find he and his men had escaped in an orderly withdrawal. After such a long and costly battle the subsequent armistice drawn up on May 5 aroused such dissatisfaction in Japan a group of armed cadets and subalterns invaded Premier Inukai's home and shot him to death.[3]

The tower of the China United Apartments, where both Snow and his charming new neighbor lived, furnished a grandstand view of the battle for Chapei. Because of the peculiar extraterritoriality protecting the position of foreigners in Shanghai, Snow recognized his unique opportunity to be intimately close to war and yet watch in relative safety. Just after the battle began he was recruited by the *London Daily Herald* as a stringer. Foster recognized this was a special opportunity for her as well. She could be "the only woman war correspondent in the whole wide world." She persuaded Snow to help her get a press card.

Their writing partnership began with a testing incident. Snow took her to the scene of battle early, and she saw what she later questionably claimed the first casualty of the war, the corpse of a Chinese bugler. Soon after she arranged for the famous Paramount News cameraman, H. S. "Newsreel" Wong, to film her interviewing General Tsai, but the interview was canceled by an explosion too close to their car for comfort. Wong was later surprised to learn Snow knew nothing of her request for the interview. Independent, competitive, and eager for public attention, Foster proved no humble apprentice.

But this battle reenforced the emotional bonding Snow had already begun with the Chinese people. Day after day he walked amid grotesque human carnage at Woosung, at Kiangwan, at Chapei, Hongkew, and Taziang. Immediately after the successful retreat of the Nineteenth Army, he described this scene to Mildred:

> I saw some Chinese with faces streaked with dirt and the char-dust from the embers, standing in the midst of chaos and distractedly looking upon the desolation of their property. They were not many, but only those who in bewilderment knew not where to flee, and had stayed, or had surged back, too tired to make the effort of migration to a new home, with thousands of other refugees. . . . As I walked I thought I heard a cry like a child's and I stopped to listen again. It came from a heap of padded cotton, where I found a girl still living, though badly bruised and wounded. I asked what I could do for her. She wanted water, which I found. Then I noticed that part of her hand had been shot away.

This same scene appears in *Far Eastern Front* and makes clear Snow's skill and care in editing his own work:

> I see the corpse of a peasant, knocked face downward, and in her back is a dark stain where a bayonet must have pierced. Near by is a child lying face downward also, with a teapot in her hand. Another and another, some with blankets thrown over them. Suddenly I heard a cry like a child's and I stop. Over by a heap of spilled tile there is a padded quilt and under it life stirs. I lift up the edge and see that under it is a young girl of fifteen or more. She is not quite dead, and weakly she cries for water. Picking up a broken piece of pottery, I dip some from the river and pour it into her burning throat. Part of one of her legs appears to have been blown off below the knee; when she lifts a hand I notice that three fingers have been shot away. It is mysterious that she still breathes.[4]

The deadly fighting in Shanghai ended, Snow wrote Mildred again in early March. The battle between his father's skepticism and his mother's faith surfaced once more as he tried to explain the post-battle letdown he experienced:

> My ideas of work and existence, of God and man, my attitudes and thought modes, have been shaken, remolded and shaken down again by the disturbing spectacle of masses of humanity being born, living, propagating and dying in an enormous irregular scheme which seems to have no sense to it, no purpose, no destiny. It is depressing no longer to be sure of anything; faiths are treacheries for the ensnarement of the naive; yet I envy with all my heart men who are not troubled by questionings.

Trying to explain his loneliness, he reviewed his acquaintances and added, "Shanghai is not conducive to making real comrades of people." Perhaps he suffered from "soul-sickness" or was caught in the "slough of despond." Then with unconvincing lightness, he offered as explanation, "Perhaps it is merely April, that comes in tomorrow. Anyway, I am not in love."

Undoubtedly, however, it did his ego, as a younger brother, some good to be able to report he had been invited to head a well-financed advertising agency and had coolly turned it down. "I should get any salary demanded, within reason, and an interest in the concern, but I think I shall decline. It would bore me and for the present I see no advantage in it, beyond the possibility of acquiring wealth."[5]

Snow soon met another extraordinary woman who had her own circle of friends, many of whom would play significant roles in his future career. In *Journey to the Beginning*, Snow noted he first met Soong Ching-ling— she preferred the use of her own name to Mme. Sun Yat-sen, her name by marriage—at the Chocolate Shop, the same popular American meeting place where Foster Snow placed her first meeting with him. The Ravens, who ran the shop, saw to it that this typical American soda fountain–confectionery shop, which also served light sandwich and salad lunches, seemed a casual bit of home in contrast to the predominance of stuffy British hotels and restaurants in Shanghai's central business district. Snow reported his lunch with Soong Ching-ling lasted on to tea, and a few days later he was invited to her modest home on Rue Moliere, but he gave no dates.

It seems likely he met Mme. Sun in late spring 1932. He closed an article datelined May 1 invoking the authority of Soong Ching-ling: "Months ago Mme. Sun Yat-sen, who is still nominally a member of the central executive committee [of the Kuomintang], declared that the Kuomintang had been knifed by reactionaries from within, and nothing could save it from bleeding to death. It had, she said, betrayed the masses and lost its mandate to govern."

Another story, datelined two days later, suggests her growing influence. He harshly criticized the Nanking government, "during the regime of which there have been more and costlier civil wars than under any previous administration," for beginning "another 'punitive expedition' against the Chinese communist armies." He noted this attack followed "the temporary cessation of Sino-Japanese hostilities at Shanghai" and marked "the fifth anniversary of the establishment of reactionary control over the Kuomintang and the beginning of the so-called 'party purgation' movement" begun by Chiang Kai-shek in April 1927.

Millions of dollars and thousands of lives had been sacrificed fighting the Reds with negligible results. He estimated the Communist army since 1927 had grown to 150,000 fighting men in fifteen divisions that held loose control over large parts of four provinces and a population of about 50 million. More than half their number was said to have been recruited from government troops sent to fight them. The Nanking government had recently thrown six divisions into the battle against Reds in central and southern China, but public confidence in the success of this campaign was low.

Soong Ching-ling was an extraordinary woman, broadly and deeply admired by many long before Snow met her. Educated in the United States, she lived in exile in Moscow and Berlin before returning to China for the dedication of the monument Chiang Kai-shek created to memorialize her late husband in Nanking.

Snow wrote his sister, "faiths are treacheries for the ensnarement of the naive," but then he also admitted envying with all his heart "men who are not troubled by questionings." His praise of Mme. Sun suggests she came to embody a resolution of this paradox:

> Almost alone, of all the once earnest patriots, Madame Sun has maintained the original stride of the Revolution. Almost alone, of all the former followers of Dr. Sun in the Kuomintang, she has fearlessly insisted upon the literal conception of his tri-principled revolutionary document, the *San Min Chu I*. She has stood steadfastly for the immediate awakening, emancipation, and enfranchisement of China's millions, the regeneration of the nation on a broad socio-democratic basis, and death to the tyranny of militarism. Her amazing struggle to uphold her husband's ideals has been a bitter one, and through it shines the radiant personality of an extraordinary woman, warmly human, indisputably sincere, intellectually brilliant, a hater of deceit and hypocrisy, but magnanimous as a Gandhi.

A page later he added:

> I have never met anyone who inspires more instant trust and affection than Madame Sun. Unquestioned integrity like hers is rare enough anywhere, but in an Orient where self-seeking intrigue, compromise and mendacity are taken for granted, such character burns like a sublime light. She seems devoid of personal ambitions, incapable of selfish acts, of half-truths, of facing any issue except squarely and with candor.

Previously he had written disparagingly of the airy vagueness of Sun Yat-sen's *San Min Chu I*. He probably had little more respect for it intrinsically than for his mother's Roman Catholicism or Gandhi's Hinduism. But Soong Ching-ling's persistent faith, and her efforts to see this high idealism grounded in real governmental and social programs, including her faith in the idealism of the Chinese Communist movement, despite real danger and even occasional hardship, made her loom large in his imagination as an extraordinary woman: caring, beautiful, and strong, a madonna not of religious myth but of secular history.

In *Journey to the Beginning* he compared his first impression of Mme. Sun with that of the romantic Vincent Sheean, who preceded him to China by a year or two:

Snow with Mme. Sun Yat-sen.

I knew that she had been Dr. Sun's "child wife" but I was not prepared
for her youthfulness and beauty. She was in her mid-thirties but she
looked ten years younger: still the pale, slender "exquisite fragment of
humanity" Jimmy Sheean had described a few years earlier. Like Sheean,
I found "the contrast between her appearance and her destiny" startling.
Mme. Sun was the conscience and the constant heart of a "still unfinished
revolution."

Even Foster Snow testified to the commanding velvet influence of Soong
Ching-ling:

As I look back now, I realize that Shanghai had only one golden glamorous
thing beyond compare. It was the brave and beautiful and lonely widow
of Dr. Sun Yat-sen, Soong Ching-ling. . . . Of course she refused to be
interviewed when I was finally able to meet her through Ed, after reading
his article about her. . . . Ed had already been influenced by Madame
Sun, and before I left Shanghai I understood why.[6]

16

A Book Rejected,
a Marriage Proposal Accepted

B Y MID-MAY, SNOW HAD a new agent, Henriette Herz, and she
had interested a publisher in his book on Manchuria. Nearly half his
story "would be devoted to Shanghai and the war here, with a concluding chapter on 'Manchukuo' under the Rising Sun, and the foreboding of
a clash with Soviet Russia. The idea would be to circumvent heavy subjects
of political controversy as much as possible but aiming to deal largely with
stories of action, dramatizing the human element in the conflict. Much of it
would be eye-witness stuff."

But he hesitated to jump into the task because Herz indicated the book
should be on the market by July, and he could not see how he could do it so
quickly. He could work on it only three to four hours a day, so he promised
her something before the end of the year. He had a second reason for delay,
six other books on the same subject already published or announced. He
wanted to see at least two of them, those by Sokolsky and Lattimore, before
he finished his own.

He was particularly grateful for his sister-in-law's work on his behalf: "she
must have disseminated some gorgeous propaganda" to interest Century
Publishing and the Dick agency. "How am I to thank her?" Her effort would
not be wasted, "for if this book doesn't materialize I'll certainly have my travel
book out before six months. And then I'll be home."

He was also happy to learn from Epes the *Sun* found his war work
satisfactory. A cable from Conso at the end of February had made him suspect

otherwise. Epes's reassurance encouraged him to send up a new trial balloon: "I have been thinking that if the Manchurian situation again develops into a major news affair it might be profitable for me to move to Peking." Fighting around Shanghai was over. He could cover political events from Peking as well as from Shanghai. If long-expected hostilities between Japan and Russia broke out, he would be in a better position to cover them from Peking. At any rate he wanted to take a trip into Manchuria again within the next few months and do a series of articles for Conso. He did not expect the press to cover all his expenses. He probably could manage satisfactorily if Conso could offer some help. He did not mention his proposed book, but he probably believed another visit to Manchuria would help him write it.

By late June, Snow took Century's expression of interest in his proposed book sufficiently seriously to cable Epes requesting forty days leave from Conso Press. He explained he had to complete the book by July 15 to make the fall publishing list, and since the news situation was quiet he decided to chance this request. He added, however, he was at the time still particularly interested in two developing stories, "the communist situation in central China, and the new state in Manchuria." He needed to travel to do both. "The communists in the Yangtze offer [a] particular lure since practically no reliable information has yet been secured from actual investigation."[1]

Shortly after his twenty-seventh birthday he described his trials with his recently completed manuscript to Howard and Dorothy. Without a clear explanation from Century of what they wanted, he had tackled the job to not let Howard and Dorothy down after all their trouble: "It was such a race against time; the odds were so against me. I had no time to get any kind of proper perspective on what I was writing . . . and no chance whatever to tear apart and reconstruct what I did." He had finished the first chapter May 20, and with "the exception of some concluding pages to the 15th chapter, and a few oddments here and there, I had everything finished by July 19th."

Meanwhile his apartment manager had decided to put in a new oak floor over old tile in the apartment immediately below, and he had "to endure the most godawful ear-splitting racket as workers pounded holes into the tile. . . . Nothing could persuade them to delay the work, or to remove the tile and lay the floors as any non-Asiatic would lay it." To make matters worse the summer heat and humidity were again the most disabling he had ever experienced. "I am sitting now with nothing on but Shan pants, which are soaked, and my body drips with sweat. This is the last summer I shall ever endure in Shanghai; indeed, I seriously doubt whether I could survive another."

He was uncertain what he would do in the fall. He wanted to come home, but news of the economy was so discouraging he had postponed his plans indefinitely. He was not making much money, but enough to live comfortably in China. He might go to Peking in the fall, get a small house, and make that handsome old city his home for a few months. The movement of war down from Manchuria to Jehol also indicated much excitement would center around Peking the coming winter. He could get "a little house on a hutung, with a large garden, four or five rooms, baths, servants quarters and sometimes all furnished for about $60 a month—the equivalent now in Peking of about $12 American money." If he rented such a house, he wanted Howard and Dorothy to come and visit for a few months. "You can't make any money in America now anyway, and you can learn much in China; what's happening in the Orient is destined to affect the whole world profoundly, and America more than you perhaps realize."

If Century did nothing with the book, he asked them to recover his manuscript and get whatever criticisms they could from Sheldon Dick and Century "so that next time I might be able to give what is wanted."

In August he sent a preface to Dorothy, noting his book in some important respect belonged to her. He had heard nothing, but he assumed the worst: "the Mss. has been put on the shelf, or in the waste basket. Anyway, doing it has been interesting and good experience." He noted with disdain and resentment the success of Sokolsky's *Tinder Box of Asia:*

> Soks for years edited a magazine called "The Far Eastern Review" in Shanghai, which gets between $80,000 and $100,000 a year from the Japanese. He also got about $60,000 from the Chinese government before he returned last year to America; he was supposed to conduct certain propaganda. The Japanese appear to have got at him in New York for his chapters on the recent events in the Far East are so obviously biased in favor of Japan that anyone who knows Soks cannot believe it was done gratuitously. However, this is between us.[2]

Foster Snow noted that sometime during the summer of 1932 she had dinner with the famous *National Geographic* explorer, Dr. Joseph Rock, just back from Yunnan. This probably was the same event that S. B. Sutton, Rock's biographer, dated in October and placed at the Rose Room, a nightclub-restaurant known for its exotic dancers. Sutton quoted from Rock's diary: "To me it was most disgusting, for everything revolved on a sexual pivot . . . so vulgar that the pen refuses to describe the scene." Rather than quote the details that followed, Sutton then edited, "but somehow accomplished the ineffable in graphic detail, breasts and pelvises included." Following which she continued the quote, "Had I known what Snow was taking us to, I would have refused. He had two American girls with us and, while he was dancing with one, I told the other to pack up and leave this town and go back to her mother." Sutton then resumed her own comment: "Two days later he was still berating Snow and the excesses of civilization upon which he blamed the odious displays of sensuality he had been forced, out of politeness, to witness. He protested the scene too much, more like a man aroused against his will than one in easy command of his passions."[3] Snow must have enjoyed evening an old score.

In September, Snow urgently expanded his previous suggestions to Epes of travel to Manchukuo or up the Yangtze and into the interior of Kiangsi or Hunan to cover the Red districts. He wanted to leave at once, returning to Shanghai in November. He cabled Epes a request that arrived before his letter. If it came to a choice between the two trips, the latter was more important:

> Probably the most significant thing happening in the Far East at present is not in Manchuria, but in the Yangtze Valley, where a civil and class war is going on between Kuomintang troops and the Soviet "armies." The outcome there may determine the fate of both Manchuria and China. Personally, I do not see any good reason to anticipate any longer that the government troops will liquidate the Reds. Everything seems to indicate that the Nanking regime and the Kuomintang are definitely moribund, and their collapse (unless improbable reforms appear in the party) is now only a matter of months.

It was not generally realized outside of China that the Communists had controlled large parts of six central provinces for four years. He then made extraordinary claims for the Communist movement at this early date:

> I do not wish to be sensational, but I think now that it is impossible for Chiang Kai-shek, even if aided by foreign troops, to put down this mass movement, which is sweeping over the whole country like a vast fever. Outside of the bankers and some of the industrialists and of course the officials and the Kuomintang, I cannot find any great antagonism against the Red idea even in the cities. People on the whole seem to believe that Communism cannot possibly result in anything worse than the present misgovernment, and many of them appear to think it might result in a decided improvement. In the country districts the landlords, usurers and officials are naturally rabid against the Reds, but the masses of peasants are either indifferent or favorable to the Communists' propaganda.

He wrote Epes on September 11. His typed profile of Mme. Sun was dated September 12.

Epes replied, "I am sorry to say there is not a chance of our financing any special travel at this time." Even if the budget permitted, "space in the papers is so tight that the material would be largely wasted." He had asked Dolan if the *New York Sun* might be interested, but his answer was also 'no."[4]

As Snow's book failed to find a publisher and the depression tightened the purse strings at Conso Press, he became increasingly restless. He began to think of major changes in his life. A move from Shanghai to Peking had been in mind for months. In November he wrote Mrs. Meloney he also was growing increasingly impatient with the transient nature of the dispatches he published in newspapers. His first effort at a book stirred his ambition: "I think soon I may give up correspondence and use all the abundant material I've authored for some more lasting and satisfactory purpose. We all say that, of course, but I really mean to do it soon. I'm planning to go to Peking shortly and there do the writing that will give me no rest till it's put down and shuttled out of my mind into print."

He apparently did not mean to give up feature articles, for he had something in mind Meloney might like very much: Madame Sun Yat-sen, "unquestionably the most interesting woman I've known in Asia." In the grand mix-up of China her story "is one of amazing bravery, adherence to principle and a rare gem-like character that burns with a true flame in all the shift and deceit and compromise that make up Asiatic ethics." He was also thinking of interviewing Lu Hsun, whose work he would eventually feature in the second book he published, *Living China*.

Mrs. Meloney replied, "I think you can get a swell piece out of Madame Sun Yat-sen. I don't think Lu Hsun is for us."[5]

It is not clear whether at this time he planned to go to Peking alone or with a wife. Foster Snow remembered Snow's appearing early for tea at the Chocolate Shop with gardenias on her twenty-fifth birthday, September 21— "the only time he was not late." Over ice cream sodas he suggested she could write her book in Peking. "Peking was cheap and quiet." But if she wanted more adventurous travel, where did she want to go?

"Borneo," she answered instantly. "That's the least explored place still— unless Osa Johnson has got there first. And Formosa. And the Celebes. And Java. And Bali. And Singapore. And every treaty port on the China coast."

"Maybe we could work something out," he said, probably quickly recognizing her suggestions were along the route he had already traveled between Shanghai and India.

Her account of what followed seems obviously romanticized, but is nevertheless revealing. He held out a silver Tibetan saddle ring, "I don't have much to offer—but try this."

After trying it on the wrong finger, she put him off, "I'll keep it in my purse for now. Books come first. You hurry up with yours and I'll hurry up with mine." He tried to persuade her this was "the real McCoy *yin-yang*" but looked trapped. After visiting a temple on Bubbling Well Road where an old priest scrambled the *pa-kua* fortune sticks and declared their destinies very good for each other, they made their way to Jessfield Park for more intimate talk. Snow reportedly confessed, "My problem is—or was—that I don't like to be tied down. . . . Until I met you, I thought of a wife as an impediment, not a helpmate. He travels fastest who travels alone."

Tempted, she was still undecided, "I had to write a book *first*, even if it was never published," but she added: "I realized that Ed had a rare—and to me, essential—characteristic. From the first, he believed in me and my talents and future. He was proud of everything I did. Up to the end, he was mystified that I did not become famous and rich, a Great Author, as each of us intended the other to be, there in the sunset of Jessfield Park."[6]

Her satisfaction in his faith in her mirrors his pleasure in her reading his writing and believing him the best-known writer on Asia except for Pearl Buck. Their common interest in writing, travel, and books promised a closer kinship of spirit than he remembered his parents having. Foster was not tied to any conventional religious faith, though she frequently voiced respect for the strengths of the early New England Puritans.

On the morning of October 27 Snow returned from a four-day trip with a Shanghai friend, probably Foster, to Hangchow and Ningpo by coastal steamer. He wrote Howard, "This is the first time I've been away from Shanghai for more than a day or two all summer and the experience infinitely refreshed me. I long now to take a real trip. But, though several are in the offing, I doubt whether any will materialize for weeks yet."

By chance Howard recently met Alfred Batson. Batson told Howard something that caused Snow to protest with suspicious righteousness. Snow insisted he did not play the "roue with the indigenes. . . . Do not worry. . . . No one could live long in the Orient and retain any pride of line if he did not confine his interests to a sphere scientific. I am happy to say that I have lived more sensibly in this respect than most. . . . Hence after four years I am still physically sound and clean and with a clear mind for work."

Howard also casually announced in a postscript he and Dorothy were expecting their first child. After noting his brother's "strange way of announcing earth-shaking events in P.S.'s," Snow offered congratulations. What followed suggests his discussions of Shaw with Foster were threatening to corrupt his style even more than his ideas:

> I think it is the most splendid thing in the world for two intelligent young
> people in this day to decide to bring a new life into the world, for never

before have people actually had the opportunity to make a choice. I have always been greatly interested in the process that has brought me up from the primeval muck to my present stature. . . . It is an overwhelming realization in a way to think that nature, through ages of selection, has chosen me to continue her experiment of evolution. I am engaged enough with the wonder and beauty of it that I wish to fulfill my natural function in it to the fullest extent. That is why I have always regarded my body with high respect; some day, with a person who feels similarly, I shall perhaps return the compliment—make you an uncle.

Howard and Dorothy's expected child occasioned another disturbed passage that probably reflected on his marriage considerations with Foster. This time he wrote his sister:

Anybody in this day who bears progeny deserves a Croix de Guerre. All social usage, at least what appears to be the best social usage, is opposed to it. Marriage seems to have moved in tempo and purpose from a thing of procreation to an arrangement for mutual recreation. Economics are all against parturition. Why bother with brats? Birth control is so much more convenient, not so messy, with none of the economic burden on man, none of the physical handicaps bringing on age and bad health to women.

His reading in eugenics made him question whether "the well-bred, the intelligent, the worthwhile element of the population is really perpetuating itself as it should?"

His eighty-three-year-old grandfather was ill, but he saw his grandfather as more capable than his half-dozen needy, hopeful, and fully grown offspring: "He is really a perfectly splendid old fellow; probably he will outwit them all yet. It's curious, the complete selfishness, indifference, egocentric attitude he manifests toward his children, but it is elemental in man of his day and he is no sentimentalist where others are concerned." He did hope, however, his father would inherit enough money to provide relief from his Gargantuan debts and perhaps even to invest to help his present income.

He also wondered if Mildred and her husband could not escape that "depressing Charlotte Street maison" and buy a decent house out south now that real estate prices were so low. He suggested they take dad along with them and let him pay them for a change rather than their paying him. He recalled one of his chief motives for leaving Kansas City was to get away from that house. The house seems a convenient means of packaging his incoherent resentments against his family.[7]

Foster Snow remembered Snow telephoning her in December, suggesting a walk on the Bund. In her memory he had just then sent off his book. In fact he had sent it off months before, and Century had turned it down. Herz was then scrambling to find another publisher. On the Bund, Ed turned her to face him, "Let's get married and make a trip to the South Seas on a Japanese ship. I've got the itinerary: every place you want to go, and Osa Johnson's never been to one of them—it says so in Japanese. We'll live in Peking while you write your book and I'll finish my travel manuscript there. Then we'll go trans-Siberian and travel in Europe."

After a half-hearted objection she fished the Tibetan ring out of her handbag and told him he could put it on now. But she had two conditions: "I don't want to be married in a filthy, dirty place like Shanghai. Tokyo is nice and clean. I want gardenias and a Japanese wedding kimono." She also insisted Snow abandon his lavender India-tailored suit for a more appropriate dark one and a Harris tweed.

On December 11 Snow wrote Epes, "Nothing exciting is happening here at present." He planned to cover the Third Plenary Session at Nanking convening December 15, but after that "a change of faces and a new environment might result in some useful copy from your correspondent." The local agent for the NYK boat line had made him a ticket offer for a trip too good to pass up. "The trip would take me for four or five days to Japan, then down to Formosa, Borneo, the Phillippines and the Dutch Indies. From there I would come back to Canton and Hongkong, to spend a week." Remembering the good mailers he had been able to send from his last trip that way, he hoped he could do so again. He had asked J. B. Powell to cover any necessary cabling. He expected to cover his own expenses, but if Epes found the work he turned in merited, he would appreciate any bonus that could help meet travel costs. He gave no indication to Epes this trip was to be his honeymoon. Two days later he wrote his father and sister:

> Oyez. I'm getting married. Do not laugh; it does look silly, but then it appears to have happened to both of you. . . . My particular Waterloo is named Helen Foster, somewhat blonde, beautiful clear blue eyes, a head that is altogether admirable except its odd little nose that wiggles, and otherwise simply splendid. We believe or disbelieve in about the same things, have similar dreams, aspirations, hopes and sinusitis. She writes wonderfully, is a poet and some of her things will make Shelly and Blake seem quite as dull as my old razor blades.

It didn't matter she could not cook. Like him she belonged to "the romantic free company": "One professor [perhaps the mysterious Dr. Frene in *Journey to the Beginning*] who knows nearly all of Europe's great and is the first to understand China psychologically recently told me that she has the ability to write a greater book than has yet been written by woman in this generation.

I daresay. Anyway we appear to be mutually necessary to each other and life can't go along that way without marriage or neurosis intervening."

He reassured them he was not doing this without premeditation. He and his bride-to-be had known each other for some months. "About a week ago a cold draught of winter blew in through Shanghai and we thought naturally of the South Seas. We decided to travel. I've written to my office for an assignment a la honeymoon and there you are." In a postscript he added:

We are to be married at sea on Christmas Eve by a Japanese skipper. Then next day we arrive in Kobe, will go up to Tokyo and get properly wed at the American Embassy. My old room-mate there, John Allison, will be my best man; he's in the Embassy now, a diplomatic career officer. Our wedding is to be on Christmas Day at High Noon—no doubt this will appeal to your sentimental, sweet hearts. You must inform all the relatives as I'm too busy making various arrangements, and I think it improbable that we'll send out any announcements.[8]

17

The Wedding and
a Repeat Journey

A S JOHN ALLISON REMEMBERED it, Snow cabled him less than a week before Christmas "with all the confidence usually found in journalists that anything they want can be produced." Allison was to arrange for the ceremony, including a preacher, at noon on Christmas Day in his apartment at the embassy.

> What Ed didn't realize was that no marriage is legal in Japan unless it is registered at the appropriate Ward Office which, for foreigners, would require complicated documents in Japanese and English, certified by the American Consul in the case of Americans. He also did not realize that in Japan Christmas was a holiday (not because it was Christmas, but because it was the anniversary of the death of the previous Emperor) and that the Kojimachi Ward Office, the one nearest the Embassy, would be closed as would the American Consulate. How could he get married on Christmas noon?

But Allison scrambled. He persuaded a young Presbyterian minister, Reverend Howard Hannaford, to perform the religious ceremony, and a young teacher in the American School, whom he was himself later to wed in a ceremony conducted by the same Rev. Hannaford, to serve as maid of honor. Ruefully Allison added, "Mr. Hannaford's efforts for both Ed and myself failed to have lasting effect, and after several years both marriages ended in divorce."

In his diary Snow described their Christmas Eve before the wedding in Kobe in as yet untroubled festive terms. At Honjo's, where they had gone for

American coffee, they came across an old acquaintance of his, Sumada, who proposed a dinner appropriate for the occasion. They decided on sukiyaki at the Kikusui, the Ciro's of Japan. After an enthusiastic description of the meal and the setting, Snow concluded, "No one can claim the title of *gourmet* . . . who has not drunk a toast to Nippon over a *sukiyaki* bowl at Kikusui." They had such a good time they missed the express evening train for Tokyo and had to settle for a slower one. They arrived at Allison's apartment in the embassy with only a couple of minutes to spare.

Once there, according to Allison, Reverend Hannaford "uttered the fateful words, Ed and Nym made the proper replies, and they were pronounced man and wife. I produced a bottle of champagne. It was drunk, the cake was cut, and off the happy couple went to a hotel, spiritually, but definitely not legally, married. The next day we made it all legal, complete with red seals." According to Snow, Allison produced Snow's first American Christmas meal in years, a magnificent Christmas turkey and a welcome, if not miraculous, cranberry sauce as well as champagne.

Two days later Snow wrote Howard on Fujiya Hotel stationery featuring an etching of famed Mount Fuji. He drew a pair of stick figures, circled them with an arrow pointing to the brink of Fuji's volcanic cone, and wrote: "Here we are on Fujiyama. Wed on Christmas Day at the prescribed High Noon. . . . A Presbyterian (I think) minister wearing a charming swallow-tail coat said the words & we echoed. Peg said I did it 'parrot-like.' It was quite impressive, except the 'till death do us part' which quite disturbed me till I thought after all a guy may get run over by a street car any day."

In the midst of these legal and religious ceremonies, on the day after Christmas, Snow also managed to squeeze in an interview, probably arranged by Allison, with a member of the ruling military clique, Shiratori Toshio. To Snow, Shiratori insisted the American assumption there was only one government in China, the Nanking government, was a mistake. There were more than a half dozen different governments on the mainland, of which Manchukuo was one. Snow recorded in his diary:

> Shiratori is [a] new type of Japanese statesman—cold, haughty, with old samurai pride and insolence, effecting what Hugh Byas calls the "Back to Asia" movement. He treated me, in my interview with him on Dec. 26, with coolness & even a trace of rudeness—the only occasion on which I felt this in Japan, except, perhaps, with my meeting with Japanese police officers & customs & passport examiners who are still as blunt, obtuse, stupid and more suspicious & ridiculous than ever.

Shiratori was tried and convicted of war crimes after World War II. He died in prison in 1949.

At Atami, where Snow had vacationed following the death of his mother two and a half years earlier, and which he later described as his "first love, and last, in dark-eyed Japan," the staff at the Kamanarea *yado-ya*, including "the *bantosan* and half a dozen blushing *nesan*," remembered him warmly, though they remembered his Japanese as better on his first visit, a tribute to his Japanese lessons from Chiyeko. "Peg saw the room where I had slept in '30 & liked it so well that we moved from the Fujiya & took up our one night residence at the Kamanarea." Indeed, Foster Snow remembered this room as "the perfect Hollywood setting for the perfect honeymoon: a paper-windowed room with bamboos on one side and the other, where the inn jutted out over the ocean, a Hokusai wave breaking underneath." Snow also noted in his diary, however, that after submitting to the allure of the hotel's wonderful bath, "Peg had quite a shock when the bath boy followed her in & gave her a cursory glance preparatory to what he thought was to be the usual rinsing-off process."

Foster Snow also later declined the communal bath, but Snow met there a Japanese businessman, Omura, who had lived for some years in London. Omura invited the couple to join him and his mother for a delicious dinner. Seventy-seven-year-old Madame Mura "possessed some indefinable charm, something that magically transformed the atmosphere, like the peal of a mellow old temple bell." Her charm and the occasion reminded Snow of his own mother's death, evoking a quote from Lafcadio Hearn, who paid tribute to the passing of such mothers: Something remains "when all the illusions fade away to reveal a reality lovelier than any illusion, which has been evolving behind the phantom-curtain."[1]

The New Year did not begin auspiciously on board the S.S. *Canada Maru*. The newlyweds were awakened at 7 A.M. The morning air severely cold, Captain Kobayashi led a ceremony on the afterdeck dedicated to the anniversary of the death of Emperor Taisho. As the ceremony ended the captain turned to the East where the rising sun appeared behind a veil of gold and crimson clouds and shouted "Banzai" (Ten Thousand Years). All assembled echoed him three times. "Peg was too frigid to do anything but chatter her teeth." Following the ceremony they drank a toast to the emperor with sweet saki, bottomed with tiny drops of gold, and used only on New Years.

Snow's diary indicates the elaborately prepared breakfast of raw fish, various pickled vegetables, herbs, roots, and warm saki was not nearly as tasteful as the meals he described with such enthusiasm in a later article for *Travel*. They went hungry most of New Year's Day. The ship boys had worked through the night on the breakfast and were allowed to sleep most of the day. But after this uncomfortable beginning, conditions on board warmed up. The captain and crew showed Foster Snow such attention the newlyweds decided from the next day on to have at least one meal a day in the dining room rather than eating exclusively in their cabin as planned.

At Keelung, Formosa, they took a train for Taihoku to stay until late the following evening before returning to the ship. Disappointed the city museum was closed, they walked through a new city park and stopped at the Lion Cafe where a *josha* named Masako-san admired Foster Snow's beauty and asked many questions. Particularly interested in Foster Snow's kimono, she also asked why her skin was so white. When Snow deflected her question by insisting she too was comely, she was pleased.

Snow's experience of European colonialism elsewhere in Asia between his two visits to Formosa made him more appreciative of Japanese rule on this trip:

> I think it obvious that the Japanese have been much more successful with their colonizing of Formosa than the British have been anywhere, or the French. . . . Though the Japanese are not without all the characteristics of imperialism, so far as the army & its methods go, the people who come to settle & trade & hold the land are a gentler folk, quieter, more courteous, less prone to effrontery, insolence & not in their hearts having the deep disdain of race and color that white men bring.

Well-planned and clean, Taihoku, as an example of Japanese colonization, was "certainly an improvement upon three centuries of Chinese rule. It has brought vices, but few as bad as the old ones of China—dirt, disorder, corruption, the Classics, Confucianism, ancestor-worship."

Coincidentally a famous fat lady, Mme. Terrell, made an appearance at their hotel with her daughter. She had been a sensation in the Orient for years, particularly with the Japanese, who had a "traditional esteem for greatness of avoirdupois." Snow had just finished a bottle of strong Japanese beer when he first saw her and her equally large daughter. For a moment he thought he was seeing double. The hotel proprietor lifted his eyebrow only so faintly before telling Snow, "She weighs 93 kan." After consulting a book and computing rapidly he added, "Say, 1,200 English pounds." School children were given special prices to encourage them to view her performance. Shopkeepers competed for the privilege of her presence an hour a day to sign autographs and attract customers. Unfortunately Olie Russell had already written up Mrs. Terrell for the *American Mercury*.[2]

The *Canada Maru* sailed from Keelung to Tawau, Borneo, January 5–10. At Tawau they called on a "cherub-faced youngster, new to the East" and to the

English civil service, who carried on "jolly well" and found living in Tawau "good sport." His mannerisms did not prevent them from quickly accepting his offer of the British Rest House.

At the government office where they went to buy stamps, they met another Englishman named Henderson who volunteered to get a car and take them to see a plantation. They drove through miles of coconut palms and saw tapioca bushes, *okbeya* (wooden potato) bananas, papayas, and mangoes, not to mention bougainvillea, hibiscus, and orchids. On their return they visited the extensive Kuhara Rubber estate owned by the ex-minister of Japan. Henderson then took them to his new home on the side of a hill for drinks and an introduction to his poetry. Snow saw in Henderson another Badock:

> Perhaps H's poetry explained him. In it he spoke often of the "faithful-ness," "submissiveness" of "little dark girls" who look upon him as "a god or supernatural person." H. enjoyed this. It fed & nourished him. Born with a sense of inferiority or one acquired, he came to the East, after a disillusion in England following the war where no one appreciated his heroism (he went over the top 14 times without a wound) & here at last found people who seemed to value him at his true worth.

Back on board the *Canada Maru*, Snow wrote Epes thanking him for his cable congratulating Snow on his marriage and authorizing his trip. He gave Epes a brief background on his new wife, before expanding on what he thought likely to happen in Japan:

> The National City Bank manager predicts that unless the military ex-pedition in Manchuria is liquidated, Japan will be bankrupt in fourteen months. Either of two possibilities may take place: Japan will become completely dominated by a Fascist government, toward which it is now headed, and that will requisition private property, heavily assess wealth and unearned incomes, and control all major profit-making industry for state benefit; or a revolution will occur, involving social and political change on a large scale, probably with a socialist form of government.

He was surprised by the anti-American sentiment he saw in Japan but suspected it was in part initiated by the military to divert public attention from the disastrous economic consequences of its Manchurian adventure. Nevertheless, the propaganda had succeeded in establishing a "war psy-chology in which conflict with America now is taken for granted by the mass of the people." He expected to arrive in Peking in February and remain there for some time, though he again hopefully suggested he would be willing to travel south to central China if Conso saw good reason for it.

The heat was intense, the sea particularly lovely, on their way to Sourabaya. The beauty of the sunsets challenged them to a writing contest:

> There are blues like Helen's eyes, reds like the lacquer on Foochow carved stuff, oranges like a debutante's favorite frappe, & a wealth of deep vermillions, purples, lavendars, cherry, lemon & orange colors. Peg & I made metaphors of the water. We called it "a hammered mace like the Greeks wore" and "a cloth of sequins," "a fabric of a million silver-winged birds," "like the sonnets of Shelley woven into a Chinese fabric," etc., "like the fluttering of a billion moths."

Both list the same books for mutual reading and discussion on the long days at sea: Shaw's *The Intelligent Woman's Guide to Socialism and Capitalism*, H. G. Wells's *Outline of History* and *The Work, Wealth, and Happiness of Mankind*, and George Dorsey's *Why We Behave Like Human Beings*.[3]

The darker side of the honeymoon indicated by Snow's later letter to Maud Russell appeared in his diary as they landed at Sourabaya, where they were to leave the ship to spend a week at Bali:

> Foster annoyed because we could not land at once; it was necessary to wait to learn whether a ship was sailing this day for Bali. Foster annoyed because we did not take more luggage ashore; also annoyed because we took too much luggage. Complained because it was too hot. Complained because I ate eggs. Complained because I tipped boy 10 guilders, with promise of more. Complained because she had not slept well, a phenomenon for which I, apparently, was in some way responsible. Foster annoyed because she got her shoe dirty on the gangway: here again I was at fault. *Je suis miserable.*

This moment is probably echoed in Foster Snow's memoir, though she places it at their docking at Tawau: "My husband looked at me without approval. He would never forgive me for bringing aboard a big black wardrobe trunk with attire for every occasion—from deck shorts to long evening gowns and gold slippers." In his eyes such trappings made clear she was no traveler, let alone an explorer.

It was an aggravating day in Sourabaya sifting through the contradictory advice they received about travel to Bali. Douglas Fairbanks recently preceded them, and the American consul gave them warnings based on Fairbanks's experience. Nevertheless they sailed that same afternoon for Bulelung, Bali, arriving the next morning. A man from the shipping lines met them with an old Dodge rented from a colorful Sudra matriarch who controlled all the automobiles in the region. In 1908 Dewa Agoong, paramount chief of the island before Dutch rule, ordered all his wives and household to commit suicide rather than surrender to the Dutch. Mah Fatimah, who served in the household, refused. She survived to become, despite her low caste, one of Bali's most prosperous citizens, trading in gold and silverware, art, and curios, besides owning and operating the motorcar agency.

The newlyweds had a pleasant and scenic drive past the Batur volcano arriving at Den Pessar late in the afternoon and booking a clean little room with a Dutch bath at the Satrya Hotel. They soon became familiar with the working order of the hotel. A man named Karson was the official manager, but the hotel was run by Matta, a slight black man who had come from the jungles of Papua fifteen years before and since had learned to speak English, German, Dutch, Balinese, Javanese, French, and Malay. Matta had married a Javanese and taught her to cook. She now presided as maîtresse d'hotel. "So much," Snow noted, "for the 'cultural tradition,' 'inheritance,' 'white superiority,' etc." Snow could not fathom why Matta stuck with Karson, who paid him very little.

On their third day Karson arranged a visit to a nearby village where he was well known. A school principal and his wife from New York City, on sabbatical leave, traveled along. At the first village they visited, Snow noted that Foster Snow and the principal's wife were strongly attracted to the adult solemnity and precocity of the dark children. It led him to speculate on why these children who seem so intelligent and civilized so often failed to develop their potential:

> There is something remote, aloof, proud and admirable about the Bali-
> nese. They do not wear the look of most conquered peoples. They have
> a frank countenance, a fearlessness, even a contempt, in the glance they
> keep for foreigners. . . . I think they are very race conscious, and that their
> tradition, religion, heroic mythology all confirms them in the belief of their
> superiority to the Dutch and to all men. It is said they have no interest
> in travelling, and exhibit little taste for modern study, though they learn
> easily and have remarkable memories.

Snow noted in his diary: "In a day's visit here one sees more breasts than Casanova saw in his life time." At one village he noted one young woman in particular:

> A leader of the dozen girls, named Lemon, seemed more personable.
> It was difficult to believe she was not at least 20 or 21; she had much
> dignity and poise and a full figure. Karson said she was 15, older than the
> rest, and their dancing instructor in the *Djangar* [a traditional Balinese
> dance]. . . . He planned to take her for a drive on the following Sunday.
> This was arranged by bribing an elder of the village to accompany him.
> In the country, said Karson, the elder would obligingly go to sleep under
> a tree or something.

As Karson sketched his plan, memories of Burma, Malami, and Ma So, though not mentioned in his diary, must have played through Snow's mind. There is a photo marked "Bali" of Snow in the midst of several bare-breasted young girls. On the back Foster Snow is indicated as the photographer.

Following a leisurely day at the beach and reading old copies of the *New York Times* at the hotel the next day, they attended a notable *Djangar* in the evening opposite the hotel. Snow described the story, the costumes, the physical movements, and the music in great detail in his diary before noting, "there were perhaps 1,500 Balinese standing in a circle round the performers." Among this large crowd a "few modern students were there in the shorts & pants Dutchmen have taught them to wear. One wonders about the dangers of Westernization destroying the beauty of this simple but in many ways perfect civilization." But the Dutchmen did not worry. They noted that even those Balinese who have traveled abroad "find nothing they want Bali to have—not even white women. They do not like motor cars, because motor cars frighten & kill the pigs & chickens. They do not care much for the cinema; a foreigner once tried to run a show in Den Pessar, and the Balinese went two nights, then found it tiresome and refused to pay, pointing out that Westerners were not charged when they came to watch Balinese shows."

Snow closed this day's diary entry with a series of observations that suggest Shaw is neither the best reading, nor Bali the happiest choice, for a honeymoon:

> I used to think my father slightly demented when he went round the house muttering lines of Shakespeare to himself, or quoting from Dante, but now I realize it was only that he was married.
>
> Every man who marries is in a sense a martyr: he marries in order to save some woman from the brutes of the world he imagines waiting to deceive her.
>
> Man marries because of jealousy; woman stays married because of it.
>
> Some women make marriage an end in life; others make marriage the end of living.

Foster Snow barely mentions Bali in her reminiscences.

Before leaving Bali, Snow regretted not having time to visit the neighboring island of Lomobok that was less modernized and less familiar to tourists. He had been told about the island by a young American in Den Pessar, who had quit the National City Bank of Tientsin after four years when he learned he had no chance of being transferred to Europe. After a week in Bali, this young man decided to make arrangements with a native family to live with them while he tried to write—"anything but be a banker again." Snow dourly warned, "there were worse things than sitting behind a cage; sitting behind a typewriter."[4]

Snow's diary peters out with his notes of their visit to Borobodur on January 24, though they remained in Java a few days longer. After landing at Sourabaya in the morning, January 23, they hired a taxi to take them to Sourakarta and Djokjakarta. In a small village where they stopped to buy new bulbs, presumably for planting by their new home in Peking, Snow was surprised to find the shop using old copies of the *New York Sun* to wrap the bulbs. He saw a page with one of his stories on it. It reminded him of the ephemerality of journalism.

At Borobodur he noted: "Buddhism once must have been a faith as vigorous and aggressive as Moslemism. Such monuments could not be put up by the passive ascetics who are the Buddhistic races of today. . . . This is the kind of God that commands respect from Americans—a God so powerful & awesome as to occasion people to erect a gigantic memorial like this to him—and men like a souvenir of it."

This reminded him of the story of an American who made a collection of stones from great monuments around the world and placed them in his garden so when his guests visited him, he could say, "Well, Bill, that's the Great Wall of China you're sitting on." This story closes book 10 of the diary and reappears in *Journey to the Beginning* as that of a Texas oilman Snow met in the Metropole Hotel in Hanoi before taking the train for Yunnanfu in 1930. The Texas oilman does not appear in Snow's diary of his Hanoi visit.

Before landing in Shanghai on their way to Peking, Snow wrote his father about a mutiny in the Dutch navy during their week in Java: "a small revolution led by Javanese and Dutch sailors. The Dutch had a difficult time putting it down; finally they used drastic measures. Some of the rebels ran away with a battle ship; Dutch naval planes bombarded the vessel, wrecked it, killed 20 sailors—their own men." He apparently did not interrupt his honeymoon to cover this story, though he pictured it to his father as part of a larger pattern of revolt in Asia.

From Sourabaya they sailed for Hong Kong, arriving by extraordinary coincidence just in time to see and hear in person the man who seemed such a strong influence on their courtship and honeymoon, George Bernard Shaw. Shaw infuriated the British by urging the students of Hong Kong University to abjure capitalism and become bolsheviks: "If you are a Red today at 20, you may be a man fit to live in the world by the time you are 40."

From Hong Kong they visited Sun Yat-sen's birthplace, Hsiang Shan, and Macao, before sailing up the estuary to Canton. Near Macao they also called on T'ang Shao-i, former secretary to Yuan Shih-k'ai, the man who so successfully finessed Sun Yat-sen's first assumption of power in China. In Canton, Foster Snow met Edward Lyon, the American lawyer whom Snow had written about on his previous visit in 1930. These were repeat visits for Snow, but for his wife they were new and imprinted themselves on her memory far more vividly than Bali.

On the *Terukini Maru* two days before landing in Shanghai, Snow summarized for his father how he expected Japanese aggression to play out. He did not look for much from the League of Nations. Mounting an economic boycott would raise the possibility of war, and none of the Western nations, including the United States, were ready to go to war for China. If Japan kept Manchukuo he would expect a war between Japan and Russia within a few years. Then he played soothsayer:

> Probably this is what will happen the next six months: 1. Japan will invade Jehol; China will put up a fight, be defeated and be crushed to below The Great Wall; 2. Japan will make certain demands on the Nanking government regarding China's relations with "Manchukuo," the result of which will be the establishment of a pro-Japan government in Peking; 3. Japan will withdraw from the League of Nations; 4. China will demand a meeting of the signatories of the Nine Powers Treaty; 5. China will demand an economic boycott by the League of Nations against Japan; the request will not be agreed to by the Powers; 6. France, England and the U. S. will profit greatly from the sale of munitions to China and Japan; the financial interests of all the Powers, with the possible exception of the U. S. A. will bring full pressure to bear on their governments to support Japanese imperialism in Asia; 7. The Filipinos will table their demands for "complete independence"—will reject any offer of it; 8. Russia and Japan *may* break off diplomatic relations; 9. China and Japan *may* break off diplomatic relations; 10. The "Reds" of China will make steady progress in Central China.

The young couple arrived in Shanghai on February 15 and stayed long enough to collect wedding gifts, including an electric coffeepot from Mme. Sun Yat-sen, and for Snow to have a satisfying interview with Lu Hsun, whom he met for the first time on February 21. Keeping in mind the prospect of war with Japan in Jehol, he also interviewed Sun Fo, now one of the presidents of the Nanking government, and Lo Wen Kai, minister of Foreign Affairs, in Nanking.[5]

Snow put the anti-American views he observed in Japan and described to Epes into an article for the *China Weekly Review*. He warned that a chauvinistic Japanese press, bent on diverting public scrutiny from the disastrous economic results of its campaigns in China, has dangerously "succeeded in establishing a real war psychology in Japan, with America as victim—or rather, with Japan as victim of American 'interference' with Japanese rights."

To incite the Japanese people the press reported an understanding had been reached between China and the United States that the latter should intervene if Japan assumed the offensive in Jehol, the last part of Manchuria yet to be annexed, and consequently the Nanking government had ordered Marshal Chang Hsueh-liang to prepare to attack.

This article was signed John Fairsworth, a slight variation of the name he used for his unpublished article on the U.S. Marines in Shanghai. Within a few weeks of its appearance he published another in the *China Weekly Review* under John Fairnsworth, C.B.E. It seems likely Snow used the pseudonym, with Powell's compliance, to protect his future opportunities to travel to Manchukuo and Japan.[6]

On their way to Peking from Shanghai the Snows made straight for ice cream sodas at Jimmy's in Tsingtao. At Weihaiwei, they observed part of the British fleet in the protected harbor behind Liu Kung Island. For several days they were stranded on the sandy Taku bar at the mouth of the river entrance to Tientsin. The wind was bitterly cold, but Foster Snow noted "the British seemed to be enjoying enough air for a change."

From Tientsin, Snow wrote Howard wondering whether he was uncle to a niece or nephew. His premonition was for the latter, and it was right. Since both Conso Press and the *New York Sun* were badly affected by the depression he was uncertain what to expect when he got to Peking. He still expected to cover the news for the *London Daily Herald*.[7]

The Snows' honeymoon ended with a ninety-mile train trip to Peking, the ancient city they would make their home until the Japanese invaded four years later.

18

A New Home and
Two Long Shots Come In

A FTER THEY ARRIVED IN Peking the Snows stayed for some weeks at the comfortable Hotel de Pekin. They did not find the home they were looking for until sometime late in March. A letter from Charles Hanson Towne, suspicious that Snow had married, belatedly caught up with them at their new home. Snow apologized for keeping him in the dark, but explained even their families read about their marriage first in their local paper because a Tokyo buddy had cabled news of the wedding home through his press association. They were having a difficult time pacifying everybody, so Snow asked Towne to prove again a true friend and understand. He was surprised how few shared their belief a marriage was and ought to be a strictly personal business. "How I wished you were here, though, to stand as my best man!" He soon dedicated his first book, *Far Eastern Front*, to Towne, perhaps in part to repair whatever damage this apparent slight had done.

He described the house they found at 21 Mei Cha Hutung to both Towne and his father. Originally he thought the street name meant "Plum Tea" Street or something equally fetching, until his cook explained it was neither that kind of *mei* nor *cha*. This *mei* meant "coal," and this *cha* meant "residue." Put together they meant "Clinker Street." If that sounded like the wrong side of the tracks, it also applied to others who were very respectable, including the American minister. He added with pride he had put into this rather swell "jernt," the "accumulations of five years' wandering in the Orient . . . spoils from China, Indo-China, India, Yunnan, Java, Japan, and so on."

The house was small but had "authentic red gates, a moon door, a high compound wall, washed white, that shuts out noise and dust, and inside a little courtyard where flowers bloom and some fruit trees that are a cloud of blossom." Although the area was not large it was divided into a number of rooms: a kitchen, dining room, guest room, bathroom, bedroom, living room, office, and library, plus three servants' rooms and a servants' bath. "We have furnished it with Peg's genius, for incredibly little, and for rent we pay 60 Mex a month—about $13 U. S. money, fluctuating with exchange." The expectations he had described to Howard from Shanghai seem to have been fulfilled.

The cook they hired rivaled "the famed I Sung," who served Snow and John Allison in Shanghai. He had been with Roy Chapman Andrews for four years in Mongolia, and Snow was sure "he could buy me out several times." But they only had to pay him, a "small-boy," and a coolie collectively the "munificent sum of $40 Mex per month! Why fry eggs when you can get them done so cheaply?"

While they stayed at the Hotel de Pekin, Foster Snow came to know Helen Burton who managed a shop on the ground floor of the hotel selling Oriental objects from jewelry to fur coats. She modeled the clothes Burton featured and tried her hand at designing both clothes and furniture. She was particularly proud of the miniature garden she created in the living room of their new home and the ultramodern half-moon willow desk with a bookcase running around it that she ordered made for her own use. When Snow one day proudly brought home many heavy pieces of furniture he had bought at bargain prices from one of the French legation men leaving Peking, she did not know how to tell him how distasteful they were to her.

They "bought a sleek Mongol racing pony and half interest in another, and joined a riding club." They "took long rides through the autumn glory to visit the temples, and across the fields and meadows to the Summer Palace and the Black Dragon Pool near the Western Hills." They named a white puppy that Sven Hedin brought back from Inner Mongolia "Gobi." It grew up to be a handsome and notable part of the household. They both made a serious effort to study Chinese.

But this golden world was threaded with risks and anxieties. Soon after they moved into their first home, three members of a radical artists' group began calling on them, making it a point to arrive and leave separately. The three had started an anti-imperialist, antifeudal society in 1925 with the innocent sounding name "Hu Tou," or "The Daubers." A year before the Snows' move to Peking a fourth member had been sent to prison for ten years for painting the Kuomintang flag lying in the mud. Foster Snow quickly took up their cause and learned what she could from them about China's contemporary art. Snow was sympathetic but otherwise preoccupied.

Agnes Smedley gave Comintern member Otto Braun a letter of introduction to the Snows that spring. He hoped to persuade Snow to accompany him on a visit to the warlord Feng Yu-hsiang, who was then playing an important role in the fate of Peking. But Snow backed away from such a trip and instead invited Braun on excursions to Peking's outskirts while each probed the other mistrustfully. Braun soon after joined the Red forces in central China as a military advisor. His advice would later become the subject of historical controversy, but he was still treated with deference when Snow visited the Red forces in 1936.

Rewriting *Far Eastern Front*, Snow became concerned his growing association with leftists might damage his credibility as a journalist. On July 5 he called on Ambassador Nelson Trusler Johnson. He told the ambassador he was friends with Mme. Sun and other liberals from Shanghai, that, like many other journalists, he had joined her civil liberties organization, but he made it clear he was not himself a subversive radical. He asked the ambassador's advice. The latter warned him against engaging in Chinese causes. That was crossing the line, but he suggested he should ignore rumors about his radicalism and let his actions and writing prove his position. Snow listened respectfully, but later did not draw the line where the ambassador advised.

Foster Snow remembered coming home one day during the summer of 1933 from riding her Mongol pony, Mist-or, to find Snow, Teilhard de Chardin, and Ida Treat in close conversation over tea. Their visit proved long and congenial, continuing "until it was too late for Teilhard to get to his monastery outside the gates." Foster Snow told their visitors about the Daubers.

Treat was immediately interested. She was an American archaelogist married to Vaillant du Courier, then head of the French Communist Party. She lived in France but often visited Chardin. She quickly agreed to arrange an exhibit for the Daubers in Paris. The paintings were to be sent to her in Shanghai, and she was then to take them to Paris. The exhibit was held at the Gallerie Billiett in Paris, March 14–29, 1934.

Snow chose to move to Peking in part because it was in the path of the Japanese encroachment from Manchukuo. He wanted to measure and warn the world of the threat it posed. But the severity of the economic depression at home threatened the delivery of his message. Horace Epes regretfully wrote Snow, "the New York *Sun* has cancelled as of April 29 the additional compensation authorized for you last Spring." Snow's salary would now revert to eighty dollars per month for his part-time work for Conso Press. Epes added, "If you have any sort of glimmering of what is going on in the newspaper world over here, however, perhaps you will not be so much surprised. The bottom has almost fallen out."

About the same time Snow also described the pitiable state of the Chinese national revolution and the Japanese menace approaching from the north to his father: "Probably not since Napoleon sabotaged the French Revolution has a people been so completely betrayed by its rulers as the Chinese have been throughout this crisis. . . . The Nanking government is still without a policy; it leans weakly upon the League of Nations and cries for the Powers to fight China's war." He disdainfully dismissed talk of economic sanctions stopping Japan. They were too little too late.

To believe Japan was heading toward economic collapse was also wishful thinking. People who clung to that hope were myopic. "The Japs have all the necessary qualifications of a conquering race: capacity for unity, sacrifice, patriotic martyrdom, organization, singleness of national purpose—it is difficult for people who know them well to believe that economics are going to baffle them in this great upthrusting moment of their history."

He made the danger even more explicit to Towne:

> People do not realize it at home, but we are rapidly being drawn toward a war with Japan. . . . The one possibility of preventing it, Japanese consider, is that America renounce her position in the Orient. Japan is determined to take no dictation, no interference, from anyone. She will fight to keep what she has, and more that she intends to take. She regards America and Russia as the two possibilities as contenders against her, and in this speculation, America comes first. . . . Russia, America, and England could break Japan, but it is obvious that at present America and England are not going to fight anybody, anywhere, over anything.

He predicted Japan would "inherit the mandate that the West was given, for nearly a century, and did not know how to use" in Asia. But he took some consolation in believing the "Japanese ascension will in the end mean the revival of the Chinese people. That is the way of China; conquests merely rejuvenate, do not destroy her. And the Chinese people today are satisfied with the outlook that in 50 years, perhaps a hundred, the little islanders will be absorbed, and the fruits of their strenuous adventures will be enjoyed by their posterity. A curiously reasonable people, the Chinese."[1]

In this bleak mood and struggling to translate Lu Hsun's darkly acerbic "Ah Q," Snow wrote a bitingly satiric, but blandly titled, article, "China Needs Healthier Leaders," for the *China Weekly Review*. He signed it John Fairnsworth, C.B.E. Traditionally "C.B.E" meant "Commander of the British Empire," but in the Snows' anticolonialist circle it meant "China's Best Enemy."

Pompously, Fairnsworth draws a relation between China's failures of public health, evidenced by its "expectorating frequency and the sickly pallor that comes upon the skin of foreign women who dwell too long this side of God's Countries to westward," and its disorganized politics.

The consequences of China's bad health were made clear by several recent incidents. The Japanese armies would not have succeeded in Manchuria but for the illness of Chang Hsueh-liang, whether pneumonia, typhoid, narcotic addiction, or more likely "bellophobia." During Japan's attack on Shanghai, Wang Ching-wei was indisposed with diabetes, Hu Han-min was recovering in Hong Kong, and Chiang Kai-shek was rest-curing in the hills of Ningpo.

During the recent fighting in Jehol, Chiang Kai-shek hurried to Paotingfu, "but due to the excruciating pain of his now famous tooth trouble he did not go on to Peking to direct operations against the Japanese as he had planned. . . . Dr. Lo Wen-kan, minister of foreign affairs, was in distress with his eye trouble, while T. V. Soong had to retire for a few days due to a disastrous struggle with influenza." Wang Ching-wei chose this historic moment to make the supreme sacrifice, but it proved a useless martyrdom. Despite returning hurriedly from Europe, "where doctors had been consulting for months over the uniqueness of his condition, he arrived in China too late to salvage Jehol. But of course General Tang Yu-lin had paralysis and some people maintain that even had Wang arrived earlier he could hardly have foreseen this intervention of the Will of Allah."

Fairnsworth concluded: "Either the guardians of the national frontiers must be chosen from healthier stock, or the hot springs of Honan and Shantung, the baths of Germany, the salubrious breezes of Hongkong and Canton, the ablest surgeons, dentists, nurses, and medicine-men must somehow be concentrated in Nanking." This grave situation particularly deserved consideration by "the youthful patriots of China, who have been foolishly advised to dabble in unconstructive speculations on socialism by a recent tourist, George Bernard Shaw."

Five months later Foster Snow first appeared in print as Nym Wales in the *China Weekly Review*. "Analyzing the 'Shanghai Mind'" complemented Snow's 1930 *American Mercury* article by indicting the British and conservative Chinese for living in the same "comfortable but hermetically sealed glass case" that Snow had indicted Americans for living within. She paralleled the fine class distinctions to which both British and Chinese unrealistically clung: "To label his position the Chinese wears long fingernails and a nob on his flat hat. The Englishman wears long coattails and a high hat on his nob."

Two years later, after the Snows had become more actively engaged in China's political life, Foster Snow explained to Herz, now her agent as well as her husband's, why she found a pen name useful:

> I use it whenever I have anything mean to say about the missionaries, the British or the local telephone company. . . . I suppose it is necessary for you to identify me somehow if we ever hope to sell any articles. I have no objection to being identified in America, but life can be very complicated in China for people who write about other people, as we live in tiny village-communities and everybody knows all about everybody else. If possible, it is certainly advisable for anyone who writes to keep his private life inviolable; life is much simpler; assassination less frequent; Chinese, Japanese, British, Nazi, Fascist etc. etc. friends more full of loving kindness.[2]

In May, Snow sent Mrs. Meloney his promised article on Soong Ching-ling. He added a nicely aimed sentence: "I do not think I have sufficiently emphasized how important she is in a China where women leaders are so vastly needed, but are so very few." He also informed Mrs. Meloney of his marriage: "You were in a manner an accomplice; the bride had once read something of mine in your magazine. Despite that she married me."

In later years Foster Snow remembered Mrs. Meloney's rejecting with "scathing thoroughness" the "juvenile attitude" of a "sweet" article her husband wrote about their wedding. She probably referred to "Christmas Escapade in Japan," eventually published in *Travel*. There Snow pictured the newlyweds standing on board ship New Year's morning, taking the shouts of the crew, *"Banzai!,"* or "Ten Thousand Years," to refer to the length of their marriage commitment: "She looked at me with eyes—never mind, they were limpid blue pools of incredible depth. As a matter of fact, I found myself very much in love with those eyes—the eyes of a new bride on New Year's dawn." Mrs. Meloney's editorial judgement seems vindicated.

But Foster Snow's view of her own role in gender politics made it a confused and sensitive issue in their marriage:

> This was the first time Ed realized how ferociously the dragonladies in control of the press guard these gates against all the "beautiful" young women and home-makers. He did not realize there has always been a civil war on between the "women's lib" warriors for identical rights with men, and the rest of womankind who run the home and social structure, never more than No. 2 in any situation usually. Ed never again mentioned his "beautiful wife," if he could avoid it. His feelings were permanently hurt by Mrs. Meloney.

Late in May, Mrs. Meloney, not yet having received Snow's Soong Ching-ling article, chided him: "Has marriage made you lazy or busy or got your mind off writing? Have you gone to war or into business or are you doing a book? There is an answer to your silence and whatever it is I hope it means you are well and happy. But, anyway, we want you to know that we would like to get a manuscript from you."

Snow sent Soong Ching-ling his typescript before sending it to Mrs. Meloney, but her corrections reached him too late to figure in the manuscript he sent, in part because of the elaborate precautions needed to be taken with her mail. He sent his own response to her letter through Victor Keen in Shanghai. Keen explained he delivered Snow's letter to Madame Sun, "but didn't get to see her personally. I telephoned her several times and left my number but could never get her so finally went out and delivered the letter to a servant at her house." He could not trust the public mail. He explained to Mrs. Meloney that Mme. Sun's "views are not popular with the present rulers of China, and publication of this may prove embarrassing."

Snow's article on Soong Ching-ling was well remembered. Rewi Alley, a friend to both Mme. Sun and Snow, told me on several occasions Mme. Sun was embarrassed by Snow's detailing of her personal and family matters. If so, the criticisms of Snow's typescript she forwarded were surprisingly mild and consenting. He accepted and forwarded them immediately to Mrs. Meloney. He then explained to Mme. Sun the "items concerning your dislike of jewelry and the scantness of your wardrobe were contributed by A.—on my request for some personal notes." "A." is not identified in the letter, but Agnes Smedley seems the obvious candidate. Smedley later fell into Mme. Sun's disfavor for such indiscretions. Snow, however, persuasively explained why he gave as much attention as he did to personal detail:

> I confess that there may be too much dramatization of your character in the story, too little of the League; it is a weakness of mine to emphasize personalities instead of principles. On the other hand there is little hope that the article would see publication if it at all smacked of "League propaganda"—the very thing I attempted to circumvent—whereas in the habiliment of a character sketch of you it will be highly acceptable, I think. Besides, I wonder if you do realize just how rare a person you are among the host of people in this East who influence the course of events.

Snow also had other news he was eager to share: "At the moment I ride on the crest of ecstacy. I have just had a cable from New York announcing that a book I wrote a year ago has finally made a dent on, nay pierced, some publisher's armor! It has been accepted, with publication date set for next October." Next October in this case meant October 1933, not 1934.

Despite his elation, he had misgivings: "I had long ago given up hope of placing it, and I am not sure now that I should let it appear. It was originally written in less than two months . . . and I have done nothing with it since. It is not the book I want to do, but perhaps it is not too bad for a beginning. I am faced now with the task of re-writing, supplementing and bringing up to date some 75,000 words, in one month."[3]

Two weeks later he cabled Horace Epes again asking for leave, this time for six weeks. His deadline for rewriting his book was July 15. Epes responded immediately. The relation between the *New York Sun* and Conso Press had ended. The *Sun* also discontinued the "World Today" column that had carried so many of Snow's travel pieces. There was no chance of Snow getting the twenty dollars more per month he requested. The next six weeks were to be decisive for Conso, but Epes thought it only fair "to let you know that the plight really is grave. It is quite possible that before you are ready to resume writing the organization will have collapsed. My personal suggestion is that you begin immediately lining up a source of income to protect yourself in case the worst happens."

Snow did not finish rewriting *Far Eastern Front* until late in July. He extended his leave from Consolidated another month. He planned to head for Manchukuo before his book came out. He expected to send Conso stories from his trip but planned to travel at his own expense. However, within a week of writing Epes, his financial anxiety was magically much relieved. He wrote his brother: "Did you ever receive the letter I wrote asking you to look after a manuscript for me? It was sold, much to my astonishment, to the *Saturday Evening Post*. For $750! Where is your depression?"

"The Decline of Western Prestige" was culled from the conclusion he had written for *Far Eastern Front*. He hoped it would prove an effective advertisement for the latter. But to gain admission to the huge reading public served by the *Saturday Evening Post* was cause for celebration in itself and marked the beginning of a long and sustaining relationship that would prove invaluable to Snow's future career, despite his enduring political differences with the magazine's editorial position. The 750-dollar payment was so unexpected it became part of a Snow legend. The check arrived in such an unpretentious envelope he and Foster Snow first thought it a subscription bill. The amount of the check seemed so unlikely they were not convinced it was real until they took it to the bank and the bank was willing to cash it.

In *Journey to the Beginning,* Snow added another story of an all-or-nothing double bet he made at the Paomachang race track shortly before receiving the check. After learning from Epes that Conso was folding—an event that in fact happened only months later—he supposedly drew out of the bank all their savings, "a pitiful sum," and split it on two desperate bets at the race track, winning both. The proceeds from this bet plus the *Post*'s 750-dollar check then provided them with a stake enabling him to turn down a secure, but distasteful, two-year desk job for the Associated Press in Peking. This is like his reported killing on Wall Street before leaving New York in 1928. There is no indication of such a race track coup in his letters home at the time. Nor does Foster Snow mention it in her memoir. The AP job does not appear in his correspondence until months after he sold his article to the *Saturday Evening Post*. Perhaps the good fortune of having the *Post* accept an article such a short time after hearing his first book was to be published years later seemed as remarkably improbable as cashing in on two long-shot bets at the track.

On September 16 Epes informed him Consolidated Press had been taken over by the North American Newspaper Alliance, but Conso was to be maintained as a separate entity "with the rights of all its present clients preserved. Just what this will mean for the future of the organization and the members of the staff remains to be seen." Epes congratulated Snow on the *Post* story: "It was by far the best exposition of the situation out there that I have seen anywhere, and I have heard a number of favorable comments on it." He also hoped Snow had finished his book on time and would write him about his future plans.[4]

19

Author of a Book

S NOW LEFT FOR MANCHURIA before receiving the discouraging news about Conso Press. He wrote Epes from Hsinking he was gathering material he expected to mail within two weeks.

Meanwhile, Foster Snow, designated "the family mail-opener" back in Peking, wrote Snow's father introducing herself and thanking him for sending clippings of Snow's *Saturday Evening Post* story. She claimed credit for convincing her husband, after much argument, to send the article to the *Post* instead of the *New York Herald Tribune,* presumably to Mrs. Meloney. Meanwhile, George Horace Lorimer, editor of the *Post,* wrote Snow's agency about the article's coming to the *Post* "unheralded and unsung," proud that "a good man can, you see, get a break with us" and suggesting their agents redouble their efforts. That, of course, did not make Henriette Herz happy.

Foster Snow told her father-in-law Snow had gone to Manchuria in part because he was "afraid he'll never be permitted in Japanese territory again after the book comes out." But the Japanese were not their only concern: "The subject of relinquishing any kind of imperialism in Asia is a very sensitive one among the local foreigners, especially the army and navy men who thrive on it, of course. The American Minister apparently is still friendly, as he has asked us for dinner next week as if nothing had happened. He is inclined toward being fairly liberal, anyway."

About this time Snow sent Mrs. Meloney a story on James Yen's Chinese Educational Movement. She had suggested it earlier. He asked Harrison

Smith to send her a copy of his book, but he again worried that it was "full of mistakes, for the Mss. had to be turned out so hurriedly, and I am so far away, that I did not even see a first proof."

When he saw the book, his fears proved accurate. He wrote his father: "I am disappointed in it chiefly because it is so full of unnecessary typographical errors which, it seems, ought not to appear in a book that is to sell for $3.75. I notice also now that words have been dropped here and there, some of them with rather tragic consequences." His father sent copies of letters from friends and relatives, and at least one of them made Snow feel he finally had done something to make his father truly proud: "I thought Merle Smith's letter a very fine tribute to you. It humbles me, and makes me wish that I could honestly survey my record and agree with his high estimate of your 'fine son.' Anything I have done or may do is to a very large extent the result of the early shaping of my mind and habit under your tutelage."

The next month his early tutor sent him a pungent paternal editorial on American depression politics:

> I am a follower of Huey Long, a sort of political brigand, who believes that swollen fortunes ought to be decentralized and the excess of wealth (more than 5 million dollars to one man) should be sent back where it is created and not used to oppress. He has been against Roosevelt policies as long as Roosevelt was surrounded by Wall Street advisers. He fired his Wall Street secretary of the treasury and other capitalistic hangers-on and now Huey and I are for him again. He has apportioned $5 billion dollars for relief and public works—an appalling mistake from a capitalistic view point. Capitalists believe a man should get his own money and keep out of jail.

Conso Press finally gave up the struggle. Snow received a cable from Epes: "Terminating January First." Snow immediately apologized to Epes for sending little or no correspondence over the last few months. After returning from Manchuria he suffered badly from sinusitis and had a slight operation performed. Nevertheless, he had intended to complete a series of articles on Manchukuo for Conso, but "all this is unnecessary explanation now. . . . Anyway, I wanted you to know my side of the thing." He hoped to be kept in mind for any opening Epes might suggest and would welcome an opportunity to work again with Epes if he made any new connection.

Epes delayed writing, hoping he could ask Snow to continue sending mail copy, but all he could offer was that Dolan of the *Sun* had asked for Snow's address. Perhaps Snow had heard from Dolan. Personally Epes was particularly sorry their association was to end. "I feel very much that I know you and that we have come to be friends." He had already spoken to Hal

O'Flaherty of the *Chicago Daily News* and passed the word to the UP about Snow's talent and availability. Dolan joined in recommending him to UP. It was a great disappointment to see thirteen years of building by David Lawrence and his associates turn out this way.

On the last day of the year Snow wrote his father: "It was kind and self-sacrificing of you to send me the $5, and I appreciate it greatly because I know how even more important it must be to you now than to me." Helen Burton had invited the Snows for Christmas to the Chinese temple she had converted into a house in Peking's Western Hills. They "stayed for three days, hiking up and down snow-covered peaks between rounds of stuffing ourselves, playing games, and otherwise being juvenile."

He gave his father a detailed accounting of his expenses writing *Far Eastern Front* and what he had received and might expect in royalties. In sum: "On a book of this type a sale of 5,000 would be the most I could hope for. So you see that if I am lucky I may break even. That is why talented people write detective stories and mystery yarns, which sell an average of 10,000 copies, when even moderately good." He did not mention he had sent a second article to the *Saturday Evening Post* at Lorimer's prompting.

He added more hopeful news in a postscript: "Did I tell you that *FEF* is to be translated and published in French?" Ida Treat, who had written several books herself besides arranging the exhibit for the Daubers, was to do the translation. No French translation was ever published.[1]

John Allison, in Tokyo, read his former roommate's *Far Eastern Front* with considerable interest and wrote Snow in detail his reaction. "Your book is fine, Ed. I think it gives a better description of what happened in Manchuria and in Shanghai than anything I have seen." He also thought Snow's assessment of events was correct, but as for Snow's solution, "all the nations agreeing to give up their colonies etc and offering a prayer that Japan will then stop her aggression on the continent, well, in the first place the nations just wont [*sic*] do it until they are compelled, and in the second place I am not sure that it would have its desired effect." To those in control in Japan it "would mean nothing more than that the West had withdrawn so that Japan could move in."

He had reservations about Snow's representation of the early history of Japan, but he thought his treatment of the Tanaka Memorial very good. "I believe it was undoubtedly a forgery but that it did express the plans and aims of the Tanaka group and the group which has been running Japan the last few years." After sharing his own speculations on Japan's future, he ended with a series of questions: "Is the war coming in 1935 or in the spring of 1934 or are we all just panicky about nothing? And if the war does come, what will the rest of the world do about it? Are we to back Japan and then watch her, after the war, wipe us off the economic map of Asia or are we all to rally round our new pals the Communists? If the latter, what will Hamilton Fish say?" He and Jeanne were planning on seeing the Snows in Tokyo in April. They could talk this all over in more detail then.

Far Eastern Front was reviewed widely and for the most part favorably. A. M. Nikolaieff praised it at length in the *New York Times Book Review*, as did Major General William S. Graves, retired commander of the American Expeditionary Force in Siberia from 1918 to 1920, in the *New York Herald Tribune*. Snow's hopes were early raised by favorable comments from Lin Yu-tang in the *China Critic* and Mauritz A. Hallgren in the *Nation*.

Lin's review was warmly personal:

> I don't read many books, and still more rarely read books on current topics, because I usually have the good sense to avoid them. But I sat up one night to read this book through . . . without having made up my mind to do so. That is how all good books should be read, accidentally, without a sense of obligation and without expectations, but with a tremendous sense of discovery. . . . I enjoyed that sense of pleasant discovery when I opened the pages of this book. It was sent me by the author. It was just like listening to him talking, telling me of what he saw personally, vividly and, at times, dramatically. But it was considerably better than his talking, and I didn't know he could write such a good book. No humbug, no heaviness; no Shanghai mind; no capitalist bias; and running through an undertone of sincere heart-felt sympathy for the Chinese people, who I know are the most misruled nation on earth. . . . An eminently human and readable book, this.

Hallgren declared *Far Eastern Front* the "most intelligent and readable" of the "fifteen or more important books dealing with the Far East that have been published since the Japanese launched their latest imperialistic drive on the Asiatic mainland two years ago." Snow had especially "sought to penetrate and understand the mentality of the Eastern peoples. In consequence he has given us a convincing picture, an account of warfare, that satisfies us much more than would a plain recital of surface facts."

Mrs. Meloney also weighed in with congratulations: "Your book is grand. I am so proud to have a mention in it. You cover the problems in that big disturbed part on this earth more completely and entertainingly than anyone who has turned out a book on the subject. It really should be a best seller."[2] It wasn't. Such praise certainly gave Snow significant confidence in his ability, and won him important respect in journalistic and literary circles, but the sale was disappointing.

In the middle of January, Snow wrote Mildred they had moved to the village of Haitien. Their new home was "next door to Yenching University,

The Snows at home in Peking.

an American-endowed institution which stands a little east of the Summer Palace and commands a marvelous view of the Western Hills. It is about eight miles outside the Peking Wall, but good bus service connects with the center of town, and we are willing to undergo the slight inconvenience because of the better air here, the inspiring view and a lower rental of a much better house than we had." The house belonged to the chairman of the Yenching University Board of Directors, who built it for his own retirement. The school needs of the last of his ten children had caused him to postpone his retirement plans, so he invited the Snows to live in the house at a rent so low they could not refuse.

There was a swimming pool on the house grounds, an independent water system, electric lights, and two modern baths, plus an acre of garden, "laid out in fruit trees, vegetables, evergreens and a fine arbor of grapes." From his study in a corner wing, Snow could look out upon the Summer Palace, "the once forbidden playground of emperors." He could also "see the sunset over the Western Hills and by day trace the patterns of willow trees against a sky that, out here away from the city, is a blue of incredible purity." All this for the equivalent of seventeen dollars a month in American money.

Although he knew his position with Consolidated Press was ended, Epes's letter of explanation had not yet arrived. This left him "with no assured income except what I manage to earn by free-lancing and my connection with the London *Daily Herald*. However, I have several prospective correspondents' posts in mind so that I am not worried." He did not mention he would also be teaching a course in magazine journalism at Yenching, but that seems almost certainly to have been part of their consideration in taking the house. He began teaching that winter semester.

He *was* ready to announce he had offers to do two more books and an invitation from a lecture agent to give a series of talks on the Far East in the fall in the United States. "Although I am afraid I shall be unconvincing on the lecture platform I intend to follow up this offer and if it develops into anything tangible I may see you next fall." He pasted up a single-page announcement of five lecture topics to be used by the booking agent, William B. Feakins. He used a quote from Charles Hanson Towne's review of *Far Eastern Front* as a lead: "If you wish to get a rushing, panoramic picture of China as it is today, and of all the political as well as the actual weapons being used against her, you will find it in Edgar Snow's *Far Eastern Front*. It brings the problems of the Far East boldly before our eyes. In sharp vivid strokes a canvas is painted, luminous and real. No thinking person should miss it."

A few days later Epes's letter describing the last days of Consolidated Press arrived. He commiserated with Epes and readily accepted his offer to forward letters to American editors. He also noted he "would be willing to go to Japan, and indeed would welcome the change, for a good assignment." He still had friends among "the Japanese official crowd who, while finding much of what I wrote about the Army in *Far Eastern Front* unpalatably harsh, nevertheless recognize it as true."

When "Japan Builds a New Colony" appeared in the *Saturday Evening Post*, his father sent him a congratulatory cable. He replied, "I'm glad you liked my *SEP* article," acknowledging somewhat wonderingly, "Lorimer actually asked me for it, which is a rare honor I imagine." He received another $750 check, but a precipitous skid in the value of the American dollar worried him. Still the *Post* check would keep them alive for some time.

He planned to go to Hsinking again for Pu Yi's coronation, and he was happy to receive a contract from Jarrolds offering to publish an English edition of *Far Eastern Front* on good terms. His book was also being translated into Chinese, but he could expect to make nothing on that. This was the good news, rather than a winning bet at Paomachang, that freed him to turn down the opportunity to become the Associated Press Peking correspondent. He did not want to commit to staying in Peking for the next twelve months.

A week earlier he shared the platform of The Men's Club of Peking Union Church with H. J. Timperley of the *Manchester Guardian* to speak on "Russia's Position in the Far East." Timperley, who was in Hankow in 1927 during the split in the Kuomintang and who had just returned by way of Russia from a world tour that allowed him to meet Howard in New York, represented the Russian point of view, and Snow who had "won recognition with his brilliant book *The Far Eastern Front*" represented the viewpoints of China and Japan vis-à-vis Russia.[3] His performance did not build confidence in his ability to speak in public.

The detailed outline and notes Snow kept for the class he taught in magazine writing at Yenching suggest he prepared with impressive thoroughness. On Friday afternoons his students were invited to his home to discuss the issues raised in class. His close relation with his students would draw him into more active participation in China's unfolding history the following year. A list of "Characteristics of great factual writers" he prepared for his students reveals his priorities:

1. Belief in importance of his work
2. Love of good writing
3. Passion for truth and social justice
4. Avidity for knowledge
5. Sense of social responsibility
6. Physical and mental vigor
7. Sympathy and unity of viewpoint with broad masses of humanity
8. Sense of humor
9. Sense of drama
10. Sincerity and courage
11. A clear and definite scientific ideology
12. Belief in the perfectibility of man

He believed "the essential thing about any writer is that he must have IDEAS of his own."

> No matter what form of writing you choose, you must first of all LIVE. This doesn't mean that you have to undergo personally all the experiences you may write about, that you must know everything, but that you *must* have given yourself up to some interest so completely, so vitally, that you can understand the consummate interests of others, and interpret them for millions without such interests, but be eager to believe, to be taught, about all phases of THE VITAL LIFE.

To achieve this goal he recommended a writer "Put himself in a new or strange environment, where life is so completely different that he will HAVE to think about everything that happens, where he will HAVE to judge and evaluate standards in his own life."

Late in March, Herz cabled Snow that Harrison Smith had offered a contract for a second book. He responded: "My own inclination is to do a travel book, and while I am writing it collect material for a work on Communism." He apparently still hoped to put together *South of the Clouds,* and he offered to send an outline for both. He also asked about the Lu Hsun stories he had sent.

Dolan soon offered Snow a twenty-five-dollar monthly retainer from the *New York Sun* for at most one travel article a month. Snow assumed that meant "or its equivalent" and happily accepted. He mentioned his refusal of the AP job to Dolan. He was still defining the role he earlier sketched for Mrs. Meloney:

> I am trying something everyone has advised against: cutting off, for a while, from routine newspaper work, and attempting to establish myself as a free-lance. I am doing this because I think there is a definite need for a writer, on the scene, who can give in magazine articles a wider interpretation of Far Eastern news events than is possible in ordinary newspaper correspondence. What I would like to develop eventually is a regular newspaper or magazine feature of a distinctly interpretative nature.

Placing a second article in the *Saturday Evening Post* undoubtedly gave him new confidence.

Even so he soon wrote Betty Keen, filling in for her husband, Victor, as the Shanghai representative of the *New York Herald Tribune,* and asked if she had any objection to his writing the *Herald Tribune* to see if it would be interested in adding a correspondent to cover north China. Victor had suggested the possibility to him before Conso Press had folded, and he would ask the *Herald Tribune* to talk to Victor about it in New York.

He was quick to tell Howard he was back on the payroll of the *New York Sun:* "It's exactly what I want; gives me the necessary newspaper connection without the toil of daily routine checking necessary to cover spot news." His new teaching experience was instructive: "I'm finding all sorts of new angles on Chinese life and that of foreigners in China." The half-American, half-Chinese nature of Yenching was unique, and the site of the campus, on a famous Ming dynasty garden, made it "incomparably more beautiful than anything in the category of University grounds" he had seen in the West.

His letter was prompted in part by a visit from Richard Walsh and Pearl Buck, a visit in turn prompted by Henriette Herz. Howard had shared Herz's reservations about Snow's independent dealing with the *Saturday Evening Post,* and Snow now conceded Howard was right. But he insisted his hesitation about sending everything through Herz was not simply because of the money: "I think the direct contact I have with editors is important. Things so often get twisted or misconstrued in passing through a third person, and I should like to feel that even though she does the actual handling of copy I still have a privilege of direct correspondence." He also complained about past mix-ups: "The book jacket and the book were humiliatingly full of errors. The article she placed with *Current History* was edited in such a way as to alter the original meaning, and I may have in consequence got into very hot water about it. It may be unjust to hold her responsible, but I cannot help thinking that if I had been dealing directly with the publishers such disasters might have been avoided."

He either conveniently forgot or may never have noticed how badly *Current History* edited the first piece he sent them. His editing problems grew primarily from his remoteness and the difficulty of timely communication. But he had considerable promotional and public relations skills of his own, and he was ambivalent about putting these matters exclusively in the hands of an agent.

Nevertheless he was excited by the previous day's visit of Walsh and Buck, and he was grateful for Herz's role in making it happen. He, Foster Snow, and Katherine Boydon, their house guest at the time, were surprised to find Buck young, personable, and modern:

> We were given quite a turn when she drank cocktails and cheerfully blew smoke rings with us. I don't know how far her reputation has spread at home, but in China she is regarded as the most interesting woman out here, and of all the writers of the post-revolutionary period she stands the greatest chance of surviving. If you haven't read *The Good Earth* I urge you to do so.
> It was very encouraging to have her express a desire to meet us. She did not call on any other foreigners while she was here, and her visit was incognito. When Walsh said that she wanted to come out, and was very interested in my writings, I thought he was pulling my leg. But she said such complimentary things to me and with such simplicity and sincerity, that I could not (it was after all no great effort) but believe her. Walsh, too, told me that my book was one of the few that he had found helpful in understanding modern China.

A year earlier Pearl Buck confronted the fundamentalist wing of the Presbyterians and wrote: "Almost every missionary who has achieved distinction in appreciation and understanding of a culture he was sent to Christianize, and who has expressed that appreciation and understanding, has been forced to leave missionary ranks." Apparently unaware of that conflict, Snow was pleasantly surprised at the rapport he felt with the noted author. Richard Walsh edited the attractive and respected *Asia* magazine and was president of the John Day Publishing company. Walsh and the future Nobel Prize winner would soon marry and become an even more formidable team influencing American perceptions of China.

Buck left early that afternoon and so missed a spectacle at the Summer Palace such as had not "been seen since the day of the Empress Dowager." The reception was held by the mayor of Peking:

> The dragon boats were taken out of their sheds and colorfully moved across the lotus lake. Old roofs brought out from the museum to be replaced in original positions, and everything was polished and shining with imperial splendor. I think Walsh was very much impressed, it brought a thrill to my heart, recalling a spent greatness that one senses in few things nowadays. Peonies and satiny yellow roses were in bloom and wisteria draped over doorways and down from curling roofs; white lilac scented one courtyard, and in another was the heavy fragrance of China magnolias, oddly voluptuous. Never mind. It was wonderful.

Snow also mentioned meeting J. P. Marquand, who was visiting China to gather background for a serial for the *Saturday Evening Post*. Howard would appreciate Marquand's droll humor, and Snow gave Marquand a letter to present to Howard when the former returned to New York. Snow gave a similar letter to Jim Mills, the Associated Press correspondent, whose former position he reported refusing under so many different circumstances. Mills was an excellent cameraman as well as a crack newspaperman, and Snow suggested Howard get Mills to show some of his cinecamera films: "Peg and I appear in some of those taken in China."

The lecture tour in the States failed to develop. Snow urged Howard again to bring Dottie and Johnnie, his young son, for a visit:

> We have this house with room for two families, and an immense garden and swimming pool. Johnnie could amuse himself with Gobi, the dawg over which Peg will otherwise go nuts. He is, it must be admitted, a remarkable animal, and can do nearly everything but talk, though his language of barks, whines, whinnies, yelps and squeals is not entirely unintelligible. He can walk on his hind legs, jump a hoop, bark at nodded direction, and so on. Do you know you can come from Seattle to Peking and return, in excellent style, for $220? Much less if you desire. No one cares how people travel out here, but I don't recommend coming as I did.[4]

Dr. Rock appeared again in Snow's life about this time. He thought of settling in Peking. Foster Snow told how Rock once regularly took advantage of Chinese superstitions about haunted houses in his travels in anticipation of describing the Snows' own next move to a haunted house with very low rent. Such houses were cheap, free of disease, clean, and safe from robbers.

Emperor Pu-yi at lunch with Japanese advisors.

Rock did this until he rented the haunted house of a big landlord in Yunnan unaware of the landlord's storied purchase and torture of slave girls. Once Rock personally experienced the icy grip of death sleeping on the assumed spot of crime, he no longer doubted Chinese ghosts.

That summer Snow added a chapter and rewrote his conclusion to *Far Eastern Front* for his British readers. He opened his new chapter with the same paragraph he had already used to open his *Post* article "Japan Builds a New Colony." He may also have used it to show his journalism students at Yenching how to win and focus their reader's attention early: "The world may decline to recognize Manchukuo as a nation, but it is impossible to ignore her as a reality, vigorous with life. Born without benefit of Geneva, and with the official disapproval of America put upon her, she is the State nobody knows, diplomatically speaking. Japan's 'love child' is a fact of such embarrassing dimensions that even a diplomat cannot entirely overlook it."

Rewriting his conclusion, he probably also had in mind John Allison's criticism of his "visionary" solution that all Western powers give up their colonial claims in Asia as a means of countering Japanese aggression. He did not weaken or withdraw his criticism of colonialism, but rather than offering such a weakly wishful prospect, he drew instead a grimly warning picture: "So the historic meaning of the Western Powers' failure now to accept Japan's challenge is more profound than mere geographical changes resulting from it. A fundamental shift in racial fronts is taking place. The rise of an Eastern Power, great and courageous, and determined enough to challenge the European Powers and America, marks the twilight of Western mastery."[5]

20

The Threat of Fascism

AN'S FATE, THE ENGLISH translation of André Malraux's Goncourt Prize novel, *La Condition Humaine,* appeared in the summer of 1934, and Snow read it with a sense of excitement. He was already questioning the relation between cultural and political revolution by his efforts to identify and translate those modern Chinese writers he thought most important to introduce to an American audience. He opened his review for the *Shanghai Evening Post and Mercury* noting, "people sickened by the glut of conventional China fiction, so much of which has been essentially vulgar or full of mendacious implication," will find this novel "arrestingly different." It is "a harsh but much needed purgative." Malraux makes China "credible in the active scheme of world logic, and for once it is seen integrally in the broad patterns of human destiny. This is the first novel to interpret the historic purpose and significance of the revolutionary events which shook China in the day of Borodin."

Snow quoted Trotsky to the effect that Malraux was "essentially an individualist and a pessimist," but with an individualism and a pessimism fully conscious of the "historic necessities" stressed by dialecticism. For Snow it was precisely this character as an imaginative artist that distinguished him from the common run of proletarian writers and enabled him to escape the restrictive confines of dialecticism to turn history into true art.

Thus Snow's enthusiastic reading of *Man's Fate,* supported by his deepening respect for Lu Hsun, who also recognized his responsibility as an artist even as he demonstrated his commitment to social revolution, helped Snow draw a clear line between his support for revolutionary literature and his disdain for Marxist dialecticism. But the events central to *Man's Fate* also provoked him to a pessimistic historical observation. He thought it "dubious whether within our time a mass revolution can again come within striking distance of success in China." In 1927 it was amazingly near triumph, but it was brought down not, in final analysis, by Chiang Kai-shek's perfidy, but by the weakness and irresolution of the Communists' own party machine. Once the Third Internationale had taken power from the workers and peasants and secured decisive economic mastery of Shanghai, "Communism in China became a broken cause."[1]

Events in China seemed to go from bad to worse. In September he gave Walsh this bleak assessment:

> China has never seemed so dead to me spiritually as at present, and in contrast to an active world elsewhere it is especially stagnant intellectually. All the Chinese intellectuals I know seem to feel equally pessimistic. But perhaps I have known only an artificial China, the revolutionary scene these six or seven years, and perhaps this old land is settling down to its ancient inertia. The placidity of the nation's greeting to Chiang's Confucian revival—which comes down to the masses like a narcotic soporific, for to them it means only the enforcement of filial piety, ancestor worship, submissive spiritual resignation—is somehow very disconcerting.

The current big story was the Sino-Japanese rapprochement. "The reopening of traffic on the Peiping-Mukden Railway, the establishment of customs stations by the Chinese along the Great Wall, the appointment of Japanese advisors to the Chinese Navy, etc. are recent indications of what has been happening." If a Russo-Japanese war came in 1935 China would probably be an ally of Japan, "at least while the Kuomintang under Chiang rules."

Along with these observations he sent Walsh an article and introductory comments to Lu Hsun's story, "Medicine," which Walsh carried away from his Peking visit to the Snows. This time Snow was careful to send his article to Walsh through Herz. Walsh was delighted with the article and the introduction. Snow was waiting for Timperley's return from Manchukuo to write a promised piece on Japanese colonization. In October, Walsh received an article from Timperley and expected another from Snow. Snow promptly responded with "Japanese Cultural Hegemony," and Walsh as promptly accepted: "I most certainly want it and I think it is the best possible way of working out the subject of Japanese colonization." He also looked forward to Foster Snow's article on modern art that Snow advised him was in the works.

The working relationship with Walsh developed promisingly. In the spring Snow recommended Walsh publish an article by Cheng Chen-tou on the tradition of the Chinese short story that Snow anticipated using as an introduction to the collection he planned as a book. He was also pleased when Walsh accepted "Ah Ao," by Sun Hsi-chen, from that collection, but Sun had recently been released from jail, so he advised Walsh "you had better cut out that item in the introduction, or at any rate put it in the past tense. Sun was given the choice of 'confessing' to Communism, or a 5–7 years term in jail." Sun's confession "aroused great amusement among Chinese intellectuals, as he has never even been affiliated with a peripheral Left society."

In November, Snow welcomed the news Mrs. Meloney had accepted "Mongolia, Pivot of Empire." He also proposed three new possible topics: "China Turns toward Fascism," "Opium's Triumph in China," and "The New Mind of China." He congratulated Mrs. Meloney on her energetic leadership in organizing the *Herald Tribune*'s Conference on Women. Foster Snow apparently had not yet revealed her resentment of Mrs. Meloney, for he suggested his wife followed Mrs. Meloney's activities with even more fervent interest than he and was eager to meet her: "Perhaps we can arrange it before very long." But for the present he and she were both wrestling strenuously with the Chinese language, written and oral, and he was in addition doing "some special work in philosophy and economics," probably research on fascism. He was soon to give a notable speech on the subject. Mrs. Meloney expressed strong interest in all three of his suggested topics, but ranked them predictably: 1-opium, 2-fascism, 3-new mind. She did not mention his wife.

While Snow referred to his refusal of Jim Mills's AP position so often it seemed a matter of pride, he restrained his envy of Demaree Bess, another Peking journalist-friend, who made the professional move Snow had strongly desired—to Moscow. In November, Bess sent him a book in Russian on Soviet China he had requested and a chatty letter on his early impressions of the challenges of his new post. Bess had succeeded William Henry Chamberlin, who moved to Tokyo.

Chamberlin loosed a highly critical flood of magazine articles and a new book on Russia before leaving: "The *Vanity Fair* reviewer called it 'slightly marred by liberal hissings,' and I think that about describes it." Chamberlin went to Russia in 1922, "hoping to discover the dawn of a new day, and was increasingly shocked and disturbed by the brutality and callousness of Russia's builders, the most energetic and ruthless since Peter the Great." In contrast Bess expected nothing and was "not displeased to see these people forging ahead, however they do it." He was annoyed by their braggart tone and contemptuous references to other countries and their hypocritical concealment of their own numerous shortcomings. "Their bland confidence that they have the last and final word from Mount Sinai irritates one's common-sense—but the damned fools are sincere and drive their third-rate millions ahead in spite of themselves and really punish corruption, which doesn't penetrate the top circles." This contrast with China drew him to the Soviets, "although the 'dictatorship of the proletariat' is at best a silly notion, capable of infinite abuse."

J. B. Powell was then in Russia, and Bess had seen a lot of him, "but he has certain prejudices which dim his view. The Russians received him very cordially, apparently believing that because he was so anti-Japanese he was therefore pro-Soviet. They are likely to be pretty sadly disappointed by his writings."

Snow and many others at this time very much feared China's attraction to fascism, a new political movement only beginning to loom hugely in world affairs. But what in substance was fascism? Italy and Germany were giving it prominence in Europe, but the particular political and economic concepts that identified it were not readily obvious. Late in 1934 John Leighton Stuart, then chancellor of Yenching University, asked Snow to address the subject before a meeting of the faculty.

Stuart may have been provoked to concern by the fighting that broke out at a remote Ethiopian outpost named Walwal, between Ethiopian and Italian forces on December 5. Mussolini would use the incident as an excuse for a deliberate build-up of troops and an eventual invasion of Ethiopia. The parallels to Japan's invasion of Manchuria would quickly catch Snow's eye. His talk was published in toto in the *Peking Chronicle*, January 8–12, 1935.

Snow began by noting that at the time: "Strictly speaking, Italy is the only country in the world where a political system known as Fascism is in operation." However, the term was in frequent use to describe characteristics of a number of governments in central Europe and Asia. Italy, Germany, and Austria were "the most completely germinative examples of this type of government." In his talk he sought to define fascism, examine its special characteristics, and finally answer the question, "How does Fascism come into power?"

He quoted several definitions beginning with Mussolini's: "The foundation of Fascism is the conception of State, its character, its duty, and its aim. Fascism conceives of the State as an absolute, in comparison with which all individuals or groups are relative." The *Fascist*, published by the Imperial Fascist League, declared: "Fascism is defined as a patriotic revolt against democracy, and a return to statesmanship. Fascism insists upon the duty of cooperation. Fascism is less a policy than a state of mind."

J. S. Barnes, an English authority, in a book prefaced by Mussolini, offered a definition that almost certainly touched Snow's feelings about Catholicism. He quoted the definition without developing the religious theme: "Fascism may be defined generally as a political and social movement having as its object the reestablishment of a political and social order, based upon the main current of traditions . . . created by Rome, first by the Empire and subsequently by the Catholic Church."

But for Snow, John Strachey, "the most brilliant of the young English Marxists," was compelling: "We must define Fascism as the movement for the preservation, by violence and at all costs, of the private ownership of the means of production. When we understand this everything else in the apparent madness of Fascism becomes comprehensible. Fascism is the enemy of science, of rationalism, of educational progress."

Fascism began as an improvisation to meet a crisis, with no substantial body of economic thought to base it on. Hence definition depended on how it operated. Snow discussed at considerable length eight characteristics: militarism; imperialism; myth of racial or cultural superiority; extreme nationalism; dictatorship; attempt to restore moribund culture; conquest of popular expression (denial of free speech); and state-controlled capitalism.

For the most part his discussion of these characteristics seemed deliberately impersonal and remote from particular references to what was then going on in China, but the threat of a fascist Japan was clear and immediate. He quoted Mussolini: "We are forty millions, squeezed into our narrow but adorable peninsula. . . . There are around Italy countries that have a population smaller than ours, and a territory double the size of ours. Hence it is obvious that the problem of Italian expansion in the world is a matter of life and death for the Italian race."

He followed that with a quote from Barnes: "Empires exhibit natural growth . . . Empires grow, filling up by *divine right* the *voids* created by states in dissolution."

Then he concluded: "This is the divine idea back of Hitler's Nordicism and Italy's new Romanism. We in the Orient are more familiar with it in terms of certain Japanese, who regard themselves as descendants of the Sun Goddess, and hence, destined to rule the earth."

To answer the question "How does fascism come into power?" Snow listed seven characteristics common to the rise of fascism in Italy, Germany, and Austria: national inferiority complex; economic crisis; failure through half-measures of socialists in control of parliament to effect complete socialist revolution; weak traditions of parliamentarism; threat of Communist overthrow; army backs the fascists; and terrorism from extralegal troops. His discussion of these characteristics led to this conclusion:

Fascism is a movement which arises when the contradictions of Capitalism under democracy reach a stage where the only solution to economic collapse seems to be the socialization of the means of production. Fascism appears primarily to have an economic basis as a Capitalist countermovement against Communism. It arises as the alternative, but this alone would not put it into power. What happens is that nationalist spirit is worked up to a high fever, and merged with this fear and ignorance of socialist consequences, and becomes a combined force that overpowers rational resistance.[3]

There is a significant parallel between the point Snow made in his review of Malraux's *Man's Fate* about the failure of the Left in 1927 in Shanghai and the preconditions he describes in his talk as necessary for fascism to come to power. When the parliamentary tradition is weak, the threat of communism strong, and the Left temporizes with its revolutionary aim, the stage is set. What followed in Italy and Germany, and what Snow sensed happening in China in the years since 1927, though he did not make it explicit in this speech, was a fearful amount of public deception and brutal terrorism by the army and extralegal forces.

Early in March he wrote to Betty Price, wife of Harry Price, professor of Economics at Yenching, in response to her request for information she might use to report to a meeting on the "pressures brought to bear" on the *Peking Chronicle*, the same paper that printed his talk on fascism. He found her question too narrowly focused. He outlined the distressingly complicated network of interests controlling the *Chronicle*:

> The paper as you probably know is owned by the Kuomintang, through a Chinese, who in turn owns it through a Britisher—the Hon. Ridge. The latter gets a monthly salary from the Kuomintang and he is there to see that nothing critical of the Party or anybody in it shall appear. On the staff also is another Englishman, who likewise draws his salary from the KMT. In addition he represents the German Transocean Agency, which is purely and simply a Nazi propaganda agency, completely controlled by Hitler. For this representation he is paid a monthly salary, gets a motor car and an occasional dinner at the German Legation. He holds this job through his ability to get into the *Chronicle* as many Transocean stories (in preference to stories by competing agencies) as possible. This explains why you often see . . . Transocean stories used in reporting events in many foreign countries, as well as Germany, instead of the agency which has, in the particular case, much better accessibility to reliable news sources, and is at least not openly a political organ.

But even the *Chronicle* had to deal with the multilayered censorship bureau of Peking, which

> consists of (1) a representative of the Central Publicity Department, (2) a representative of Huang Fu, (3) a representative of Chiang Kai-shek

through Ho Ying-chin, (4) a representative of Mayor Yuan Liang. For a while a Japanese was actually on the bureau, too, but I am told that he has now been withdrawn, and Yuan Ling's censor carries out Japanese instructions with regard to any news which the Legation or Japanese military attache wants suppressed. Sheldon Ridge now and then breaks through with a harsh editorial against the Japanese (he is really very anti-Japanese), but as regards news the censorship of the *Chronicle* is almost as severe as over the Chinese press.

He found it telling that "nothing has appeared in the *Chronicle* about the extensive red-hunting campaign which has been going on during the last three months in Tientsin and Peking, and which has resulted in the arrest and imprisonment (and in some cases executions) of more than 200 middle school and college students and professors." Only recently while out walking he had seen a squad of gendarmes marching "with sixteen or seventeen young men and one woman, apparently students, all with their hands bound with ropes and tied together. Not a line appeared in any press about it next day—though this would be a front-page story elsewhere."

He also cited the deaths of Sze Liang-tsai, the owner of the *Shun Pao, Sin Wen Pao,* and other papers in Shanghai, and Yang Chien, a friend, as evidence of what happened when one took an interest in news the authorities wanted suppressed.

Near the same time Foster Snow, using her pen name, sent an article, "Fascism in China," to Henriette Herz. She noted that twelve student members of a "Sit and Talk Club" dedicated to discussing social problems at nearby Tsinghua University were arrested by police. The police also came into the girls' dormitory at Yenching looking for a "revolutionary girl," but she had escaped in her nightgown five minutes before. In this case two of the girls, who had fathers in high official positions, refused release unless the entire group were freed, and the students thus won the day.

Wales was very explicit about the Fascist threat from within China:

Although Chiang Kai-shek established what was really in effect a Fascist military dictatorship in 1927 when he outlawed all other political constituencies . . . the first evidence of his Mussolinian aspirations came with the assassinations and kidnappings of the Blue Jackets shortly after the Shanghai War, in March, 1932. The Blue Jackets and the Er Chen Pai (CC Brothers Party) seem to have been organized almost simultaneously after the Manchurian Incident of 1931, and especially after the student demonstrations in Shanghai and Nanking in December caused the Kuomintang to lose so much "face," and after the Shanghai War in February showed the need for better and more centralized government control. Both are Fascist parties, the Blue Jackets representing the military wing and the Er Chen Pai the civil, apparently.

Wales also pointed out the Kuomintang's New Life Movement was modeled after Mussolini's "Nuova Vita" and "Confucianism, with its old tradition of a hierarchy of personal loyalties and blind obedience to elders and superiors is being desperately called in as an aid to dictatorship and pacification." But if fascism came into being in part as a reaction to the threat of communism, Wales had no problem pointing to the Russian Communist Party itself as a disturbing model for fascism: "It is important to note also that the Kuomintang Party dictatorship nominally now in effect was modelled after the Communist Party of Russia and lends itself rather well to the establishment of Fascist dictatorship."

In March, J. B. Powell attacked the "liberal and radical press in America" for the articles it published on the Red movement. The attack and the subsequent argument published in the *China Weekly Review* provoked Snow to write to the editors of both the *Nation* and the *New Republic*:

> The missionaries are terribly depressed about your attitude and I gather that they plan to set you aright on the "truth about the Chinese Reds." There is a bloodthirsty man-hunt on in North China at present to discover who is hiding under the name "Crispian Corcoran," for it is suspected that he is the vile beast who is misguiding you and supplying all the false information. . . . It so happens that I stumbled upon this young man from Tientsin a few days ago, and for your information I wish to record the fact that I found him a very brilliant, alert journalist unquestionably responsible, and that it is my impression that his information is as reliable as it is possible to get from the chaos in China today. . . . I don't have to tell you, of course, that all news "from China" is garbled, superficial and contradictory, especially at present when censorship is watertight. Authentic news about the Communist movement is so difficult to get that scarcely anyone attempts to go after it.

"Crispian Corcoran" was the name a young Israel Epstein assumed to write an admiring article about the Long March. The name was playfully made up from British adolescent fiction. As a Chinese citizen Epstein could not count on extraterritorial protection from the severe political censorship of that time. He began a lifelong friendship with Snow after reviewing *Far Eastern Front*.

About Powell, Snow continued: "The editor, who attacked you so heartily, is that rare creature, an idealistic American Don Quixote gone out to make the world safe for democracy. Like the missionaries he has staked his fortune upon General Chiang and cannot fail him now, even though he should violate all that Mr. Powell once held dear. He hates Reds with a childlike naivete, and hasn't the vaguest idea of what Communism is."[4] Relations between the Snows and Powell were cool for months until Powell witnessed the December 1935 student demonstrations in Peking and strongly supported their anti-Japanese theme.

With Japanese fascism threatening China from without, and Kuomintang fascism threatening China from within, Snow became increasingly eager to learn more about the alternative Communist movement. While researching his talk on fascism, or possibly just before, Snow was encouraged to apply for a Guggenheim Fellowship to study "The Agrarian Crisis in China" with particular reference to communism. From our post–Cold War perspective there is an almost refreshingly telling ingenuousness about Snow's application to the Guggenheim Foundation for a grant to study whether the Communist movement in rural China was a local revolt or "a genuine social *revolution.*"

His proposal began with the assumption that since 1927 the rural economy of China was in complete collapse. That gave urgency to the study of the relatively unreported but surprisingly persistent and sizable Communist movement in rural China. In his plan he posed many of the same questions he would pose a year later when he left Peking to enter Red territory in the Northwest: What kind of men are Red leaders, what is their background? What explains the enigmatic tenacity with which this revolt of the masses has resisted all attempts at liquidation by the Nanking troops under Generalissimo Chiang Kai-shek? . . . How are their armies organized? . . . What is Soviet Russia's role in the movement? What of the Third International?

Recognizing that China is overwhelmingly agricultural, the question became not so much "whether the 'so-called' Communists can physically conquer China as whether under present circumstances such a triumph could have any hopeful meaning, whether it would not be altogether disastrous, putting the final touches upon a scene of chaos and dissolution, or whether it could with greatest dispatch bring about the regeneration of a people."

The purpose for his study echoed his 1930 report on the Communist movement and in substance would be repeated in *Red Star over China*:

> The raison d'etre of my own work is that no documented study, no coherent and integrated history, is yet available in English concerning Communism in China. . . . There is no book analyzing the causes of Communism, the validity of the movement from the standpoint of Chinese history of the recent past and the present, nor one which examines the character it has taken on in its indigenous growth. No one has combined this sort of treatise with a clear, uncolored report of conditions prevailing in rural and urban China, or scientifically studied the reasons for the rise of the Reds, and the disintegration of the Kuomintang. No one has attempted to report on life in "Red China" as a result of personal investigation.

The only hint he recognized the Red armies were even then engaged on the Long March was his proposed itinerary. He planned to visit Szechuan, Hunan, Hupeh, Kiangsi, Fukien, Chekiang, and Kiangsu and to seek personal interviews with Red leaders. He had a contract with Harrison Smith and Robert Haas in New York to publish the results of his research in a book.

In *Journey to the Beginning*, Snow listed several supporters for this project led by (Jimmy) Yen Yang Chu, head of the Ting Hsien rural education experiment that Snow featured for Mrs. Meloney. He admitted his other sponsors "made strange company": Dr. J. Leighton Stuart, Dr. Amadeus Grabau, Lin Yu-tang, Lu Hsun, and J. P. Marquand.

Curiously he omitted C. Walter Young, author of several books on Manchuria and Peking friend of the Snows. Young wrote a very strong letter of recommendation for Snow: "If such a study could be seriously tackled and carried through to conclusions I think it would be a very valuable contribution not only to knowledge of contemporary China but to that broader subject of agrarian movements in relation to present-day capitalism, with all the political manifestations, including revolution, which are involved."

About Snow himself, Young offered: "I can think of only two American journalists in China whom I would describe as having scholarly capacities, and Mr. Snow is one of them. Snow's qualifications here are a keen sensitivity to details that may describe the reality, an inclination to concentrate time and effort on the literature of a subject, and a somewhat philosophic bent which encourages him to weigh the values of his discoveries."

Young urged the foundation be discreet: " 'Communism' is a touchy subject in China, as it is elsewhere, and the less one advertised the fact that he were pursuing a serious study of it the better. University professors here in Peking have been detained by police authority on the ground that they were 'Communist' suspects when the only justification for the accusation lay in an academic interest in the subject—or perhaps a travel trip to the Soviet Union."

He added, however: "I cannot believe that he would have any objection to your making all the inquiries you and your Committee desired to make privately about him, except for his caution against letting more into this matter than necessary."

Snow apparently was initially very hopeful of Guggenheim support. At least he seriously discussed a trip to the interior with close friends. Hsiao Chien, a young writer whom Snow helped introduce to world readers and who was then helping Snow with the translation of contemporary Chinese stories, spent a sleepless night thinking of Snow's prospective trip, and the next day proposed he go along:

> Somehow I saw there is not much difficulties for me to join you. A person like me doesn't cost people much. I can travel on any class. On the way,

> I not only can act as your interpreter in interviews, but also your Chinese teacher . . . we can do the translations face to face. It would save a lot of time. . . . That part of the country has always been a mystic corner to me. . . . It will certainly broaden my horizon, enable me to comprehend [in] what a land I am living. It may help to decide the path for my life.

Horace Epes also noted, "Dolan tells me you are considering a trip into the interior of China for the London *Herald.*" A little later Epes gave Snow encouraging news about the Guggenheim. But by late April, though he did not yet have a definite decision, Snow was no longer hopeful:

> I have learned that five others in China are asking help from the Foundation, and I suppose others in America have the same idea. Guggenheim grants only one fellowship for China, and often not that. Their preferences are usually for men with the highest academic degrees, and like most foundations they generally choose projects that are pretty safely moss-covered, and unlikely to get anyone agitated one way or another, save a few intent scholars.[5]

A short time later he wrote Epes he planned to leave for Japan soon and would be back in July: "The future of China is rapidly being decided by Japan, so that the China question is increasingly becoming the Japanese question. Despite some much advertised superficial gains, notably the increased spread of Chiang Kai-shek's power, the suppression of the Reds in Kiangsi, and considerable military road building, the country as a whole is worse off than at any time in recent history."

Japan's control of Manchuria, and hence of virtually all the mineral resources of China, made clear her determination to keep China a market for the goods she produced from Chinese raw materials. This meant one must "no longer think of Japan as an island power, but as a continental power, the strongest in Eastern Asia. Think of the center of Japan no longer as Tokyo, but Mukden or Hsinking." The political map of this area that underlay the Washington conference is now ancient history:

> The conquests of Japanese capitalist-imperialism seem to have eliminated definitely the historical possibility of the development of a strong China on a capitalist basis, leaving but two choices: continued impoverization as a backward agricultural country, and as economic and political colony of Japan—or a mass revolution which will shake Asia to its depths. The possibilities of a successful mass revolution do not seem likely to develop until the industrialization of Manchuria produces a proletarian leadership for the backward peasant millions of China. What is likely in the immediate future is the continued extension of Japanese, and to some extent other foreign, domination of Chinese economic life, with the ultimate result of further intensification of the eternal crisis of over-population and under-production in China.

The continuing drastic drop in the exchange value of the dollar made Snow think urgently of finding another news connection. He was happy to learn Epes was hopeful Colonel Knox of the *Chicago Daily News* would offer Snow a position. He wrote Colonel Knox the following week suggesting that because of the connection between the *Daily News* and the *New York Sun* and his own six-year relationship with "that well-loved journal" they would get on very well: "I am prepared to go almost anywhere the story goes. I like travelling and don't mind the inconvenience of it. I like entering and analyzing new situations. However, since my experience has been chiefly in the Orient (Japan, Indo-China, China, India) I naturally feel that I can be of greatest usefulness to you in this part of the world."

Knox did not offer Snow a job, and the chairman of the Yenching University Board of Directors was ready to reclaim his comfortable house in Haitien. Late in May the Snows moved back into the city, to the haunted house near the Fox Tower. Dr. Rock's storied conversion did not dissuade them.

However, before the move Snow received a note from Smedley forwarding a request from Vanguard Press for translations of Lu Hsun and Mao Tun. Snow wrote Vanguard about the collection he had now gathered, including works by Lu Hsun and Mao Tun. He stressed his intent to present writing by Chinese "about themselves as they really think, as they really talk, and as they really are," as an alternative to the deceptively romantic picture of China written by outsiders.

Since art in modern China was inseparable from politics, he admitted: "The thing of chief interest about these stories is in fact probably not their 'art,' for that is perhaps of necessity raw and formless, but the vast change of outlook they reflect, the sharpness of the break Chinese intellectuals are making with the past." If the American readers could not accept this, then he could only say, "the real heart and mind of living China itself" was of no interest to them.[6]

Vanguard did not publish *Living China*, but Richard Walsh at John Day, after a long period of skepticism, did.

21

From the Academy into the Cause

AFTER THE SCHOOL SEMESTER ended, Snow left for Manchuria in search of material for articles. He also took along his *South of the Clouds* manuscript to finish up for his contracted second book. While he was away, Foster Snow vacationed in a cottage at the seaside resort of Peitaiho, the guest of Harry and Betty Price.

Foster Snow was back in Peking by early July when she wrote her husband that Wang Chun-chu, one of the Daubers they had befriended, feared arrest and had to leave Peking immediately. The political war in China was tightening. She had made the mistake of sending an article on China's modern art to *China Today* in New York, knowing no one on its staff. Despite her warning, the artists' names had been published on the photographs, jeopardizing their safety.

Wang's position had been politically dangerous for some time. The police now had an excuse to arrest him. He wanted to go to Moscow but did not have the necessary Party contacts. She gave him the money he could expect from the magazine and the Shanghai address of Yao Hsin-nung, a writer and editor collaborating with Snow on translating Lu Hsun. Yao had met the Daubers on an earlier visit to the Snows. Wang left on a train for Shanghai late in the afternoon of July 8. Foster Snow also explained the situation to Smedley and asked her help for Wang.

Yao wrote Foster Snow a coded message describing Wang's arrival. Both Mme. Sun Yat-sen and Smedley wrote about the difficulties posed by Wang's not being a member of "the organization." Smedley suggested Japan was probably the cheapest and most practical refuge. Mme. Sun promised to put him in touch with Father and Son (Lu Hsun and Mao Tun) and to see if he might get a recommendation from the organization even though he was not a member. Mme. Sun noted: "Father's health is very bad, as is Son's." Leftist politics were at a low point in Shanghai, as elsewhere in China at this time.

Snow responded from Dairen with both a telegram and a letter. He was "worried as hell about Wang" and suggested he stay in their pavilion. "He can sleep in my office and work there too." They could decide on the best haven after Snow got back, but Wang probably could not stay in North China much longer in any case. Snow had planned to stay in Dairen until he finished his book, but now he would return on July 20 after flying into Mukden.

Foster Snow had forwarded a batch of mail along with her letter about Wang. Snow was disappointed at the news from the *Chicago Daily News*. "Epes [had] seemed pretty positive that an appointment would be offered in due time." He advised Foster Snow to stop work on the introduction to the Chinese stories since it caused her to neglect her own work. He also advised her to keep Gobi out of their bed. "Not only fleas but you will likely get a louse carrying typhus, or you may get cholera or something."

On July 14 Foster Snow wrote Smedley again. She described Wang as anxious to join the organization and to meet Father, whom he greatly admired. She also assumed, probably wrongly, Smedley would take her side of a running contest with her husband over clothes: "You should see the cute new suit I have had made from one of Archibald's [Snow's] old ones, patched at the seat. It's a darling and everyone, including the tailor, looks upon me as a very canny person in the sartorial line. . . . A. will be sore when he gets back—I'm always stealing his clothes when he goes away and can't protect his wardrobe."

She also tried to interest Smedley in the case of a young woman writing under the name of Shih Ming, but Smedley considered her a Trotskyite and was unsympathetic. Walsh published Shih Ming's "Fragment from a Lost Diary" a few months later after both Snows recommended it. Shih Ming, known as Yang Kang and Yang Ping, later worked many years for the respected paper *Ta Kung Pao* and was given a high governmental post after 1949.

The Snows received a letter from Wang Chun-Chu announcing his arrival in Paris on October 15. He was well received by writers and artists there and hoped quickly to prepare exhibits of his work for the following spring. Lu Hsun also relayed a message to Smedley from Wang that the suitcase she sent with him on his voyage from Shanghai to Vladivostok was not picked up, and Wang had to carry it along with him. The Snows heard from Wang sporadically. After studying in the Soviet Union he eventually reappeared in Yenan in 1939.[1]

Snow returned to Peking two days early, to be filled in on all the drama of the previous week. Over the next two days he wrote three long and revealing letters respectively to C. Walter Young, Richard Walsh, and his brother, Howard, all of whom had significant personal experiences while Snow was in Manchuria. The Youngs left for the States following the death of their young son; Walsh married Pearl Buck; and Howard was appointed to a new position with the National Association of Manufacturers.

After expressing his condolences over the "shocking fate of little Carl," Snow reported at length his experiences in Manchuria, a land that Young knew well. He was surprised at how freely he could travel, with little of-ficial suspicion or surveillance. The Japanese seemed indifferent to what foreigners wrote and thought about them and their program. Changchun (Hsinking) had more than doubled its population since 1931, and 50,000 of the 150,000 increase was Japanese. He was in Changchun the day the new Japan-Manchukuo Economic Bloc agreement was signed, an agree-ment that gave the army dominant industrial and economic control over civilian Japanese capitalists. The army was planning to extend its control throughout North China through the S.M.R. (South Manchurian Railway) Commission.

While the transfer of the railway to the control of Manchukuo officially was seen as minimizing the possibility of conflict between Japan and Russia, there was hardly a single kilometer of the three-thousand-kilometer border between Manchukuo and Russia agreed upon; and the Japanese were building enor-mous fortifications all the way from Manchouli to the Korean border. They were treating Outer Mongolia as if it were a state completely independent of Russia to establish an open door to this little-known neighbor.

He speculated:

> it is quite possible the Japanese may send a little expedition into Urga before long, not with the idea of provoking a war with Russia, but antic-ipating resistance from the Mongols, the creation of an incident, and then the necessity for calling a real conference between Manchukuo and O. M. [Outer Mongolia], which will, they hope, result in opening up the country. The Russians seem to be quite aware of this possibility and are, if reports are correct, rapidly preparing O. M. to give a good reception to the Japanese "surveying party" that first attempts to penetrate Urga.

Snow risked addressing Walsh with the familiar "Dear Dick," citing his congratulations on Walsh's June marriage to Pearl Buck as appropriate grounds for initiating this friendlier address. He was pleased Walsh had accepted two stories from his collection of Chinese writing and sorry Walsh could not publish the collection as a book. He was happy Walsh was publishing Lin Yu-tang's book, but Walsh should know Lu Hsun was writing a special and rival book on China for the American public that will "make a large dent in sinological cerebrums":

> It will amuse me to see how much of it will contradict the whimsical views of Lin Y. T. Lu Hsun, as you probably know, is considered the master of humor and satire in Chinese that Lin is looked upon to be in English. What a wonderful, if also terrible, place China. Not only do no two foreign writers agree about what the country is, but neither do the Chinese. Grand, enigmatic, paradoxical, absurd and sublime China! It is good to get back to her after a sojourn among the darkly sane and regimented Japanese.

The Snow brothers were both achieving success, but on disparate paths. Howard's latest success posed a question of how far the brothers could move apart politically yet retain their brotherly bond:

> It is interesting to hear your comments on the economic and political conditions of American life, especially since you now speak, I note, more or less ex cathedra from the high-sounding quarters of the National Association of Manufacturers. You tell me nothing of your job, but such an Association, I take it, does not exist for the purpose of providing salary checks for non-manufacturing young men. So I suppose you are busy. I would be very interested to know just what you are doing. Is it your task to get more manufacturers to associate or to promote company unions among the workers? In either case I smell no good in it for Mr. Roosevelt, poor muddled lad. Meanwhile it is a very impressive job and I hope the pay is commensurate with the title of the organization.

His concern was not just inspired by Howard's new position. Howard had also heard indirectly that Snow was becoming "leftist" or "communistic." That alarmed Snow, and he wanted to know where the rumor came from. Hardly an editor in America would print his work if he were thought a communist. And for Howard's satisfaction, he was not. He did not believe in interpreting facts according to "any ready-made economic or political doctrine, whether Marxist or Leninist or Mussolinian or Rooseveltian." He did have "a lingering belief in such things as the rights of men to equal opportunity, a belief in the fundamental soundness of such concepts as freedom of speech, freedom of press, freedom of assembly, and a somehow undying faith in the notion that the highest degree of individual freedom (in the largest political sense) is not necessarily incompatible with democratic political forms." Sarcastically, he added, he might "get over this when I see Huey Long seriously on the way to the White House." Meanwhile he believed it possible, though by no means probable, that Americans would be able to "work out a decent civilized system of life and economics which will fairly soon put the control of the means of production in the hands of the people, and for the widest social benefit." If this was treason, Howard could tell the Liberty League to prepare the noose.

China was different from America. "There is no voting for officials here; there is no voting for anything. The man with the biggest pile and the biggest army casts all the votes, and the only way to get him out is to collect a bigger pile and a bigger army." It had been so for so long that "some millions of the starving peasantry and workers who support the whimsical structure are now sufficiently exasperated about it to try organizing their own armies and make an attempt to seize the power." While revolution was never a pleasant thing, it was sometimes needed to save a people. Revolution was occurring in China only after every other means of resolving intolerable situations had been exhausted. The Red Army was "simply the technique the peasants and workers—who produce all the wealth there is in this amazingly topheavy country—use to cast their vote in the national will."

If Howard came to China, he would not see much resemblance between the Red Army and an American election. But when he had been in the country as long as Snow had, he would see this revolution was "merely an expression of a historic need of the masses, too long suppressed, too long denied, and now become volcanic and catastrophic in its manifestations. It is the people's thumb-down on the rulers of the realm."

This passionate argument is followed by a renewal of his previous invitation: "And the offer of the guest room still goes; we have a wing of the house with bath that we could let you have. Why not put Jimmie with his grandmama for a season and come to visit us? China isn't nearly as far as you think." He closed with another family question, "What has happened to Dad? He owes me several letters. Mildred too. I hope this finds them in good health and in no difficulty."[2]

Walsh thanked Snow for his congratulations and wrote separately to Foster Snow to congratulate her "on that splendid poem 'Old Peking'" that he was happily accepting along with Shih Ming's "Notes of a Young Revolutionary." He still "could not see the book of Chinese stories as a good commercial prospect." But he would be glad to reconsider it in six months if it did not find a publisher. He hoped books by Lin Yu-tang, Lu Hsun, and Mao Tun would all greatly widen the market for Chinese writing.

He also wondered if Snow had discussed Walsh's idea of a series of articles on comparative imperialisms with Timperley. Timperley was then advisory editor to *Asia* among his many other professional posts. Walsh suggested comparing "what Japan has done in Manchukuo and Korea and Formosa, England in India, France in Indo-China, the Dutch in the Netherlands Indies, the Americans in the Philippines and the Russians in the outlying republics of the Soviet Union." If anyone could do such a study, he thought Snow the one: "Your article on Formosa showed that you have the insight and the grasp of the whole subject."

Walsh supposed one would need a year of travel and study combined to do this job properly, and the cost in time and money would be prohibitive without some subsidy. Neither *Asia* nor the John Day Company could afford it. But if Snow felt as he did last year, and was considering cutting loose from Peking, he wondered whether between them "we could not figure out a way in which you could take a swing all around the Orient and do this big job that needs so badly to be done?" He was thinking of the Guggenheim Foundation in addition to *Asia* and the John Day Company. Perhaps a scheme could be put together. Was it too wild for Snow to consider?[3]

Such a proposal seemed tailor-made to arouse Snow's interest, but he was slow to respond. And before he did the political scene in China erupted. That very summer Ho Ying-chin, chief of staff of China's armies, signed a truce with General Umetsu, Japan's commander in North China, agreeing to withdraw not only Chinese troops but also central government civil officers and local Kuomintang officers from Peking and Tientsin, setting up a buffer zone administered by officials and local troops, acceptable to Japan. The agreement was not at first publicly acknowledged, but its implementation could not be hidden, and the secrecy about the agreement only added to the anger and resentment deeply felt, particularly by the students of Peking and Tientsin, when it became obvious.

On October 28 Japanese premier Hirota formally announced his famous Three Principles providing a basis for a Japan-Manchukuo-China axis devoted to the opposition of communism and the development of North China. General Kenji Doihara, whom the Snows believed the mastermind behind the Ho-Umetsu agreement, threatened invasion unless General Sung Cheh-yuan, the Nationalist leader chosen under the agreement, declared North China an autonomous region independent of the Nanking government. The Nanking government offered little support to strengthen Sung's will to resist. Doihara seemed very close to turning North China into a second Manchukuo. The Snows and close associates among whom they later sent coded messages would mock Snow's own behind-the-scenes role with dark humor by code-naming Snow "Doihara."

Just before Hirota's proclamation Snow wrote Walsh his deep appreciation for the latter's expression of confidence in his ability to do a study of comparative imperialism and for the generosity of his offer to help make it possible financially. But he wanted time to think about it. He sent Walsh instead another article for *Asia*, "The Economics of Slavery," a chapter from *South of the Clouds*.[4] With both *South of the Clouds* and *Living China* still uncertain of publication, he probably was reluctant to begin another large book.

The impotence of the League of Nations, first revealed in Manchuria, was brought home to the Western world by events in Europe during the summer and early fall of 1935. On October 2 a clumsy series of diplomatic maneuvers reached a decisive point. Mussolini told the Black Shirts of the Revolution, men and women of all Italy, and Italians scattered throughout the world that since 1915 they had waited patiently enough for the Allies to grant Italy her fair place in the sun, her fair share of "the rich colonial loot."

Instead of recognizing Italy's claim, the League of Nations talked only of sanctions. Until proved wrong, Mussolini refused to believe that "France . . . or the people of Great Britain, with whom we have never quarreled, would risk throwing Europe into catastrophe to defend a country in Africa well known to be without the least shade of civilization." Italy would reply to economic sanctions with discipline, sobriety, and a spirit of sacrifice. But to military sanctions "we will reply with military measures! To acts of war we shall reply with acts of war!"

The next day Italian troops began their "civilizing mission" by crossing the Mareb River and advancing into Ethiopia. That afternoon Count Aloisi told the League of Nations that "the warlike and aggressive spirit of Ethiopia" had succeeded in "imposing war" on Italy. The parallels Snow had drawn between Italy and Japan in his talk on fascism were now forebodingly real.

Snow sent another piece from *South of the Clouds* to Mrs. Meloney in October, reminding her November 11 would mark the seventh anniversary of her publishing his first article about the Orient, and thanking her for her long-standing support. However, for the moment he was depressed, "the world is not round but flat."[5]

It was against this background of ominous political rumblings both at home and abroad and his professional anxiety and frustration that one of his journalism students, who was then head of the Yenching Students' Self-Government Association, came calling late in October. Chang Chao-lin was from Dairen. The Manchurian (Tungpei) students were particularly frustrated and shamed by the appeasement of the Japanese, who were even then consolidating and buffering their control over Manchuria by extending their control over North China. Chang hoped Snow could give him encouraging news of resistance in his homeland. He believed the Peking newspapers dared not print the truth. But that day not only was Snow unable give him hopeful news, but Chang also had to endure a lecture from Foster Snow on the threat of fascism implicit in Japanese aggression.

On November 1 the students publicly addressed a petition "For the Right of Free Speech, Press, and Assembly and against the Illegal Arrest of Students." Protesting censorship and asserting their civil rights seemed appropriate themes to expand public support beyond Yenching and Tsinghua Universities. The students petitioned the Sixth Plenary Session of the CEC of the Kuomintang ostensibly convened to honor the rights of free speech, press, and assembly guaranteed by the National Government itself on June 1, 1931.

After noting the slaughter of more than three hundred thousand young people and an untold number imprisoned and disappeared, not to mention instances of torture and live burial, the students charged that formerly "under the pretext of the Red danger, and now, under the pretext of 'injuring international friendship,' any activity might be branded a crime. Anyone stood in danger of losing his life." They cited the arrest of Dr. Fung Yu-lan, a noted scholar, and the trial of Tu Chung-yuan, a patriot, as of special recent concern. "Who would expect that the old 'burning of books and burying of scholars' (as in the days of Chin Shih Huang Ti) would reoccur in China today!" The petition was signed by the Students' Self-Government Association of Yenching University and ten other student organizations, including Tsinghua University.

A spark from the historic May 4 student revolt of 1919 now smoldered in the dry tinder. A gusty wind of public frustration and anger soon blew across, and it quickly flamed into the December 9 student revolt. While perhaps not as clear an ideological turning point as its predecessor, it was still a very notable chapter in the history of China's student rebellions. Both Snows fanned the flames as recognized friends of the students.

Foster Snow tried to get the international news services to carry the story and was refused by Frank Oliver of Reuters, who criticized the petition as mere propaganda, but F. MacCracken Fisher of United Press, a Yenching graduate himself, was more sympathetic and sent the news to Earl Leaf in Tientsin. Foster Snow also sent the petition on to J. B. Powell along with an article for the *China Weekly Review* on the students' concerns. Powell was deeply sympathetic with the antifascist, anti-Japanese themes of the movement. His sympathy and cooperation restored much of the good feeling between him and the Snows.

On November 25 General Doihara inaugurated the East Hopei Autonomous Council under a puppet chairman, Yin Ju-keng, naming Tungchow, only thirteen miles east of Peking, the capital of this "autonomous federation." The danger was obvious.

Foster Snow later frequently represented the students as being political innocents awakened and energized by her and Snow. One of the 1935 innocents was Wang Ju-mei, chairman of the Executive Committee of the Yenching Student Council and roommate of Chang Chao-lin. By May 1985, when he remembered his Yenching student days in an interview, he had become better known to the world as the distinguished diplomat Huang Hua, the first ambassador to the United Nations from the People's Republic of China. His remarks made clear he believed Foster Snow in 1935 the more innocent, that there had in fact been much leftist organizational activity prior to the November petition and the students' first discussions with the Snows.

He particularly remembered that Northeastern University students, experienced in the earlier guerrilla resistance in Manchuria, helped train other students in the use of small arms and hand grenades. He personally brought concealed arms from Northeastern University to Yenching University on a bus in the summer of 1935. Yenching and Tsinghua students practiced throwing grenades in the nearby grounds of the old abandoned Summer Palace. With a smile he remembered a policeman once grumbling, "You made a big noise." He also later acknowledged he was the principal author of the students' November 1 petition.[6]

Regardless of their previous organization, the students sought the Snows' advice and help, particularly in the early stages of the movement, and both clearly and forcefully urged dramatic public action. Snow wrote Smedley he had advised the students they needed to demonstrate no later than December 10, the deadline Doihara had given Sung to declare North China's autonomy. The demonstration should: protest "against an autonomous N[orth] C[hina], or any other camouflaged device for yielding territorial, political or economic rights of the Chinese people in the northern provinces"; "demand that the National Government make known in clear language the policy it expects to follow to save the sovereignty of the people in this area"; declare the united students "will support any government and any army which offers revolutionary resistance to the impending conquest of North China"; and demand "the restoration of all civil rights of the people."

Foster Snow advised Chen Han-po, who was to address the gathered students, what to say and how to say it. She also suggested a mock funeral with North China as the corpse being buried by Japanese and Chinese officials to keynote the demonstration. Her suggested mock funeral seemed too bizarre to the students, but the need for some public demonstration became very clear when General Ho Ying-chin arrived in Peking on December 3. His visit appeared to be an ominous prelude to Nanking's surrender of North China. The Student Union voted to demonstrate the evening General Ho arrived. On December 9 the students confronted the authorities in large-scale rallies that turned into parades. They marched to General Ho's headquarters and presented him petitions aimed at keeping North China from becoming another Manchukuo.

The Snows had taken a significant step beyond disinterested, observing journalists. Snow later remembered telling his wife, "Now I know why people like W. H. Donald, Putnam Weale, Tom Millard and other newspaper men mixed up in China's internal affairs in the past. You can't just stand by and watch a lady you love being ravished and do nothing about it. And Peking is a nice old lady indeed."

Both seemed to accept a reasonably clear division of their labor. Foster Snow, lesser known and writing under a pseudonym, was free to advocate the students' cause openly. Snow was to be more dispassionate, thus guarding his valuable public reputation for objectivity, particularly with the editors and readers of the *Saturday Evening Post,* where two more of his articles on the international significance of Manchuria were soon to appear, and *Asia,* which increasingly valued his insight and writing. In her memoir, Foster Snow drew this distinction:

> Ed hated propaganda—he never in his life wrote any that I know of—but he allowed me to do it, even though it was dangerous for us both in several ways. He taught his journalism students to hate propaganda, too. At the same time, I was teaching them how to *make* propaganda. I was naturally an activist and had always been a student leader, from grade school to the University of Utah, just as Ed was naturally a real journalist, always on top of his subject and nearly always minding his own business, except to support me at strategic moments.[7]

22

The Students Demonstrate, and a Door Opens

O N DECEMBER 9, WHEN the students arrived at General Ho's headquarters, they were met by an aide who told them the general was spending the day at the Tangshan hot springs resort, but the aide accepted the students' petition. From there events went from bad to worse. In the early stages of the students' organizing, the situation of Yenching and Tsinghua Universities outside the city gates offered protection from police scrutiny, but on this day it also made it easy for police to lock marching students outside of Hsichihmen, the gate where they planned to enter the city and join students from other universities. When the students inside learned of the lockout, they spontaneously shouted "To Hsichimen!" and tried to join forces. They were met by soldiers with broad swords and armed police at Hsitan Pailou. Blocked, the students decided to move into the eastern section of the city only to be sprayed by fire hoses in the freezing cold as they approached the Legation Quarter along Wangfuching Street.

That evening student leaders met and angrily called for a general student strike. Indignation spread rapidly among the students, and sympathy grew within the people. On December 11 police and soldiers surrounded several campuses. They arrested nine students at Northeastern University, the pride of Young Marshal Chang Hsueh-liang. On December 14 the chancellors of the universities within the city tried to end the strike, arguing most of the arrested students had been released the day before. But hope for a settlement was dashed when plans for the inauguration of the Hopei-Chahar Political

Council, the suspected puppet regime, were announced the same day. On December 16 the demonstrations were so massive they made the week-earlier protests seem only minor incidents. One campus newspaper estimated 7,775 students from twenty-eight schools took part.

Snow bought his first movie camera to record these events and sent strongly worded international cables explaining the students' effort to halt Japanese encroachment and to awaken the Chinese national spirit. Foster Snow wrote an indignant report of the suppression and intimidation of the students for the *China Weekly Review*. She cabled J. B. Powell in Tientsin to come and see the December 16 demonstration for himself, and he did. Coincidentally William Allen White, the famed Kansas journalist, visited Peking at the time. He too was deeply impressed and encouraged public support for the students.

A single incident on December 16 captured the attention and sympathy of a world audience. About one hundred students from Yenching and Tsinghua entered the city December 15, the night before the demonstration, to avoid being locked out as they had been the week before. The main body of demonstrators from these two universities once again were to enter the city at Hsichimen. The authorities again locked the gate. This time the long column of students made its way southward along the outer city wall until the students found a Peking-Hankow Railroad gate they could break through. Inside the outer wall the column picked up five hundred more students from Normal University and thousands of Tienchao residents. Now stretching to nearly three-quarters of a mile, the column approached a barred Chienmen to enter the inner city. After some turmoil and spirited negotiation, the police permitted several hundred marchers to enter through Chienmen and sent the bulk of the demonstrators to enter the western quarter of the city at Shunchihmen.

When the demonstrators arrived at Shunchihmen they found it barred, contrary to police promises. Inside a contingent of Peking University students defied police beatings and shouted encouragement to the outside demonstrators to join forces. A slight but fiery and strikingly attractive young woman from Tsinghua, Lu Tsui, suddenly broke from the crowd and rolled under the gate. To her dismay she found the two iron rings inside the gate doors bound shut with wire. While she struggled to unwind the wire the police came up and brusquely took her into custody. Foreign correspondents rushed to her side to restrain the police by their witness. They heard the young woman lecture the police furiously on their patriotic duty. She was dragged off to police headquarters for questioning, and her followers quickly began a sit-down strike demanding her release.

At the station she was ordered to stand in a corner near a window apart from the confusion of groups of military police rushing in and out. The window was coated with thin ice from the subzero temperature. When the police looked away she cleaned a portion of the window with her fingers and found herself looking directly into the smiling eyes of Edgar Snow, who gently asked if he might come in. She whispered a quick "Of course, please come in!"

Snow introduced himself and quietly asked who she was and why she was demonstrating. The police at first did not interfere but after a short time interrupted the conversation, ordering Lu into the back of a truck outside the station. Snow walked beside her to the truck, offering reassurance as she was driven away. At 7:30 P.M. she was released and allowed to roll back under the gate and lead her followers in a triumphant return to Tsinghua University. The story of her dramatic act was quickly featured in newspapers around the world, and the Western press soon gleefully referred to Lu Tsui as China's "Joan of Arc."

A few weeks later, in March, Lu found refuge in the Snows' home from the threat of arrest. They put her on a train to Shanghai where she helped reorganize the National Student Association. That summer she represented China at the World Youth Congress in Geneva. Later in Paris she helped establish an overseas branch of the Federation of National Salvation Associations. She became one of several Peking student leaders who found it made sense to join the Communist Party in 1936.[1]

The Chinese students' protest against Japanese encroachment in North China was in part greeted with considerable sympathy on the world stage because a parallel political drama was playing at the same time in Europe and Africa. Just two days before the Peking students called on the absent General Ho, Sir Samuel Hoare, representing the English Conservative government, met with Pierre Laval, the French foreign minister, in Paris to draw up a proposal for the League of Nations intended to halt Italy's massive invasion of Ethiopia. Consulting no one representing Ethiopia, they proposed ceding a sizable amount of Ethiopia to Italy and in effect making Ethiopia a protected state under Italy's paternal authority. The English and French desperately wanted to keep Italy as part of a European alliance believed necessary to contain the threat of growing German military might and aggression. They thought the sacrifice of distant Ethiopia a small price to pay.

When the Hoare-Laval proposal became public, it was greeted by an angry and indignant reaction that forced the resignation of Hoare from office, but it did not save Ethiopia. Nevertheless the brutal spectacle of modern industrialized Italy invading ancient, but economically underdeveloped, Ethiopia in pretense of civilizing it created a backdrop for widespread international sympathy for the Chinese students' protest against Japanese aggression and Nanking appeasement.

Initially the Peking student demonstrations claimed at least a partial victory. The immediate Japanese plan for declaring North China an autonomous area was withdrawn. The students then tried to build on their success. They took their message to the people every way they could. Twenty Tsinghua students planned to bicycle more than six hundred miles to Nanking in the winter cold to spread their message. More than half completed the mission. The Peking Student Union organized an arduous campaign to reach nearby villages. Students in other cities—Hangchow, Canton, Shanghai, and Sian— voiced public support in various forms. By the end of the month approximately sixty-five demonstrations took place in thirty-two different areas.

The noted philosopher Hu Shih, then dean at Peking University, aged and now considered conservative, sparked widespread critical debate with an article, "A Word on the Student Movement." Opposition within the student ranks struggled to make itself heard, often encouraged by government and university officials. But the appeal to national pride to resist Japanese encroachment overrode for most such fine critical reservations. Shortly after the December 9 demonstration Tao Hsing-chih initiated the National Crisis Education Society in Shanghai. Among the founders were four of the "Seven Gentlemen" who were to become martyrs of the National Salvation Movement in November. Two of the four, journalist Tsou Tao-fen and banker Chang Nai-chi, established the Shanghai Cultural Circles' Education Society. Soong Ching-ling joined the cause. National Salvation Associations of women, teachers, cultural workers, and filmmakers followed. The Workers' Anti-Japanese National Salvation Association suffered particularly harsh persecution from both Chinese and Japanese authorities, and so fed public indignation.[2]

Several of the students who led the demonstrations in Peking immediately influenced the lives of the Snows, particularly during the next several months. But a few of the relationships begun then assumed even greater significance in the distant future as these same young people assumed key roles in the modern China struggling into existence. Wang Ju-mei, chairman of the Executive Committee of the Yenching Student Council, came early to the Snows' home. Foster Snow remembered he "spoke in a slow, quiet, deep voice and flushed easily," but he "had pride and dignity and was much admired for his 'courage.' " The relationship begun late in 1935 would last the full course of Edgar Snow's life. Just after being named China's first ambassador to the United Nations, Wang Ju-mei, by then better known to the world as Huang

Hua, would stand in fellowship and grief by Edgar Snow's bedside during the latter's dying days in Switzerland in 1972.

On December 6, just before the first demonstration, Wang published an article, "The Present State of the Chinese Fascist Movement," in the *Yentochoukan (Yenching Weekly)*. The Snows early shared their concern about fascism with the students. Wang argued that Chiang Kai-shek was trying to follow Hitler's and Mussolini's example in establishing a fascist state but predicted Chiang's failure: "Aside from squeezing out the last few drops of national territory and the lives of four hundred million people to give to the imperialists, Chinese Fascism has no future. It lacks a mass base, its structure is extremely unstable; its political and economic contradictions deny it any possibility of development." Although Wang's words show him already familiar with marxist rhetoric, he, like Lu Tsui, did not join the Communist Party until later the next year.

Wang was not as dashing as his friend Chang Chao-lin, but he was a thorough organizer and effective strategist. He kept in touch with the Snows during the students' harsh and dangerous trips to the countryside to enlist villagers' support in early 1936, and on March 31 he was among fifty-four students arrested in a Peking demonstration. He was imprisoned for two weeks and upon his release first checked to see if a friend was also free and then went to the Snows to tell his story. By the time he finished his tale it was too late for him to return to Yenching by bus. Snow took him to the home of another sympathetic Yenching faculty member, Ran Sailer, who drove Wang back to Yenching, where the students still waited at the gate to receive him.

This is the story he told the Snows. On March 31 he and about fifty other students fled into a *hutung* to escape police attack, but there they were trapped. While arresting him the police beat him with belts and poked rifle butts into his stomach. When he tried to protect himself from the rifle butts, he was thrown to the pavement and injured his head. The demonstrators were tied together in twos and threes and taken to prison, where they were put in heavy iron leg manacles. After the first week the manacles were released from the women students. During the first few days there were not enough beds, so the students had to sleep wherever they could find space on the cold damp floor. Sleep did not come easily because they feared and anticipated torture. Many were physically abused, but Wang knew only one who suffered deliberate physical torture.

The police wanted information about secret organizations and the names of student leaders, so they tried to persuade the students they had become tools of Communists who never attended meetings or demonstrations. They warned Wang he could be in serious trouble and sternly advised him to work on his thesis and graduate. He responded by circulating a secret newspaper written in English and titled "Prison Flowers," with poems and short pieces contributed by several of the student prisoners.[3]

Ironically the police charge that the demonstrations were planned and organized by Communists later also became the claim of Party historians, not to mention Wang Ju-mei himself. But American historians have more commonly leaned toward the Snows' account that the Party was then in such a state of disorganization that it struggled to catch up with the spontaneous widespread patriotic response of university students to the threat of Japanese encroachment. Leftist politics then seemed right for a variety of historical reasons, and it was not always clear whether the Chinese Communist Party was leader or follower. But even in the Snows' accounts an important lone romantic Party figure emerged, a very capable young man who joined the student movement soon after others set it in motion, and who at key moments provided the students with effective leadership and advice.

David Yu, as he became known to the Snows, was a student at Peking University. He was twenty-five, six years younger than Snow and only four years younger than Foster Snow, but already significantly more experienced than both in revolutionary politics. He was born in Shaohsing, the birthplace of Lu Hsun. His family was influential. One uncle held cabinet posts in the Nationalist government, and a second became an adviser to the Hopei-Chahar Political Council, the target of the student demonstrations. A third uncle, Tseng Chao-lun, was a famous chemistry professor at Peking University and supported the student movement. Yu's younger sister became an actress while he became a Communist. He was imprisoned in Tsingtao for his activities as chief of the local Party's Propaganda Department. After his release on bail, he traveled to Shanghai, where he became a familiar figure in the city's dramatic circle.

When he returned to Tsingtao, he married and introduced to secret Party circles an ambitious young library clerk named Li Yun-he, who subsequently gained fame in Shanghai as the actress Lan Ping and eventually moved on to Yenan and Peking to gain international recognition as Chiang Ching, wife of Mao Tse-tung and one of the principal leaders of the Cultural Revolution. Yu had apparently left Li Yun-he behind by 1935. He attended classes in mathematics at Peking University and was one of only a few active Communists then out of jail in North China. In February 1936, Liu Shao-chi, the future president of the People's Republic and eventually the most prominent victim of the Cultural Revolution, was released from prison in Kiangsi. He moved to Tientsin to lead the North China Bureau of the CCP. David Yu worked directly under Liu. Yu himself achieved considerable prominence in later years under the name Huang Ching, serving briefly as mayor of Kalgan in the late forties and after 1949 as mayor of Tientsin. He became a member of the CCP Central Committee and held two ministerial positions. Chronic ill health led to his early death in 1958.

Yu came to the Snows with four other students sometime shortly after the December 9 demonstrations. Foster Snow was immediately struck with his appearance: "He was fairly tall for a Chinese, pale, tired and ill-looking, a little unkempt in his long Chinese gown, which all the student leaders wore at that time. His face was handsome and expressive, with an easy smile and good teeth. He had a grandfatherly air toward the other students." The Snows did not ask if he were a Party member. Such knowledge openly expressed would be dangerous for him and for them. But they quickly understood. Foster Snow asked him to stay after the others left, and she later wrote: "David was the first real Marxist I had ever really had a chance to talk with. I thought then that he had the most remarkable mind of anyone I had ever met, but attributed this to my youthful inexperience."

Yu came often to the Snows' house after that. He succeeded in making friends with their chow, Ginger, "a real Fascist who bit all the students he could get hold of." Gobi, their Irish wolfhound, on the other hand was all for the Student Union. In March, Yu told the Snows he had to leave Peking. To his discomfort, they transformed him into a "gentleman," putting him in Snow's pepper-and-salt tweed suit, and then placed him on a train for Tientsin.

He carried with him an urgent request from Snow to Liu Shao-chi for an invitation to visit the Red forces in the northwest. On March 22 he wrote from a hotel in Tientsin: "I shall write to you again at to-night or tomorrow, and it shall bring you some news about Ed's business." He wrote again on March 25:

> I shall go to the south at to-night. I think I shall be all right at anywhere. Don't take care on me, because I am a "gentleman" now!
> The problem of Ed's shall be settled a few days later. One of the both men shall tell you this consideration. On this problem, I have explained to them as possible as I can. I think they have no reason to refuse your requirement. I hope it shall be realized. Please write to me before your travelling.[4]

Yu went south to Shanghai. After several weeks, when Snow did not receive Yu's promised response, he too went to Shanghai, to press his case with Soong Ching-ling. This Shanghai visit in early May was brief, sensitive, and apparently successful. Snow left no detailed account, but there are scattered intriguing references. There is little doubt he saw Soong Ching-ling and received her support. However, a meeting with Smedley was not so happy. In November he explained to Randall Gould why he didn't know Smedley's whereabouts: "We had a small battle during my last trip to Shanghai, of which you may have heard, and since then, apparently, I have been off her calling list."

Just before heading for Shanghai, Snow wrote L. M. MacBride, his editor at the *London Daily Herald*, that Dr. T. T. Li, the chief censor in the Chinese Foreign Office who had been giving Snow much trouble with his press credentials, had shown him a letter seized by Shanghai police from Smedley to a friend in New York. The letter was chiefly an attack on Kuomintang apologist Tang Liang-li, then on a tour of Europe, but it also embarrassed Snow.

He wrote MacBride:

> After advising her friends in the West to prepare a threatening "rotten-egg" reception for Tang, and describing his corruption, bribery, activities, etc., Miss Smedley informs her correspondent that Edgar Snow (in addition to herself being persecuted by Tang) has had his press privileges revoked by Nanking, and she implies that Tang was responsible. She states that because Tang was once correspondent for the *Daily Herald* (which is news to me), he intends to induce the *Herald* to sack me. She tells of his activities in Europe in effecting close relationships between Fascist groups in China and those in Germany, Italy and England, etc. The letter contains some references to me for which I cannot take responsibility.

Dr. Li advised Snow he had to send a copy of this letter to Tang to warn him. Thus Snow wanted to anticipate the possibility that Tang might bring this letter to MacBride and to disavow having any hand in preparing the letter or providing information in it. He explained: "Agnes Smedley is an old friend of mine, and I occasionally help her out with news or information which she finds useful, and in exchange for that she sends me data difficult to procure elsewhere." He closed the subject making sure MacBride in fact received the warning he said he had no need to give:

> Personally, what Tang does in Europe or America, or whether he calls on the *Daily Herald*, or the New York *Sun*, or Oswald Mosely or my maiden aunt, for that matter, is no particular business of mine. It would never have occurred to me to "warn" you about him, as I consider him quite harmless. But, especially, I have no interest whatever in becoming involved in Miss Smedley's personal feud with Tang, for those taking sides in these theological disputes in China brings about endless embarrassment.

Besides this conflict with Snow, Smedley passionately wanted to visit the Red forces. Because of her unabashed published support for the Communist movement, she felt she deserved the chance more than Snow. It seems likely she suspected, if she did not know, Snow's purpose in coming to Shanghai, and her resentment poisoned their meeting. Smedley probably hurt her own cause by quarreling with Manny and Grace Granich, who had been brought to Shanghai to publish *Voice of China*. Soong Ching-ling sided with the Granichs. In addition Soong Ching-ling had come to resent the frequent reference to Smedley as her secretary. She eventually made clear Smedley was not and never had been so employed.

It also at first seems odd on this Shanghai visit Snow was not introduced to Dr. George Hatem, a good friend of Smedley's, certainly well known to Soong Ching-ling, and within a few weeks to be his traveling companion in the northwest. In the spring of 1985 when asked about Snow's May 1935 Shanghai visit, Dr. Hatem confidently insisted Snow could not have made such a visit or they would have met. Snow did make the visit, but since his northwest journey was not yet approved, his visit to Shanghai was brief and deliberately quiet. Personal relations between local leftists were obviously touchy. This seems sufficient explanation why they were not then introduced.

David Yu returned to Tientsin from Shanghai. The Snows received a letter from him dated May 19 with no reference to Snow's trip. However, since the trip was finally authorized by Liu Shao-chi, then serving as head of the North China branch of the Party in Tientsin, it seems likely Yu's efforts on Snow's behalf were not useless. By June 1 Snow was able to propose to MacBride an exclusive contract for British rights on any articles he might write on his historic journey to interview such Red leaders as Mao Tse-tung, Chu Teh, Hsu Hsiang-chien, Liu Chih-tan, and others: "If I succeed in seeing them, as I may, it will be a world scoop on a situation about which millions of words have been written, based only on hearsay and highly colored government reports." The barely restrained exuberance in his proposal to MacBride suggests by this time he had received his introductory letter to Mao Tse-tung written in invisible ink from Tungpei University faculty member Hsu Ping.[5]

23

Where Journalism Meets Literature

I N THE SAME MONTH Snow's trip to the northwest was finally approved *Asia* published what the editors believed "to be the first thorough and completely impartial story of the Red Army in China" by a young Canadian named Norman Hanwell. Edgar Snow forwarded these articles to *Asia* and introduced Hanwell by letter to Richard Walsh in January while the Peking students were spreading their message to the countryside. Snow had known Hanwell since he first came to China more than two years earlier. His interest was in political economy, particularly rural or village structures. His research brought him into contact with the Communist movement in the southwest, and his interest in the latter was beginning to pose some strain on his ambition to turn his research into a doctoral dissertation either at the University of California or Chicago.

Snow wrote Walsh: "The attached article is something of a scoop for you: Hanwell wrote it, by the way, especially for *Asia*. It is one of the few pieces I have seen in English giving a picture of the Red Army, without being colored by blatant prejudice." Snow found the piece of special interest because Hanwell came out "imbued with Christian reformism," which he "overcame" to secure valuable information presented with "scrupulous honesty" and "painstaking labor." He sent the article just as Hanwell wrote it, though Hanwell had suggested they collaborate—"he deprecates his abilities as a writer." But there was little Snow could add, and he found the piece engaging enough as it stood.

Snow also arranged for one of Hanwell's pieces to be published in the *China Weekly Review*, much to the latter's surprise and delight, and forwarded others to *China Today*, where in the interest of a future academic career Hanwell requested his name be withheld.

Another young academic, a New Zealand Rhodes scholar from Oxford University destined to write several impressive books on his China experiences, arrived in Peking early in 1936. James Bertram quickly proved to the staff at the Language School in the eastern part of the city that his conversational Chinese was adequate for him to move to Yenching University to study Chinese history and philosophy. Fortuitously his roommates at Yenching became Chang Chao-lin and Wang Ju-mei. In 1985 Huang Hua (Wang Ju-mei) remembered giving Bertram custody of his Communist reading material whenever he thought their room might be searched. Before leaving England, Bertram prudently made his trip to China known to a few newspaper editors, and Douglas Pringle of the *Manchester Guardian* particularly expressed interest in firsthand material on the Chinese Red Army. Thus Bertram quickly moved into the Snows' orbit in Peking. From then on he and the Snows shared much of their work and adventure until the Snows left China and Bertram was subsequently imprisoned by the Japanese.[1]

Snow's more than seven years' experience reporting on China, his ready access to the pages of the *China Weekly Review, Asia,* and the *Saturday Evening Post,* as well as to such important newspapers as the *London Daily Herald* and the *New York Herald Tribune,* made him an invaluable mentor to the young New Zealander, as he had been for Hanwell. But both Hanwell and Bertram were drawn to the American journalist, not just by his professional success, but also by the reach of his imagination beyond the ordinary concerns of journalists.

Living China makes the point. British publisher George G. Harrap finally agreed to bring the book out in 1936, even as Snow was arranging his trip to the northwest. Richard Walsh then agreed to bring out an American edition the following year. Snow's introduction is dated "Peking, July, 1936." On that date he was in fact in the northwest becoming acquainted with the Red Army. Obviously it was postdated to comply with the book's date of publication. But his explanation of why he put this book together indicates the large dimension Snow gave to his role as a journalist in China: "The motivation for it derives from a mixture of curiosity and experiment, but chiefly an intense interest on my part both to find out and to make available to Western readers the answer to the question, 'What is happening to the creative mind of modern China?' "

To interest Vanguard Press in publishing his book a year earlier Snow had written:

It is true not only in literature but also in the drama and music and painting that the only creative and original work being done in China is finding its material in the life of the masses—in itself a revolutionary idea in Chinese art—and since the masses today are revolutionary it is natural that some of the modern art must be informed with revolutionary ardor. This may be a good thing or a bad thing for art, but it is at any rate a fact.

Before Snow met the Red Army he assumed revolutionary change was necessary, desirable, and inevitable. He was not convinced revolution would follow a marxist formula, but his personal and professional experience of Kuomintang repression and his disdain for Kuomintang appeasement of Japanese aggression increasingly pushed him to view the Chinese Communist movement as the principal promise of necessary revolutionary change.

Pearl Buck wrote of *Living China*, "It is undoubtedly true that the editor's personal bias has made him omit some of the finest stories because they are not by Leftist writers and this is a pity." Richard Walsh, her husband, quoted Lin Yu-tang on the book jacket of the John Day publication, "With two exceptions, the writers included represent the leftist school which is now dominant."

Foster Snow responded indignantly to such criticism by pointing out neither Shen Tsung-wen, Hsiao Chien, Yu Ta-fu, nor Lin Yu-tang were leftists. Kuo Mo-jo and Lu Hsun only became leftists after 1927 and all their work included in *Living China* was written before then, during what she labeled the early "bourgeois Renaissance period." Pa Chin, an anarchist, and Sun Hsi-chen were not true leftists, but could only be called fellow travelers. Clearly the center from which one measured Left and Right shifted with the perceiver, and, particularly during the thirties, "leftist" was a far more ambiguous and inclusive term than "marxist." Lu Hsun openly became a leftist, but Snow insisted in his introduction Lu was not a marxist, except in the most general terms.

When Snow first suggested *Living China* to Walsh he described Lu Hsun as "the master of humor and satire in Chinese that Lin [Yu-tang] is looked upon to be in English." Lin was a personal friend of both Snows, and his recent book *My Country and My People*, published by Walsh, posed a personal and professional challenge. Lin took exception to Snow's review of *My Country and My People*. I have not been able to locate this review, but Snow did reply to Lin's complaint, "Your letter troubled me a little, for I fear you misunderstood my review; but then of course you also think I misunderstood your book."

Snow insisted despite his reservations, the praise in his review was "heartfelt and sincere, every word," but such matters could not be settled in a letter or two. He suggested Lin visit Peking soon, "before it is necessary to get a Japanese visa." Since the letter was written just after the student demonstrations, he also noted with a mixture of excited admiration and foreboding: "The students are marvelous. . . . You should be proud of these youths and their courage and their sincerity and their sharp intelligence. Do what you can to help them; in a few weeks, when the reaction begins, and the purge and the arrests, they will need every friend they can get."

Snow wrote Lin again in March, this time in response to the latter's request for information on censorship, about which Snow was clearly happy to inform him. *Current History* had recently published a "somewhat bowdlerized" version of a piece Snow had sent them under "the unforgivable title, 'The Ways of the Chinese Censor.'" This time he did not blame Herz for *Current History*'s flagrant editorializing. He sent Lin notes he had from several other sources and a bibliography of recent articles on the subject. But he could not resist adding:

> For the I.P.R. [Institute for Pacific Relations], however, I fancy that you will not be required to delve too deeply into the sordid facts of newspaper life. Such as the recent death of the *Peiping Chen Pao*? Or the present censorship arrangement here? Or what happens to critics of the N.L.M. [New Life Movement] in regions beyond the control of the Hopei-Chahar Council? Or the exact rules prescribing the limits of expression of public opinion in this area, or Shansi, or in the East Hopei Anti-Communist Self-Governing Council's jurisdiction?

He congratulated Lin again "on the rapid and deserved success of *My Country and My People*. I admire much of it, endorse most of it, and can forgive the rest, except the chapter on women." He then added,

> You don't know much about Communism, I see, or you didn't then, and neither did I. Have you read Strachey's "Literature and Dialectical Materialism," or his chapters on literature in the "Coming Struggle for Power"? Then you might read "Problems of Soviet Literature" also the next time you are out looking at the moon that all those meanie proletarian writers want to keep you from eating the green cheese thereof.

He was planning his trip south by this time, and according to his lunar reckoning "the moon will be favorable on that night . . . I intend to spend in Shanghai."

Apparently Snow did not meet either Lin Yu-tang or Lu Hsun on his Shanghai visit in May. He was too preoccupied with arranging his trip to the northwest. Lu Hsun was then in the terminal stage of tuberculosis, though in April he had been able to get up from his sickbed and carry on a minimum of correspondence. Smedley was persuaded to call Dr. Thomas Dunn to the author's bedside in May. Dunn diagnosed the author's condition as critical. In *Living China*, Foster Snow quoted Lu Hsun's assessment of contemporary Chinese writing as if it were from a prior interview with Snow. In fact it was probably taken from a preface Lu Hsun had written for *Living China* but the Snows had judged too long. But it was clearly Lu Hsun himself who most significantly shaped Snow's view of modern Chinese writing:

> Our best writers are at present almost without exception Leftists. This seems to be because their writings are the only ones of sufficient vital content seriously to interest intellectuals. . . . China cannot go through a period of true *bourgeois* literary development, any more than it can go through a period of independent *bourgeois* political development. There is no time for it, and no privilege of choice before us. The only possible culture for China to-day is Left revolutionary culture, the alternative being colonial acceptance of an invading imperialist culture, which means to have no independent or national culture at all. . . .
>
> It is precisely because of that great leap from feudal social concepts into proletarian cultural concepts that the foundations of modern Chinese literature are poor. Chinese literary development is probably unique in this respect. Even in the earliest beginnings of the renaissance movement there was a strong inclination to the Left. It is a curious fact that China has produced no important *bourgeois* writer. Even Lin Yu-tang cannot be classed in that way, for he belongs more to the literary tradition of old scholasticism, which grew out of a feudal background, than he does to modern *bourgeois* concepts—which in fact he satirizes. . . .

At the same time Lu noted it was also true no genuine proletarian writers had yet emerged in China from the peasants and workers. Left literature was still confined to the realm of the revolutionary intellectuals and the "petty-bourgeoisie."[2]

The achievement of Snow's *Living China* was dwarfed by the publication of *Red Star over China* the following year, but *Living China* was a critical, if modest, success. The *London Times Literary Supplement* noted: "Books out of China are rare enough, and a book of modern Chinese short stories is something of an event. This volume edited by the *Daily Herald* correspondent in Peking, has very definite distinction." Since 1917 literary activity in China had largely centered on the short story, but few of these stories had been translated into English. "Mr. Snow now fills the gap with some remarkable examples of the art, which provide a virile interpretation of the impact of Western civilization on the oldest culture in the world."

M. P. W. in the *China Weekly Review* wrote of Snow's editorial achievement:

> in addition to being a prolific writer himself, [he] is definitely gifted with unlimited patience and [a] sensitiveness to his environment, not

shared by many foreigners residing in China. It is understandable, if he even surprised himself, with his sure skill in translating, condensing and interpreting for the reader the very life of the "present-day upper-and-lower-class Chinese, how they, among themselves, really work, act, play, and socialize their role in the design of things."

The reviewer accepted Snow's focus on Lu Hsun, "one of the most celebrated modern Chinese writers," as appropriate, singling out "Medicine" as a veiled attack on government for not more actively combatting the superstitious practices described in the story. He concluded with a tribute to Lu Hsun's grim yoking of humor and death.

Randolph Bartlett in the *New York Sun* found Jou Shih's "Slave Mother," by all odds the greatest story in the book, a story "De Maupassant would have been proud to have conceived, or Poe, Strindberg, Wedekind, or Schnitzler." But Bartlett particularly found the stories collectively a healthy antidote to the preoccupation with the "boy-gets-girl" formula of popular American magazines. "Search as you will, you cannot find the account of the shipping clerk who marries the proprietor, nor that of [a] lad whose One Great Mistake taught him the lesson that led him to fame, fortune, and a blonde wife immortalized by Neysa McMein."

Snow must have been pleased by Bartlett's suggesting *Living China* illustrated Lin Yu-tang's argument, "that it is neither desirable nor possible to remold the Chinese consciousness in conformance with Occidental ideas and definitions of civilization, not because the Oriental scheme of life is superior, but because it is different." Bartlett also found "the great virtue of the stories which Mr. Snow has collected, with so much toil, is that almost all are expositions of the Chinese soul and not of Chinese politics."

Randall Gould, who a few years earlier went after Snow with hammer and tongs for his "Americans in Shanghai" article in the *American Mercury*, paid extensive tribute to *Living China*. Ironically his review opened with his repeating Snow's charge of cultural insulation leveled against Shanghai Americans years earlier:

> Few Shanghailanders have any real idea what expression, if any, the creative mind of modern China is seeking and finding. Few realize that there is any such creative mind, or the terrific struggle and repression which has been in progress—despite the fact that it was at Lunghwa, no longer ago than February 7, 1932, that the execution of six Leftist writers stirred excitement virtually everywhere in the world except in Shanghai.

After extensively summarizing the collection, Gould focused on the problem of literary translation and called particular attention to Lu Hsun's essay on "Mother's," the title of an "oath very common in Chinese and ranging from the literally unprintable to the equivalent of a mild 'My dear!'" Lu Hsun gives sharp political point to his droll review of the various uses of this notable Chinese eloquence, particularly in his explanation of its most popular use. Gould also congratulated Snow on his ability to translate the living speech, "preserving its flavor of quaintness without unduly contributing to the superstition of the 'queer' or 'heathen' Chinese." Snow successfully avoided "the usual mealy-mouthed approach to certain fundamentals which, while they should not be given any prominent place, cannot be entirely eliminated without emasculating the language of this very old, very realistic people."[3]

After reviewing Lu Hsun's career as leader and organizer of the League of Left Writers in the early thirties, the murder and torture of many of his colleagues and friends that followed, and Lu's own subsequent constant fear of assassination and arrest in *Living China*, Snow still earnestly argued Lu Hsun was no more a proletarian writer than Upton Sinclair. An intellectual reformer in the revolutionary politics of China was not to be confused with an authentic proletarian writer in revolutionary politics. Like Gorki,

> Lu Hsun has always been more at home in the social and cultural phases of the revolution than in its politics. In life and work he remains essentially an individualist. His belief in the socialist state is based on deep personal realizations of the economic and spiritual needs of the masses, rather than on any academic concern with dialectical materialism. He scoffs at art for art's sake, and believes writing is of value only for its propagandistic message; but, whether he wills it or not, much of his work is art, and as near great art as anything produced in modern China.

Snow singled out the genius of Lu Hsun's laughter, his "Attic humour, poised between pathos and mirth" as the unique quality of China no foreign writer had ever quite grasped. He deftly quoted Lin Yu-tang's magazine, the *Analects*, to support his point:

> Like Chekhov's intellectuals of old Russia, like Dickens' classtypes of nineteenth-century England, Lu Hsun's characters will continue to live in the future because of their basic soundness and reality. . . . The depth of his portrayals is such that he not only makes us feel the truth and realism of his stories, and provokes mirth with every line, but he brings to us a new realization of our social conditions. . . . Our amusement when reading him is not merely superficial, but rather complex. In the midst of laughter we suddenly comprehend the inevitability of the obliteration of our feudal society in which his characters live. He is a subtle artist.[4]

On October 19, 1936, at the age of fifty-five, Lu Hsun died of tuberculosis. Snow was then with the Communist forces in the northwest, but well before his death Lu Hsun had joined Pandit Nehru and Soong Ching-ling, to whom *Living China* was dedicated, as a member of Edgar Snow's pantheon of historic figures personally met who he believed would live long in world history for their exemplary passion for social justice. In Snow's effort to recognize and understand the soul of the people among whom he had lived for eight eventful years, Lu Hsun's dark but impassioned vision provided a "shock of recognition," even as Hawthorne's writing once struck Melville. Lu Hsun, like Hawthorne, could say "no" in thunder.

Living China was an important prelude to *Red Star over China* in one other respect. Compiling the stories of *Living China*, Snow worked diligently to let Chinese writers whose work had been suppressed for political reasons address a Western audience as directly as possible. To do that and yet give the collection impact required both writing and translating skills as well as rare editorial gifts in identifying and choosing appropriate material. He drew heavily upon what he learned from composing *Living China* as he set himself a new and grander, but similar, task in the northwest of allowing the leaders of the Red Army, whose story had also been suppressed for political reasons, to speak as directly as possible to a world audience.

24

To Sian
Stage One

U NAWARE HISTORY WAS ALREADY opening its curtain for her brother to appear on the world's stage, Mildred thought he needed a helping hand. She persuaded her employer, Powell G. Groner, to suggest to Harry Payne Burton, the editor of *Cosmopolitan* magazine, that Snow was working on two books, *Living China* and *South of the Clouds,* that might contain material of interest to *Cosmopolitan.* Snow was dubious about the fit, but he outlined for Burton a potentially suitable article on Doihara as the "Lawrence of Asia."

On May 28, only days before he left Peking for Red territory, he belatedly responded to a telegram from Burton inviting him to make additional suggestions for articles. He made two: the first, "New Styles of Conquest," outlined Japan's innovative imperialism in North China; the second, "Will Japan and Russia Fight?," outlined the ideological conflict between the "Red Idea" and the "Imperial Idea" as a basis for war between these two great Pacific powers. But these negotiations were quickly lost in the flurry and excitement of his new opportunity.

On June 1 Snow wrote MacBride that an apparent months-long truce between the Red forces and those of Yen Hsi-shan and Chang Hsueh-liang indicated a new interest in a united front and offered a very special opportunity:

> If these reports are true it is of great significance and it is partly to confirm them that I am going to Sianfu. During my trip I intend to

interview Marshal Chang. I have made arrangements to get permission, and possibly the use of a plane, to fly to the front in Shensi. I have been assured, by men in whose word I place confidence, that it may be possible for me even to enter the Red districts of Shensi and Kansu, and interview important Communists, including Mao Tse-tung, the Lenin of China.

To underline the historic potential of this opportunity he pointed out no foreign journalist had penetrated a Red-controlled region since the Reds had organized in central China. This meant

No interviews with any of the famous Red leaders—Mao Tse-tung, Chu Teh, Hsu Hsiang-chien, Liu Chih-tan and others—have been published. If I succeed in seeing them, as I may, it will be a world scoop on a situation about which millions of words have been written, based only on hearsay and highly colored government reports. What are these men made of that they can stand such punishment? How do they live? What kind of administration do they give the peasants? How "Communist" are they? These and many other questions are subjects of wide controversy, but no one has been able to answer them with first-hand information.

Snow offered to contract with MacBride for exclusive British rights on any articles from his trip in addition to any straight news coverage. He explained at the same time he would be writing for the *New York Sun* for American publication. He expected the *Herald* to bear its share of his travel expenses, which he anticipated would be modest. He was taking both a movie and a regular camera with him. He would turn over any shots of value to MacBride for whatever he considered a fair price. The trip would last at most two months, possibly less, and he would arrange for adequate news coverage in Peking during his absence.

Do not, however, consider this trip a certainty. All sorts of upsets may occur. Reports reaching here tonight for example, describe a serious plague in Shensi, and war between the Moslems in Kansu and the Reds on their west is said to have been renewed. However, if the idea interests you, you might send me a cable, simply "Trip approved" when you receive this. The journey to Sianfu, and a visit to the front, if nothing else develops, should be worthwhile.

Snow took threats of plague and other diseases in Shensi seriously. He took so many inoculations in a short span of time he actually made himself ill and once again almost missed his train. It would be more, rather than less, than two months before he returned to Peking. He later described his state of mind on setting out to Ambassador Johnson:

If I succeeded in getting into the Soviet areas, I was not entirely sure that I would get out. I had ceased believing in the general propaganda handed out about the Reds long ago, which simply didn't make sense: one could not believe that mere bandits, interested only in loot and slaughter, could defy all Nanking's forces for nearly 10 years, there must be a powerful something holding them up: but at the same time there was always the possibility that my investigation to find out what it was might be rudely interrupted by my demise. . . . There was also the certainty that if I did come out, and was able to report anything favorable about the Reds, I would at best antagonize Nanking, and at worst be attacked as a trouble-maker, an agent of the omnipresent Comintern, a propagandist, etc.

He assured Johnson he had early determined to make no agreement about what he would or would not write, and he was surprised no one asked him to do so, "nobody examined my notes, I was allowed freely to photograph whatever I chose, and I got every cooperation possible in collecting information, getting interviews, etc." He was on occasion subjected to doses of propaganda, "but nothing compared to what I have been accustomed to receive in non-bandit quarters, and for this I was grateful." He reminded the ambassador, whatever his personal sympathies, he was decidedly from Missouri.

He also pointed out the *London Daily Herald*, which was featuring articles and photographs from his trip, was the official British Labour Party newspaper, as strongly anticommunist as it was antifascist. The *New York Sun*, which he believed had just begun running his articles, was "the most conservative paper in New York."

He acknowledged Johnson's kind comments on *Living China*. That book "grew out of a struggle to understand many inexplicable things I saw happening around me," out of personal contact with some of the authors, and "out of opening doors onto the tragedy and courage of their lives. I am thinking of Lu Hsun especially—one of the finest men I have ever known." He understood one "cannot enter into a thing like this very deeply without coming to share some of the feeling that produces it and to begin to have feelings about a country and its people may prove a good road to ruin for a 'foreign correspondent.' "[1]

Political events playing out elsewhere on the world stage also influenced his coming adventure. Early in May the Italians were completing their conquest of Ethiopia. Haile Selassie left Addis Ababa for exile May 2. On May 9 Mussolini announced the war was over and named General Badoglio, the commander of the invading Italian army, viceroy of Ethiopia. On June 30 Haile Selassie made an address to the League of Nations that evoked deep sympathy and indignation throughout the world. Snow was then waiting in Sian to cross into Red territory.

Meanwhile civil order in Spain rapidly broke down and provided another arena for Italy, Germany, and Russia to test their international reach. In the second week of July, just after Snow crossed into Red territory, General Francisco Franco y Bahamonde was flown in a speedy, rented English plane, the *Dragon Rapide*, from his assignment in the Canary Islands to Morocco to take command of the Spanish army and make it the military backbone of a rebellious coup plotted by Monarchists and Falangists. The geopolitical groundwork for the 1937 anti-Communist Tripartite agreement between Germany, Italy, and Japan was rapidly prepared, and Snow was amazed how clearly these events were recognized in the remote loess hills of China's northwest provinces.

In the *Saturday Evening Post* as he began his journey, Snow made two challenging predictions. First, that Japan, in her "effort to master the markets and the inland wealth of China," was "destined to break her imperial neck." This would happen "because the conditions of suzerainty which Japan must impose on China will prove humanly intolerable and will shortly provoke an effort of resistance that will astound the world." Second, that the United States would be maneuvered into assuming "the burden of chastising Japan," probably not out of loyalty to China, but rather out of loyalty to Western colonial powers. If that occurred then the Russian bolsheviks "are convinced that Eastern war will bring the Chinese Communists into power. And their prophecies, even when due allowance is made for wish fancy, are heavily freighted with historic logic."[2]

As Snow boarded the train for Sian in Peking early in June he believed the force he was about to see firsthand was already significantly positioned to play a major role in the history not only of China but also of Asia and the world. If the broad themes of history seemed clear, he was, however, by no means so confident about what to expect immediately in Sian. Shortly after registering at the Sian Guest Hostel, he was surprised by a Lebanese-American doctor from Buffalo, New York, who introduced himself by announcing he knew Snow's mission and hoped they were going across the line together.

The doctor's name was George Hatem, and he subsequently played a key role in many major events of Snow's life. In 1961 Snow himself published a vivid account of his fellow adventurer. In a brief period of prosperity in the twenties Hatem's immigrant father struggled to save enough to start his son in medical school. Hatem paid for much of his own schooling with hard work. After finishing three years of premed studies, he won a scholarship to American University in Beirut and once there earned another scholarship to medical school at the University of Geneva. Without money for railway fare to cross southern Europe, he happily bicycled from the Mediterranean to Geneva.

Graduating from medical school, he and two fellow students decided to open practice in Shanghai. Hatem looked for a place where basic medicine was needed, but in Shanghai the three new graduates found the quickest way to get started was to specialize in venereal disease. One of the partners went home because of family troubles, and the other married a rich girl and became a society doctor. Hatem became a staff doctor for the Shanghai International Settlement police force, examining brothel women and cleaning them up till the next dose.

Hatem wrote a pamphlet on health conditions in Shanghai that brought him to the attention of Agnes Smedley. Once convinced he sincerely wanted to make the world better, she introduced him to Liu Ting, a young Red engineer, who told him of the egalitarian life in Communist areas, where doctors were sorely needed. Liu later helped arrange the passage of Hatem and Snow from Sian across the line. Hatem's distaste for both Shanghai and his job, which he described as "Fighting V. D. with a pea shooter," led him to conclude, "I could make a fortune there treating nothing but chancres and blueballs for the rest of my life. . . . But I didn't spend my old man's money learning to become a V. D. quack for a gangster society."[3]

Hatem and Snow spent nearly a month in Sian. Besides playing a lot of gin rummy, Snow talked to missionaries, government officials, and Red representatives. He did not get a chance to interview Chang Hsueh-liang, but he did interview General Yang Hu-cheng, named pacification commissioner of Shensi Province by Chiang Kai-shek. The interview got stuck on Yang's problem of deciding which wife, if either, was to live in his new house. Yang was very closemouthed about political affairs, but he assigned his secretary to show Snow the historic aspects of this ancient capital. On June 14 Snow recorded in his diary a visit to the Tang dynasty pagoda. One of his companions was Anna Wang, wife of a very special secretary to Yang, Wang Ping-nan.

Wang Ping-nan's father was a rich landlord and blood brother to Yang. Wang had only recently returned from Germany where he had been sent by Yang to prepare for service. In Berlin, Wang had become active among radical students and met Anna, a talented linguist from a conservative German family, who became his wife. In the spring of 1936 the Wangs spent several days in Moscow on their way to Sian from Berlin. There Wang Ping-nan discussed the political situation in the northwest thoroughly with Wang Ming, nominally the most important Chinese Communist in Moscow. Wang Ming, however, played a very equivocal role in Chinese history over the next several years. Wang Ping-nan agreed to persuade his benefactor Yang to join a united front with the Communists and the Manchurian forces.

In Sian, Wang was surprised at how amenable General Yang was to the idea, and he quickly established a covert liaison with both Red forces and the Manchurians. The Reds' argument that Chinese should not fight Chinese but join in a united front to drive the Japanese from their land grew more persuasive every day. Like Wang Ju-mei become Huang Hua, Wang Ping-nan later became another of the People's Republic's best-known diplomats. As China's ambassador to Poland, and its senior diplomat in Europe, he represented China in its later acknowledged offstage discussions with the United States from 1955 to 1964.[4]

In Sian, Snow carefully noted the many signs that the Communist push for a united front was far more advanced than the outside world realized. Pastor Wang, no relation to Wang Ping-nan or Wang Ju-mei, had flown to Yenan in Young Marshal Chang Hsueh-liang's plane to open negotiations for forming a united front months before Snow arrived. The Young Marshal himself shortly after flew to Yenan and met with Chou En-lai. This meeting made possible the truce between the armies that in turn provided the opportunity for Snow and Hatem to cross into Red territory. Wang told Snow it was now potentially too embarrassing for Snow to fly to Yenan in the Young Marshal's plane, so he was to leave Sian by less conspicuous means.

Soon after, Wang and a Tungpei officer called on Snow to take him to visit the ancient Han capital outside of Sian. There they overlooked the site since excavated to reveal to millions of tourists the burial place of the famed terra-cotta warriors. On arriving, the Tungpei officer took off his dark glasses, put his face close to Snow's, and laughingly challenged, "Look at me! Do you recognize me?" He was Teng Fa, chief of the Chinese Red Army's Security Force, a man for whose capture the Kuomintang had advertised a fifty-thousand-dollar reward. When Snow overcame his surprise and asked if Teng was not afraid for his head, the latter responded, "Not anymore than Chang Hsueh-liang is. I am living with him."

While still in Sian, Snow learned some news that disappointed him and more that excited him. The Red leader, Liu Chih-tan, who welcomed the Red forces to Shensi at the end of the Long March, and who appeared on the list of hoped-for interviews Snow sent to MacBride, was killed in action before Snow could cross the line. But the details he began to put together of the Red Army's Long March, even then still being concluded, excited him. He early learned at least the bare outlines of the desperate battle to cross the Tatu, and he began to recognize something of the enormity of the army's passage through challenging geography and hostile peoples. The battles going on in Kansu and further west were current topics of conversation. The Red Army loomed large in deed, if not in numbers, even before he met its main force.

Before leaving Peking, Snow had asked Wang Ju-mei if he would like to travel with him as an interpreter. But for some reason he first invited another student from Szechuan. When that student at the last minute backed out, he sent a coded message from Sian to Foster Snow indicating he wanted Wang. Demonstrating his potential diplomatic talents, Wang appealed to the Yenching University secretary to provide him a letter authorizing him to investigate banking institutions in the northwest. President John Leighton Stuart signed such a letter. Wang never wrote up his research on banking, nor did he ever graduate from Yenching, but like Hatem, he received a uniquely valuable education traveling with Edgar Snow in the northwest.

Wang arrived in Sian while Snow and Hatem were still there, but he did not travel with them to Pao An. With the help of Liu Ting and Teng Fa he left Sian with a second group. His learning to defend his rights in the recent student demonstrations, however, drew his mission into jeopardy at a crucial moment. Two men assigned to guard him forced their way into his room. He protested their entry. His hotel room was for the time his private home. He insisted they needed his permission or appropriate legal documents to enter. The men then quietly informed him they were in fact from the Shensi Communist Headquarters. Suspicious, he tested them by asking if they knew who a particular young woman from Yenching was going to marry. They knew the right answer, a young man from their own province. Wang's transfer through the lines to rejoin Edgar Snow was then arranged without serious incident.[5]

25

Chou and Mao, in Person

O N THE ANNIVERSARY OF America's independence from Great
Britain, Snow and Hatem began traveling by truck for two and a half
days from Sian to Yenan. After an overnight stay in Yenan, then the
crossing point into Red territory, led by a single guide, their gear loaded on
mules, they walked into the loess hills toward An Tsai, where they hoped to
meet Mao Tse-tung. They were briefly threatened by nearby "white bandits,"
armed men hired by those hostile to Communist-led change, but they did not
learn of the threat until it was over. They found An Tsai almost completely
devastated ten years earlier by flood. Neither Mao nor hardly anyone else
was there. But at nearby Pai Chia Ping their ambitious hopes revived when
Chou En-lai himself came calling their first evening. Soon after Snow also
met Wang Ling, the young student from Tientsin who had given the letter
introducing Snow to Mao Tse-tung to Hsu Ping to pass on to Snow.[1]

Chou invited Snow to his nearby office the day after calling on him, and
Snow immediately began gathering firsthand answers to the questions about
the Red leaders he had posed to MacBride: "What are these men made of that
they stand such punishment? How do they live? What kind of administration
do they give the peasants? How Communist are they?"

Chou surprised Snow by suggesting a tour of Red territory that would last
ninety-two days, considerably longer than Snow had projected to MacBride
and thus strongly implying there was more that Snow could and should see
than he had originally hoped. Chou's suggested schedule did not provide

for Snow to stay in Pai Chia Ping long enough to gather a detailed story of Chou's life, as Snow later was able to do with Mao Tse-tung in Pao An, but Chou did answer Snow's wide-ranging questions frankly and in considerable detail in long interviews held on July 9 and 10. Snow used the information principally for Chou's brief biography in "The Insurrectionist," in his later account of the Long March, and in his descriptions of various aspects of life under Communist rule. He also listened with special interest to Chou's account of the catastrophe that befell the Communists in Shanghai the year before Snow arrived, including Chou's personal escape from near execution. Snow later retold Chou's story so vividly in *Red Star over China* that J. B. Powell mistakenly assumed in his own memoir that Snow must have arrived in Shanghai in time to be a firsthand witness.

Initially Snow ran into a cultural barrier that brought his goal of examining the revolutionary movement through knowing its leaders into question. Those he first met were reluctant to talk informatively about their personal lives. Only after Mao Tse-tung broke the ice by telling Snow his life story, which became a special event attracting an audience of interested comrades, and even Mao's wife, who had never heard such information, was Snow able to persuade others to tell their stories. Traditional Chinese suspicions of the individual who separated himself from his social group as well as more recent marxist teaching minimizing concern for the individual in history's impersonal class struggle clashed with Snow's American humanist assumptions that history was shaped by individuals who often represented a thitherto unrealized potential in the group. Fortunately he persuaded Mao that a wide public audience could better understand the forces of history by learning the personal stories of representative individuals. *Red Star over China* grew from Snow's carrying this point.

In *Red Star* he followed Chou En-lai's story with "Something about Ho Lung." Ho Lung was the legendary commander of the Second Front Army, who maintained the soviet area in northern Hunan for approximately a year after the larger body of Red forces further south began their Long March. His Second Front Army had joined the Fourth Front Army in Szechuan, but had not yet arrived in the northwest. The chapter is a collection of personal anecdotes about Ho Lung told Snow on his two-day journey from Pai Chia Ping to Pao An by Li Chiang-lin, a commander in Ho's army. It becomes an exuberant double portrait, Ho's and Li's, the subject and the teller. The warmly vivid respect Li felt for Ho, big and strong as a tiger, caring for no personal possessions except horses, willing even to fight a major battle to recapture a beautiful horse, but otherwise personally humble and ever faithful to the Party, all these admired personal characteristics revealed something significant to Snow, and he believed to his readers, about the Red Army and the men who led it.

But the army was not only leaders. In the next chapter Snow added the stories of young, ordinary soldiers—Old Dog, Local Cousin, and Iron Tiger—who traveled with him on this two-day journey. He also asked the peasants through whose land they traveled such questions as "What is a Communist?" and "What is a capitalist?" and reported their answers. Persistently personalizing to make his story graphic, Snow also saw these interviews as a means of shaping, testing, and validating whatever generalizations he might come to about the Communists as a revolutionary force in history.

Parts 3 through 6 of *Red Star over China* are written from Snow's interviews and experiences during his slightly more than two-week stay in Pao An during the latter half of July. Part 4 is Mao's autobiography, and part 5 is the story of the Long March, which in part also brought Mao's life story up-to-date. Parts 3 and 6 give a more extended picture of life in the Communist capital, but the opening chapter of part 3, "Soviet Strong Man," is Snow's evaluation of Mao's personality and his leadership, and in effect precedes and introduces Mao's autobiography. Thus the personality of Mao is put vividly before the reader early and dominates all four parts concerned with soviet life in the capital.

In his editorial chapter on Mao, Snow staked a claim for the life of this "gaunt, rather Lincolnesque figure," as "a rich cross-section of a whole generation, an important guide to understanding the sources of action in China." He thus forewarned his reader that the "full exciting record of [Mao's] personal history, just as he told it to me" will appear in part 4. While he acknowledged there would never be any one "savior" of China, he also insisted "whatever there was extraordinary in this man grew out of the uncanny degree to which he synthesized and expressed the urgent demands of millions of Chinese, and especially the peasantry. If their 'demands' and the movement which was pressing them forward were the dynamics which could regenerate China, then in that deeply historical sense Mao Tse-tung might possibly become a very great man." This was the humanistic and democratic touchstone by which he believed history would measure and in turn be shaped by Mao's leadership.

Snow also posed Mao for a photograph. Mao seldom wore a cap, and his hair was then long and unruly. To tidy up his image Snow persuaded Mao to put on the Red Army cap Snow had been given. In 1960 George Hatem reminded Snow he was "the only person around who managed to put a hat on Mao Tse-tung." Snow was then even more surprised to find his photo became one of the most popular photos ever taken of Mao, winning a

The photo that later became an icon.

place in the Revolutionary Museum as soon as it was constructed. In 1964 Snow faced this same photo blown up to a gigantic thirty-foot poster opposite Tienanmen Square. But at this original meeting in 1936 he had little reason to imagine the heroic portrait he drew of Mao in words and in photographic image would decades later become a significant element in the political cult worship of Mao that eventually transformed him into a new-style emperor.[2]

Part 3 closes with Snow describing an evening of Red theater. He recognized several important leaders and their wives, including Lo Fu, Lin Piao, Lin Po-chu, and Mao Tse-tung, scattered in the crowd, "seated on the springy turf like the rest." The performance was full of overt propaganda, and the props were primitive, but it had the advantage "of dealing with living material rather than with meaningless historical intrigues that are the concern of the decadent Chinese opera." Snow applauded this "naive art" as suitable for a mass audience indifferent to distinguishing art from propaganda, thus stretching his argument from *Living China* to its thinnest. He was also pleased to find that Ting Ling, represented in *Living China*, had authored several skits popular with the people's theater.

He saw in the enthusiastic theater audience a possible explanation for the Reds' surprising ability to resist and survive for so long against the superior numbers and arms of the Kuomintang:

> I often had a queer feeling among the Reds that I was in the midst of a host of schoolboys, engaged in a life of violence because some strange design of history had made this seem infinitely more important to them than football games, textbooks, love, or the main concerns of youth in other countries. At times I could scarcely believe that it had been only this determined aggregation of youth, equipped with an Idea, that had directed a mass struggle for ten years against all the armies of Nanking.

This observation set up a series of rhetorical questions to be answered by the autobiography of Mao in part 4: "How had the incredible brotherhood arisen, banded together, held together, and whence came its strength? And why had it perhaps, after all, failed to mature, why did it still seem fundamentally like a mighty demonstration of youth? How could one ever make it plausible to those who had seen nothing of it?"

As night after night Snow wrote down the story Mao told him, he realized "this was not only his story but an explanation of how communism grew—a variety of it real and indigenous to China—and why it had won the adherence and support of thousands of young men and women." If Snow had recently been reading Strachey, Shaw, Marx, and Lenin in an effort to understand the revolutionary force communism might have in Asia it is clear Ralph Waldo Emerson's belief in a history shaped by *representative* men responding to imperative ideals profoundly predetermined his own journalistic premises.

Snow was deliberately an intellectual amateur in the most favorable sense. It was a matter of journalistic conscience for him not to be pinned down to any particular school of thought, though he recognized his responsibility to be aware of modern ideas. A good listener, he also was often an acute psychological observer. At this early time he had not read Freud with the diligence he read Marx, but later in *Journey to the Beginning* he observed, "An Oedipus pattern runs through the lives of many Chinese revolutionists. Mao simply seemed franker about it than most." In *Red Star over China* he left this theme implicit, without mention of Freud or the behavior patterns he made famous. While belatedly he clearly identified this theme in Mao's life, he probably never fully recognized the significant parallels between the Oedipal drama in Mao's life and his own.

Red Army class at cave entrance—Pao An.

Mao's father was far more tyrannical than Snow's, but both were stern taskmasters, harshly skeptical of religious beliefs. Both mothers were more sympathetic religious believers, one a Buddhist and the other Roman Catholic, but neither seemed to their sons able to stand up to their husbands. Mao learned to fight his father by using the same Chinese classics his father respected, but he also developed a strong taste for Old China's stories of romantic rebellion. Mao struggled through long years of adolescence and young adulthood searching for a belief or a commitment that would focus his talents. He hungered for travel, and when Snow met him he had just completed a wondrous journey far more adventurous and taxing than Snow's own treasured caravan trip, but unlike Snow, Mao found his native land a sufficiently unknown and challenging world to explore. He declined the opportunity to study and travel in Europe when it was offered.

Snow almost certainly felt ambivalent about his own more privileged upbringing and travel. He had seen much more of the world than Mao, but he deeply respected Mao's nativist focus. He may have even felt relatively embarrassed about his own long exile from his native land. He was often defensive about it in his letters home. That the revolution China needed to take its place in the modern world should be profoundly Chinese followed from Snow's deepest anticolonial commitment. He happily recorded Mao's difficulties with Comintern advisers and representatives and more particularly his development of a peasant-based revolutionary line in long and harsh conflict with the more conservative marxist insistence on the requirement of an urban-based proletariat for a successful revolution.

He wanted to believe Mao an authentic national revolutionary, not a mere puppet of the Stalin-dominated International Comintern. Mao's struggle to use the best of his native cultural tradition to fight against first his father's greed and oppression and then to transform that struggle into a broader social struggle to free his people from the greed and oppression of a feudal capitalism only too spinelessly willing to accede to the demands of a new fascist imperial threat appealed strongly to Snow's own pattern of belief. As he noted in *Journey to the Beginning*, "Mao's impact on his American Boswell" became part of his own story. Consciously he acted as a scrupulous journalist; nevertheless, deep currents in his own nature created a strong empathy with Mao at this stage of the revolution.

The story Mao told covered the Long March and the arrival of the Red forces in the northwest with only three anticlimactic paragraphs. That left Snow the opportunity to cap and expand Mao's autobiography with a lengthy, sometimes stirringly melodramatic, narrative, culled from all he had learned from Mao and other sources, of the Red Army's truly epic military exodus. But before beginning that narrative he briefly reviewed "the six years of the Soviets of South China" preceding the Long March. This was the world Snow had sought to penetrate with a curiosity that increased in intensity with growing disillusion and frustration at the Kuomintang's censorship and oppression of dissent, both artistic and political, and its subservient accommodation to Japanese aggression.

He noted sardonically it was "one of the amazing facts of our age" that no single outside foreign observer had entered Red territory during these years despite the fact that this territory was then the only Communist-ruled nation in the world outside of the USSR. A few salient points about life in these Chinese soviets had now become "confirmable from accounts both friendly and inimical," and "these clearly indicate the basis of the Red Army's support":

> Land was redistributed and taxes were lightened. Collective enterprise was established on a wide scale; by 1933 there were more than 1,000

Soviet co-operatives in Kiangsi alone. Unemployment, opium, prostitution, child slavery, and compulsory marriage were eliminated, and the living conditions of the workers and the poor peasants in the peaceful areas were greatly improved. Mass education made much progress in the stabilized Soviets. In some counties the Reds attained a higher degree of literacy among the populace in three or four years than had been achieved anywhere else in rural China after centuries.

In 1968, revising *Red Star over China,* Snow acknowledged history had changed by inserting this qualifying reservation:

> "Revolution," observed Mao Tse-tung, "is not a tea party." That "Red" terror methods were widely used against landlords and other class enemies—who were arrested, deprived of land, condemned in "mass trials," and often executed—was undoubtedly true, as indeed the Communists' own reports confirmed. Were such activities to be regarded as atrocities or as "mass justice" executed by the armed poor in punishment of "White" terror crimes by the rich when they held the guns? Never having seen Soviet Kiangsi, I could add little, with my testimony, to an evaluation of second-hand materials about it, or to the usefulness of this book, which is largely limited to the range of an eyewitness.

Snow followed his summary of the Kiangsi soviet years by noting that speculation on what the Reds might have accomplished had they been able to hold their bases in the south became only of academic interest after Nanking's fifth and greatest anti-Red campaign forced the Reds to carry out a retreat that began as if it were the Red Army's funeral march. However, the Long March, or the "Chang Cheng," as the Reds termed it, not only became moving evidence of the extraordinary dedication and courage of the Red forces, but also something more. "However one may feel about the Reds and what they represent politically," Snow insisted, it was "one of the great exploits of military history," surpassed only by the Mongols. "Hannibal's march over the Alps looks like a holiday excursion beside it." Snow saw Napoleon's retreat from Moscow, when the Grand Army was utterly broken and demoralized, the more interesting comparison.

Unquestionably begun as a strategic retreat, when the Reds finally reached their objective on October 20, 1935, in Shensi with their nucleus intact, after a year of epic military battles and fantastic struggle through some of the most remote and forbidding geography of the world, it was transformed from a demoralized retreat into a spirited march of victory to the anti-Japanese front. Mao had correctly foreseen, as had Snow when he moved to Peking in 1933, that the northwest was "to play a determining role in the immediate destinies of China, Japan, and Soviet Russia." The arrest of Chiang Kai-shek in Sian and the Japanese resort to open warfare by invading Peking months later, even as Snow wrote his story, confirmed their jointly held convictions.

Snow had space for only the "briefest outline" of the Long March. The Communists had begun to collect accounts from marchers already totaling more than three hundred thousand words, and they recognized the march itself was not yet complete. He chose to skim quickly over the early stages of confusion and hardship and focus on the battle he had first learned about in Sian, the battle to cross the Tatu River in the remote mountains of Szechuan. His story of that pivotal event blended revealing history with agitprop drama more effectively than anything he had observed at the outdoor theater in Pao An. When Snow's reports of his northwest journey began to reach readers in China even before *Red Star over China* was published in English, this story would stir the passionate idealism of a generation of young people hungry for an authentic national political force to believe in. And for generations after the Communists came to power, songs, films, and endless political rhetoric would celebrate the battle over the Tatu. Edgar Snow gave the crossing of the Tatu a giant push into the same realm of legendary history as the Battle of Valley Forge occupies in American history.

The Red forces rehearsed their crossing of the Tatu by first making fools of the Kuomintang crossing the Yangtze in Yunnan, a land that lived vividly in Snow's memory. Once the Red forces entered this wild mountainous province, Chiang Kai-shek believed he had them trapped. He expected the Reds to attempt a crossing at Lengkai, but a Red battalion unobtrusively reversed direction and caught government forces by surprise at Chou Ping Fort. There government troops were easy prey and quickly disarmed. A vanguard of the Red Army arrived at noon the next day and easily crossed in great good humor at the enemy's expense.

Furious, Chiang Kai-shek then flew to Szechuan, where he planned a doom for the Red forces similar to the fate of the heroes of the classic *Three Kingdoms* and the Taiping rebels. But Mao knew the story of the Taipings as well as Chiang and avoided their fateful delay. Again moving more swiftly than the government believed possible, the Red forces entered the tribal territory of the fierce people, then known as Lolos. Today these people prefer to be known as Yi. A Red commander, Liu Po-cheng, understood the tribals' hatred of the Chinese. Speaking their language he explained how the Red Chinese differed from the White by favoring autonomy for all the national minorities of China. When the Reds agreed to give the Yi arms and bullets to guard their independence, they believed Liu.

Liu Po-cheng and the high chief of the Yi sealed a pledge of brotherhood by drinking the blood of a freshly killed chicken, and many tribals joined the Red forces as invaluable guides and soldiers. Thus a vanguard division led by Lin Piao was able to descend upon the Tatu River town of An Jen Chang just as surprisingly as previously Red troops had descended upon Chou Ping Fort.

Red soldiers crossed the river in a commandeered boat and after a short but fierce battle captured the enemy position on the north bank. But it was May, and the Tatu was swift and wide, filled with floodwater from the mountains above. By the third day of laboriously ferrying troops across the treacherous river, it was clear it would take weeks to carry the whole army with its supplies across. A hurriedly called military council quickly decided on a desperate alternative.

Four hundred *li* to the west was a famous iron-chain bridge, Lu Ting Chiao, the "Bridge Fixed by Liu," suspended high above a gorge through which the Tatu flowed turbulently far below. Snow had marveled at such bridges on his caravan journey from Yunnanfu into Burma years before. It was the last possible crossing east of Tibet. The division that had already crossed set out along the north bank, while the main force strung out along the south bank, each moving at forced march through rugged mountainous terrain. On the second day the north bank division was delayed by skirmishes with Szechuan troops. Then White reinforcements were observed also hurrying toward the bridge.

The Red vanguard on the south bank, the pick of the Red Army, soon outpaced the enemy's tired soldiers. They arrived first to find the Szechuanese had not destroyed the bridge but had removed the southern half of the wooden flooring. Only bare iron chains swung to a point midway above the stream. The enemy assumed a machine-gun nest on the northern bridgehead covering bare chains over half the bridge would be sufficient deterrent.

The Reds had no choice and little time. Thirty volunteers armed with grenades and mausers swung out on the bare chains above the boiling water. Red machine guns provided covering fire, but they did not quiet the enemy's machine guns or snipers. Several volunteers were hit and dropped to the river below, but the remaining planks on the northern half of the bridge provided minimal cover from enemy fire.

Snow paid tribute to the power of the revolutionary ideals motivating the Red fighters:

> Never before had the Szechuanese seen Chinese fighters like these—men for whom soldiering was not just a rice-bowl, but youths ready to commit suicide to win! Were they human beings or madmen or gods? wondered the superstitious Szechuanese. Their own morale was affected; perhaps they did not shoot to kill; perhaps some of them secretly prayed that

they would succeed in their attempt! At last one Red crawled up over the
bridge flooring, uncapped a grenade, and tossed it with perfect aim into
the enemy redoubt.

The enemy desperately tried to tear up the remaining planks, but it was
too late. Kerosene was then thrown on the planks and set ablaze, but the
volunteers moved forward implacably lobbing their grenades, their courage
and determination too much for the enemy. The Szechuanese fled in consternation. The bridge was secured, and within an hour or two the Red Army was
exultingly crossing the Tatu. "Far overhead angrily and impotently roared the
planes of Chiang Kai-shek, and the Reds cried out in delirious challenge to
them. As the Communist troops poured over the river, these planes tried to
hit the bridge, but their torpedoes only made pretty splashes in the river."

In Szechuan the Reds found welcome respite. The Fourth Front Army
of Hsu Hsiang-chien and Chang Kuo-tao joined the survivors of the Tatu
crossing at Mokung. For three weeks the armies rested, and military councils
were held. Snow reported the disagreement between Chang Kuo-tao and
Hsu Hsiang-chien, who favored staying in Szechuan and building a base,
and Mao Tse-tung and Chu Teh, who were determined to continue into the
northwest to open a Japanese front. Snow's information was understandably
sketchy at best, and his account only hints at the depth of the political and
personal conflict between Chang Kuo-tao and Mao Tse-tung.[3]

He followed the journey of Mao and the main Kiangsi force northward
through Mantzu tribal territory. The Mantzus hated the Chinese, whether
Red or White. They refused to meet with the Red forces, but their own
guerrilla attacks with snipers and boulders in narrow passageways were
fiercely effective. The Reds were able to capture a few Mantzu to serve as
guides and gleaned green Tibetan wheat and huge beets and turnips to serve
as their major food supply for crossing the notorious Great Grasslands ahead.
The severe weather and treacherous pathways through the high-altitude
"weird sea of wet grass" claimed many victims, but the Long Marchers shed
the far less resolute White forces who tried to follow and attack them in their
weakened state. In Kansu on the last leg of their epic journey they broke
through every blockade the native Muslim forces set in their path to finally
reach the welcoming Red armies operating in Shensi since 1933.

Since Mao Tse-tung had defeated his father with classical Chinese poetry,
he believed, unlike Lu Hsun, such poetry could express modern revolutionary
themes. He won admiring respect from his American Boswell because he
could write such poetry while leading an epic march. Snow made a free translation of a poem by Mao as a fitting epilogue to his story of the Long March:

The Red Army, never fearing the challenging Long March,
Looked lightly on the many peaks and rivers.
Wu Liang's Range rose, lowered rippled,
And green-tiered were the rounded steps of Wu Meng.
Warm-beating the Gold-Sand River's waves against the rocks,
A thousand joyous li of freshening snow on Min Shan,
And then, the last pass vanquished, Three Armies smiled!

26

Measuring the Revolutionary Force

PART 6, "RED STAR IN THE NORTHWEST," principally describes how the new soviet society in Pao An was organized. But again Snow could not resist telling the story of a representative leader to focus his broader social analysis. Liu Chih-tan was the original leader of the Shensi soviet who welcomed the Long Marchers and who died a hero's death while Snow waited in Sian to cross the line. Liu's story raised a question of Party discipline that ultimately reassured Snow of the healthy independent judgment of the Red leaders Snow was only then coming to know.

Liu was born in Pao An, which was subsequently renamed to honor him. Snow pictured him a "modern Robin Hood, with the mountaineer's hatred of rich men." After Hsu Hai-tung brought his Twenty-fifth Red Army to Shensi from Honan and the Twenty-fifth, Twenty-sixth, and Twenty-seventh Armies were reorganized into the Fifteenth Red Army Corps in July 1935, Liu became vice commander of the new army under Hsu Hai-tung. In August a mysterious Mr. Chang (nicknamed Chang the Corpulent) appeared as a kind of superinspector empowered to reorganize the Party and the army. He charged and tried Liu for failure to follow the Party line. He also imprisoned more than one hundred other "reactionaries."

Mao Tse-tung, Lin Piao, Chou En-lai, and Peng Teh-huai found this surprising situation on their arrival in October. They promptly ordered a reexamination of the evidence, reinstated Liu and his confederates, and arrested, tried, and imprisoned Chang the Corpulent. Liu was freed only a short time before he distinguished himself on a two-month anti-Japanese expedition and suffered a fatal wound leading a raiding party against an enemy fortification, the capture of which enabled the Red Army to cross the Yellow River. Carried back to Pao An, he died "gazing upon the hills he had roamed and loved as a boy."

To complete his transition Snow, like a shrewd country lawyer, disarmingly discounted the significance of the personal story he had just told: "But, although Liu Chih-tan was the personality round which these Soviets of the Northwest grew up, it was not Liu, but the conditions of life itself, which produced this convulsive movement of his people."

Chapter 2 is principally taken up with Snow's summary of a report by Dr. A. Stampar, a health expert sent by the League of Nations to advise the Nanking government in 1934. Stampar's report provided objective scientific evidence to ballast Snow's personal observation. But this time Snow used a memory from his own personal experience to focus his readers' attention. He recalled the emotional shock he had experienced on his 1929 visit to the nearby area of Suiyuan, then plagued by brutal drought and famine. Young and searching for the "glamour of the orient," for the first time in his life he had come abruptly upon men, women, and children, dying because they had nothing to eat. Now that early image becomes a vivid illustration of the impotence of the Chinese people in desperate need of regaining control of their destiny.

> Have you ever seen a man—a good honest man who has worked hard, a "law-abiding citizen," doing no serious harm to any one—when he had had no food for more than a month? It is a most agonizing sight. His dying flesh hangs from him in wrinkled folds; you can clearly see every bone in his body; his eyes stare out unseeing, and even if he is a youth of twenty he moves like an ancient crone, dragging himself from spot to spot. If he has been lucky he has long ago sold his wife and daughters. He has also sold everything he owns—the timber of his house itself, and most of his clothes. Sometimes he has, indeed, even sold the last rag of decency, and he sways there in the scorching sun, his testicles dangling from him like withered olive seeds—the last grim jest to remind you that this was once a man!

He now more clearly understood circumstances that compounded his sense of moral outrage:

> in many of those towns there were still rich men, rice-hoarders, wheat-hoarders, money-lenders, and landlords, with armed guards to defend them, while they profiteered enormously. The shocking thing was that in the cities—where officials danced or played with sing-song girls—there was grain and food, and had been for months; that in Peking and Tientsin and elsewhere were thousands of tons of wheat and millet, collected

(mostly by contributions from abroad) by the Famine Commission, but which could not be shipped to the starving. Why not? Because in the Northwest there were some militarists who wanted to hold all of their rolling-stock and would release none of it towards the east, while in the east there were other Kuomintang generals who would send no rolling-stock westward—even to starving people—because they feared it would be seized by their rivals.

The passion in this writing suggests Snow was not merely employing a clever journalistic trick to key the reader's response to a duller corroborating statistical report made by a neutral professional. Years later he began *Journey to the Beginning* with this same experience to explain in part the beginning of his own strong identification with China as a second home, a land he belonged to. His moral outrage had clearly embedded itself deeply in his consciousness. It also, however, made his summary of Dr. Stampar's report on the victimization of the northwest peasants seem little more than a long, detailed supporting footnote to his personal statement.

The Red Army with its supply and equipment needs was an industrial force moving into a fossilized feudal culture in Shensi. The communism Snow was able to observe seemed yet a far cry from "anything Marx would have found acceptable as a model child of his own." The Reds focused on two key immediate problems: land distribution and taxes. They abolished the exploitative feudal tax system and in effect shifted the tax burden onto the rich by seizing their land and excess personal property. Redistributing land to the peasants helped them build a mass base for the development of their revolutionary struggle. Rhetorically they referred to their soviets as made up of peasants and workers, but they were in fact overwhelmingly peasants turned into, not dedicated marxists, but happy new private land owners grateful to a Communist army that freed them from an oppressive burden of taxation and feudal tyranny.

Sixty-one-year-old Hsu Teh-li, former president of a school in Changsha, now in effect minister of Education in Pao An, earnestly instilled basic principles of marxism into his peasant students while teaching them how to read. In Lenin clubs, Communist Youth leagues, partisans, and village soviets Shensi Dick and Jane learned from *Shih-tzu* ("Know Characters") texts:

"What is this?"
"This is the Red Flag."
"What is this?"
"This is a poor man."
"What is the Red Flag?"
"The Red Flag is the flag of the Red Army."
"What is the Red Army?"
"The Red Army is the army of the poor men!"

Thus young and old began to absorb appropriate soviet ideas as they became basically literate.

In the midst of a predominantly youthful Red Army, Snow found another dignified old man, Lin Tsu-han, presiding as commissioner of Finance. He had been treasurer and chairman of the General Affairs Department of the Kuomintang when Sun Yat-sen was its leader. It was Lin who explained the "tax-shift" to Snow. Snow told the personal life stories of both Hsu and Lin, their pre-Communist experience and their personal and professional journeys to communism and the positions they then held, before discussing their policies of education and money management.

While cultural progress, judged by advanced Western standards, was negligible, "certain outstanding evils common in most parts of China had definitely been eliminated." Opium was gone. Official corruption was almost unheard-of. There were no signs of beggary and unemployment. Foot binding and infanticide were criminal offenses. Child slavery and prostitution had disappeared. Polyandry and polygamy were prohibited. New marriage regulations provided relatively greater protection for the rights of women and children.

Snow marveled that the soviet economy worked as well as it did so soon after the Communists had moved in, but he inserted here reservations he had written in his diary after his interview with Lin:

> Nevertheless, it is perfectly clear that the situation is extremely grave, even for an organization that exists on such shoe-strings as the Reds feed upon, and one of three exchanges must shortly occur in Soviet economy: (1) some form of machine industrialization, to supply the market with needed manufactures; (2) the establishment of a good connection with some modern economic base in the outside world, or the capture of some economic base on a higher level than the present one (Sian or Lanchow, for example); (3) the actual coalition of such a base, now under White control, with the Red districts.

By the time he had returned to Peking and was writing *Red Star over China*, he believed the way out for the economy was in fact found by the formation of a united front following the dramatic events in Sian in December 1936.

It was clear to Snow in sum that abolition of a cruelly exploitative tax system, land redistribution, and a strong insistence on the Red soldier's respect for the personhood and property of the peasant population had won for the Red Army the strong support from the people a partisan army depended upon.

By this point in his journey Snow realized he had already accumulated a rich harvest of publishable information about the Red forces. When he heard

Chiang Kai-shek was preparing to launch a major offensive from the south, he thought it might well be the better part of valor to cross the line while he still had a chance with his valuable notes. When he told Wu Liang-ping, an official who also often served as his interpreter, what he was thinking, the latter was dumbfounded. "You can't go back without seeing the *real* Red Army!" Wu's statement of disbelief appealed to a presumption Snow shared with most good war correspondents: that the battlefront was the testing ground for what is real, not headquarters. Snow quickly dismissed the thought of heading back to Peking and later underscored Wu's point by titling the first chapter of the story of his stay at the front "The Real Red Army."

Snow left Pao An to visit the western front at Yu Wang Pao about the end of July. His nearly two-week journey is reported in a short part 7, made up of three chapters, two of which concern his three-day stop at the primitive Red industrial community, Wu Chi Chen. He traveled with Fu Chin-kuei, a young Communist who regarded him "frankly as an imperialist" and viewed his whole trip with open skepticism.

In Chou Chia, a village near the Kansu border and the end of their journey, a number of peasants came to visit the foreigner with numerous questions of their own. Snow took advantage of the occasion to ask them what they thought of the Red Army. They complained the Red cavalry's horses ate too much. Fu defensively demanded, "Didn't they [the cavalrymen] pay you for what they bought?" The peasants admitted they had, but they were still worried about the dent in their supplies for the winter ahead, and they were not confident soviet money would buy what they needed. To drive home their concern, one old man complained, "We can't even buy opium!" Their host chipped in against Fu, holding up a cheap red Japanese-made celluloid bowl and asking if they could buy another like it.

Fu had to admit the cooperative did not stock opium or cheap red bowls, but insisted it had plenty of grain, cloth, kerosene, candles, needles, matches, and salt—"what did they want?" He then lectured them on the sacrifices the Red Army made for them and closed his tirade with a rhetorical challenge: "Suppose you can't always buy all the cloth you want, and you can't get opium, it's a fact you don't pay taxes, isn't it? You don't go in debt to the landlords and lose your house and land, do you? Well, old brother, do you like the White Army better than us, or not?" At this, all complaints appeared reluctantly to melt away, though the discussion went on heatedly for some time.

Snow was impressed the farmers had not hesitated to challenge a Red official. He closed his chapter noting the last to leave was the old man, who whispered to Fu on his way out, "Old comrade, is there any opium at Pao An; now, is there any?" As soon as the old man was out the door Fu turned to

Snow in disgust, "Would you believe it? That old defile-mother is chairman of the Poor People's Society here, and still he wants opium! This village needs more educational work."

The industrial community of Wu Chi Chen was "remarkable, not for any achievements in industrial science of which Detroit or Manchester need take note—but because it was there at all." To find a colony of workers turning out the goods and tools needed by the army and the soviet on machines in the middle of this barren, medieval world was astonishing. Snow's wonder began the night he arrived, very late, very tired. The *yao fang* (cave home) in which he was put up was clean, with freshly whitewashed walls. Hot water, fresh towels, an ample dinner with good baked bread, and then surprise of all surprises, rich brown coffee with sugar, just what he had been hopelessly longing for.

> "Products of our five-year plan!" the commissar laughed.
> "Products of your confiscation department, you mean." I amended. I think it must have been stolen fruit at that, for it had all the charms of the illicit.

Wu Chi Chen included a substantial arsenal, cloth and uniform factories, a shoe factory, a stocking factory, and a pharmacy and drug dispensary with an attending doctor. A hospital with three doctors was nearby. Most of the workers, except in the arsenal and uniform factories, were young women, all with bobbed hair, a readily understood sign of their emancipation. A policy of "Equal pay for equal labor" protected against pay discrimination by gender but did not prevent workers from being better paid than soldiers.

Pretty, twenty-nine-year-old Liu Chun-hsien, returned student from Moscow's Chung Shan University, and former friend of Rayna Prohme, to whom Vincent Sheehan paid romantic tribute in *Personal History*, was director of the women's department of the trade unions. She outlined women workers' benefits: four months' rest and pay for pregnancy, a crude nursery for workers' children, and a small "social insurance" pay supplement for mothers. The government also contributed 2 percent of the entire wage output for education and recreation for all workers. An eight-hour day, six-day week was standard. Three shifts a day kept the factories in continuous operation for six days.

Conditions were primitive but progressive. Why did these workers choose to work so hard in such an out-of-the-way place? Again Snow invoked a personal memory, his experience of the brutal, disease-ridden conditions of factory work in Shanghai. In contrast, "here was a life at least of good health, exercise, clean mountain air, freedom, dignity and hope, in which there was room for growth. They knew that nobody was making money out of them, I think they felt they were working for themselves and for China." Seeing themselves as part of a revolution, they took seriously their daily two hours of reading and writing, political lectures and dramatic groups, even the "miserable" prizes offered for competition between groups.

Chu Tso-chih, a very serious-minded engineer, knew English and German well, had written a textbook widely used in China, and had been a successful consulting engineer and efficiency expert earning ten thousand dollars a year, working for such firms as the Shanghai Power Company and Andersen Meyer and Company. He left his family and successful practice to offer his services to the Reds because a beloved grandfather, a famous philanthropist of Ningpo, had given his grandson a deathbed injunction to "devote his life to raising the cultural standard of the masses."

Chu had the solemnity of a martyr. He was shocked to find so much happiness and horseplay around him. He gravely told Snow he had but one serious criticism of his community, "These people spend entirely too much time *singing*! This is no time to be singing!" In honor of Chu's solemnity Snow titled his chapter, "They Sing Too Much."

As he was about to leave Wu Chi Chen, Snow wrote his wife he had been working on his "botanical collection. There is a tremendous number of wholly new specimens here unknown to the scientific world & the project is a much greater one than I had imagined." He was planning a long journey of up to two months to some unknown territory where he hoped to find "some rare peppers of a strange hue." His present living conditions were austere, no creature comforts at all, of course, but the food, though monotonous, was ample, and so far he suffered nothing serious. His chief worry was "bugs, which I am also collecting for the Smithsonian Institute: fleas, ants, spiders, bedbugs, lice, mosquitoes, flies, etc." He was being "devoured by epidermal inches."

His experience, however, was worth all that and much more. He was particularly exhilarated by "contact with heroic young scientists working under conditions just as bad for them (or worse) as for me." Optimistic and cheerful, "they go at the difficult labor of discovering a new scientific world like schoolboys to a football match."

He asked her to send copies of Malraux's *Man's Fate*, Smedley's *China's Red Army Marches*, and issues of *China Today* and *Voice of China*. He listed several other items including an article on chemical farming from *Harper's* that he put much value on and a mapmaking instrument she might buy at an optometrist shop. He let her know that Jimmy (Wang Ju-mei) had arrived and was now at work. He was traveling with Snow and would probably spend the winter there. Jimmy sent an accompanying letter for "the big fellow C [Chang Chao-lin]."

He was uncertain whether she would be home to receive his letter. She had her own plans for travel during the summer, but he wanted his letter forwarded wherever she was. He hoped someone would fill his requests. Wang Ling, who carried the letter, would be in the north two or three weeks. He was sorry he could not send her any of the specimens he had collected. "Some are very rare, unknown in Europe & unique. However, because of difficulties in packing, climate, transportation etc. it is best not to try transportation now." He did wish she were there. "What lively conversations and discussion you could have here; the air sparkles with intelligence. But then the bugs and filth you despise."[1]

27

The Real Red Army

P ARTS 8 THROUGH 10 OF *Red Star over China* synthesize a wide variety of Snow's travel experiences into a portrait of the Red Army at the front, but as a side effect the reader may find it difficult to recognize clearly the chronology of his travel. He arrived at Yu Wang Pao, where Peng Teh-huai, the soldier's general, was in command, about August 11. He stayed slightly more than two weeks before leaving for Yu Wang Hsien, a short distance away, to visit Hsu Hai-tung and the Fifteenth Red Army Corps. After five days in Yu Wang Hsien, he rode back to Yu Wang Pao, while Hsu Hai-tung and two of his divisions traveled westward to Ninghsia and Kansu to help clear a path for the arrival of Chu Teh and Ho Lung and their armies. A day or two later he followed Hsu westward with Peng Teh-huai and additional troops. He returned to Yu Wang Pao on September 7, struggling to stay in the wooden Chinese saddle astride the splendid Ninghsia pony that Hsu Hai-tung mischievously loaned him in response to Snow's grumbling about walking with the cavalry. He left the western front September 8 on his two-week return journey to Pao An.

The front turned out to be a misnomer in one respect. Because the Red leaders were underlining their call for a united front against the Japanese at the time, Snow saw no major military battle. Peng Teh-huai made the army's priorities clear in a speech to his frontline troops: first "to enlarge and develop our Soviet districts; secondly, to co-operate with [the] movement and advance of the Second and Fourth Front Armies (in south Kansu); thirdly, to

Riding the Ninghsia pony Hsu Hai-tung provided.

liquidate the influence of Ma Hung-kuei and Ma Hung-ping in these regions and form a United Front directly with their troops." Meanwhile Peng Teh-huai and Hsu Hai-tung were particularly valuable tutors in the principles of partisan, or guerrilla, warfare that made the Red Army a novel modern fighting force.

Parts 8, 9, and 10 each feature a distinctive battle-tested general's biography, Peng Teh-huai, Hsu Hai-tung, and Chu Teh, respectively. Knowing much of Peng's long history of struggle, Snow expected to find a "weary, grim, fanatical leader, perhaps a physical wreck," but instead found "a gay, laughter-loving man in excellent health except for a delicate stomach," a man who ate and lived sparingly and simply with happy conviction. He was particularly fond of children and was especially proud and supportive of the "little Red Devils," or *hsiao kuei*, that Snow found such an attractive feature of the Red Army. Unlike Mao Tse-tung, Peng retired late and rose early, seeming to need no more than four or five hours sleep per night.

Like Mao, Peng came from the rich peasant class and early rebelled against parental authority, but his father was more indifferent than tyrannical. As Snow told the story, Peng's grandmother was a particularly vicious, self-serving defender of traditional authority. Rewi Alley, who later also wrote a biographical portrait of Peng, claimed Snow must have misunderstood. Peng's grandmother was not so spiteful. But Snow accurately recorded Peng's early formative act of impetuous leadership of half-starved peasants against a rich man's hoard of rice, Peng's later capture and torture in Changsha, and his subsequent search for a political movement that could promise his people hope for a more just and prosperous future, a search that led him to join the Communist Party in 1927.

Snow questioned Peng particularly about partisan warfare, but Peng very deliberately bracketed his list of ten principles of military tactics basic to partisan warfare with forthright statements of political conditions necessary to make them work. He explained, "partisan warfare in China can only succeed under the leadership of the Communist Party, because only the Communist Party wants to and can satisfy the demands of the peasantry." Since "the masses are interested only in the practical solution of their problems of livelihood," successful partisan warfare depends upon "the *immediate* satisfaction of their most urgent demands. This means that the exploiting class must be promptly disarmed and immobilized."

Peng's list of tactical principles that explained the Reds' success included such hallmarks of guerrilla warfare as: partisans must refuse engagement unless there are strong indications of success; static warfare is to be avoided; superior maneuverability depends upon thorough planning and detailed knowledge of the enemy; and numerical superiority is desirable in any engagement, but a surprise "short-attack" well directed at a vital point can be very effective against a numerically superior, but unprepared, enemy. He emphasized to be successful these principles demanded "fearlessness, swiftness, intelligent planning, mobility, secrecy, and suddenness and determination in action."

Ultimately, however, this veteran campaigner returned to the political theme with sober conviction. It was absolutely "necessary for the partisans to win the support and participation of the peasant masses. If there is no movement of the armed peasantry, in fact, there is no partisan base, and the army cannot exist. . . . The Red Army is a people's army, and has grown because the people helped us. . . . We are nothing but the fist of the people beating their oppressors!"

Reminding himself he had been seeing too much of commanders and party leaders, Snow imposed upon a serious-minded young Party worker named Liu to take him to a Lenin Club meeting where he was able to question the young soldiers about how the Red Army was different from other armies and how they could be certain the peasants truly supported them. So

One of the Red Army's hsiao kuei, *or "little Red Devils," that caught Snow's eye.*

much testimony was eagerly volunteered Snow unwittingly kept them long beyond their dinner call as he wrote down their answers. He apologized, but one *hsiao kuei* stood up and proclaimed with patriotic fervor: "Don't worry about ceremony. We Reds don't care about going without food when we are fighting, and we don't care about missing our food when we can tell a foreign friend about our Red Army!" Snow finished the story: "It was a nice speech, and probably the *hsiao kuei* meant every word of it. But it did not in the least interfere with him putting away at terrific speed an enormous bowl of steaming millet which, a few minutes later, I saw served to him in the company mess."

Yu Wang Hsien was an ancient walled Muslim village that fell to Hsu Hai-tung and his troops after a ten-day siege. During his five-day stay there Snow gathered the story of Hsu Hai-tung, the only "pure proletarian," with the exception of Ho Lung, among the Red Army commanders. Hsu was the most "strongly 'class-conscious' man—in manner, appearance, conversation, and background" of all the Red leaders Snow had met. He often grinned proudly as he referred to himself as a "coolie." His education in "class" began early when his proud but illiterate family sent him to school with the sons of landlords and merchants who scorned and beat him, though he gave as good as he got in face-to-face combat. At the age of eleven, in battle he threw a stone that cut the head of a landlord's son. The landlord kicked and beat him for forgetting his birth. His teacher then reenforced the landlord's message with a second beating. That was enough. He was convinced it was impossible for a poor boy to get justice in school.

Hsu learned the potter's trade, but after a bout of cholera wiped out his savings he joined the army of a warlord. Some soldiers caught propagandizing for the Communists were beheaded. That aroused Hsu's interest in their cause. Shortly afterward he skipped from the warlord's army to Chang Fa-kuei's Fourth Kuomintang Army in Canton, where he became a platoon leader. By the spring of 1927 when the conflict between Right and Left forces came to a climax, he had become an active Communist and had to flee the army. He returned to Yellow Slope where he had worked as a potter and openly organized the first worker and peasant army of Hupeh. Originally it was an army of seventeen men with one revolver and eight bullets, Hsu's own. By 1933 it was the sixty-thousand-member Fourth Front Red Army.

Snow reserved the most powerful implications of Hsu's class conscious-ness for the chapter titled "Class War in China," where he told the story of what happened to Hsu's extended family after he became famous as a Red Army commander. Twenty-seven near relatives and thirty-nine distant relatives—old and young, women and children, everyone living in Huangpi Hsien named Hsu—were deliberately executed by Generals Tang En-po and Sha Tou-yin. Thirteen escaped the village and fled to Lihsiang Hsien. They were arrested there and the men beheaded, the women and children shot. This wiped out the entire Hsu clan except for Hsu's wife, three brothers in the Red Army, and himself. Two brothers died later in battle. His wife was captured when the White troops took Huangpi Hsien. His brothers told him she was sold as a concubine to a merchant near Hankow. He had no news of her after that.

Noticing Snow's shocked look, Hsu grinned mirthlessly, "That was noth-ing unusual," he said. "That happened to the clans of many Red officers, though mine had the biggest losses. Chiang Kai-shek had given an order that when my district was captured no one named Hsu should be left alive." Chiang's Fifth Campaign to defeat the Red forces was an effective campaign of deliberate extermination. Snow collected many corroborating stories of such atrocities from other Red leaders. It was clear the war had not always been fought exclusively on the battlefield.

The large Muslim community that spread over the provinces of Chinghai, Ninghsia, and Kansu was ruled like a medieval sultanate by a family of Muslim generals named Ma: Ma Hung-kuei, Ma Hung-ping, Ma Pu-fang, and Ma Pu-ching. Ma Hung-kuei, who ruled Yu Wang Hsien before Hsu Hai-tung and his forces captured it, held a monopoly on the distribution of salt. Every person was required to buy half a pound per month and to pay tax on its purchase to boot. Reselling the salt was a crime punishable by whipping or even death. The Government Bulletin of Ninghsia issued a long list of other taxes collected by General Ma: sales, domestic animals, opium lamps, sheep, merchants, porters, pigeons, land, and twenty other items. This heavy burden of taxation was oppressive, but military conscription added insult and was even more hated. Every family with sons had to contribute or hire a substitute at a current cost of 150 dollars. The conscripts received no pay and had to furnish their own food and clothing.

Such ruinous oppression offered the Communists an opportunity to shape a minority group policy that successfully brought converts to their cause. It promised

> To abolish all sur-taxes.
> To help form an autonomous Muslim Government.
> To prohibit conscription.
> To cancel old debts and loans.
> To protect Muslim culture.
> To guarantee religious freedom of all sects.
> To help create and arm an anti-Japanese Muslim army.
> To help unite the Muslims of China, Outer Mongolia, Sinkiang, and Soviet
>   Russia.

Snow did not comment on what the Comintern might have thought of the last promise.

At the time of Snow's visit to the Kansu-Ninghsia border area the Fourth Front Red Army had crossed the Yellow River, moved two hundred miles farther west, and reached Hsuchow in Ma Pu-fang's territory astride the main road to Sinkiang. Enough soviets were thus added in Muslim territory in Ninghsia to warrant the convening of a meeting in Yu Wang Pao of over three hundred Muslim delegates from soviet committees elected by the villages then under Red Army control. They voted resolutions "to co-operate with the Red Army and accept its offer to help create an anti-Japanese Muslim Army, and to begin at once the organization of a Chinese-Muslim unity league, a poor people's league, and a mass anti-Japanese society." Their last item of business was the remarkable case of a much hated Kuomintang tax collector who had avoided the Red Army by fleeing to hill country where he continued to collect taxes, and even doubled his levies while claiming to represent the Red government. The delegates unanimously decided to execute him. He became the only civilian shot during Snow's two-week stay in Yu Wang Pao.

Just before Snow left Yu Wang Hsien to travel to the Kansu front by way of Yu Wang Pao, a whole division of Ma Hung-kuei's Chinese troops had turned over to Chu Teh's Fourth Front Red Army. This political and military victory set off a melon feast celebration in Yu Wang Hsien. But regretfully Snow had to leave for Yu Wang Pao before Chu Teh arrived.

In the not too distant past, when news about the Red "bandits" in Kiangsi had largely depended upon hearsay, Chu-Mao was often assumed to be the name of a single leader. Snow had gained a wealth of anecdote and information about the Chu half of this fabled figure from Li Chang-lin, who was on Chu's staff from the earliest days in Kiangsi. He supplemented that with briefer data from interviews with Mao Tse-tung, Peng Teh-huai, and others to build an impressive biographical sketch.

In classic contrast to Hsu Hai-tung's proletarian beginnings, Chu Teh was "the scion of a family of landlords, rising to power and luxury and dissipation while still young." Most notable about his career was that past middle age, he was able "to discard the degenerate environment of his youth, to break, by a superb act of human will, a life-long addiction to narcotics, and finally even to forsake his family, and devote his entire fortune to a revolutionary ideal which he believed to animate the highest cause and purpose of his time." Thus he earned the name Chu Teh, "Red Virtue."

He distinguished himself as a soldier in Yunnan in the 1912 overthrow of the Manchu dynasty. By 1916 he had become a brigadier general, and his Yunnanese troops under Tsai Ao were the first to raise the banner of revolt that doomed Yuan Shih-kai's attempt to restore the monarchy. He gained a place in the public mind as one of the "four fierce generals" of Tsai Ao. Corruption and opium smoking were endemic, and Chu Teh was addicted to both. He was said to have housed nine wives and concubines in a palatial home in Yunnanfu, the provincial capital Snow remembered well from his protracted stay prior to his caravan journey.

But another addiction turned Chu around. He liked to read books. Slowly his reading and conversation with a few returned students made him aware the revolution of 1911 had meant nothing to the mass of people in Yunnan. The deplorable social conditions in Yunnanfu, a city of forty thousand slave girls and boys, aroused a sense of shame in him and awakened a desire to emulate the heroes of the West he read about by "modernizing" China. He wanted to study and travel. By 1922 he pensioned off his wives and concubines and moved to Shanghai where he met many young Kuomintang revolutionaries. He broke himself of his opium habit by booking passage on board a British steamer on the Yangtze, where opium was not available, and sailing up and down the river between Hankow and Shanghai for weeks until he could leave the ship with clear eyes and a confident step, his addiction cured.

With other Chinese students young enough to be his sons he went to Germany, where he joined the Chinese branch of the Communist Party. He later moved to a school for Chinese students in Paris, where he was repeatedly told by his instructors, "To be modern, to understand the meaning of the revolution, you must go to Russia. There you can see the future." He took their advice, studying marxism at Moscow's Eastern Toilers' University under Chinese teachers. He returned to Shanghai in 1925 to work under the direction of the Party, to which he soon gave his fortune.

Chu Teh went to work for his fellow Yunnanese and former superior, General Chu Pei-teh, second in power in the Kuomintang army only to Chiang Kai-shek. On August 1 he faced the fateful decision whether to follow the order of General Chu to suppress the famous August Uprising in Nanchang led by Ho Lung or to come out openly as a Communist and join the insurrectionists. He chose the latter and after Ho Lung's defeat led his training regiment southward through the city gates in a final open break with the security and success of his youth.

Renaming his regiment the National Revolutionary Army, he had only brief success before accepting an offer to join with another Yunnan commander, General Fan Shih-sheng, who, though not a Communist, tolerated Communists in his army. Chu Teh then became chief political adviser to the Sixteenth Army.

Communist influence in the army rapidly increased and provoked an anti-bolshevik faction to secretly plan a coup against Chu. After a colorful escape from being assassinated Chu notified General Fan he was withdrawing his forces. His army endured a harsh winter on a diet of squash with side dishes of intense political debates. Meanwhile Mao Tse-tung had found a sanctuary on nearby Chingkangshan. Mao sent his brother with Party directions for Chu to unite his army with Mao's along with a program of partisan warfare, agrarian revolution, and the building of soviets. The Chu-Mao combination that became legendary over the next six years began at Chingkangshan in May 1928.

In 1931 at the First Soviet Congress, Chu Teh was unanimously elected commander in chief of the Red Army. The early growth of the army in numbers, firepower, and fighting efficiency was spectacular. In combat he repeatedly proved his superiority to every general sent against him in "tactical ingenuity, spectacular mobility, and richness of versatility in maneuver." He established beyond doubt the formidable fighting power of Red Chinese troops in partisan warfare. His extraordinary generalship was vividly evidenced even as Snow traveled across the northwest. Chu rallied his weary, but hardened, troops to complete their Long March by driving a brutally effective wedge through the defense lines of enemy troops that had prepared for months against his advance.

These three Red leaders were generals fighting men anywhere would choose to have. They encouraged Snow to believe the Red Army was a truly new and revolutionary force in China.

On his return journey to Pao An, Snow stopped for three days at the Red Army supply center of Holienwan. A resident couple repeated the French-style meal he had experienced on his way to the front, and he savored it. He gathered the story of proud sixty-four-year-old Li, who for the present took good care of Snow's horse, but made clear despite his age he thought himself an active Red soldier. He also noted the huge landholdings of Belgian missionaries who took advantage of the Reds' deliberately tolerant northwest religious policy.

The rich supply of anecdotes Snow collected suggests he again was enjoying the open road. In no great hurry, good-humoredly disregarding the frequent lack of personal comforts, he gained weight on a steady diet of millet. Occasional personal danger seemed only a tonic, or a brief reminder of his personal inconsequence in the large affairs of the world.

Back at Pao An for about three weeks late in September and early October he "collected enough biographies to fill a *Who's Who in Red China*," but he also had time to play a trilingual (Russian, English, and Chinese) game of tennis most every morning with three faculty members of the Red Army Academy: the enigmatic German Li Teh and Commissars Tsai and Wu. He taught Commissar Tsai to play rummy, and the wives of the Red leaders picked up the game with astonishing enthusiasm. He then taught his tennis partners poker. They played for very high stakes, in matches. He plotted to get his hands on some cocoa Po Ku had been hoarding to try a simple recipe for chocolate cake he had come across. The baked cake had a "two-inch layer of charcoal on the bottom, and a top still in a state of slimy fluidity," but was nevertheless consumed with great relish. His culinary flop led to Li Teh's inviting him to a much better prepared "foreign meal" by Li's Chinese wife.

Snow used the story of Li Teh, except for the deliberately unmentioned Ma Hai-teh the only Westerner in Pao An, as the occasion in *Red Star over China* to comment on the controversial issue of the Russian role in Chinese Communism. Li Teh had called on Snow early in 1933 in Peking representing himself as a German correspondent named Otto Stern and carrying a letter of introduction from Agnes Smedley. His real name was Otto Braun, but that was not publicly revealed until 1964.[1] In his interviews with Mao, however, Snow was told Li Teh was a German military officer and had been sent into Kiangsi as a Comintern delegate. That fact had given him considerable status as a military adviser, and according to Mao the Reds had disastrously followed his advice, responding to Chiang Kai-shek's Fifth Annihilation Campaign planned by another German officer, General Von Seeckt, with traditional military tactics. As Otto Braun, Li Teh published a much different version of these events in 1975.

The Soviet Union as an existing example of a state established by marxist revolution was a potent source of hope and faith for the Chinese Communists. Snow recognized that the tactical line and theoretical leadership of the Chinese Communists "have been under the close guidance, if not positive detailed direction, of the Communist International, which during the past decade has become virtually a bureau of the Russian Communist Party." Because Stalin's insistence on giving priority to building a model soviet state in Russia had effectively triumphed over any previous Comintern pretension that the class revolution should be fought simultaneously throughout the world, "the policies of the Chinese Communists, like Communists in every other country, have had to fall in line with, and usually subordinate themselves to, the broad strategic requirements of Soviet Russia, under the dictatorship of Stalin."

But Snow pointed out that the Chinese Reds were effectively cut off from all but the most minimal contacts with the Soviet Union for more than a decade. The Reds had built their soviet in Kiangsi independent of any direction or guidance from Moscow. Physical support from Russia—money or supplies—was practically impossible to ship in. The Reds had no foreign adviser of any kind until Li Teh was smuggled in from Shanghai in 1933. Contrast that with the prominent advice, military supplies, and huge financial aid Chiang Kai-shek openly received from several foreign nations. General Von Seeckt and his staff were an obvious example. In his later memoir, Li Teh noted he understood "a group of Chinese comrades with radio equipment and codes made its way from the Soviet Union" to arrive at Chinese Red headquarters just weeks prior to Snow's arrival. This was not made public and in no way contradicts Snow's conclusion that "the

Reds have fought with less foreign help than any army in modern Chinese history."

Anecdotally the isolation of the Chinese Reds was brought home to Snow when copies of *Inprecorr*, the Russian Soviet publication, arrived in Pao An while he was there. Lo Fu, the secretary of the Central Committee of the Party, read them avidly, while casually explaining to Snow he had not seen a copy for three years. The Chinese did not receive a detailed account of the proceedings of the Seventh Congress of the Communist International until September 1936, a year after the Congress was held. This was the Congress that developed the united front tactics that were to guide the Chinese Communists through the tumultuous political events immediately ahead, particularly the Sian Incident and the Japanese invasion of Peking.

While the Chinese Reds did not have ready detailed communication with Moscow, they saw their own revolution within an international context and were keenly curious about events in other parts of the world that might bear on their struggle. Snow reported special lectures given on the "significance of the Spanish war, and the 'People's Front' in Spain contrasted with the 'United Front' in China." He was surprised to find "even far back in the mountains, Red farmers who knew a few rudimentary facts about such things as the Italian conquest of Abyssinia and the German-Italian invasion of Spain, and spoke of these powers as the 'Fascist allies' of their enemy, Japan!"

Just a few days before Snow left Pao An a radio message carried the news of "the successful junction at Huining of the vanguard of the Fourth Red Army with Chen Keng's First Division of the First Army Corps," and a few days later Chu Teh, Hsu Hsiang-chien, Ho Lung, Chang Kuo-tao, Hsiao Keh, and others were welcomed in a joyous reunion.

About that time Snow was called in by Mao Tse-tung for an important interview in which, for the first time, Mao laid out "concrete terms on the basis of which the Communists would welcome peace with the Kuomintang, and co-operation to resist Japan." Snow clearly understood his role as a journalist now carried significant diplomatic responsibilities. He sent the full text of this interview to be published as an "Open Letter Addressed to the Kuomintang" in the *China Weekly Review* as soon as he reached Peking.[2] This would not be the last time Mao Tse-tung used Edgar Snow to send an important message to the world outside his control.

Twenty years later, in the midst of the Cold War, he somewhat defiantly wrote in *Journey to the Beginning* how he felt about the Red forces he had come to know as he prepared to leave Pao An:

> What I can say is that the four months I spent with the Red Army were a highly exhilarating experience. The people I met in it seemed

the freest and happiest Chinese I had known. I was never afterward to feel so strongly the impact of youthful hope, enthusiasm and human invincibility in men dedicated to what they conceived to be a wholly righteous cause. . . .

The setting here was not Missouri but the poverty, ignorance, filth, brutality, indifference, chaos and general hopelessness which I had seen and felt in Eastern Asia for seven years, and which now largely environed my own thought. By contrast with the corruption and demoralization the "in-office" oligarchies and the small and greedy possessing groups I knew, both the white and the brown, the Reds were men of probity and selflessness. Compared to their countrymen who also despised both the Japanese and the Kuomintang, yet docilely accepted living under either, they were at least ready to die to affirm the worth of an ideal they cherished more than personal survival.

I also felt an affinity to them because of their enthusiastic espousal of science, the practice of equality and fraternity among men and women, their insistence upon racial equality, their positive attitude toward the future. In contrast to the inert fatalism of old China, all this seemed to me on the good side. The reforms they enforced or advocated were not the country-club ideals of political freedom by any means. But they did offer the essential satisfactions of food, shelter and some kind of democratic equalitarianism for all, which I now knew to be the first demands of Asia. Perhaps their strongest appeal to me as a Westerner was their decisive rejection of mysticism and the gods that had failed the poor, in favor of the rationalist's faith in man's ability to solve the problems of mankind.[3]

By early October, Chiang Kai-shek grew increasingly suspicious of the loyalty of Chang Hsueh-liang and his Manchurian troops. They were being replaced all along the line bordering Red territory. This made Snow's departure complicated and urgent. At nine in the morning on October 12 he walked down the main street of Pao An waving an emotional farewell to many of the friends who came to see him off. As he passed the Red Academy, Lin Piao and his class rose and shouted, "Peaceful good road, Comrade Snow! Ten thousand years!" Mao Tse-tung did not disturb his daily routine; he slept on.

The Manchurians still guarded one point of the line near Lochuan, roughly halfway between Yenan and Sian, where Snow was to cross. He reached Anchiapan on October 16 and loafed there until October 19 when he was directed across the line to a group of Manchurian soldiers led by an immaculate young officer wearing a gold sword and white gloves. He had dinner that evening with the officer's regimental commander, and the next morning he was hidden in a Kuomintang army truck and driven to quarters arranged by Marshal Chang Hsueh-liang in Sian.

His exit was relatively uneventful except for one final near catastrophe. When he got out of the truck in Sian he discovered the bag containing all his interviews, diaries, and notebooks was missing. It had been stuffed inside one of many sacks of broken rifles brought in for repair on the truck. All the sacks had been dumped at an arms depot twenty miles before their final stop in

Sian. Snow argued forcefully and persistently to persuade the officer in charge and the driver to return that same night for his missing bag. Worry that his invaluable records might be discovered or lost kept him awake throughout the night, until his friends stumbled in at dawn with his bag intact. Shortly after their return the city gates were closed and all traffic stopped as the roads leading into Sian were lined with Chiang Kai-shek's bodyguards. The "Generalissimo" was flying in that day for a surprise inspection visit. The god of good fortune smiled on Edgar Snow one more time.

Snow stayed in Sian for at least one more night. There was a well-remembered dinner party at the home of a German dentist, Dr. Herbert Wunsch. Wunsch was the Young Marshal's personal dentist, but he also served as a conduit for medical supplies to the Red Army. Ting Ling was then hiding at his home disguised as his servant. Agnes Smedley was summoned from nearby Lintung, where she was nursing her troublesome back and her ambition to visit the Red forces. Wang Pingnan and his wife, Anna, were also present. Ting Ling carefully prepared chicken and remembered the evening as a joyful occasion to hear a preview of the material Snow collected for his yet to be written *Red Star over China*. A few weeks later she too slipped out of Sian to join the Red Army. Dr. Wunsch became a much lamented casualty of the Sian Incident.[4]

28

The Home Front

SNOW DEDICATED *RED STAR OVER CHINA* "To Nym." Since Nym Wales was only beginning to be known to American readers, he probably intended to boost Foster Snow's professional name recognition and obliquely acknowledge their marital partnership as writers. He may also have been making amends for an unintentional injustice. Foster Snow had done a considerable amount of work for *Living China*, but the public recognition was almost exclusively his. She later gave a strong hint of pent-up frustration when she described how she felt as he left for Red territory: "I sat down and wrote up a quantity of articles, once my husband was out of the way." Later she compared the impact of China's turbulent politics on her and her husband: "My personality was changing—the impact of China was tremendous on me. I was intensely concerned with everything, great and small, that came up—but my husband had a different attitude—he was a reporter first and only second a participant. After I had done the legwork, he would make a report on it and write letters. He was easy-going and casual and did not take things so seriously as I did."

In June she finished her account of China's modern literary movement that concluded *Living China* as well as a shortened version to be published in London's *Life and Letters Today* with stories by Pa Chin and Chang Tien-yi. She was particularly proud of the July 1936 issue of *Asia* that featured her article on the student movement and her cotranslation of "Poems from Revolutionary China" plus several of her photographs. She saw this issue in print about the same time she learned from Walsh that her poem "Old Peking" was included in the 1935 *Anthology of Magazine Verse and Yearbook of American Poetry*. In June she also sent two articles to the *Nation* along with an accompanying suggestion she would be happy to send regular news stories from China from time to time. That same day she wrote Henriette Herz: "I am very much interested in doing regular work for the *Nation* if possible. . . . When I came to the Far East, you know, I hoped to become somewhat of an expert on this and that and return to New York and get a job as editor of a magazine like the *Nation*, so I should like some such loose connection very much indeed."

She had plans for a book of essays divided into three sections: China and revolution; youth and revolution in China; and art and revolution in China. These essays would give her own explanation of a paradoxical thesis presented by Meadows in *The Chinese and Their Rebellions*: "The Chinese are the most rebellious and the least revolutionary people of all."

At the end of June she attended a memorable picnic at the Summer Palace for Yenching's graduates, minus those who had already gone to Sian and beyond. Then the Snows' Yenching friends, the Prices, invited her to their cottage at Peitaiho again. Jim Bertram was at the Summer Palace picnic and at Peitaiho. Most friends seemed to understand they were not to ask about Snow's absence, still it was inevitable that as his absence lengthened speculation widened. Bertram was chivalrously attentive, and Foster Snow enjoyed his talk of Rilke and poetry. The restful beach did its work, and she felt much restored.

Back in Peking she found Li Min, one of her most loyal admirers among the student activists, in the hospital having her appendix removed. Li's condition was not dangerous, however, and Foster Snow proceeded to plan an adventurous climbing trip of her own to the Diamond Mountains of Korea. Growing up in Utah gave her an appetite for climbing, but she may also have remembered Snow's Yunnan-to-Burma articles that inspired her to seek out their author. On the way to Korea she stopped for a few days at the Allisons, who hosted the Snows' Tokyo wedding and now were posted in Dairen. In Mukden she met John Paton Davies, stationed there as vice-consul, and he gave her a quick tour before taking her to the local club to view a tennis match. A monstrous typhoon gave more than sufficient adventure and danger to her climb of Korea's highest mountain.

Bertram returned to Peking from travel within China about the same time Foster Snow did. She remembered talking with him "of everything under the sun. . . . Jim was far from talkative, he was quite reserved, but he missed not an overtone."

But Foster Snow could not have been home from Korea more than a week or ten days before Wang Ling came calling with Snow's letter from Wu Chi Chen. Wearing a broad grin and conspicuous knickers designed to make him pass for a bourgeois, he quickly won her confidence with a welcome invitation to Red territory. She wasted no time deciding to go back with him. To her surprise Wang was not only pleased but also automatically assumed Snow would be too.

"No, he won't be glad. He'll only be surprised," she responded. "In fact, he'll probably want to turn you over to the police himself for spoiling his vacation."

Wang enjoyed her humor and either deliberately ignored or did not hear her underlying complaint. "He thought of taking me back with him as a surprise for Snow and a favor to him—not in terms of bringing another reporter to the scene."

When she asked if the Red Army would allow her to come, Wang assured her that because of her articles on the student movement she was most welcome. She asked how they knew she wrote them. Wang replied, "We didn't until Snow told us. We used to wonder who wrote them because they were quite sympathetic. Snow made a lot of face for himself, when he told us you were his wife." She suspected teasing humor in Wang's voice.

Her sudden decision forced several other decisions. Jim Bertram was now told about Snow's trip and her plans to join him. He was himself eager to go, both for the journalistic opportunity and to provide her male protection. She wanted him to come, but could not tell him so. His traveling with her would quickly be known and might be misunderstood. "Thus Jim had to be sacrificed on the altar of conventionality." Bertram gave her a red shirt he had worn at Oxford for luck. Eventually she was able in turn to pass the shirt on to Bertram's former roommate, Wang Ju-mei, but that would be on another trip the following year.

She had her hair cut short and permanent-waved, and, like her husband, took several inoculations. The one for typhus caused a severe reaction. She wrote Henriette Herz:

> I have simply tons of good material for articles and for my book and can't wait to work on it, but feel too strong an imperative to take this trip to resist it. Anyway it's all in the line of my said magnum opus, so the time will be valuably spent. . . . I have started at least four books since I arrived in China; and now I thank all the literary gods that I didn't finish with any of them as I hope I have evolved out of the various stages that produce such attempts.

Herz had forwarded letters from Wang Chun-chu, the Dauber, and Foster Snow thanked her.

Finally one evening late in September, Bertram came to call at 13 Kuei Chia Chang to escort her by ricksha to the railway station. She was to meet Wang Ling but not show him any recognition. He would be on the train, but they were not to sit together. He gave her the name of an inn to stay at on their one-night stopover. He would be there too, but they were still not to know each other. She was to go to a particular guest house in Sian, and a Red Army representative would call on her. At her convenience she could look up Chang Chao-lin, the former Yenching student leader now editing the Young Marshal's newspaper.

Liu Ting, who had helped engineer Snow's passage through Sian, called on her soon after she arrived at the Guest House. His dress, golfing tweeds and cap, was as colorfully bourgeois as Wang Ling's, but his reaction to her plans for crossing into Red territory was much cooler. If a truck could get through to the front, she could hide herself in it. If not, she was to go back to Peking and try again later. He seemed to doubt she was strong enough for the journey.

She waited restlessly day after day, hoping there would be space on the "single little conspiratorial truck" that made its way every ten days or so through the Kuomintang police network with its precious baggage. Chang Chao-lin escorted her around the tourist sites of Sian. After two weeks Liu called on her again to say the truck was held up on the other side of the lines and, though he had been unable to find out definitely when Snow was to come out, he was reasonably certain he would have to come out soon. If he did, it would be best for her to have left Sian as her presence might lead police to Snow and endanger all the notes, films, and other items he might be carrying out.

Liu offered her a compensating opportunity, an interview with Chang Hsueh-liang. She quickly came to understand his primary purpose was for her to carry the story she would get from the Young Marshal beyond the control of the Kuomintang censors to the outside world, but she did not want to leave Sian. She sensed some kind of political crisis building. She only later learned Smedley was staying in nearby Lintung, soon to be the site of Chiang Kai-shek's Chaplinesque capture in his nightshirt. It soon became clear she had to accept the offer of the interview and leave Sian.

On October 3, with Chang Chao-lin as interpreter, she called on the Young Marshal and was greeted by his secretary, Ying Teh-tien, who later became one of the Three Musketeers planning Chiang Kai-shek's arrest. The official reporters for the Central News Agency and *Ta Kung Pao* were also present to give her interview the appearance of a news conference. Chang asked her to let him check her copy before she sent it out, and she agreed. The next morning he checked and authorized his answers to her questions. The Sian Telegraph Office, under Nanking control, bluntly refused to send her story, so she took the first train for Peking.

In response to her question about relations between Japan and China reaching a new crisis, the Young Marshal said: China had reached the last extremity, and peace would be decided by Japan; rumors that five northwestern provinces would claim independence and ally with Soviet Russia were false; and he and his officers absolutely supported the movement for the unification of China and would obey the leader—Chiang Kai-shek—in any program of unified resistance against aggression. In response to a question about the student movement that she had loaded by referring to his initiative in the release of forty-six Tungpei students in Peking the previous winter, she reported he laughed and did not seem displeased but said only, "So long as this movement is reasonable and lawful the government must permit it." The next morning he added, "But sometimes the Government has its own particular difficulties in this connection."

In other answers Chang made clear the people would not let the government accept Japanese General Hirota's program for North China and that China could be united only by resistance to foreign aggression. As for civil war, "if the Communists can sincerely cooperate with us under the leadership of the Central Government to resist the common foreign invader, perhaps it is possible that this problem can be settled peacefully as in the recent Southwest case."

She left Sian either on the evening of October 4 or the morning of October 5. Snow arrived in Sian on October 21 from Lochuan. Chiang Kai-shek arrived in Sian on October 22 to meet with Chang Hsueh-liang and his officers and to bolster his campaign against the Reds. Snow would hear about her trip when he arrived in Lochuan, and he would note and quote her interview with the Young Marshal in *Red Star over China*.

Chang Chao-lin returned with Foster Snow to Peking, and on the train both were heartened by the chance company of Colonel Wan Yi, a Tungpei officer who spoke his mind freely and loudly about his deep feeling for the student movement, the need for cooperation with the Red Army against Japanese aggression, Chang Hsueh-liang's indecision, and Chiang Kai-shek's opportunism. Foster Snow published a report of this conversation under a second pseudonym in *Voice of China*, but she resented how it was cut.

Back in Peking she cabled a report of her interview to MacBride in London and wrote "Northeastern Exiles Prepared to Fight Back to the Old Home" for the *China Weekly Review*. In the waiting mail Maxwell S. Stewart of the *Nation* rejected her two articles, chiefly because of the limited interest in China but concluded, "we are greatly in need of a good China correspondent and I am hoping that you will be able to help us out." Henriette Herz had also written. She was soon to marry, and she enclosed a photograph. She was very attractive with beautiful brown eyes. Her comment on the American mood revealed how difficult the home audience might be for the disturbing news both Snows were writing: "If you were here you would find a fairly healthy attitude in the people toward war. You could not sell them the idea of a war for democracy. I think if they fight again they will know what they are fighting for."[1]

In little more than two weeks Snow too returned to Peking with his compelling story of the Red forces that would capture worldwide attention, but that would also overshadow her work even more than anything he had previously written.

29

History and His Story

I am not the person best suited for this enterprise, but circumstances have bestowed it upon me, and I intend to have a stab at it.

—Edgar Snow to U.S. Ambassador Nelson Trusler Johnson

FOSTER SNOW HAD BARELY settled in at home before her husband, still scraggly bearded, surprised her at their side door. Once inside he took a battered cap with a faded red star out of one of the many bundles he carried, put it on, and capered about the room. Home after months of hardship, diligent note-taking, and testing adventure he was happy and triumphant. He knew he carried information of extraordinary historic value. But most immediately he wanted scrambled eggs, Camel cigarettes, Maxwell House coffee, canned peaches, and the mail.

Foster Snow took his films to Hartung's and worried. Hartung was German, but the films were developed with professional care, no questions asked. Snow hoped to keep his return quiet so he could concentrate on mining his rich trove of notes. But just two days after he returned, Jimmy White called from Associated Press. He asked Foster Snow when she last heard from her husband. She told him she heard from him that very day. White said a report had appeared on the AP wire in the States that Snow had been caught writing in his notebook about the Red bandits and had been shot. Snow's father in Kansas City had immediately requested that the AP check in China. That gave Snow no choice.

This was not just a matter of concern for his family. Such incidents could rapidly escalate into matters of international governmental concern. He took the phone and reassured White he was indeed alive. A few hours later he went to the American Embassy to tell his hastily summoned press colleagues he now understood how his fellow Missourian Mark Twain felt upon hearing exaggerated rumors of his death. He had not been shot by the Reds. Indeed he had been treated with great consideration.

Snow's need to acknowledge publicly his return against his own wishes hinted at a larger writing problem. He was an actor in a historical drama whose plotline was even then developing toward a climax he could not control. The Sian Incident and the subsequent Japanese decision to invade Peking, and thus in effect openly declare war on China, were then in the making and would become the appropriate conclusion to the book he had not yet begun to write.

He wrote Randall Gould about the challenge he faced putting on paper what his "still small voice" told him should be written: "Fortunately the *Herald* is liberal and anti-Fascist, though almost as anti-Red, and at any rate will have to pay for what it ordered, whether they like it or not." The Japanese-financed White Russian Press of Tientsin had already libeled him, alleging he was in the "joint pay of Wall Street and Stalin." He recognized many would believe it, but fortunately Harrison Smith had given him a generous advance on the book, "and that at any rate will be an unbowdlerized version."

Immediately after his return he sent a complete transcript of his final interview with Mao to the *China Weekly Review*. Believing it potentially of interest to the American government, he also sent a copy to American Ambassador Johnson, noting the ambassador might like to read what was inside a head for which rewards of two hundred thousand dollars were offered.

Johnson replied the next day:

> I have read the interview with great interest, and am sending a copy along to Washington, where I know it will also be read and appreciated.
> It seems to me that Mr. Mao Tse-tung talks very much like a lot of other Chinese leaders that I have met. But then, after all, his case is not as bad as some of the others, for he has less access to information about conditions in the world than do others that I have met and talked with.

For the next several weeks Snow balanced his need for privacy to write his story against a pressing number of calls from students, friends, and reporters wanting to hear about his trip. Foster Snow remembered he ordinarily did not talk about his writing, but after this trip he was unusually eager to talk. She pressed him particularly about Mao Tse-tung, "Did you *like* him? Was he friendly to you?" "I was his first foreign newspaperman," Snow replied. "I didn't make any enemies that I know of."

She read from his teasing raised eyebrows that of course he had got on famously with Mao, but she only discovered how much the troops he visited respected and liked him when she visited Red territory herself the following year to fill out the collection of biographies he had begun in *Red Star over China*.[1]

Snow left Red territory at the last point guarded by Manchurian forces. Chiang Kai-shek had reason to be suspicious of the Manchurians' devotion to his program of eliminating the Communist opposition, and he was rapidly moving in replacements loyal to his priorities. After Snow returned to Peking, Chiang's program met with snowballing reaction.

In October, Japanese-led Mongol and Chinese puppet troops began invading northern Suiyuan. Predictably a wave of strong anti-Japanese feeling swept the country. The Japanese demanded the suppression of the National Salvation Movement that had grown from the Peking student strikes. Nanking obliged by arresting seven of the most prominent leaders of the organization, including a banker, a lawyer, educators, and writers, all men of national stature. Anti-Japanese strikes took place in Shanghai and Tsingtao. The Japanese brought in their own forces to break them, and Nanking looked the other way. The government suppressed fourteen nationally popular magazines because of their anti-Japanese statements.

In November Chang Hsueh-liang felt compelled to dispatch an appeal to Chiang Kai-shek at the Suiyuan front. It concluded:

> In order to control our troops we should keep our promise to them that whenever the chance comes they will be allowed to carry out their desire of fighting the enemy. Otherwise, they will regard not only myself, but also Your Excellency, as a cheat, and thus will no longer obey us. Please give us the order to mobilize at least a part, if not the whole, of the Tungpei Army, to march immediately to Suiyuan as enforcements to those who are fulfilling their sacred mission of fighting Japanese imperialism there. If so, I, as well as my troops, of more than 100,000, shall follow Your Excellency's leadership to the end.

The Generalissimo rejected the Young Marshal's request. Soon afterward the latter flew to Loyang to repeat his plea in person and to intercede for the arrested leaders of the National Salvation Association. He told Chiang at Loyang, "Your cruelty in dealing with the patriotic movement of the people is exactly the same as that of Yuan Shih-kai or Chang Tsung-chang."

The Generalissimo replied, "That is merely your viewpoint. I am the Government. My action was that of a revolutionary."

When the Young Marshal asked his audience, "Fellow countrymen, do you believe this?," the reply was loud and angry. The Generalissimo made one significant concession. He agreed to visit Sian and explain his plans and strategy in detail to the Tungpei division generals.

Just after Snow arrived back in Peking, Franco called in German and Italian bombers to pulverize Madrid. Night after night the Madrileños responded to the radio voice of *La Pasionaria* chanting "No pasaran! No pasaran!" Just as all seemed lost units of the International Brigades made up of a motley mix of volunteers from many countries, even some from Germany and Italy, came marching to the rescue. It was the high point of the war for the Spanish Republican cause.

Germany and Japan signed an anti-Communist agreement with Italy's unofficial adherence. Italy's opening of relations with Manchukuo particularly angered the Young Marshal. Count Ciano, now the Italian foreign minister, once was a personal friend who had persuaded Chang to admire several aspects of the Italian fascist movement. In a speech to his cadets the Young Marshal declared, "This is absolutely the end of the Fascist movement in China!" The German and Italian military advisers training Chiang's army and air force subsequently became another source of resentment.

But it was a stinging classic defeat the Red partisan forces administered to General Hu Tsung-nan's famed First Army that most convinced the Tungpei army of the folly of civil war. For weeks Hu's army had moved into north Kansu meeting little resistance other than Red propaganda leaflets urging his troops that "Chinese must not fight Chinese." Hu took this as evidence of his enemy's weakness and boldly marched his army as far as Holienwan, where Snow recently visited. There at dusk in a loessland valley the Reds silently surrounded Hu's troops. After the Nationalist bombers were forced by evening darkness to return to their landing fields, the Reds attacked with bayonets and hand grenades from both flanks. Zero-degree weather made it often impossible for the Reds to pull the caps from their potato-masher grenades, so they used them as clubs. The fierceness of the attack caught Hu's army by surprise and resulted in the complete destruction and disarming of two infantry brigades and a regiment of cavalry and the capture of thousands of rifles and machine guns. One entire government regiment was turned over intact to the Reds.

George Hatem wrote Snow with relish about the details of this battle early in December. Hatem was clearly elated at witnessing a real battle and did not mind pointing out what Snow had missed: "I spent four months travelling with 1st, 2nd, and 4th Front armies and this is the only way to see revolution in action." Too bad Snow could not make the trip, "for it was a real life's experience." This trip would have made Snow's material "live." It would have given him "a complete conception of the whole." But Snow was already a famous character at the front. Since Hatem had grown a beard he was often mistaken for Snow, "No harm?"

Just before writing, Hatem was present when Mao read the first part of Snow's interview in the *China Weekly Review*. Mao was pleased but contradicted Snow's report, "we are insisting on universal suffrage which is a fundamental condition of Dem. Govt." Mao also had some reservations about Snow's representation of his views on "class struggle." He insisted, "We Communists will not abandon our fundamental principle of class struggle," to which Hatem added with practical ideological irreverence, "Just don't bring up for emphasis that question, is his diplomatic opinion now." The central concern at the time was the united front. This made old forms of reference to class struggle inappropriate. Nevertheless, Hatem closed with a compliment: "Your work is great on the English side in the publication and it certainly is very timely."

Near the end of November, Snow gave Harrison Brown, visiting from British Columbia, a letter of introduction to Chang Chao-lin, then editing the Young Marshal's newspaper in Sian. The former Yenching student leader arranged for Chang Hsueh-liang to call on Brown the night before Brown left Sian December 9. This was probably the last interview the Young Marshal had with a foreigner before the fateful action December 12. "He [Chang Hsueh-liang] was very steamed up and talked excitedly for nearly an hour," explaining, "even school children are forcing my hand." Brown liked Chang "better than any other prominent figure I met in China but I always regretted he did not give me a hint to stay on!" He doubted Chang knew for certain what was to happen in the next few days, but "he took the trouble to see me as the only opportunity available to emphasize his views to a stranger who was going out."[2]

Before the fall semester Chang Hsueh-liang moved Northeastern University from Peking to Sian. On December 9, the same day Brown left Sian, Tungpei students celebrated the first anniversary of the student movement in Peking with a demonstration. Before daybreak three days later in Peking, completely unaware of the plan to arrest Chiang Kai-shek that same day at Lintung, Peking students began assembling their own demonstration to express their solidarity with the Sian Tungpei students and renew their demands for resistance to Japanese encroachment. Snow, Wales, Bertram, and Mac Fisher were all up with the sun to cover the more than six thousand students who that afternoon marched to Coal Hill, where Mayor Chin Teh-chun spoke for forty minutes with respect and sympathy for their concerns. The students left singing a song new to the streets of Peking, a song that had become the marching song of the Red Army and the "Volunteers Song" of the Manchurian guerrilla forces.

Sometime that evening one of the students brought a hastily printed broadsheet to Bertram. The student's hands trembled as he asked, "Have you heard? Chiang Kai-shek was killed by Northeastern troops in Sian, early this morning."

Bertram brought the news to a dinner party that included the Snows at the home of Ran and Louise Sailer. They were all stunned. Rumors of Chiang's death were common and obviously not always to be trusted, but recent events seemed more and more eerily like Chinese opera, designed for great incidental surprise within a plot that was inevitable. Reassurance that Chiang was not dead followed relatively quickly; but since everyone understood how carefully news was controlled, no one was certain what to believe. Bertram and Fisher both began thinking immediately of going to Sian and contacting their friend, Chang Chao-lin, to get the real story.

In the next few days the Snows were dismayed to see Chang Hsueh-liang cast as a villain in world reaction streaming in via the news services. The Western world seemed to understand little about particular current events in China, but Chiang Kai-shek was simplistically represented as a leader attempting to unite China in a modern government against the opposition of feudal warlords. Chiang's arrest by Chang Hsueh-liang was thus generally seen as a setback to this progressive purpose. The world did not yet have *Red Star over China* to read and little respected and much feared the Communist movement as a factor in the political equation. The Young Marshal's effort to force a united front of all Chinese parties against Japan was ironically seen by much of the rest of the world as only a reversionary step to feudal warlord rule.

For days Snow made several attempts to send out at least the eight demands Chang and his cohorts had agreed upon as necessary to the general's release and basic to a new anti-Japanese united front. But he could not get even these past the censors. It was no surprise when the Japanese suggested the sinister hand of the Soviets behind this event, but on December 16 when Tass reported an editorial from *Pravda,* it was a stab from Brutus. *Pravda* strongly suggested "the well-known Japanese agent, Wang Ching-wei," was behind the Young Marshal's action, and that the latter raised the banner of struggle against Japan, "while in reality he assists the dismemberment of the country and sows further chaos in China."

Foster Snow showed the report to David Yu, then in Peking. Appalled at such a topsy-turvy reading of events, she immediately called the Tass correspondent V. J. Albotin to try to set Moscow straight. Frustrated by the unsympathetic response at the other end of the phone, she insisted Yu go personally to the Tass office and tell Albotin the truth. Overriding his protests that as a Chinese Communist he was not allowed to have any public contact with representatives from the Soviet Union, she convinced him the issue at stake was far more important than ordinary rules of Party discipline. Together they called at the Soviet Embassy, but predictably Yu's written explanation of the true anti-Japanese rationale behind the arrest of the Generalissimo had little effect. It is unclear how far Yu's message penetrated the Soviet bureaucracy, but Stalin had publicly invested too much of his prestige in Chiang Kai-shek as his best bet to keep the Japanese at bay for him to pay much heed.

Another man of mystery entered the plot at this stage. Miao Chien-chiu, also known as Miao Feng-hsia or Miao Feng-shan, had been secretary to the Young Marshal and a leader of the younger officers who early rebelled against Chiang Kai-shek's commands to destroy the Communists before fighting the Japanese. He had openly challenged the Generalissimo on his October visit and in November had first proposed to the Young Marshal the arrest of Chiang Kai-shek as a means of compelling a united front. After Chang initially rejected his plan, Miao left Sian fearing arrest by Chiang's secret police. In Peking, Miao, as soon as he heard his plan had in fact been put into operation, got in touch with Snow. He planned to return to Sian as quickly as possible and asked Snow to go with him providing cover.

Snow already had a load of historical information demanding narrative shape for the world to ponder. He could not afford to put off one task to follow another. Knowing Bertram and Fisher wanted desperately to get into Sian and were unable to find a means of entry, Snow deputized Bertram a special correspondent for the *London Daily Herald* and introduced Miao to Bertram and Fisher only as a friend named Chou who knew Chang Hsueh-liang and was going to Sian. On their first meeting Bertram noted Chou's incongruous lavender-colored spats, but did not suspect his important and dangerous position.

Miao admitted his true role only after they reached Taiyuan where he hoped to arrange for the three to fly to Sian on Chang Hsueh-liang's own plane. Fisher immediately recognized accompanying Miao was both dangerous and could compromise his employer, Associated Press. He decided to make his way on his own, but without success. Bertram stuck with the intense and temperamental Miao and after several risky adventures finally made it to Sian on December 28. It was just three days after Chiang Kai-shek flew out with Chang Hsueh-liang, who had surrendered himself to the Generalissimo in a dramatic gesture of Chinese political fealty that has intrigued the world ever since. Snow sent a packet of introductory letters with Bertram. One, to Mao Tse-tung, was hastily destroyed when Bertram feared he would be searched. A copy of another, to "Dear Charles" [Liu Ting], survives. Snow introduced Bertram as a British journalist whom Foster Snow told Liu about during her previous trip to Sian. "He is one of the family and a fine person. Please give him all the news you have and help him to get it out." Noting "the press is fed with rumors and propaganda which everybody, left and right both, is swallowing completely," Snow typed: "IT IS IMPERATIVE TO GET NEWS OF THE TRUE SITUATION IN SIAN OUT TO THE WORLD. IT IS ABSOLUTELY IMPOSSIBLE TO RALLY ANY SUPPORT FOR THE MOVEMENT UNTIL SUCH NEWS IS FORTHCOMING."

Snow described the *Pravda* and Izvestia reports as evidence Moscow was uninformed, but he worried their reports might demoralize Chang Hsueh-liang. He put the best face possible on the situation and asked Liu to assure Chang this was put out only to try to counteract fascist propaganda that his act was backed by the USSR.

> The important thing for Chang Hsueh-liang and the defense government bloc is that it hold its position solidly, without wavering, until the situation develops to a point where Nanking is forced to let out the real story behind the movement. If Chang falters now, especially if he releases the tiger, not only is he ruined, not only the rest of you are ruined, but the whole united front is shattered beyond repair, and the result can be nothing but disaster for China. If Chiang returns to Nanking without any fundamental change having taken place in the whole situation his prestige will enable him to complete his dictatorship to the point where any sort of opposition in China will be absolutely smothered, and the open announcement of his adherence to the Japan-German-anti-Communist pact and the preparation of China as a battleground for war against Russia will become a fact.

Snow indicated the Sian crisis had moved most "neutral students" to the side of Chiang because they identified the fate of the Nanking government with him, thus leaving students of all persuasions about evenly divided. But he felt strongly if the Young Marshal remained firm, insisted upon his original points, and Nanking began to negotiate, the students would line up behind him. So far Nanking had effectively dominated the news, representing Chang's position as "a rebel bent on destroying unity and the united front, and determined to achieve personal power even at the expense of the downfall of the country." He must give every cooperation to these two newspaper men and see that their news gets out to the world. Snow apologized for being so disorganized and explained he knew only a half hour before writing his letter that Bertram was going. He asked Liu to introduce Bertram to "A.," presumably Agnes Smedley.

On January 2 Smedley wrote. Bertram was a sincere chap, and before long would be sending them "good things—perhaps more to your liking than these things of mine." She advised them not to be discouraged: "I for one was opposed to the release of that bastard [Chiang]. But I am not alone nor are others. I take comfort in knowing that his confidence was broken and his prestige gone. Also—vast supplies of arms, ammunition, foodstuffs lost to him—enough to keep things going for months here. He can't do anything now even if he tries."

Like Snow she recognized an outlet for information from Sian was desperately needed, but the movement there was "very deep." She pleaded to know if the reports she and Bertram were sending were being heard. "We are both broadcasting and we hope against hope you and your friends hear. There is a deep and broad ferment going on beneath the surface. Before long there will be unbreakable force here."

She was half-dead, working from early morning until past midnight "collecting, translating, and putting out 15 to 20 pages of broadcast news reports" each day. She and Bertram were assisted by "two rotten translators who know as much English as I do Chinese . . . one a kid of 18 who wants to be killed on the battlefield right now, the other a gentleman who speaks under the imaginative illusion that each word he utters is addressed to an audience of 100,000 in a high shrill voice, impossible English and grand gestures. Your friend Jim goes nuts, but I went that way long ago." Could Snow please send a translator-typist to help?

She had sent extensive news, including reports from Dr. Ma, in the last mail. "The reports and rumors put out by Tass angered us ALL here. Silence would be OK, or a denial, but why the dirty lies?" She asked them to listen particularly to her and Bertram's coming broadcast of extracts from some of the plays given there. "Did you get the news that Dr. W[unsch] was accidentally killed? A terrible tragedy. The only one. Why just him!" She sent her love and signed, "GOERING."[3]

Early in January Snow wrote MacBride of his disappointment at the *Herald*'s handling of his cables about the Sian affair, but he blamed the censors. He also enclosed a story from a young Englishman in Sianfu, whose "sympathies are obvious in this report, but I have checked the facts with our Embassy, and find that it is substantially correct." At the same time MacBride wrote about the excellent series of twenty-five articles Snow proposed doing on "Red China." On January 14 Snow sent MacBride another story from Bertram and asked MacBride to send him an extra ten copies of any issue of the *Herald* that carried any of the stories from his own series. He had requests from many people to see them, and one or two foreign papers wanted to reprint them if the *Herald* did not object.

Henry Luce was just beginning a news-photography venture that would achieve world recognition as rapidly as had his innovative *Time* magazine. *Life* was still so new and unknown Foster Snow initially confused it with its predecessor *Showbook*. Luce surprised the Snows by paying a thousand dollars for more than forty of Snow's photographs and featuring them in two early issues. Walsh also bought several photos at fifty dollars each for *Asia*.

On January 10 Smedley wrote again sending photos she had taken with film Snow had provided. She asked Snow to have them developed and marketed for her. She also proudly announced her long-awaited entry into Red territory: "I am going in to see my family for two weeks and I take the 5 films with me. These are not enough, perhaps. I will write out things, send to Jim and have him send them to you. Give them publicity. Jim is writing you of Lantien and today's mass meeting. No need for me to do so."

Bertram wrote to "Dear Editor," apologized for being a rotten correspondent, and explained he had been preoccupied with "another job," his radio broadcasts. It had become a bit warm for Smedley, so friends recommended a trip to a cooler region three days ago. Chang Chao-lin had been promoted to a bigger paper, and Chen Han-po was taking over Chang's former job. "And the third of the gang [Wang Ju-mei] may blow in any time—had a letter yesterday." He closed wondering what happened to Fisher.[4]

Snow decided to give a lecture on his own journey into Red territory to answer many of the repeated questions he was getting from friends and acquaintances. Late in January, Foster Snow sent Randall Gould a copy of the talk Snow had already given twice, "once before a discussion group of sinologues and students of Chinese history, etc. and again on January 21 before the Men's Forum of the Peking Union Church."

Gould had pressed Snow for something from his trip, and Foster Snow sent him the speech so he could choose to excerpt what he wanted. Gould surprised them by publishing the entire speech in two long sections, February 3 and 4. The speech divided readily into two parts, a fairly detailed history of the Chinese Communist movement through the Long March and then a description of the life Snow discovered in the soviet districts on his visit. He divided the second part into four sections: social and political organization; economy; character of the Red Army; and policies of the Soviet government. The speech contains the gist of *Red Star over China* minus the biographies and Snow's personal narrative.

About the same time, Snow's stories on the events in Sian brought a charge from T. T. Li, director of Intelligence and Publicity for the National

Government, that Snow too was writing "propaganda" and warning him that appropriate measures might be taken. Snow delayed responding until February 4 by which time he had received copies of the *Herald* carrying his stories. He was also careful to copy his letter to Ambassador Johnson. He found it very ironic his reports were singled out as propaganda when major agencies had carried reports

> that the chief of police of Sianfu was nailed to the city gate by the rebels, that Chang Hsueh-liang demanded 10,000,000 ransom for the release of the Generalissimo . . . that Marshal Chang Hsueh-liang had announced over the radio from Sianfu that he had murdered the Generalissimo . . . that Marshal Chang Hsueh-liang had made a secret pact with Soviet Russia during his last trip to Europe, that Marshal Chang would be executed in Nanking, [and] that America and Great Britain had secured the release of the Generalissimo.

After his long list of sensationalized uncensored news, his protest grew even more telling:

> I question (especially from the government's viewpoint) the wisdom of suppressing entirely the eight-point program of the Sianfu demonstrators. I honestly believe it cannot much help China's prestige abroad to convey the impression that a high official like Marshal Chang Hsueh-liang (whose record of loyalty to the government for ten years has been unquestioned) should suddenly seize the chief executive only out of a whim of personal grievance or the need for ready cash—which as we both know quite well, was not the case.

In his letter to Johnson, Snow suggested Li was in fact more concerned with his stories about the Communist forces than those he filed about the Sian Incident, but to Li he brought in the former only as a secondary concern. Snow closed with an offer that implied the information he now possessed placed him in a very strong negotiating position: "Before you take any irrevocable steps along the lines indicated in that last paragraph in your letter I would appreciate the opportunity of a personal talk with you and with H. E. Chang Chun, for I believe there may be angles to this whole situation (and even about the Northwest) which you may not fully comprehend, which will clarify any doubts you may have concerning the authenticity of my dispatches."

He wrote Johnson with strong conviction:

> After four months with the Reds I have become convinced that it cannot possibly injure China or the Central Government to know what kind of people Nanking has been fighting for a decade, and on the contrary the

lending of a little light may actually hasten some amicable settlement of long-standing disputes. . . . I do believe in my right as an American journalist to tell the truth as I have found it—just as a Chinese journalist is entitled to do in America. In my case I believe it quite enough to describe what I have seen and explain this phenomenon of the Red Army—a task which I feel will supply some much-needed materials of history. I am not the person best suited for this enterprise, but circumstances have bestowed it upon me, and I intend to have a stab at it.

Snow also explained to Johnson he had not expected Gould to publish the whole of his Men's Forum talk, but only to use excerpts: "It was prepared hurriedly, and wasn't meant to contain final conclusions, but to impart the information requested on the subject, 'from the viewpoint of the Chinese Communists'—a qualification mentioned in the introduction, but I'm rather afraid that may be lost sight of." C. E. Gauss, then consul general in Shanghai and later U.S. ambassador to China, had sent Johnson a copy of Snow's talk immediately after publication with this comment: "Apparently written from a standpoint sympathetic to Chinese Communist aspirations, this is the most comprehensive, authoritative and up-to-date account of the Chinese Soviet movement to come to the attention of this Consulate General. It is accordingly believed that it merits the close attention of the Embassy."[5]

Bertram returned to Peking in February. On February 7 Snow sent photos Bertam had taken while in Sian to MacBride. He also told MacBride that he had had "a nasty attack of flu," and was now trying to work overtime on his articles to make up for it. Snow debriefed Bertram on February 11 and took notes. While Snow was writing *Red Star over China,* Bertram began writing *First Act in China: The Story of the Sian Mutiny.* Both essentially finished their books shortly before the Japanese invasion of Peking. Snow arranged for Herz to represent Bertram in the United States, and the American edition of Bertram's book was published by Random House, Snow's publisher. In September, Snow and Bertram left Peking together to find Foster Snow, who by this time had been in Yenan for months significantly adding to Snow's biographies of Red leaders.

Chang Hsueh-liang's price for the release of Chiang Kai-shek, a united front, was essentially met. The danger from Japan was acknowledged as primary, and uneasy terms were arranged for the Communist forces to work within the united front acknowledging Chiang Kai-shek as the supreme commander. The Young Marshal's own fate was not so clear, but for the time he voluntarily surrendered himself to the leader to whom he had persistently proclaimed his loyalty, even while placing him under arrest. The outside world breathed easier again, but those close to the scene recognized this resolution had created many smaller, yet just as troublesome, knots to be tied and untied before the enigma of China's national future was to be made clear.

In *Red Star over China*, Snow told as much of the story of elaborate personal diplomacy and international political pressure as was then available to him, clearly much aided by the information Bertram brought back to Peking. He paid tribute to the political shrewdness of Chiang Kai-shek's maneuvers during the months following his release. Just as those who arrested Chiang in Sian were forced to admit his leadership was essential to China's unity, so by offering his resignation as premier he forced his Kuomintang opponents also to acknowledge publicly there was no one of sufficient stature to replace him. Thus he was able to force through the Central Executive Committee a nationally popular united-front program that made him appear to the watching world a national statesman at the political expense of others less publicly visible.

The potential threat of forces controlled by Chang Hsueh-liang and Yang Hu-cheng joining the Communists to create a powerful northwest bloc was averted. Without the Young Marshal the leadership of the Manchurian forces broke into open conflict. Miao and his fellow young radical officers could not accept the continued leadership of older officers, Wang Yi-chih and Ho Chu-kuo, whom they blamed for their army's shameful role in the loss of Manchuria and who seemed all too willing to cooperate with Chiang Kai-shek's plan to neutralize the Manchurian army by moving it into territory away from any meaningful action. Wang was assassinated, and Ho barely escaped with his life. Nationalist forces assumed complete supremacy in Sian. Bertram recognized it was no longer safe to remain in Sian, and after a final farewell dinner with his old Peking classmates, Chang Chao-lin and Chen Han-po, took a midnight train for Peking.[6]

Snow still saw new opportunities for the Red forces in the ending of civil war: "a certain degree of liberalization and tolerance in Nanking's national internal policies, a stiffening towards Japan, and a partial release of the Soviet districts from their long isolation." The Reds had occupied large new areas during the Sian Incident, including most of Shensi Province north of the Wei River. It was the largest realm they had ever controlled, roughly twice the size of Austria. Though poor, this area was strategically important, providing the Reds opportunity to fight the Japanese to the east and receive Russian supplies from the west. Their leadership and armies were now collected and concentrated.

The short final chapter of *Red Star over China* begins with Lenin's acknowledgment that history often thwarts marxist and nonmarxist prognosticators alike, since even communists are subject to "emotional wish-fancy."

Although the Chinese Communist movement Snow discovered was far more substantial and promising than the Nanking government had wanted the world to see, it still lagged far behind the apparent swift success of its Russian counterpart. Possibly blinded by "wish-fancy," conservative marxists had badly overestimated the revolutionary capacity of the industrial proletariat in such foreign-controlled Chinese cities as Shanghai: "Here you can see British, American, French, Japanese, Italian, *and Chinese*, soldiers, sailors, and police, all the forces of world imperialism combined with native gangsterism and the comprador bourgeoisie, the most degenerate elements in Chinese society, 'co-operating' in wielding the truncheon over the heads of the hundreds of thousands of unarmed workers."

Unable to establish a sufficiently broad base in cities under such domination despite years of frustrating effort, the Communists had been forced to go into the rural districts where "the Communist movement, while retaining the aims and ideology of Socialism, in practice assumed the economic character of an agrarian revolution." This deviation from marxist orthodoxy contributed to a significant diversion of support from the Soviet Union:

> the great help, amounting to intervention, which the Soviet Union gave to Chiang Kai-shek until 1927 had the objective influence of bringing into power the most reactionary elements of the Kuomintang. Of course, the rendering of direct aid to the Chinese Communists after 1927 became quite incompatible with the position adopted by the U.S.S.R.—and here is the well-known contradiction between the immediate needs of the national policy of the Soviet Union and the immediate demands of the world revolution—for to do so would have been to jeopardize by the danger of international war the whole program of Socialist construction in one country. Nevertheless, it must be noted that the influence of this factor on the Chinese revolution was very great.

The price imperialist power, particularly Japan, claimed from the Nanking government for its support in effectively destroying any Communist movement in the cities was the ceding of authority and territory. Japanese aggression thus made it impossible "for the Kuomintang to introduce in the rural areas the necessary capitalist 'reforms'—commercial banking, improved communications, centralized taxing, and policing power, etc—fast enough to suppress the spread of rural discontent and peasant rebellion." Thus the Reds were able through land revolution to take the leadership at least in parts of rural China.

This led to a peculiar ideological stalemate. The Communists argued that Nationalist attacks on the Communists at the expense of liberating China from Japan proved the bankruptcy of bourgeois leadership. The Nationalists retorted that Communist efforts to overthrow the government prevented them from resisting Japan and retarded the realization of internal reforms. But Japan's increasingly aggressive demands made the stalemate too costly to continue and forced an unstable united front, its inner contradictions temporarily minimized.

To attain this united front the Reds recognized the national leadership and authority of the Kuomintang while retaining leadership and authority on problems within the soviet districts and the Red Army. The Reds, however, made clear they were not giving up their ultimate goals of socialism and communism. Whether the truce would work to the advantage of the Communists or the Kuomintang depended upon a great many factors, but Japan's response was crucial. In the spring of 1937 Japan seemed to slow, if not halt, its aggressive moves. This suggested the Communists might have miscalculated the price of the political concession they had made.

But the incident at Lukochiao Bridge, better known to the world outside China as the Marco Polo Bridge, and the subsequent Japanese march into Peking early in July made clear there had been no significant change in Japanese policy. Snow had already sent off what he considered a complete manuscript before the Japanese attack. Thus he wrote his final chapter, trying to understand and explain the implications of the attack in light of what he had already written. Open war between China and Japan previously thought likely now seemed inevitable. Although never openly declared, it had in fact begun.

Consequently Snow speculated the Communists' calculated gamble on the united front might well yet pay off. A war for national independence would empower the Chinese people and destroy a significant base for imperialism. The war was likely "to assume the character of a world war, [that] will release the forces that can bring to the Asiatic masses the arms, training, the political experience, the freedom of organization, and the mortal weakening of the internal policing power which are the necessary accessories for any conceivably successful revolutionary ascent to power in the relatively near future." Whether the USSR would be drawn into such a war and whether it consequently would abandon its program of socialism in one country for socialism in all countries, or world revolution, might well determine whether the Chinese Communists would ascend to power following such world conflagration.

These were speculations. Another of Lenin's observations expressed a safer certainty: "Whatever may be the fate of the great Chinese revolution against which various 'civilized' hyenas are now sharpening their teeth, no forces in the world will restore the old serfdom in Asia, nor erase from the face of the earth the heroic democracy of the popular masses in the Asiatic and semi-Asiatic countries." The social revolution in China might suffer defeats, but Snow believed eventually it would win. If his book proved anything, it proved "the basic conditions which have given it birth carry within themselves the dynamic necessity for its triumph."

He closed, however, with a characteristic step back from such absolutism by reminding those who found such conclusions too alarming that he had begun his chapter with Lenin's skeptical note that those who write the history of revolutions almost inevitably reveal subjective faults.[7]

30

Amid Challenging Distractions

D URING THE MONTHS THAT Snow was writing *Red Star over China* he not only had to wrestle with a rush of significant historical events in China and in Europe, but also endured a host of personal distractions. Perhaps the most bizarre was a macabre murder that took place too close to the Snows' home for comfort. On January 8 the mutilated body of nineteen-year-old Pamela Werner was found in a deep ditch along the road that ran by the ancient Tartar City wall. Foster Snow frequently rode her bicycle along this road on her way home at night.

Pamela was the daughter of the deceased wife of E. T. C. Werner, seventy-two-year-old former member of the British Consular Service and now reclusive writer, and another man. Pamela's heart and lungs had been removed through a surgically neat circle cut in her diaphragm. There was evidence of recent sexual intercourse. She reportedly had an appointment with a dentist, Dr. Prentice, who was rumored to belong to a love cult, and whom the elder Werner accused of the murder. Others suspected Werner himself. Still others noted the body carried the hallmarks of a ritual Chinese murder. The crime was never solved. It did, however, generate a potent mix of gossip and speculation that made the Snows question their earlier decision to take advantage of the were-fox legend in moving into their home on Kuei Chia Chang and lose a little faith in the sense of security and privilege that Westerners characteristically enjoyed in Peking.[1]

On a happier note the reviews of *Living China* appeared over the winter months, and as noted earlier they were a source of pride for Snow to read.

Ambassador Johnson sent a personal congratulatory note. The Snows were invited to become members of a newly formed Lu Hsun Memorial Committee, and Snow wrote a new tribute to the writer whose ironic honesty he found so penetrating and insightful. But he had little time to savor reviews of a book long since finished.

In late January or early February an energetic missionary, J. Spencer Kennard, called on the Snows with what at first seemed a curious request that they edit a "journal of applied Christian ethics." Kennard had one thousand U.S. dollars in pocket contributed for the purpose. Snow was preoccupied. He had given his talk to the Peking Men's Forum on January 21 and was working the material from his trip into a series of articles for the *Herald* and for eventual book publication as *Red Star over China*. But Foster Snow saw an opportunity to test her own editorial ambitions and to take advantage of the wealth of written material being generated immediately around her. Snow's forum talk was originally scheduled to be in the first issue. Bertram could be counted on for something on the Sian Incident, and there were many other possible contributions from the Yenching faculty and writers nearby, not to mention her own unpublished articles and poems piling up.

Organizing clear lines of editorial authority and policy was an expected initial challenge. Ran Sailer talked to Harry Price and then wrote Snow suggesting a realistic understanding:

> I remember your passing remark in answer to mine that you and Peg really *are* the paper, to the effect that if you were you wouldn't run it this way. Can't we have the understanding that you two *are* the paper as far as final authority and leadership are concerned—that the rest of us are most eager to help just as much as we can? The amount of work that you two are doing in trying to work with Kennard and the rest of us can't be as well spent as if you put it into getting things the way you want them, telling us where to get off, where you want us and where you don't, and all that.

Kennard's purpose to establish "a journal of Christian ethics" became comically divisive. Both Snows were skeptical of Christian missionaries, but they believed strongly that democracy was, or at least should be, an evolutionary goal of history, even if they recognized considerable difficulty in defining what democracy might mean in China's then-turbulent politics. Kennard was apparently willing to accept the Snows' democratic beliefs as part of the meaning of applied Christian ethics, but for some time he insisted on "a journal of Christian ethics" as part of the title.

In the midst of this early confusion another young Englishman, in a turtleneck sweater, carrying a long cigarette holder, strongly anti-Nazi and anti-Franco, a former secretary to Labor M.P. Hugh Dalton, appeared. He was traveling through Peking without occupation, and his name was John Leaning. He had never edited a journal, and he certainly had no intention of editing one with the subtitle "Journal of Christian Ethics." Foster Snow liked him immediately. He laughed at the Ogden Nash–style puns then featured in her political poetry, and more importantly since she had also become seriously committed to making her own journey into Red territory, someone else would have to be in charge in Peking.

Leaning was named editor. His religious reservations and lack of experience were disregarded. Although Foster Snow considered him "one of the favored and pampered youths of his generation in England," he was willing to move into a cheap little house that served as both his office and residence. But he drew the line at Kennard's moving in with him to save funds. He and Foster Snow were to make up the dummy for the first issue of the magazine then officially titled *Democracy*, deliberately lowercased and without a subtitle, about two weeks before she was to leave Peking for Yenan. Leaning at the time did not know what a "dummy" was.

That same night Snow went to the hospital to have painful kidney stones removed. Foster Snow and Leaning sat on the floor at the Snow home pasting up the dummy. Leaning persisted in telling Foster Snow why he could not come to terms with Kennard on any matter great or small. Foster Snow began to cry and could not stop. She wept copiously all the while they completed the dummy and then took a ricksha to the Peking Union Medical College (PUMC) to find out how Snow's operation had gone. Her anguish was still vividly remembered decades later:

> I wept for John's cavalier blue-pencilling of my carefully diplomatic sentences that tried so hard to build our little anti-Fascist front among conflicting elements. I wept for China. I wept for the future of England, facing such Labour party fastidiousness while the boots of Hitler's Brown Shirts echoed through Europe. I wept for "The Story of Sian," Jim Bertram's contribution, as I handed it to John to paste up. As for Dr. Stuart's article, I pasted that up myself to keep John's selfish heathen hands off this holy writ.[2]

Snow's operation brought only temporary relief from his kidney stones. Foster Snow left for Yenan on April 21. And the first issue of *Democracy* appeared May 1.

Instead of Snow's forum speech it contained his portrait of Mao Tsetung. This was politically balanced by J. Leighton Stuart's "The Outlook for Democracy in China." Stuart, then president of Yenching University and future American ambassador to China, was a staunch supporter of

Chiang Kai-shek, though he shared the Snows' deep concern with Japanese aggression. In the middle of Snow's interview with Mao, the editors boxed this lonely comment: "In this space was a photograph which we have not been permitted to publish." Hubert Liang, head of Yenching's journalism department, added an article on "Japanese Diplomacy—Dr. Jekyll and Mr. Hyde." Bertram contributed part 1 of "The Story of Sian," and Ida Pruitt added a telling case history from her social work at PUMC titled "The Dowager."

Democracy was intended to provide a forum for democratic ideas ranging across the United Front political spectrum, but to create a vigorous public dialogue the magazine had to challenge government censorship and the threat of fascism that loomed behind:

> Democracy is not now the bright thing it was when Jefferson and his friends penned the Constitution of the United States; or when the British broadened down to the British Commonwealth of Nations. But in the ranks of the great democracies there is now one new member, and the strength it may bring to the World Peace Front is immeasurable. Democracy still means freedom to develop, to move forward; Fascism is reaction, is the negation of freedom. In the struggle of these two forces, there can be no middle way. Democracy for China is not an academic ideal. It is the condition for her national existence, no less of her national salvation. China must have a Democratic united front, or become a colony.

At the bottom of the page concluding J. Leighton Stuart's article the following boxed quotes drove the challenge home:

> The democracies are done for. They are, consciously or unconsciously, centres of infection, carriers of bacilli, and the hacks of Bolshevism.
> > —Mussolini in an interview with the
> > "Volkisher Beobachter," January 1937

> National Socialism is one of the few bulwarks against world Bolshevism—, democracies are only the channels in which the poison runs.
> > —Hitler, in his speech before the Nazi
> > Party Congress at Nuremberg, September 1936

Snow's "Salute to Lu Hsun" was published in the third issue. He called attention to the "rare spectacle" of a man whose death was mourned by people of all classes and political persuasions in China. At his Shanghai funeral: "Thousands of ragged men and women, child workers, their hands roughened by toil in the silk filiatures, the cotton mills, and the dark workshops of the noisome city, mingled with the thousands of soft-handed, educated people— writers, editors, journalists, scientists, teachers, and a vast throng of devoted students, who followed Lu Hsun's wasted body to its grave." He quoted a well-known Shanghai financier, Chang Nai-chi: "Lu Hsun is great because he spoke for the oppressed, and pointed the way for the oppressed to follow. He did not write to vindicate his own grievances. He did not write to amuse the leisure class. He wrote only what the oppressed would want to say."

But in his more personal tribute Snow bluntly described Lu Hsun's position on the issue so sensitive to *Democracy*'s origins, Christian ethics:

> From the beginning he hated feudalism, he hated cant and hypocrisy, he hated corruption. He hated falsehood and pretence, he despised bourgeois complacency and every form of slavery. He knew all these were evil, just as he "instinctively realized" when he first read Dante, that he was "a very evil man." He hated cruelty and injustice, he hated ignorance, he hated compromise, but above all he hated the kind of "tolerance" that excused these crimes of society as "natural." And it was because of this, he once said, that he loved Christ but hated Christianity. Christ, he believed, was as intolerant as Lenin, while the Christian Church was more tolerant than the devil himself.

Ran Sailer's "Christians and Communists" immediately followed and made clear Snow's views on religion were not editorial policy.

The third issue of *Democracy* also contained a book review by M. G. Shippe of *Die Grosse Luge (The Great Lie)*. Shippe was not further identified in this issue, but in the next he also authored an article titled "Sun Yat-sen as a Democratic Leader." There M. G. Shippe is identified as the pen name of a refugee journalist from Hitler's Germany.[3] This seems almost certainly to be the same man that Snow later identified as Heinz Shippe, who also wrote under the alias of "Asiaticus," and who from an orthodox marxist position sharply criticized the political theory underlying *Red Star over China* as Trotskyist.

Just before Kennard approached the Snows to edit his journal of Christian ethics, Snow was also asked to edit a new magazine, *Amerasia*, in New York. Cyrus Peake led a small group of Asian specialists attending the Yosemite Conference of the Institute of Pacific Relations in planning the new magazine, and it was he who extended the invitation that Snow declined.

On April 30, just after Foster Snow had herself left Peking for Yenan, Lu Tsui, the student leader whom Foster Snow dubbed the "Chinese Joan of Arc," unexpectedly renewed correspondence with the Snows from New York. She wrote about *Amerasia*'s new managing editor, Philip J. Jaffe, whom she had only recently met and who himself hoped to meet the Snows soon. Jaffe, his wife, Owen Lattimore, and T. A. Bisson passed through Peking in June on their way to a two-day visit to Yenan. Snow helped arrange their trip, and they carried news and supplies to Foster Snow and Smedley as well as other friends Snow had made among the Red forces.[4]

Foster Snow left Peking for Sian on April 21. David Yu arranged her trip, but passage through Sian to Red territory was now much more difficult than when Chang Hsueh-liang was still in power. Yu traveled on the same train, but in the now-familiar pattern as if they were unknown to each other. He was on his way to a May conference in Yenan. Wang Fu-hsih, the son of the president of Tungpei University, was to be Foster Snow's interpreter and like Yu traveled separately on the same train. The week before she and her friends arrived in Sian a truck in which Chou En-lai was traveling was ambushed. He barely escaped with his life. The United Front had many enemies.

From Chengchow, her first stop, Foster Snow wrote that Wang was "train sea-sick," but she slept like a top and enjoyed her first first-class train travel very much. Reassuringly, Yu was there. She had been reading *40 Days of Mussa Degh*, but found the Armenians horrible people. She hoped Snow would get over his spleen and kidney trouble soon and advised him to take atebrin for his malaria and not to drink beer for at least a month. "You must not think of coming here until all these diseases are cleared up."

On April 24 she wrote again from Sian. After fleeing the Guest House because of strict police surveillance she had been caught and returned: "They know I am E.S.' frau and don't like it & they are furious about the 3 others who slipped out. . . . If you come you must do so with all preparations to leave *immediately* upon arrival. . . . You'd better *not* come in fact. Everything will be done to cause you harm. It's not worth an accident." David Yu, Wang Fu-hsih, and Chen Han-po all were then forced to break contact with her. But she was still determined not to return to Peking without visiting Red territory. Snow's interview of Mao Tse-tung was widely reprinted in Sian. She urged him to get his book out that spring and translated immediately into Chinese before political reaction could make it forbidden to be read.

On April 26 she wrote again. No development, except she had met Kempton Fitch, whose father was a long-established YMCA leader in China, who took her out in a car. The police insisted one of her bodyguards ride in the car with them. "We had a fight with the police captain. The Orientals are extremely unchivalrous." She described what she had learned of the central government's rapid assumption of power from the forces of Yang Hu-cheng and Chang Hsueh-liang. It was rainy, and she felt miserable. "How's Ginger & Gobi? I wish Ginger were here to sink his teeth into my unwanted friends. Well—no more—be sure to get your book out immediately & don't waste any more time because I'm leaving China after this experience!"

Fitch was eventually stirred to anger by the heavy-handed police watch on Foster Snow. He agreed to take her to visit the Red Army office, still allowed to function because of the United Front. There he listened while she was told nothing could be done at the time because of the sensitive negotiations then going on with Chiang Kai-shek. The Red Army had its hands full with the delegates, such as Yu, then coming through to their May conference in Yenan. They would, however, secretly advise their office at Sanyuan of her plans, and if she could get there she had a chance to get through.

Now convinced of the legitimacy of Foster Snow's journalistic interests, though still by no means sympathetic with her political views, Fitch took matters into his own hands. He took her to call on Effie Hill, who was ill in a local hospital and who had previously been driver-mechanic for the famous explorer Sven Hedin. Hedin's well-known fascist sympathies would likely make such a visit politically safe. Hill accepted the challenge and planned to arrange a general's car to take Foster Snow to Sanyuan. She and Fitch were responsible for arranging her escape from the Guest House and making their way to a meeting point near the Drum Tower.

After much confusion Foster Snow made a testing escape from the Guest House and with great good luck met Fitch on a bicycle after both believed their plan had failed. The driver Hill hired refused to go to Sanyuan unless Fitch went too. So Fitch bundled Foster Snow up to look like a man and drove with her to Sanyuan where he insisted on delivering her to the Red Army office. Although he returned to Sian in time to pretend he was still sleeping, his role in her escape was strongly suspected, and Standard Oil decided shortly after to transfer him to Changsha.

Late on the same day of his ride to Sanyuan, Fitch wrote Snow. He enclosed a note from Foster Snow and informed Snow his wife "arrived safely in Sanyuan, and the last I heard expected to go on into Red territory the same day, and on to Yenan the next." Snow would no doubt be amused if he gave "even a slight idea of how burned up the local so-called secret service are here, but not so amusing was the difficulty I had of keeping my own good name here."

Then he good-humoredly complained of the chivalrous role he felt obligated to assume because of Snow's carelessness as a proper husband:

> I have heard that there are women who are good travellers and make the grade in a bit of adventure—but I hope you will pardon me for observing that your wife is not one of these, if such exist, and should not be allowed to run around without the gentle hand of restraint at her elbow. Incidentally, if you ever mention a word of this letter to her, from what I hear here, it would be a very easy matter to have you assassinated

by a Blueshirt—also, if you learn my name, you will recognize the fact that
we are not supposed to be good friends, but of course, political opinions
aside, a lone American always sticks up for another lone American, and
it seems that a young man always assists a lady in distress, so far be it
from me to stray from the path of custom.

Foster Snow wrote her husband from Peng Teh-huai's headquarters near
Sanyuan the next day: "I had a terrible time trying to get here but arrived
successfully. Today I am going to see Ho Lung and then to Y[enan]." She had
only a minute to write and still get her note off, but she assured him she felt
swell, "not sick at all." Peng Teh-huai and Lo Ting-yi sent their regards.

On May 3 Snow complained he had not yet received any of her letters
but did receive a wire designed to mislead the police. He addressed a coded
letter to "Pat" and noted the writer had received letters from "Arthur." It also
noted Pat might be seeing Jim before she finished her holiday, which Foster
Snow took to mean Bertram might be on his way. But then he playfully tried
to further confuse the police by adding to her fiction:

> It's certainly amusing that the police dog *your* footsteps! You know the
> manager there in your place, Chou, even wrote to Leaf down here that
> you had arrived and intended to go to the Red districts. This is just as well;
> let them go on thinking so, and the police, too: as long as they think that
> you are the one to look after, and not Arthur, everything should be okay.
> Arthur says that the police don't even know he is there in Sian; they think
> he is still in Peking. In fact I think you had better encourage the police to
> stay around you. One thing is certain, as long as they keep men watching
> you, they will never find Arthur. Meanwhile Arthur can arrange his trip
> to Yenan, and all the time the police will be watching you, and when
> you return to Peking they will think they have accomplished something.
> Apparently they think you really want to go there, eh the fools.

Earl Leaf, another American correspondent had recently visited Sian and
Yenan, and Foster Snow's early letters often referred to the reports he made,
which at the time threatened to rival Snow's.

Snow closed his letter expressing concern for his wife's health and then
buttered his complaint with extravagant sentiment: "I wish you would write
to me once in a while, and tell me your exact condition. Do you think I could
possibly help any if I came up to see you, or do you think it would just decoy
the germs from you to me. That would be good, if possible. Ah, I love you so."

In May, Foster Snow wrote from Yenan. She had had a septic sore throat
and spent two days in bed but was better when she wrote. Many there were
eager for Snow to come and be "grounded in the present denominational
situation," in effect to hear their side of the confusing United Front politics.
A different route into Red territory could be arranged for him, but she questioned whether it was worth his while considering how quiet things were. She

urged him to send food for Ma Hai-teh, whatever Smedley had requested, and parcel post for Mao. She complained there was no one to translate for her and wondered if he could send someone.

A few days later she advised him that Cheng Ken, once a noted officer in the Kuomintang Northern Expedition and a Whampoa graduate, was concerned about what Snow might say of his role in Chiang Kai-shek's arrest. He particularly did not want Snow to mention his role in once carrying Chiang Kai-shek off the battlefield. Although still very uncertain about her plans, she suggested she might come home in two weeks. She urged him to send his *Herald* articles and photos, "They want 'em."

Snow continued to complain he had not had a letter from her since her arrival at "threeyuan" (Sanyuan). He had hoped to leave for Yenan on May 15. Dave's friend had come to see him, but had no "constructive suggestion." He doubted whether he could get sufficient information to justify the trip, but he was trying to arrange for "L." and "B." to go. "L." and "B." referred to Lattimore and Bisson, who traveled to Yenan with the Jaffes. Leaf was "the foliage man," already glutting the market with his reports of his recent visit.

He sent the second issue of *Democracy*, but the magazine was facing a serious financial crisis unless an angel appeared: "Ask our friends in there whether they are sufficiently interested to contrib anything to save the life of our child." It had received damned good reviews, and subscriptions were coming in. Powell was also in Peking and very curious about her absence. "Poor old JB actually thinks we're a coupla conspirators I fear and lost souls. Has become more rabidly antichrist than ever."

Snow had finished a draft of his book, but it needed editing, probably taking out about thirty to forty thousand words. "Now that I've done I'm afraid I can't say much for it. Bits are surprisingly good reading, other parts trite. I'll try to eliminate the latter in editing."

He wished he knew how long she planned to stay. His own plans were held up. If she were going to remain in Yenan for some time he might come for a month or so, but he was not eager. He advised her to collect all the material she could on "the long hike." Walsh indicated great interest in this topic at home.

He was sending edibles, books, magazines, and newspapers. He closed: "We miss your companionship, criticism, and help and are all tired of this single existence. Gobi and Ginger insist on coming with me if I go; otherwise we expect you to hurry home."

Wang Fu-hsih carried to "Fasuta" a long list of items for Marie (Smedley) and Shag (Hatem). But the long separation and the apparent failed delivery of mail was taking an emotional toll:

> Wang tells me you got your stuff through from Sian so I suppose you're
> not in need of anything especially. At least you could write me for it if
> you were, and till you do to hell with you. You might at least have sent
> me a note to say you arrived in Y. okay. Haven't had a word for nearly
> a month and I'm getting disgusted; worried like hell after I heard about
> the incident of Chou and the tufei [bandits], and not till yesterday did I
> definitely hear you'd arrived safely. . . . Would appreciate a note, if only
> a few scribbled lines, telling me how long you intend to stay, so I can
> make my plans accordingly.

Late in May after finally receiving one of her notes that he complained said very little, he told her *Democracy* had been "warned by the highest authority it was publishing material 'favorable to the uni front.' " That this was cause for complaint made clear the repressive policy then in force against publications, and "anybody who imagines the large fellow isn't behind it is cockeyed or a liar." Chang Chao-lin was back in Peking. "I never saw him so deeply in the doldrums."

While Snow did not believe things were as bad as they seemed, he was not happy with the public statements coming out of Yenan. He was concerned the Reds' political base had eroded severely in the last four months, and this fit neatly Chiang Kai-shek's policy to reduce them to a mere "military problem." He asked Foster Snow to question whether the Red leadership realized this: "Can you stop their diarrhea of vapid manifestos for a while and get a realistic reply to such questions?" He closed: "Come back soon, before the new weipao [encirclement] begins. I don't want to go to Turkestan after you."

On June 9 Snow wrote Jaffe in Sian. He had just learned Jaffe had been told Foster Snow was in Yenan. Snow had been careful to follow his wife's stern command to tell no one, but now that Jaffe knew, he was sending a note for the latter to carry to her in Yenan. He also asked Jaffe to buy chocolate, tinned fruit, coffee, a flashlight, batteries, and other supplies for her. He planned to send Jaffe a twenty-dollar check, but then thought better of it and expected Jaffe to make the purchases and accept payment later when he could mail him the money more safely.

He wrote Foster Snow that since he had received no more news from her, he had drawn money to fly to Sian and go into Yenan with the Jaffe party when a girl, An, appeared with a letter from Mason. An apparently reassured him his wife was all right and "didn't wish to bother to write." That sparked more indignation: "That's all right if you go somewhere else but damned inconsiderate and selfish under present circumstances. I can believe you are busy but not that busy. Anyway, I assume you need nothing or you'd have written for it. An and Wu tell me nearly everything can be bought there now.

If you want to come back you'd better return with the friend who brings this, as it should be safer that way; the roads none too secure I hear."

He was busy revising the last four chapters of his book to fit recent developments:

> The obvious historical meaning of the twelvetwelve [date of the Sian Incident] is now very clear: direct transfer of leadership and upgiving of it in the natmovement and the bourg rev for possibly many years to come; that, and nothing more. It weakens the whole structure of my book very much, but that's nothing. Ck's diary reveals very clearly the whole situation and the decisive vic[tory] of his position is now abundantly manifest. Perhaps unavoidable; anyway the xians could not do much to alter it; only no use not recognizing what's happened.

He wondered again when she was coming home and closed:

> This one-sided correspondence is becoming tedious so I'll write no more till I hear from you. But if I don't hear from you by the end of June I'll send the marines in after you. Tell the folk there to send me some news once in a while. Have had nothing for weeks, but maybe it's being seized. Regards to marie [Smedley], lt [Li-teh], hai [Ma Hai-teh], mausie [Mao Tse-tung], wu [Wu Liang-ping], etc. No need to come back till you get everything you want but let me know your will and when you are returning. Love you mug. Esther[5]

31

More Mixed Messages
between Yenan and Peking

W HILE THE LETTERS OF the Snows reveal their mounting frustration and anxiety, Brian Hall, Snow's London agent, sent initially discouraging news about the prospects of *Red Star over China* in England. Jarrolds declined their option, and Routledge, frightened of its length, could not come to a decision until they saw the whole text: "I am not altogether happy about the prospects of 'selling' China at the present time. Interest in Europe is so much greater, and though a certain number of books on China have appeared, they have not done well, and publishers are a little shy. Routledge said that if they made an offer for the book, it would probably be dependent on their coming to terms with Random House for the production costs."[1]

But just around history's corner events in Asia were about to explode. The unexpected savagery of the Japanese war on China that began less than a month after Hall's letter—the invasion of Peking, the bombing of Shanghai, the sinking of the U.S. gunboat *Panay*, and the internationally shocking rape of Nanking—all backgrounded by the movie version of Pearl Buck's bestseller, *The Good Earth*, just making its way before an almost compulsively sympathetic public, made 1937 a turning point in world attitudes toward China. *Red Star over China* would benefit hugely from this attention and give it new energy and focus.

On June 14 Foster Snow sent fourteen boxes of film to her husband: "A. has many good pictures. Mine not good." She complained she had not yet seen

Mausie but might the next day. The whole previous month had been devoted to conferences. She felt sidelined. She did not know whether to advise him to join her or not. A history of the Red Army was to be ready in August. She hoped to get some part of it. *Democracy* was well received, but she thought the second issue rather dull. She hoped he might consider renting a temple in the western hills for a month where she could rest and eat canned American food on her return: "I am very afraid of getting sick here—typhus or dysentery etc. as the town's full of disease so I'm very careful about eating & hence hungry. I am going to fry a chicken now as the potatoes are all gone here now. The rest of the non-Christians here live exactly like the Chinese & like it but I am not yet an expert at this life."

On June 18 Foster Snow wrote that the four missionaries from Peking were expected any day. Cheng Ken had again expressed concern about what Snow might publish as his biography. He was going into United Front work and did not want his role in the arrest of Chiang Kai-shek published. Chou En-lai arrived by plane that day in Yenan. The Red Army history was going to be twelve volumes and not available until August 1. A Nanking delegation came to Yenan on May 29 and viewed the Red districts for two days. Rain had cooled off the hot weather and brought relief. She had collected thirteen life stories but was unhappy she had nothing more for her time and effort.

Snow learned Jaffe had all his luggage sent to Shanghai, indicating he was not coming back through Peking. He sent Jaffe ten dollars, which he hoped would cover the purchases he had asked him to make in Sian. Snow was glad he had not traveled with Jaffe and his friends, because this "damned kidney of mine has been leaking ever since you left." He was still chagrined that many people knew his wife was in Yenan while he had carefully guarded her secret. Jaffe left him thirty dollars to line up something promising for *Amerasia*, but he had not yet found anything suitable. He was turning over another thirty dollars Jaffe had left to *Democracy*, "which seems to be the worthiest cause at the moment."

Late in June, Foster Snow received the angry letter her husband sent with the Jaffe-Lattimore-Bisson group, and she responded in kind. She did not understand why he had not received the letters she sent to the box, but there was no news in them anyway. She had been lucky to meet Hsiao Ke, Hsu Hai-tung, and others from the front when they came in May, but endless conferences left no time for her to get personal interviews. On June 10 Mao had promised to write a short handbook of the Chinese Revolution with her, but he since had had no time. Her first appointment with him was at nine o'clock on the morning the foreigners came. He also had promised her the last chapter of his autobiography, but she had not yet received it. She had been waiting without results for thirteen days, but he now promised to work with her as soon as the foreigners left.

She had meant to leave with the Jaffe group, but there was no room in their car, and "they don't especially want me to travel with them apparently for political reasons, and I can't get the interviews I want in time." She hoped to take three days to visit Ho Lung before she left Red territory. She was sending thirteen notebooks, with other things inside, and some films back with the foreigners. She then detailed her frustrations and complaints:

> My trip from a news point has been ruined completely by various things, also my pictures etc because I could not get any local cooperation to get the work finished and away. I dope it out that the Chinese thot the foreigners were helping me (which they have not in the least) and the foreigners thought the Chinese were, so as a result nobody has done anything much. As I thot when I left Peking, one would not be very welcome here without bringing a lot of tinned goods to the local Aryans, and you have not sent anything to HT [Hai-teh] for a year particularly, nor the things Marie asked for by mail. Nor have you sent any of your articles nor any big pictures. I asked you a hundred times to send your articles here and you have done nothing about it. PJ [Philip Jaffe] bought the things for me you asked him to in Sian but you didn't give him any money so he gave them to Marie instead as a personal gift. I have not seen anything whatsoever to eat here except the local food except the chili and fruit which you sent with WL [Wang Ling], and I can't imagine where you get the idea that "everything" can be bought here or that when I climbed out of a window I was able to take a truckload of food with me. However, as you know, I pay no attention at all to what I eat so except for starving it doesn't bother me in the least.

She described living in a compound with Li Teh, Ma Haiteh, Wang Ju-mei, five bodyguards, two mafus, and two horses. The others ate together. She ate at the restaurant when she was hungry. Smedley was ill and lived separately in a cave on a hill. She had shown not the least sign of wanting Foster Snow to live with her, so Snow's idea "of having me move to a more respectable place because of your personal satisfaction is not feasible as well as a nauseating and sickening and typical remark." Furthermore she did not have the slightest idea who An, Mason, or any of his other funny friends were. He should give up their Peking house and store the furniture as she had done the previous summer. She did not want to spend the summer in the house and was in no condition after this trip to do so.

Without skipping a beat she attacked the political thesis he outlined for his book's conclusion:

> I don't know what you did to the last chapters of your book about Sian, but you will make a lot of enemies if you say what you did in your letters

about the UF position here and it may be very harmful for them also. They depend a lot on international support for this line and in fact it has little other meaning now. They here regard Sian as a "military plot," both Mao, Chou, Po Ku, etc. all of them, and leftists are called Trotskyists now. They here are optimistic about the negotiations with Nanking and think no mistakes have been made in the Northwest except minor ones.

Warming to her task, she added: "Chou En-lai was irked that you published the interview with him stating the information about radio stations and that the R [Reds] had discovered all Nanking codes, etc. He said this was meant to be secret and he did not personally give it to you that he remembers anyway. He is afraid you are going to publish names of commanders and forces which he gave you confidentially, so be careful about this."

Since he had been forced to wait in Yenan for a month before leaving she thought he should be more understanding of why she did not know when she could leave. Since mail could no longer be sent he would have to wait to learn about her return until she could wire him, probably from Chengchow: "except that I have no money for this now but only barely enough to get home by train left and don't [want] to borrow after you didn't pay back what you borrowed yourself before in a similar situation."

Foster Snow's "doping out" of the situation for her being so neglected seems revealingly innocent in retrospect. There was another, and more cogent, reason for her being isolated. In addition to the increasingly ominous threat of Japanese invasion, Mao had something else on his mind, something Foster Snow glimpsed but thought trivial at the time. Late in May she was a guest for dinner in Smedley's cave along with Smedley's notable translator, Wu Kuang-wei, or Lily Wu, and Mao Tse-tung himself. Wu cooked peppers and scrambled eggs while Smedley ordered "cabbage soup and such," and small *shao-ping* cakes from the restaurant. Foster Snow roasted potatoes outside. Viewed from Smedley's cave, dusk that evening seemed as pretty as a Maxfield Parrish painting. Mao watched Smedley sprinkle her flower garden. Savoring the smell of cut roses in two vases, he asked Foster Snow which flowers were most prevalent in America. She told him roses.

A company of troops drilled bayonet practice in the square below, their shouts ringing across the valley. The troops singing "Dixieland" prompted Foster Snow to teach her present company the Stein Song, but Wu already knew it. Then Foster Snow recorded an unmistakable scene briefly: "We sing a lot of old songs & Mao lies on the kang on Sm. roll of bedding which is Jim Bertram's (I gave Wang Ju-mei his red shirt.) When food ready we drink pai kerh & Lily gets tight & I & Mao says he has had too much & holds hands with Lily all evening & she leans on his knee in a very familiar way

& S coughs all time but wants to try to cure it & always has good black tea—Lipton's."[2]

A month earlier Smedley sent Snow a gossipy letter that backgrounds this scene. To bring a little life to Yenan's social scene Smedley taught Ho Lung to fox-trot. Other Red leaders quickly became willing students, but their wives, led by Chu Teh's, rebelled and tried to get the dancing stopped. Smedley wrote of Chu Teh's wife, "She's peasant, like most women here, so I suppose she considers it a kind of public sexual intercourse." Smedley had little sympathy for these wives and was clearly proud when Chu defied the proposed ban: "It takes someone as strong as a commander-in-chief to defy some of these women here." Mao still seemed a "damned lovable sort," a "dear brother," to Smedley: "He says that if he ever goes abroad, he will go to study dancing and singing,—that he wishes to learn the latest fox-trots!" She added sardonically, "I think he should leave his wife here if he does."

Snow apparently heard more about the consequences of these developing conflicts when he came to meet his wife in Sian in September but did not publish the story until many years later. Soon after the scene noted in Foster Snow's diary Mao's domestic life blew up, and Smedley was banished from Yenan as a consequence. She resented Mao's role in that banishment the rest of her life and probably did not hesitate in September to give Snow the details of what she considered his unmanly behavior. Before sending the story to the Japanese magazine *Chuo Koron,* in 1954, Snow sought the advice of friend and fellow writer Berry Berrigan. Berrigan recommended publication. Perhaps because the story was published in Japanese, and Japan was then still far from being the world power it is now, the story received very little attention. Foster Snow apparently never learned of it. By that time she and Snow had been divorced for five years.

Snow began his story with a tribute to Smedley, who had died in London a few years before and named him her literary executor. Angry at the gender barriers that had restricted her freedom, she could not respect women who defined their life roles as selfless supportive wives, content to remain in the background of their husbands' achievements. Such women were an insult to their husbands as well as to themselves.

Lily Wu also saw herself as an emancipated woman. Foster Snow recorded Wu's own description of her separation from her husband: "We are still married. My husband is progressive but inactive, like so many other Chinese. However, I feel that I cannot waste my life on ordinary family affairs. House-work is trivial, and there are important things to be done in China, requiring that women take leadership in action, as well as men. It is better for both the husband and wife in progressive circles to do their own separate work."

Wu was an actress and teacher trained in traditional Chinese drama who became more and more interested in modern theater and particularly "dramatics as a form of mass education." She arrived in Yenan on February 19 without the wear and tear of the Long March. She quickly became notable for her acting talent, her relative cultural sophistication, and her beauty. Both Foster Snow and Jaffe commented on her performance in the lead role of Gorky's *The Mother* in June. Jaffe published her photo in his *New Masses* article resulting from his Yenan visit. She also served as translator for Earl Leaf on his earlier visit to Yenan. With such views and background she probably became a friend and ally to Smedley as well as an interpreter. She was a willing and able partner in teaching the male Red leaders how to dance.

In her May 31 diary entry, after noting Mao told her he was too busy to see her for ten days, Foster Snow wrote, "A. is always playing solitaire—she tells fortunes & is very amusing & *we can't find a single 'dangerous' woman in Yenan as rival to Lily* except Ting Ling who is too fat now & A & I fight over Hsu Hai-tung—Mao is amused" (italics added). Foster Snow drew a questionable conclusion from this and the previous quote from her diary in *My China Years*: "Lily Wu was . . . looking at Mao with hero-worship. A bit later I was stunned to see Lily walk over and sit beside Mao on the bench, putting her hand on his knee (very timidly). Lily announced that she had had too much wine, and, as she appeared to have been affected to the point of foolishness, it seemed to be a simple fact to me then; I could have remembered that she was a professional actress."

Foster Snow represented Mao as in effect an innocent victim of a designing Lily Wu. There were few women then in Yenan among a multitude of eligible bachelors. Her account suggests strongly she was not aware, even in 1972, of the story Snow told in *Chuo Koron* in 1954 of Smedley's sleepily hearing Mao padding into Wu's cave late one night only to be rudely awakened later by Mao's wife's shrill vituperation as she followed and confronted the two. It was clear to Smedley that Mao was very curious about the Western concept of romantic love. He questioned Smedley closely about her own relation with Chattopadhyaya, and, in her eyes, his poetry markedly improved as he explored the subject. Lily Wu officially served as translator for these conversations, but Smedley distinctly felt Mao's words were frequently directed *at* Lily rather than *through* her.

Snow also noted in *Chuo Koron* that Dr. Shag Hatem had been courting Lily Wu until he was called upon to treat her following the incident in her cave. Realizing his courtship was getting him into politically deep water, he then backed off. Snow does not identify Hatem further here. His nickname was probably used as a thin veil to those not in the know. Snow publicly explained Hatem's presence in Yenan later in his 1958 revision of *Red Star over China.*

Mao's wife, Ho Tzu-chen, was pregnant with Mao's child and became bitterly distracted by what was happening to her marriage. She would not be silenced or mollified. The crisis that ensued led to harsh consequences for herself, Wu, and Smedley. Smedley's biographers refer to the Lily Wu affair as taking place in July. Mao canceled an interview with Foster Snow on July 7, the day of the Marco Polo Bridge incident. Her observation of Mao and Wu's hand-holding was probably near the beginning of the affair. By September, Ho, Wu, and Smedley knew they were banished from Yenan. Smedley told Foster Snow she was ordered to leave with the first group out. This was part of the Party's price for Mao to receive his divorce.

This event takes on greater significance for the future history of Mao and China, because another actress, then known by the name Lan Ping, entered Yenan just as the Mao–Lily Wu affair reached its crisis. Within a year Lan Ping would become Mao's next wife and eventually one of the most powerful women in the history of modern China. Ironically Lan Ping had been introduced to communist political thought in 1933 by the same David Yu who helped smooth Snow's way into Red territory. Yu and Lan Ping lived together in Tsingtao for some time in a nonregistered marriage. They separated amicably, and Yu would provide a key recommendation for Lan Ping as she moved into important political circles in Yenan. Ross Terrill described the relation between the two romantic episodes in Mao's life: "At first by chance, later consciously, she [Lan Ping] profited from the breakdown of the Mao-Ho marriage. And she built upon the ruins left by Lily Wu's fall; Lan became a shrewder and luckier successor to Wu, a fresh 'embodiment of Western romantic love.'"

Foster Snow was also distracted from Mao's womanizing by the story of Kim San, a Korean Communist working and studying with the Chinese Communists in Yenan. She first met him in the Lu Hsun Library where she was surprised by his omnivorous reading. When she learned he was Korean, she was intrigued and cultivated his confidence by questioning him about his homeland and its modern history. Sometime in July she persuaded him to tell his personal story, which she recorded in seven notebooks. John Day published *Song of Ariran* by Nym Wales and Kim San in 1941. It became Foster Snow's best-selling book.[3]

Shortly after the Jaffe-Lattimore-Bisson group brought Foster Snow's letter and notebooks to Snow in Peking, the Japanese, impatient with signs that Chiang Kai-shek might change his appeasement policy, created the incident on July 7 at Marco Polo Bridge that served as an excuse to invade Peking in force. After an exchange of claims and counterclaims, Chiang Kai-shek on July 19 astonished many of his critics with a surprisingly strong declaration:

> Now the point of conflict—Lukouchiao [site of the Marco Polo Bridge] —has reached the very gates of Peking. If we allow Lukouchiao to be occupied by force . . . the Peking of today would become a second Mukden; the Hopei and Chahar provinces would share the fate of the four Northeastern Provinces. . . . *We seek for peace, but we do not seek for peace at any cost. We do not want war, but we may be forced to defend ourselves.*

Red policy following the Sian Incident, of which Snow was so originally skeptical, now seemed vindicated. On July 26 the Japanese bombed the village of Lanfang and presented General Sung Che-yuan in Peking an ultimatum for the withdrawal of Chinese troops from much of north China. A day later General Sung rejected the ultimatum as unreasonable, and military war between Japan and China, though still undeclared, began.

It quickly became too late for Snow to take his wife's advice and close up their home. It was sorely needed as a place of refuge for professors and students on Japan's blacklist. Among them was Wang Fu hsih's father, the president of Tungpei University. Snow also soon agreed to let the Manchurian students set up a shortwave radio in the compound. Number 13 Kuei Chia Chang became something of an underground headquarters.

Nevertheless, by July 23, just before the Japanese invaded Peking in force, Snow arranged to send a large shipment of canned food to "Peg and/or Marie." He sent only a brief accompanying note trying to restore a tone of civil good humor to their correspondence, but he clearly had read her grievances:

> The local office complains of the large shipment, and hereafter I will be able to send only small quantities, mostly condensed food. Let me know what you want most. Of the above items I got the sausages especially for LT and the coffee for HT., but you will all have to share it according to the principle from each according to his ability to each according to his need. There are also two combs and two knives inclosed. Please give one of the knives to Wang Ju-mei. Let me know whether you receive this okay. Did you get the last lot I sent July 5, and the shipment before, about June 15? Please give something out of this to mauzzie and wife from me. Tell mauzzie also I'm sending him the money earned by his biography— which will be considerably better than his $5 monthly. Will write him by the next courier. Thank him for his letter.

Snow wrote a much longer letter just a few days later, July 26, the day before the Japanese began heavy bombing of the last military outpost protecting

Peking. He wanted Foster Snow to reassure Cheng Ken he had cut out the chapter describing his role in the arrest of Chiang Kai-shek. She should also reassure Chou he had cut the chapter about him as well. These changes might delay publication in America until next spring, and he might have to pay for the changes: "Too bad that of all your letters *that* one had to reach me."

Cheng Ken's story is published many years later by Snow in *Random Notes on China*, where his name is corrected to Chen Keng. Chen was a Whampoa graduate and once a well-recognized leader of the Northern Expedition. His story is rich in details of arrest, torture, and oblique forms of bribery and appeals to Whampoa loyalty. Snow intended it as an example of the "tactics and kindly treatment and persuasion" Chiang used to turn Red officers, particularly Whampoa cadets, back to the Kuomintang. His story included the tidbit that Chou En-lai had criticized Chiang as such an inept horseman his presence on the battlefield proved more an embarrassment than an inspiration. Snow obviously regretted omitting such colorful material, but rather than endanger the budding United Front he chose to make such journalistic sacrifices.[4]

Snow now realized and admitted he probably had received all the messages his wife had written, but he had expected fuller letters rather than brief memoranda and could not yet make out either her plans for leaving or her current health. It was probably better she had decided to stay on. It was witheringly hot in Peking and now impossible to move into the Western Hills because of the war. He had to cover the fighting for the *Herald*. He had resigned from the North American Newspaper Alliance in protest over what he thought was their refusal to print any of his stories from his trip. He learned later his stories were not being printed because of a dispute between the *Sun* and the *Times* in New York, both of whom claimed exclusive rights.

He advised Foster Snow he was still living at Kuei and invited her "to come up and see him sometime." He sent her another seventy dollars in case she had not received the last one hundred dollars. He also sent a check for one hundred dollars to the Sian Guest House for her expenses. He would send more, but he had no great confidence she would receive it. He enclosed a clipping about the purges in Moscow and suggested: "Here is a good story, if you can get an interview from someone there answering questions of attitude toward this, and what it means . . . and why this wouldn't happen in China."

By August 12 Foster Snow had received his letter and the money he sent, but the food had not yet arrived—no truck had come through for some time. She was worried her letters had been intercepted, and there was now a file in Sian "to prove something or other when I get there. A cameraman was taken in custody three weeks ago and everything removed." She had only sketchy information about the routes available for her to get out and where it was safe for her to go after she did get out. Maizie (Mao) had asked her to wait three weeks for an important statement, but she did not have much confidence in his promise. Maizie would also like Snow to come and work in the field for several weeks. She did not know what to advise but thought Yenan might become the center of the situation. She asked if they could continue to live in Peking or had to move to Shanghai. If the latter she suggested he might store their things and come to Yenan. No transport would be available for three weeks, and she still hoped for the important information Mao promised. "I have had chronic dysentery and been miserable generally for different reasons, but am not sick at the moment."

On September 3 she was able to send him Mao's promised news:

> The name is the "8th Route Army" of the National Revolutionary Armies of China, just like all others. CT [Chu Teh] is Commander in Chief (this was a moot question for a long time as Nanking wanted their own man and also their own political head), and Peng TH is Vice-Commander. All are wearing KMT hats now. The whole army is now clothed and fed by the KMT—and no more star or insignia, nor will the rouge flag be used at the front. The elections began July 15 slowly and will be completed about the end of October, at which time the "Shen-Kan-Ning" Bordering Districts Government will be inaugurated. Election is universal suffrage. (Incidentally M and the political people are not yet wearing KMT mautzers [*mao tzu* or hats, in contrast to the military people who were already wearing KMT hats]. M. gave me an interview two weeks ago but still it can't be published—it says nothing anyhow of great importance. I send herewith the ten point program as given by M. to me at that time. . . . The Jap advance has electrified this place and solved all political problems. The army is prepared to go to the field any day—if not sooner.

She was not able to send her letter immediately. It had been raining steadily for four days and promised the best harvest in thirty years if the rain did not ruin it. On September 6 she typed more on the same page. She reviewed her food problem and how it led to her dysentery and then added another version of how Smedley wound up with the food Jaffe bought in Sian: "I gave what J. brought to Marie, for which she didn't even thank me but thought it was brought by him for her of course." This was followed by the handwritten note: "Here I left for Sian."

Just before her final note she received a radiogram from Snow from Tientsin reading: "YOU CAN STILL RETURN VIA TSINGTAO BUT URGENT YOU LEAVE IMMEDIATELY OR CANNOT RETURN THIS YEAR." He and Bertram had then just arrived in Tientsin en route to Sian hoping to locate her. Bertram also hoped to cross into Red territory. The two had provided cover on the train from Peking to Tientsin for two Red political refugees, one a cadre who posed as Bertram's secretary, and the other, Teng Ying-chao, the wife of Chou En-lai. The latter traveled disguised as Snow's amah and clearly would have been a distinguished political prize for the Japanese if discovered. She had been recuperating from tuberculosis in Peking's Western Hills when the Japanese took over the city. Israel Epstein, who had kept close touch with the Snows and the student movement, arranged passage for Snow and Bertram from Tientsin.

After finishing his book on the Sian Incident, Bertram traveled with Pruitt through Dairen and Seoul to Tokyo. Bertram stayed in Tokyo after Pruitt returned. He was still there at the time of the Marco Polo Bridge incident but hastily returned to Peking just in time for the Japanese march into the city. On the evening of July 27 he had dinner with Ivor and Dorothea Richards, who were staying in Owen Lattimore's home in the inner city. Richards read aloud from a recent William Empson poem appropriately foreshadowing the occasion:

> It is the Chinese tombs and the slag hills
> Usurp the soil, and not the soil retires.
> Slowly the poison the whole blood stream fills.
> The waste remains, the waste remains and kills.

They talked of Julian Bell, mortally wounded in Spain just a week earlier. Bell drove an ambulance picking up casualties in the battle of Brunete. A Frenchman interrupted their talk carrying a leaflet advising them to take shelter in the British Embassy at once. They awoke next morning to the Japanese bombardment preceding the invasion of Peking.

Bertram remembered that during the strange interlude following the Japanese entry into the city on August 7 Snow had somehow obtained the use of a handsome limousine that he decked out with American flags and enjoyed driving past Japanese sentries. He also remembered Snow keeping plunder from a Manchu tomb under his bed, plunder taken by the Chinese resistance who then asked Snow's help in turning it into hard cash for their cause. Snow accepted the task in return for the resistance fighters' freeing some Italian friars they had captured in the Western Hills.[5]

While in Tientsin waiting for a ship to Tsingtao from which he and Bertram planned to go by rail to Sian, Snow wrote a by then rare letter to his father. Apparently to keep his father from worrying he wrote he was heading for Shanghai rather than Sian. Perhaps that was also why he made no mention of Foster Snow. But he was broodingly dour as he once more tried to explain to his father why he had not yet kept his many promises to come home. The war "doomed" him to life as a newspaper correspondent. He had to stay and see it through, but he was tired, not just of war, but especially of the Orient. He could

> remember how two or three or four years ago the prospect of covering this epoch in history, of being in it and perhaps in a small way helping to make it, would have gripped me as no other writing assignment I could think of; but since then I have seen so much of little wars, and come to realize that all wars are much alike, so far as human suffering and brutality and stupidity are concerned, whether big or small, that reporting one seems a rather sordid and unglorious business. And especially this one. Here you can't hope for any spectacular and just victory on the side that should win, but at most only for a display of greater endurance at hardship and misery, of one lot of wretched human beings sitting on its dunghill without completely suffocating, longer than those on the equally fetid opposing dunghill can do. And yet to be ruler of one's own dunghill is important I suppose, and worth dying for, because if the other people win one is simply ground down into and becomes something indistinguishable from the dung itself.

He thought the future course of the war fairly obvious. China could not hope quickly to confront and defeat Japan's modern military machine, but with its huge extent and population it could make the war an economic disaster for Japan through long, tenacious resistance. He thought it likely a third power or powers would intervene in the second year of the war. That third party might well be the United States:

> but the real key to the situation will lie with Russia. Whether Russia will use that key, whether it will intervene to the point of risking war with Japan, depends very much first of all on developments in the Soviet Union itself, and then in Europe, and finally in China. But I think Russian intervention, in one form or another, will come, and be decisive. Very much however depends upon the endurance and staying power of the Chinese; it is a war of exhaustion, and if China collapses too quickly (as Japan confidently counts upon her doing) the possibilities of the war developing tangents in the form of third-power participation will be ruled out.

He did not expect to be home before the war ended. He still had *his* house in Peking, and he probably would keep it despite Peking's occupation by the Japanese who had no love for him. He tried to assure his father he knew as well as anyone how to avoid unnecessary risks, and he warned him against thinking the worst if he did not hear from him over long stretches of time. "Though we have been separated a great many years, you and Mildred and Howard are closer to me than anyone else, and I shall prove it by staying alive and coming home shortly for a reunion."[6]

Before leaving Yenan, Foster Snow talked to Mao about visiting the Shansi front and persuaded him to write a letter for her to Teng Hsiao-ping. She was then provided with a bodyguard, a military escort, a pony, and two mules to carry her baggage. Smedley suffered a painful back injury when her prized horse, a gift from Chu Teh, fell sometime in August. Her back needed to be X-rayed, but she doubted she could take being carried on a litter for ten days. Nevertheless, she was ordered to leave with Foster Snow. Smedley had already given Foster Snow "her few small treasures with instructions for their disposal, bequeathing her silk stockings to me personally. (I still have them.)"

Despite her troubles Smedley was still an intimidating figure to Foster Snow. She not only appropriated one of her suitcases but also bluntly asked how much money she had. When told one hundred dollars, Smedley demanded it, saying, "You can borrow some here but I can't." Her closest supporters, Chu Teh and Ting Ling, were at the front. Foster Snow meekly handed her money over and borrowed another sum from Chou En-lai, unaware her husband was even then performing a more than compensating service for Chou's wife.

Their traveling party swelled to about thirty, excluding the armed escort and those in charge of the horses. The wives of Chu Teh, Hsiao Ke, and Po Ku among others went with them to join their husbands at the front. During the trip to Sian by way of Sanyuan relations between Foster Snow and Smedley warmed considerably.

In Sian their party went directly to the Eighth Route Army headquarters where Foster Snow met Teng Ying-chao and learned of her brief masquerade as amah to Snow. Teng invited Foster Snow to share her small room that night. Concerned that her Sian visa expired September 18 Foster Snow moved the next day to the Guest House where the manager, Mr. Chou, welcomed her now as a romantic celebrity.

After she confirmed Snow's message that the railroad to Tsingtao was still open, Foster Snow gave up all further thought of going to the front as a war correspondent. The Eighth Route Army arranged a special permit for her to travel on a troop train, and she left Sian on her thirtieth birthday, September 21. She wrote a note to her husband before she left reassuring him that two weeks on wonton during her trip from Yenan to Sian had cured her dysentery. She was amply protected by one Red bodyguard and three "spies from the Sian police." Her train was headed for Hsuchow, Tsinan, and Tsingtao, but she wondered how they could get through since the Japanese had bombed Taiyuan a day or so ago and Chengchow and Hsuchow expected the same. She might stop in Tsinan to visit Allison Davis. She was not sure where Snow was or when she would see him.

Even as she wrote, Snow and Bertram were on a train heading for Sian. They arrived four hours after she boarded the train in the opposite direction. When Snow learned at the Guest House she had just left, he called ahead to Tungkuan to arrange for her to return to Sian. Tungkuan was Chiang Kai-shek's military headquarters for the northwest. When Foster Snow was ordered from her train, she feared the worst. She was wearing a life belt of notes and films under her coat, and those who came for her refused to even look at her special pass from the governor.

A half-hour ricksha ride through dark and desolate streets ended not at some secret Gestapo outpost as she feared, but at the China Travel Service Guest House. The manager rang Sian and handed her the phone. It was her husband's welcoming voice asking if she was all right and telling her to take the next train back to Sian. She later wrote this "reprieve from terror" was the best birthday present she could have received.

Snow and Bertram's entry into Sian also had its complications. At the railway station they were asked for their visas. Bertram still had his endorsed by the old Hopei-Chahar Political Council, which was by then defunct, but the police were happy to accept it. Snow, however, had a brand new passport from Peking with no visa for Sian. He patiently explained since there was no Chinese government functioning in Peking, he could not get a visa. This satisfied the military but not the civilian Special Police. He was told he must leave without delay on the next train. As his resentment and frustration began to wear thin, he suddenly thought to ask when the next train left. After admitting it was not until late afternoon, the detective consented to let them go to the Guest House. It was the break he needed. Once inside the city he counted on and received the help he hoped for from the Eighth Route Army.

At the Guest House, Manager Chou welcomed them with the news of Foster Snow's recent departure and Smedley's present residence. This prompted Snow's call to Tungkuan. Chou called the Eighth Route Army headquarters, and Smedley, proudly wearing her army uniform, soon entered the Guest House to greet them. She asked about their plans and told Bertram the difficulties he would face getting into Yenan. She hoped to go to Taiyuan where Chu Teh had his headquarters. Her respect for Chu had not diminished.

Snow and Bertram met Foster Snow's train at 2 A.M. the next morning. Chou waited up for them at the Guest House and proudly gave Foster Snow the same room she had escaped from months before. They broke out a bottle of brandy Bertram was carrying to Li Teh and celebrated their reunion.

The Snows left Sian the next day on a train headed for Tsingtao, much to the relief of the Special Police. The *London Daily Herald* expected Snow to get down to Shanghai where the Japanese had already opened a major second front in the spreading military conflict. At Hsuchow the Snows changed trains. They asked about a wrecked train they had seen not far from the city. The wreck was the result of Japanese bombing, and many passengers had been killed. It was the train Foster Snow would have been on if Snow had not had her called back to Sian from Tungkuan.

At Tsingtao they decided they deserved and needed a vacation. As the only guests at the Edgewater Beach Hotel they enjoyed the good food and the beach for ten days before Snow went on to Shanghai and Foster Snow returned to Peking to see what had happened to their home and possessions at Number 13 Kuei Chia Chang and to get medical treatment for her troubled stomach. But even in Tsingtao the war was too close to ignore completely. Snow called on the mayor, Admiral Shen Hung-lieh, in part to ask why he was not moving valuable Japanese industrial machinery inland before the inevitable Japanese takeover of his city. Snow received an evasive answer, but after he arrived in Shanghai he was gratified to learn the Chinese did demolish Japanese industries estimated at a value of about 200 million yen with dynamite and had set fires before evacuating the city. It was the first evidence the government's much talked about "scorched earth" policy was put into practice. Snow's concern with the value of this industrial machinery was also a harbinger of a new, grandly ambitious venture that he, Foster Snow, Rewi Alley, and friends would within a few months begin planning in Shanghai: the Chinese Industrial Cooperative Association.[7]

32

Seeds Planted in
Shanghai's Garden of War

FOSTER SNOW SPENT HER first few days back in Peking at the German Hospital where the doctors found that she suffered from amoebic and four other kinds of dysentery. Despite the glare of Hitler's portrait hanging in her room she recovered. Malcolm MacDonald, a *London Times* correspondent, like Snow, had been ordered to Shanghai to cover the Japanese attack, and his wife invited Foster Snow to move in with her from the hospital. MacDonald was on board the USS *Panay* on the Yangtze in December when it was sunk by Japanese bombers. His story of that attack appeared on the front page across the world, stimulating particular national indignation in America. At the MacDonalds, Foster Snow packed the invaluable collection of notes and papers she and her husband had accumulated into forty boxes to take with her late in November to Shanghai.[1]

Snow arrived in Shanghai about the same time that the *London Daily Herald* announced the publication of *Red Star over China,* a "historical document of the first order . . . as exciting and enthralling a tale of exploration as anyone can want to read."

About two weeks later Bennett Cerf confirmed rumors that Random House "was preparing a sensational book that would make the entire Chinese-Japanese situation completely clear to American readers." A few excerpts from the book had appeared in the *Saturday Evening Post,* and the *New Republic,* while *Life* had printed several pages of the author's photos, but the most sensational parts of the book were still to appear, and Random

House had rejected all offers for further serialization. Although Gollancz already had its Left Book Club edition on the market, Cerf announced *Red Star over China* would be published in England and America on the same day.

Shanghai in 1937 quickly reminded Snow of Shanghai in 1932. He saw the Japanese again making a tactical blunder in opening a second southern battlefront. Despite their previous experience they were once more surprised by the stubborn resistance of Chinese troops defending the city.

This time, however, the Japanese commitment to invasion was total. When the flank of the Chinese forces defending Shanghai was finally turned, the Japanese army marched straight on to Nanking. There the army began an orgy of rape and looting in Nanking on December 12 that obscenely exposed the official Japanese pretence of entering China in Pan-Asian friendship to liberate it from European colonial power and save it from communism. For Snow the barbarous behavior of the Japanese soldiers made clear the "physician and the headhunter still exist side by side" in the Japanese army. Japan was attempting "to colonize not a semi-civilized people but a nation in many respects more advanced than herself." Its triumph could bring China nothing but degradation.

Meanwhile Snow was again reminded that war in Shanghai was unique because of the strategic position of the International Settlement. Nowhere else could a journalist have a "ringside seat at a killing contest involving nearly a million men." Foreign military observers, with cameras and notebooks, flocked to the scene. One could even take a city bus to the front.

But in this war, as in most, the combatants were not always the master of the technology they used. Early on, Chinese planes mistakenly dropped their bombs on innocent crowds of people gathered in the city's main shopping areas, many naïvely gawking at the aerial warfare as if it were a heavenly spectacle. More than two thousand were killed or injured. Photos of this carnage shocked the world, even as *Red Star over China,* often coupled with Bertram's story of the Sian Incident, *First Act in China,* began receiving very favorable reviews throughout England and in much of the rest of the British empire.[2]

Soon after Snow arrived, he learned an old friend, Marine Captain Evans Carlson, had returned to Shanghai. Carlson's original assignment to China in 1927 was a last-minute surprise. He landed, like Snow, with no special interest in this strange land. But by the time he and Snow became friends during the next year, his curiosity had been stirred. In 1929 he was sent to Nicaragua to combat the guerrilla forces of Augusto Calderon Sandino, for which service he won two distinguished decorations. In March 1933 his request for reassignment to China was honored, and he was quickly en route to his old job as intelligence officer of the Fourth Regiment in Shanghai. However, Shanghai, dominated by its International Settlement, no longer satisfied his curiosity about China any more than it did Edgar Snow's. He moved to Peking, where he and his wife, Etelle, were soon happy to rejoin Snow and meet his new wife.

The Carlsons particularly enjoyed the high culture of Peking. He and Etelle joined the Snows as guests of Helen Burton in the Temple of Flowering Fragrance that she rented during the summer in the Western Hills. He became adept at polo and taught a class in American literature. He started a class in Chinese language, history, and culture for the Peking Legation Guard and was happy to learn the incidents of men subject to disciplinary action dropped from one hundred a month to ten, and morale dramatically improved.

Before the student movement erupted, Carlson was returned to the United States, promoted to captain, and made an aide to Major General Charles Lyman, and second in command of President Roosevelt's Warm Springs detachment. He was allowed to return to China in the spring of 1937. President Roosevelt personally asked Carlson to send him his private observations. For Roosevelt it was not an unusual request, but the president's expression of interest heightened Carlson's sense of mission as he again met Snow in Shanghai.

During the night of November 8 the bulk of the Chinese army evacuated its positions on the Shanghai front and retired toward Soochow. The next day Carlson inspected the military situation along the front with U.S. Naval Attache Commander Overesch. He was surprised and stirred to find five or six thousand Chinese troops continuing to resist the Japanese in what was then a hopeless military situation. After an hour and a half of fierce battle a few of the Chinese successfully crossed a creek at great risk and escaped into the French Settlement to be interned. Those who did not surrender then retired to the east.

Returning to the International Settlement for lunch, Carlson found a message from Snow inviting him to the latter's hotel. He found Snow with MacDonald and insisted on taking both Snow and MacDonald to the site of the battle he had just witnessed. MacDonald in particular was eager to follow the retreating Chinese forces to see if any of the battle continued. At the southern end of the French Concession they climbed to the first of two platforms on a water tower to look over a wall to the south just as firing again broke out. The Chinese were in the open while the Japanese had taken cover inside nearby buildings. After several minutes of brisk battle they realized a steady stream of machine-gun fire played on the side of the tank above. No matter the tower was within the supposed sanctuary of the French Concession.

Carlson circled the base and saw from a second platform above, the toes of Western shoes pointing down indicating their owner was flat on his stomach. He wondered who the shoes belonged to, but the intense firing continued for another twenty minutes before the Chinese wheeled about, dashed for the wall, and made their way through a maze of barbed wire into the arms of waiting French troops to whom they willingly surrendered their weapons. It was only then both Snow and Carlson noted blood dripping from the upper platform. Carlson quickly climbed a ladder to find seven men laying flat and motionless, heads buried in their arms. He spoke testingly. One raised his head slowly and whispered, "Are the Japanese here?"

After Carlson reassured the speaker it was safe, five of the others, over-hearing, got warily to their feet and descended without a word. Carlson and the man who spoke bent over the remaining body laying in a pool of blood. The latter pronounced the prone man dead before producing with surprising decorousness a visiting card that introduced him as Dr. Richer. Carlson respected Dr. Richer's civility and handed his own card in return. At that point another young man approached and identified the body as Pembroke Stephens of the *London Daily Telegraph*, his boss.

Both Snow and Carlson knew Stephens only slightly, but they understood the occasion of his swift death only too well. They toasted Stephens that evening with a bottle of Napoleon brandy Soong Ching-ling had sent Snow a week earlier when she was forced to evacuate her home in the French Concession. Their conversation turned to how China could effectively resist a modern army such as Japan's after losing most of her industrial capacity concentrated in the cities along her eastern coast. Snow had probably not yet seen a published copy of *Red Star over China*. Nevertheless, he eagerly told an interested, but skeptical, Carlson about the Red guerrilla tactics and the Red leaders he had met. Carlson had grudgingly admired the military shrewdness of Sandino even as he chased him around Nicaragua, but it was Snow's enthusiastic description of the social commitment of the Red generals that seemed to Carlson too good to be true. But Snow knew his man, saying, "Why don't you go and see for yourself?"

Carlson's blue eyes narrowed as he thought if only it were possible. Then Snow made it possible. He sent a query to Mao Tse-tung. A response came quickly. Carlson was welcome if Chiang Kai-shek consented. Commander Overesch readily authorized Carlson's plan. In Nanking, on Thanksgiving Day, only three or four weeks before the Japanese attack on the city turned into infamous pillage and rape, Carlson had in hand an impressive document, fourteen inches long and sixteen inches wide, with the great red seal of the Nanking government's Military Affairs Commission at the bottom authorizing his visit to the Communist forces.

By Christmas, behind Red lines at Hungtung, where Chu Teh had established his headquarters, Carlson overcame Agnes Smedley's initial suspicions and played "The Marine Hymn" and "Silent Night" on the harmonica while she sang. He had been given permission to go to Wutaishan, where Peng Teh-huai's forces were fighting fiercely, while Smedley once more had to resentfully endure being refused the same opportunity because she was a woman. For Carlson it began an eventful journey that would lead to his becoming a legendary American hero in the South Pacific fighting the Japanese in World War II.[3]

Back in Shanghai, Snow wandered through the devastation with another old acquaintance who would also soon become a significant friend for the rest of his life. Rewi Alley, originally from New Zealand and tellingly named by his parents for a Maori chieftain, had first arrived in Shanghai in 1927 just days after the massacre of Red leadership. Snow first wrote about Alley in 1929 while witnessing the nightmare effects of drought and famine in Inner Mongolia. Alley's selfless commitment to helping others impressed him deeply.

Alley later appeared often in Snow's published accounts of his China experiences, usually cast in a role deliberately contrasted to Snow's own. Snow portrayed himself as the morally stunned, ingenuous writer-observer; Alley, the capable and experienced, but unselfish and dedicated, volunteer. While Snow came out of Saratsi to write about his shock and indignation at the human devastation he observed, Alley came out of Saratsi with an adopted son orphaned by the disaster. Two years later Alley, helping rebuild the Yangtze dikes after a monstrous flood, added a brother for his son to his family. Alley's first son, Alan, eventually was elected president of his class at Shanghai's St. John's University and was in Peking applying to Yenching University when the Marco Polo Bridge incident triggered the Japanese invasion.

Alan returned to Shanghai just two days before the bombs first fell on Shanghai's downtown. He and Mike, the second son, were caught in the bombing as they returned from Medhurst Academy where Mike was going to school. Alan caught a fragment in his left arm and was separated from Mike. Each feared the other dead in the carnage, but both found their way to the home of Manny and Grace Granich, editors of the *Voice of China*, with whom they had been staying while Alley was on his tour of factories in England and America. Alley returned to Shanghai about the same time Snow arrived from Tsingtao. Shortly after Alley returned Alan and Mike told him they were leaving school to go to the northwest to fight the Japanese. Alley could only give them his blessing. Snow obviously admired, and maybe even envied, Alley's bachelor family.

As Snow and Alley walked among the factory ruins the latter made the story of the devastated machinery vividly personal:

> "That's Chang Chi-lin's new boiler," he would dourly observe. "I made him put it in not long ago; the old one was a menace. Wonder if the poor devil is under that mess?"
> Or we would come to a pile of quite undistinguished bricks through which you could see broken furniture or a torn wheel or lathe. "Yang Hsin's electric goods shop," Alley would volunteer. "I told him to put guards on his machines a few months ago. He waited till two of his workers lost their fingers. Suppose it doesn't matter now."

Alley knew the personal history of hundreds of the little workshops destroyed and the life stories of thousands of workers in them.

In *Battle for Asia,* his next book, Snow would blame China's loss of industrial capacity in Shanghai in 1937 on the rightist massacre of 1927 by explaining how the earlier devastation of labor leadership left the workers of Shanghai impotent and leaderless ten years later with costly consequences: "Had the workers been mobilized and properly led, thousands of tons of machinery, tools, and metals could have been carried out of Shanghai between July 7th and the fall of the city."[4]

J. B. Powell was with Snow on the Shanghai customs jetty to greet Foster Snow in a cold late November wind when she handed her husband her luggage manifest. He whistled his disapproval, "You've got nearly forty boxes of useless stuff here. Who's going to pay all the transportation and storage on this junk?" It had become a familiar complaint since their honeymoon. Snow introduced his wife to Alley the first Sunday after she arrived, and Alley in turn took her on a tour of the devastation as soon as the Japanese allowed. Foster Snow was immediately impressed: "He was modest, diffident and sweet-natured, though always he was God's Angry Man in the John Brown tradition, anxious to free slave labor however it might be done."

The shared concern of all three for China's industrial capacity became gathered tinder waiting for a spark, and the spark came from John Alexander, a young British consul, who one night over dinner drew on his experience in Scandinavia to emphatically declare: "Cooperatives are a democratic base in any kind of society—capitalist, socialist, communist, or what have you. There's no argument against them, for anything can be built on such a base." Foster Snow apparently shared the initial skepticism and indifference of the others at the dinner, but that night she dreamed about cooperatives and awoke the next morning seized with the idea as a democratic means of renewing China's industrial capacity.

She took the idea forcefully to both Snow and Alley, and they too soon began to find authority and reason in the idea. An October 25 interview of Mao Tse-tung that Bertram sent from Yenan on November 3 provided political encouragement. It was a lengthy policy statement, thirty-five typed pages, carefully phrased and translated. Alley acknowledged to Ida Pruitt many years later it was one of two documents that made him believe in the value of industrial cooperatives. The second was Mao's statement, "Urgent Tasks following the Establishment of Kuomintang-Communist Co-operation," dated September 29, 1937.[5]

Bertram forwarded his interview to Snow to be published and later noted: "I do hope you got the interview all right; it will break my heart if you didn't." Since there also was a large section of the interview devoted to the Eighth Route Army and its tactics, it seems likely Snow shared the typescript not only with Alley but also with Carlson.

The interview opened with a soft-pitch question from Bertram: "What was the response of the Communist Party to the outbreak of war between Japan and China?" Mao's answer made clear Japanese aggression had to be the overriding concern of all the Chinese people:

> We repeatedly pointed out the errors, both of those who believed the Japanese assurances of peace, and thought that war could be avoided; and of those who believed that without the mobilization of the Chinese masses, this country could resist Japanese aggression. . . .
> All this indicates that our line of strengthening the United Front, and realising a revolutionary policy in the anti-Japanese war, has been maintained consistently and without relaxation. In this spirit, all our slogans and manifestos have been concentrated on this one point—to realise a *nationwide, inclusive war of resistance* against Japanese imperialism.

Bertram added a note: "The word 'inclusive' is used here to signify a war in which *all elements* of the people take part; it is not to be confused with General Goering's doctrine of 'total war,' of which the basic feature is the indiscriminate slaughter of 'enemy' civilians, women and children."

Bertram's second question was in fact two: What should be China's foreign policy, and what was Mao's opinion of the policies of Great Britain and the United States toward the Far East situation? Snow drew a line next to Mao's answer, giving it special prominence on the typescript. Mao noted the generally favorable international attitude toward China and cited "the friendly atmosphere at Geneva, the speech of President Roosevelt on October 5th," as particular instances. But he also noted that so far this goodwill had been expressed only in words, not action. Great Britain and the United States were particularly important, and, notwithstanding their supportive words, they had in fact aided the fascist aggressors by not backing their words with action. Now that fascism threatened the democratic powers themselves, an international peace front was needed. He hoped in the interest of international peace the favorable public disposition toward China in these countries would be intensified and widened "to influence the governments of these countries towards some positive action to restrain Japan."

Later, speaking of the lessons to be learned from the first few months of the war, Mao noted the political weakness of China: "The *elements* participating in the war are still one-sided, because we have still only a war waged by the government and regular troops, not a war of the whole people . . . there is still no common program of consolidation for the whole nation." The war had to "be waged with every means at our disposal—military, political, economic, educational, diplomatic, propagandist, etc."

Mao's insistence that the Communist Party's primary mission under these circumstances was to strengthen the United Front prompted a tougher question from Bertram: "What is the precise meaning of the Communist slogan of 'Democracy' at the present time; and is this compatible with war-time government in a time of crisis?" When Mao answered with three Party policies, including one that called for a government structured by "democratic centralization," Bertram persisted, "But is not democratic-centralization a contradiction in terms?"

Mao denied it, saying both were then necessary for China: "The government we desire must be thoroughly representative of the people; it must have the full support of the broad masses of the Chinese nation." In war, policy needed to be executed quickly, but the government executing the policy needed to be representative of the people. Only then could it be strong. As Bertram continued probing this question, Mao observed all wars could be divided into "revolutionary" or "counter-revolutionary" wars. When people are forced to fight against their own interests the result is a "counter-revolutionary" war. World War I was for him an example of an "imperialist," counterrevolutionary war. But there had been revolutionary wars, "the first wars of the French Revolution, the war of the Soviet Union against foreign intervention, and the war of the Spanish people today. . . . If the aim and object of the war is in the direct interest of the masses, then the more democratic the government, the better the war will go." To support this belief and despite the Kuomintang's calling off a proposed meeting of the National Congress, the Communist Party was then calling for an emergency meeting of a more broadly representative National People's Congress as a transitional measure to the establishment of a more permanent democratic government.[6]

Mao Tse-tung's endorsement of a democratic United Front to resist Japanese aggression highlighted the potential value of an industrial cooperative movement. As Alexander had emphatically declared over dinner, cooperatives are intrinsically democratic, both economically and politically, no matter what kind of society within which they are incorporated. They could appeal both to the Kuomintang and the Communists. They could provide practical technical training and employment to a desperate, displaced people and so give the Chinese people an "inclusive" sense of national purpose and unity in resisting Japanese economic and military encroachment. They could be an institution foreign governments and peoples could support without taking sides in China's internal political contest.

Organizing such cooperatives quickly became an ambitious dream of the Snows, Alley, and others, though most of those initially involved were wise enough to recognize they were putting their idealistic faith into a political arena notorious for chewing up innocents. Almost from the beginning it was tacitly acknowledged the movement would have to be built around Alley. He had the practical experience. His integrity and dedication were tested and widely acknowledged. It was to be his life and career most immediately on the line, though if the movement were to grow and ultimately have the hoped-for national and international impact it would require extraordinary dedication and sacrifice from many. So for the next three years it also became an idealistic tar baby from which Edgar Snow could not, or would not, free himself. While much of his support for the movement was open and public, he also very deliberately kept much of his extraordinary activity behind the scenes.

33

Snow's Star Rises in the West

THE *LONDON TIMES LITERARY SUPPLEMENT* sniffed only a grudging respect for *Red Star over China*, finding it "repetitive, ingenuous and far too long," but admitted it was "of considerable interest to the student of Far Eastern politics."

> Mr. Snow struggles gamely to be objective, but can be held to have succeeded only on the assumption that every Chinese who follows Lenin is "cute, hilarious and indomitable," whereas the three or four hundred millions lead miserable and degraded lives under the Nanking Government. For all that, he is a competent reporter, with exclusive access to some highly valuable information; he will be read with interest—and a grain of salt.

But *Red Star over China* proved its popular appeal by rapidly going through three English printings in its first month. Reviews almost immediately appeared in town and city newspapers throughout Britain, even throughout the British empire, and most were far less grudging in their respect than the *London Times Literary Supplement.*

Random House brought out its American edition in January 1938. The *Saturday Review of Literature* carried a photo of a youthful and handsome Snow on the front page of its January 1 edition. Inside David H. Popper wrote:

> *Red Star Over China* deserves the accolade which will be bestowed upon it by students of social experiments, Far Eastern experts, and devotees of

journalistic reminiscences. It would be a significant book if it were simply the saga of the Chinese Communists' dramatic struggle to maintain their beleaguered government against five smashing Kuomintang offensives. It would be a first-rate tale of heroic adventure if it did no more than chronicle that master military achievement of modern times—the incredible six-thousand-mile march across all China to the far Northwest. It would be an illuminating social document if it were only a biographical account of the Chinese Soviet leaders, a record of the evolution of Soviet policy, and a description of the Reds' achievements. In all these fields it blazes new trails for the historian.

Popper included Bertram's *First Act in China* in his review, noting it described "an isolated though crucially important episode in Chinese history," but he concluded it was inevitably overshadowed by Snow's work.

Popper's praise was by no means exceptional. A week later Clifton Fadiman in a *New Yorker* review titled "A Marco Polo out of Red China" wrote:

At any rate, whatever one's feelings about Communists or one's notions about the rights and wrongs of the present Sino-Japanese struggle, Mr. Snow's story should stand as one of the most important and readable pieces of fundamental journalism of the last decade. I should say offhand that it is impossible to understand today's headlines from the East without having read "Red Star Over China," and I recommend it without reservation.

Malcolm Cowley followed soon after in the *New Republic*: "To Edgar Snow goes credit for what is perhaps the greatest single feat performed by a journalist in our century."

The best-known authority on China then for Americans was Pearl S. Buck, recent Nobel Prize winner and author of *The Good Earth*. Buck began her "Asia Book-Shelf" column noting that *Far Eastern Front* was so good she had felt compelled to watch and heed closely the articles its author subsequently wrote. Edgar Snow "writes as he does because he knows what he is talking about—he's been there. When he tells about a thing, he has seen it." She thought it likely that the form of communism that ruled the territory where Snow most recently journeyed must have been less severe than in violent-natured Hunan, but *Red Star over China* was an intensely readable book. Snow writes "amazingly well, by natural gift." She particularly respected him because he "seems to have been genuinely interested not in himself at all, but absorbed in the people about whom he went to learn."

Red Star over China read for her "like a modern version of that old Chinese Robin Hood novel, *Shui Hu Chuan*," which only a few years earlier she had translated as *All Men Are Brothers*. Whether China went communist or not, she found it "incontrovertible that modern Chinese Communism has accomplished something which nothing else has done—it has awakened, in so far as it has gone, the common people." And, "This in itself is a tremendous thing in a country where a corrupt governing class is a tradition, which modern times have done nothing to destroy." She concluded: "Except for the last chapter, which turns rather surprisingly heavy-handed, *Red Star Over China* measures head and shoulders above any journalist's book of recent years."

Joanna McGaughey called on the cartoonist Milton Caniff shortly after *Red Star over China* was published and asked him why on earth his popular *Terry and the Pirates* was set in China, which seemed to her then out-of-bounds for most Americans. Caniff answered, "Because nobody can make a liar out of me," and pointed to a nearby copy of *Red Star over China* before continuing, "There is THE accurate book on China."

Bennett Cerf, as president of Random House, exuberantly explained how "for once, an author's failure to deliver a manuscript on time was a major blessing." Cerf noted the sales of *Far Eastern Front* were so disappointing to Harrison Smith and Robert Haas that the latter wrote Snow, "It seems that the only books on China that can succeed here are novels, but I do believe that soon some writer, and I don't see why it shouldn't be you, will write a book that is not fiction, but of such compelling interest that this strange taboo will be broken!"

Smith and Haas had signed a contract with Snow offering an advance for a book to be delivered December 1934 on "Red China, or another topic." Cerf then rehearsed Snow's efforts to find a way into Red territory and particularly noted his disappointment when the Guggenheim went to a Columbia professor for "a study of Chinese emotional reactions in relation to the general subject of culture." But Snow meanwhile found a ready market for his work in the *Saturday Evening Post, Asia,* and others.

Finally Random House received a letter dated June 2, 1936, marked "Strictly Confidential," announcing Snow had found a way to visit the Communist forces. Smith and Haas was then merging with Random House in New York. When Cerf originally asked Bob Haas about Snow's promised book on Red China, then a year and a half overdue, Haas replied, "I've got a very definite feeling about that book. Let's just be patient." When he first returned from Red territory, Snow believed strongly his book had to be published in the spring of 1937 to secure his scoop and to avoid being outdated by rapidly developing events. "Even Snow didn't realize just *how* rapidly the whole situation was reaching a climax—nor how long it was going to take him to put the final touches to his manuscript." *Red Star over China* was published three years behind its original schedule but "just in time to have the headlines on the front page of every newspaper in the country act as an advertisement for our book!"

Cerf wrote four weeks to the day after *Red Star over China*'s publication date. It had already sold twelve thousand copies, with orders arriving at the rate of about six hundred a day. A total sale of five hundred thousand copies was well within the range of possibilities. Concluding his remarks he happily turned Haas's earlier discouraged statement about the popularity of journalism versus fiction on its head: "How can fiction hope to compete for intelligent reader interest with books that are so closely tied up with the most important happenings of the day?"[1]

Back in Shanghai, Snow seemed unaware of the success his book was having in Britain and the United States. By mid-January he had heard nothing from his father, brother, or sister for weeks, not even Christmas greetings, and he worried he was becoming more and more remote from them. He hoped he had not offended his father, "you know your approval is very important to me—and your correspondence more so."

He still wrote as if his father were one of his most concerned and informed readers, though before writing a prescient summary of the war and its consequences, he now took the precaution of adding "not for publication."

> From here it seems that the war may drag along for another year or more, with Russia becoming more deeply involved as it develops, and with England and America taking a more decided stand as Japan's warlords and admirals become more reckless and provocative in their anxiety to conclude their adventure quickly, by isolating China and blockading its lines of supplies with the West—to do which they must violate foreign neutral shipping, trading and diplomatic rights. We shall become involved in the war probably not later than 1940—and possibly next year.

He believed Japan had in effect already lost the war even though it would probably for some time win many battles and so postpone the realization of defeat for many years. Meanwhile "terrific suffering will have to be inflicted on China, and ultimately on the Japanese people." He predicted that Americans too would endure hardship for the later phases of the Japan-China war would phase into the beginning of a new world war. Japan missed its chance to win "when her warlords destroyed the compradore-bourgeoisie in Shanghai, robbing it of its economic base, and hence its power of political decision in the government, by invading Kiangsu and Chekiang." The deeper the war went inland "the more inextricably Japan flounders in the mud of China, and the greater becomes her impotency to withdraw."

He asked if his father had read his new book. He wanted to hear his opinion. He intended another soon, but probably not until he left China.

He and his wife wanted to get away for a change and planned to return to the United States by way of Europe some time in the spring. But he readily admitted he had broken many such promises in the past. He enclosed a check to cover the cost of planting two dwarf evergreens, or, if that proved impractical, some perennial flower, on his mother's grave.[2]

By late spring he must have been informed that *Red Star over China* was winning far more readers than either *Far Eastern Front* or *Living China*, yet he was still sensitive to negative criticisms where he expected friendly support. He wrote a delayed, but carefully detailed and strongly indignant, rebuttal to Harry Howard's review that appeared in the *China Weekly Review*. Howard had become so caught up in criticizing Snow's views on the United Front, he had slighted the achievements of *Red Star over China*. J. B. Powell subsequently refused to print Howard's angry rejoinder, which prompted Howard to accuse Snow of influencing Powell's decision.

Snow then privately reminded Howard they both knew Powell too well to believe an author could so readily influence Powell's editorial decision. He explained his first reaction to Howard's review had been "it was lamentably misleading," but decided against writing a rebuttal. However many Chinese wrote him that Howard's review was sowing much confusion and needed correction. Only then did he decide to respond publicly:

> I have had a lot of silly charges hurled at me, from being an agent of Moscow to being an agent of Wall Street, and have regarded them as too ridiculous to dignify by a reply. You called me no names, but something much more serious, used my book in connection with your own statement implying that the United Front was a surrender, that the "Communists had abandoned the struggle for social revolution," etc. etc. I was not thinking of my selfish interests in the matter but only that I did not want to have my book utilized to slander the heroic efforts and idealism and sacrifice of some of the finest human beings I have known.

Months later Powell made clear to Snow that Howard was not easily appeased, but Powell considered the dispute a regrettable, but all too common, conflict between reviewer and author: "I have had no further repercussions from Harry Howard. Chamberlain of the *Monitor* was here recently and he also is gunning for Howard because of Howard's review of his book."[3] The *China Weekly Review* had long been important to the professional careers of both Snows, and they continued to count on it as an important resource for their reporting of China's war with Japan and now for their efforts to build Indusco. Snow still had a strong interest in making certain the *China Weekly Review*'s readers knew his position.

Just before Howard's review appeared in print, Snow also learned from Herz that the Left-leaning Book Society, after ordering fifteen hundred copies of *Red Star over China*, had suddenly canceled its order on instructions from the American Communist Party. *New Masses* had also refused Random House's advertisement. Snow wrote directly to Earl Browder, then secretary of the American Communist Party, calling these facts to his attention. He argued General Yakhontoff's review, which made clear the Party's criticisms of *Red Star*, did not seem sufficiently damning to justify a ban against American Communists' reading his book.

He noted *Red Star over China* had been favorably reviewed by British and Chinese Communists, so he was puzzled why it should be regarded as dangerous for American Communists:

> I would be dull indeed if I did not reflect that, had the decision rested with those responsible for the boycott I have mentioned, the book would never have been published at all, and probably the manuscript would have been burned. And it is just possible that its author might have been shot. It's a melancholy thought not because my own life is of much value to anyone but myself . . . but because it would have been a monstrous crime to waste and destroy the materials Red Star contained, and which have on the whole done very much good to the Chinese revolution.

He noted it was understood by Browder and other Party leaders when Snow went into the Red area that he was not a communist and hence his report would not be that of a Comintern delegate. No foreign communist had gone in to visit the Red Army to counteract the vicious lies circulated concerning the army during the years it struggled for life. So he found it strange "when at last an outside journalist does go in, and returns with a sympathetic report, he is rewarded for his efforts by being boycotted by those very foreign comrades [to] whom the Chinese were so anxious that he should communicate their good wishes—and need for help."[4]

There was, however, hard-line communist criticism outside America as well. Heinz Shippe, the Comintern member who used the pen name "Asiaticus," came calling on the Snows in Shanghai after publishing a long letter in *Pacific Affairs* claiming Snow, under Trotskyist delusions, misrepresented the theory and practice of the Chinese Communist Party during the United Front period in *Red Star over China*. As mentioned earlier Shippe had published in *Democracy*, but Snow probably knew little about him at the time. Beginning in 1934, apparently unknown to Snow, Shippe led a marxist study group in Shanghai that included Hatem, Alley, and sometimes Smedley, among others. Foster Snow expressed indignant surprise years later when she read Alley's account of his early friendship with Shippe.

Shippe seemed to have assumed the Snows knew more about him than they did. He wrote as if he even thought of them as recruits, like other members of his study group, eager for his instruction. His letter is ideologically dogmatic but less hostile and threatening than Foster Snow pictured his personal call: This total stranger "pranced into the room like gangbusters. . . . His deep blue eyes blazed with adrenaline. . . . I had a sense of true evil—not entirely explicable. What he said was this: I am 'Asiaticus.' Your new book is very harmful. It is necessary for me to destroy both you and your book."

Shippe began his letter cordially: "Many thanks for your note enclosing your reply to *P.A.* . . . We are now certainly on a higher level in our discussion, as you agree that at least there is a deep difference in both our viewpoints on the essential Comm. tactics since 1927." He then tried to distinguish between *Red Star over China* as journalism, which he admitted had "great and permanent value," and *Red Star over China* as political theory and method, which he found dangerous. He accused Snow of separating his theory on the Russian Revolution and the Communist International from his theory on the Chinese revolution, and then dealing with the United Front period only on the basis of the Chinese revolution.

Shippe, however, did not let the matter rest. He wrote a second letter to *Pacific Affairs* and had both translated into Chinese and sent to Mao Tse-tung. He then went to Yenan personally to press his case. He first received nothing but silence from Mao in response to his charge. Dissatisfied he insisted on a second interview. Mao then reportedly cut him short, telling him it was a serious mistake for him to attack *Red Star over China*. Alley later told Snow of Mao's rebuke to Shippe, and his report was confirmed by another from Smedley, who met Shippe just after his interview with Mao. Snow was clearly relieved and gratified by Mao's reported response.[5]

Red Star over China was attacked not just from the Left, but also from the Right. One such attack, a letter from Dr. A. J. Brace, a "Christian worker with the Y.M.C.A." who claimed also to be an Associated Press correspondent, appeared in Snow's hometown newspaper, the *Kansas City Star.* This provided Snow a suitable stage to dramatize his moral indignation for the benefit of his skeptic father. Dr. Brace wrote that Chu Teh and the Chinese Red Army had a three-point policy in west China to kill all who had money; all who had any office; and all who had any religion. Brace also claimed to know of graves in Szechuan holding the bodies of as many as forty innocent children murdered in cold blood by Chu Teh and his men.

Snow wrote he cared little what Dr. Brace thought of *Red Star over China*, but he deeply resented the charges of Red mistreatment of children. After spending many months with these Reds, he could assure his readers "nowhere else in China did I see youth so glorified, so happy and so free. Thousands of little children had run away from slavery to join the Reds, and everywhere they were welcomed. I never saw a child struck nor bullied in all my travels with the Chinese Reds. I never anywhere in China saw children with such dignity and personality."

To refute the charge the Reds wanted to kill all who had any religion he noted the many former Christians he found in the Red Army, pointing in particular to Dr. Nelson Fu, for many years head of the Red Army Medical Service, who remained consistently devout, never renouncing his faith. He also noted many Christians, including missionaries, had expressed high opinion of the Reds, citing as a notable example Episcopal Bishop Logan Roots of Hankow, who had spent a lifetime in China. Snow was then planning a visit to Hankow, where he hoped to enjoy the good bishop's hospitality, famous for its stimulating political diversity.

He also checked with both the YMCA and the Associated Press on Brace's credentials. Brace's ties were misleadingly overstated but had thin justification.

The *Kansas City Star's* review of *Red Star over China* was much more appreciative than Brace's letter. Mildred also made available to the *Kansas City Star* an early letter Snow had written from on board the *Radnor* just as he was leaving New York in 1928. The *Kansas City Star* used it for an independent story on how this favorite son's expressed desire to experience the beauty and adventure of far-off lands before "the imagination and spirit of his youth had dimmed" led to the success of his latest book and his recognition as an authority on "a confusing and complex country."[6]

34

Seeding Indusco
in Besieged Hankow

WHILE *RED STAR OVER CHINA* was reaching a worldwide audience surpassing its author's expectations, the Snows and Alley began promoting industrial cooperatives. Soong Ching-ling gave strong support from Hong Kong, where she was organizing her own response to the Japanese invasion, the China Defense League. She saw no reason why the league could not work in happy parallel with the proposed cooperative movement, and her support was crucial to cooperation from the Left. Mao Tse-tung also offered support but not with high priority.

John Alexander left Shanghai on professional leave shortly after the dinner where he ignited Foster Snow's imagination. He returned early in 1938 and ran into her in the hall of the Medhurst Apartments. Good-humoredly surprised at her turnaround, he did not hesitate to add his support but insisted his role be hidden from public view to not compromise his diplomatic position. He quickly termed Alley indispensable as administrative head of the project but questioned whether Alley would or should leave an important civil post in Shanghai that carried a secure lifetime pension to lead an ambitious, but still very nebulous, utopian project.

On March 19, at 6 P.M. in the Snows' apartment, Alexander, Alley, Snow, and H. J. Timperley convened the first formally recorded meeting dedicated to the establishment of the industrial cooperative movement in China. Foster Snow, apparently angry at an agreement to submit an initial skeleton plan to the Military Council in Hankow, did not attend the first meeting.

Alexander presided and kept minutes, his presence disguised under the initials "A. C." It was formally decided if the Military Council supported the plan, Alley was to lead the movement. He was willing if he could be released from his present position on reasonable terms.

A detailed plan for the revival of *Democracy* was attached to the minutes. The need for such a magazine was just as urgent as when it was first published. This was a new opportunity for its original editors, "Edgar Snow, Hubert Liang, Nym Wales, James Bertram, John Leaning, and possibly Ida Pruitt," dispersed by the events of last summer, to come together again, along with such new friends as Wen Yuan-ning and H. J. Timperley.

The original editors, however, never came back together. Both Wales and Bertram were writing books on their visits to the Red forces in the northwest. Snow had begun to brood on an appropriate sequel to *Red Star over China*. Leaning and Bertram soon traveled to Hong Kong to work with Soong Ching-ling's China Defense League. Ida Pruitt would meet Rewi Alley later that year and immediately volunteer to work for Indusco. Harry Price and Ran Sailer had already returned to the United States. The proposal to revive *Democracy* languished until its original sponsor, J. C. Kennard, tried once more in 1939, but Humpty Dumpty could not be put back together.

The Military Council never responded to the original cooperative proposal, but the small group of founders continued to meet and attracted a number of impressive new members. Hubert Liang brought in Hsu Hsing-lo, a respected Shanghai banker, whose service and life was regrettably cut short when his plane to Hankow crashed only a few months after his first meeting with the group. Randall Gould, Anna Wang, Dr. J. B. Grant from the Rockefeller Foundation, and a growing number of other professionals and activists attended early meetings.

On April 20 at an informal meeting of organizers Snow read parts of a letter from Bertram describing the formation of Soong Ching-ling's new China Defense League and the league's quick and formal decision to support industrial cooperatives. Bertram's letter also included a long message from Smedley who was then in Hankow. Smedley was already an imposingly effective one-woman organization providing medical support for the Eighth Route Army. She suggested Indusco set up a cotton-spinning and weaving plant at Yunyang, near Sanyuan, to make jobs for six hundred wounded or crippled Eighth Route Army men.

Bertram's new book had been delayed two valuable months by his Hong Kong sojourn and a misunderstanding about when his publisher wanted a finished manuscript. He still wondered what to write in his story about Snow and Foster Snow, and he might well end up writing nothing since personal references were likely to get an author in trouble: "A[gnes] will never forgive me for making her so tough. And what can one do with 'Nym'?" He was happy to hear Snow was doing another book and assumed it was for the fall. That made it more urgent for him to get his own out before then. He did not want to compete with Snow for public attention again.

Bertram was leaving soon for the United States, expecting to land in California on May 14. He felt stifled, too close to China and its problems. He apologized for the expenses Snow had borne for "the world's worst sub-correspondent." Perhaps one day he would write a novel and repay his debt. He hoped they might soon meet in Europe but later added a more accurate premonition, "I've a feeling, you know, that we're all going to meet again *in China*, and before so very long."

Both Snows wrote to another *Democracy* founder, Harry Price, who was looking forward to seeing Bertram in New York. The Snows expected Price to join eagerly in organizing American support for Indusco. But his lengthy and reserved reply disappointed them. He found *Red Star over China* better and far more significant than he had anticipated. He was impressed by the public praise it had won, particularly from the right-wing press, and suggested Snow not be overly concerned with criticism from the Left. No book was discussed with more genuine appreciation for the new insights it gave into the significance of the Chinese Communist movement. "Time and time again I have heard people say: 'Well, I had no idea that the Communists in China were really like that! Is it a fair picture?' And our reply is: 'We believe that it is.' "

Price was skeptical about the fledgling industrial cooperative movement. He was already involved in a growing complex of Chinese relief organizations, and his offer of help fell far short of what the Snows hoped: "After something is definitely under way, please let me have details, and I will see what can be done to generate further interest on this side."[1]

Both Snows saw the need of winning the support of the National Government and actively supported new overtures by bankers Hsu and Wang by writing under their respective pseudonyms for the *China Weekly Review*. Foster Snow was almost certainly well recognized by this time, at least among their writer friends, as Nym Wales, but Snow probably still hid more effectively behind his infrequent use of John Fairnsworth. This time it was just plain John Fairnsworth, no "C.B.E." behind it.

Foster Snow reported her tour of the devastated industrial areas of Shanghai and built a plea for industrial cooperatives as a means of defending China against the second front of the Japanese invasion, the economic front. Snow followed up a month later, arguing the Chinese people were threatened with being "forced back into agricultural feudalism as a colony for Japan to exploit" if they did not find a means to answer the economic aggression implicit in Japan's military strategy. He reassured his readers industrial cooperatives were not in competition with private industry, but on the contrary would supplement and stimulate its development. Such cooperatives would be, however, most importantly a rear line of defense necessary to China's strategy of using its large land mass to frustrate and ultimately defeat Japan's superior modern military technology: "Scattered throughout the hinterland, industrial cooperatives can become the economic basis for prolonged resistance in every hsien, every town, every important village. They can alone maintain a market for China's farming population, even if China's cities and railways are all lost."

The National Government showed little interest until Sir Archibald Clark-Kerr, the new British ambassador, arrived in May. The liberal ambassador had been Lytton Strachey's friend for years. John Alexander had no trouble persuading him to meet the author of *Red Star over China* for lunch. Within a few days W. H. Auden and Christopher Isherwood, visitors whom the ambassador prized, also arrived in Shanghai at the end of a months-long China tour. They had met Smedley, whom Auden described as "one of the great melancholy domineering frumps," in Hankow. In Shanghai they called on the Snows and were introduced to Alley, who took them on the now de rigueur tour of Shanghai's devastated industrial area. They closed their published account of their Chinese *Journey to a War* with a tribute to Alley and his work. The end result was that Ambassador Clark-Kerr, or Archie, as Snow was requested to call him, was quickly enlisted in the effort to win government support for Indusco.[2]

In *Journey to the Beginning*, Snow reduced what was probably the result of several conversations to a single friendly, but dramatic, encounter between him and the ambassador. Although not literally factual, the dialogue accurately represents the issues. The dialogue drew on a booklet Snow and Alley prepared early in the movement. Clark-Kerr eventually provided the political clout to arrange Alley's release from his Shanghai post and to have him invited to Hankow to meet with W. H. Donald, Mme. Chiang Kai-shek, and Finance Minister H. H. Kung.

Since Snow arrived in Hankow on June 29, a few days before Alley, who arrived on July 2, he could not have been summoned by Alley as he represents in *Journey to the Beginning*. The battlefront then between Shanghai and the new capital apparently made direct rail travel difficult, if not impossible, so it was common to travel first to Hong Kong by ship from which one could fly or travel by train into Hankow. Snow spent at least a week in Hong Kong meeting with many of his old friends before traveling to Hankow. From there he wrote Soong Ching-ling:

> I had a piece of luck when I arrived and managed to get the flat of the Y director who is on leave, and as ra [Rewi Alley] had no place to stay he naturally moved in. This looked like prearrangement I suppose, and I warned ra it would do him no good. It hasn't. D [Donald] and S [*soeur*, Mme. Chiang—Snow frequently referred to Mme. Sun's brother, T. V. Soong, as *frère*] hate me apparently and look upon hutung [Alley] evidently as being instigated by me or some such thing. He's moving out as soon as possible.

Housing was very scarce in the new capital, still adjusting to the sudden influx of governmental offices from occupied Nanking and their myriad supplicants and observers.

Early in July, Snow asked Hollington Tong, another Missouri alumnus, then serving as the Generalissimo's press secretary, to arrange an interview with Mme. Chiang so he might make a pitch for Indusco. But between his request and the interview an unexpected breakthrough occurred. Alley received a clear signal of approval from the top and prepared an outline plan for Kung minus the names of Soong Ching-ling, T. V. Soong, or any mention of the Eighth Route Army. Snow explained, rather wishfully, to Soong Ching-ling that her brother-in-law, H. H. Kung, "expects according to D[onald]'s promise that you and tv [T. V. Soong] will be added later at his discreet recommendation."

Kung was at the time acting-president of the National Government. Chiang Kai-shek was in the middle of another of his political maneuvers designed to make clear he was the indispensable leader. Kung remained the official at the top of Indusco's organizational chart from then until the end of World War II, but he never accepted Indusco as a principal part of China's defense against Japan's economic aggression. At best he could only see it as a means of supporting China's "cottage industries" and a favorable means of winning international support, both financial and political.

Donald, upon learning of Snow's scheduled interview with Mme. Chiang, warned if Snow brought up the cooperatives he would only spoil the cozy new arrangement. Under this restriction Snow's interview with Mme. Chiang was strained and empty, but he still happily, if somewhat satirically, reported to her sister:

> Mrs. C. saw Ra yesterday and impressed upon him that this was just the thing they had been hoping and dreaming and planning for all these years. It seems that it is what D has also had in mind for many years, and

they were glad when they found someone (ra) who had the same vision. Etcetera. Their main effort now is devoted to keeping it from becoming public property until it can be announced in its proper setting as an offspring of the divine brain. Also to keep it away from the Min. of Econ., where Laurel and Hardy are maneuvering to develop it as a monopoly in the rear provinces with Gov. and foreign money used by private banks.

A couple of days after writing Soong Ching-ling, Snow wrote his wife with mistaken resignation: "I have seen Mrs. C. and we had a minor bout. She and hh [Kung] have taken over the icm [industrial cooperative movement] as their own and ra seems on the way to being adopted into the *chia-li* [the family] to carry it out. It appears our work is done." There is no hint he was pressured by Donald, as he represents in *Journey to the Beginning*, to write something to placate Mme. Chiang for his caricature of her husband's flight from arrest in Xian in *Red Star over China*.

Alley remembered Mme. Chiang's role in Hankow differently. According to Alley, Dr. Kung arranged a meeting in the boardroom of the bank on the Hankow Bund with Donald in attendance. The meeting was intended to organize a committee of old-time industrialists under the leadership of Mou Ouchu, one of their own, "to consider what industry might be set up in safe regions of unoccupied China, as a sound banking investment." Alley saw the idea of Indusco slipping away.

But Mme. Chiang swept into the room before the discussion could start and summoned Alley and Donald downstairs. From there she asked Donald to invite Dr. Kung to join them. When he came in

> she flew at him and said, "You have spoiled every project that I tried to carry out. But you will not spoil this one." She demanded that the green light be given immediately to Gung Ho to get on with its work. She said, "Tomorrow morning Alley must have full authorization," and with that determined outburst, she sailed out of the room and down the steps into the dust and heat of the crowded bund, with Dr. Kung in a blue silk gown padding after her trying to say something and waving his fan, for it was a very hot Wuhan afternoon.

Alley remembered then returning to his room in the Navy YMCA. This apparently was the breakthrough preceding Snow's interview with Mme. Chiang.

Apparently Mme. Chiang did not carry her resentment against Snow into her relation with Alley. Snow had another reason, however, to fear his relation to Indusco might endanger its support by the Generalissimo and his wife. He probably had already sent off to *Foreign Affairs* an article titled "China's Fighting Generalissimo" that appeared in print about the time of these events.

It was a serious critical appraisal of Chiang's leadership role, not a cartoon of Chiang featuring his dropped false teeth, but it was at least as unlikely to warm either the Generalissimo's or his wife's feelings toward its author. Snow repeated his long-held reservations about Chiang's leadership:

> Chiang's persistence in power can readily be analyzed step by step; but the mystery of his personal leadership is not so easily explained. He lacks the long-range vision and the unity of concept necessary to make a military genius. . . . There are in China half a dozen military tacticians more competent than he. Mao Tse-tung and Pai Chung-hsi are by many observers conceded to be at least his equals intellectually and as political leaders. . . . In one talent alone history has demonstrated his consummate skill: his mastery of the art of political manoeuvre. Yet despite the richness of rival talent, it is Chiang alone who has the prestige   . of having ruled a united China.[3]

Even after Indusco was officially accepted by the National Government, finding funds to get it started was a constant worry for Alley, and he in turn continually pleaded with his good friend Snow not to abandon their struggling newborn. Contrary to his account in *Journey to the Beginning,* Snow arranged a discreet loan from T. V. Soong for Indusco's initial expenses only after he returned to Hong Kong from Hankow. The loan was not easily obtained. Soong was politically at odds with his brother-in-law, H. H. Kung, at the time, so a nominal supportive committee in Hong Kong was arranged to disguise the source of the loan. It was not until the next year that Snow returned to Hong Kong to play a leading role in organizing a more permanent and fully credentialed Hong Kong Promotion Committee to meet some of Alley's most crucial financial needs for Indusco.

Indusco was not Snow's exclusive concern while in Hankow. He called upon the Communist delegation as soon as he arrived. He particularly wanted reassurance that Heinz Shippe's criticism of *Red Star over China* had not damaged his relation with the Red leadership. Foster Snow had written about the negative reaction of the Communist Party in America, but he found her warning happily unnecessary: "upon arrival here I find the whole thing has been engineered over there [in the United States] and has no support here. I've seen pk [Po Ku] and cel [Chou En-lai] and wm [Wang Ming] and all are quite emphatically enthusiastic about the opus."

Snow had pointed out to Po Ku Shippe's statement in his *Pacific Affairs* letter that "competition for leadership has never been a main question." Po Ku laughingly replied:

> This is nonsense. We must struggle for leadership everywhere and at all times. We do not deny that. A political party that does not lead has

Snow calls on Chou En-lai and Teng Ying-chao in Hankow.

no reason for existence. Of course, right now we cannot talk about the struggle for proletarian leadership. (But) every Kuomintang leader knows that Stalin said, "The struggle for proletarian leadership is the first stage in the struggle for proletarian dictatorship."

To his wife, Snow added, "57 varieties [*Heinz* Shippe] failed to report the full humiliation of his reception in y [Yenan] and no wonder he came back somewhat crestfallen." Snow also noted he had seen Smedley a couple of times wearing a bright red suit. It was probably in these early days in Hankow that he was reassured by reports from both Smedley and Alley of Shippe's disappointment with his Yenan mission.

Smedley became close friends in Hankow with Freda Utley, an English journalist, whose recent book *Japan's Feet of Clay* was one Foster Snow had read with enthusiasm on the train to Sian. Utley's personal story aroused strong sympathetic interest. Once an English Communist and a Comintern

Freda Utley and Agnes Smedley—friends in Wuhan.

courier, she had lived in the Soviet Union from 1930 to 1936 until her Russian husband became a purge victim and she "a fugitive from Stalin's tyranny." When Utley insisted she knew the Chinese Reds in Hankow would have nothing to do with her, Snow disagreed and bet they would. Respecting her talent as a journalist as well as her strong antifascist politics, he suggested to Po Ku and Chou En-lai "they see their exiled comrade." To show they were interested in fighting the Japanese and not the battles of the Comintern, they surprised Snow by arranging a tea party in Utley's honor. She too was surprised and impressed, then acknowledging the Chinese Communists "really were a different breed," a position quite different from what she would assume in later Cold War years.

Sometime later Snow also met two of China's Japanese allies whose stories he found worth reporting to his American audience. Wataru Kaji and his pretty wife, Ikeda Yuki, both writers and survivors of years of physical and mental abuse in Japanese prisons, were now working as liaisons between the Chinese government, its Japanese prisoners, and rebellious elements within the invading Japanese army. They survived a deliberate Japanese bombing attack on their home in Wuchang to meet Snow over chocolate nut sundaes at the Hankow Navy YMCA. Snow met them again a year later in Chungking and was reminded "Japan was full of decent people like them who, if they had not had their craniums stuffed full of Sun Goddess myths and other imperialist filth, and been forbidden access to dangerous thoughts, and been armed by American and British hypocrites, could easily live in a civilized co-operative world—if any of us could provide one."

Wang Fu-hsih, who published much of Snow's story of his trip into Red territory in Chinese and who accompanied Foster Snow on her Yenan trip, also remembered a surprise encounter with Snow in Hankow. Wang and a friend entered a fashionable Western restaurant seeking funds to support the guerrilla army. They were told in no uncertain terms by the management to leave until Snow, who just happened to be dining there, recognized what was going on and interceded. They were then allowed to make their pitch.

The summer heat of Hankow was oppressive. It reminded Snow how bad Shanghai could also be. Neither he nor Foster Snow had yet recovered fully from their long sojourns in the northwest. His weight was down to 136 pounds. He wrote his wife: "Please take care of yourself and if the heat is intolerable go down to the Philippines as you planned. All here send their regards and seemed disappointed that you did not come; but things being as they are it would have been extremely foolish. I'll be along in three or four weeks. Love you, mug."[4]

If Snow was quick to make certain of his credit with Red representatives in Hankow, he also was careful to maintain cordial relations with U.S. Ambassador Johnson. Shortly after arriving in Hankow he sent Johnson copies of articles he had recently published in the *Saturday Evening Post* and in the *Hong Kong Sunday Herald*. The first spelled out in richer detail the thesis he summarized in his letter to his father from Shanghai that the Japanese had lost the war by expanding their front and unifying disparate factions within China with their brutal inland invasion culminating in the rape of Nanking. The title of the latter, "Total War, Total Resistance," made clear its primary concern.

Johnson read them both and responded the same day. He thought Snow overly optimistic in the *Saturday Evening Post* article, probably because of the early dramatic victory for United Front forces at Taierchuang. He thought Snow's idea for uniting China behind a "total war, total resistance" policy excellent, but doubted it could be carried out by "the individualistic Chinese." He concluded: "They are going to fight this out on a Chinese basis . . . and I expect that you and I will just have to sit and watch it, vent our disappointments upon the bacon in the morning and try to report the results, with as little rancor as possible."

Snow wrote again nine days later to inform the ambassador about Indusco, enclosing the pamphlet he and Alley had prepared. He described the movement's gathering support from the League of Nations, the British, and the Rockefeller Foundation: "One of our representatives in America writes that Mrs. Roosevelt is also keenly interested. As you've probably heard, the Chinese Government has adopted the plan and intends to carry it out. What do you think of it?"

Again the ambassador responded promptly: "I think the plan a good one. I wonder still whether the carrying out of such a plan is not contingent upon the existence of a much more highly organized and integrated government than anything China has ever known or had any experience with. It would be my hope that something of the sort might come out of the present necessity. If only part can be done I would feel that much had been done."

Snow then called personally on the ambassador and was subjected to "an incredible panegyric" of Chiang Kai-shek. But Johnson also "impishly" brought up the fact that his letter about *Living China* had gone unanswered and wondered whether his praise for Nym Wales had caused a split in the family. Snow wrote his wife that underneath his jocularity, the ambassador seemed a little peeved she had not replied. To make amends he told Johnson she was publishing a book of her own and he would ask her to send him a copy.

Anna Wang brought news from Shanghai that Doubleday had accepted Foster Snow's *Inside Red China*, though the title had not yet been decided. The news called for congratulations:

> Considering the vast quantity of books on China emerging this fall I think you should feel very proud that DD [Doubleday and Doran] are taking yours; and I believe it will be one of the two or three of any value. It's wonderful news, and I think a book that will at once establish your name and reputation. Followed up by your Korean opus [*Song of Ariran*, 1941] it should put you in the top flight. So what? Your dream come true. I suppose you'll be impossible for a common mortal like your measly petty lollypop to live with henceforth. But I intend to assert my rights and make you support me from now on.

The publication of Foster Snow's first book by a well-recognized American publisher promised the realization of both their original acknowledged ambitions for their writers' marriage. Snow nevertheless warned his wife with good reason, "If you have time you'd better go over your whole mss. and improve its style and diction—which is very rough in spots, as you know. You can send this mss. revised in ink in time for the publishers to make changes before publication." Foster Snow herself often later acknowledged her impatience with editing her own work. It became an important, but by no means the only, reason why her writing career would stall far short of the eminence then so promising. Snow's uneasy humor, however, also suggests her success stirred unresolved questions about the terms on which they lived together. But for the time historic events made it convenient to shelve personal marital concerns far back in their minds.

By the end of Snow's stay it was clear Hankow was doomed to fall to the advancing Japanese. The city's plight attracted an intriguing collection of journalists from all over the world, several fresh from the fighting in Spain, some hoping Hankow might become a second Madrid, defiantly offering resistance to the end. Snow saw little likelihood of that. Meanwhile the manager of the YMCA was expected back any day to claim his flat, and Snow knew how hard it was to find a decent place. Wang Ping-nan and Anna had been able to find only a single room in the wretched Italian Hotel.

Snow briefly thought of visiting Red territory again. The Eighth Route Army people had been too preoccupied with United Front politics to give him much time. He closed a letter to his wife, "If I decide to make a trip anywhere I'll wire you in four or five days, and you'd better leave Sh[anghai] for the Ph[ilippines] where you can rest; otherwise wait there for me, as I shall leave here at the end of July."[5] Evans Carlson had been in Hankow since March, but both he and Snow were too preoccupied to spend much time together. Hollington K. Tong threw a final party for Snow and sent him on his way.

35

All These Irons in the Fire

I NDUSCO'S FIRST OFFICIAL ASSIGNMENT was to keep as much heavy industry as possible from falling into the hands of the Japanese by moving it from Wuhan to Paochi, the last stop available by rail in the northwest inland from Wuhan. Just before leaving Hankow for Paochi, Alley wrote ominously to Snow, then in Hong Kong arranging the loan for Indusco from T. V. Soong: "L. T. Chen is in charge of our files in Chungking. . . . Don't let me fall between two stools. We are a tender plant, the bulk of the pop[ulation] do not recognize our beauty yet." Months later, Chen, H. H. Kung's personal secretary, insisted on a kickback that was the first of many tests of who would control the growth of the new and tender plant.

Meanwhile in Hong Kong, Snow called on T. V. Soong for financial help to tide Indusco over its initial budget problems. Late in August, Snow was able to write Alley that Soong, with other bankers, was willing to loan Indusco two hundred thousand dollars as long as Alley and Snow took personal responsibility. Neither hesitated to accept such responsibility.

Snow cleared the matter with Hsu Hsing-lo and received several names for a proposed Hong Kong committee to support Indusco. He expected to visit Alley in September with Ambassador Clark-Kerr, but was otherwise uncertain where he would head next.[1]

He wrote his wife:

> In Hankow I met Han Ying and had a grand time with him. He was one of the few bright spots of my trip: another Peng Teh-huai, a real army man,

but have not yet had time to write it up. He asked me to go back with him to the front, and I tentatively agreed. . . . I think I could do the trip in three weeks or a month and come out through Wenchow to Shanghai. The only rubs are two: (1) I'm not very well; (2) I'm afraid you'll be utterly disgusted.

He asked her to wire if she was willing to holiday in Baguio while he made this trip; otherwise he would not do it.

Foster Snow did not respond. A week later he thought it likely he would travel to the northwest with some Ford trucks he expected to purchase for Indusco and then visit Peng Teh-huai's army, but he was still also much drawn to visit the newly formed Fourth Route Army,

because if I'm to write anything I must have something original in the vol and this is about the only story left now that hasn't been hackneyed by all the tourists, students, etc. who are flocking to the nw [northwest] like flies. Although I've plenty of material to write a book about the situation in gen I've nothing happy to say and feel like touching none of it, but I've a notion some direct contact with the 4ra [Fourth Route Army] might change my outlook.

Snow was particularly impressed that the January 1938 reorganization of the New Fourth Army rejoined two able commanding officers, the senior general Yeh Ting and Field Commander Han Ying, whom Snow relished meeting in Hankow. Yeh had commanded the Twenty-fourth Division of the old Fourth Route Army known as "Ironsides" at Wuhan just before the 1927 split between the Left and Right factions of the Kuomintang. He had then given Han Ying, in charge of the city's workers, one thousand rifles to police the city. These workers later carried their rifles into the countryside to become some of China's first Red partisans. Yeh Ting also later joined his men with the forces of Chu Teh and Ho Lung in the Nanchang uprising, which marked the beginning of the Red Army.

But Snow made neither visit behind the lines. Instead he invited Foster Snow to Hong Kong and proposed they head for Europe after a few weeks in the Philippines: "A trip through the canal in September or October is certainly better than going in this heat, anyway; and autumn is generally better for travelling in Europe."

He complained again of not having heard from her for weeks. "N.Y people know your book is coming out, and have written here about it. They have a fine opinion of it, say you've profited from all my mistakes, and think it's going to make you famous." He also mentioned that Smedley's *China Fights Back* was out, though he had not yet seen a copy. "AS [Agnes Smedley] told me ALS

[Anna Louise Strong] had edited the whole thing, taken out 'everything vital' from it, and ruined it; but I imagine on the contrary it's probably benefited."

Foster Snow arrived in Hong Kong the same day a plane carrying Hsu Hsing-lo to Hankow was shot down by the Japanese near Macao. Snow wrote J. B. Powell: "his death shocked me beyond expression, as I had a very warm affection for him; he was a rare personality of his class indeed, a generous and sincere and honest man, and one of the few first class financial brains in China. I talked with him only a few hours before his departure and came away feeling that his sanity and intelligence and feeling were qualities making him one of the big men of his country."

The Snows did not head for Europe but spent much of the next month on the beach at Repulse Bay recuperating. Late in September, Snow wrote the *London Daily Herald* this seemed an opportune time for him "to take a much-needed and much-delayed holiday" in the Philippines. J. B. Powell would assume his routine duties. Snow expected to be gone three or four weeks, returning in time to cover the climax of the Hankow campaign. Hankow fell in October with such little resistance there was no incentive for Snow to return from the Philippines.

Soong Ching-ling, whose Philippine contacts were extensive, encouraged him to speak freely after he arrived in the islands: "I hope you will agree to deliver as many addresses as possible . . . for your words will carry great weight everywhere." She made clear Snow should not fear preempting her audience, since she had decided not to leave China this year. While she and he had disagreed over the trucks he planned to purchase for Indusco, she playfully reassured him that if she came to the Philippines, "it would only be to bathe in the sunshine of your charming smiles, and not to plant deadly denunciations on your pathway or accuse you of fantastic misdeeds."

She also tartly commented on Evans Carlson's recent resignation from the marines: "Think it ill-advised . . . and I bet Lizzie [Smedley] was the adviser, for it sounds like her." During Carlson's visits behind the lines to the Red forces he became strongly convinced war between the United States and Japan was inevitable and China's partisan forces needed and deserved American support. Scrupulously respecting the United Front he reported his observations to newsmen. His published views then became an embarrassment to official U.S. policy toward Japan. As an American marine officer he was ordered to stop taking his views public.

About the time the Snows arrived in the Philippines, Carlson, as a matter of conscience, chose rather than obey such an order to travel to the American Embassy in Chungking to formally and officially resign before returning to the States to write and lecture about the threat to international peace posed by Japanese aggression. To make his decision morally unambiguous, he gave up the pension he had earned with twenty-five years of service. Contrary to Mme. Sun's suspicions, Smedley advised him his decision was crazy, even if he was right.[2]

Another Missouri alumnus then edited the *Manila Bulletin* and welcomed the Snows into Manila's harbor. That same evening he escorted them to Malacanang Palace where President Manuel Quezon was entertaining with traditional Philippine lavishness. Foster Snow, pinned into a hastily prepared dress sufficiently frilly for the occasion, was reminded of happier ball days in Peking. Snow, in a comfortable, native pineapple-gauze shirt, enjoyed the public attention. They immediately made friends with William and Polly Babcock, who just as quickly invited them to move out of the hotel their editor friend had chosen for them and into the Babcocks' ample and comfortable house, the former residence of the commander of the American occupation force.

They enjoyed the large quiet garden shaded by banyan trees and the daily spectacle of servants polishing the handsome native narrawood floors by skating over them on half-coconut husks. But Manila was sultry and busy, so after only a few days they moved to the congenial American community in the pine-forested mountains of quieter, cooler Baguio.

They quickly found another sympathetic friend and hostess in Natalie Crouter, who gave comfortable parties and generous support for Indusco. Their stay in the Philippines lasted far longer than originally intended. Snow returned to China for a few months in 1939, but Foster Snow lived in Baguio continuously, except for occasional trips to Manila, until she returned alone to the United States in 1940. The Babcocks generously made their Manila home available to the Snows whenever they returned to the island capital.[3]

The Snows quickly became influential in collecting money from the Philippine Chinese community to support specific Indusco projects. Some of the early contributions were sent through the China Defense League for Indusco so that it would not disappear into the private pockets of National Government officials. Late in November, Snow wrote Soong Ching-ling again to head off some problems of rivalry over foreign support beginning to develop between the China Defense League and Indusco. Surprisingly the Snows were even able to tap the Chinese Women's Relief Association, which had been organized by Mme. Chiang Kai-shek and was hence politically conservative. Since the Philippine Chinese had strong family ties with Fukien Province, the Snows parlayed this connection with some of the community's more progressive sentiment to support the partisan forces, by designating this financial support for Indusco projects in western Fukien, where they would be available to the New Fourth Army.

Keeping such funds intact and documenting their application to the designated projects was a severe challenge for the rapidly growing but still loosely organized patchwork that was then Indusco. The China Defense League had its own organizational problems, but it also had the advantage of not being under the direct control of the National Government. Snow, however, explained in great detail and with obvious sincerity to Mme. Sun that their fund-raising efforts in the Philippines were not designed to take support away from either the China Defense League or the Eighth Route Army. Had this money not gone to Indusco projects in Fukien, "it would have gone *only* to Mme. Chiang for relief and other purposes."

If their attempts "to divert at least some of this money from Mme. Chiang's soup kitchens" had led to what Mme. Sun euphemistically described as "a number of misconceptions concerning an effective social and political program for the P. I.," then they would have to reconsider the weeks of work they had devoted to win this financial support. If some better method were found "for mobilizing the economic and human resources of the hinterland, in order to prepare in advance adequate bases for the guerrillas who will ultimately inherit it," it would be a relief. It would greatly simplify his life if he had only to ask people to aid the Eighth Route and New Fourth Armies directly, and if they declined, placidly watch them send all their gifts to Mme. Chiang for purposes of her own. Finally if CIC was complicating CDL affairs, it would be better for him just to drop it.[4]

True to his early writer-traveler commitment, Snow quickly looked at the Philippines as a subject as well as a place for retreat. Soon after arriving in Baguio he proposed to Herz an article titled "Little Brown Brother, What Now?" aimed at the *Saturday Evening Post*. His thesis: "Faced with independence, the F[ilipinos], after demanding . . . freedom for years, and unexpectedly getting their way, are now in desperation about the future of a Philippine Republic to be set loose for a sink or swim performance in the midst of a sea full of hungry Japanese sharks." By late October, Herz had an encouraging response from the *Post,* and he began research and writing in earnest.

In the middle of November, Herz suggested his article might be important and long enough to be a booklet after it appeared in the *Saturday Evening Post.* By early December he had nearly finished the article and was planning a second on Japanese economic penetration of the Philippines. But in January the *Post* rejected both, and Herz forwarded them to *Collier's.* She explained Martin Sommers felt several books had already covered the Philippines from the same angle as Snow. She added, "the *Post* is an anti–New Deal outfit, and anything that supports Roosevelt measures in behalf of the Philippines is something they frown upon." Sommers did not think this way, but his support was not strong enough to overcome the prevailing political position.

Just before this bad news the *London Daily Herald* took Snow's Philippine holiday as an opportunity to change his contract, making his three-pounds-a-week retainer fee a minimum lineage fee instead. Events in Europe then so commanded its readers' attention, the *Herald* required little news cabled from China. *Red Star over China*'s success did not yet make Snow feel financially secure. He tried unsuccessfully to restore his previous contract with the *Herald*

He also sent Herz two additional articles on the Fourth Route Army and wondered whether there was enough interest in America for him to win a contract for his Philippine book. He planned to return to China on March 10 if nothing intervened.

Snow took heart from Sommers's explanation for the rejection of his Philippine articles. In early February he cabled Herz he was sending a new article, hoping the news would forestall the magazine from accepting anything else on the Philippines in the interim. *Collier's* meanwhile also rejected his two articles, and Herz sent them on to *Ken*, an ambitious new magazine edited by Arnold Gingrich that regrettably proved short-lived. Robert Haas at Random House was not encouraging about the Philippine book. He felt the American public expected something more ambitious from Snow following *Red Star over China*. Barring some extraordinary happening in the Philippines, Snow should abandon that project.

Snow suggested to Sommers he might follow up his Philippine article with a discussion of Anglo-French complications in the Far East as a result of the war. He noted in particular:

> There are some fascinating aspects to Britain's China predicament. One of them is the extraordinary Sir Archibald Clark-Kerr, the most remarkable diplomat I have met. In a year he has upset most of the precedents of Chinese diplomatic history, has acquired more personal influence in Chinese affairs than any foreigner probably since the days of Sir Robert Hart, and keeps Chiang and the Madame wondering, on tenterhooks, what's coming next. I might call this, "Britain's Other Cheek in the Orient."

If Sommers approved, he proposed writing this article on the spot when he returned to Hong Kong and Indochina. He also noted that along with eight other foreign correspondents he was marked for death by the "Society of Honorable and Righteous and True Chinese," a Japanese assassination gang.

Snow thought Haas might wrongly think his Philippine book was intended to substitute for the contracted China book. He asked Herz to "shed a little enlightenment on Haas' attitude, which you apparently share." He had several short articles outlined for early work but was anxious to hear she had been able to place at least some of those he had already sent.

Simultaneously Herz wrote better news. The *Saturday Evening Post* not only bought his new Philippine article but raised his fee to one thousand dollars. Herz quoted their letter: "We do want to give him regular raises steadily, but we should like to do that on some article which we like a lot." They also encouraged him to write about Ambassador Clark-Kerr. In September the *Saturday Evening Post* published an article by Snow on how British appeasement at Munich provoked Japan to dramatize the weakness of the British colonial position in China and other nearby territories. This article did not feature Clark-Kerr, and the *Post* paid Snow only nine hundred dollars. The *Post* also asked Herz to withdraw the two other Philippine articles from *Ken* until after their publication. *Asia* bought the two articles on the Fourth Route Army.

Richard Walsh wrote separately a few days later, assuming mistakenly Snow was back in Hong Kong. He thanked Snow for sending *Asia* an article on China's Japanese allies as well as the two on the New Fourth Army. He also noted his wife had sent her thanks for his congratulations on her recent Nobel Prize. The visiting Hubert Liang had so stirred her with his account of Indusco's work she had written an article endorsing the movement for *Asia*'s April issue. Walsh also could not resist continuing his friendly quarrel by boasting of the success of the supplement to Lin Yu-tang's *My Country and My People* in the March issue of *Asia*.

Late in March, Herz wrote Snow that Random House had changed its mind and was now interested in a book on the Philippines. Among the reasons she gave for her original skepticism was his proposal to do the book with his wife: "Such collaborations are not wanted by publishers, because each publisher wants to keep his respective author."

But the news came too late. In April he wrote Herz: "I have already made plans to leave Manila on the 22nd, and cannot change them now. Had I got word in January or February I might have had the book completed by now." He sent the promised *Saturday Evening Post* article along in a messy state, asking her to have someone retype it at his expense. He expected to return to Baguio in June or July, once more underestimating his travel plans.

After Snow arrived in Hong Kong, Herz forwarded Brian Hall's opinion that Gollancz would also have almost certainly accepted Snow's book on the Philippines and probably would have made it a Left Book Club

Supplementary Volume. But the English preferred he cover the whole Pacific question, not just the Philippines, with a chapter or two on the British strategic position. Herz also reported that though Doubleday had not sold more than three thousand copies of Foster Snow's book to date, they were the only firm to publish a book on China that did not lose money that year. Bertram sailed for China in the middle of April.[5]

Herz and the Snows knew each other only through written correspondence, but that correspondence indicates she served them well professionally and often helped with personal matters. However, managing both their rapidly expanding literary careers became more and more demanding, and it is not surprising small cracks in their mutual trust threatened to expand into fissures.

After Herz returned from England where she had conferred with both his British agent and publisher, she tried to reassure Snow that Hall was not charging an exploitative commission and there was no way to exempt Snow from an English income tax he strongly objected to: "As agents go, I found Brian Hall a very good one, and certainly a thoroughly honest and conscientious person."

Late in October the Snows' complaints provoked Herz to write that she would call it a red-letter day when either acknowledged she remained the same "obliging stranger" they had termed her five years ago: "the two of you have to get it out of your heads that I am willfully disregarding your instructions and doing all sorts of 'mean' things to upset you."

Snow complained a letter he had sent to be forwarded to Jaffe had not been delivered. Herz assured him it had, but with the result "Jaffe goes around foaming at the mouth." The *Daily Worker* had reviewed the new edition of *Red Star over China,* and the Communist Party had lifted its ban on its sales from the Workers' Bookshop. Herz had complained to Paul Draper, a decent guy with a sense of humor, of words like "malicious" and "slanderous" appearing in the *Daily Worker* review. He laughed at her taking such words so seriously and insisted the review on the whole was very favorable.

Herz denied showing Snow's confidential letters to others. She admitted answering general questions from the Wittfogels and Harry Price about the Snows when asked, but insisted she had not shown them any letters. "Frankly, the letters that have passed between us in the last few months I wouldn't like anyone to see." She defended her fees again, insisting the "type of agency I run barely succeeds in being self-supporting."

Not all the people she met through the Snows were disasters. She and her husband liked Bertram "tremendously." He stayed with them for two weeks, and they now missed him much. He is "a most devoted friend of yours and

Peg's." She hoped "the next guests we are going to have will be you and Peg. Don't you think it's time for you to see your country again?"

Herz acknowledged Snow's cable about the Philippine article for the *Saturday Evening Post* and cuts made in Foster Snow's book. Sales of *Red Star over China* were still moving steadily. It "is still the one book that overshadowed all others on the same subject!" She added Owen Lattimore, a very grand person, to her list of the Snows' friends she had come to appreciate, but she was more ambivalent about Timperley, who was hanging around New York: "I think he has a very good head on him. I like talking to him quite a lot, but in accordance with my ideas and your warnings, I do not bring the Snows in except to say they are well and doing nicely."

In early December, Foster Snow sent two articles to Herz, one on the significance of Munich to China and the other on Indusco's importance to China's defense. She hoped Herz could place them in the *Nation* or the *New Republic*. She did not mention she had just published the Munich article in the *China Weekly Review*. The second, on Indusco, appeared in the *China Weekly Review* late in December.

Foster Snow was disappointed Gollancz had refused to publish *Inside Red China* in England, but happy with the outline of contents that survived at Doubleday: "I expected the publisher to cut out all the ANATOMY OF REV. stuff. And it's marvelous to get so many words in it." Their stay in the Philippines was proving no vacation: "Have been giving talks on Spain and China etc. to wake these sleepy Filipinos (lousy with money) up. They're all pro-Franco and not a bit anti-Japanese—think China is saving the PI by letting Japan take China instead of the south seas!"[6]

Inside Red China was officially published February 3, about the same time Herz delivered a welcome baby boy. Some reviews coupled *Inside Red China* with Bertram's latest, *Unconquered*, but more often reviewers compared it with *Red Star over China*. After approving the author's light touch in describing her melodramatic escape from Sian and life at Yenan, T. A. Bisson gave one of the more favorable descriptions of the relation between the two books: "This study must henceforth be bracketed with the earlier work of Edgar Snow, which it supplements in substantial respects. Aside from their interest as vivid personal narratives, the two volumes constitute an invaluable source book of historical materials on the Chinese communist movement."

R. L. Duffers, on the other hand, was more sardonic:

> After Mr. Snow's book, Miss Agnes Smedley's *China Fights Back*, and other testimony the existence of Soviet China is not now news. . . . If so many astounding happenings were not clamoring for attention in our

times the Red Army's story would be one of the tremendous epics of all time. Its degree of redness, its doctrinal background and development, and its links with Moscow will not interest everyone as much as they do Miss Wales.

He did, however, offer some balm: "Her observations of the character and position of women in the Soviet movement are illuminating—more so, in some respects, than those of Agnes Smedley."[7]

Inside Red China did not do for Foster Snow what *Red Star over China* did for her husband. War clouds in Europe effectively dimmed the significance of the profuse detail she recorded of the Chinese Communist movement that most of the Western world yet refused to take seriously.

In January, Alley wrote that a news release, supposedly from Foster Snow, had put him "in bad again with the powers that be, so that my position is as before." At this point the National Government had given him neither an official title nor a salary. Israel Epstein, working in the Hong Kong office, saw Alley's letter and chided Foster Snow for her indiscreet outspokenness: "There is stuff in your letters to Ida [Pruitt] which would blow local committee, Rewi, and everything and everybody else sky-high."

Snow came quickly to his wife's defense. To Alley he denied she had anything to do with the troublesome release that came out of Shanghai: "It is singularly putrid for such people to be griping about P's work on such trumped up nonsense." He noted only he knew how much work she had done for Indusco in Shanghai, the Philippines, and abroad, "and none of it has done a dot of harm to the movement at all." So he requested Alley "just put a bug in one or two HK ears to the effect that you did not mean that the Snows would 'ruin the movement' when you commented on that UP thing."

To Epstein he wrote a more legalistic defense, but concluded with a heavy-handedness equal to Epstein's original charge: "Finally, let me as an old friend suggest that you overcome your pontifical tendencies, and a kind of patronizing overconfidence of manner which, I have long observed, often creates umbrage where I am sure you do not really desire it."

The dispute cooled after Epstein wrote a fuller explanation for his charge and admitted he had not been aware of Foster Snow's large role in getting Indusco started. But he did not completely back down. Acknowledging that "Peg has done a tremendous job in hustling the CIC into being," he still insisted "there are elements in her activity which carry the possibility of unfortunate results in the present circumstances of the U[nited] F[ront]," elements borne out not only by her letters but also by her book. He was being "straightforward and not self-righteous, in token of which I now offer my chin for the stiff socks, which, though on other counts, it no less richly deserves."

Alley's final words on the subject were buried amid a host of other more important concerns in his correspondence with Snow:

> My apologies to Peg. My friends will have to put up with my short-comings these days of rough and scurry. I know that I am too hasty in many things I say and do. . . . But we must all realise that our plant is a very tender one still, and not by a long way yet able to stand on its own legs. Must be careful not to give N. Shensi and Anhwei offices publicity inside China these days. They are still outlawed, more or less.

Indusco's troubles compounded during the early months of 1939. Alley was nearly asphyxiated in his sleep when the charcoal stove in his cave room at Shwangshihpoo burned up the oxygen vital to human life. Subsequently he came down with typhoid and was immobilized for weeks. Ida Pruitt was to leave for New York to head up fund-raising in the United States for Indusco, but her credentials and authority were questioned by the Rockefeller Foundation's J. B. Grant, to whom, among many others, Snow had appealed for support. Without consulting Snow, Hilda Selwyn-Clarke, the forceful wife of the British health commissioner in Hong Kong, proposed to Gollancz that Snow was exactly the right person to come to England for a lecture tour to raise money for Indusco, and Gollancz encouraged the idea. Snow at the same time was arranging a visit to Indusco sites for Philippine businessman Mike Appleman that would prelude the latter's fund-raising journey through the Chinese communities of Southeast Asia. All these events occasioned lengthy and numerous letters and draining emotional concern.

By late March, Snow was convinced Indusco was about to fall into the hands of a particularly venal political faction within the National Government's Ministry of Economy through a proposed "reorganization." Indusco had now grown beyond the capacity of Mme. Chiang to watch over personally, and Dr. Kung, "having had the whole thing dumped in his lap by circumstances beyond his control, is perhaps ready to heave a sigh of relief if responsibilities are shifted elsewhere." To prevent this disaster, Snow and Alley agreed it was necessary to establish a more substantial organization in Hong Kong through which aid from the international community could be funneled more directly to Alley, and hence to areas where it was most needed behind the Japanese lines. Snow also assumed the task of publicizing Alley's dedication and achievements to the international community. It was these concerns as much as his search for a new book subject that brought him back to mainland China late in April.[8]

36

Distant Thunder in Europe

J UST BEFORE SNOW LEFT the Philippines for Hong Kong, the Northwestern Youth National Salvation Congress met in Yenan to encourage
the young people of the rest of the nation to unite and mobilize all their
resources against the menace of Japanese aggression. Mao Tse-tung gave
the opening address, and Smedley sent Snow an enthusiastic report of the
speeches and collective actions. Such a public gathering of young people
from across the nation made clear the status of the Communist movement
had markedly improved since Snow's visit three years before. *Red Star over
China* played a significant role in the creation of that new understanding and
respect. It also stimulated such a parade of Western journalists and observers
to Yenan that Snow could no longer confidently expect another visit would
be particularly newsworthy.

But even before he left the Philippines events in Europe were rapidly
escalating to set an explosive background of world history for Snow's next
visit with Mao Tse-tung. Hitler took advantage of the Munich pact to invade
Czechoslovakia in March. Italy took over Albania in April. Germany and Italy
signed a full military alliance in May. In August, Hitler and Stalin agreed to
a mutual nonaggression pact, and, in September, Germany invaded Poland,
provoking England and France to declare war. World War II was no longer
deniable as Snow would sit face-to-face with Mao Tse-tung one more time.

Still in Hong Kong, however, he felt no great urgency to visit Yenan. He
had another prior job to do, and it took longer than he expected. He called

on Soong Ching-ling and T. V. Soong soon after settling in at the Gloucester Hotel. They were the keys to establishing an international committee for Indusco to channel funds raised abroad directly to Alley for use behind the Japanese lines.

In late November or early December of the previous year, L. T. Chen tested Indusco's integrity by demanding a fifty-thousand-dollar kickback before he would advance Indusco's budgeted money. K. P. Liu, whom Alley left in charge in Hankow during his journey to Paochi, refused. In retaliation Chen discredited Liu to Kung. Liu told his story to Alley and asked Alley to make everything clear to Kung. Alley could not bring the matter directly to Kung but sent the story through Ida Pruitt, whom he met for the first time in Chekiang in November and immediately recruited to the cause, on to Ambassador Clark-Kerr in Shanghai.

Alley described what followed to Pruitt, who sent the letter on to Snow:

> Now what a hell of a row. But I am tickled to death. All the stuff you told the Ambassador he promptly put on paper and sent on to our big chief [Kung], names and all. Of course there has never been such a frank undiplomatic document and department people are horrified. I have just come back from L. T. [Chen] who had to draft an answer. They all look at me as though I was the worst kind, etc. some more in pity than anything else. I apologise profusely. But it has made the whole lot sit up and take a very considerable amount of notice . . . please warn Ed of what has happened and guard against anything that will sink the ship.

Pruitt arrived in Hong Kong in February with a charge from Alley to build international support for Indusco. She became acting chairman of the Hong Kong Promotion Committee that eventually merged with the International Committee that Snow was engaged in setting up. She and Snow must have worked together in this effort, but neither later acknowledged the work of the other, probably as a consequence of Pruitt's siding with Foster Snow in her quarrel with Snow over their separation and divorce.

From early May until well into June, Snow worked at persuading an impressive array of recognized leaders to serve on a board for the newly proposed Indusco support organization. His task was complicated by an ambiguity in his own role. Many questioned why he too should not be a board member. He countered he was not a Hong Kong resident and that his journalistic support could be much more effective if he was not publicly identified with the organization. While he took the initiative for organizing the new international board, he at the same time kept his own role publicly and legally marginal.

His correspondence concerning this affair makes clear, however, he felt deeply Indusco was at a critical moment in the history of its development. Late in May he wrote Clark-Kerr there was strong circumstantial evidence that Indusco was "about to fall into the hands of the monopolists operating under the Ministry of Economics." This was "the culmination of a long behind-the-scenes struggle which began last July in Hankow—and with the first act of which you are pretty familiar." Alley had a recent bout with typhoid that provided these schemers a dangerous opportunity. "When he returns to Chungking the whole 'reorganization' will be presented to him as a fait accompli." The consequences could be tragic.

Snow detailed his plan to prevent or at least stall this reorganization until Alley could get out of the hospital and back to work. He must be given an important voice in any reorganization or outside support "could quickly turn to disgust, if not active hostility." Alley soon afterward sent word from Chungking that Snow's letter to Clark-Kerr had paid off: "Saw Bonaparte [Kung] today who was very friendly having apparently seen bdip [British diplomat Clark-Kerr]."

Snow also advised Alley if worse came to worst, to resign. But Alley felt his official position, though awkward and at times embarrassing, enabled him to visit work being done in the field more freely than he could without official title. He also noted if he resigned, he would "let all the rats get in on the dough. And these things will fall apart in a way that we'll never get them together again. See what frere [T.V. Soong] thinks."

Two weeks after Snow's letter to Clark-Kerr he made a final, urgent, but for the time unsuccessful, appeal to Soong Ching-ling to accept a place on the international board he was setting up. She continued to support CIC, but that support seemed more and more at the expense of her own China Defense League. Snow listed these counterarguments:

> (1) CIC offers the best means of broadening the basis of support for CDL and its friends. (2) This CIC support can only be fully mobilized if you, as a personality but also as head of CDL, will take nominal responsibility on the Board. (3) The Philippine Chinese have already promised their support, on the basis of your letter announcing the Board and the Trustee Fund, in which you promised to serve on the Board. It may badly confuse them if you withdraw just now, and spoil the campaign there.

On June 22, 1939, S. J. Chen, manager of the Bank of China, in the capacity of acting chair and convenor, announced the organization of the board of trustees for the Chinese Industrial Co-operatives Productive Relief Fund. Neither Soong Ching-ling nor Snow were board members.

While still in Hong Kong, Snow also received a long letter from Jack Belden, recovering from a draining bout with malaria and looking for a job, as well as hinting for help in finishing and placing a manuscript that seems a preliminary exercise for his masterpiece, *China Shakes the World,* which appeared more than a decade later. Belden wanted to write about "100–150 tableaus of 1,000 to 2,000 words apiece—perhaps less—mostly picture—for this I need a wealth of intimate detail that my own personal experiences don't sufficiently cover." He detailed the material he had and what he needed. If he could only find a publisher to stake him for a year he believed he could write a story more dramatic than Prescott's *Conquest of Mexico.*

While visiting the New Fourth Army, Belden had seen Smedley. She was rather lonely because she was not allowed to visit the battlefront, but she was just as passionately true to herself as ever. He was surprised by Carlson's resignation and skeptical of its good sense. He had read Snow's *Saturday Evening Post* articles with great interest and added, "Your industriousness is embarrassing to me."

Snow soon learned his wife did not share Belden's view. She minced no words: "EXACTLY WHAT IN HELL ARE YOU DOING THERE for three months? I cannot understand how you can waste so much time and never do a thing to show for it." Petulantly, and inaccurately, but with enough truth to hurt, she added, "It has been going on now for a year and a half—you haven't written a thing."[1]

Snow responded by filling out and sending her his Last Will and Testament. A few months earlier he had purchased his first life insurance. His life was now taking on value in terms of money. Then, late in July, he flew to Chungking where, deep in the mountains of remote Szechuan, Chiang Kai-shek had regrouped his government to survive relentless Japanese aggression.

Chungking was a jerry-built "utterly planless overgrown medieval town." While the National Government tried to impose some modern order, the Japanese frustrated this effort with punishing air raids that took a barbaric incendiary toll on the flimsy wooden construction of much of the city. But catastrophe, whether natural or man-inflicted, was hardly novel to Chungking. By the time Snow arrived its citizens were already adapting to the new circumstances with stoic resolution.

Tillman Durdin, *New York Times* correspondent, and his wife, Peggy, the latter newly arrived from Shanghai, invited Snow to stay at their home. Snow quickly grew accustomed to scuttling into a nearby bomb shelter that offered crouching room to their party and about two hundred Chinese for two- and three-hour stints while Japanese planes unloaded their lethal burden.

After Snow endured four sleepless nights in the shelter, General Yeh Chien-ying and Teng Ying-chao came to the Durdins' for dinner. Everyone was so fatigued the conversation was listless. The guests left early, and Snow and his hosts fell gratefully into deep sleep. When the midnight alarm sounded, Snow, with suspicious promptness, proposed, "Let's sit this one out." He rapidly calculated they had only one chance in 2,231 of even being scratched. Peg Durdin, however, skeptical of his suddenly awakened math, firmly insisted they go to the shelter.

Inside the shelter heavy tremors warned them bombs had fallen nearby. After the all-clear signal they hurried up the dirt path to the Durdins' cottage to find a one chance in 2,231 bomb had hit just outside the kitchen. The house was a total wreck. A piece of Snow's underwear "was blown out of the bathroom window and ended up on a bush on the opposite side of the house, to do which it had to pass through an iron-barred window—the walls of the bathroom were intact—and curve around two corners of the house."

Other correspondents hearing of their close call quickly came round to investigate. Surprisingly two bottles of liquor on the bottom shelf of a bookcase survived intact. With a little search Peg Durdin also found a few glasses still whole. As a toast Snow offered to "take back the whole goddamned law of probabilities." The survival party lasted till dawn.

The very next night, however, a two-hundred-pound bomb added an exclamation point to the lesson of such massive impersonal malevolence by landing at the bottom of the flight of stairs leading to the shelter Snow and the Durdins had huddled in, this time without hesitation or debate. Half a dozen loiterers at the entrance were killed as Snow and his friends crawled deeper into the shelter's bowels.[2]

Bertram arrived in Chungking on an ambitiously improbable, but ultimately successful, mission for the China Defense League shortly before Snow was to leave. Bertram was escorting a team of volunteers delivering a cumbersome Thorneycroft ambulance, donated in England, from its point of embarkation at Haiphong over a route that paralleled much of the Long March to the Eighth Route Army in Shensi. He remembered ruefully Snow had a distinct advantage when both were invited to speak before the Foreign Relations Association on the eve of the Hitler-Stalin pact: "he had been able to commend his own President Roosevelt; I could only attack Britain's fumbling Chamberlain."

There was little time, however, for Snow to spend with his friends in the wartime capital before he found an opportunity to travel by truck with Lu Kuang-mien on an inspection tour of Indusco facilities on the road from Chungking to Chengtu to the Indusco center at Paochi. From Paochi he could travel by train to Sian and then make his way once more into Yenan. Snow left Bertram his sleeping bag, but after being routed by bugs his first night in a country inn, he made sure he borrowed another from Spencer Kennard, the missionary sponsor of *Democracy,* then living in Chengtu.

The lush fertility of the Szechuan land as he left Chungking seemed in sharp contrast to the poverty and backwardness of the people. "Szechuan," he noted sardonically, "is feudal Europe connected with the modern world by American trucks and trimotored Japanese bombers." But the city of Chengtu, wartime host to American-mission-sponsored Nanking University, offered more congenial social fellowship. Dr. Lewis Smythe, survivor of the savage Japanese occupation of Nanking, proved a different kind of missionary than those Snow had lampooned early in his writing career. He took Snow to visit a nearby cooperative machine shop and put into words the dilemma he felt as an American missionary: "We [Americans] collect millions from Japanese aggression and then send a few dollars to China to patch up some of the mangled bodies. We talk about brotherly love and peace but the Chinese see Christ as a 'front' for foreign participation in Japanese aggression. How can we answer them?"

Nanking University put its considerable experience supporting spinning and weaving handicrafts before the war at the disposal of Indusco in Chengtu, and thus played a key role in the winning of an army order for 1.5 million woolen blankets from Indusco weavers in 1940. In *Battle for Asia,* Snow credited such courage and devotion with saving much of whatever face Americans had left in China.

Snow's travel by truck ended in Paochi, rapidly becoming known as Kung-Ho Cheng, or Indusco City. The early effort in 1938 to save as much as possible of Hankow's industrial machinery by sending it to the end of the railroad line at Paochi had blossomed into the capacity to make shoes, canvas bags, clothing, tools, soap, dyes, electrical goods, confectionery, military uniforms, leggings, canvas cots, tents, blankets, and so on. Its success even merited the attention of Japanese bombers, but its growth was sufficient to encourage workers to jokingly claim the Japanese had only saved them the trouble of pulling down buildings already too small.

The success Snow observed, achieved with such little government support, encouraged him to believe the movement could eventually be self-supporting and thus free itself from the invidious politics and corruption then emanating from Chungking. He titled the chapter in *Battle for Asia* describing what he saw in Paochi "Tomorrow's Hope?" He and others by this time had begun to lobby the American government to earmark part of its funding for China for Indusco.[3]

He arrived in Sian on the night of September 5 in a pouring rain. He wrote his wife he was lucky to get a room in the Guest House where they had been reunited almost two years earlier. It was now sadly dilapidated, its dining room destroyed, and the building badly shaken. He had only the most fragmentary news of events in Europe, but he understood England and France had declared war on Germany, and he assumed Germany was at war with Poland. He found it difficult to believe Chamberlain really meant to engage in a major war if given the faintest trace of a road out. "However, when great war machines start rolling it is not easy to stop them, even when their drivers on all sides are evidently so reluctant to break their necks over comparatively trivial issues as in this case." He did not mention the Hitler-Stalin pact preceding these events, but it became an important topic in his conversations with Mao Tse-tung.

War in Europe complicated his personal plans: "If the war goes ahead, there will be no market of importance for writing on the f[ar] e[ast] for some months to come. My opus would fall with a faint thud into a marshland of disinterest." It also made their travel plans uncertain. He felt compelled to make one more trip to Shanghai before they left China, but perhaps he ought to return to Baguio first so they could talk over their future. A few days later he wrote his father he knew Foster Snow was disappointed that war had in effect canceled their long-held plans for Europe. To her he said only: "Should conditions necessitate your early departure from the Ph., do not hesitate to go ahead without me."

Bertram had wired from Chengtu he was leaving on September 29. But there had been heavy rains, and Snow feared he might be stuck in the mud or delayed by avalanches on the mountainous route: "Poor kid, he has had a bellyful of bad luck and trouble and discouragement on this trip."

He apologized to his father for not writing for months but gave a composed assessment of the impact of the dramatic events in Europe on China. "The Russo-German non-aggression pact, and Russia's neutrality declaration, would seem to leave Russia's hands freer for action here, and aid to China. But the physical difficulties of extending that aid are enormous." After listing the three-thousand-mile central Asian road across deserts, the railway from French Indochina to Yunnanfu, and the Burma Road, he noted that European war would mean that Russian supplies over such routes would dwindle. England and France would have to bring their forces home, giving Japan a splendid opportunity to exploit. China's "main hopes must now lie with the USSR and America." He looked for a prolonged European conflict, though a quick German defeat would be most welcome. Like many, he assumed the Maginot line was a substantial defense and did not foresee France's quick defeat or Germany's blitzkrieg sweep through Belgium and the Netherlands.

He offered his father a melancholy personal assessment of his long stay away from home: "I am in good health, but growing older and full of groans and protests at the hard life, which formerly did not bother me. I look forward to a 'settling down' period in the not too distant future. Never did I dream, when I set out 11 years ago, that my wanderjahr would last this long. I have become a Marco Polo indeed, and my own land will seem strange to me as a new world, when I return."

Meanwhile Foster Snow, thinking his family might be worried about his safety, reassured them he had cabled her from Sian on September 10. "He had two narrow escapes in Chungking in bombing raids but wasn't bothered by them." She explained why she wrote so seldom:

> I have too much writing to do to expend my limited energy in social correspondence, and always expect Ed to do the family correspondence with you, but we are always happy to hear from you and people there. Ed gets a little homesick once in awhile, but we don't have much time for such things in the middle of this mess in the Far East. I am afraid to start any personal correspondence with the Snows—you have so interminably many aunts and uncles and various degrees of relatives that I was lost in the shuffle long ago.

Bertram arrived at the Sian Guest House only a few days after Snow and later remembered Snow's eagerly telling him they could travel with a Red Army convoy to Yenan the next week. Snow was surprised when Bertram replied, "Fine. I only wish I were going with you." Bertram then explained he was going back to New Zealand to join the war effort either in the ranks or as a correspondent.

Snow in turn answered with an indifference that surprised Bertram: "Well, it's your war. Or Chamberlain's, don't forget. I suppose I might feel the same way, if we were in it."[4]

Snow may have seemed distant from British feeling about war with Nazi Germany, but Bertram would have been even more dismayed had he sat with Snow to hear Mao Tse-tung's views of the British following these history-making events in Europe. Late in September, Snow had two formal interviews with Mao and saw him informally on several other occasions. He published a fairly complete text of his interviews in two installments of the *China Weekly Review:* one, under the heading "The United Front and Problems of Policy" on January 13, 1940, and the second headed "International Questions" on January 20. Wang Ju-mei, now known as Huang Hua, "greatly matured" and "now a man of quiet self-confidence," served as interpreter.

Mao saw the effect of the Hitler-Stalin pact and the outbreak of war in Europe as a simplification of international conflict. To him these events made clear the prime issue all along was colonialism. Chamberlain and Britain were now Public Enemy Number 1, leading a coalition of "so-called democratic" countries in defense of imperialism and capitalism. To Mao the two were synonymous. Stalin had outmaneuvered Chamberlain, who had previously appeased Hitler in the hopes of forming an anti-Soviet coalition. Nazi Germany as an imperialist threat would soon be severely weakened by war against other colonialist powers, Britain and France. Mao rightly blamed Chamberlain for the breakdown in British-Soviet negotiations.

When an incredulous Snow asked if Mao saw "no difference between Fascism and the cause of the democracies of England and France," Mao blandly explained there was no difference in their positions in this war. Britain was being driven primarily by her imperial interests, which were threatened by China's defeating the Japanese, Germany's recovering her colonies, and India's winning her independence.

To Snow's question about the effect of the European war on Japanese strategy, Mao offered Japan would stay out of that war to continue trade with Britain, France, and the United States, but she would be keeping a covetous eye on the Dutch East Indies. He then added a vivid cartoon of world politics that Snow at the time could hardly have found to his taste: "Japan hopes to get rich in this world war. Roosevelt is also hoping to get rich. Roosevelt wants to win leadership in the capitalist world. He wants Chamberlain for a secretary and Japan for part of his guard, his rearguard—with Hitler and Mussolini in the vanguard." Germany's attack on Russia two years later made clear Mao severely underestimated the Nazi threat and overestimated Stalin's shrewdness.

Snow interrupted an answer Mao made to a later question to ask how Mao could excuse the Soviet Union's making available to Germany's imperialist adventure Russia's wheat, oil, and other war materials, or Russia's continued leasing of oil lands in Sakhalin and fishing rights elsewhere to Japan. After Mao responded rather lamely, Snow pushed him to distinguish between the United States' supplying Japan with war materials and Russia's supplying Germany with similar war materials. Mao replied what mattered was "whether the country in question was really supporting imperialist war as a matter of policy, or whether it was supporting revolutionary wars of liberation." He insisted the USSR had established a clear record in support of liberating revolutions.

Since Snow had asked this question off the record, by which he apparently meant he had not submitted it in writing, he offered not to publish Mao's response. But Mao did not hesitate to put his answer on record, and Snow did not hesitate to publish it.

Finally Snow suggested the Hitler-Stalin pact would greatly weaken communist parties in England, France, and America, drive away sympathetic liberals, and sow much confusion in the ranks of the working class. Reactionary elements would be strengthened, and the chances for a future anti-Soviet combination would be much improved. Mao serenely disagreed, asserting flatly, "Hitler is in Stalin's pocket."

For his own readers Snow then added: "So all is well—unless it turns out that there is a hole in Stalin's pocket."

Back in Chungking, Snow noted in his diary that Po Ku, after hearing Snow's account of his interview with Mao, thought Mao attacked the British too strongly and that Britain and the USSR might still team up against Germany. Po Ku also told Snow the Chungking Party office had wired Mao to "leave America out" in his attack on imperialist warmongers. The Party had only recently declared the United States the only capitalist democracy genuinely antifascist. When Snow quoted Mao's remarks about Chamberlain and Roosevelt, Po Ku wondered if it was necessary for Snow to publish the quoted comments. Snow concluded:

> As Communist representative on the spot, who had to answer criticisms of non-Communist Chinese, as well as Westerners, who felt Stalin had betrayed the cause of progress and enlightenment by his cynical deal to swallow one half of Poland while Hitler was inhaling the other, Po Ku was (it seemed to me) more keenly aware of the "contradictions" in the Kremlin's turncoat policy than Mao, whose views went unchallenged in Yenan.

Mao's harsh and open criticism of Britain and America published in the *China Weekly Review* provoked angry reaction in Chungking and brought new strain to the United Front. The Kuomintang was still courting aid from both countries.

When Snow wrote about his Yenan visit a year later in *Battle for Asia,* he omitted Mao's pungent personal references to Chamberlain and Roosevelt and his indictment of American capitalism. He put the interview in the context of a larger discussion of Mao as a prophet. Mao's leadership was in part built upon his past ability to foresee events others found incredible. Snow remembered the faith Mao had in China's ability to survive Japanese aggression when others, including Snow, were so much more dubious. Snow acknowledged the belatedly proven wisdom of Mao's policy through the turbulent events in Sian late in 1936. He also had to admit visiting Yenan for the second time he found the Communists in a stronger political and military position than he realistically expected after his first visit. On the other side of the ledger he noted only Mao's early prophecy that Japanese aggression would drive China to "complete internal mobilization" was still far from being realized.

Mao's view of the British role in the Hitler-Stalin pact and the invasion of Poland was an example of predictions Snow found very dubious in 1939. But months after his Yenan visit, he read Sir Nevile Henderson's memoirs, which revealed the persistence of Chamberlain's dream of appeasing Hitler until the very last moment. And even more telling and more recent, in July 1940 Britain closed the Burma supply route to China in an effort to appease Japan. The Burma Road had not been reopened when Snow wrote. Snow clearly implied Mao's harsh indictment of Britain's role in these events a year later seemed again to reveal shrewd insights he had not originally appreciated.

Snow also understood Mao's primary concern with colonialism: "Nationalist sentiment seems more pronounced in Mao Tse-tung and his followers than among Communists in advanced capitalist countries. It must be repeated that in Communist theory China is a semi-colonial and semi-feudal country struggling *not* for immediate socialism but to achieve national emancipation on the one hand, and to liquidate 'remnants of feudalism'—to achieve social democracy—on the other." Nevertheless he insisted this was no reason to doubt the revolutionary nature of their communism.[5]

Snow frequently criticized both British and American policies toward China for being inconsistent with their democratic traditions, but his criticisms were based on his own strong faith in those traditions. Mao Tse-tung was far more likely to judge these traditions by the behavior of their representative governments, and he had seen the colonialism of these democratic nations firsthand. Democracy, like communism, in its fullest sense seemed some ultimate, but remote, prize following several necessary political stages. Mao was even then on the eve of defining a "new democracy" in his own national revolutionary terms. "Fascism" was useful to him primarily to describe the corrupt use of arbitrary power by the Kuomintang against the interests of the Chinese people or as the most urgent threat from Japan in a long series of colonizing invaders.

Snow might not have seen the war with Hitler in quite the immediate national terms Bertram did, but he certainly viewed Hitler and fascism as a far more dangerous threat to world civilization than did Mao Tse-tung. That Stalin should go to bed with Hitler shocked him. Never a fan of Stalin's, he frequently seemed to resent Stalin's lack of support for Chinese communism more than Mao did. He clearly was disappointed by Mao's ingenuous defense of Stalin. He was, however, sufficiently a journalist to report Mao's views in all their revealing frankness in the *China Weekly Review*, but his report of the interview in *Battle for Asia* was more carefully diplomatic and hence regrettably less responsible.

Chou En-lai was in Moscow while Snow was in Yenan, but Mao with his new wife, who would later give yet another cruel face to political tyranny, was surprisingly sociable, inviting Snow to play bridge and poker for pretend stakes several nights in a row. The European war was still too new and distant to totally displace Snow's concern for Indusco, and he persisted in asking Mao's support. The Chairman finally signed a statement Snow could use to persuade overseas Chinese to support Indusco behind the Japanese lines:

> We support the idea of building many small industries as an important part of economic reconstruction during the war. Even if Chinese Industrial Cooperatives can do nothing for front-line areas and the guerrilla districts behind enemy lines, the work they are doing is very important in helping to restore industry in the rear. But it is in the war areas and the guerrilla districts in the enemy's rear that industrial cooperatives are most needed and will find the warmest welcome from our troops, from the people, and from the government. . . . All friends of China should support this progressive movement.[6]

Snow's first visit to the Red forces in 1936 had led a stream of Western journalists looking for something to add to his extraordinary scoop. His brief visit to Yenan in 1939 was the last by a foreign journalist for the next five years. His two visits thus serve as curious bookends to three tumultuous years of history for the communist movement in China's modern national revolution.

37

Clearing the Way for *Battle for Asia*

MAO OFFERED SNOW A LOAN to cover his return to Hong Kong, but Snow assured him he could manage. His smoothly arranged two-day return trip to Sian contrasted pleasantly with his rough ten days by motor convoy on his way up. He arrived on September 30 in time to make the Eurasia flight for Chungking, but the plane bypassed Sian because of a Japanese bombing raid. The delay gave him time to write his thanks to Mao.

Even though his stay in Yenan had been short, the opportunity to interview the Chairman had made it very worthwhile. He was particularly pleased with Mao's support for Indusco. He emphasized the importance of keeping the outside world informed of the progress of co-ops and medical work within the domain of the Frontier Government. He suggested Ma Hai-teh might be just the person to make a monthly report to the China Defense League, which would also in effect inform Indusco contributors.

As his wait dragged on, he added a second letter October 2, suggesting a new and grandly ambitious proposal for raising guerrilla industry funds involving American and Russian cooperation that apparently came to no consequence. Finally he flew to Chengtu, stopped overnight, and next morning caught another flight to Chungking to be greeted by Corin Bernfeld, a New Zealand journalist he had recommended to Indusco, and Anna Wang at the entrance of the Guest House. Alley came by shortly after. Snow's stay in Chungking this time was brief and free from Japanese bombs.

The war in Europe still seemed more of proclamations than bullets. He wrote Sommers of the *Saturday Evening Post:* "I hope I can get something to you about this part of the world by the end of the year. Or do you think you can get your readers' minds off the sound-accompanied diplomatic war in Europe long enough to read about any place so remote? After all, when we start an undeclared war here we mean it, which appears to be more than can be said for some the declared wars elsewhere." He flew back to Hong Kong on October 10.[1]

The International Committee was on hold when he arrived. Chen Han-seng, administrative head, was in Shanghai, and Bishop Hall, chairman of the board, was in the hospital. Bertram's decision to return to New Zealand and volunteer for the war also stalled activity in the China Defense League. Some supporters even doubted the existence of the International Peace Hospital, then the focus of CDL's medical mission. Snow described this lack of faith to Alley to reenforce the importance of those in the field keeping Hong Kong informed of work done.

For a time Alley seriously considered whether he should not leave his post with Indusco and volunteer his services to the Red forces. He wrote Snow: "Should I go to the missionaries, it would have to be done very quietly. But I still think the best thing is to hold the thing together somehow. Its fall would mean so much— and the tragedy is the babies here would not have sense to realise just how much." In another letter he added: "Wish you would give my very best to Aunt [Mme. Sun Yat-sen] and tell her that the savages have not got me yet, though they are doing their damndest—and that I'm with the missionaries no matter what." He shared Snow's enthusiasm for establishing a strong Indusco presence in the southeast that would support the New Fourth Army.

Chen Han-seng returned to Hong Kong and a meeting of the board of the International Committee was called October 30. Snow was now an official board member. He persuaded the board to allocate a substantial loan for guerrilla industries in the northwest to establish a new International Co-op Center that would attract funding from abroad. He assured the board this had Alley's approval and wrote Alley immediately of the board's action.

The next day he wrote Ma Hai-teh telling him the good news and asking him to inform Mao Tse-tung. He wanted most of all to avoid the publicity problems of the International Peace Hospital. He also told Ma, in case he had not already learned, that CDL had appointed him its representative in Yenan, and he suggested Huang Hua would be a good man to get interested in CIC: "Talk to him about it will you?"

After Snow left for the Philippines, Chen Han-seng received a note from Alley apparently written before Alley learned of Snow's board motion for the International Co-op Center in Yenan. Alley's note suggested he would be satisfied with a far more modest appropriation to begin cooperative work in the guerilla war region. *"Other projects* could follow." Chen quoted Alley's letter to Snow, making clear the dilemma this created for him following the board's approval of Snow's far more ambitious proposal.

Snow felt betrayed and embarrassed. He wrote Chen offering his resignation if Alley and he were truly working at cross-purposes, and he wrote Alley indignantly questioning how Alley could have written what he did.

> I went all the way to the Northwest to get a collective opinion from Lu Kuang-mien, Wu Chu-fei, the Yenan depot, and yourself, on this matter. I spent hours explaining the situation to all of you. You personally have no reason for not understanding the position completely. I returned to Hong Kong, and submitted a plan, according to our understanding, and with great difficulty got the IC's agreement on this matter. I wrote to you in detail about it, and told you just what was necessary. Chen Han-seng was even more explicit. . . . And your final word is given in such a manner as to leave us both without any basis for further insistence that the I.C. support this terribly urgent—as fully agreed by you—program.

Chen kept Alley's more modest request quiet and persuaded him to make another more in keeping with the board's action. Chen then wrote Snow: "With such a triumph I now hold your letter to Rewi and will destroy it when I hear from you. The old horse, as he chooses to call himself, has enough troubles and worries and I think I am right in not forwarding something which is already a bygone."

Before leaving Hong Kong for the Philippines, Snow sent Herz some short articles he hoped she could place and proposed spending the next four months writing in Baguio. He denied the rumor he was returning to the United States soon and promised to give her plenty of advance warning before he did. He asked the *Daily Herald* for an extension of his leave of absence without pay, explaining he had to fulfill a book contract or lose his advance.

Meanwhile Pruitt began organizing support for Indusco in the United States amid another snarl of confusing and conflicting interests. She stayed a few days with Eleanor Lattimore in Baltimore at the end of October and early November and left much of her personal belongings stored with the Lattimores. She saw Mac Fisher and Evans Carlson in New York. Fisher was looking for a job, and she found Carlson feeling low: "He cannot see things clearly ahead of him. I think he is very low in funds." She was getting early encouragement from Pearl Buck and John Hersey, but she was finding it difficult to work with Edward Carter from the Institute of Pacific Relations. She wrote Foster Snow: "There seems to be some hitch about the committee that I do not understand. Carter does not like me and resents me as too small a potato for him to bother with, I think. Apparently he told Ed something like that or rather that I was not the right person to send."

With some pride she insisted: "Small as I am I am getting some things done and could do more if they would use me as a messenger and not as a prize exhibit, which Ed would be if he should come." She believed strongly "the committee is something that needs doing," but she postscripted her letter with, "I wish Ed had told me about Carter's attitude or advised me not to come if he thought I would not get anywhere as he seems to have done."

When Alley heard Snow might return to the United States to build support for Indusco, he thought well of the idea. But Snow was clearly embarrassed by the rumor's spread. It was one more sore spot with Alley:

> Why you should take I.P.'s word on such a matter, rather than my own, I do not know. We discussed this thing at length, and I said, as I have told you repeatedly, that I could not go to the U.S.A. in the near future, and in any case not on a lecture tour or for C.I.C. I.P. has evidently informed Carter that I am coming to U.S.A.; yesterday I had a cable from him asking me to cable him the date of my arrival. As a matter of fact I have not had a single note or even a P.S. from I.P. since she left, and I have not written her myself, so she has no authority for her statement to you.

The idea Snow might return to the United States and spark a campaign to support Indusco was nurtured by wishful thinking from a variety of sources. Carter wrote Snow after receiving the latter's cable terming the report of his return a canard: "I am not at all grateful for the cable because I thought you were coming to the United States and on the basis of this news, [Henry] Luce and I started in to organize an American cooperating committee for the C.I.C. Can't you reverse your decision and come right along?"

Hubert Liang, who had only recently returned to China after an American tour in which he had aroused considerable interest in Indusco, wrote from Lanchow: "I certainly hope you can make a trip to the States this spring and spend at least three or four months there. The earlier you can be there the better. I feel sure you can do a great deal in getting the interest aroused crystallized along some concrete and definite lines. The American situation is extremely important and has a tremendous bearing on the course of development of our Movement on this side."

Before Liang had flown from Chengtu to Lanchow with Alley, he, Alley, and Spencer Kennard had also discussed the possibility of reviving *Democracy*.

They already had in mind an appropriate person to produce a Chinese edition and a young Harvard graduate, Hugh Reade, whom Kennard considered a "several hundred percent improvement on John Leaning for office editor." Frank Price would join Kennard and Liang in sponsoring the venture. Yet needed were a Hong Kong office and cash. Kennard hoped Snow might help with both of these as well as contributing articles. It would also help if Foster Snow could come to Chengtu to help. Living there was very inexpensive. Kennard was sufficiently impressed with Liang's belief that *Democracy* once had "a very profound influence," and could again, that he was now in favor of relaunching the publication at the earliest date Snow thought practical.

Ma Hai-teh wrote early in December, not long after Dr. Norman Bethune died tragically from infection while operating in the combat field. Ma still had no request from the China Defense League to write regular reports, but he was willing to send a report directly to Snow every two weeks or each month. He included a report on Bethune's work from February to July and considerable information about the hospital stations and medical training going on. He had much less to report on Indusco, though he had an instructive letter of Snow's translated into Chinese and distributed and had talked personally to CIC representatives about informing overseas funding sources how their money was being used. A CIC industrial exhibition was planned for January, and he had enlisted an American Chinese, Chen Sze-kuen, whom Snow had met, to report on Indusco work.[2]

In Baguio the Snows leased a three-bedroom house with a small office room for Snow at 2 Outlook Drive until April 1. He invited Kuo Ta, a former Yenching student who had earlier done some translation work for him, to come from Hong Kong to stay in the house and work as his secretary. He expected to begin writing his new book in earnest at the beginning of the year. Until then he would be reading, researching, and outlining. Foster Snow had finished *A Song for Ariran* just before his return. Herz thought its chances of a good sale were much better than *Inside Red China*'s. She expected Doubleday to take it, but John Day became Foster Snow's latest publisher instead. She was not having much luck placing Foster Snow's poems. She also noted the *Saturday Evening Post* frequently asked about Snow and his plans, particularly if he was coming back to the States soon.

That stirred Snow to query the *Saturday Evening Post* about its interest in an article on future Russian-Chinese relations. Herz cabled a reply: "Sommers very interested would like emphasis Mao Stalin aspect." Hallett Abend had proposed a similar article to the *Post*, but Sommers told her "of all the Far-Eastern writers you're his favorite." Since Sommers understood

Mao to be in Russia at the time, Snow's proposed article seemed especially timely.

Snow dourly responded Mao was not in Russia, and such false information was part of the battle he had continually to fight.

By December 12 he sent twenty pages titled "Will Stalin Sell Out China?" to Sommers and asked whether the *Post* might also be interested in a general roundup describing the Chinaman's chances, after thirty months of war, based on several thousand miles of recent travel.

The *Saturday Evening Post* printed Abend's article instead of Snow's. When Snow saw it he was angry and disappointed, not just for the fate of his first article, but also for his proposed second. He wrote Herz:

> Good heavens, I see from Abend's article that he swallowed all that *Domei* bull about the Sinoreds taking over the Northwest and acquiring wings from Stalin. I wonder if that will cook my article [his second] with the *Post*, they certainly wouldn't want to contradict themselves, and will, I suppose, have to stand by Abend's yarn, having published it. Still I am amazed that the *SEP* published that stuff, as it could easily have checked the statements by a few inquiries at Washington. Or is it so bad that people have really lost all interest in any truth about anything named red any more?
> If so Stalin has nobody to thank for it more than himself.

Abend's piece did not cook his second article. On the contrary, "The Dragon Licks His Wounds" became one of the most successful articles Snow published in the *Saturday Evening Post*. He also significantly rewrote "Will Stalin Sell Out China?" for spring publication in *Foreign Affairs*.[3]

Spencer Kennard wrote a second letter urging some response from the Snows about *Democracy*. The *Daily Herald* accepted Snow's request for leave, but would pay only space rates to Powell as Snow's replacement. Snow wrote Powell if this was not satisfactory to him, perhaps Jack Belden might be interested.

He asked Chen Han-seng to write Carter urging that he and Luce go ahead with organizing an American support group for CIC. He wrote Carter a flattering letter encouraging his efforts on behalf of Indusco: "Beyond any question in my mind, now, the movement could become one of the greatest epics of modern war-time China, perhaps the greatest one, if it is given the support it merits by the Government." He wished he could be more encouraging about the government's support, but Indusco, with courageous and honest leadership, was persisting.

Late in February, Mildred Sayre, the wife of the new American high commissioner in the Philippines, published the text of a radio broadcast, carried over a national hookup in the United States, in which she noted that "Every cooperative worker is an owner and, therefore, a leader in his new task. A new social consciousness is evident in the vicinity of each unit. The Chinese loyalty to family and clan is spreading to what might be called in the west 'community welfare.' The nation is being bound together by a common, unified economic program." The new industrial cooperatives "are directly in line with the promotion in China of democracy on a grand scale."

Snow sent Sayre's comments to Ambassador Johnson in Chungking, who knew the Sayres well, adding that Mrs. Sayre's enthusiasm probably "had a good deal to do with Mrs. Roosevelt's recent decision to sponsor as honorary chairman, the American committee for C.I.C." He then noted: "I remember talking to you about our Indusco scheme in '38, it seems only a few months ago, when Alley and I brought our little booklet up to a rather hostile Hankow. Your belief in the plan was an encouragement. I think you must feel gratified now to know that it hasn't worked out quite such a crack-pot idea as most people there felt."

Ambassador Johnson promptly thanked Snow and acknowledged diplomatically: "There seems to be no doubt that China's intellectual leaders in all fields who have been driven back into the interior by the present emergency are getting a foothold and discovering that they can use their minds on the solutions of problems here which should result in great progress in developing Chinese resources in China's interests."[4]

Late in 1939 Snow restated to Charles Hanson Towne the claim he earlier made to Sommers that the only real war going on then was the war in China:

> I'm not complaining, nor do I join with the smart-alecs in sneering at Europe for its so-called "phoney war." The phonier they are the better; though I suspect it can't remain thus for long. What we've seen so far is but the preliminary to a first-rate cataclysm, and I very much fear our own messiahs will succeed in dragging us into the center for a kay-oh of our own. . . . I am opposed to our going to war with Japan, or any other power, however great the moral provocation, but it is high time we went to war against traders in death who make this wholesale murder possible. We can at least clean our hands by stopping this criminal and stupid trade [in scrap iron].

To Evans Carlson he handed on greetings from his friends in Yenan and Chungking and asked what he was going to do next. He hoped Carlson had made more progress on his book than he had. His comment on events in Europe implied he may have absorbed a good bit of Mao's argument on the Hitler-Stalin pact:

The European war does not interest me greatly—as a military affair, I mean. It is largely political. Chamberlain and Co. still hope to make an arrangement with the Nazis, and the present is largely a period of diplomatic maneuver (with sound accompaniment) in which British and French imperialism are trying to change the character of the combination from an inter-imperialist war into a joint imperialist war against Russia. The Soviets' blunder in Finland has raised Chamberlain's hopes. American excitement helps to encourage the old gent, who thinks we will come in, if he can collect a few more atrocity tales about the bolos. What about it? Are we going into the holy war to save British imperialism again?

He wrote his father about his China trip, and particularly his brushes with Japanese bombs. If the *Herald* did not grant his request for transfer to Europe, he intended to come home, but that would not be earlier than next summer: "The odds are at least 50–50, in my opinion, that we'll be tied up in war of our own, out here (more likely than in Europe) by then."

The phrase "phoney war" to describe events in Europe during this period was not original with Snow. Because there was relatively little fighting in western Europe until the German invasion of Denmark and Norway in April 1940, the grand declarations from governments were open to much wishful skepticism. Herz wrote in late December: "Anna Louise Strong, who is in town now together with her Russian husband, feels that the attitude we are taking regarding Finland will lead us to war and Fascism within a few months. I still cling to my belief that we'll be able to stay out of it, although underneath I am as fear-ridden as the majority of people."

Snow reported to Alley that Bertram had not joined up because there "was no need for more rookies just then." He was fattening himself up on a farm but was sick about leaving China. "Seems pretty swamped by it all, as who is not? Finland is a frightful mess, and impossible to defend. What bothers me is how sinister a picture of internal conditions in Russia it suggests." He strained to put a positive face on the universal malaise: "But the world is dynamic now as never before, and the wisest man cannot say whether a catastrophe anywhere is not historically the 'good' thing to happen."

Kennard invited Epstein to organize the Hong Kong office he needed to publish a new edition of *Democracy*. Epstein asked Snow's advice about the project. Snow repeated what he had told Kennard. He had no time to take an active part in the venture, but if democratic elements in Chengtu and Chungking felt a strong-enough need to start the magazine and if they believed it could fulfill its role under present conditions, he believed it should be supported. He would "contribute a piece now and then, try to get subscribers, and maybe buy a share. . . . But the initiative must definitely come from there, backed by people who will have to fight the magazine's battles on the spot."

He sharpened this statement in reply to a later query from Selwyn-Clarke, insisting the magazine "had to be published in Chengtu not Hong Kong (as was suggested) and could survive and be of value only if the Chinese liberals would make a fight for its right to present valid news and views which could not get a hearing elsewhere."[5]

He wrote Ma Hai-teh on January 15 he was "tickled to death" to get his letters and the report on Bethune, which "has already been published by cdl [China Defense League]." Yet that same day he wrote Soong Ching-ling, enclosing Ma's Bethune article, which he had somewhat revised, and requested her approval of his revisions. He suggested: "With Bethune's end, it would seem that a Bethune Memorial Medical Indusco might receive a good response as a project," and she might then issue an appeal for financial support in booklet form, featuring Ma's article. He enclosed a check for $130 Chinese "to cover Hai-teh's salary for November and December."

To Ma he also said he "was sorry after coming out that I had not spent more time in Y. [Yenan], I could have learned more there than outside without doubt, moussy [Mao] being quite right. However, I'm attached to the old world, and it makes demands."

Mme. Sun thanked him for the check for Ma's salary and for editing the articles. She found Ma's article on Bethune "especially useful for reproduction." But she also warned Snow of some reactions to his recent interview with Mao: "Many complaints have been lodged against you by different agents doing publicity work abroad for China. Your article to the LDH [*London Daily Herald*], they claimed, has damaged China's cause. Some one told me mau [Mao] is issuing a public denial of that interview, that he has to do this in view of many T. [?] papers utilizing it to attack the x [Communist] people. . . . When I obtain a copy, I shall mail it to you."

Snow immediately detailed for her his justification for publishing the interview. He had sent Mme. Sun the full manuscript that was the basis for "the offending dispatch to *LDH*," even before the complete interview was published in the *China Weekly Review*. He reached back to a long letter he had received a year earlier from "Earl Yeh, of Dies fame," who begged him not to even mention the Communists when he wrote about China. This seemed the same as Chiang Kai-shek's idea: "If people stopped writing about them the powers would forget that there were any, etc. He thinks it's all done with mirrors."

Snow believed, however, such tactics merely tended to give China's worst enemies a monopoly on interpreting a complicated situation: "For their own protection, now and in the future, the Xians [Communists] must let the world know what is happening, and what their program is. The latter will not scare off friends of China, but will arouse them to the necessity for greater effort, and will win new friends as well."

He was confident Mao "was fully aware of repercussions his comment might create. He knew he was speaking for publication, and asked me where the interview would appear. When I suggested that it would create a sensation he only smiled." Snow thought Mao judged plain-speaking necessary, and simply took the opportunity to broadcast warnings he could not publish otherwise. For a while Snow had doubted Mao's wisdom but in the end entirely agreed with him. "I can see that if an issue is made of it it might become necessary for Feathers [Mao] to issue a 'public denial.' Feathers and I both know privately that it is the truth, which is all that matters to me."

Mme. Sun's warning caused him to advise Powell the Mao interview was not liked in "certain quarters" and to ask if Powell had heard any repercussions. By this time he was well into writing "The Dragon Licks His Wounds," so he also noted concerning Chungking: "I have a few things on schedule that should make them feel better about me I hope."[6]

He wrote Pruitt a tentatively supportive letter. He shared with her the code names he and Alley had devised to get significant information past the scrutiny of government security agents, warning she must not use them with anyone other than him and Alley. He, for one, thought she had done splendidly in her beginning efforts, but she probably read his added advice with suspicion: "You are handling a big job, on a national scale, and have to feel your way carefully. . . . Take your time and get the right people."

He paid passing tribute to Alley's work for Indusco in "The Dragon Licks His Wounds," but he was already planning another piece to draw international attention to Alley as the selfless organizer of a timely effort to save China's wartime industrial capacity.

He offered to send Mildred, who had divorced and remarried, a movie NBC made of him and Foster Snow while he was doing a radio broadcast on the Philippines. He had several copies, and he thought this might be a means of paying his family a visit. His father sent a piece of advice concerning public sentiment in the United States that drew a prickly response:

> I have never subscribed to the dictates of any particular party or pub-
> lication, but have been mainly interested in presenting facts and in
> interpreting them as well as my equipment permits. I have a fairly good
> reputation for accuracy and honesty and that is the reason I can publish
> what I write. It would not do to repudiate anything I have written, unless

new facts proved it in error; and there are no such new facts. Therefore I write what I think, let the chips fall where they may.

He added greetings to his unmet new brother-in-law, Claude Mackey.[7] In December, Snow wrote his agent:

> Quite *confidentially*, Peg and I are thinking of doing a small book on Indusco. It would not interfere with my other book. I'm sorry to admit I've not started on the latter. It's terribly difficult to write anything as permanent as a book in these days, and hard to find a form for it. But I have five months leave from the *Herald*, now, and intend to do that book before that leave is up. I've asked for a transfer to Europe, after that period, and the *Herald* is "considering it."

Herz promptly warned: "The majority of publishers would reject it unless it were written as a human interest story, or perhaps as a courtesy to you because of your name. Everybody is so frightened and confused with the upheaval in this country and European events, that publishers take it for granted that no one would be concerned with Cooperatives in China."

Encouraged by a cable from Herz, he sat down to write "The Dragon Licks His Wounds," finishing it in roughly a week. He wrote Sommers that Abend had used the "international politics" angle, while he had deliberately confined himself to eyewitness stuff for the most part. He also noted he had "got quite a chuckle out of your picture of Ida Pruitt 'springing to her reticule' to write to me to do an article for you on the co-ops—which indeed she did. 'Indusco' really is a dramatic and wonderful thing, and so is Miss Pruitt, but somehow when the two combine it always makes me feel vaguely that I must be in the wrong church."

Early in February he had Herz advise Haas he would begin writing his book and hoped to have it ready for fall publication. Sommers was quick to tell Snow how pleased he was with his latest article: "This is simply to congratulate you on THE DRAGON LICKS HIS WOUNDS, which we all thought a magnificent job. I personally admired and envied the deft way you leavened international politics with good, vivid reporting. And you certainly covered ground. I think I've read a couple of dozen articles on the state of China in the last year or so, but the sum total didn't give me as clear a picture as your one piece did."

The article was a confidence builder for beginning *Battle for Asia*. The *Saturday Evening Post* paid Snow a "handsome price" for it and illustrated it with several of his photos. Herz was particularly pleased that for the first time Snow's name appeared on the cover of the magazine. Since the article appeared she had "heard from many people about it; they all think it's about the best thing the *Post* has carried for a long time."

Hollington K. Tong proved Snow right in believing his article would improve his status in Chungking:

> I do not hesitate to say that it is one of the best analyses I have seen of the present situation between China and Japan. It should emphatically give the lie to the rubbish which the American public has seen so much of late. You sized up the situation very well and while the things you say of China are not all favorable, they are the things you have seen with your own eyes and therefore factual. They are quite different from the things penned by observers who sit tight in Shanghai or Hong Kong and who have no use for personal experience or close-range studies.

Tong was particularly pleased by Snow's statement that "Chiang Kai-shek believes that Stalin is still more concerned with military security than political evangelism." Such a statement should help many to recognize that Russian assistance for China was not based on doctrinaire considerations.

Foreign Affairs published Snow's revised "Will Stalin Sell Out China?" a week after "The Dragon Licks His Wounds" appeared in the *Saturday Evening Post*. Richard Walsh was impressed with both and a little jealous he did not have the former for *Asia*. He was pleased, however, with the prospect Herz offered of publishing some of the chapters from Snow's forthcoming book. Walsh, Pearl Buck, and Sir Stafford Cripps spoke in support of the Chinese Industrial Cooperatives at a big meeting in New York on the same day "The Dragon Licks His Wounds" was published. He wrote Snow: "There isn't any doubt in our minds that the Cooperatives are the most important thing now being done in China."

Snow's persistent public-relations work had created a bandwagon in New York he might have hoped for but hardly could have fully anticipated. On April 22 Henry Luce's *Time* carried a brief, but very supportive, article on the success of the Chinese Industrial Cooperatives. In addition to the Snows and Alley, it named John Alexander, the British diplomat who had thitherto kept his role hidden, as one of the four Westerners who advised the Chinese in beginning the movement. The article carried a photo of Snow over the caption: "His factories cost $7 a man." Thus all within ten days, "The Dragon Licks His Wounds" appeared in the *Saturday Evening Post*; "Will Stalin Sell Out China?" appeared in *Foreign Affairs*; Pearl Buck, Richard Walsh, and Sir Stafford Cripps took Indusco's case before a large New York audience; and the *Time* article gave substantial national recognition to both Edgar Snow and the cooperatives. It is hard to imagine he could have done much better if in fact he had been personally present in New York.

All this publicity obviously made his publisher happy. Robert Haas wrote promptly: "I just want to tell you that I've read THE DRAGON LICKS HIS WOUNDS, and I think it's a perfectly fine piece. My congratulations! . . . You may imagine how eager we are to see you taking your place on our list again with a new volume."[8]

38

Asia Hears the Thunder in Europe

WHILE SNOW WROTE *Battle for Asia* in the Philippines, Hitler made what Churchill later described as his "tiger spring at the throat of western Europe." This was no "paper tiger," safely stuffed in Stalin's pocket. Norway and Denmark fell in early April. French and British forces swallowed the German bait of a fierce attack on Holland and Belgium and were subsequently trapped when a major German armored force threaded the supposedly impenetrable Ardennes Forest to sweep easily past the vaunted Maginot line and humiliate France once more at Sedan where the Third French Empire was brought to an end. Encircled Allied troops were forced to evacuate at Dunkirk late in May. France fell like a tethered goose, and a new government was set up quickly in Vichy. The clash of official pronouncements was replaced by very real and massive carnage that stunned the residents of Baguio. The rush of Allied defeats in Europe ominously also made the threat of Japanese attack in the Pacific both more likely and more imminent.

Kuo Ta arrived by ship in Manila in the middle of April to resume working for Snow as secretary and translator. Snow asked Lim Sian-tek of the *Manila World* to meet Kuo, as he was busy preparing to move into what Bertram described as "an improbable timbered chalet called 'Wor-ces-ter Cottage.'" Snow had written the first chapters of *Scorched Earth*. Gollancz, his British publisher, would choose to retain this title while enduring the full fury of the Nazi bombing of London, but Random House and Herz preferred instead the more distantly descriptive *Battle for Asia*.

By May 24, just before the disheartening evacuation at Dunkirk, Snow had an outline and twenty-two chapters, not necessarily consecutive, to put in the mail to Herz. He wrote Haas he expected his book in all to have about fifty to sixty short chapters, totaling about 150,000 words:

> There is no special theme to the book; it is a continuation of *Red Star Over China*, history as I saw it, the story of the war seen through its impact on one nosy foreign devil and his friends, living and dead. There are a few heroes in it; there is one hero in particular, Rewi Alley, whose effort to build guerrilla industry in China, as much of an epic as Lawrence's organization of guerrilla war in Arabia, provides a kind of ribbon of hope throughout the latter part of the book, making it a little different from most memoirs of war correspondents.

Herz quickly read fifteen of the twenty-two chapters at one sitting and wrote with enthusiasm, "my education on China stopped with *Red Star Over China* and yours and Nym's articles. I have read a lot of odds and ends that have come out, but I didn't get anything from them that continued the background you gave me through your first book." She saw no reason to worry his book would be "snowed under" or get a dismal reception because of events in Europe. She expected it to "meet with tremendous acclaim. It is sound, objective work and 'history,' in contrast to all the other sightseeing books on China and other places that are being written and published now." If he could send a complete manuscript in July the book could still be published that fall; if September, it would be published in January. "Ordinarily I would say that a book of 150,000 words might be too long, but after reading what you have to say I am inclined to say 'the more the better.' "

Haas wrote with similar, if more succinct enthusiasm, finding Snow's chapters "what we expected, vivid, dramatic and obviously well-informed. Were they consecutive, it would be easier to evaluate the book as a whole, but we have seen enough to be convinced that it will be a valuable contribution to an understanding of the tremendous events now shaking Asia."[1]

At the same time Alley wrote Indusco's situation was again desperate. He asked Snow to airmail T. V. Soong an urgent request to warn H. H. Kung that the promising new American support would be in jeopardy if political "adventurers on the side line" took over in Chungking.

Alley invited Snow "to see all the lads before they dispersed" at an upcoming seminar in Chungking. He had no letters from Pruitt for some time and hoped she had not deserted them. Two days later Alley wrote he was not sure Indusco would last. He identified a new political threat: "Attacks vicious, and YPM trying to battle in." YPM was Y. P. Mei, former leader of Chiang Kai-shek's Blue Shirts, who was then positioning himself to take effective control of Indusco's national headquarters. Alley wondered if the Hong Kong committee "should move—or if records should be sent to Manila or not."

By July 13 Snow had reshaped the structure of his book and made a new table of contents. He sent the revised manuscript with eleven new chapters to Herz on the chance she might place some of the chapters with magazines. Foster Snow had taken over the book on Indusco, and he hoped to send her manuscript with his new chapters.

Writing "with the world tottering all around one" was not easy. It was "terribly difficult to concentrate on the fate of a small part of it, or to feel any certainty in writing about it, when tomorrow may bring international changes which invalidate all one's own opinions and conceptions." Nazi troops marched into Paris with dismayingly little effective resistance. *Scorched Earth* was turning into neither fish nor fowl: "My book mixes up objective reporting of political and military events and conditions with sometimes extremely subjective comment and sometimes mere travel commentary. . . . Perhaps I would have done better to make it either one or the other . . . instead it is becoming one of those Mexican jumping bean affairs. But *again* I say, what a time to choose for making a book!"[2]

Herz took the chapters he sent her first to the *Saturday Evening Post,* without much luck. She then took them to Walsh, who promised to use a minimum of four articles for which he would pay $225. She passed on the comments of Elsie Weil who read the chapters for *Asia.* Weil feared "readers now harassed with Europe and domestic problems and personal worries" were readily bored with China, and she wanted them "to read Edgar Snow's book because he has a real message and an important one—and it must be got across to as many as possible." She urged him to "steam up his chapters on what America has done to help Japan wage this war on China . . . to make Americans writhe and be ashamed, arise and take action." She was much moved even though she was "reading this on thin paper in the small hours of the morning after I had done a more than daily manuscript stint . . . with the perspiration rolling down my cheeks and neck. It's splendid stuff! All power to Edgar Snow!"[3]

On July 22 the Philippine Indusco Committee submitted a substantial petition to President Franklin D. Roosevelt requesting a loan of fifty million U.S. dollars to support the Chinese Industrial Cooperatives. Three weeks earlier, on the same day Alley wrote Snow requesting his intervention with T. V. Soong, Foster Snow wrote Alley:

> I feel so unhappy about China lately that I want to chuck the whole thing and go home and do something really important where there is a real

power for progressive movements. You ask why we don't come there. I couldn't bear the suffocation. . . . I can't decide whether it is worthwhile to make one grand effort more to get $50,000,000 from the US Govt. for this work—or just skip it and let matters take their course. Yet I feel history is at a crucial moment in China when such a loan might change the whole situation there. . . . Actually in writing about China I (and Ed) have reached a blind alley—we don't know what to say. I feel like a potential criminal in recommending help for a Govt. that may start slaughtering its own people again any time.

Early in August, Chen Han-seng described the reorganization of Indusco recently completed in Chungking. Y. P. Mei had been named to head the Secretariat: "The natural tendency at present is that Mei will become Secretary-General, de facto but not de jure." Then he concluded with sardonic realism: "Rewi thinks that if we could build up a strong field force with good coops, we will be all right. I hold a different opinion because I think good coops are eggs of the hen, which, however, now approaches infertility."[4]

A trio of old friends rendezvoused with the Snows in the Philippines in August. Snow and Alley had arranged for the Hong Kong International Committee to employ Carlson as a frontline advisor to Indusco. He was to meet Alley in the Philippines and return with him particularly to visit the area behind the Japanese lines commanded by the New Fourth Army. Bertram, meanwhile, had tired of waiting in New Zealand and Australia for an appropriate role in the European war. In June, Mme. Sun cabled the China Defense League needed him urgently. When his application to become an official war correspondent for the state news agency 2NZEF was turned down, he chose the war in Asia over that in Europe. Before boarding ship from Wellington to Sydney, he had a second cable from Mme. Sun: "Please stop over in Manila and try to form a CDL Branch there."

It was a welcome reunion of Westerners who cared deeply for China, but this was not the happiest moment in Snow's writing schedule for it to happen. His work was interrupted by the comings and goings of these good friends for three weeks. Even so Snow sent Herz five more chapters on August 22 along with revisions of "Rip Tide" for Asia. He knew he had much more work to do, but he still hoped to see the book out by January. Bertram spent a week with them before returning to Manila. Alley arrived the day after Bertram left. Snow planned to use Alley's visit to work on the Alley article. By this time he had decided to limit Alley's role in Battle for Asia in favor of featuring his story in the Saturday Evening Post.

He wrote Herz: "I am anxious to get this book off my hands and do a tour for the SEP. Whatever people may say against this journal it is in my experience the only one which will publish any information in an article." The

Reunion in the Philippines—James Bertram, the Snows, Rewi Alley, and Evans Carlson.

Post, however, could not yet see its way to name him a foreign correspondent. It took Pearl Harbor to change its mind.

Polly Babcock apologized to the Snows for causing Alley's visit to be brief, but it was important to hold a fund-raising meeting at the home of the Sayres in Manila on August 29. Mrs. Sayre had to leave for Mindinao on August 31. Babcock invited the Snows to come down to Manila with Alley and stay at her home.

Just before Alley arrived Snow described for his sister how he saw the national revolutions in Asia figuring in the drastic reshaping of the world's political alliances:

> Japan will break up before long: within a couple of years, I think. Rev-
> olutions are coming all over the world, but will probably start in Asia;
> indeed are already beginning. The political remapping will extend from
> Mongolia through China down to Burma and India, the Dutch Indies
> and the Malay States, Indo-China and Siam. Australia and New Zealand
> may follow Canada in making a mutual defense pact with the U.S.A., if
> the British lose control of the North Sea and the Meditterranean. I don't
> think Hitler will attempt a blitzkrieg against Britain but will confine his
> work chiefly to air bombing with the objective of immobilizing Britain as
> a possible base of attack for invasion of the continent: crippling British
> industry and communications, terrorizing the countryside, doing as much
> damage as possible to shipping, and sowing all the seas around England

with bones as thick as wheat. If and when he has immobilized Britain as a base he will move on down into the Balkans and try to get control of adequate oil reserves—either with or without Soviet consent. Seems to me he must inevitably clash with Russia. Only after he succeeds in pushing the Russians back behind the Ukraine will he set out in earnest for the destruction of Britain, it appears, and mastering the eastern Atlantic. But who knows?[5]

The *Saturday Evening Post* was not happy with the article Snow sent them on Alley and asked for substantial revisions before eventually publishing it the following February.

Late in September Snow was finishing his book, but the "last chapters are most important and I must take some time to think and coordinate these with the rest of the book." About this time he came up with the title *Battle for Asia* that quickly pleased Herz and Random House. On October 5 he sent Herz a complete manuscript except for the last chapter. He promised that would be on the mail-carrying Clipper on October 11. He closed his letter: "War may come here any day. I hope to get out; don't want to be interned here. But there are few ships. If I should for any reason be unable to get the last chapter to you the book could be published as it stands."

Foster Snow finished her book on Indusco and decided to have Kelly-Walsh, a scholarly publishing firm, print it in Hong Kong or Shanghai and then try to sell the sheets to an American and English publisher. The Snows wanted the book published quickly as part of the campaign for American support for Indusco. They enlisted Carlson to help explain to the American people that Indusco was part of American self-defense. Foster Snow wrote: "It is worth $200 to Ed and me to get the thing printed, for we spend that much on typing alone in writing up reports for various people, on the subject. This book will serve to put a stop to all these long conversations, and questions people ask, for it contains all the answers."

Herz recognized Snow's stress finishing his book but still felt obligated to tell him of a request from a new progressive magazine, *Who*, with reputable editors and substantial backing that wanted him to do an article on the Soong sisters for their opening January issue. Snow questioned why *Who* did not ask Emily Hahn, who was writing a book on the subject, but eventually he shouldered this task as well.

Sometime during this busy period he also found time to read and comment on a collection of essays by Philippine writer Salvador P. Lopez, just then being published. Grateful, Lopez asked if he could send Snow's comments on with a review copy of his book to Elsie Weil at *Asia*. Lopez also noted a series of recent events he would like to discuss when Snow had time: "The prospects for the 'Free Asia' of which you speak rather glowingly are just now not exactly bright. The Pact of Berlin and the French Indo-China 'Incident' have cast a gloom upon the Orient that is most ominous. The sharpening crisis in Japanese-American relations and the opportunist policy of the Soviet Union do not encourage the hope that the march of aggression in Asia will soon be stemmed." Snow praised Lopez for opening new doors of political and cultural dialogue between East and West in his review of the book.[6]

Early in October their landlord, Elizabeth Worcester, wrote from Zamboanga that her husband Fritz was insisting she join a growing exodus of Americans from the Philippines to the safety of the States. She did not plan to return to their Baguio cottage and was grateful for the care the Snows had taken of it.

As he sent the last section of *Battle for Asia* to Herz he told her he had much difficulty persuading Foster Snow to get on a ship for home without him, but he felt he ought to stay and cover the naval war he expected in the Pacific for the *Saturday Evening Post*. He would probably have to set up in Singapore or India to cover it. "Mentally and physically very tired and a bit surfeited with war," he also worried about what he could do when he arrived home.

"Home" suggested "family." Howard wrote in February, and Snow did not immediately reply. After completing his book manuscript, he apologized for his long silence. He commented on the war and the coming presidential election in the States and added: "Peg is not well and has not been for months. I have been trying to get her to go home but she is an obstinate woman and has refused. Now I have a reservation for her at the end of the month, and if she does not go then she may leave early in November. I may come on to New York in December or January, if I can get away then." He could summon little enthusiasm for his book's near-publication: "It is not at all satisfying to me. But it is a hell of a time to write a book. It will be no worse than those written by other swine, I suppose." His emotional resources seemed worn thin.

While Snow was writing the conclusion for his book Hitler's blitzkrieg drastically foreshortened the time America had to choose and shape the terms under which it would enter the international conflict. Snow wrote Herz his worry: "The forces in the world are now so evenly matched that the most unexpected things may happen in the search of each side for an improvement in its strength. Everything I have written may look completely silly by the time it's published. I shall at least have the consolation of being in a huge company of discredited prophets." He did have the article on the Soong sisters for *Who* nearly ready to send.

He asked Gollancz to send his reaction to *Scorched Earth* as soon as he could read it, but he had no idea where he would be: "I am trying to get a visa for a trip to India and the Near East right now." If revisions were needed immediately he would be happy to do them provided Herz could get in touch with him. Otherwise he would be happy if Gollancz would have his own staff read proofs as he did for *Red Star over China*.

With the revised Alley article he wrote: "Personally I thought the original article was better than this one, so I have not much hope for it, in this form. However, since Sommers said they were really interested, here is the attempt. They must admit at least that it is full of Alley, this time. Of course the story of Alley is the story of Indusco—which is really only a kind of fulfillment of all the early experiences of his life."

Foster Snow was leaving on November 14 on the *President Taft* for San Francisco. He would probably accompany her to Shanghai, stay there for ten days, and then sail to Indochina and Siam on a ship that would first return to Manila. He wanted to go back to India through Siam. There might be a story there for the *Saturday Evening Post*. He asked Herz to forward suggestions from the *Post* of any other Far Eastern stories they might be interested in. He also, however, applied for a visa to Moscow, and if he got it, would fly by way of Chungking and Turkestan.

The next day he wrote hurriedly to Herz, upset by Lewis Gannett's suggestion in his review of Carlson's *Twin Stars over China* that he and others had picked Carlson's brains to write their books. He noted Carlson himself indicated in his book it was the other way around. Although he seemed to recognize he was being petty, he compounded his complaint wondering, "if for the rest of my life my name is going to be linked with Agnes Smedley's every time it is mentioned."[7]

The world was well into a massive global war that would drastically threaten and change the organization of human civilization. Snow felt small in his efforts to understand and warn his fellowman of all he had seen. But he was stubbornly proud he had tried to picture what he had seen and understood with integrity. At the very moment his emotional exhaustion seemed to swamp him with self-doubt and raw sensitivity to others' criticism, he in fact enjoyed enormous respect in America for the very integrity he took such pride in. The public response to *Battle for Asia*, even as its author returned to his homeland, would make that clear, but he left his Philippine mountain retreat uncertain of his personal and professional future, groping for a map of the historic events that might give direction to his journalistic talent.

39

An Alien Corn Adrift. . . .

P RESUMABLY SNOW LEFT THE Philippines with Foster Snow on
board the *President Taft* for Shanghai in mid-November. He probably
stayed a short time in Shanghai before moving to Hong Kong. There
he halfheartedly mapped out southern and northern routes through Asia to
Europe to finally complete his twice-delayed education as a world traveler
before abruptly deciding to return to the United States instead. Documents
of his movements during this period are very sparse.

He wrote a brief note to Foster Snow across the top of a letter to Chen Han-
seng on December 22. The International Committee had borrowed money
from the funds earmarked for Carlson's advisory work to pay Kelly-Walsh to
print Foster Snow's book on Indusco. This created a problem when Carlson
rather abruptly decided to abandon his plan to visit Indusco in the northwest
in favor of returning immediately to the United States to warn Americans
against an imminent Japanese attack.

Snow insisted Carlson should be paid the full sum originally promised
in one payment rather than in installments as the committee proposed. He
enclosed a personal check for $740 as a loan to the committee to cover
the costs of printing Foster Snow's book and thus enable the committee
to make immediate full payment to Carlson. His loan was to be repaid to
Foster Snow from the sales of her book. His handwritten note to her said
only: "Dear Peg—Please write to I. C. what disposal you want to make of
royalties."[1]

Bertram placed Snow at a 1940 Hong Kong Christmas party organized by Hilda Selwyn-Clarke, which he described as resembling a scene from a later novel by John le Carré. Bertram was in part prompted to this analogy by Smedley's current friendship with David MacDougal, "ostensible head of the Ministry of Information in Hong Kong, but in fact resident chief of the British Secret Service." Bertram noted that after World War II, Smedley was sensationally charged with being part of an alleged Soviet spy ring run by Richard Sorge. Chen Han-seng remembered Sorge and Smedley spent much of the late spring and summer of 1930 together in south China, and he believed them "romantically involved." Smedley's frank and open espousal of her radical beliefs, however, made those who knew her smile at the thought of her as a professional spy. But Smedley was not the only prompt to the analogy with le Carré.

Anna Louise Strong had just flown in from Moscow. Charles Boxer, openly in charge of British Army Intelligence in Hong Kong, was prominently present in the company of Emily Hahn, the author of *The Soong Sisters*, who was also to become the mother of his child before he had divorced his previous wife. Hahn had also begun a warm friendship with Smedley, who at the party "harshly crooned cowboy ballads," while "Anna Louise seized a lily and danced a ponderous *pas seul*. Selwyn [husband of the hostess] looked in politely for a few minutes, stroking his grey moustache, then withdrew to his desk and a mountain of papers. None of us, fortunately, knew what would be happening to Hong Kong just a year from that night."

The day after the Christmas party Snow gave added point to Bertram's analogy by sending a story to the *New York Herald Tribune* that opened: "Tension in the interior of China between the Kuomintang and the Communists is continuing to coincide with aggravated economic troubles, and the result is the gravest crisis since the beginning of China's resistance to Japan." The tension was brought to crisis stage particularly by a November order from the National Government's General Ho Ying-chin, minister of War, for the Communist New Fourth Army to move north of the Yangtze River from the area it had been assigned for the last three years.

Apparently unknown to Bertram, if not to Snow, Strong had been briefed by Chou En-lai on this same developing conflict in Chungking on her way to Hong Kong. When Chou handed her twenty-six pages of documentation about the growing tension, he also warned, "Do not publish this material unless I send word to do so. We do not want to increase friction by prematurely revealing these clashes." Chou charged Chiang Kai-shek with giving the order for the New Fourth Army to move on December 10, and he outlined the danger of splitting the country between north and south, leaving the Communist-held northern territory an easier target for the Japanese.

Strong told Liao Cheng-chih, the Red Army's liaison officer in Hong Kong, about the material she carried from Chou. Liao told her he would signal her when to release the material. The story Snow filed shortly after the Christmas party made essentially the same point as the material Strong carried from Chou. The most likely source for Snow's story was Liao—he later named Liao as his source for the story of the Kuomintang attack on the New Fourth Army that took place only a few days later. Either Strong must have left Hong Kong just prior to Liao's orders to release the story or Liao for some reason decided Snow was the preferable medium for releasing the story.

Snow apparently sent the story from Hong Kong by Clipper. It did not appear in the *New York Herald Tribune* until January 7. By that time government troops had attacked and Liao had also given Snow the story of the climactic battle. Bertram remembered coming upon Liao in the China Defense League office one morning early in January with the wife of General Yeh Ting, commander of the New Fourth Army. They had just heard the general had been taken prisoner and that his second in command, Han Ying, had been killed in the clash with Kuomintang troops. A lightly armed headquarters company of the New Fourth Army, reluctantly fulfilling its order from the National Government to move north of the Yangtze, had been ambushed.

Strong's biographer places her on a steamer between Japan and San Francisco when she first heard fragmentary word of the attack on the New Fourth Army.

For Snow, still in Hong Kong, the threat of renewed civil war in China was the last straw added to his burden of disillusionment. The attack on the New Fourth Army echoed in minor key Chiang Kai-shek's 1927 surprise move against the Reds in Shanghai that ended an earlier promising United Front. Snow had stumbled into the aftermath of that tragic political breakdown thirteen years earlier as a wide-eyed youthful vagabond. He had since painstakingly established a substantial professional career discovering and telling the story of the Chinese people's modern national aspirations. Now those aspirations seemed likely to fall victim again to the same deadly fratricidal conflict.

As later remembered in his autobiography, this was the moment an *"urgent sense of neglect and failure in my personal life came over me"* (italics added). He abruptly cabled Joe Barnes, his *Herald Tribune* editor, that after extending his originally intended "six weeks" stopover in China into thirteen years, he was coming home on the next Clipper. His Clipper left Hong Kong on January 8.

Chungking issued its version of the military clash on January 17. It accused Yeh Ting of "lengthily preparing for revolt" and "ambitiously attempting to increase the number of his own troops." When it became evident the government would use its much larger army to enforce its order for the New Fourth Army to move north of the Yangtze, Yeh Ting, according to this report, sent the families of his men across the river and attacked the government's Fortieth Division. Han Ying was missing, and a search for him was in progress, but the New Fourth Army was now disbanded. The *Herald Tribune* carried the government's story January 18.

On January 22 the *Herald Tribune* carried another story by Snow placed and dated Hong Kong, January 21. This story was probably carried by the same Clipper that carried him from Hong Kong to the Philippines on January 8. It opened: "The first reliable account of the recent clashes between the Chinese New 4th Route Army (Communist) and the Central armies of Generalissimo Chiang Kai-shek revealed today that the Communists had fought Chungking's 9th Army, supported by the 40th Division, for nine days, losing 4,000 casualties, 2,000 prisoners and their commander and vice-commander." Both Yeh Ting and Han Ying were seriously wounded and captured, the latter later murdered.

It was probably this story that caused Snow to write in *Journey to the Beginning* that Dr. Hu Shih, the Chinese ambassador in Washington, insisted the *Herald Tribune* editors apologize and publish Hu's statement branding Snow's account completely false.

Strong reached New York late in January to read these accounts. Early in February she received an unsigned letter telling her, "The time has come to publish what you know." With the letter came the text of the Chinese Communists' official order recognizing the continued existence of the New Fourth Army and a charge by the Revolutionary Military Committee of a fifteen-step plot by which pro-Japanese elements in Chungking planned to take China into the Nazi-Fascist Axis. The *New York Times* declined her story, so she took it to the same Joe Barnes, who had already published Snow's story. She made clear in *Amerasia* that she took the threat of renewed civil war as seriously as did Snow.[2] Thus history sometimes competes even with le Carré's fiction.

Mme. Sun made a last-minute effort to persuade Snow to stay in Hong Kong, but it was no use. She insightfully insisted, however, that part of him would forever belong to China. Despite the profound disillusion in which he left, the rest of his life became identified with the cause of China. But he "would never again imagine that I personally was anything more to China than an alien corn adrift on vast tides of history with a logic of its own and beyond my power to alter or my birthright to judge."

The night before his flight homeward he had a final dinner with Bertram laced with sardonic forecasts over champagne about the opportunities China's internal conflict created for the Japanese. They may also have compared stories about W. H. Donald's break with Chiang Kai-shek and consequent departure from Hong Kong just a few months earlier. Snow later noted the parallel in *Journey to the Beginning.* The Australian, like J. B. Powell, was a respected, if distant, mentor in Snow's career.[3]

Snow apparently did not remind Bertram, or mention to any of the others at Selwyn-Clarke's party, that Christmas also happened to be his wedding anniversary. But long-suppressed concern about his marriage, probably enhanced by longer-standing questions about his relation to his family, was clearly one of the more significant factors in the middle-age crisis then overwhelming him. By the time the Clipper reached Manila his acute depression produced obvious physical symptoms. The Babcocks remembered him as "so distraught he could barely string coherent sentences together." He phoned Foster Snow from the Philippines and again from Hawaii.

At Midway on January 13 he wrote in his diary: "Surely this whole period must remain the darkest in my life. Never have I been through the depths of despondency and despair in which my own role has appeared so altogether despicable & contemptible." He followed that with a passage in which he blamed himself with abject self-denigration for the problems in his marriage:

> First of all the long record of my abuses & lack of appreciation of Peg—failure to understand her & properly to value her in every way: first, the treasury of her love as a wife; second, the beauty of her character as a woman; third, the brilliance of her mind as an intellectual. How early and quickly I forgot the hard struggle I fought to win her & how quickly I gave up the effort to keep her after the first victory. Because she would not submit—which I took for granted—because she would not praise me & flatter me (when I offered her no praise & no credit) because I considered the mere payment of bills sufficient to claim her affection, but never gave her any money for her own use; because I foolishly spent money on my own needs & then complained about her extravagance (a myth) because I blamed everything on the purely sexual relationship (my own failure) and took no account of my own role in the cause of its failure; because of my niggardliness about money she spent on work done for other people; because . . . (the entry ends here)

On another page he listed Captain W. D. Barrows and the other flight officers of the Clipper, indicating his flight began in Hong Kong on January 8.

Many years later, in 1968, almost two decades after he and Foster Snow were divorced and he had finally established his own family, Snow tried to comfort his nephew, Toby, in the aftermath of a near-fatal auto accident. He described to Howard's son two close calls of his own, the first when he was sixteen and crashed Mildred's boyfriend's car into a tree beside the driveway of their Kansas City home, and the second when he was flying home from China and felt such "deep depression and despair over guilt feelings in relation to others, or over my own weaknesses and failure" that he was at the point of suicide. He did not further explain his depression to Toby, but told instead a story within a story of how the Clipper captain, sensing his mood on a stopover at Wake Island, told Snow of crashing a one-seater mail plane over a disappointing love affair. "He was not killed but the shock restored his sense of proportion—and falling in love with his nurse helped!" Snow wrote Toby that hearing the captain's story helped him snap out of his depression, and he realized: "once an event occurs it could not possibly be prevented or happen in any other way. *I had been enormously exaggerating my own share of the guilt,* which arose from a combination of circumstances really beyond my control—chance or luck" (italics added).

Snow pulled out the pages quoted above from his diary and gave them to Foster Snow as part of his effort to renew their marriage when he rejoined her in the States. The whole diary is not available. But with regard to his story in his letter to Toby, Midway is a later stop than Wake Island on the flight home, and there is no indication in Snow's diary entry at Midway that he had already experienced the therapeutic relief of the captain's story indicated in his letter to his nephew. That relief should come so readily from such a story stretches belief, even though Snow's own recovery from acute depression was in fact strikingly rapid after reaching the States. His diary indicates he arrived in Los Angeles on or just prior to February 17.

A later *Saturday Evening Post* article indicates he spent some time with military personnel talking about the conspicuous American buildup in military force then going on in the South Pacific but does not indicate how much time he divided between Midway and Hawaii. He may have taken time out on either island to recoup his emotional health. In any case it seems likely the captain's story, while clearly having some basis, was primarily another fiction, this time well intended, to help his nephew through a dangerous emotional crisis. The lesson he drew for his nephew not to exaggerate his sense of responsibility and guilt, seems also a clear later judgment on his emotional state during this crisis.[4]

The Snows tried to renew their marriage after his return, but he later indicated the effort was brief. His travels for the *Saturday Evening Post* quickly took him away from the Connecticut home they purchased except for brief writing periods during World War II. By 1945 a separation agreement was drawn up and signed, but negotiations over a final divorce quickly became bitterly antagonistic.

This antagonism climaxed with the bizarre event noted earlier of Foster Snow's leading a late-night search in the company of Pruitt, Susan B. Anthony, and three Connecticut bailiffs of the home of a friend of Snow's on July 21, 1948. Snow was with Lois Wheeler, who had already agreed to be his second wife. That raid caused Snow to write Maud Russell, Pruitt's roommate, the painful story of his marriage to Foster Snow. By then his frustrating dealings with her over the terms of their separation made him gropingly aware of their shared responsibility for the failure of their marriage:

> I won't trouble to review the history of my mistakes with Peg Snow, which is a tragedy that may or may not be fully exposed to public view. It is enough here to say that I married her in all good faith in 1932 and that soon afterward difficulties and incompatibility developed which proved fatal to the union. I blame myself for my own faults and for my own contributions to the failure, but not beyond that; I cannot assume responsibility for all the conditions of birth and early history which shaped Peg's faults and account for her contributions to the fiasco. In view of her own emphatically expressed dissatisfaction with our marriage, as early as 1933, she should have deserted me then, or divorced me, for from that time on we never had a physical life together, except for a couple of very brief intervals. The last was in 1941, seven years ago, which was ended by Peg in a scene of violence.

Snow filed suit for divorce in Connecticut following the raid on his friend's home. Foster Snow counterclaimed, and he accepted her counterclaim to bring the case to court in Connecticut. The first hearing was held in New Haven on November 19, 1948. The divorce was not finally decreed until May 1949.

Snow had met Wheeler, a talented actress and again a beautiful woman, in the spring of 1946. They were sure of their love and had decided on marriage by the time of the raid and Snow's subsequent filing for divorce in Connecticut. Wheeler's father, a staunch Catholic, was concerned about his daughter's marrying a divorcé, so they had made application to the Catholic Church to have Snow's first marriage annulled. But Mr. Wheeler's unexpected death in an automobile accident and the Connecticut divorce proceedings ended that effort. They married within a week after Snow's divorce became final at an attractive old Georgian home in Sneden's Landing, New York. Agnes Smedley filled the house with mock orange blossoms, and Snow's brother, Howard, served as best man. Snow had finally pieced a home and family together.

The suppressed problems in Snow's marriage were clearly an important, but by no means the sole, cause of the middle-age crisis he experienced on his return journey to America. The hint to his nephew Toby that the flight captain's recovery was significantly aided by his falling in love with his nurse could well have been prompted by Snow's own feeling at that late date that his second marriage was solace and recompense for his first. It also echoes his romantic creation ten years earlier in *Journey to the Beginning* of the beautiful Batala, who in fantasy nursed-loved him to recovery from a leg injury at the end of his caravan.

Snow also explained the acute depression he experienced on his return to the States in yet other terms in *Journey to the Beginning:*

> Poverty is relative to time and place, and in the dying world of Western power in the Orient no white man was ever really poor; but as I drew closer to America, where success was the shadow of the figures behind your own dollar value, I regretted my improvidence. I had frittered away my savings on "war work," on a book that would earn nothing and on keeping two households going. I was "worth" less than when I had first touched Shanghai, in 1928, and the values I had lived by in China now seemed hardly convertible to gold. What, after all, was I taking home? I had no honor to show for my years but the physical ravages of malaria, dysentery and nephritis—not even an honest wound as souvenir. I was, I thought, a failure.

Still later he came to believe the principal cause of his depression was something completely unsuspected at the time, "a kind of slow starvation; avitaminosis had gradually seized me over a period of months." His weight had fallen from a healthy normal 165 to 125. After eating fresh, nourishing California food and vacationing on a ranch in Arizona, where he "forgot all about China," he regained thirty pounds and one morning "woke up a whole man again."[5]

None of these later efforts to explain the acute depression he experienced and his quick recovery can be completely dismissed. His passage home and recognition of his middle age was truly storm-troubled. The colorful world he originally had planned to vagabond through had turned into a searing lesson in humankind's inability to govern its more cruelly aggressive instincts. His personal attempt at romantic love had turned into a marriage chronically troubled by problems of sex, money, and denial. Only his writing proved commensurate to his early dreams, and on his journey homeward he was by no means confident of that.

Snow's letters home had grown more and more infrequent over the years he was away. Latterly he often seemed to picture his family according to his own needs as the middle-class family he was writing for in the *Saturday Evening Post*, a Norman Rockwell caricature that failed to account for many of the distinctive personal details of their lives. But a stern, judgmental father was often part even of the Rockwell picture. So it is not surprising to find Snow's return causing an old problem of sibling rivalry to kick back into play. Howard was now a successful representative of the National Association of Manufacturers and not only apparently a happy husband, but a happy father as well.

Snow returned to the United States with less than two thousand dollars ready money in his bank account. Even if *Battle for Asia* proved as successful as *Red Star over China* he could not be confident of financial security. By remaining in China he had foregone many of the opportunities to capitalize in the United States on the success of *Red Star over China* with promotional lecture tours and the like. He was only dimly aware of how the system worked. He was also by no means confident *Battle for Asia* would sell as well as *Red Star over China*. There was nothing in it to match the exciting adventure of the Long March or the surprising revelation of the Communist army's social and political success with the people among whom they lived. But *Battle for Asia* was at least some tangible reward he could bring to the family from whom he had been so long absent. *Red Star over China* was dedicated to Nym, his writer-wife, *Battle for Asia* "To my Father and Mother."

The value of his life depended on the success of his writing, and Hitler's recent European surprise made him acutely aware how whimsically history betrayed journalists. He had also taken much time from his profession, with a recurrent sense of misgiving, to help establish and build Indusco. He particularly hoped Indusco would help the Communist guerrilla forces establish a substantial and internationally recognized position within China's United Front. He had made Indusco's story a significant part of his new book, *Battle for Asia*, then being readied for publication. He had written and rewritten an article on Rewi Alley he was by no means confident the *Saturday Evening Post* would publish. He hoped to give Alley's position such international recognition that political factions within the Kuomintang would hesitate to move against him. But he knew only too well how fragile his hopes were.

Returning home as he did, instead of continuing his voyage around the world by way of Europe, also made Snow professionally vulnerable in another sense. He had always asked the obvious question: What was the relation between Russian and Chinese Communists? He early and often felt the need to visit Russia to answer that question by personal investigation. He made repeated efforts to travel there. Early on, Chinese Communism seemed to him as to most others only a footnote compared to the major historical event of the Communist revolution in Soviet Russia. As he returned to the United States, having just finished his third book about war in Asia and particularly having made clear to the world the distinctive nationalist nature of Chinese Communism, he still had not visited the land from which communism as a modern force had sprung.

Nor did he know Europe firsthand. Even as he wrote *Battle for Asia,* he was aware events in Europe were not only center stage in world history, but indirectly shaping the course of war in Asia. The threat of Nazi-fascist victory in Europe and North Africa continued to spread and escalate rapidly as he journeyed homeward and unquestionably would test particularly the concluding chapters of *Battle for Asia* in which he tried to foresee where the battle was leading. But Europe, like Russia, was still a part of the world he knew only through what he could learn from reading and what others told him. If events there could astonish longtime resident observers, what faith could he have in his own efforts to predict the influence of European affairs on Asia?

It is hardly surprising, with all these contingencies darkly looming, he was in such emotional distress as the Flying Clipper carried him homeward across the Pacific to the bay of Los Angeles early in 1941.

40

The Returning Author
Challenges America

D ESPITE HIS EMOTIONAL DEPRESSION, Snow took careful note of the massive American military preparations underway on the Pacific island bases where his Clipper stopped. He talked to military men, and his long-held fear of the probability of war between the United States and Japan hardened into something close to a sense of inevitability. He described what he saw and its significance in an article he personally delivered to the editors of the *Saturday Evening Post* in Philadelphia.

Guam, Wake, and Midway all stirred with plans and new construction, but he was most impressed by what he observed in Hawaii. The navy was spending 100 million dollars to modernize and enlarge Pearl Harbor. There he saw "the largest single collection of modern hangars of my life, acres and acres of them." The romantic South Seas he had seen and written about thirteen years earlier, when the American military presence seemed inconsequential, now existed "only in stage backgrounds for the crooning of Bing Crosby to La Lamour." And the buildup in the Pacific was matched by an impressive new American commitment to provide military support, particularly airpower, to its allies in Southeast Asia, including China. A high American naval observer told him bluntly, but honestly, "we are sending our stuff to China to keep the Japs off the necks of the British, and all other reasons are eyewash." Recent conferences at Manila between Dutch, American, and British military officials made it very clear to the Japanese that the "white men are getting together to defy her at last."

These observations led him to the following conclusions:

> Nothing is certain these days, and least of all in the Orient, but three things now seem to me reasonably probable—though by no means probably reasonable. The first is that the United States will fight, if necessary, to prevent Japan from securing bases in the British and Dutch colonies of Southeastern Asia and Malaysia. The second is that Japan must pounce on these colonies soon—I believe this year—or abandon her whole dream of southward expansion and mastery of the Western Pacific. And the third, that what Japan does in the next few months can decisively influence the outcome of the battle for Europe itself.

He speculated Japan would take decisive action if in cooperation with Germany and Italy it could lure or force America to divide its naval power equally between the Atlantic and the Pacific and if it could secure some kind of resolution to its war in China. Japan's recent signing of a neutrality pact with the Soviet Union gave it limited security on its rapidly expanding Asian land borders, but as long as China was united in its hostility to Japan, the war on mainland China would likely be a serious deterrent to Japan's expanding its aggression. Snow saw the renewed threat of civil war in China playing into the hands of Japan and thus possibly unleashing Japanese aggression elsewhere. He confidently predicted if and when, "those two conditions are realized there will be a blitzkrieg in the Pacific."

By the time he met face-to-face in Philadelphia with the editors who had given him opportunity over the last eight years to reach a large segment of the American public, not to mention providing him with the most substantial part of his income as a writer, his emotional and physical health seemed much restored. His editors asked the obvious question: How does it feel to be back home?, and then published his answer in "Keeping Posted," thereby acknowledging he was one of their own.

Arriving in Los Angeles, he was initially struck by American streamlining and by the extravagant waste and plenty. Everything had speeded up by about thirty miles since he had left. He and Foster Snow were fascinated by seasonal oranges selling for five cents a bucketful. But American packaging evoked a more quizzical response: "after the shopping, there was the business of paring off yards of paper bags, lovely brown wrapping paper, fine twine, rubber bands, advertising folders, fancy jars, tin boxes and cans, but we could never bear to throw away the costly packaging until the piles got so high we could not wade through them." In the used-car lots there were thousands of virtually new cars selling at give-away prices. "In other countries, government officials would be proud to be seen in any one of these chariots which Americans discard as nonchalantly as a year-old hat."[1]

Foster Snow had become involved in organizing support for Indusco in Los Angeles before Snow arrived. Lin Yu-tang, his old friend and sometimes cultural antagonist, agreed to chair the local organization, and John Garfield, the actor, served as vice chairman. An Indusco commitment kept Foster Snow from meeting his plane the evening it landed at the San Pedro docks, but she sent Richard Nickson, a young poet she had met through Anna Louise Strong, in her stead. Nickson took Snow to his own apartment at the Brevort, a comfortable hotel owned by his family, conveniently located in Hollywood. There Nickson patiently and willingly answered on into the early morning hours Snow's many questions about the country from which he had been so long away. The next day the Snows rented an apartment of their own at the hotel.

Even before he arrived, the February 1 issue of the *Saturday Evening Post* relieved one of his most immediate worries by announcing it would carry "China's Blitzbuilder, Rewi Alley," in its next issue. The story was printed with a photo of Alley handsomely shadowed by the bronze bust done by Francis R. Shurrock from the London Royal Academy. Seeing his story in print, while he sat in Hollywood, was probably as much a tonic to Snow's depressed spirit as California's fresh fruits and vegetables were to his deprived body. Hollywood provided just the audience to believe Snow's grand claim that Alley meant to China what Colonel T. E. Lawrence once meant to the Arabs, "and perhaps more. Where Lawrence brought to Arabia the destructive guerrilla warfare, Alley is teaching China the constructive organization of guerrilla industry."

Several years later Graham Peck wrote about Alley and his Indusco mission with clarifying hindsight. Having traveled and lived with Alley, his respect for Alley's personal commitment was as fervid as Snow's; however, his melancholy assessment of Indusco proved Snow's worst fears ultimately realistic. After noting many signs of its almost-certain failure, he concluded the cause of its success was also the cause of its decline. The popular foreign influence Snow had so diligently cultivated and organized to protect Alley from the corruption of national government politics had kept CIC alive and even growing, but that also sharpened the avidity and resentment government forces felt toward it. When the American government failed to recognize Indusco officially, the Kuomintang felt free to reduce its support and slowly strangle this unwelcome experiment in economic democracy.[2]

But early in 1941 back in the States, with the glossy popularity of his *Saturday Evening Post* article and Evans Carlson's carrying to President Franklin Roosevelt the Philippine petition requesting 50 million dollars to be earmarked for Indusco from American aid, Snow still had good reason for renewed optimism. The attention of Hollywood celebrities certainly helped, as did being invited to argue with Theodore Dreiser on national radio. Then the first reviews of *Battle for Asia* probably provided even more effective tonic by quickly signaling the book's substantial success. Henry Luce added a gratifying personal stroke by writing, "I want to tell you how deeply indebted I feel to you for that masterly book."

The *Saturday Review of Literature* carried a photo of Snow on its cover, and inside Random House purchased a three-page foldout advertising *Battle for Asia*. Miles Vaughn, a fellow midwesterner who as former UP Tokyo bureau chief was far more sympathetic with the Japanese than Snow, wrote the review. Vaughn particularly praised the portions of *Battle for Asia* dealing with the Communist movement, describing it as "the most authoritative ever penned . . . to be commended to all who seek a realistic understanding of the forces at work in China and the outlook for that country after the conflict with Japan ends." He only briefly commented on the final section of *Battle for Asia* over which Snow had so long agonized: "In the latter chapters Snow sets forth his ideas for a new world order which are provocative whether one agrees with them or not."

The *New York Herald Tribune* carried prominently a worldly wise and weary review by Rodney Gilbert that focused on Snow's conclusion. It opened suggesting Snow's readers should be prepared for a surprise: "Those who have followed him hitherto know him as an original, enterprising, conscientious and very readable reporter of events in the Far East, who usually has something new to tell, which all others have overlooked or would not take the pains to learn." For the first nine sections of his book Snow met these expectations, but in the final section he caught his unsuspecting audience offguard by introducing himself as the prophet of a new social order in China that was an essential precedent to Japan's defeat, a new order for colonial Asia that was an essential precedent to the defeat of totalitarianism at large, and a new world order, which, as Gilbert understood it, was to be "a federation of states that have made capitalism over into 'democratic socialism.'" After indulgently summarizing what he considered Snow's overambitious efforts at reshaping the world, Gilbert concluded, "But it's a good book on China, anyway."

William M. Reddig, book editor of the *Kansas City Star*, better known a few years later as author of *Tom's Town*, began his review noting Snow's new book "may well serve as a major source of general enlightenment on the far eastern struggle," but he assumed Snow's final thesis, "that greater political reconciliation between the East and the West is the key to successful resistance of the new Japanese advance," was indeed the book's central argument. He criticized Snow for neglecting "to explore the factor of Britain's ability to meet the Japanese threat with its present setup" and for greatly oversimplifying "an enormously complicated problem when he proposes that the British empire structure be dismantled in the midst of war." He found it both naïve and despairing "to suggest that the new world democratic order must be brought into being in one dramatic leap or the Nips and the Nazis will take over. . . . To insist on the impossible for the democracies is to give an unjustified advantage to the totalitarians." Nevertheless, he too praised Snow's reflective, analytical, and objective talents as a reporter.[3]

But retrospectively it is the review by Freda Utley in the *New York Times* that carried with it the richest personal and historical ironies for Snow's writing career then and for the future. Her review was in effect extended in time and print by an invitation from Richard Walsh for her to answer an article drawn from *Battle for Asia* on the threat of the resumption of civil war in China. This gave Utley a chance to expand her political argument with Snow free of the necessity she felt in her review to recognize his considerable talents as a journalist. Walsh printed the two articles in *Asia* side by side under the comprehensive title "China at War."

Snow first crossed paths with Utley in Hankow in 1938. She was then so impressed by the tea Chou En-lai arranged for her at Snow's instigation that she questioned Snow's insistence the Chinese were true communists. She was personally grateful for Snow's intercession on her behalf.

Many years later, after World War II, Utley would become particularly indignant over Snow's book *Stalin Must Have Peace*. She would then spearhead the Cold War attack on Snow, by publicly questioning why the ostensibly conservative *Saturday Evening Post* kept "one of the cleverest, smoothest, and most subtle advocates the Kremlin has ever had on its side" on its editorial staff and allowed him to propagandize for Russian tyranny within its pages.

In 1941 her view of Snow had not yet come full circle. She still acknowledged personal and professional respect even while attacking his political assumptions.

She began her review accurately recognizing his journalistic strengths: "The author's long residence in China, his generous human sympathies, and his complete lack of any feeling of racial or cultural superiority have brought him into closer personal contact with the Chinese than other foreign journalists. Combined with his first-hand experiences of the war on many fronts and his understanding of its causes and implications, this imparts to his narrative an intimate and realistic quality." She described Snow's account of the Japanese terror as "terse and terribly authentic," and she particularly complimented his account of Indusco that, like so much else of a progressive nature in China, "has received too meagre support from the Chinese capitalists and landowners and little financial backing from abroad."

Then she turned to her attack: "Edgar Snow is one of those Communist sympathizers who is essentially a liberal and a humanitarian but who, no doubt because he has lived in the Far East throughout the past decade, is not yet disillusioned. Consequently he is still able to write of revolutionary movements with zest and youthful hopefulness and has no misgivings concerning Soviet Russia's role in the East or in the West." Like Vaughn and others, she noted to Snow's credit his rebuke of liberals who denied the Chinese Communists were either revolutionary or marxist. She noted also he recognized Comintern policy gave Russian national interests priority over international class revolution.

But she charged despite these insights Snow completely ignored "the complication introduced into the Chinese political scene by the fact that the Communists are under the orders of a foreign power." Her *Asia* article made clear she had read Snow's 1939 interview with Mao Tse-tung in the *China Weekly Review* with close and shocked attention. Mao's apology for Stalin's pact with Hitler convinced her Mao was completely controlled by the Comintern.

Before that her firsthand experience of Stalin's dictatorial terror also convinced her that Nazi and Soviet statism were essentially similar, and thus the Hitler-Stalin pact appeared to her only the most visible evidence of a more profound alliance dangerous to Western democracies. Hitler's blitzkrieg in western Europe sealed her conviction, but Hitler's surprise invasion of Russia, a dramatic challenge to her belief, was yet three months in the future.

She accused Snow of failing to recognize "both the pressures which Nazi Germany can exert upon Russia, and the inducements which Germany and Japan may be able to offer to Stalin in the shape of further territorial gains for the U.S.S.R." She pointed out Snow had never visited the Soviet Union and his knowledge of the Comintern was based exclusively on "the as-yet-uncorrupted Chinese Communists."

Thus Utley saw Snow's "eloquent plea in the final chapters of his book for a new dynamic conception of capitalist democracy which could transform the undemocratic rule of the Western imperialist powers over the peoples of Asia" as fatally flawed with unwitting contradictions. Nevertheless, she concluded: "The criticisms which Mr. Snow's political chapters provoke do not, however, detract from the essential value of his exhaustive account of the situation in China, nor from the truth of his argument that Britain must abandon the undemocratic concept of Empire if India and China and the other Asiatic peoples are to be saved from the Fascist tyranny, and the British Empire preserved from the Nazis and the Japanese."

While Utley may well have understood Stalin's Soviet Russia better than Snow, she did not know or understand Asia, and particularly not China, as well as he. Her belief in the Comintern's control over Mao Tse-tung has hardly been substantiated by history. Snow too had been shocked by Mao's easy apology for Stalin's pact with Hitler in 1939, but he found it best explained by Mao's deeply rooted antagonism to European colonialism rather than evidence of his obedience to Comintern policy.

For most of Asia colonialism was the most obvious and long-entrenched enemy to national self-determination, and Great Britain was imperialism's principal model and apologist. The Japanese threat was essentially an imitation of British imperialism dressed up in the flimsy disguise of pan-Asian patriotism. European democracies had two faces: one they saw in their own mirror and another was seen by the colonial peoples subject to their rule.

Snow's concluding section of *Battle for Asia*, "Empire or Democracy?" challenged his readers to face the questions colonialism posed for the future of democracy, not only for the colonized nations but also for the integrity of the democratic nations themselves. Snow had spent thirteen years in Asia, principally in China, trying to understand what his own passion for democracy meant in what he increasingly believed to be an extraordinary historical necessity for democratic revolution in modern Asia. His passion was shaped more by Emerson and Jefferson than by Marx, though he unquestionably was very favorably impressed by the ability of the Chinese Communists to win the hearts and minds of the people they lived among.

The United States was sliding rapidly into a world war already spreading in Europe and Asia. He had seen enough of war to recognize its terrible costs not just in terms of immediate cruel human pain and suffering but also in its unpredictable anarchic violation of the social fabric that provides much of the meaning of human life. He believed if the American people were finally to be drawn into this worldwide cataclysm—and at this point he had little hope they would not be—then it was important for them at least to understand and declare the terms on which they should fight. America should fight for democracy, but European democracies were also colonial powers. America could most effectively counter the Comintern's influence in Asia by dissociating itself from complicity with imperialism, even while supporting democracy against fascism in Europe.

Today ironically it is fashionable to contrast the clarity of moral purpose with which Americans fought in World War II with the moral ambiguity with which Americans fought later in Vietnam and to a lesser extent in Korea.

In the conclusion for *Battle for Asia,* Edgar Snow reminds us while there was no moral ambiguity about the right of the United States to defend itself against a massive Japanese attack, Pearl Harbor in effect allowed us to leave the question of our relation to imperialism in Asia and Africa halfheartedly unresolved. America's answer to that question became even more confused as it was overridden by the Cold War effort to contain communism. Much of the moral ambiguity of our later participation in wars in Asia stemmed from our inability or unwillingness to answer the challenge Snow posed before we entered World War II in the conclusion of *Battle for Asia:*

> Our decisive frontier is not in China, and it is not in England. It is in our own soul and on our own soil. . . . History is dynamic, it will not long permit static objects to obstruct its movement. Regimes which have exhausted the positive possibilities of their political slogans will eventually be obliterated. . . . Democracy, if it is to survive, must pose a mightier antithesis which can capture the political will and invoke the courage of the peoples.

Snow applied these Emersonian strictures on moral and political integrity to Mao's blunt charge that England was Asia's most dangerous enemy to produce a more velvet-gloved, but rootedly American, warning:

> Democracy in England in particular needs to reinforce itself with something no less than a new charter of human liberty, a new declaration of the rights of man. Rulers in England may not see this, but men in England's colonies do; and it is there in her flanks that England is weakest. . . . It will be suggested that the emancipation of India would mean the end of British "unity." It may be the only way to create it. The strongest allies democratic England has today are Canada, Australia, and New Zealand, and without the help of a certain former colony south of Canada she might not survive at all. A Free India could become as valuable an asset as a free America.[4]

The months between Snow's landing in Los Angeles and the Japanese attack on Pearl Harbor, when *Battle for Asia* was being debated and absorbed by the American people, were filled with angry political debate in the United States frequently outdated by the next day's historical events. Soon after arriving in Los Angeles, Snow followed Theodore Dreiser on a Hollywood radio show. Dreiser attacked British colonialism more savagely than did Mao Tse-tung and all but implied Hitler was doing the free world a favor by warring against this arch colonial power. Roosevelt was a monster for taking Britain's part. Snow and the seventy-year-old author, whose work the younger writer deeply respected, argued heatedly over the next three days without either convincing the other.

Dreiser, nevertheless, arranged for Snow to be invited to address the American Writers Congress meeting in New York's Madison Square Garden in June. But the invitation was abruptly withdrawn when Snow refused to delete his plea for American support for Britain and China in their fight against fascism and his speculation that Russia would soon be drawn into the merging struggle against Nazi-fascist imperialism. Since the Hitler-Stalin pact was still in effect, the leadership of the Writers Congress, sympathetic to, if not controlled by, the American Communist Party, requested Snow omit such offending opinions.

Twelve days after the scheduled address "Hitler's heretical tanks crashed into the Ukraine, taking Stalin's minions by surprise." If the far Right thought Snow an apologist for communism, the far Left continued to find him far too independent for its tortured party line.[5] And history with another of its astonishing lurches proved Snow had good reason to wonder at the terrible responsibility a journalist assumed as he tried to alert his readers to the political challenges of the future.

41

From Hot to Cold War

S YNDICATED REVIEWS OF *Battle for Asia* appeared in small-town newspapers across the United States, as they had for *Red Star over China*. It made the nonfiction best-seller list. But this time Snow could feel the praise and respect of his readers personally, looking them in the eye and shaking their hands, no longer confined to reading their responses at great distance in time and place.

The day after the Snows arrived in New York City, Random House staged a well-attended press conference for its prized author. Harrison Smith, half of Snow's first publisher, Smith and Haas, and president of *Saturday Review of Literature,* came calling. Eleanor Roosevelt noted in her popular syndicated column, "My Day," that she had met the Snows in Washington. Charles Hanson Towne happily reintroduced the Snows to the best of New York's restaurants. And Kelley Graham, Snow's first big client at Scovil before he abandoned his advertising career, now took pleasure in hosting a substantial dinner party in honor of the successful author. Snow had loyally kept his account in Graham's bank throughout his long absence. On the whole it was a confidence-building, triumphant return to the city he had left as a little-known deckhand on the SS *Radnor* thirteen years earlier.

The Snows did not choose to live in New York City itself but wanted to be nearby. Richard Walsh and Pearl Buck encouraged them to think of settling near them in Pennsylvania, but they chose a small house built in 1752 in Madison, Connecticut, a short way up the Atlantic coast. Snow refurbished

Journalist

two corncribs to use as his office and bought a red convertible as part of the furnishing appropriate to a modern young couple rediscovering their native America.

Meanwhile the news from Kansas City was not so upbeat. Snow's father suffered from a debilitating flu and the discouraging news the *Kansas City Star* had found cheaper and more efficient printing services elsewhere. The elder Snow no longer had the will or the energy to keep up with the new commercial challenge of this "beggarly business." A legal squabble about his handling of his deceased father's farm also caused hard feelings within the family.

The Snows had not stopped in Kansas City on their way from Los Angeles to New York. They stayed south from Arizona, visiting New Orleans before going on to Philadelphia and then New York. Snow and his brother implicitly staked a claim for New York as the home of the reigning generation of the family by inviting their father, sister, and Claude Mackey, the brother-in-law Snow had never met, to New York for a family reunion at the end of April. Proud of his son's success, Snow's father quietly acknowledged the end of his paternal authority, noting he would make no more suggestions about his son's writing: "Your style and subjects have improved so much that I do not think I could say anything that would help you."[1]

As he had in China, Snow, upon his return to America, wanted to talk to the men in uniform. What motivated them to serve? What were they willing to risk their lives for? He wrote a series of articles for the *Saturday Evening Post* published over the next several months: "They Don't Want to Play Soldier," "What Is Morale?," and "Made-In-America Blitz." He no longer had to worry about what he could do in America. His opinions were now news. The *Philadelphia Evening Bulletin* published with respect his prediction the United States would be at war with Japan before the end of the year.

When the Japanese did in fact attack Pearl Harbor, Will and Polly Babcock from Manila were visiting the Snows in Madison. The two couples heard the news on the radio on their way to the bus station. Back in the Philippines their close friends, the Crouters, were soon interned by the invading Japanese. Bertram in Hong Kong and J. B. Powell in Shanghai were also quickly taken prisoners as the well-planned Japanese attack unfolded. Snow later admitted to being as surprised as anyone else that the Japanese had "returned our scrap iron to us with compounded interest at Hawaii." He had expected Japan to hit the British and Dutch first and then exploit American isolationist sentiment for a time. He believed the Japanese made a major blunder in precipitating the United States into war *and* national unity.[2] What had grown into a dread conviction over the last several years of his Asian experience now became a not-so-welcome climax to his return and another turning point in his life.

His authority with the American public had reached a high plateau that would extend through the years of World War II and then rapidly dissipate for a long period as the Cold War chilled the never very substantial American concern for understanding the diversity and complexity of Asian national aspirations.

Immediately after Pearl Harbor he was offered a position as an intelligence officer by the U.S. government and was recruited as a radio news analyst for NBC. However, the *Saturday Evening Post* not only wanted to name him its first foreign correspondent, but also offered him financial terms and a freedom to choose his own assignments that fulfilled the ambitious dreams he had left New York with thirteen years earlier. The war and his new post again provided direction for his talents and offered the opportunity for him to finally complete his journey around the world.

In February 1942 he requested and was granted a meeting with President Franklin Roosevelt. He had accepted the *Saturday Evening Post*'s offer before meeting the president, though he often later represented Roosevelt as advising him to accept his correspondent's role rather than enter government intelligence. Encouraged by the president, he submitted to him a plan for decolonization that expanded on his argument in the conclusion of *Battle for Asia:* "To conduct effective political and psychological war in Asia it is necessary for us to convert the defensive have-got and mean-to-hold strategy of the Western colonial powers into an offensive war of liberation, promising the colonial peoples full participation in a post-war democratic world—and giving them all possible immediate aid and arms." Like his good friend Carlson, who would soon become a nationally celebrated war hero, Snow was invited to correspond directly with the president as he continued his travels. Subsequent American policy toward China, however, made clear the president, while vaguely sympathetic with Snow's anticolonialist views, was not inclined to let such sympathies interfere with the tough domestic political decisions he had to make.[3]

Snow's first year home was happily preoccupied with his professional travel and success. The house in Connecticut, like their temporary homes in Peking and Baguio, belonged principally to his wife. He used the corncribs for a refuge in which he could work.

By April he was back in Asia covering the story of Britain's effort to enlist the Indian people in its war against fascism without giving in to their desire for national independence. He found the political insularity of key British officials, such as Sir Stafford Cripps and Lord Linlithgow, incredible, even as the Japanese were proving how easy it was to exploit colonial resentment in neighboring Burma. But he was also dismayed by Gandhi's faith that his program of nonviolence would prove India had nothing to fear from the Japanese. He met M. Thein Pe, a popular Burmese writer and joint secretary of Burma's extreme nationalist party, a portion of which had bargained for Japan's support. Pe published a chilling story of Burma's occupation by Japanese troops, *What Happened in Burma,* to which Snow added an introduction.

Gandhi's flat insistence that Britain was India's principal enemy echoed and reenforced from a very different perspective the message Snow had heard from Mao Tse-tung, but Snow in his introduction underscored Pe's public warning that "Mr. Gandhi must realize that it is very dangerous to underestimate the ferocity and black-heartedness of the Fascist beasts. They are capable of catching you by the neck with your own consent and with the help of your own doctrine of *ahimsa.*" As in 1931 Snow found Nehru's more pragmatic contemporary point of view more sympathetic than Gandhi's religious pacifism. Nehru, however, was for the moment paralyzed by the obtuseness of British policy and the simplistic integrity of Gandhi's popular appeal.

Snow did his best to sort out the complexities of Asian politics for the American public. He wrote privately to the president of the United States, and he shared his experience and his questions extensively with military and diplomatic leaders from many countries, particularly and repeatedly with those from his own. His next book, *People on Our Side*, written and published in 1944, after victory for the Allied forces seemed realistically probable, was a popular success and a choice of the Book of the Month Club. He closed that book with yet another appeal for the democracies to consider and plan for an end to imperialism in Asia. Roosevelt reported he stayed up half the night reading Snow's book on board the *Quincy*, the ship on which he traveled to the Yalta Conference.

At the end of World War II, the European powers withdrew from many of their former colonial possessions more from exhaustion than conviction. In January 1948 Snow was in New Delhi happily covering the story of India's newly won independence. Gandhi rebuked Snow: "You were not very kind to me in your last book," but as he took Snow's hand in his own he added, "You are more ready to listen to me now, I know." Only a few days later the Mahatma was gunned down by a religious fanatic. Snow sent a report from the scene to the *Saturday Evening Post* that William Shirer would later describe as "one of the classics of American journalism." Snow acknowledged a wisdom in Gandhi's position he had originally failed to appreciate. He now understood Gandhi "was talking about the atom bomb and the far worse bacteriological weapons, and a world arbitrarily 'divided into two irreconcilable camps,' that we had all got as our answer in the war he wouldn't fight."[4]

During the war Snow finally made three extended visits to Russia, the first from October 1942 to April 1943; the second from April through December 1944; and the third during the war's conclusion from June through September 1945. His first visit was dominated by the siege of Stalingrad; his second by the confident anticipation of Allied victory; and his third by Hiroshima and the end of the war. During his first two visits Stalin and Russia were yet prized members of the Allied team. By his third, he could sense the growing suspicions that were to develop into the Cold War. Despite repeated efforts Snow was never permitted to meet Stalin. He never gained anything like the personal access he enjoyed in China to the leaders of the Soviet Communist Party. He was viewed by the latter, as well as their loyal American followers, with great suspicion, if not open hostility. He did what he could to break out of the heavy restrictions the pool of foreign journalists in Moscow had to work under, but he had no chance to get to know Russia and its people as he had the land and the people of China.

While Snow was finally learning about Russia firsthand during his first two visits, an extraordinarily lengthy and fateful struggle was going on in China between a tough and pragmatic General Joseph W. Stilwell, designated to lead and coordinate the American and Chinese military response to the invasion of Japanese ground forces into Southeast Asia, and a proud and defensive Chiang Kai-shek, who seemed determined to let the Americans fight the Japanese while he strengthened his position for a later struggle with the Communists in his own country. Stilwell tried every means he could think of to shape Chinese Nationalist troops into an effective fighting force against the Japanese. With Allied support he hoped to retake Burma and reopen the Burma Road as a supply route to China. He planned to reestablish a substantial land base in China from which Allied forces could launch the final invasion of Japan that then seemed necessary to end the war. Barbara W. Tuchman has told in great detail the story of Stilwell's frustrating and tragic effort to push Chiang Kai-shek into a more active and aggressive engagement of the Japanese that eventually led to his own humiliating recall from command on October 19, 1944. Most of the best-informed members of the press and the diplomatic service sided with Stilwell, but in the interest of Allied unity the story was muted at the time. It was, however, another significant cause of the schism opening among American experts on East Asia, and particularly on China.

Snow, preoccupied with the dramatic events happening in Russia, returned to America to find what had once been sharp, but still civil, quarrels about Chinese politics between personal friends now a matter of more serious public concern. In his latest book, *The Vigil of a Nation*, Lin Yu-tang defended the cause of the Kuomintang with a surprising zeal, claiming that most Chinese feared and abhorred the Communists. He designated Snow one of the chief propagandists for the Chinese Reds. In a review of Lin's book for the *Nation*, Snow questioned the reliability of Lin's sources and charged he paid inadequate attention to the Kuomintang's failures. Snow's review provoked an angry response from Lin, which Snow was allowed to answer. The *Nation* printed both responses.[5]

J. B. Powell suffered such severe malnutrition in Japanese prisons that the forepart of both his feet had to be amputated, but fortunately he was included in an exchange of prisoners in 1943. He was hospitalized in New York, and Agnes Smedley became one of his most regular and faithful visitors. They argued heatedly about politics but apparently their personal friendship was never threatened. Powell was influential in founding the American China Policy Association, which later became a key part of the pro-Nationalist China Lobby. With Max Eastman, like Freda Utley a reformed Communist, Powell wrote an article for the *Reader's Digest* itemizing Chinese Communist deceits. The article referred to Edgar Snow as the "best-known popularizer of the pro-Communist view." Powell's "popularizer" was less objectionable than Lin's "propagandist" to describe Snow's role with the Chinese Communists, but the serious charges of both old friends against the Communists fed an increasingly anticommunist popular sentiment that made their designations seem more sinister than in fact they were. Snow did not reply to the glancing attack by Powell.[6]

While dealing with these public attacks, Snow also took steps to recognize legally the failure of his marriage. He and Foster Snow drew up and signed a formal agreement of separation early in 1945, and Snow once again took an apartment in New York. At the urging of his editors, he then returned to Russia for the concluding events of the war.

The atomic bombing of Hiroshima and Nagasaki gave a devastating American answer to Pearl Harbor that would raise a whole new generation of questions about humankind's ability to survive its own destructive capacity, but Snow's most immediate concern was to get back into China. He went to Japan, expecting to enter China from there. The Nationalists, however, wanted no part of him and denied him, along with several other American reporters, a visa. Ambassador Patrick Hurley's incendiary charge that "a considerable section of our State Department is endeavoring to support Communism generally as well as specifically in China" as he announced his surprise resignation, provided the Nationalists considerable cover for their blatantly political action. Snow indignantly protested the act as a serious violation of the freedom of the press, noting in particular, "It is ironic that I who for many years advocated abolition of extraterritoriality should now be among the first excluded as a result of full restoration of sovereignty under the Chungking government."

The American press stood up for Snow but in the process began to make his greatest claim to fame his most serious Cold War political liability by repeatedly referring to him as the writer most noted for making the case for the Chinese Communists. General George C. Marshall, during his 1946 mediation efforts between the Nationalists and the Communists, finally arranged for the Nationalists' ban to be lifted, but by then it was clear to Snow that the civil war he feared when he left China in 1941 was now in fact breaking out on a grand scale. He told his editor at the *Saturday Evening Post* he should send someone else: "If we are to remain and back the Kuomintang with armed forces then it would be necessary for me, if I went there, to take sides in support of a regime and a policy with which I would be out of sympathy."

In Tokyo in December 1945 Snow had a happy reunion with Jim Bertram, only recently released from his long and grueling ordeal as a prisoner of war. To Bertram's surprise he seldom saw Snow at the Press Club "without a group of Japanese publishers besieging him, pressing their demands for translation rights of *The Battle for Asia* or *People on Our Side.*" He wondered at their motives. Snow explained to Bennett Cerf: "My books were banned in Japan for years because they were supposed to be pro-Chinese and anti-Japanese. Since the defeat, there is a hot demand here for American literature; the Japanese haven't had any for years." He happily arranged for the Japanese publication of four of his own books and of three by "Nym Wales." He apparently still felt loyal to their writers' contract. He sent advance royalties from two of his books to Mme. Sun Yat-sen, relishing the idea his Japanese readers would pay for the support of a Chinese boy and girl in her Defense League orphanage.

By New Year's Eve, Snow was with his *Post* editor, Martin Sommers, on the Thirty-eight Parallel in Korea. He was dismayed by the partition of Korea and the unpreparedness of either the American or the Soviet forces to listen, let alone respond, to the needs of the Korean people. He believed only a quickly arranged national election would keep the division of Korea from hardening: "The longer the bargaining [between Americans and Soviets] is prolonged, the more the two zones draw apart, the more each tends to reflect the social pattern typified by its occupying power."[7] The tragic consequences for Korea of the incipient Cold War were already becoming all too clear.

Meanwhile back home the debate over American postwar China policy continued to heat up. Snow supported the formation of the Committee for a Democratic Far Eastern Policy. Its purpose was to organize public support for a democratic China, which frequently meant in practice challenging the Henry Luce umbrella organization, United China Relief, and lobbying against the Kuomintang. Evans Carlson became its first president. Carlson had reenlisted in the U.S. Marines a few months before Pearl Harbor and subsequently was chosen to develop and lead a crack marine commando group that became a legendary force in America's retaking of the Pacific. Ironically the popular movie in which Hollywood sanctified Carlson's use of Mao's guerrilla tactics was still playing as Cold War politics began reshaping American public opinion. Carlson had also adopted Indusco's slogan, "Gung Ho," "Work Together," for his Marine Raiders. It became the title of the movie and so entered the American language to eventually become transformed into an English expression in ironic contrast to its original Chinese significance.

In March in Fulton, Missouri, with Harry Truman as proud host, Winston Churchill gave stentorian voice to the memorable public image of a Soviet Iron Curtain descending on eastern Europe. Joseph Stalin then declared Churchill's words "a call to war with the Soviet Union." The civil war Snow dreaded in China was now in effect subsumed into a worldwide Cold War, but while the latter's principal antagonists were to be Russia and the United States, many of its most devastating battles would be fought in Asia. Snow had been far more prescient in predicting World War II than he was in foreseeing the Cold War that followed. He could not believe America had moved so far away from its own anticolonial revolutionary past.

Joseph Stilwell died suddenly of a heart attack October 12, 1946. A few months later Evans Carlson suffered a similar fate. In a memorial tribute to Carlson, Agnes Smedley remembered her dead friend's description of Churchill's speech at Fulton as "the most arrogant insult to the American people from an Englishman since the time of George III," an attempt to arouse support for the "bankrupt policies of colonialism, special privileges, human exploitation, and military balance-of-power alliances." The full dimension of Stilwell's bitter experience with Chiang Kai-shek began to open to public view with the publication of *The Stilwell Papers*, edited by Theodore White two years later, in 1948.

Early in 1946, back in the States, Snow met Lois Wheeler, the strong-minded American actress who was to become his second wife. One of the first questions she asked him was why he did work for such a conservative publication as the *Saturday Evening Post*. Somewhat indignantly he replied: "The *Post* prints any article I want to write. They don't change my material. They pay me very well and they send me places I want to go. And the magazine gets into many houses." Almost to emphasize Snow's point, the *Post* soon afterward published Snow's highly complimentary portrait of Archibald Clark-Kerr, who since his China assignment had become Britain's ambassador to Russia; and *Post* editor Ben Hibbs suggested Snow do a series of articles on Russia, even though editorially the *Post* was strongly concerned about "our inane surrenders at Yalta."

Snow accepted Hibbs's invitation, deciding to write a series that would "lift the lid from Ivan Ivanovich's skull." Looking at the world through the turbulent violence of recent Russian history, particularly of the Soviet revolution and the terrible price of resisting and defeating the Nazi invasion, he identified "insecurity" as the principal determinant of Soviet foreign policy. Continuing the logic of his conclusion to *Battle for Asia*, he believed American failure to be clear early about our postwar priorities, and our newly announced containment policy added to that sense of insecurity. Ivanovich had good reason to feel hopelessly muddled as he saw himself surrounded. Snow believed our recent cooperation with the Soviets in war proved the possibility of our working with a hostile Communist political system, and he called for greater American understanding of the Soviet history and point of view.

The *Saturday Evening Post's* editors, divided in their view of Snow's articles, nevertheless published them with only minor changes that Snow approved. Hibbs wrote a qualifying open letter to Generalissimo Stalin and other *Post* readers to accompany the series. The articles aroused immediate intense praise and criticism. Patrick Hurley focused the hostile reaction by taking indignant exception to Snow's description of Hurley's leaving an April 1945 meeting with Stalin believing the Soviets would follow the American lead on China. Snow had substantial evidence to stand by his account, but Hurley charged Snow with being "pro-Communist" and alleged his story came from confidential reports "given or sold to Communists by State Department officials."

Random House, taking advantage of the strong public interest, then brought the series out as a book, *Stalin Must Have Peace*, with an introduction by Martin Sommers. It became a selection of the Book Find Club and fueled Freda Utley's attack on Snow and the *Post* in *Plain Talk*. The attack on Snow spread in conservative publications. Ironically, but consistently, the Soviets were no more pleased than American conservatives. Snow was refused a visa to return to Moscow, and Soviet officials made clear to him his *Post* series was "positively unsatisfactory." He would become even more resentful of Soviet policy when Anna Louise Strong was arrested in Moscow and accused of being an American spy in 1949. He angrily resigned from the Committee for a Democratic Policy in the Far East for its failure to defend Strong. Snow's rich personal experience vividly told him again and again communism was not globally of one mind.

Snow would continue to maintain an editorial position on the *Saturday Evening Post* until February 1951, though his relations with the other editors were often strained. Twice the chief editors refused his offers to resign. When the United States entered the war in Korea in June 1950 the stakes became high and, because of his long residence in China, personal. Eventually he came to believe it was a matter of his own political integrity to divorce himself from a magazine with whose official editorial opinion on foreign policy he was so starkly at odds. At a painful final luncheon with Snow at the Down Town Club in Philadelphia the *Saturday Evening Post* editors reluctantly agreed to accept his resignation from the editorial staff. Hibbs encouraged

Snow to continue to send freelance articles, and Snow did. Some were even published.[8]

The prudence of Snow's decision both economically and politically is open to question. After considerable legal wrangling, he and Foster Snow had divorced in 1949 and he had married Lois Wheeler. By now he was father to one child with a second soon to be born and still obligated to pay alimony to his first wife. The *Saturday Evening Post* had long been his financial mainstay, and there was nothing in sight to replace it. Besides financial support, it provided him with a conservatively safe and substantial platform to present his liberal views to middle America. The magazine became a far less broadly representative American magazine without him. Nevertheless, convinced continuing as an editor compromised his personal and professional integrity, he resigned. His new wife never wavered in support of his decision. But for the next decade his voice was effectively marginalized in the shaping of public opinion on American foreign policy issues.

42

The Ghost at the Banquet

I N NOVEMBER 1949 THE newly married Snows put a rug over Agnes Smedley in the back seat of their car to evade FBI surveillance and drove to a New York City pier. There they waved good-bye to the woman who had added her own inimitable flair to their wedding. No longer able to afford living in the States, Smedley was on her way to England. Knopf had insisted on significant editorial changes in her contracted biography of Chu Teh. Snow advised Smedley that Knopf's editorial requests were reasonable, but she chose to abandon her contract. The House Un-American Activities Committee, planning to question her and perhaps bring her before a grand jury, made it difficult for Smedley to obtain even a passport restricting her travel to England, Italy, and France. A few months after arriving in England, Smedley had a serious abdominal operation that unexpectedly proved fatal. The task of editing her Chu Teh manuscript and finding a publisher for it fell largely to Snow. Over the next few years it became a frequent reminder of a world from which he was increasingly isolated by Cold War politics he considered mistaken, if not mad.[1]

Early in 1951, soon after resigning his editorial position with the *Saturday Evening Post,* he proposed writing an autobiography, and Random House readily offered a contract. The project dragged on fitfully for years, he frequently apologizing for his tardiness. During this time he experimented with a wide range of literary activities trying to find new outlets for his talents that would finesse the political barrier his long and public association with

Chinese Communism created for him during the Cold War. His hopes for a break in the polarized international scene were briefly boosted in 1954 when Senator Joseph McCarthy so overplayed his demagogic anticommunism before a Senate subcommittee that the whole Senate condemned his behavior. But the Cold War survived McCarthy's humiliation.

During this long dry period, Wheeler Snow's earnings as an actress became the mainstay of the family finances, and Snow fell behind in his alimony payments to Foster Snow.

In 1956 John King Fairbank arranged a modest stipend for him as a research associate at Harvard so he could mine his papers to produce *Random Notes on Red China, 1936–1945.* It was an academic addendum to *Red Star over China* and *Battle for Asia* that contained significant information for East Asian scholars but had little appeal to Random House as a commercial publication.

It was also, however, useful review and research for his long-delayed autobiography. The death of McCarthy in 1957 again encouraged Snow to believe his own story could help expose the irrationality of the Cold War. He began his final chapter:

> There has seldom been such successful demagoguery, conspired in by a responsible American political party, as the "twenty-years-of-treason" hoax which helped carry the Republican party to power in 1952. Nor was there in our history any campaign more costly to the American people, to our prestige abroad and to our internal unity and self-respect, than the triumph of lies and slander, spearheaded by McCarthy and Nixon, which charged Roosevelt, Marshall, Stilwell, Truman, Acheson and loyal men of the U.S. Foreign Service with betrayal of our country and "selling China to the Russians."

With a proud sense of historical vindication he recalled the answer he had published in 1949 to the question "Will the Communist-led government inevitably mean that China must fall under the absolute domination of the Kremlin?" Besides the obvious facts of China's immense size with a population double that of the Soviet Union, he had pointed out that the Chinese Red Army had fought its major battles for survival before World War II without significant Soviet aid and that it was led by Mao Tse-tung, who remained in power despite a Comintern demand for his removal, and whose personality and writings had deeply Sinicized the marxism of a generation of Party leaders strongly conditioned by long years of developing their movement in independent isolation.

> Mao Tse-tung and his followers were the first to prove that Communist-led revolutions in semi-colonial countries can conquer by combining the

role of national liberation with anti-feudal social reform movements. In a setting quite unforeseen by the Kremlin hierarchy they proved that such revolutions can succeed without depending upon urban proletarian insurrections, without help from Russia or the world proletariat, and on the basis of the organized peasantry as a main force.

Thus in 1949 he foresaw as a result of the Chinese Communists' victory that "Moscow must deal with a major foreign power run by Communists possessing all the means of maintaining real equality and independence." Far from being a Russian satellite, the Chinese saw "their country as the potential focus of a new federation of Eastern Socialist states." While this would please the Kremlin no more than Tito's Balkan federation theme, Snow did not expect the Soviets to repeat their mistake in Yugoslavia. They will tolerate China's independence so long as Americans retain their position of China's Foreign Enemy Number 1 by supporting the defeated Nationalists.

He then shrewdly and accurately speculated: "Peking might eventually become a kind of Asiatic Moscow, an Eastern Rome preaching a kind of 'Asiatic Marxism' out of Moscow's control . . . the symbol of the overthrow of the European colonial system in Asia, as well as the denial of our own principles of democracy bound up with ideas of private property rights in the ownership of the means of production." He ended his autobiography suggesting if we could recognize that colonialism was truly finished and convince China and other Asian states we were free of any neocolonial designs it might still be possible to contain Soviet Communism with Chinese Communism.[2] Snow would have to wait fourteen years before the team of Henry Kissinger and Richard Nixon would surprise the world and essentially embrace the realpolitik he first suggested in 1949 and reiterated in 1958, but the wait would prove too long for his life.

Journey to the Beginning was a moderate critical success. It was nominated for the National Book Award. But its sales were disappointing. It came out to the sound of big guns aimed at two little-known islands, Quemoy and Matsu in the Taiwan Straits, that again politically inflamed the China question in the mind of the American public. But perhaps more fundamental to aborting Snow's hopes for an end to the Cold War in Asia, the United States was already deeply engaged in resisting the Communist-led national rebellion in Vietnam. That engagement would escalate over the next few years into a war rending the fabric of American society even more divisively than Senator Joseph McCarthy and his witch-hunting compatriots.

Snow returned to America in 1941 to escape being an Ishmael. Now almost two decades after passing through his first middle-age crisis Snow once more shared the damp drizzly November of Ishmael's soul. America's single-minded foreign policy reduced the rich and various national histories and aspirations of Asian peoples to simplistic counters in a global political contest between superpowers. That violated all he had learned and tried to explain to the American people during his long journey among the peoples of Asia. While his second wife did not share his Asian experience, she quickly came to share his sense of political alienation as she found herself unexplainedly "black-listed" from acting jobs previously a readily available staple of her professional career.

Then in 1959 Snow-Ishmael came upon a surprising opportunity to go again to sea. Karl Jaeger, an eccentric but wealthy young man from Columbus, Ohio, invited Snow to be the social studies professor on a five-person faculty of the International School of America. It was an educational experiment in uniting international travel with learning, an experiment for which Snow obviously had impressive credentials and that probably combined happy memories of the SS *Radnor* and Yenching University. But perhaps even more persuasive was a chance to arrange the school's itinerary so he might renew contacts with his friends in China.

He contracted to teach from September 1959 through June 1960. Wheeler Snow and their two children rented a house in Switzerland from a doctor who had treated Snow years earlier. Their residence in Switzerland became a happier and more permanent family move than originally intended, but the final choice of a home would take several years to make. The first seven months of his new teaching experience provided sufficient adventurous experience to make him think of turning it into a book, but in April he excitedly wrote Random House from Paris that inquiries made in Hong Kong had now paid off in assurances he could get a three-month visa to return to China. He eagerly bought his way out of the remainder of his school contract so he could leave for China in June and return to Europe in August to write a short book about the new China, with photos, that could be published late in 1960 or early 1961.[3]

Random House quickly approved the proposal, but Cold War politics made getting the necessary travel documents more complicated than he expected. With the active sponsorship, however, of Random House and, even more effectively, Gardner Cowles from *Look* magazine, the passport difficulties were resolved in time for him to wave good-bye to his family in Geneva on June 28 and return to his second homeland. Once more he felt the excitement of his twenty-four years earlier crossing into unknown Red territory. Both visits began in June and ended in November.

But both Snow and his Chinese Communist hosts were fundamentally changed by all that had happened in the years between these journeys.

Instead of a dedicated revolutionary guerrilla army, the Communists were now the ruling power of mainland China. Mao Tse-tung, who seemed so clear-sighted and modest in his leadership role in 1936, was now the hero of a burgeoning cultlike political mythology. Snow was first surprised and proud to find a photo he had taken in Pao An of Mao had become a national political icon. But he could not be comfortable with Mao as a cult figure and questioned him about it directly and repeatedly.

Two years earlier Mao had initiated a national program, the Great Leap Forward, to transform China rapidly into a modern industrial nation. It was a mix of willful politics and incredibly naïve economics that focused the nation on creating vast amounts of crude and essentially useless homemade cast iron. Chinese agricultural production was consequently disastrously weakened just as it was to be severely tested by a three-year drought that began before Snow's visit. Peng Teh-huai, the Red commander with whom Snow traveled in 1936 and whose loyalty to the national revolution he deeply respected, had written a letter to Mao on July 14, 1959, at a fateful Party meeting at Lushan, calling attention to some of the failures of the Great Leap Forward. In September, Peng had been replaced by Lin Piao as minister of Defense and ousted from the Party. The full extent of the famine that had begun in China and the details of Peng's criticism of national policy were at the time of Snow's visit still carefully shrouded from public view and from Snow. He attempted to find out more about both, but was easily put off.

The rivalry between Nikita Khrushchev and Mao Tse-tung as world communist leaders came to a climax during Snow's visit, with the Russians in August abruptly pulling out their large contingent of technicians supporting Chinese efforts to industrialize their economy. The Chinese took pride in marching on independently. Snow had no trouble believing in China's independent capacity, but this Sino-Soviet split now seemed important to him principally for what it implied about China's nuclear capability. Unenthusiastically, but accurately, he predicted China would have its own bomb by 1964.

While he tried earnestly to maintain his independence as a journalist by meticulously insisting on paying his own travel expenses, there was no escape from being the guest of a ruling power. He could ask questions freely. He could travel extensively to places he himself chose. But he no longer had the independent contacts and resources for informing himself that in 1936 he had built up by years of residence and reporting within China. He stayed in Alley's apartment and saw much of Ma Hai-teh and his family. He took special pleasure in publicly acknowledging Hatem as his unnamed traveling companion in 1936 and writing about his impressive role in ridding modern

China of prostitution and venereal disease. These old China friends told him much of what they knew, but they too could often only guess at what happened within the inner circles of the Party. And they were sufficiently experienced and politically committed to be careful about making dangerous guesses public information.

There were, on the other hand, very real and publicly obvious achievements of the revolution as yet little known to the outside world that deserved to be celebrated. The public order, cleanliness, and industry were all truly impressive compared to the China that Snow had last seen before the Communists came to power. The physical health and national pride of the people excited and moved him Even though in hindsight it became clear the full extent of hunger caused by drought and mistaken public policy was hidden from him, he saw an enormous number of ordinary people going about their everyday lives in towns and cities across a large and various nation, and they were obviously and significantly better fed and clothed than the people he had seen as he traveled a troubled China before the Communists came to power.

He was truly exhilarated by his visit and eager to get his story to the public. Both Chou En-lai and Mao Tse-tung gave him long and significant interviews to lend international political weight to his report. John F. Kennedy defeated Richard Nixon in the American election while Snow was in China. After a brief reunion with his family in Switzerland, Snow flew to New York, hoping a new Democratic administration would welcome the information he brought from China. Bennett Cerf arranged an early morning meeting with Dean Rusk, newly named secretary of state. The brush-off Snow received from Rusk rudely deflated any hope he had of a fresh initiative in Asia from the new administration. It was also an ominous portent of the public reception of the story of his trip.

The Other Side of the River: Red China Today—later editions would revert to Snow's original order: *Red China Today: The Other Side of the River*—was not the short quick book he first projected. There were many delays and much rewriting before it turned out the longest book he ever published. It was no *Red Star over China*. He rightly believed the American public needed a historical education on how China came to be where it was. Understandably, he also hoped to restore his own once-prominent position of authority in the public eye. To these ends he buttressed what he observed on his trip with large borrowings from his previous writings. Dressed up, however, in words borrowed from Walter Lippmann, his familiar challenge to the American people now seemed a little weary and discouraged. The issue "is not communism but whether we can 'to ourselves be true,' and whether we can 'find our strength by developing and applying our principles, not in abandoning them.' " The American public was no more ready to accept such a challenge as the basis for determining our policy toward the culturally distant nations of Asia in 1962 than it had been in 1941. The Kennedy administration, mindful of its slim electoral victory, shared only the rhetoric.[4]

Publication of his book brought Snow face-to-face with another unhappy domestic reality. Foster Snow attached his royalties for his failure to pay alimony. Eventually he worked out an agreement to end his alimony obligations in exchange for royalties from his book.

Early in 1964, while the reviews of *Red China Today* were still in the public mind, the Paris newspaper *Le Nouveau Candide* sent Snow to Conakry, Guinea, to interview Chou En-Lai, then on a ten-country African tour. France was preparing to resume diplomatic relations with China, while the United States found itself increasingly isolated, recognizing only the Taiwan regime. To the envy of Snow's fellow reporters, Premier Chou gave Snow a five-hour interview he was able to publish in the *New York Times* and *Washington Post*. Chou also made it clear Snow was welcome to visit China again.

Late in October, sponsored by France's *Le Nouveau Candide*, Germany's *Stern*, and Italy's *L'Europe*, with a book contract from MacMillan arranged by a new agent, Mary Heathcote, and supplied with the latest in handheld television cameras, Snow was back in China for a visit that lasted until mid-January. China's agricultural production had recovered. The famine was over. But the cult of Mao was even more conspicuous than before. Again both Mao and Chou gave Snow interviews that indicated how special they still viewed his role in interpreting their cause to the Western world.

This time as Snow entered China, Lyndon Johnson was selling himself to the American public as a peace candidate against "the mad bomber" Barry Goldwater. Mao gave Snow a potentially significant assurance, on the record, that Chinese troops would not intervene in Vietnam. Snow had great difficulty coordinating the release of his Mao interview in major newspapers around the world and in keeping his promise the interview would not be cut. Mao's pledge was published in February, but Johnson, now elected, had already made a fateful decision. Under the legal cover of the Tonkin Gulf resolution from Congress he ordered the bombing of North Vietnam to begin that same month.

The war in Vietnam entered its most violently destructive phase shortly after Snow's return to Switzerland and eventually provoked him to write a spoof for the *Columbia University Forum*, "Barkinson's Law on Bombing," reminiscent in its bitter satire of "China Needs Healthier Leaders," written more than thirty years earlier by China's Best Enemy, John Fairnsworth.

Lyndon Johnson's later American hubris seemed even more brutally and directly destructive than the earlier British variety. In June, Snow wrote Howard: "Johnson seems to have gone mad with power. Maybe he will blow us all up before we can come back to the goddess liberty. I think I liked it better when we were not trying to run everybody. I remember the twenties now as a good time when we were satisfied just to be ourselves without so much preaching with bombs and so on. How did we get to be god so quickly?"

Snow's trip to China was delayed by a blockage in his bladder requiring surgery. Despite considerate treatment from his hosts, the trip exhausted him. Shortly after he returned to Switzerland he had to check into a Bern hospital with an infection. His body was beginning to show the severe tests he had subjected it to. He and MacMillan tangled over the kind of book his contract called for. He bought his way out of the contract, and after much time and effort produced instead a television documentary, *One Fourth of Humanity*, badly flawed technically, but still shown widely in Europe.[5]

In the summer of 1966 the Cultural Revolution reared its dragonhead in China. Snow's minor, but still disquieting, physical problems, the bitter political divisions in the United States over the Vietnam War, and now this portentous political drama in his second homeland made Switzerland a welcome haven of sanity and security. In 1968 the Snows bought an old farmhouse just outside the village of Eysins that presented a welcome challenge to restore.

Reuters correspondent Anthony Grey was held in China under house arrest for two years at the beginning of the Cultural Revolution. His copy of *Red China Today* was confiscated, and he was told it was "unfriendly to the Chinese People's Republic." Snow learned from "several people he was bound to believe" he was "no longer considered a friend of China." After several unsuccessful efforts to return to China, he wrote with some feeling to Israel Epstein, unaware the latter was already in prison charged with spying for the CIA. If he were to be judged and condemned on the basis of hearsay or slander, he wrote, he would have to reassess his friendship for China. His record was clear for all to see, and though his writing might be full of faults in detail, it was honest and independent journalism. He was "not a writer who changes his political views to suit a weather vane."

In 1967 and 1968 he revised *Red Star over China* for a new Grove Press edition, adding a substantial appendix of biographical sketches drawn from his notes. He dedicated the book to Grenville Clark, active in the cause of world government and sufficiently wealthy to provide Snow with needed capital to produce *One Fourth of Humanity*. Before his death in 1967, Clark generously informed Snow he was not to worry about repayment. The public reception of the revised *Red Star over China* was a pleasant surprise. The reviews were favorable and respectful, many acknowledging *Red Star over China* as a classic of American journalism. The *New York Times* covered a talk he gave in Hartford arguing for the credibility of Mao's assurance he would not send Chinese troops into Vietnam. He lectured for two months in Japan to sizable and enthusiastic audiences.

In the summer of 1969 he wrote directly to Mao Tse-tung requesting permission "to see for myself the results of the Great Proletarian Cultural Revolution." He had no response for almost a year, much of which he spent coping with a recurrence of old illnesses, malaria, and a bladder infection. The latter he now traced to the cystoscopic removal of his kidney stone in Peking during the thirties. Then in June 1970 the Chinese Embassy in Paris informed him not only he but also his wife was welcome to visit China.

This time Wheeler Snow decided to finesse the problem that had prevented her from accompanying her husband on his past visits by simply not applying for a visa from the State department. Snow arranged for her to do a book on Chinese opera and ballet with Random House as a surprise birthday gift. Their joint visit took on symbolic political significance to both countries. No resolution was then in sight for the Vietnam War ever more deeply dividing America. Mao Tse-tung recognized the need to normalize conditions in China after the brutal excesses of the early years of the Cultural Revolution. China's relations with the Soviets had again become ominous. Both China and the United States watched each other warily, hoping to find appropriate terms and conditions to restore relations.[6]

Chou En-lai called Huang Hua from the May 7th School, where he was being retrained in revolutionary political correctness, to plan and coordinate the Snows' visit. The student leader Snow had summoned to Red territory to translate for him in 1936 had risen to high diplomatic posts before experiencing the arbitrary authority of the Cultural Revolution. Two days after the Snows arrived in Beijing, Chou summoned them to an international table tennis tournament attended by many prominent foreign diplomats. He took Snow into a side room and questioned him extensively about the United States, candidly acknowledging his interest in a resumption of contact between the two governments. At the time Chou had no suspicion "ping-pong diplomacy" would within a year become a catchphrase bringing a smile of satisfaction to much of the rest of the world.

The twenty-first anniversary of the founding of the People's Republic was publicly celebrated October 1 by a huge parade reviewed by Chinese and foreign dignitaries gathered on the balcony of Tien An Men and made visible to China and the world by national television. At a strategic moment in the long parade, Chou En-lai touched Snow's arm and motioned both him and his wife from their already prominent seats to stand alongside Mao Tse-tung. The latter dryly acknowledged Snow's long unanswered request to see the Cultural Revolution: "It pays to complain. So now you are here?"

He told Snow the ultraleftists who opposed him were all cleared out. He had read Snow's articles, including criticism of the Mao cult, and he reassured Snow: "We do not expect you to agree with everything we say. You have a right to your own opinion. It is better to keep independent judgment." After the parade, in a room inside the gate, the Snows had tea with Chou En-lai.

Years later Henry Kissinger confessed the Chinese "overestimated our subtlety, for what they conveyed [bringing Snow to stand with Mao on Tien An Men] was so oblique that our crude Occidental minds completely missed the point."

On December 18 Snow had a long conversation with Mao over breakfast. Mao told Snow messages were being exchanged with the United States and that an American envoy might soon come to Peking. China was considering ways of admitting Americans. President Nixon himself would be welcome "either as a tourist or as President." He admitted recent widespread use of force and maltreatment of captives violated the spirit of the national revolution. Snow took the opening to tell the Chairman he had never known Israel Epstein to be disloyal to China. Mao said he did not know of Epstein's imprisonment.

A photo of Snow and Mao standing side by side at Tien An Men, with Snow described as a "friendly" American, appeared on the front page of the *People's Daily* on Christmas Day. The Snows had no way of knowing then what hope and reassurance that photo brought Epstein when he saw it in prison. Snow saw both Hatem and Alley were worried about their Chinese families, but he had no idea how cruelly Alley's son and daughter-in-law had been made to suffer. He understood enough, however, to respond to Huang Hua's bland assurance that the Cultural Revolution was creating a healthy spiritual transformation by quoting the exchange between Alice in Wonderland and the White Queen:

> "I can't believe that!"
> "Can't you? I dare say you haven't had much practice. When I was your age, I always did it for half-an-hour a day. Why, sometimes I've believed as many as six impossible things before breakfast."[7]

Wheeler Snow left China to spend Christmas with their daughter, then in her freshman year at Antioch College, while Snow remained for the promise of another interview with Chou En-lai. The interview did not take place until mid-January, and then approval of Snow's rendering and addenda was long delayed. He suffered severely from bronchitis, at least once coughing up blood, but turned aside Hatem's advice to see a doctor. He also appreciatively declined China's offer to provide him and his family a home for the remainder of his life. Because China and the United States did not yet officially recognize each other, it was difficult for him and his wife to keep in touch by mail. Anxious also about money problems and eager to begin writing his projected book, he flew to Hong Kong in early February without the approved Chou interview. It was forwarded to him in Switzerland.

He laid over two days in a Hong Kong hospital for a checkup and to avoid the press eager to question him about his five-month stay on the mainland. Back in Switzerland he was happy to have his son, Chris, as buffer from yet more reporters. The lengthy Chou interview when it finally came also proved difficult to place along with the demand it be accepted in its entirety. A misunderstanding with the *New York Times* caused him angrily to direct his agent to have no further dealing with the paper. The interview ran in five installments instead in the *New Republic*.[8]

Shortly after it began running the Chinese invited an American table tennis team then competing in Japan to visit China. The novel, but extraordinary, symbolic significance quickly caught the imagination of the world. *Life* magazine, known for its Cold War patriotism until the death of its founder Henry Luce in 1967, happily gave twenty-one pages to Snow's interview with Mao Tse-tung accompanied by appropriate photos. Its editors coolly proclaimed the time ripe for rapprochement. Snow was deluged with public attention after President Nixon in July publicly accepted China's invitation to visit. The new paperback edition of *Red Star over China* sold 11,500 copies within two months.

Life was now ready to meet any reasonable demand from Snow if he would represent the magazine and cover Nixon's visit. In the midst of clamorous demands for opinions, advice, and intercession with the Chinese, both the Snows worked on completing their books. Snow, however, was seriously troubled by constant fatigue and back pains. When his wife came down with infectious hepatitis and entered the hospital, they suspected Snow suffered the same illness. Hospital tests revealed something much more serious instead: his liver was gravely enlarged from cancer of the pancreas. An exploratory four-hour operation in December left little room for hope, but chemotherapy was ordered and tried.

With the help of devoted friends and family members, a still-recovering Wheeler Snow did her best to care for her dying husband whose determination to finish writing his last book seemed an important part of his will to live.

Mary Heathcote came to help. Unwilling to accept his cancer as inevitably fatal, Wheeler Snow wrote desperately to friends for advice. The Chinese quickly organized a professionally sophisticated medical team appropriately led by Dr. George Hatem to fly to Switzerland and bring Snow back to China for treatment. A government plane was specially equipped and designated for the task.

On January 24 the Snows awaited the arrival of this remarkable delegation with mixed feelings of awed gratitude and fear of losing Snow's prized independent control over his life. After Snow's death Wheeler Snow would write in wonder and deep gratitude at the care and sensitivity with which this team entered their home, quickly recognized it was too late to return her husband to China, and accommodated themselves to their dying friend's needs and persistent ambition. The personal bond first formed between two adventurous young Americans, one a doctor and the other a reporter, as they crossed into unknown territory in 1936, had grown over the years into a resourcefully deep understanding and respect between two men of remarkable human experience. Hatem and the proficient, caring team he brought with him knew how to enter his friend's family without displacing anyone. They extended the basic family and freed its closest members of many onerous and dispiriting responsibilities. For Wheeler Snow it seemed a marvel of the best of ancient and modern Chinese culture, and she later told the world so in a second book, *A Death with Dignity*.

Snow's fatal illness was a public event at yet another dramatic moment in human history. Huang Hua, reassigned from his ambassadorial post in Canada to represent the People's Government newly seated in the United Nations, spent two days during the final week of Snow's life at the side of his friend and mentor. Richard Nixon sent his prayers for Snow's recovery, adding, "I can only hope that it will strengthen you to know that your distinguished career is so widely respected and appreciated." Snow did not choose to respond, but the American president's words may not have been as empty as they seemed at the time. Kissinger later indicated Snow's writings were among the briefing materials Nixon "read with exquisite care."[9]

John Service, who first met Snow in Peking in 1935 when Service was beginning a distinguished career in the State department later tragically disrupted by the McCarthyism of the Cold War, reflected most tellingly on the ironic coincidence of Snow's death and Nixon's China visit. His first reaction was to think Snow's not being able to cover Nixon's historic visit tragic. Snow deserved the opportunity "as a kind of recompense for the long years in the wilderness," and Snow "would certainly have savored the historical significance (and irony, after all that had happened in the past twenty-three years) of an American president shaking hands with Mao Tse-tung and Chou En-lai."

But later and wiser thoughts caused Service to wonder:

> what could be done with a "correspondent" who was much more than that, who was really a ghost at the banquet? How could he be expected to be one of the horde of confused and frustrated news and television men, watching from afar and gleaning little? He could hardly be a member of the President's party (though that might be fitting). And his presence could only have posed awkward problems for the innate courtesy of his old (and very important) Chinese friends.

In the end Service preferred to remember his friend, "as we see him in that magnificent picture taken with Mao Tse-tung on Tien-an-men. Surely in the animated look on his face, we see the flash of fulfillment and the awareness of destiny achieved."[10]

Snow's last book, published posthumously as *The Long Revolution,* fittingly enough occupied his mind almost to his last moment of consciousness. His struggle to finish it was painful for his wife and his friends to witness even though it was clear to all it was part of his valiant will to live. Finally he admitted what he had written was enough to publish and soon after lapsed into a coma. He had begun a journey to see the world and write about it forty-four years earlier, in another February, as a deckboy on board the SS *Radnor.* His disappointments were many and trying; however, his deeply felt, but youthfully vague, aspirations were early and lastingly transformed into substantial historic issues in his journalism. He ended his journey quietly in his sleep at 2:20 A.M. on February 15, 1972.

Notes

1. Setting Out on a Second Life

1. Edgar Snow, *Journey to the Beginning*, 3, 11–15, 28–30; Charles White, interview by author, January 20, 1986; John Maxwell Hamilton, *Edgar Snow*, 1–11.

2. The *Collegian*, the Kansas City Junior College paper, August 27, 1924, 2; transcripts from Columbia University, Edgar Snow Collection, University of Missouri–Kansas City (hereafter all letters, diaries, and typescripts referred to will be from the Edgar Snow Collection unless otherwise designated); Hamilton, *Edgar Snow*, 11–13; ES to sister, August 8, 1926; ES to father, March 21, 1927.

3. ES to father, October 3, 1927; ES to mother, November 10, 1927.

4. ES to mother, December 2, 1927; ES to father, December 16, 1927; ES to family, January 9, 1928.

5. ES to mother, January 31, 1928; ES to parents, February 17, 1928.

6. Typescript, autobiographical sketch for Paul Freye, January 1946, Tokyo; ES to family, March 7, 1928; Snow, *Journey*, 28–30.

2. First Success—and a Great Job

1. ES to Charles Hanson Towne, March 7, 1928, Charles Hanson Towne Papers, manuscript division, New York Public Library; ES to family, March 7 and March 16, 1928.

2. ES to brother, March 26; ES to parents, May 11 and July 9, 1928; ES to Towne, June 26, 1928, Towne Papers; Edgar Snow, "In Hula Land."

3. Edgar Snow, "Kansas City Boy Stowaway"; ES to Towne, June 26, 1928, Towne Papers; ES to Al Joslin, June 21, 1928; Hamilton, *Edgar Snow*, 35–36.

4. In *Journey*, 35–37, Snow tells a rather hard-to-believe story of his friend Larry taking a naïve young Edgar to visit a well-appointed geisha house under the pretence of introducing him to two young Japanese "modern girl" banker's daughters. Snow does not clearly date the event but implies it took place when he arrived in Yokohama from Honolulu. It seems more likely that it never happened but is instead a deliberate fiction designed to memorialize a later romantic visit to Japan and an intimate relation with a Japanese woman that followed in Shanghai. See also text p. 54.

5. ES to parents, July 9, 1928; ES to mother, July 26, 1928.

3. The China Maelstrom

1. ES to father, August 15 and September 24, 1928; ES to brother, September 28, 1928; ES to mother, August 21, 1928.

2. John B. Powell, *My Twenty-five Years in China*, 154, 158–60; Snow, *Journey*, 26–27.

4. Manchuria and the Threat from Japan

1. ES to mother, July 28, 1928; ES to brother, January 17, 1929; ES to family, February 20, 1929; Edgar Snow, "Why the Rolling Stock Isn't Rolling out of Tsinanfu."

2. ES to father, March 21, 1928; ES to mother, November 4, 1928; Snow, *Journey*, 13–14.

3. Edgar Snow, "Hangchow and Beyond," "Journeying through Kiangsu," "Through China's 'Holy Land,'" and "Beyond the Great Wall"; ES to brother, May 3, 1929; ES to mother, June 2, 1929; Snow, *Journey*, 205; Edgar Snow, "Son of the Grand Marshal," 14–15, 25.

4. Edgar Snow, "Which Way Manchuria?"

5. The Cost of "a line or two that may not die"

1. ES to mother, June 2, 1929; ES to father, July 1, 1929.

2. Snow, *Journey*, 7; Edgar Snow, *Red Star over China*, 205–6; Edgar Snow, *The Other Side of the River: Red China Today*, 47; Edgar Snow, "Saving 250,000 Lives"; "Who's Who in China."

3. Janice R. MacKinnon and Stephen R. MacKinnon, *Agnes Smedley, the Life and Times of an American Radical*, 140–41; Gertrude Binder, phone interview by author, September 10, 1985; Snow, *Journey*, 25.

4. Edgar Snow, "The American College Boy Vagabond in the Far East"; ES to father, November 3, 1929; ES to family, September 6, 1929; ES to sister, September 14, 1929; Edgar Snow, "Entering the Notorious Yunnan Province in South China and Planning a Caravan Trek across This Mysterious Bandit Ridden Region."

5. ES to father, November 3, 1929; ES to mother, November 12 and November 22, 1929; John Powell, "My Father's Library," 36; Edgar Snow, review of *Chiang Kai-shek: The Builder of China*.

6. ES to mother, November 22 and December 19, 1929, and January 7, 1930; father to ES, March 15, 1930; John M. Allison, *Ambassador from the Prairie or Allison Wonderland*, 9–10; Snow, *Journey*, 33–34. Ida Pruitt, who grew up in China and whose life would begin to significantly touch Snow's after he moved to Peking in 1933, coincidentally soon published a more cruel, but more searching, explanation of the comparative value of human life and property in China than his story of rescuing a man in flames with his coat, but she had the advantage of many more years of experience living in China. She first described one day being struck by the sight of a condemned man, drunken but amply guarded, being carted to his execution, probably for thievery. Soon afterward her assistant told the story of an apprentice who killed his master in an irrational fit of rage and frustration. After being told the apprentice had been caught, Pruitt assumed he would be executed. Her assistant, however, was surprised by her assumption and quickly informed her, "He will probably get several months or perhaps a year or two in prison. There was no robbery, you see."

She then concluded: "This little dialogue brought an overwhelming realization of the sanctity of property and the need for that sanctity. With millions living each day on what each day brings forth,—two meals or one, or none,—with millions who literally never have been really full but once or twice in their lives, while human beings teem on every hand, is this attitude any wonder? He who takes a life merely reduces the consuming population, of which there are millions too many anyway. He who takes that takes that of which there is much too little to go round" ("Day by Day in Peking," 618–19).

6. Mother's Death and Escape

1. ES to mother, November 12, 1929; ES to family, December 2, 1929; ES to father, February 15, 1930; ES to Horace Epes, February 28, 1930.

2. ES to father, March 28, 1930; ES from father, May 12, 1930; Anna Snow's medical records, St. Mary's Hospital; Helen Foster Snow, interview by author, Madison, Conn., May 20, 1986.

3. ES to brother, May 17, 1930; "Snow Diary Transcript, Book II," 15–18; Snow, *Journey*, 14, 35–37; Edgar Snow, review of *Infidels and Heretics*, 386.

7. Good-bye Shanghai

1. He used this pseudonym on at least three other later occasions, including twice for brief articles in the *China Weekly Review* early in 1933, shortly after he married. In one of these the last name appears without the "n," *Fairsworth*. In the other, John Fairnsworth is followed by C.B.E., suggesting the assumed persona was very

acceptably British. The final instance is a 1938 article in the *China Weekly Review* plumping Industrial Cooperatives, a cause Snow believed in deeply but wanted to represent as having support from others than himself. ES to brother, May 17, 1930; Edgar Snow, "Marines at Peace."

2. ES to father, April 11, 1930; "The *American Mercury* Takes Up China," 372; Edgar Snow, "The Americans in Shanghai"; *Shanghai Evening Post and Mercury,* August 16, 1930, 2; copy of Snow's letter to the editor dated August 17, 1930, as printed in the *Shanghai Evening Post and Mercury,* undated; *Shanghai Evening Post and Mercury,* August 21, 1930, copy in Edgar Snow Collection, University of Missouri–Kansas City.

3. ES to Epes, July 18, 1930; ES to James Bertram, April 5, 1959; MacKinnon and MacKinnon, *Agnes Smedley,* 151.

4. Edgar Snow, "Change Enters the Chinese Pear Garden," 14–15, 25.

5. ES to editors of *Current History,* August 17 and September 1, 1930; Edgar Snow, "Communist Strength in China"; Snow typescript, "The Strength of Communism in China."

The editors at *Current History* significantly changed Snow's numbers for the damage done by the Communists. "*350* cities and towns" became "*250* cities and towns." The 45 of 83 hsien in Kiangsi Province captured by the Communists is changed to 55. Where Snow writes, "in Kwangsi, Hupeh and Honan, lawlessness has prevailed over such wide areas that it is impossible to estimate the extent of the damage actively directed by Communists," *Current History* edited, "in Honan, Hupeh, Kiangsu, and Suchuan, outlaws and marauders were everywhere, but their activities were not communistic, although in some instances village soviets were established."

8. Formosa, Canton, Hong Kong, and Macao

1. ES to Epes, September 17, 1930; Transcript of diary 1a: 1; Robert M. Farnsworth, ed., *Edgar Snow's Journey South of the Clouds,* 27–55; Edgar Snow, *Far Eastern Front,* 304.

2. Farnsworth, *South of the Clouds,* 32–38; Snow, *Journey,* 38; transcript of diary 1a: 8–34.

3. Transcript of diary 1a: 34–66; Farnsworth, *South of the Clouds,* 39–42, 56–61; Edgar Snow, "Protecting the Morals of the Formosans," 429.

4. Snow, *Journey,* 38–39; transcript of diary 1a: 74–82; Farnsworth, *South of the Clouds,* 69–73, 80–82.

5. Farnsworth, *South of the Clouds,* 74–78; *China Weekly Review,* September 5 and September 12, 1931.

6. Farnsworth, *South of the Clouds,* 83–97.

7. Ibid., 98–118.

9. The Embrace of France

1. Transcript of diary 3: 1–14; Snow, *Journey*, 43–45; Farnsworth, *South of the Clouds*, 119–36.

2. Transcript of diary 3: 5–6; Farnsworth, *South of the Clouds*, 137–49.

10. Within the Shadows of the Golden Horse and the Jade Phoenix

1. Transcript of diary 3: 9; Bruce Chatwin, *What Am I Doing Here?*, 206–15. See also Wendy Stallard Flory, *Ezra Pound and "The Cantos,"* 275–78.

2. Transcript of diary 3: 9–26; transcript of diary 4: 3–11; Rock, diary 16: 4–6; ES to brother, December 8, 1930; ES to sister, January 22, 1931; S. B. Sutton, *In China's Border Provinces: The Turbulent Career of Joseph Rock, Botanist-Explorer*, 208–11; Farnsworth, *South of the Clouds*, 122–26, 175–80.

3. Transcript of diary 3: 10–27; Snow, *Journey*, 49–50; Edgar Snow, "Celestial Poppy Smoke"; ES to Richard Walsh, Lois Wheeler Snow, *Edgar Snow's China*, 44; Farnsworth, *South of the Clouds*, 150–61.

11. On Caravan South of the Clouds

1. Snow, *Journey*, 54–59; transcript of diary 4: 18–30 and transcript of diary 5: 1–12; Sutton, *China's Border Provinces*, 214.

2. Transcript of diary 5: 17; Farnsworth, *South of the Clouds*, 221–24.

3. Transcript of diary 5: 29–31; transcript of diary 6: 2–28; Farnsworth, *South of the Clouds*, 208–9.

4. Transcript of diary 6: 28–49; Farnsworth, *South of the Clouds*, 210–16.

5. Transcript of diary 6: 28–49; Farnsworth, *South of the Clouds*, 221–29.

12. Compelled by the Golden Spire

1. Farnsworth, *South of the Clouds*, 229; transcript of diary 2: 4–6; transcript of diary 6: 56–60.

2. Transcript of diary 2: 4–6; transcript of diary 6: 56–60; transcript of diary 8: 1; Snow, *Journey*, 63–70; Farnsworth, *South of the Clouds*, 256–60.

3. Transcript of diary 7: 1–2; Farnsworth, *South of the Clouds*, 210–16.

4. ES to sister-in-law, March 20, 1931; Farnsworth, *South of the Clouds*, 221–24.

5. Snow, *Journey*, 68.

13. India: The Challenge of Yet Another National Revolution

1. Transcript of diary 7: 13–25.

2. Transcript of diary 7: 26–37; Snow, *Journey,* 74; Farnsworth, *South of the Clouds,* 273–80.

3. William Shirer, *Gandhi: A Memoir,* 231–32; Edgar Snow, "The Message of Gandhi"; Edgar Snow, "Gandhi Asserts American Visit Impossible"; ES to sister, May 29, 1931; Epes to ES, June 23, 1931.

4. Transcript of diary 7: 43–44; transcript of diary 8: 11; MacKinnon and MacKinnon, *Agnes Smedley,* 139; Edgar Snow, "The Trial of British Communists at Meerut, India"; Farnsworth, *South of the Clouds,* 269–72; Snow, *Journey,* 78.

5. ES to father, June 13, 1931.

6. Transcript of diary 8: 38–42.

7. Snow, *Journey,* 79–81; Edgar Snow, "The Revolt of India's Women"; transcript of diary 8: 2–9, 34.

8. Transcript of diary 8: 12–19.

14. An Attractive Woman and Hopeful Writer Lands in Shanghai and His Life

1. ES to father and Epes, August 5, 1931; Epes to ES, July 24 and August 20, 1931; ES to Towne, August 6, 1931, Towne Papers.

2. Edgar Snow, "Indo-China Now Hotbed of Reds"; Snow, *Journey,* 46.

3. ES to editor of *Current History,* September 18, 1931; Snow, "Revolt of India's Women."

4. Helen Foster Snow, *My China Years,* 24–32.

5. Snow, *Journey,* 102–6; ES to Maud Russell, July 21, 1948, Maud Russell Papers, manuscripts and archives section, New York Public Library.

6. Edgar Snow, "In the Wake of China's Flood," 4–5, 21. See also Snow, *Far Eastern Front,* 18–20.

7. Epes to ES, September 11, 1931; ES to Epes, October 25, 1931; Edgar Snow, "Why Lindbergh Plane Crashed"; Snow, *Far Eastern Front,* 24.

15. War's Obscenities and a Secular Madonna's Grace

1. *China Weekly Review,* November 14, 1931, 428; Snow, *Far Eastern Front,* 83, 99–112, 227–28; ES to brother, December 7, 1931.

2. ES to brother, December 7, 1931; ES to father, January 2, 1932.

3. Snow, *Far Eastern Front*, 180–220.

4. Foster Snow, *My China Years*, 51–53; ES to sister, March 4, 1932; Snow, *Far Eastern Front*, 215–16.

5. ES to sister, March 31, 1932.

6. Edgar Snow, "Profile, Mme. Sun Yat-sen"; Edgar Snow, "Kuomintang May Be Eliminated"; Edgar Snow, "Chinese Communists Make Gain"; Edgar Snow, "Mme. Sun Yat-sen, Leader of China's Youth"; Snow, *Journey*, 82–83; Foster Snow, *My China Years*, 43. Information about the Chocolate Shop is courtesy of John S. Service, who reviewed this manuscript.

16. A Book Rejected, a Marriage Proposal Accepted

1. ES to brother, May 17, 1932; ES to Epes, June 27, 1932.

2. ES to brother and sister-in-law, undated; ES to sister-in-law, August 17, 1932.

3. Foster Snow, *My China Years*, 67–70; Sutton, *China's Border Provinces*, 107–8.

4. ES to Epes, September 11, 1932; Epes to ES, October 15, 1932.

5. ES to Mrs. Meloney, November 23, 1932; ES from Mrs. Meloney, December 27, 1932, respectively.

6. Foster Snow, *My China Years*, 71–73.

7. ES to brother, October 27; ES to sister, November 22, 1932.

8. Foster Snow, *My China Years*, 73–74; ES to Epes, December 11, 1932; ES to father and sister, December 13, 1932.

17. The Wedding and a Repeat Journey

1. Allison, *Ambassador*, 17–19; Edgar Snow, "Christmas Escapade in Japan," 35–36; ES to brother, December 27, 1932; Foster Snow, *My China Years*, 75; transcript of diary 10: 2–4.

2. Transcript of diary 10: 1–6.

3. Ibid., 6–10; ES to Horace Epes, January 11, 1933; Snow, *Journey*, 107; Foster Snow, *My China Years*, 73–74.

4. Transcript of diary 10: 10–26;

5. Ibid., 27–28; Snow, *Journey*, 46–47; ES to father, February 16, 1933; ES to brother, February 25, 1933; Ling Yue-lin, vice director of the Lu Hsun Museum, Shanghai, provided the date for Snow's meeting Lu Hsun from the latter's diary (Hsun to author, December 12, 1987).

6. John Fairsworth, "How Anti-American Sentiment Is Fostered in Japan," 475.

7. Foster Snow, *My China Years*, 79–80; ES to brother, February 25, 1933.

18. A New Home and Two Long Shots Come In

1. ES to Towne, March 30, 1933; ES to father, April 11, 1933; Epes to ES, April 8, 1933; Foster Snow, *My China Years*, 91–93, 100, 107–10; Helen Foster Snow [Nym Wales, pseud.], *Historical Notes on China*, 1–2, 9; Hamilton, *Edgar Snow*, 53–54; Snow, *Journey*, 123; Otto Braun, *A Comintern Agent in China, 1932–1939*, 24.

2. John Fairnsworth, C.B.E. [pseud.], "China Needs Healthier Leaders"; Nym Wales, "Analyzing the 'Shanghai Mind,'" 57–58; Foster Snow, *Historical Notes on China*, 33–34.

3. ES to and from Mrs. Meloney, May 7, May 26, and June 1, 1933; ES to Soong Ching-ling, May 13, 1933; Victor Keen to ES, July 21, 1933; Snow, "Christmas Escapade," 47; Foster Snow, "Introduction to Edgar Snow," Nym Wales Collection, 5–6.

4. Letters to and from Epes, June 17, August 17, and September 16, 1933; ES to brother, September 6, 1933; Snow, *Journey*, 123–26; Foster Snow, *My China Years*, 122–24.

19. Author of a Book

1. Foster Snow to ES's father, September 27, 1933; Epes to ES, October 25, 1933; ES to Mrs. Meloney, October 28, 1933; ES to father, November 10, 1933; father to ES, December 4, 1933; ES to Epes, December 9, 1933; Epes to ES, December 18, 1933; ES to father, December 31, 1933.

2. John M. Allison to ES, December 20, 1933; Mrs. William Brown Meloney to ES, February 1, 1934; A. M. Nikolaieff, "The Undeclared War in the Far East," 11; William S. Graves, "An Arraignment of Japan," 2; Lin Yu-tang, review of *Far Eastern Front*; Mauritz A. Hallgren, "The Undeclared War in the East."

3. ES to sister, January 17, 1934; ES to Epes, January 21, 1934; ES to father, March 3 and 21, 1934; pasteup of lecture topics in Edgar Snow Collection; "Men's Club of Union Church to Hold Its First Forum on Monday."

4. Class notes for Yenching course in Edgar Snow Collection; ES to Henriette Herz, March 30, 1934; ES to Peter A. Dolan, May 7, 1934; ES to Betty Keen, June 19, 1934; ES to brother, May 8, 1934; Stanley J. Kunitz, ed., *Authors Today and Yesterday*, 107–8.

5. Foster Snow, *My China Years*, 131; Sutton, *China's Border Provinces*, 241–42; Snow, *Far Eastern Front*, 262. See also Edgar Snow, "Japan Builds a Colony," 12.

20. The Threat of Fascism

1. Edgar Snow, "Malraux's Revolutionary Novel an Epochal Work of China Fiction."

2. Letters to and from Walsh, September 6, October 17, and December 17, 1934, and April 17, 1935; ES to Mrs. Meloney, November 18, 1934; ES from Mrs. Meloney, December 19, 1934; Demaree Bess to ES, November 4, 1934.

3. *Peking Chronicle*, January 8–12, 1935, clipping in Nym Wales Collection.

4. ES to Betty Keen, March 7, 1935; Helen Foster Snow [Nym Wales, pseud.], *Notes on the Chinese Student Movement, 1935–1936*, 7–8; ES to editors of the *Nation* and the *New Republic*, April 1, 1935, Nym Wales Collection; Israel Epstein, interview by author, Beijing, November 30, 1984; Epstein to author, March 16, 1995.

5. Proposal to Guggenheim Foundation to study "The Agrarian Crisis in China"; Snow, *Journey*, 147; C. Walter Young to Mr. Henry Allen Moe, The Guggenheim Foundation, December 20, 1934; Hsiao Chien to ES, February 7, 1935; Epes to ES, March 30, 1935; ES to Epes, April 7, 1935.

6. ES to Epes, April 25, 1935; ES to Colonel Knox, May 2, 1935; ES to Mr. Henle, May 10, 1935, Nym Wales Collection.

21. From the Academy into the Cause

1. Foster Snow, *My China Years*, 148; Helen Foster Snow [Nym Wales, pseud.], *Notes on the Left-Wing Painters and Modern Art in China*, 30–48; Lu Hsun to Yao Ke, October 20, 1935.

2. ES to C. Walter Young and Walsh, July 19, 1935; ES to brother, July 20, 1935.

3. Walsh to ES, August 21, 1935.

4. ES to Walsh, October 25, 1935. The manuscript Snow was working on regrettably has not survived. I collected Snow's travel articles and supplemented them with information from his diaries to give readers a good sense of the raw material Snow originally intended to write into his first book, *Edgar Snow's Journey South of the Clouds*.

5. A. J. Barker, *The Civilizing Mission: A History of the Italo-Ethiopian War of 1935–1936*, 141–43; ES to Mrs. William Brown Meloney, October 14, 1935.

6. Huang Hua, interview by author, tape recording, Palace of the People, Beijing, May 20, 1985.

7. Snow, *Journey*, 139–43; Foster Snow, *My China Years*, 154–62; Foster Snow [Nym Wales, pseud.], *Chinese Student Movement*, 1–17, 193–95; John Israel, *Student Nationalism in China, 1927–1937*, 111–18.

22. The Students Demonstrate, and a Door Opens

1. Israel, *Student Nationalism*, 118–29; Foster Snow [Nym Wales, pseud.], *Chinese Student Movement*, 108–11; Lu Cui, "We Shall Forever Remember Edgar Snow with Gratitude."

2. Hubert Freyn, *Prelude to War: The Chinese Student Rebellion of 1935–1936*; Israel, *Student Nationalism*, 129–34.

3. John Israel and Donald W. Klein, *Rebels and Bureaucrats, China's December 9'ers,* 32–36; Foster Snow [Nym Wales, pseud.], *Chinese Student Movement,* 112–17; Huang, interview.

4. Israel and Klein, *Rebels and Bureaucrats,* 72–75; David Yu to the Snows, March 22 and March 25, 1936, Nym Wales Collection.

5. ES to Randall Gould, November 24, 1936; ES to L. M. MacBride, April 28 and June 1, 1936; MacKinnon and MacKinnon, *Agnes Smedley,* 168–69; George Hatem, interview by author, Beijing, April 1985. In the 1968 revised edition of *Red Star over China,* p. 477, n. 1, Snow indicated Hsu Ping was from Tungpei University, but in 1983 in "How Edgar Snow Arranged to Make His Trip to the Northwest, 1936," Foster Snow wrote: "Ed had a poor memory and 'Hsu Ping' must have been someone I remember as from possibly P'ing Ta University, not Tungpei, named 'Peter Wu,' who called on us only once or twice that I know of."

23. Where Journalism Meets Literature

1. ES to Walsh, January 11, 1936; ES to Norman Hanwell, November 8, 1935; Hanwell to ES, October 5 and October 17, 1935; Norman Hanwell, "The Chinese Red Army"; Norman Hanwell, "Where Chinese Reds Move In"; James Bertram, *Capes of China Slide Away;* Huang, interview.

2. ES to Henle, May 10, 1935; undated typescript of letter to Walsh from Foster Snow, Nym Wales Collection; ES to Lin Yu-tang, December 23, 1935, and March 29, 1936; Wang Shiqing, *Lu Xun: A Biography,* 317; Edgar Snow, *Living China; Modern Chinese Short Stories,* 346–49. I cannot locate Snow's review of *My Country and My People* referred to in Snow's letter to Lin Yu-tang.

3. Letters between Yao Hsin-nung and Foster Snow, June 22 and July 3, 1936, Nym Wales Collection; S. E. R. W., review of *Living China;* M. P. W., review of *Living China,* 155; Randolph Bartlett, review of *Living China;* Randall Gould, review of *Living China.*

4. Snow, *Living China,* 25–27.

24. To Sian: Stage One

1. ES to sister, March 17, 1936; ES to Mr. Burton, May 28, 1936; ES to MacBride, June 1, 1936; ES to Nelson Trusler Johnson, February 8, 1937.

2. Edgar Snow, "The Coming Conflict with Japan," 85, 92.

3. Snow, *Other Side of the River,* 261–65.

4. Snow, *Red Star over China,* 1968 rev. ed., 43–44, 505–6; transcript of diary 11: 24–27, 44–48; Edgar Snow, *Random Notes on Red China, 1936–1945,* 4–5.

5. Huang, interview.

25. Chou and Mao, in Person

1. Snow, transcript of diary 12: 8. The quotations from *Red Star over China* that follow will be from the first American edition of 1938 unless otherwise indicated.
2. Wheeler Snow, *Edgar Snow's China*, 132.
3. See Harrison Salisbury, *The Long March, The Untold Story*, 242–52, for a fuller account.

26. Measuring the Revolutionary Force

1. Foster Snow, *My China Years*, 188–96; Snow, *Red Star over China*, 396–97; Helen Foster Snow [Nym Wales, pseud.], *Notes on the Sian Incident, 1936*, 22–23.

27. The Real Red Army

1. Snow, *Red Star over China*, 1968 rev. ed., 479.
2. Braun, *Comintern Agent*, 167–68; *China Weekly Review*, November 14 and 21, 1936.
3. Snow, *Journey*, 178–79.
4. MacKinnon and MacKinnon, *Agnes Smedley*, 173.

28. The Home Front

1. Foster Snow [Nym Wales, pseud.], *Sian Incident*, 4–51; Foster Snow, *My China Years*, 152–53, 175–77, 188–89.

29. History and His Story

1. Foster Snow [Nym Wales, pseud.] *Sian Incident*, 51–54; Foster Snow, *My China Years*, 197–99; Snow, *Journey*, 183; Hamilton, *Edgar Snow*, 78–79; MacBride to ES, October 31, 1936; ES to Gould, November 24, 1936; ES to Johnson, November 13, 1936; Johnson to ES, November 14, 1936.
2. Snow, *Red Star over China*, 395–402 and Ma Hai-teh [George Hatem, pseud.] to ES, December 3, 1936. I have also received a copy of a letter sent to Snow from Mao Tse-tung, March 10, 1937, in Chinese. The translation provided for me by Liu Liqun, former general secretary of the Strong, Smedley, Snow Society of China, reads: "I've missed you a great deal ever since you left. You are getting along fine, I suppose? I dwelt upon a few fresh steps in our policies in my conversation with Agnes Smedley,

a copy of which is now, by taking a convenient chance, forwarded to you for your perusal and dissemination. We are all grateful to you. Wishing you good health." The copy of the policy changes referred to did not accompany the copy provided me. Letter to friends signed John [Chang Chao-lin], December 10, 1936, Nym Wales Collection; Foster Snow [Nym Wales, pseud.], *Sian Incident*, 6.

3. Snow, *Red Star over China*, 409–10; Foster Snow, *My China Years*, 204–12; James Bertram, *First Act in China*, 8–16, 28–40; Foster Snow [Nym Wales, pseud.], *Sian Incident*, 77, 92–102, 129–30; Hamilton, *Edgar Snow*, 81; ES to Charles [Liu Ting], December 16, 1936. Braun gives a very different view of these events: *Comintern Agent*, 182–90.

4. Letters to and from MacBride, January 5, 1937; ES to MacBride, January 14, 1937; Foster Snow to Herz, January 14, 1937; Bertram to editor, January 15, 1937, Nym Wales Collection; Hamilton, *Edgar Snow*, 80; Foster Snow [Nym Wales, pseud.], *Sian Incident*, 130.

5. Foster Snow to Gould, January 26, 1937, Nym Wales Collection; ES to T. T. Li, February 4, 1937; ES to Johnson, February 6, 1937; C. E. Gauss to Johnson, February 9, 1937, State Department files, National Archives; Edgar Snow, "Reds and Northwest, I and II."

6. ES to MacBride, February 7, 1937; "February 11. Notes of a talk with J. Bertram who left Sianfu Monday night, the 8th," Nym Wales Collection; Bertram, *First Act in China*, 257–61, 276–79; Snow, *Random Notes*, 5–14.

7. Snow, *Red Star over China*, 431, 436–50; there is a strong hint in a letter from Henriette Herz, November 12, 1937, that suggests that "Red Horizons" may have been written at the request of Random House after *Red Star over China* was near publication. Herz wrote: "Mr. Haas wanted to know whether you wouldn't write a conclusive chapter for RED STAR OVER CHINA. Since the book is coming out in January and has to be off the press the middle of December, it seemed impossible of course, to get it from you. Furthermore I feel that no conclusive chapter can be written about the present Sino-Japanese situation. What has happened before—up to date—and what may happen in the future, you have indicated well enough in the book. A made-to-order final chapter would only 'date' your book." Snow may have steered a course between the needs of his publisher and Herz's concern in writing "Red Horizons" as a conclusion after leaving Peking.

30. Amid Challenging Distractions

1. Foster Snow [Nym Wales, pseud.], *Sian Incident*, 156–57; Foster Snow, *My China Years*, 217–19; the *China Weekly Review*, January 16, 1937, 248.

2. Foster Snow, *Sian Incident*, 173–78; Foster Snow, *My China Years*, 220–27.

3. *Democracy*, May 1, 1937, 5, 10, 22; *Democracy*, June 8, 1937, 85–87; Foster Snow, *Sian Incident*, 185.

4. Foster Snow quotes a letter from "a professor at Columbia University," written January 18, 1937, in *Sian Incident*, 158. In a letter to me, June 18, 1992, she identified

this letter as from Cyrus Peake. This is the text: "Dear Ed, Your cable came two days ago. Of course, we are all extremely sorry that you found it impossible to accept. I realize of course how unattractive our offer was, but I was betting on the possibility that you might be wishing to come back on a 'furlough' and this offer would have made it possible. I can readily understand how deeply tied you are by now to China and your as always meaty and interesting articles attest to that. The next best thing to having you for our editor-in-chief is to have a contribution from you now and then . . . write us a 2,500 word article on the implications of the United Front in China for American Far Eastern policy. We have adopted as yet no policy of paying for contributions . . . I am almost ashamed, or should be at any rate, to offer you the small sum of $35 for such an article, but it appears that that is all our budget allows at present . . . I trust this finds you and Peg in the best of health, with best wishes to you both." Letter to Snows from Suzie, April 30, 1937, Nym Wales Collection.

5. The messages between Edgar and Helen Snow are all in the Edgar Snow and Nym Wales Collections. The letter from Snow to Phillip Jaffe is in the Phillip Jaffe Collection, Robert W. Woodruff Library, Emory University, Atlanta, Georgia. Their dates are indicated in the text. Supplemental information can be found in Foster Snow, *My China Years*, 231–73, and in the Da Capo edition of Helen Foster Snow's *Inside Red China*, New York, 1979, xxxix, xlii–xliii, xlv, xlvii–xlix, lix.

31. More Mixed Messages between Yenan and Peking

1. Brian Hall to ES, June 11, 1937.

2. Messages between ES and Foster Snow are in the Nym Wales Collection. Dates are indicated in the text. ES to Phillip Jaffe, June 22, 1937, Phillip Jaffe Collection; Helen Foster Snow, *Yenan Diary*, May 31, 1937, Nym Wales Collection.

3. "Mao's Love Affair: The Women of Yenan and Agnes Smedley," 54–61; Agnes Smedley to ES, April 19, 1937; Berry Berrigan to ES, June 1, 1954; Helen Foster Snow, *Chinese Communists, Sketches and Autobiographies of the Old Guard*, 250–61; Ross Terrill, *The White-Boned Demon*, 139–46; MacKinnon and MacKinnon, *Agnes Smedley*, 187–94; Braun, *Comintern Agent*, 249–50; Helen Foster Snow and Kim San, *Song of Ariran*, 31. Snow noted in the 1968 revised edition of *Red Star over China* that Mao's wife, Ho Tzu-chen, had formally charged Lily Wu with having alienated her husband's affections. Foster Snow used this as a reason to discuss what she knew of Lily Wu and to publish Wu's biography in book 2 of *Chinese Communists*. Ross Terrill saw an early manuscript version of the *Chuo Koron* article among Snow's papers and used it significantly in *White-Boned Demon*. This manuscript is not presently in the Edgar Snow Collection. The MacKinnons printed an extensive translation of the *Chuo Koron* article in their biography of Smedley.

4. Snow, *Random Notes*, 90–99; Hamilton, *Edgar Snow*, 94–96.

5. Bertram, *Capes of China*, 195–98, and Snow, *Journey*, 190–91. Ida Pruitt saw Snow, Bertram, and their Chinese secretary and amah got on the train in Peking. She was surprised to recognize the cadre as someone she believed a Red general who

had survived the Long March and who for a time was one of many guests who had taken shelter in her home after the Japanese occupied Peking. She also helped the resistance market some of the plunder they took from western hill tombs. Marjorie King, *Missionary Mother and Radical Daughter: Anna and Ida Pruitt in China, 1887–1939*, 386–88.

6. ES to father, September 8, 1937.

7. Foster Snow, *My China Years*, 280–93; Agnes Smedley, *China Fights Back*, 17–50, 93–95; Snow, *The Battle for Asia*, 27–29; James Bertram, *Unconquered*, 75–79.

32. Seeds Planted in Shanghai's Garden of War

1. Foster Snow, *My China Years*, 297–98.

2. Snow, *Battle for Asia*, 45–50, 60–77.

3. Michael Blankfort, *The Big Yankee: The Life of Carlson of the Raiders*, 135–89, 210–12, 244–64, 280–92; Snow, *Battle for Asia*, 50–54; Snow, *Journey*, 195–97; Evans Fordyce Carlson, *Twin Stars of China*, 26–35, 49, 83–86; Hugh Deane, "Letters to FDR: Evans Carlson on China at War, 1937–1941."

4. Snow, *Battle for Asia*, 80–85, 93; Rewi Alley, *At 90: Memoirs of My China Years*, 99–101.

5. Foster Snow, *My China Years*, 299–302; Helen Foster Snow [Nym Wales, pseud.], *Notes on the Beginnings of the Industrial Cooperatives in China*, 1–5; Douglas Robertson Reynolds, "The Chinese Industrial Cooperative Movement and the Political Polarization of Wartime China, 1938–1945," 66.

6. Bertram to ES, November 3, 1937, and typescript, "Interview with Mao Tse-tung." The first twenty-seven pages of this interview is reprinted in slightly different form in *Selected Works of Mao Tse-tung, II*, 47–59; Bertram gives a much fuller account of the interview in *Unconquered*, 110–24. Bertram to ES, November 14, 1937, Nym Wales Collection.

33. Snow's Star Rises in the West

1. Review of *Red Star over China*, 771; David H. Popper, review of *Red Star over China*, 6–7; Clifton Fadiman, "A Marco Polo out of Red China," 63–65; Malcolm Cowley, review of *Red Star over China*, 287; Pearl S. Buck, "Asia Book-Shelf," 202–3; Memo from Joanna McGaughey to Diane McGrew (Edgar Snow Fund research assistant), December 25, 1985; Bennett Cerf, "A Matter of Time," 238–40.

2. ES to father, January 18, 1938.

3. Harry Howard, "New Books of Interest in the Far East," 110–11; Edgar Snow, "Of Red Stars and Red Herrings," 271–72; ES to Harry Howard, May 30, 1938; Powell to ES, September 22, 1938.

4. ES to Earl Browder, March 20, 1938.

5. Alley, *At 90*, 78–79; Heinz Shippe to ES, February 27, 1938; typescript from Helen Foster Snow, "Who Was Hans Shippe"; Snow, *Random Notes*, 20–21.

6. ES to *Kansas City Star*, June 23, 1938; "Former Westport High Student Lives Life of Adventure in China," undated copy of article.

34. Seeding Indusco in Besieged Hankow

1. Foster Snow [Nym Wales, pseud.], *Industrial Cooperatives*, 1–10; Foster Snow, *My China Years*, 299–306; letter plus enclosures from Bertram, April 9, 1938; Harry Price to Snows, May 28, 1938, Nym Wales Collection.

2. Helen Foster Snow [Nym Wales, pseud.], "An Industrial Line Defense for China," 314–15; John Fairnsworth [pseud.], "Why Industrial Cooperatives?," 88–89; Humphrey Carpenter, *W. H. Auden: A Biography*, 236–40; W. H. Auden and Christopher Isherwood, *Journey to a War*, 245–53.

3. Snow, *Journey*, 203–8; ES to Foster Snow, July 3 and July 12, 1938; ES to Soong Ching-ling, July 10, 1938; Alley, *At 90*, 106–7; Edgar Snow, "China's Fighting Generalissimo," 615–16.

4. ES to Foster Snow, July 3, 1938; Snow, *Random Notes*, 22; Snow, *Battle for Asia*, 187–95, 289–90; Freda Utley, *Odyssey of a Liberal*, 210–12; Wang Fu-hsih, interview by author, Kansas City, Mo., March 1, 1993.

5. ES to Johnson, July 8 and July 17, 1938; Johnson to ES, July 8 and July 18, 1938; ES to Foster Snow, July 22, 1938.

35. All These Irons in the Fire

1. Foster Snow [Nym Wales, pseud.], *Industrial Cooperatives*, 35–36; Reynolds, "Chinese Industrial Cooperative Movement," 133–39; ES to Rewi Alley, August 24, 1938.

2. ES to Foster Snow, August 12 and 18, 1938; ES to Powell, August 28, 1938; ES to foreign editor, *London Daily Herald*, September 28, 1938; Soong Ching-ling to ES, date smudged but September 30, 1938, seems likely; Snow, *Battle for Asia*, 134.

3. Hamilton, *Edgar Snow*, 108–9; Snow, *Journey*, 208–11.

4. Soong Ching-ling to ES, date smudged but September 30, 1938, seems likely from internal evidence; ES to Soong Ching-ling, November 27, 1938.

5. ES to Herz, October 2, 1938, and January 23, February 12, March 5, and April 14, 1939; Herz to ES, October 25 and November 17, 1938, and January 17, January 24, February 7, March 8, March 20, March 27, May 2, and July 21, 1939; Foster Snow to Herz, December 4, 1938; William Towler, foreign press editor, *London Daily Herald*, to ES, December 22, 1938; Walsh to ES, March 10, 1939; Snow, "Peeling John Bull's Skin."

6. Herz to ES, July 29, August 25, October 25, and November 17, 1938; Foster Snow to Herz, December 4, 1938; Helen Foster Snow, "Chamberlain's Betrayal of

Democracy and the Far East," 342–44; Helen Foster Snow, "Industrial Cooperatives Needed to Strengthen China," 119–20.

7. T. A. Bisson, review of *Inside Red China,* 10; R. L. Duffers, review of *Inside Red China,* 6.

8. Rewi Alley to ES, January 19, February 16, March 7, March 8, and March 9, 1939; ES to Alley, one undated, but probably late in February, March 6, and April 14, 1939; Epstein to Foster Snow, February 14; Epstein to Snows, March 15, 1939; ES to Epstein, February 25 and March 7, 1939; ES to J. B. Grant, February 28; Grant to ES, March 16, 1939; ES to Soong Ching-ling, February 26 and March 6, 1939; ES to Morris (Mike) Appleman, March 2 and March 3, 1939; ES to Ida Pruitt, two letters dated March 6, 1939; Victor Gollancz to Hilda Selwyn-Clarke, February 6, 1939; from Selwyn-Clarke to ES, February 17, 1939; ES to Selwyn-Clarke, February 25, 1939.

36. Distant Thunder in Europe

1. Typed report from Agnes Smedley, April 19, 1939; ES to Soong Ching-ling, May 2 and June 13, 1939; ES to T. V. Soong, May 2, 1939; ES to Ambassador Clark-Kerr, May 31, 1939; Alley to ES, undated, but probably sometime in July from internal evidence; Jack Belden to ES, June 28, 1939; Foster Snow to ES, July 7, 1939; typed "Announcement, Board of Trustees for Chinese Industrial Co-operatives Productive Relief Fund," signed by S. J. Chen, Hong Kong, June 22, 1939; Reynolds, "Chinese Industrial Cooperative Movement," 133–39, 228–32; Snow, *Battle for Asia,* 148.

2. Snow, *Battle for Asia,* 156–58; Hamilton, *Edgar Snow,* 113; ES to Herz, December 12, 1939.

3. Bertram, *Capes of China,* 254–55; and Snow, *Battle for Asia,* 216–38.

4. ES to Foster Snow, September 6, 1939; ES to his father, September 9, 1939; Foster Snow to the Snows, September 17, 1939; Snow, *Battle for Asia,* 281–82; Bertram, *Capes of China,* 257–58.

5. Edgar Snow, "The Chinese Communists and Wars on Two Continents: Interviews with Mao Tse-tung," 277–80; Snow, *Random Notes,* 24–25; Snow, *Battle for Asia,* 283–88.

6. Snow, *Random Notes,* 71–73.

37. Clearing the Way for *Battle for Asia*

1. ES to Mao, September 30 and October 2, 1939; ES to Meng and to Martin Sommers, October 6, 1939.

2. ES to Alley, October 18, October 27, October 30, and November 16, 1939; ES to Ma Hai-teh, October 31, 1939; Alley to ES, October 19 and 28, 1939; ES to Herz, October 31, 1939; ES to foreign editor, *London Daily Herald,* November 10, 1939; Chen Han-seng to ES, November 10 and 27, 1939; ES to Chen, November 16, 1939; Edward

Carter to ES, November 21, 1939; Hubert Liang to ES, December 2, 1939; Spencer Kennard to ES, November 25, 1939; Ma Hai-teh to ES, December 5, 1939; Pruitt to Alley, November 1, 4, and 11, 1939; Pruitt to Foster Snow, November 11, 1939.

3. ES to Kuo Ta, November 16, 1939; Herz to Foster Snow, November 6, 1939; Herz to ES, December 4, 1939; ES to Herz, December 12, 1939, and February 17, 1940; cable from Herz to ES, November 23, 1939.

4. Kennard to ES, December 13, 1939; ES to Powell, December 14, 1939; ES to Chen, December 15, 1939; ES to Edward Carter, December 15, 1939. ES to Johnson, March 1, 1940, and from Johnson, March 9, 1940, plus copy of "Cooperatives in China," *Herald Mid-Week Magazine*, February 28, 1940, Johnson Papers, Library of Congress.

5. ES to Towne, December 16, 1939; ES to Evans Carlson, first page with date missing; ES to father, December 16, 1939; Herz to ES, December 22, 1939; ES to Alley, December 23, 1939; Kennard to ES and Israel Epstein, January 3, 1940; Epstein to ES, January 9, 1940; ES to Epstein, January 31, 1940; ES to Selwyn-Clarke, March 5, 1940.

6. ES to Ma Hai-teh, January 15, 1940; ES to Mme. Sun Yat-sen, January 15, 1940; Mme. Sun Yat-sen to ES, January 24, 1940; ES to Mme. Sun Yat-sen, January 31, 1940; ES to Powell, February 25, 1940.

7. ES to Pruitt, February 5, 1940; ES to sister, February 15, 1940; ES to father, March 5, 1940.

8. ES to Herz, December 16, 1939; fragment of letter from Herz with postscript dated January 8, 1940; ES to Herz, January 28, 1940; ES to Sommers, February 5, 1940; ES to Herz, February 6, 1940; Sommers to ES, February 22, 1940; ES to Herz, April 2, 1940; Herz to ES, April 22, 1940; Hollington K. Tong to ES, March 19, 1940; Harrison Brown to ES, May 6, 1940; Walsh to ES, April 29, 1940; *Time*, April 22, 1940; Robert K. Haas to ES, April 16, 1940.

38. Asia Hears the Thunder in Europe

1. ES to Lim Sian-tok, April 15, 1940, ES to Haas, May 24, 1940; Herz to ES, June 10, 1940; Haas to ES, July 1, 1940.

2. Alley to ES, July 1 and 3, 1940; ES to Herz, July 13, 1940.

3. ES to Herz, July 31, 1940; Herz to ES, July 17 and August 5, 1940.

4. "Petition to the President of the United States for a Loan of U.S. $50,000,000 to the Chinese Industrial Cooperatives"; Foster Snow to Alley, July 1, 1940; Chen to Foster Snow, August 7, 1940; Y. P. Mei to Alley, August, 23, 1940, Nym Wales Collection.

5. Bertram, *Capes of China*, 265–70; ES to Herz, August 22, 1940; Polly Babcock to Foster Snow, August 26, 1940, Nym Wales Collection; ES to sister, August 20, 1940.

6. ES to Herz, September 5, 1940; Herz to ES, September 9, 1940; Alley to ES, September 13, 1940; ES to Herz, September 22, 1940; ES to Herz, October 5, 1940;

Foster Snow to Herz, September 21, 1940; Herz to ES, September 30, 1940; Salvador P. Lopez to ES, October 5, 1940; Edgar Snow, "A Free Filipino Speaks."

7. Elizabeth M. Worcester to Foster Snow, October 9, 1940, Nym Wales Collection; ES to Herz, October 17 and 20, November 8 and 9, 1940; ES to brother, October 19, 1940; ES to Victor Gollancz, November 8, 1940.

39. An Alien Corn Adrift. . . .

1. ES to Chen, December 22, 1940.

2. Bertram, *Capes of China*, 279–81; MacKinnon and MacKinnon, *Agnes Smedley*, 146–48; Emily Hahn tells of her relation to Charles Boxer in *China to Me*; Snow, *Journey*, 235–41; Tracy B. Strong and Helene Keyssar, *Right in Her Soul: The Life of Anna Louise Strong*, 195–98; Anna Louise Strong, "The Kuomintang-Communist Crisis in China," 11, 21–23; *New York Herald Tribune*, January 7, 18, and 22, 1941. Otto Braun supports the Kuomintang's version of these events many years later in *Comintern Agent*, 86–87.

3. Snow, *Journey*, 238–41; Bertram, *Capes of China*, 281.

4. Hamilton, *Edgar Snow*, 123; January 13, 1941, pages from diary; ES to Toby, July 11, 1968; Edgar Snow, "Showdown in the Pacific," 4+.

5. Letter to Russell, July 21, 1948, Maud Russell Papers; ES to sister, February 17, November 3 and 23, and December 16, 1948, and May 31, 1949; Hamilton, *Edgar Snow*, 191–92; Snow, *Journey*, 241.

40. The Returning Author Challenges America

1. Foster Snow to author, June 10, 1993, and "Showdown" and "Keeping Posted," 4, 27, 40, 43, 44, 47.

2. Hamilton, *Edgar Snow*, 124–25; Edgar Snow, "China's Blitzbuilder: Rewi Alley," 12–13+; Graham Peck, *Two Kinds of Time*, 197.

3. Henry Luce to ES, February 25, 1941; Miles Vaughn, "The Inner Drama of China," 5; Rodney Gilbert, review of *Battle for Asia*, 3; William M. Reddig, "The Fight for a New World Order that Spreads from 'Free' China," 14.

4. Freda Utley, "Red Star over Independence Square, the Strange Case of Edgar Snow and the *Saturday Evening Post*"; Freda Utley, "A Terse, Authentic Report of the Terror in China," 9; Edgar Snow, "Is It Civil War in China?"; Freda Utley, "Will Russia Betray China"; Snow, *Battle for Asia*, 416–17.

5. Hamilton, *Edgar Snow*, 132–33; Snow, *Journey*, 245–50.

41. From Hot to Cold War

1. Hamilton, *Edgar Snow*, 126–27; father to ES, April 28 and November 19, 1941.

2. Edgar Snow, "They Don't Want to Play Soldier," 14+; Edgar Snow, "What Is Morale?" 16+; Edgar Snow, "Made-in-America Blitz," 12+; Snow, *People on Our Side*, 5.

3. Hamilton, *Edgar Snow*, 127–32; Snow, *Journey*, 253–58.

4. M. Thein Pe, *What Happened in Burma*, 76; Snow, *People on Our Side*, 8–57; Snow, *Journey*, 268–72, 341, 398–403; Snow, "Message of Gandhi," 24–25; Shirer, *Gandhi*, 227.

5. Barbara W. Tuchman, *Stilwell and the American Experience in China, 1911–1945*, 302–509; Lin Yu-tang, *The Vigil of a Nation*, 111, 125, 224–42; Snow, "China to Lin Yu-tang," 180–83; Lin Yu-tang, "China and Its Critics," 324–27; Edgar Snow, "China to Lin Yu-tang—II," 359. For a full discussion of Snow's troubles with America's Cold War policies as they developed, see also Hamilton, *Edgar Snow*, 155–81.

6. Powell, *Twenty-five Years*, 355–416; Max Eastman and J. B. Powell, "The Fate of the World Is at Stake in China," 16.

7. Hamilton, *Edgar Snow*, 171–72; James Bertram, *The Shadow of War*, 313; ES to Bennett Cerf, February 12, 1946, Random House Collection, Columbia University Library; Edgar Snow, "We Meet Russia in Korea," 18–19.

8. MacKinnon and MacKinnon, *Agnes Smedley*, 314–17; Hamilton, *Edgar Snow*, 170–81; Edgar Snow, "Why We Don't Understand Russia," 18–19; Edgar Snow, "How It Looks to Ivan Ivanovich," 23; Edgar Snow, "Stalin Must Have Peace," 25.

42. The Ghost at the Banquet

1. MacKinnon and MacKinnon, *Agnes Smedley*, 337–46; Lois Wheeler Snow, *A Death with Dignity*, 21–22.

2. John King Fairbank, "Foreword"; Hamilton, *Edgar Snow*, 191–211; Snow, *Journey*, 413–23.

3. Hamilton, *Edgar Snow*, 209–11, 215; Snow, *Journey*, 240; Wheeler Snow, *Death with Dignity*, 24–25, 38; ES to Donald Klopfer, April 15, 1960, Random House Collection.

4. Hamilton, *Edgar Snow*, 222–47; Peng Dehuai, *Memoirs of a Chinese Marshal*, 485–520; John King Fairbank, *The United States and China*, 422–26; Snow, *Other Side of the River*, 12, 217–18.

5. Hamilton, *Edgar Snow*, 248, 253–58, 264; Snow, "Barkinson's Law on Bombing," 309–14; Fairnsworth, "China Needs Healthier Leaders," 338–39; ES to brother, June 1, 1965.

6. Hamilton, *Edgar Snow*, 258–67; Wheeler Snow, *Death with Dignity*, 33; Fairbank, *United States and China*, 457–62.

7. Hamilton, *Edgar Snow*, 267–72; Epstein, interview; Rewi Alley, interview by author, Beijing, November 6, 1984.

8. Hamilton, *Edgar Snow*, 272–74; Wheeler Snow, *Death With Dignity*, 26–32.

9. Hamilton, *Edgar Snow*, 274–82; Wheeler Snow, *Death With Dignity*, 35–48, 79–135.

10. John S. Service, "Edgar Snow, Some Personal Reminiscences," 218–19.

Bibliography

T his bibliography is a listing of only the works cited in this book. It is
not a complete listing of Edgar Snow's published works or a complete
listing of all works consulted during the writing of this book. It is meant
to supplement and complete the information contained in the endnotes and
to serve as a convenient list of the principal sources for this study. For most
magazine citations I have given the volume, year, and page numbers.

The letters I have quoted and many miscellaneous papers are to be found
in two major collections: the Nym Wales Collection at the Hoover Institute in
Palo Alto, Calif., and the Edgar Snow Collection at the University of Missouri–
Kansas City.

Books by Edgar Snow

Far Eastern Front. New York: Smith and R. Haas, 1933; London: Jarrolds,
1934.

Living China: Modern Chinese Short Stories. New York: John Day, 1936;
London: G. G. Harrap, 1936.

Red Star over China. New York: Random House, 1937; London: Gollancz,
1937; rev. ed., New York: Grove Press, 1968.

The Battle for Asia. New York: Random House, 1941; *Scorched Earth*, London:
Gollancz, 1941.

People on Our Side. New York: Random House, 1944.

The Pattern of Soviet Power. New York: Random House, 1945.

Stalin Must Have Peace. New York: Random House, 1947.

Random Notes on Red China, 1936–1945. Cambridge: East Asian Research Center, Harvard University, 1957.

Journey to the Beginning. New York: Random House, 1958.

The Other Side of the River: Red China Today. New York: Random House, 1962.

The Long Revolution. New York: Random House, 1972.

Articles by Edgar Snow

1928

"In Hula Land." *Harper's Bazaar* (September 1): 98–99+.

"Kansas City Boy Stowaway." *Kansas City Journal-Post Magazine* (November 14): 4–5.

"Lifting China out of the Mud." *China Weekly Review* 46: 84–91.

"Chinese Woolworth in the Clock and Watch Business." *China Weekly Review* 46: 214.

1929

"Why the Rolling Stock Isn't Rolling out of Tsinanfu." *China Weekly Review* 47: 274–75.

"Which Way Manchuria?" *China Weekly Review* 48: 333–40.

"Saving 250,000 Lives." *China Weekly Review* 48: 418–24.

"Hangchow and Beyond." *China Weekly Review* 48: supplement.

"The American College Boy Vagabond in the Far East." *China Weekly Review* 49: 279–81.

"Journeying through Kiangsu." *China Weekly Review* 49: supplement.

Review of *Chiang Kai-shek: The Builder of China. China Weekly Review* 50: 392.

"Through China's 'Holy Land.' " *China Weekly Review* 50: supplement.

"Son of the Grand Marshal." *New York Herald Tribune Magazine* (December 15): 14–15+.

1930

[John Fairnsworth, pseud.] "Marines at Peace." Typescript. February 12. Edgar Snow Collection, University of Missouri–Kansas City.

"Beyond the Great Wall." *China Weekly Review* 52: supplement.

"The Americans in Shanghai." *American Mercury* 20: 437–45.

Review of *Infidels and Heretics. China Weekly Review* 53: 386.

"Change Enters the Chinese Pear Garden." *New York Herald Tribune Magazine* (November 16): 14–15+.

"Protecting the Morals of the Formosans." *China Weekly Review* 54: 428–29.

"Communist Strength in China." Typescript. Edgar Snow Collection, University of Missouri–Kansas City.

1931

"The Strength of Communism in China." *Current History* 33: 521–26.

"Celestial Poppy Smoke." *Asia* 31: 164–69+.

"Entering the Notorious Yunnan Province in South China and Planning a Caravan Trek across this Mysterious Bandit Ridden Region." *New York Sun* (June 23): 19.

"Gandhi Asserts American Visit Impossible." *New York Sun* (datelined June 24): Snow scrapbook. Edgar Snow Collection, University of Missouri–Kansas City.

"The Trial of British Communists at Meerut, India." *China Weekly Review* 58: 106.

"Indo-China Now Hotbed of Reds." *New York Sun* (datelined September 28): Snow scrapbook. Edgar Snow Collection, University of Missouri–Kansas City.

"The Revolt of India's Women." *New York Herald Tribune Magazine* (October 25): 14–15+.

"Why Lindbergh Plane Crashed." *New York Sun* (datelined November 20): Snow scrapbook. Edgar Snow Collection, University of Missouri–Kansas City.

"In the Wake of China's Flood." *New York Herald Tribune* (December 6): 4–5+.

1932

"Mme. Sun Yat-sen, Leader of China's Youth." Typescript. April 23. Edgar Snow Collection, University of Missouri–Kansas City.

"Kuomintang May Be Eliminated." *New York Sun* (datelined May 1): Snow scrapbook. Edgar Snow Collection, University of Missouri–Kansas City.

"Chinese Communists Make Gain." *New York Sun* (datelined May 3): Snow scrapbook. Edgar Snow Collection, University of Missouri–Kansas City.

"Profile, Mme. Sun Yat-sen." Typescript. September 12. Edgar Snow Collection, University of Missouri–Kansas City.

1933

[John Fairnsworth, C.B.E., pseud.] "China Needs Healthier Leaders." *China Weekly Review* 66: 338–39.
[John Fairnsworth, pseud.] "How Anti-American Sentiment Is Fostered in Japan." *China Weekly Review* 66: 475.

1934

"Japan Builds a Colony." *Saturday Evening Post* 206: 12–13+.
"Malraux's Revolutionary Novel an Epochal Work of China Fiction." *Shanghai Evening Post and Mercury* (August 11), Edgar Snow Collection, University of Missouri–Kansas City.

1935

"Christmas Escapade in Japan." *Travel* 64: 35–36+.

1936

"The Coming Conflict with Japan." *Saturday Evening Post* 208: 14–15+.

1937

"Reds and Northwest, I and II." *Shanghai Evening Post and Mercury* (February 3–4). Edgar Snow Collection, University of Missouri–Kansas City.
"Portrait of a Rebel." *Democracy* (May 1): 11–13+.
"Salute to Lu Hsun." *Democracy* (June 8): 85–87.

1938

"Of Red Stars and Red Herrings." *China Weekly Review* 84: 271–72.
[John Fairnsworth, pseud.] "Why Industrial Cooperatives?" *China Weekly Review* 85: 88–89.
"China's Fighting Generalissimo." *Foreign Affairs* 16: 612–25.

1939

"Peeling John Bull's Skin." *Saturday Evening Post* 212 (September 2): 23+.

1940

"The Dragon Licks His Wounds." *Saturday Evening Post* 212 (April 13): 9–11+.

"Will Stalin Sell Out China." *Foreign Affairs* 18: 450–63.

"The Chinese Communists and Wars on Two Continents: Interviews with Mao Tse-tung." *China Weekly Review* 87: 277–80.

1941

"China's Blitzbuilder: Rewi Alley." *Saturday Evening Post* 213 (February 8): 12–13+.

"Is It Civil War in China?" *Asia* 41: 166–70.

"A Free Filipino Speaks." *Asia* 41: 207.

"Showdown in the Pacific." *Saturday Evening Post* 213 (May 31): 20+.

"They Don't Want to Play Soldier." *Saturday Evening Post* 214 (October 25): 14–15+.

"What Is Morale?" *Saturday Evening Post* 214 (November 15): 16–17+.

1942 and after

"Made-in-America Blitz." *Saturday Evening Post* 214 (February 7, 1942): 12–13+.

"China to Lin Yu-tang." Review of *Vigil of a Nation*. *Nation* 160 (1945): 180–83.

"China to Lin Yu-tang—II." *Nation* 160 (1945): 359.

"We Meet Russia in Korea." *Saturday Evening Post* 218 (March 30, 1946): 18–19+.

"Why We Don't Understand Russia." *Saturday Evening Post* 219 (February 22, 1947): 18–19+.

"How It Looks to Ivan Ivanovich." *Saturday Evening Post* 219 (February 22, 1947): 23+.

"Stalin Must Have Peace." *Saturday Evening Post* 219 (March 1, 1947): 25+.

"The Message of Gandhi." *Saturday Evening Post* 220 (March 27, 1948): 24–25+.

"Mao's Love Affair: The Women of Yenan and Agnes Smedley." *Chuo Koron* (July 1954): 54–61.

"Barkinson's Law on Bombing." *The Columbia University Forum Anthology*. New York: Atheneum, 1968.

Books by Others

Alley, Rewi. *At 90: Memoirs of My China Years.* Beijing: New World Press, 1986.

Allison, John M. *Ambassador from the Prairie or Allison Wonderland.* Boston: Houghton Mifflin, 1973.

Auden, W. H., and Christopher Isherwood. *Journey to a War.* London: Faber and Faber, 1939.

Barker, A. J. *The Civilizing Mission: A History of the Italo-Ethiopian War of 1935–1936.* New York: Dial Press, 1968.

Bertram, James. Typescript. *Capes of China Slide Away.*

———. *First Act in China.* New York: Viking, 1938.

———. *The Shadow of War.* London: MacMillan, 1947.

———. *Unconquered.* New York: John Day, 1939.

Blankfort, Michael. *The Big Yankee: The Life of Carlson of the Raiders.* Boston: Little, Brown, 1947.

Braun, Otto. *A Comintern Agent in China, 1932–1939.* Stanford: Stanford University Press, 1982.

Carlson, Evans Fordyce. *Twin Stars of China.* New York: Dodd, Mead, 1940.

Carpenter, Humphrey. *W. H. Auden: A Biography.* Boston: Houghton Mifflin, 1981.

Chatwin, Bruce. *What Am I Doing Here?* New York: Viking, 1989.

Fairbank, John King. *The United States and China.* 4th ed. Cambridge: Harvard University Press, 1980.

Farnsworth, Robert M., ed. *Edgar Snow's Journey South of the Clouds.* Columbia: University of Missouri Press, 1991.

Flory, Wendy Stallard. *Ezra Pound and "The Cantos."* New Haven: Yale University Press, 1980.

Foster Snow, Helen. *Chinese Communists, Sketches and Autobiographies of the Old Guard.* Westport, Conn.: Greenwood, 1972.

———. *My China Years.* New York: William Morrow, 1984.

———[Nym Wales]. *Historical Notes on China.* Nym Wales Collection. Hoover Institute, Palo Alto, Calif., 1961. Includes *Notes on the Left-Wing Painters and Modern Art in China; Notes on the Chinese Student Movement, 1935–1936; Notes on the Sian Incident, 1936;* and *Notes on the Beginnings of the Industrial Cooperatives in China.*

———. *Yenan Diary.* Nym Wales Collection. Hoover Institute, Palo Alto, Calif.

Foster Snow, Helen [Nym Wales, pseud.], and Kim San. *Song of Ariran.* New York: John Day, 1941.

Freyn, Hubert. *Prelude to War: The Chinese Student Rebellion of 1935–1936.* Reprint, Westport, Conn.: Hyperion, 1977.

Hahn, Emily. *China to Me.* Garden City, N.Y.: Doubleday, Doran, 1945.

Hamilton, John Maxwell. *Edgar Snow.* Bloomington and Indianapolis: Indiana University Press, 1988.

Israel, John. *Student Nationalism in China, 1927–1937.* Stanford: Stanford University Press, 1966.

Israel, John, and Donald W. Klein. *Rebels and Bureaucrats, China's December 9'ers.* Berkeley and Los Angeles: University of California Press, 1976.

King, Marjorie. "Missionary Mother and Radical Daughter: Anna and Ida Pruitt in China, 1887–1939." (Ph.D. diss., Temple University, 1984).

Kunitz, Stanley J. *Authors Today and Yesterday.* New York: H. W. Wilson, 1934.

Lin Yu-tang. *The Vigil of a Nation.* New York: John Day, 1944.

MacKinnon, Janice R., and Stephen R. MacKinnon. *Agnes Smedley: The Life and Times of an American Radical.* Berkeley and Los Angeles: University of California Press, 1988.

Pe, M. Thein. *What Happened in Burma.* Allahabad: Kitabistan, 1943.

Peck, Graham. *Two Kinds of Time.* Boston: Houghton Mifflin, 1967.

Peng Dehuai. *Memoirs of a Chinese Marshal.* Beijing: Foreign Languages Press, 1984.

Powell, John B. *My Twenty-five Years in China.* New York: Macmillan, 1945.

Salisbury, Harrison. *The Long March, The Untold Story.* New York: Harper and Row, 1985.

Selle, Earl Albert. *Donald of China.* New York: Harper and Brothers, 1948.

Shirer, William. *Gandhi: A Memoir.* New York: Simon and Schuster, 1979.

Smedley, Agnes. *China Fights Back.* London: Victor Gollancz, 1938.

Strong, Tracy B., and Helene Keyssar. *Right in Her Soul: The Life of Anna Louise Strong.* New York: Random House, 1983.

Sutton, S. B. *In China's Border Provinces: The Turbulent Career of Joseph Rock, Botanist-Explorer.* New York: Hastings House, 1974.

Terrill, Ross. *The White-Boned Demon.* New York: William Morrow, 1984.

Tuchman, Barbara. *Stilwell and the American Experience in China, 1911–1945.* New York: Macmillan, 1970.

Utley, Freda. *Odyssey of a Liberal.* Washington, D.C.: Washington National Press, 1970.

Wang Shiqing. *Lu Xun: A Biography.* Beijing: Foreign Languages Press, 1984.

Wheeler Snow, Lois. *A Death with Dignity.* New York: Random House, 1974.

———, ed. *Edgar Snow's China.* New York: Random House, 1981.

Miscellaneous by Others

"*American Mercury* Takes Up China, The." *China Weekly Review* 52 (1930): 372.

Bartlett, Randolph. Review of *Living China.* *New York Sun* (March 20, 1937).

Bertram, James. "The Story of Sian: I. Prelude to Mutiny." *Democracy* (May 1, 1937): 16–18+.

Bisson, T. A. Review of *Inside Red China. Saturday Review of Literature* 19 (February 25, 1939): 10.

Buck, Pearl S. "Asia Book-Shelf." Review of *Red Star over China. Asia* 38 (1938): 202–3.

Cerf, Bennett. "A Matter of Time." *Publishers Weekly* 833 (1938): 838–40.

Cowley, Malcolm. Review of *Red Star over China. New Republic* (January 12, 1938): 287.

Deane, Hugh. "Letters to FDR: Evans Carlson on China at War, 1937–1941." *U.S.-China Review* (summer 1992): 12–18.

"Democracy for China." *Democracy* (May 1, 1937): 5.

Duffers, R. L. Review of *Inside Red China. New York Times* (July 23, 1939): 6.

Eastman, Max, and J. B. Powell. "The Fate of the World Is at Stake in China." *Reader's Digest* 46 (1945): 13–22.

Fadiman, Clifton. "A Marco Polo out of Red China." *New Yorker* (January 8, 1938): 63–65.

Fairbank, John King. "Foreword." *Random Notes on Red China, 1936–1945.* Cambridge, East Asian Research Center, Harvard University, 1947.

Foster Snow, Helen. "Chamberlain's Betrayal of Democracy and the Far East." *China Weekly Review* 86 (1938): 342–44.

———. "How Edgar Snow Arranged to Make His Trip to the Northwest, 1936." Nym Wales Collection. Hoover Institute, Palo Alto, Calif., 1961.

———. "Industrial Cooperatives Needed to Strengthen China." *China Weekly Review* 87 (1938): 119–20.

———[Nym Wales, pseud.]. "Analyzing the 'Shanghai Mind.' " *China Weekly Review* 1933: 57–58.

———[Nym Wales, pseud.]. "An Industrial Line Defense for China." *China Weekly Review* 84 (1938): 314–15.

———[Nym Wales, pseud.]. "Introduction to Edgar Snow." Nym Wales Collection. Hoover Institute, Palo Alto, Calif.

———[Nym Wales, pseud.]. "Reflections in an Old T'ang Mirror. . . ." *Democracy* (May 1, 1937): 22.

Gilbert, Rodney. Review of *Battle for Asia. New York Herald Tribune, Books* (February 23, 1941): 3.

Gould, Randall. Review of *Living China. Shanghai Evening Post and Mercury* (December 1, 1936).

Graves, William S. "An Arraignment of Japan." Review of *Far Eastern Front. New York Herald Tribune, Books* 7 (1932): 2.

Hallgren, Mauritz A. "The Undeclared War in the East." Review of *Far Eastern Front. Nation* 137 (1933): 629.

Hanwell, Norman. "The Chinese Red Army." *Asia* 36 (1936): 316–22.

———. "Where Chinese Reds Move In." *Asia* 36 (1936): 631–36.

Howard, Harry. "New Books of Interest in the Far East." Review of *Red Star over China. China Weekly Review* 83 (1938): 110–11.

"Keeping Posted." *Saturday Evening Post* 213 (May 31, 1941): 4.

Liang, Hubert S. "Japanese Diplomacy—Dr. Jekyll and Mr. Hyde." *Democracy* (May 1, 1937): 7–8+.

Lin Yu-tang. "China and Its Critics." *Nation* 160 (1945): 324–27.

———. Review of *Far Eastern Front. China Critic* (December 14, 1933).

Lu Cui. "We Shall Forever Remember Edgar Snow with Gratitude." Biannual Edgar Snow Symposium, July 1992, Beijing.

"Men's Club of Union Church to Hold Its First Forum on Monday." *Peking Chronicle* (February 24, 1934): Edgar Snow Collection, University of Missouri–Kansas City.

Nikolaieff, A. M. "The Undeclared War in the Far East." Review of *Far Eastern Front. New York Times Book Review* (October 29, 1933): 11.

Popper, David H. Review of *Red Star over China. Saturday Review of Literature* 17 (January 1, 1938): 6–7.

Powell, John. "My Father's Library." *Wilson Library Bulletin* 60 (1986): 35–37.

Pruitt, Ida. "Day by Day in Peking." *Atlantic Monthly* 147 (1931): 611–19.

———. "The Dowager." *Democracy* (May 1, 1937): 20–22.

Reddig, William M. "The Fight for a New World Order that Spreads from 'Free' China." Review of *Battle for Asia. Kansas City Star* (February 22, 1941): 14.

Review of *Red Star over China. London Times Literary Supplement* (October 23, 1937): 771.

Reynolds, Douglas Robertson. "The Chinese Industrial Cooperative Movement and the Political Polarization of Wartime China, 1938–1945." Ph.D. diss., Columbia University, 1975.

Sayre, Mildred. "Cooperatives in China." *Manila Herald Mid-Week Magazine.* (February 28, 1940).

Service, John S. "Edgar Snow, Some Personal Reminiscences." *China Quarterly* (April–June 1972): 218–19.

Shippe, M. G. "Sun Yat-sen as a Democratic Leader." *Democracy* (June 22, 1937): 114–17.

———. "When Japan's Ally Goes to War." *Democracy* (June 8, 1937): 95–98.

Strong, Anna Louise. "The Kuomintang-Communist Crisis in China." *Amerasia* (March 1941): 11+.

Stuart, J. Leighton. "The Outlook for Democracy in China." *Democracy* (May 1, 1937): 9–10.

Utley, Freda. "Red Star over Independence Square, the Strange Case of Edgar

Snow and the *Saturday Evening Post.*" *Plain Talk* (September 1947): 416–17.

———. "A Terse, Authentic Report of the Terror in China." Review of *Battle for Asia. New York Times Book Review* (March 9, 1941): 9.

———. "Will Russia Betray China." *Asia* 41 (1941): 170–73.

Vaughn, Miles. "The Inner Drama of China." Review of *Battle for Asia. Saturday Review of Literature* 23 (March 1, 1941): 5.

W., M. P. Review of *Living China. China Weekly Review* (March 27, 1937): 155.

W., S. E. R. Review of *Living China. London Times Literary Supplement* (no date): Edgar Snow Collection, University of Missouri–Kansas City.

"Who's Who in China." *China Weekly Review* (December 7, 1927).

Index

B
S6726 F

PROVIDENCE ATHENAEUM

3 1753 00166 9933

JUN 2 8 1996

PROVIDENCE ATHENAEUM